Be a Fodor's Correspondent

Your opinion matters. It matters to us. It matters to your fellow Fodor's travelers, too. And we'd like to hear it. In fact, we need to hear it.

When you share your experiences and opinions, you become an active member of the Fodor's community. That means we'll not only use your feedback to make our books better, but we'll publish your names and comments whenever possible. Throughout our guides, look for "Word of Mouth," excerpts of your unvarnished feedback.

Here's how you can help improve Fodor's for all of us.

Tell us when we're right. We rely on local writers to give you an insider's perspective. But our writers and staff editors—who are the best in the business—depend on you. Your positive feedback is a vote to renew our recommendations for the next edition.

Tell us when we're wrong. We're proud that we update most of our guides every year. But we're not perfect. Things change. Hotels cut services. Museums change hours. Charming cafés lose charm. If our writer didn't quite capture the essence of a place, tell us how you'd do it differently. If any of our descriptions are inaccurate or inadequate, we'll incorporate your changes in the next edition and will correct factual errors at fodors.com immediately.

Tell us what to include. You probably have had fantastic travel experiences that aren't yet in Fodor's. Why not share them with a community of like-minded travelers? Maybe you chanced upon a beach or bistro or B&B that you don't want to keep to yourself. Tell us why we should include it. And share your discoveries and experiences with everyone directly at fodors.com. Your input may lead us to add a new listing or highlight a place we cover with a "Highly Recommended" star or with our highest rating, "Fodor's Choice."

Give us your opinion instantly at our feedback center at www.fodors.com/feedback. You may also e-mail editors@fodors.com with the subject line "Bahamas Editor." Or send your nominations, comments, and complaints by mail to Bahamas Editor, Fodor's, 1745 Broadway, New York, NY 10019.

You and travelers like you are the heart of the Fodor's community. Make our community richer by sharing your experiences. Be a Fodor's correspondent.

Happy traveling!

Tim Jarrell, Publisher

CONTENTS

Fodor's 2009

BAHAMAS

Where to Stay and Eat
for All Budgets

Must-See Sights
and Local Secrets

Ratings You Can Trust

Fodor's Travel Publications   New York, Toronto, London, Sydney, Auckland
www.fodors.com

917. 296
FOD
[handwritten]

FODOR'S BAHAMAS 2009

Editor: Molly Moker
Editorial Contributors: Chelle Koster Walton, Kevin Kwan, Jessica Robertson, Patricia Rodriguez Terrell, Ramona Settle, Stephen F. Vletas

Editorial Production: Carolyn Roth
Maps & Illustrations: David Lindroth, *cartographer*; Bob Blake, Rebecca Baer, *map editors;* William Wu, *information graphics*
Design: Fabrizio LaRocca, *creative director*; Guido Caroti, Siobhan O'Hare, *art directors*; Tina Malaney, Chie Ushio, Ann McBride, Jessica Walsh, *designers*; Melanie Marin, *senior picture editor;* Moon Sun Kim, *cover designer*
Cover Photo: Lucayan National Park, Grand Bahama Island: Ian Cumming/Axiom
Production/Manufacturing: Matthew Struble

COPYRIGHT

Copyright © 2009 by Fodor's Travel, a division of Random House, Inc.

Fodor's is a registered trademark of Random House, Inc.

All rights reserved. Published in the United States by Fodor's Travel, a division of Random House, Inc., and simultaneously in Canada by Random House of Canada, Limited, Toronto. Distributed by Random House, Inc., New York.

No maps, illustrations, or other portions of this book may be reproduced in any form without written permission from the publisher.

ISBN 978-1-4000-1953-3

ISSN 1524-7945

SPECIAL SALES

This book is available at special discounts for bulk purchases for sales promotions or premiums. Special editions, including personalized covers, excerpts of existing books, and corporate imprints, can be created in large quantities for special needs. For more information, write to Special Markets/Premium Sales, 1745 Broadway, MD 6-2, New York, New York 10019, or e-mail specialmarkets@randomhouse.com.

AN IMPORTANT TIP & AN INVITATION

Although all prices, opening times, and other details in this book are based on information supplied to us at press time, changes occur all the time in the travel world, and Fodor's cannot accept responsibility for facts that become outdated or for inadvertent errors or omissions. So **always confirm information when it matters,** especially if you're making a detour to visit a specific place. Your experiences—positive and negative—matter to us. If we have missed or misstated something, **please write to us.** We follow up on all suggestions. Contact the Bahamas editor at editors@fodors.com or c/o Fodor's at 1745 Broadway, New York, NY 10019.

PRINTED IN THE UNITED STATES OF AMERICA

10 9 8 7 6 5 4 3 2 1

MAPS

ABOUT THIS BOOK

Sometimes you find terrific travel experiences and sometimes they just find you. But usually the burden is on you to select the right combination of experiences. That's where our ratings come in.

As travelers we've all discovered a place so wonderful that its worthiness is obvious. And sometimes that place is so unique that superlatives don't do it justice: you just have to be there to know. These sights, properties, and experiences get our highest rating, **Fodor's Choice**, indicated by orange stars throughout this book.

Black stars highlight sights and properties we deem **Highly Recommended**, places that our writers, editors, and readers praise again and again for consistency and excellence.

By default, there's another category: any place we include in this book is by definition worth your time, unless we say otherwise. And we will.

Disagree with any of our choices? Care to nominate a place or suggest that we rate one more highly? Visit our feedback center at www.fodors.com/feedback.

Hotel and restaurant price categories from ¢ to $$$$ are defined in the opening pages of each chapter. For attractions, we always give standard adult admission fees; reductions are usually available for children, students, and senior citizens. Want to pay with plastic? **AE, D, DC, MC, V** following restaurant and hotel listings indicate whether American Express, Discover, Diners Club, MasterCard, and Visa are accepted.

Unless we state otherwise, restaurants are open for lunch and dinner daily. We mention dress only when there's a specific requirement and reservations only when they're essential or not accepted—it's always best to book ahead.

Hotels have private bath, phone, TV, and air-conditioning and operate on the European Plan (aka EP, meaning without meals), unless we specify that they use the Continental Plan (CP, with a Continental breakfast), Breakfast Plan (BP, with a full breakfast), or Modified American Plan (MAP, with breakfast and dinner), or are all-inclusive (AI, including all meals and most activities). We always list facilities but not whether you'll

be charged an extra fee to use them, so when pricing accommodations, find out what's included.

Many Listings

★	Fodor's Choice
★	Highly recommended
⊠	Physical address
✛	Directions
⌂	Mailing address
☎	Telephone
🖷	Fax
⊕	On the Web
✉	E-mail
🖃	Admission fee
☉	Open/closed times
Ⓜ	Metro stations
▭	Credit cards

Hotels & Restaurants

🏨	Hotel
⇨	Number of rooms
⌂	Facilities
⦿	Meal plans
✕	Restaurant
⌂	Reservations
⌇	Smoking
🆈	BYOB
✕🏨	Hotel with restaurant that warrants a visit

Outdoors

🏌	Golf
⛺	Camping

Other

☯	Family-friendly
⇨	See also
⊠	Branch address
☞	Take note

NEW PROVIDENCE ISLAND

To some, New Providence has come to be associated largely with Paradise Island—the skinny islet connected to its larger neighbor by bridge (Paradise Island is home to some of the Bahamas' priciest vacation homes and splashiest resorts, including the megaresort and water park, Atlantis, and the new, even more upscale Cove Atlantis with a signature restaurant by star chef Bobby Flay). But New Providence Island is also the site of Nassau, the nation's capital. As a historical and cultural center, Nassau is packed with tour-worthy mansions, churches, government buildings, gardens, forts, museums, and monuments, many with a distinctly British accent left over from the old colonial days. As the nation's largest city, Nassau also offers sophisticated shopping and dining, flashy casinos, hot nightlife—and some of the less-pleasant aspects of big city living, including crowds, traffic, pollution, and, despite a crackdown and cleanup, some petty crime. Not to be outdone, Cable Beach is undergoing a multimillion dollar renovation, part of Baha Mar's plan to rival Paradise Island—and Las Vegas. By 2011, the megaresort complex will include more than 3,000 rooms in six upscale hotels, a casino, a Jack Nicklaus golf course, a spa being billed as the largest in the Caribbean, and an entertainment complex to satisfy every whim and fancy.

GRAND BAHAMA ISLAND

Grand Bahama has struggled to reclaim the glory it knew in the Rat Pack era, but thanks to extensive investment and a determined marketing campaign, it is now the quieter alternative to fast-paced New Providence. Established in the 1950s and 1960s, the twin cities of Freeport and Lucaya can't match Nassau's colonial charm or Paradise Island's upmarket chic. But as the second-largest population center in the islands, Grand Bahama does offer a good variety of places to shop, gamble, or golf, and beautiful beaches where you'll often leave the first footprint, no matter what time of day you get there. Some properties, closed for years because of hurricane damage, have finally changed hands, with the promise of much needed rejuvenation and class. But there's still a wild side to this island, the fourth-largest in the chain: visitors can escape their fellow tourists by choosing from a growing list of soft-adventure and ecotours, including kayaking, exploring old-island fishing settlements, and bird-watching.

WHAT'S WHERE

THE ABACOS 	If you're a sailing or yachting aficionado—or if you'd like to be one for a week or two—the Abacos is the place to be. A slim string of small cays, the Abacos were once the nation's boat-building capital. Today, shallow, translucent waters and top-notch marinas make them a hot spot for pleasure boating and fishing. If you don't bring your own catamaran or powerboat, plenty of places here rent them by the day or week, and idle sails between cays, stopping for picnics on uninhabited islets or for tours of small settlements, are a popular pastime. British Loyalists fleeing the newly independent America first settled here about 225 years ago, and many surviving structures, including candy-color clapboard houses on Green Turtle Cay and Elbow Cay's famous striped lighthouse, make a visit to these isles something of a time-traveling experience. However, that also extends to some of the lodging options. Although there are some spectacular homes and vacation rentals, hotels here in general tend to be not as sophisticated as elsewhere in the nation. Perfect for vacationers who seek isolated beaches by day and unmatched stargazing by night, these islands might not be for you if you crave nightlife, brand-name shopping, or beaches with a full retinue of Jet Skis, parasailing boats, and hair-braiders.
ELEUTHERA & THE EXUMAS 	Harbour Island, with its pink-sand beaches; quaint Cape Cod–style architecture; upscale restaurants; and intimate, luxurious hotels, makes many "best-of" lists among travelers and travel writers alike. Chic but still friendly, popular but still small enough that a "crowded" stretch of beach might contain a few dozen sunbathers, Harbour Island has grown into something of a celebrity magnet with resorts like Pink Sands and Rock House, and prices have risen accordingly. If you're not a supermodel or an investment banker, you might get sticker shock. On the "mainland" of Eleuthera, visitors will also enjoy friendly hosts, gorgeous beaches, bounteous bougainvillea, and fine diving—but at a lower price. Here the hotels tend to be simpler motels, B&Bs, and cottages, with a handful of luxurious digs interspersed throughout.
	The hundreds of little cays that make up the Exumas are prime cruising ground for yachters. Though some fans worried that the 2003 opening of the luxurious Four Seasons Resort Great Exuma at Emerald Bay hotel and spa would ruin the region's laid-back charm, the Exumas remain a quiet

destination, albeit with a slowly growing number of options for those who enjoy other active pursuits.

THE OTHER OUT ISLANDS

The remaining Out Islands are often lumped together as the "Family Islands," since many Bahamians have roots on these smaller and less-populated cays. Each has a casual, small-town atmosphere and abundant natural beauty, but the similarities end there. For deep-sea fishing, head to Bimini, once famous for its connections to Ernest Hemingway and illicit rumrunners. For bonefishing, try Andros, a lush, green island that's also a lure for bird-watchers. For a glimpse of the past, visit Cat Island, where remnants of mansions and slave quarters provide a historical backdrop to a quiet community of farmers and fishermen. To really get away from it all, the Berry Islands or Crooked and Acklins Islands are among the least developed in the nation. In general, there are far fewer tourist amenities in the Out Islands, and hotels and restaurants tend to be rustic. (Bimini, with its loads of hotels, restaurants, and bars, and San Salvador, with its large and unusually luxurious Club Med, are among the exceptions.)

TURKS & CAICOS

The Turks and Caicos, two groups of islands that lie at the bottom edge of the Bahamas, were long considered country cousins to the other Bahamian islands. But in recent years, T&C has upped the glitz factor, especially in the capital of Providenciales (known to all simply as Provo) and tiny Parrot Cay, which is popular with celebrities. New and newly renovated resorts, spas, and restaurants attract a chic, well-heeled clientele who come for the stunning beaches and terrific diving and snorkeling on the outlying coral reefs (however, the islands' terrain tends toward the dry and scrubby rather than the lush and tropical). Still, many spots in the Turks and Caicos remain charmingly "undiscovered."

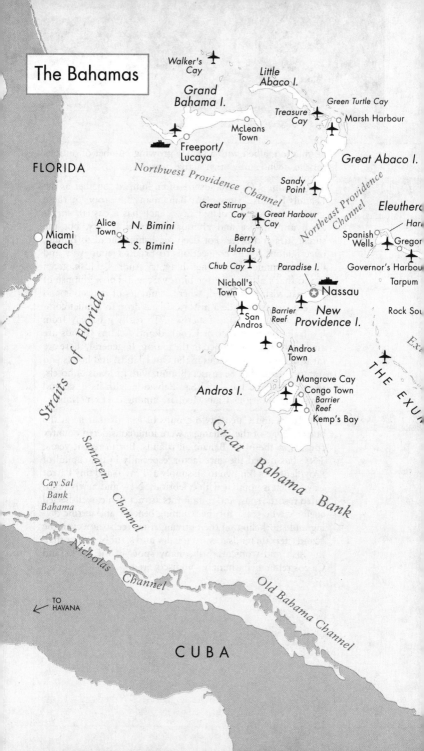

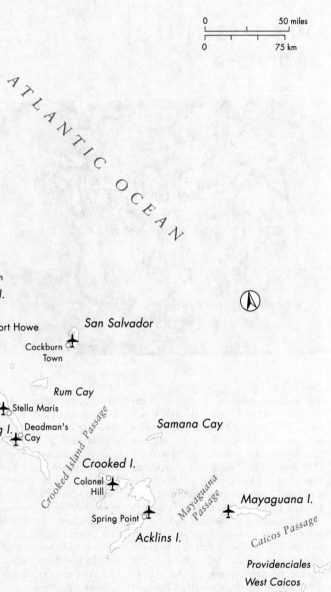

ATLANTIC OCEAN

0 — 50 miles
0 — 75 km

✈ Arthur's Town
Cat I.
. Alvernia ▲
New Bight ✈
Port Howe
San Salvador
✈ Cockburn
Town

Rum Cay

✈ George
Town
Great
Exuma I.
✈ Stella Maris
Long I.
Deadman's
Cay
✈
Samana Cay

Crooked I.
Colonel ✈
Hill
Spring Point ✈
Acklins I.

Mayaguana
Passage
✈ Mayaguana I.

Caicos Passage

Providenciales
West Caicos
Little
Inagua I.
TO
TURKS AND
CAICOS
ISLANDS

Great Inagua I.
Matthew ✈
Town
Lake
Windsor

ound

Crooked Island Passage

QUINTESSENTIAL BAHAMAS

Junkanoo

The Bahamas's answer to Rio de Janeiro's Carnaval and New Orleans's Mardi Gras, Junkanoo is a festival of parades and parties held annually on Boxing Day (the day after Christmas) and New Year's Day. Rooted in West African traditions kept alive by slaves, today's Junkanoo is a raucous, joyful celebration of freedom. Groups create a theme, complete with elaborate, colorful costumes and choreographed routines. Winners receive not just cash prizes but a full year's worth of bragging rights. More than just a parade, Junkanoo is a moveable, danceable party, fueled by distinctly Bahamian music created by goatskin drums, clanging cowbells, conch-shell horns, shrieking whistles, and brass bands. Although Junkanoo festivals occur throughout the islands, the biggest celebrations are in Nassau. And the real fun starts long after midnight, so rest up.

Conch

Conch, pronounced "konk," is popular for more than just its distinctive, spiral-shape shells; this sea creature, essentially a giant snail, is one of the mainstays of Bahamian cuisine. Firm white conch meat is tenderized, then turned into a variety of dishes. There's cracked conch, fried in seasoned batter and served as a main dish or a sandwich; conch salad, the Bahamian version of ceviche, with raw conch marinated in lime juice with onions and peppers; conch chowder; and the popular appetizer, conch fritters. Head to Potter's Cay in Nassau to watch fishermen get the meat out of the shells—it makes for a great photo opportunity. Islanders often claim that conch has two other magical powers—as a hangover cure (when eaten straight from the shell with hot peppers, salt, and lime) and as an especially tasty aphrodisiac.

eautiful beaches, crystalline water a dozen shades of blue and green, ixurious resorts — sure, these images are all trademarks of the Bahamas, ut to really get a sense of the islands, you'll want to experience a few f these culture highlights.

ake 'n' Scrape

amaica has reggae, the Dominican Republic has merengue, and the Bahamas as rake 'n' scrape, its own lively brand of raditional music. Generations ago, many ahamians didn't have the money to buy istruments, so they would make music sing whatever was at hand. Someone night have played a saw, someone else nade a bass out of string and a tin tub, nd another musician kept time by shaking a plastic jug filled with rocks or dried eans, or by beating a goatskin drum. rom those humble beginnings came this lting, highly danceable music, a version f which is often played by bands in nightlubs or at local festivals. Today the best lace to hear authentic rake 'n' scrape is n Cat Island, where the style is said to ave been born, or during Junkanoo celbrations throughout the islands.

The Straw Markets

Perhaps best known for its hair braiders and aggressive vendors, the Nassau straw market is a bona fide Bahamian tradition. The market was established in the '40s, when Bahamian women looking for an income began making and selling baskets, bags, and dolls made from dried palm fronds and sisal leaves. Now, many of the products are imported or made in the Out Islands. As of this writing, the Nassau market is still in a temporary, tented location, after a fire in 2001 destroyed the permanent market. Officials vow the market will be rebuilt, but it's unclear when, if ever, it will happen. Still, for colorful personalities and an array of souvenir choices, this market shouldn't be missed. Be prepared to haggle, and don't be afraid to say no (nicely) to the many vendors who will approach with a "Hi, sweetie," or a "You all right?"

IF YOU LIKE

Beaches

The Bahamas has more than 800 mi of beachfront, more than any other Atlantic or Caribbean nation. Theoretically, it's all yours to explore, since all Bahamian beaches are public up to the high-water mark. In practice, private homes and resorts can make it difficult to reach some stretches of sand, unless you arrive by boat. The best stretches, such as Cabbage Beach on Paradise Island and Cable Beach on New Providence Island, are packed with resorts and resort guests, but there are plenty of more secluded beauties.

Guana Cay Beach, Great Guana Cay. The lightly visited, 7-mi-long western shore of this cay is probably what you envision when you imagine running away to a tropical isle.

Harbour Island Beach. Perhaps the single most famous beach in the Bahamas, thanks to its unusual pink-powder sand, this 3-mi stretch is also among the best spots in the islands to spy Hollywood stars—and the occasional bikini model (part of the 2006 *Sports Illustrated* swimsuit calendar was photographed here).

Old Bight Beach, Cat Island. Lined with coconut palms and shade-casting casuarina trees, this rustic (read: no facilities) white-sand beach gives you 5 mi of opportunity for a private picnic, a shell-searching stroll, or a snooze.

Treasure Cay Beach, Great Abaco. This 3½-mi, sugary white-sand beach borders a shallow, turquoise bay that's perfect for swimming, even for kids. One end brims with vendors hawking water-sports equipment, while the other end is often nearly deserted.

Underwater Sports

Surrounded by some of the most beautiful water in the world—and lots of it—it's no wonder that much of the activity in the Bahamas centers on water sports. And although many think of fishing and sailing first, snorkeling and scuba diving are just as spectacular here, with wrecks and reefs, blue holes and drop-offs, and sea gardens and shallow shoals. Thanks to a vast system of coral reefs, diving and snorkeling are good just about everywhere, but the quality of instruction and rental equipment can vary, especially in some of the Out Islands where there are a limited number of operators. Be sure to check out the condition of masks, fins, and dive computers before plopping down your money.

Pelican Cays National Park, Great Abaco. Turtles, spotted eagle rays, and tarpon are among the common sightings in this shallow (25 feet) marine park; you'll need to take a boat to one of the three moorings for the best spots.

Thunderball Grotto, Staniel Cay. Beneath a three-story curved limestone ceiling, this domed cave at the northern end of the Exumas chain has some of the best snorkeling and diving in the Family Islands. James Bond aficionados will recognize it from one of the boat chase scenes in the movie *Thunderball.*

UNEXSO (Underwater Explorers Society), Grand Bahama. The offerings are vast at this famous outfitter: learn to dive, get certified, check out reefs and wrecks, swim with dolphins, and, if you're an experienced diver, witness a shark feeding frenzy.

olf

ourses designed by some of the biggest
ames in the game are scattered through-
ut the islands—and, thanks to consis-
ntly sunny weather, you can squeeze
a round nearly every day. Green fees
sually remain well under the $200-and-
p heights common in Hawai'i and Las
egas, and most courses offer terrific
ater views.

baco Club on Winding Bay, Great Abaco.
he only Scottish-style links course in the
ahamas wins rave reviews for its beauty
nd drama, with an 18th hole that plays
ut ocean side, 60 feet above the crashing
irf. Now managed by Ritz-Carlton, it's
ill a private club, and although you're
lowed one visit before joining, member-
iips start at $75,000.

our Seasons Golf Club Great Exuma at Emer-
d Bay. Pro golfer Greg Norman designed
iis 18-hole ocean-side course, attached
） the exclusive Four Seasons resort.

ne & Only Ocean Club Golf Course, Paradise
and. Michael Jordan holds his celebrity
ivitational tournament at this course
ach winter. Part of the posh One & Only
)cean Club, play here is limited to the
lub's guests and several others; green fees
re among the highest in the Bahamas.

easure Cay Golf Course, Great Abaco. This
8-hole course, designed by Dick Wilson,
as a relaxed, friendly atmosphere. No tee
mes are required, and afternoon golfers
ften get the course all to themselves.

Vestin and Sheraton Grand Bahama Island
esort Lucayan Course. This challenging
cean-side course, the most acclaimed on
irand Bahama Island, was designed by
)ick Wilson.

One-of-a-Kind Resorts

Spurred partly by competition from other
tropical destinations, the luxury market
in the Bahamas has grown substantially
in the past several years; it's now possible
to dine at restaurants opened by internationally famous chefs, relax with a signature treatment at an Eastern-inspired spa,
and luxuriate in a $2,000-a-night suite—
all without leaving the resort premises.

Atlantis, Paradise Island. You either love the
sprawling Atlantis resort for its 35 restaurants, casino, constant activity, and
water park and walk-through aquarium
with kitschy Lost City theme—or you
hate it, for exactly the same reasons.
Adding more than 1,000 luxurious suites,
the Cove and the Reef joined the Atlantis offerings in 2007, bringing even more
dining, pool, and beach options.

One & Only Ocean Club, Paradise Island.
Much smaller and not as busy as its
neighbor Atlantis, this exclusive resort
is for those who want to relax in luxury.
It also played a starring role in the 2006
Bond flick, *Casino Royale*. Enjoy a complimentary yoga class or shell out for an
ocean body wrap at the spa, then dine at
Dune, the restaurant by famed New York
chef Jean-Georges Vongerichten.

Pink Sands, Harbour Island. Founded by
Chris Blackwell, the Island Records exec
who also has luxe properties in Jamaica,
this chic, cozy retreat pampers high rollers with things rarely found in the Out
Islands, including imported Indonesian
furniture, DVD players, and French
presses. Favored by guests in the record-
ing, film, and fashion industries, the resort
will roll out the welcome mat for you,
too—if you can afford the $500-and-up
nightly room rates.

GREAT ITINERARIES

WEEKEND IN PARADISE (ISLAND)

Day 1: Beach It

With lots of direct flights from major U.S. airports, Paradise Island is the perfect long-weekend getaway for those who want their beach with a side of big-city culture. On your first day, get settled into your hotel, then hit the sand. If you'd like a game of pickup volleyball or a parasailing excursion, head to Cabbage Beach, where the music and the crowds are hopping; if you're after more sedate sunbathing, just walk along the beach away from the hotels. For dinner, try Dune at the One & Only Ocean Club or one of the 35 restaurants in the Atlantis complex. Finish the night at Atlantis's casino or at the pulsating nightclub Aura, just upstairs. The bars and dance clubs on Bay Street in Nassau, such as the massive indoor/outdoor Club Waterloo, also promise to be a great time.

Day 2: City Break

Get oriented with downtown Nassau. In Rawson Square, a popular meeting place between the wharf and the bridge, skip the horse-drawn surreys and go on one of the daily walking tours; official guides dressed in traditional batik vests offer a choice of three itineraries that recall the city's colonial past as a British outpost, touring mansions, cathedrals, forts, and prim-and-proper government buildings. In the afternoon, type-A personalities who can handle noise and crowds should do some friendly haggling with the hair braiders and souvenir sellers at the straw market; others might be better off ducking into some of the chic boutiques and duty-free shops along Bay and Parliament streets. For dinner, instead of a five-star extravaganza, try one of the local haunts at Arawak Cay, where cooks pull conch from their shells and make fresh conch salad as you watch.

Day 3: Sporting & Relaxing

Depending on whether you prefer land- or water-based adventures, book an early tee time at one of Nassau's championship courses, or a morning snorkel or scuba tour. Beginners will enjoy the shallow reefs near Rose Island, though expert divers may prefer a more challenging dive, such as the cliff at Lyford Cay's Dropoff, where your dive partners might include giant grouper, hogfish, and rockfish. After all that strenuous activity, an afternoon at the spa is in order, and you'll still have plenty of time to get back to your room and dress for dinner.

Optional Add-Ons

Everyone except die-hard city slickers will have seen enough of Nassau and Paradise Island after three days, so head for one of the remote Out Islands if you have another few days to spend in the Bahamas. Our top picks are Eleuthera and Harbour Island. On the morning of Day 4, catch the fast ferry that delivers you to Harbour Island in about two hours, then walk, rent a golf cart, or catch a taxi to the Harbour Island resort where you'll base yourself for the next few nights. On Day 5, stick around pretty, serene Dunmore Town, which could pass for a New England village if it weren't for all the palms and hibiscus. On Day 6, explore the neighboring island of Eleuthera, making sure not to miss the famous Glass Window Bridge, a narrow strip of the island where the Atlantic meets the Caribbean in a swirl of turquoise, indigo, and aqua waves. On Day 7, you'll have time for a leisurely breakfast—perhaps at local favorite Arthur's Bakery & Cafe—before catching a puddle jumper for Nassau and connecting to your flight home.

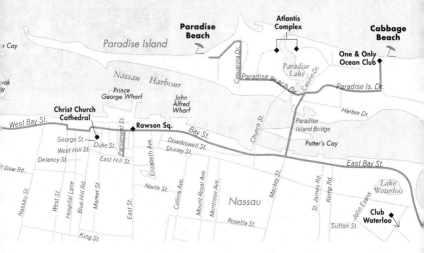

our Out Island leg is at the end of your
cation, book the earliest possible flight
ck to Nassau so you'll have time to make
ur connection back home; Out Island air
vice has improved in recent years, but
ays are still frustratingly frequent.

Green

e Tiamo Resort in Andros sets the stan-
rd for eco-resorts in the Bahamas and
e Caribbean. Guests of the resort, which
s designed to have minimal impact on
e environment, can indulge in a pleth-
a of eco-activities including bone fishing,
orkeling, biologist-led nature walks, and
ean kayaking.

w large Bahamian resorts can be con-
ered eco-friendly, but the mega Atlan-
has coined its own phrase and concept:
ie Tourism. They've teamed up with
al dive operator Stuart Cove's to pro-
le marine-based activities, and a portion
revenue from the Reef Atlantis complex
l go towards the restoration of a nearby
al reef.

e Family Islands offer the kind of scen-
most eco-friendly tourists are look-
; for, and more and more of the small
orts there are doing what they can to be
re environmentally sustainable.

Contact the Bahamas National Trust
(☎242/393–1317, *www.bnt.bs*) to find
out about nature walks, or try one of Bahamas Outdoor Ecoventures' hiking, biking,
or bird watching expeditions (☎242/362–
1574, ⊕*www.bahamasoutdoors.com*).

TIPS

■ Water taxis are a fun way to travel
between Paradise Island and Nassau, but
the departure schedules are definitely on
island time—rather than sticking to posted
schedules, many operators seem to wait
until the boat is full. Also, water taxis only
run during daylight hours.

■ For taxi fares and for shopping at places
like the straw market, bring lots of small
bills; drivers and vendors either won't have
change for big bills—or will claim not to in
hopes of getting a bigger tip or a higher
price for that T-shirt.

■ U.S. money is used interchangeably with
Bahamian dollars on a one-to-one exchange
rate, but spend any Bahamian dollars you
get as change first; you'll lose money when
you convert Bahamian bills back to U.S. dollars on the way home. Don't try to haggle
at upscale Nassau shops, including those at
the resorts; prices are set and not subject to
being talked down.

ISLAND FINDER

	NEW PROVIDENCE & PARADISE ISLANDS	GRAND BAHAMA ISLAND	THE ABACOS	ELEUTHERA	HARBOUR ISLAND	THE EXUMAS	THE OTHER OUT ISLANDS
Beaches							
Activities & Sports	●	●	●	◐	◐	●	●
Deserted		◐	◐	●		◐	●
Party Scene	●	◐			●		
Pink Sand				◐	●		◐
City Life							
Crowds	●	◐			◐		
Urban Development	●	●					
Entertainment							
Bahamian Cultural Events & Sights	●	◐	◐		◐		
Hot Restaurant Scene	●	◐		◐	●		
Nightlife	●	◐			◐		
Shopping	●	●	◐		◐	◐	
Spas	●	◐				◐	
Casinos	●	◐				◐	
Lodging							
Luxury Hotels & Resorts	●	●	◐	◐	●	◐	◐
Condos	●	◐	◐	◐	◐	◐	◐
Nature							
Wildlife	◐	●	●	◐		◐	●
Eco-tourism	●	●	●	◐		●	●
Sports							
Golf	●	●	◐			●	
Scuba & Snorkeling	●	●	●	●	●	●	●
Fishing	●	●	●	●	●	●	●

●: noteworthy; ◐: some; Nothing: little or none

CTIVITY	SAVE	SPLURGE
Dining on Paradise Island	So long as everyone in your group can settle on a dish or two, **Carmines** (242/363–3000 ext 29, www.atlantis.com) in Marina Village is a great deal. Italian food is served up family style, which means huge portions to share. Desserts, like the chocolate cannoli and the tiramisu are wonderful, so save room and order your own.	For the ultimate in fine dining, try **Café Martinique**, also in Marina Village. Select your courses from the exquisite menu which includes a market price mixed seafood appetizer and Chateaubriand (130) for two. Or order the chef's tasting menu for $145 per person.
Underwater Adventures	Pick up a snorkel and mask from your hotel kiosk or nearest beach stand and hit the nearest beach. The northern coast of New Providence, where most resorts are located, is lined with easy-to-access coral reefs.	Experienced divers can explore the 25 mi Tongue of the Ocean. This span of water just off the east coast of Andros gets up to 3,000 ft deep and can be seen from space. **Stuart Cove's Dive Bahamas** (800/879–9832 www.stuartcove.com) offers a one-of-a-kind Out Island Seafari for $185 per person.
Shopping	Hit the **Straw Market** on Bay Street where bartering for a good deal is all part of the fun. It's the only place in the islands where negotiating the price is accepted. Straw bags, beaded necklaces, t-shirts, fun souvenirs, and shells abound.	**Bay Street, Marina Village** on Paradise Island, and the main shopping court at **Atlantis** are lined with stores selling many of the world's most exclusive brands. A duty-free regime ensures that even when splurging, you'll often land a deal.
Night on the Town	Most of the big resorts on Paradise Island and Cable Beach have live entertainment in their lobby or bars. Drinks can be a bit pricey in these properties, but there's no charge for admission and usually no obligation to order a round.	**Aura Nightclub**, upstairs from the casino at Atlantis, is one of the hottest night spots in the country. Admission can range from nothing to $100, drinks cost a pretty penny, and tables are only available to groups buying a bottle of top shelf liquor.
Romantic Sunset	Order a drink and sit outside at **Compass Point Restaurant and Hotel**. Overlooking the ocean, their extended bar serves up great drinks and food, as well as the best vantage point for a romantic Bahamian sunset Nassau has to offer.	Sign up for one of the various evening boat cruises along **Nassau Harbour**. The romantic night time sailing with **Flying Cloud** is relaxing and romantic. Hot and cold hors d'oeuvres are served, but private dinner cruises can be arranged by special request.

WHEN TO GO

The Bahamas enjoys sunny days, refreshing breezes, and moderate-to-warm temperatures with little change from season to season. That said, the most pleasant time to visit is from December through May, when the temperature averages 70°F–75°F. It stands to reason that hotel prices during this period are at their highest—around 30% higher than during the less popular times. The rest of the year is hot and humid and prone to tropical storms; the temperature hovers around 80°F–85°F. Hurricane season is from about June 1 through November 30, with greatest risk for a storm from August through October. Meteorology being what it is, you generally know days in advance if the area you're traveling to will be affected. Check with your hotel if a storm is on the horizon—the islands are so spread out, that one island could be experiencing hurricane force winds, while it's nice and sunny in another.

Whether you want to join it or avoid it, be advised that spring break takes place between the end of February and mid-April. This means a lot of vacationing college students, beach parties, sports events, and entertainment.

Climate

What follows are average daily maximum and minimum temperatures for Nassau. Freeport's temperatures are nearly the same: a degree or two cooler in the spring and fall, and a degree or two warmer in the summer. As you head down to the more southern islands, expect temperatures to be about a degree or two warmer than the capital year round.

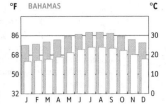

The Bahamas is known for its fishing tournaments and sailing regattas, but it's a uniquely Bahamian event—the Carnaval-like Junkanoo—that many travelers plan their trips around.

December

The **Authentically Bahamian Christmas Trade Show** on Cable Beach showcases conch shell jewelry, straw handbags, batiks, and other island-made crafts. Other Christmas traditions include **Festival Noel**, an annual holiday fest featuring music, crafts, wine tastings, and food at the Rand Nature Center on Grand Bahama Island, and the **Abaco Christmas Festival** in Marsh Harbour, where the highlight is a parade of boats decked out in lights and tropical flowers.

Junkanoo is held on Boxing Day on Bay and Shirley streets. Parades start just after midnight and typically carry-on well into the late morning.

The **Bahamas International Film Festival** in Nassau celebrates cinema in paradise, with screenings, receptions, and movie-industry panels.

Christmas Day and **Boxing Day**, December 25 and 26, are both public holidays. Other annual December doings in Nassau include the **Police Band Beat Retreat, Night of Christmas Music, Junior Junkanoo Parade,** and **New Year's Eve Party.**

January

Most churches ring in the New Year with a **New Year's Midnight Service.** Afterward, the Junkanoo festivities continue with the **New Year's Day Junkanoo Parade** in downtown Nassau. Less extensive celebrations take place in the Out Islands and in the Turks and Caicos—also on January 1, a public holiday. Later in the month, kids get into the act with the **Junior Junkanoo Parade** on Grand Bahama and in the Out Islands.

The **New Year's Sailing Regatta** at Montagu Bay, Nassau, features competition among Bahamian-built sloops, whereas the **Staniel Cay Annual New Year's Day Cruising Regatta** in the Exumas marks the finale of a five-day celebration.

Pomp and pageantry take over when the **Supreme Court** opens in Nassau with the Chief Justice inspecting the Royal Bahamas Police Force Guard-of-Honor, accompanied by the acclaimed Bahamas Police Force Band.

ON THE CALENDAR

	Basketball legend Michael Jordan hosts his annual **Michael Jordan Celebrity Invitational Golf Tournament** at the One & Only Ocean Club on Paradise Island. The **Breitling Golf Tournament** is a week of meets on Grand Bahama Island that draws a roster of professional and amateur golfers.
	The second installment of the **Bahamas Wahoo Tournament** draws competitive anglers from the Bahamas and Florida.
February	**Miami to Nassau Race Week** comprises three days of international sailboat championship racing. The **Valentine's Day Sailing Regatta,** a weekend-long event at Montagu Bay in Nassau, is a smaller, yet still competitive race.
	The **Bahamas Wahoo Tournament** concludes, with the last of its three legs.
	Also in the Out Islands, in late February or early March, Exuma begins its **George Town Cruising Regatta.**
	Beginning in February and continuing through April, **whale-watching trips** depart from several islands in the Turks and Caicos.
	At the end of February, the **Annual Alton Lowe Art Exhibition** in Nassau features pieces by the famed Bahamian painter; sometimes guest artists also display works.
	The **E. Clement Bethel National Arts Festival,** a show by one of the islands' foremost painters, kicks off a nationwide series of events spotlighting music, dance, drama, and Junkanoo; the festivities take place throughout spring.
SPRING	The tourism ministry sponsors beach parties, music, games, and other celebrations on Grand Bahama and Paradise Island during **spring break** for vacationing college students.
March	The annual **Red Cross Fair** at the Queen Elizabeth Sports Centre entertains kids and adults with games, carnival rides, local delicacies, and entertainment.
	In Nassau, watch dogs of all classes compete at the **International Dog Show & Obedience Trials** at the Botanical Gardens.
	The weeklong **Bacardi Rum Billfish Tournament,** which rotates around Grand Bahama and the Out Islands, kicks off the Bahamas billfish season.

Local musicians, Junkanoo groups, and special cultural demonstrations are on tap at the three-day **Bahamian Music and Heritage Festival** in the Exumas.

Hope Town's annual **Heritage Day** celebrates the history of the Loyalist settlement on Elbow Cay, with traditional songs, speeches and exhibits on historical topics, and a boat parade. In Nassau, there's more historical reflection at the **Fort Charlotte Heritage Festival,** a two-day series of events sponsored by Bahamian museums and the tourism department.

April	Port Lucaya Marina hosts the **Dolphin/Tuna Classic Tournament** on Grand Bahama.

The annual **Bahamas White Marlin Open** at Treasure Cay, Great Abaco, is an all-release tournament, with plenty of parties to complement the fishing. The **Bahamas Billfish Championship,** consisting of several tournaments throughout the Out Islands, also begins this month.

The **Coconut Festival** in Grand Bahama's Pelican Point settlement includes coconut food sampling, coconut tree climbing, and other activities.

The Royal Nassau Sailing Club presents the **Snipe Bacardi Cup & Dudley Gambling Series,** an annual race.

A Junkanoo rushout (parading in the streets), live music, fashion shows, and, of course, traditional foods are all part of the agenda at the **South Eleuthera Homecoming Festival** in Rock Sound. The **Bahamas National Youth Choir** puts on its annual concert of classical, gospel, and original and traditional Bahamian songs at the Dundas Centre for the Performing Arts in Nassau.

Develop a strong case of yacht envy at the **International Yacht and Jet Show** on Providence and Paradise islands, where multimillion-dollar craft are on display.

One of the biggest annual festivals in the Bahamas, the **Exuma Family Island Regatta** attracts native sloops from all over the nation for races in Elizabeth Harbour; parties and festivals abound.

May	There are several fishing tournaments in the Out Islands this month, including the continuation of the **Bahamas Billfish Championship** and the **Bimini Festival of Champions.**

ON THE
CALENDAR

		The **Island Roots Festival** celebrates Bahamian traditions with an outdoor party on tiny Green Turtle Cay, while the **Cat Island Heritage Festival** brings a weekend of performing arts and Bahamian food to Arthur's Town on Cat Island.
SUMMER	June	**Labour Day,** the first Friday of the month, and **Whit Monday** are public holidays in the Bahamas. Labour Day is marked by parades and picnics throughout the nation.

Yes, more fishing tournaments: the continuation of the **Bahamas Billfish Tournament** is a major one this month.

The **Long Island Sailing Regatta** in Salt Pond, Long Island, has sloop races, a yacht parade, and lots of activity—both on and off the water.

The **Cat Island Rake 'N' Scrape Festival** celebrates the Bahamas' indigenous rake 'n' scrape music.

Three days of crab races, cook-offs, live rake 'n' scrape music, and a performance by the Bahamas Police Band comprise the **Crab Fest** in Fresh Creek, Andros.

Nassau/Paradise Island Junkanoo Summer Festival has become the premier island event of the summer, with two months' worth of festivities starting in June, including live performances, crafts, kids' programs, fabulous local dishes, and a costumed Junkanoo Rushout each night. The main venue is Arawak Cay, which is transformed each weekend into a heritage village.

Town is the scene of the four-day **Eleuthera Pineapple Festival,** with a Junkanoo parade, crafts displays, tours of pineapple farms, games, contests, and sports events—as well as an opportunity to sample what Eleuthera natives proclaim to be the sweetest pineapple in the world.

Sailing sloops from throughout the country meet at the **Grand Bahama Sailing Regatta,** in the exciting "Championship of the Seas." On-shore festivities take place at Taíno Beach and include Junkanoo Rushout parades, dancing, music, and food.

Grand Turk's **Conch Carnival** celebrates the Turks and Caicos' favorite culinary icon with four days of music, dancing, kayak races, and conch-fritter eating contests.

July	The Bahamas' most important public holiday falls on July 10—**Independence Day,** which was established in 1973 and marks the end of 300 years of British rule. There's a progression of flag ceremonies on each of the islands, beginning the week before the holiday and culminating in New Providence on July 10. **Independence Week** is celebrated throughout the Bahamas with regattas, fishing tournaments, and a plethora of parties.
	Eleuthera offers three **Homecoming Festivals** in Savannah Sound, Governor's Harbour, and Bluff; all are great ways to mingle with locals over food, drink, games, and general partying.
	Regatta Time in Abaco is an eight-day event stretching over several islands, with races and plenty of onshore parties.
	Goombay Festivals—traditional summertime parties with dance troupes and musical groups—take place throughout the summer in Andros and Abaco.
August	**Emancipation Day,** which marks when the English freed Bahamian and Turks and Caicos slaves in 1834, is a public holiday celebrated on the first Monday in August (always August 1 in the Turks and Caicos).
	In the Turks and Caicos, August brings the monthlong **Caicos Classic All-Release Fishing Tournament. Provo Summer Festival** spans a week of pageants and cultural shows in Providenciales. The **Turks and Caicos Music and Cultural Festival** brings together international and Bahamian music stars for several days of outdoor concerts.
	The Nassau **Fox Hill Festival** pays tribute to Emancipation with church services, Junkanoo Rushout parades, music, cookouts, games, and other festivities.
	The annual **Cat Island Regatta** includes parties, fashion shows, live music, games, dancing, and lots of island cooking.
	Swimming, biking, and running make up the **Great Nassau Triathlon,** which draws more than 200 international competitors.

ON THE CALENDAR

FALL	
September	More than 200 contestants participate in the grueling **Great Abaco Triathlon,** which includes swimming, running, and biking. The Abaco islands are also the setting for the **All Abaco Sailing Regatta,** a weekend event highlighted by native sloop racing, Junkanoo festivities, dominos competitions, and a food fest.
October	The **Annual Kalik Junkanoo Rushout** gives islanders and visitors on Grand Bahama a reason to party without waiting for the Junkanoo holidays on Taíno Beach.
	The annual **McLean's Town Conch Cracking Contest,** which includes 20 days of conch-cracking competitions, games, entertainment, and good eating, takes place on Grand Bahama Island as it has for more than 30 years. Eat and drink your way around the world at the **International Cultural Weekend,** hosted at the Botanic Gardens the third weekend of October.
	Discovery Day, commemorating the landing of Columbus in the islands in 1492, is observed on October 12, a public holiday. You may hear some refer to this holiday as National Heroes Day, intended to honor a wider range of explorers and adventurers. (On Turks and Caicos Islands, it's known simply as Columbus Day.)
	The **North Eleuthera/Harbour Island Sailing Regatta** occupies five days of busy sailing.
November	Top chefs turn native ingredients into haute cuisine at the **Bahamas Culinary Wine & Food Festival** in Nassau, with many Bahamian resorts and restaurants among those competing and also sharing dishes with visitors. **Christmas Jollification** is an ongoing arts-and-crafts fair with Bahamian Christmas crafts, food, and music held at the Retreat in Nassau.
	On Grand Bahama the annual **Conchman Triathlon** is a swimming-running-bicycling competition for amateurs that raises funds for local charities. Miss it? The **EnduraSport Grand Bahama Triathlon** is also in November.
	The **Bahamas Wahoo Tournament,** a series of three fishing tournaments in the waters around Grand Bahama and the Abacos, begins its winter run.

New Providence Island

WORD OF MOUTH

"We were at Atlantis in January. It reminded me of a combination of Disneyland and Las Vegas, but about twice as expensive."

—margyb

"A short walk from Atlantis will get you to the Potters Cay (dock area) where they will prepare a fresh conch salad before your very eyes. I mean pull the conch out of the shell, dice it up along with veggies, and then squeeze the fresh lime over the top. It was a cheap lunch with some built in entertainment. VERY casual and very 'local.'"

—Michaelpl

Updated
by Jessica
Robertson

AN INCONGRUOUS MIX OF GLITZY casinos and quiet, shady lanes; trendy, up-to-date resorts and tiny settlements that recall a distant, simpler age; land development unrivaled elsewhere in the Bahamas and vast stretches of untrampled territory. This is New Providence Island, a grab bag of everything one could hope for in a vacation destination. The island, home to two-thirds of all Bahamians, offers fast-paced living, nightlife that goes on until dawn, and high-end shopping strips that feature the most exclusive brands found anywhere. And when all the hustle and bustle becomes too much, there are hundreds of years of history to explore at leisure in art galleries, and quiet stretches of sandy white beaches where the only noise is the waves rolling in and out and the occasional seagull flying overhead.

In the course of its history, the island has weathered the comings and goings of lawless pirates, Spanish invaders, slave-holding British Loyalists who fled the United States after the Revolutionary War, Civil War–era Confederate blockade runners, and Prohibition rumrunners. Nevertheless, New Providence remains most influenced by England, which sent its first royal governor to the island in 1718. Although Bahamians won government control in 1967 and independence six years later, British influence is felt to this day.

Nassau is the nation's capital and transportation hub, as well as the banking and commercial center. Visitors need look no further than Nassau's many duty-free shops for proof of the island's commercial vitality. The fortuitous combination of tourist-friendly enterprise, tropical weather, and island flavor with a European overlay has not gone unnoticed: each year more than a million cruise-ship passengers arrive at Nassau's Prince George Wharf, on short trips from Florida or as a stopover on cruises to ports farther south in the Caribbean. In keeping with New Providence's commercial spirit, Festival Place on Prince George Wharf offers much more than maps and information—it was designed to showcase the work of Bahamian artisans, and exhibits the handmade arts and crafts of more than 45 vendors. Another joy for hard-bargaining shoppers is Nassau's Bay Street shops. A 2001 fire destroyed the Straw Market, a premier Nassau shopping attraction, and it still has not been rebuilt. In the meantime, you can spar with many of the same vendors at a temporary straw market site, housed under a huge tent on the western end of Bay Street.

A mile or so east of town, under the bridge from Paradise Island, Potter's Cay Dock is another colorful scene: boats bring catches of fish and conch, and open-air stalls carry fresh fruit, vegetables, and local foods—freshly made conch salad predominates. If the daytime bustle isn't enough, the nighttime action at the island's nightclubs and casinos can keep you going into the wee hours of the morning.

Be sure to leave some time for outdoor activities, one of the area's major draws. From shark diving and snorkeling to bicycle tours, horseback riding, tennis, and golf, active pursuits abound in Nassau. Avid water-sports fans will find a range of possibilities, including water skiing, sailing, windsurfing, and deep-sea fishing. Or simply cruise the

NEW PROVIDENCE'S TOP 5

Changing of the Guard. Every other Saturday, enjoy the pomp and pageantry at Government House, including the music of the world-renowned Royal Bahamas Police Force Band.

Conch Salad. Order a bowl of this spicy national dish and watch in amazement as the fresh ingredients are sliced and diced at a dizzying pace. Enjoy the tasty treat at the Arawak Cay fish shacks.

Junkanoo. If you can't make it for the Christmastime parades, join the

rush at Marina Village on Paradise Island Friday and Saturday nights for a smaller-scale celebration.

People-to-People Program. Your Bahamian hosts will share their favorite island experiences and often invite you home for a truly authentic meal.

Surrey Tour. Pick your favorite horse and carriage and enjoy a casual tour through the streets of historic Nassau.

clear Bahamian waters for a day trip or an evening ride. Although the resorts have a great deal to offer, it would be a shame not to venture into the incredible alfresco world that is the Bahamas' calling card.

Most hotels are either in Cable Beach or on Paradise Island; just outside downtown Nassau, these tourist areas offer unfettered beach access and proximity to casinos. Cable Beach, so named because the Bahamas' first transatlantic telegraph cable was laid here, is a crescent-shaped stretch of sand west of Nassau, rimmed by resorts and the Crystal Palace Casino.Although by no means secluded—a string of high-profile resorts rub up against each other on the shore—Cable Beach is one of New Providence Island's prettiest stretches. The strip is undergoing a major transformation: Over the next few years, roads will be relocated, canals dug, and new hotels, shops, and entertainment centers created. Once completed, the Baha Mar complex is expected to rival megaresort Atlantis on Paradise Island.

P.I. (as locals call the island) is connected to downtown Nassau's east end by a pair of bridges, one leading to the island, and the original, just east, heading back to Nassau. Its status as an unspoiled alternative to the glitz of Cable Beach is long gone; Paradise Island has been irrevocably changed by Atlantis. The tallest building in the Bahamas is home to a beachfront resort complete with a gamut of dining options, the largest casino in the Bahamas or the Caribbean, and some of the region's fanciest shops. Most memorable, however, are the water-based activities, slides, and aquariums. Love it or despise it, it's today's face of Paradise.

PLORING NEW PROVIDENCE

Tourist action is concentrated on New Providence's northeastern side, mostly in the capital city of Nassau and nearby Paradise Island and Cable Beach. You could easily spend your entire trip in those three areas, but if you're staying for more than a few days, you may want to see the rest of this 7- by 21-mi island. This can even be done in a single day, making occasional stops. The terrain is flat, and getting around is easy, except in the Old City of Nassau, where many sights such as Government House and the National Art Gallery are up a steep hill. Renting a car is your best bet for trips around the island—or pick up a scooter for a more adventurous ride. Traffic in Nassau is bumper-to-bumper except on Sunday and after 7 PM weekdays. The frequent jitneys, 32-seat air-conditioned buses, are a better and cheaper choice on routes such as Cable Beach to downtown Nassau. Fare is only $1 each way, and it's a nice way to see the sights and chat with other riders.

ABOUT THE RESTAURANTS

New Providence's high-caliber dining ranges from Continental fare to ethnic specialties, including Bahamian, Mediterranean, Asian, Latin, and European eats. Dining out is a major activity, especially now that internationally renowned chefs have started moving to the Bahamas to hone their skills. Fresh fish is the staple for tourists and locals alike. Most popular are grouper, snapper, and dolphin (the fish, not the mammal; also called mahi-mahi), but tuna, wahoo, and conch are also well liked. Restaurateurs rely on local fishermen and Nassau wholesalers to stock their kitchens.

ABOUT THE HOTELS

Accommodations in New Providence cater to myriad tastes and budgets, from swanky luxury hotels on Paradise Island to small guest houses in the western and southern reaches of the island. Consider what type of vacation you want—the ambience, amenities, service, and activities—then study the options to determine which best suits your style and needs. Do you prefer to be in the middle of the action or on a secluded property away from the hubbub? Must the beach be outside your doorstep, or are you willing to drive or take public transportation? Are on-property restaurants and a casino essential to your vacation? If convenience and luxury are your top priorities, an all-inclusive on Cable Beach or Paradise Island is probably best for you. If you want to mix with the locals and experience a little more of Bahamian culture, choose a hotel in downtown Nassau.

WHAT IT COSTS IN U.S. DOLLARS				
	¢	$	$$	$$$	$$$$
RESTAURANTS	under $10	$10–$20	$20–$30	$30–$40	over $40
HOTELS	under $100	$100–$200	$200–$300	$300–$400	over $400

Restaurant prices are for a main course at dinner, excluding gratuity, typically 15%, which is often automatically added to the bill. Hotel prices are for two people in a standard double room in high season, excluding service charges and 6%–12% tax.

IF YOU LIKE

BEACH BUMMING

Bahamian beaches make an indelible impression: think warm, blue-green waves lapping up against powdery white- or pink-sand beaches. New Providence beaches, though less secluded than those on the Out Islands, still tempt travelers with their balmy breezes and aquamarine water. Choose between the more remote beaches of the western end of New Providence Island, action-packed strips on Cable Beach, or public beaches in downtown Nassau, such as the Western Esplanade at the mouth of the harbor where you can watch the cruise ships and Haitian sloops come in, and the road-side Saunders Beach (just east of Cable Beach), lined by shady casuarina trees. Try Love Beach for snorkeling—here you'll find 40 acres of coral and forests of fern known as the Sea Gardens.

A CULINARY PLAYGROUND

New Providence is paradise for seafood lovers, adventurous eaters, gourmands, and meat-and-potatoes people alike. The island has a restaurant for every price range—and most every palate. Fresh seafood abounds, in addition to world-class Continental fare and ethnic eateries, including Bahamian, Indian, Chinese, French, and Greek. The beauty of dining in New Providence is that you can eat at a grungy local dive for one meal, and feast in a celebrity-chef restaurant for the next.

A FEAST FOR THE EYES

Downtown Nassau intrigues travelers of all types. Shoppers, history buffs, culture mavens, and strollers all seem to find their niche in the blur of colors and aromas. Wander through the straw market, chat with the vendors, then bargain for a hat to shield yourself from the midday sun. Linger in Parliament Square, where pink, colonnaded government buildings from the late 1700s and towering palm trees create an old-world ambience. Immerse yourself in the world of booty and high-seas adventures at the Pirates of Nassau interactive museum. Visit Festival Place, adjacent to the Prince George Wharf, to buy handcrafted souvenirs or designer purses. Or sample local culinary specialties such as conch fritters, and take a stroll in one of the lush public gardens.

TIMING

With the warm Gulf Stream currents swirling and balmy trade winds blowing, the Bahamas is an appealing year-round destination. The temperature usually hovers in the 70s and 80s, and rarely gets above 90°F on a midsummer's day or below 60°F on a winter's night. June to October tend to be the hottest and wettest months, although rain is often limited to periodic showers.

The best time to visit New Providence is December to May, especially if you're escaping the cold. Be aware that tropical depressions, tropical storms, and hurricanes are a possibility in New Providence during the Atlantic hurricane season from early June to late November.

AROUND THE ISLAND

Life in the Bahamas is not *all* about glorious laziness. Nassau, th country's capital, is a bustling city on New Providence Island wit shops, nightclubs, and an enviable array of restaurants, glitzy casino and posh hotels. Even in Nassau, though, there are quiet byways an shady lanes where you can escape the main tourist drags' tumult. Sho 'til you drop or wander past buildings that reveal the capital's coloni history. Dine on French cuisine in an elegant restaurant or rub shou ders with Bahamians at Arawak Cay, or the "Fish Fry," as they call i Drop your dollars in a clangorous casino or escape to Paradise Island secluded Versailles Gardens. Boogie the night away in a rowdy club o take a nighttime stroll along the lush landscaped median along Cab Beach, the daytime crowds just a memory.

Of course, you can flee the hurly-burly altogether and head straight fo the water. You'll be hard-pressed to find yourself alone on a stretch c sand, but take heart—relatively secluded beaches do exist, they're ju harder to come by.

NASSAU

Nassau's sheltered harbor bustles with cruise-ship activity, while block away, Bay Street's sidewalks are crowded with shoppers wh duck into air-conditioned boutiques and relax on benches in the sha of mahogany and lignum vitae trees. Shops angle for tourist dolla with fine imported goods at duty-free prices, yet you'll find a hanc ful of stores overflowing with authentic Bahamian crafts, food suj plies, and other delights. Most of Nassau's historic sites are centere around downtown.

With its thoroughly revitalized downtown, and the revamped Britis Colonial Hilton leading the way, Nassau is recapturing some of its pa glamour. Nevertheless, modern influences are very apparent: fancy re taurants, suave clubs, and trendy coffeehouses have popped up ever where. These changes come partly in response to the growing numbe of upper-crust crowds that now supplement the spring breakers an cruise passengers who have traditionally flocked to Nassau. Of cours you can still find a wild club or a rowdy bar, but you can also sip ca puccino while viewing contemporary Bahamian art or dine by candl light beneath prints of old Nassau, serenaded by soft, island-inspire calypso music. Coffeehouses advertise art exhibitions and bistro night and along the streets you'll find elegant stores that many bigger tow would be lucky to have.

SIGHTS TO SEE

⓭ **Bahamas Historical Society Museum.** For those interested in the country origins and life before European settlement, this small collection co tains archaeological, historical, and anthropological artifacts. Th museum is staffed by volunteers and is often closed during posted op hours, so call ahead. ⊠ *Shirley St. and Elizabeth Ave.* ☎ 242/322–42

GREAT ITINERARIES

Numbers in the text correspond to numbers in the margins and on the Nassau and Paradise Island map.

IF YOU HAVE 3 DAYS

You can take in most of the markets, gardens, and historic sites of **Nassau ❶–⓰** in a single day. A good starting point is **Rawson Square ❶**, in the heart of the commercial area. Do your shopping in the morning, hitting **Bay Street,** the capital's main street, and Festival Place at **Prince George Wharf ❷**. To avoid the afternoon heat, visit the **National Art Gallery ⓰**, checking out the colonial architecture along the way. Or sit in the shade at one of Nassau's lush public gardens. For a change of pace, spend the next day relaxing at the beach. Decide whether you'd prefer a secluded stretch of sand or a beach right in the middle of the action, such as **Cable Beach**—New Providence has both. Tour Paradise Island on the following day. Try your luck at the casino, and explore the giant aquariums (non–resort guests will have to pay a hefty $32 for adults or $22 for kids 12 and under to tour them), shops, and restaurants of the **Atlantis ⓱** megaresort.

IF YOU HAVE 5 DAYS

Follow the suggested three-day itinerary, and on Day 4, head north for lunch and a bit of local flavor at **Arawak Cay**. Visit nearby **Potter's Cay**, where you can find the freshest seafood and produce on the island. On your final day, drive to **Western New Providence**, stopping for lunch at Goodfellow Farms on your way to quaint **Adelaide Village**.

IF YOU HAVE 7 DAYS

A week will give you plenty of time to explore most areas of New Providence and **Paradise Island ⓱–⓴**. For your first five days, follow the itinerary above. On Day 6, go on a sailing cruise or a guided tour—choose your outfitter and trip based on which area you'd like to see: **Eastern New Providence** or **Western New Providence** and the **South Coast**. Or keep it mellow and spend more time at the beach and in the water. For your final evening, splurge at one of New Providence's fancier restaurants or hit the Nassau nightclub scene. Spend the next day at a spa, finish up that last-minute shopping, or take in your final rays before the trip home.

⊕ *www.bahamashistoricalsociety.com* ✉$1 ☉ *Mon., Tues, Thurs, Fri. 10–4, Sat. 10–noon.*

★ ❽ **Balcony House.** A charming 18th-century landmark—a pink two-story house named aptly for its overhanging balcony—this is the oldest wooden residential structure in Nassau, and its furnishings and design recapture the elegance of a bygone era. A mahogany staircase, believed to have been salvaged from a ship during the 19th century, is a highlight of the interior. A guided tour through this fascinating building is an hour well spent. ✉*Market St. and Trinity Pl.* ☎*242/302–2621* ✉*Donations accepted* ☉ *Mon.–Wed. and Fri. 9:30–4:30, Thurs. 9:30–1.*

❾ **Central Bank of the Bahamas.** The Central Bank of the Bahamas monitors and regulates the country's financial institutions. The building's cornerstone was laid by Prince Charles on July 9, 1973, during the

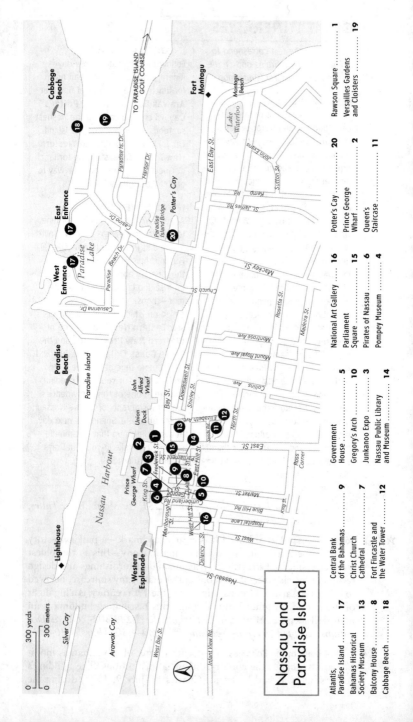

Nassau and Paradise Island

0 ___ 300 yards
0 ___ 300 meters

Silver Cay

Arawak Cay

Lighthouse

Nassau Harbour

Western Esplanade

Paradise Beach

Paradise Island

Union Dock

John Alfred Wharf

Prince George Wharf

Cabbage Beach

West Entrance

East Entrance

Paradise Lake

Paradise Island Bridge

Potter's Cay

TO PARADISE ISLAND GOLF COURSE

Fort Montagu

Lake Waterloo

Montagu Beach

Casuarina Dr.

Paradise Beach Dr.

Casino Dr.

Paradise Is. Dr.

Harbour Dr.

East Bay St.

John Evans

Sutton St.

St. James Rd.

Kemp Rd.

Mackey St.

Church St.

Rosetta St.

Madeira St.

Montrose Ave.

Mount Royal Ave.

Collins Ave.

Shirley St.

Dowdeswell St.

Bay St.

East St.

North St.

Ross Corner

Elizabeth Ave.

Sands Rd.

East Hill St.

Parliament St.

Frederick St.

King St.

George St.

Market St.

Cumberland Rd.

Deveaux St.

Blue Hill Rd.

Market St.

Hospital Lane

Delancy St.

West Hill St.

Marlborough St.

West St.

Nassau St.

West Bay St.

Infant View Rd.

Blue Hill Rd.

Legend

Atlantis, Paradise Island 17
Bahamas Historical Society Museum 13
Balcony House 8
Cabbage Beach 18

Central Bank of the Bahamas 9
Christ Church Cathedral 7
Fort Fincastle and the Water Tower 12

Government House 5
Gregory's Arch 10
Junkanoo Expo 3
Nassau Public Library and Museum 14

National Art Gallery 16
Parliament Square 15
Pirates of Nassau 6
Pompey Museum 4

Potter's Cay 20
Prince George Wharf 2
Queen's Staircase 11

Rawson Square 1
Versailles Gardens and Cloisters 19

country's Independence celebrations, and the bank was opened by Queen Elizabeth II in February 1975 (you can find commemorations of these events at the back of the building). Periodically, exhibits on two floors of the lobby display emerging and established Bahamian artists' work. ⊠ *Market St. and Trinity Pl.* ☎ *242/322–2193* ⊕ *www.centralbankbahamas.com* ⊘ *Weekdays 9:30–4:30.*

> **DID YOU KNOW?**
>
> Over 35% of Bahamians are Baptist (the islands' number-one religion), but many government ceremonies—including the opening of the Supreme Court—are held at the Anglican Christ Church Cathedral (Queen Elizabeth II has attended services here).

★ **7** **Christ Church Cathedral.** It's worth the short walk off the main thoroughfare to see the stained-glass windows of this cathedral, which was built in 1837, when Nassau officially became a city. The white pillars of the church's spacious, airy interior support ceilings beamed with dark wood handcrafted by ship builders. The crucifixion depicted in the east window's center panel is flanked by depictions of the Empty Tomb and the Ascension. Be sure to spend a few minutes in the small, flower-filled Garden of Remembrance, where stone plaques adorn the walls. Sunday mass is held at 7:30, 9, 11:15 AM, and 6 PM. Drop by the cathedral Christmas Eve and New Year's Eve for the 11 PM services to see the glorious church at night, and hear the music and choir. ⊠ *George and King Sts.* ☎ *242/322–4186* ⊘ *Daily 9–5.*

12 **Fort Fincastle and the Water Tower.** Shaped like the bow of a ship and perched near the top of the Queen's Staircase, Fort Fincastle—named for Royal Governor Lord Dunmore (Viscount Fincastle)—was completed in 1793 to be a lookout post for marauders trying to sneak into the harbor. It served as a lighthouse in the early 19th century. ⊠ *Top of Elizabeth Ave. hill, south of Shirley St.* ⊘ *Daily 8–5.*

★ **5** **Government House.** The official residence of the governor-general of the Bahamas, the personal representative of the queen since 1801, this imposing pink-and-white building on Duke Street is an excellent example of the mingling of Bahamian-British and American Colonial architecture. Its graceful columns and broad, circular drive recall the styles of Virginia or the Carolinas. But its pink color, distinctive white quoins (cross-laid cornerstones), and louvered wooden shutters (to keep out the tropical sun) are typically Bahamian. Here you can catch the crisply disciplined but beautifully flamboyant changing of the guard ceremony, which takes place every second and fourth Saturday of the month at 10 AM. The stars of the pomp and pageantry are members of the Royal Bahamas Police Force Band, who are decked out in white tunics, red-stripe navy trousers, and spiked, white pith helmets with red bands. The drummers sport leopard skins. The governor's wife hosts a tea party open to the public from 4 to 5 PM on the last Friday of the month January–May as part of the People-to-People program. Dress is casual but elegant—no shorts, jeans, or tennis shoes. Musicians, poets, and storytellers provide entertainment. ⊠ *Duke and*

George Sts. ☎242/356–5415 *ceremony schedule, 242/323–1853 tea party, 242/322–1875 Government House.*

⑩ Gregory's Arch. Named for John Gregory (royal governor 1849–54), this arch, at the intersection of Market and Duke streets, separates downtown from the "over-the-hill" neighborhood of **Grant's Town,** where much of Nassau's population lives. Grant's Town was laid out in the 1820s by Governor Lewis Grant as a settlement for freed slaves. Visitors once enjoyed late-night mingling with the locals in the small, dimly lighted bars; nowadays you should exhibit the same caution you would if you were visiting the commercial areas of a large city. Nevertheless, it's a vibrant section of town where you can rub shoulders with Bahamians at a funky take-out food stand or down-home restaurant.

③ Junkanoo Expo. Handmade floats and costumes used by revelers during the annual Bahamian Junkanoo celebration are exhibited in an old customs warehouse at the wharf's entrance. Junkanoo, which is celebrated yearly on Boxing Day (the day after Christmas) and New Year's Day, can be likened to Carnaval in Rio de Janeiro and Mardi Gras in New Orleans—although Junkanoo is family-oriented, with children in the parades and families in the stands. Visiting the Expo is the next best thing to seeing the festivities in person. The accommodating staff will tell you everything you want to know about Junkanoo, and the colorful displays speak for themselves. ⊠*Prince George Wharf* 🎟*$1* ⊙*Daily 9–5:30.*

⑭ Nassau Public Library and Museum. The octagonal building near Parliament Square was the Nassau Gaol (the old British spelling for jail), circa 1797. You're welcome to pop in and browse. The small prison cells are now lined with books. The museum has an interesting collection of historic prints and old colonial documents. Check out the small native fruit and flower museum on the second floor, and ask to see the dungeon (usually locked) under the library where you can see wall etchings of clipper ships created by prisoners. ⊠*Shirley St., between Parliament St. and Bank La.* ☎242/322–4907 🎟*Free* ⊙*Mon.–Thurs. 10–8, Fri. 10–5, Sat. 10–4.*

★ ⑯ National Art Gallery of the Bahamas. Opened in July 2003, the museum houses the works of esteemed Bahamian artists such as Max Taylor, Amos Ferguson, Brent Malone, John Cox, and Antonius Roberts. The glorious Italianate-colonial mansion, built in 1860 and restored in the 1990s, has double-tiered verandas with elegant columns. It was the residence of Sir William Doyle, the first chief justice of the Bahamas. On Thursdays during the summer, join locals on the lawn for movie night under the stars. Don't miss the museum's gift shop, where you will find books about the Bahamas and Bahamian quilts, prints, and crafts. ⊠*West and W. Hill Sts., across from St. Francis Xavier Cathedral* ☎242/328–5800 ⊕*www.nagb.org.bs* 🎟*$5, 12 and under free* ⊙*Tue.–Sat. 10–4.*

⑮ Parliament Square. Nassau is the seat of the national government. The Bahamian Parliament comprises two houses—a 16-member Senate (Upper House) and a 40-member House of Assembly (Lower House)—

and a ministerial cabinet headed by a prime minister. If the House is in session, sit in to watch lawmakers debate. Parliament Square's pink, colonnaded government buildings were constructed in the late 1700s and early 1800s by Loyalists who came to the Bahamas from North Carolina. The square is dominated

> **DID YOU KNOW?**
>
> Judges and barristers still wear wigs in court. Each Supreme Court judge has two wigs—one for the court room and one for formal occasions that require pomp and pageantry.

by a statue of a slim young Queen Victoria that was erected on her birthday, May 24, in 1905. In the immediate area are a handful of magistrates' courts. Behind the House of Assembly is the **Supreme Court.** Its four-times-a-year opening ceremonies (held the first weeks of January, April, July, and October) recall the wigs and mace-bearing pageantry of the Houses of Parliament in London. The Royal Bahamas Police Force Band is usually on hand for the event. ⊠ *Bay St.* ☎ *242/322–2041* 🔲 *Free* ⊗ *Weekdays 10–4.*

🍼 ❻ **Pirates of Nassau.** Take a journey through Nassau's pirate days in this interactive museum devoted to such notorious members of the city's past as Blackbeard, Mary Read, and Anne Bonney. Board a pirate ship, see dioramas of intrigue on the high seas, hear historical narration, and experience sound effects re-creating some of the gruesome highlights. It's a fun and educational (if slightly scary) family outing. Be sure to check out the offbeat souvenirs in the Pirate Shop, and the Pirate Pub next door. ⊠ *George and King Sts.* ☎ *242/356-3759* ⊕ *www.pirates-of-nassau.com* 🔲 *$12 adults, $6 children under 18, under 3 free* ⊗ *Mon.–Sat. 9–5.*

❹ **Pompey Museum.** The building, where slave auctions were held in the 1700s, is named for a rebel slave who lived on the Out Island of Exuma in 1830. Exhibits focus on the issues of slavery and emancipation and highlight the works of local artists. A knowledgeable, enthusiastic young staff is on hand to answer questions. ⊠ *Bay and George Sts.* ☎ *242/356-0495* ⊕ *www.antiquitiescorp.com* 🔲 *$3 adults, $2 seniors, $1 under 14.* ⊗ *Mon.–Wed. and Fri. 9:30–4:30, Sat. 10–1.*

❷ **Prince George Wharf.** The wharf that leads into Rawson Square is the first view that cruise passengers encounter after they tumble off their ships. Up to a dozen gigantic cruise ships call on Nassau at any one time, and passengers spill out onto downtown, giving Nassau an instant, and constantly replenished, surge of life. Even if you're not visiting via cruise ship, it's worth heading to Festival Place, a Bahamian village-style shopping emporium. Here you'll find booths for 45 Bahamian artisans; Internet kiosks; vendors selling diving, fishing, and day trips; scooter rentals; and an information desk offering maps, directions, and suggestions for sightseeing. You can also arrange walking tours of historic Nassau here. ⊠ *Waterfront, at Rawson Sq.*

⓫ **Queen's Staircase.** A popular early morning exercise regime for locals, the "66 Steps" (as Bahamians call them) are thought to have been carved out of a solid limestone cliff by slaves in the 1790s. The staircase

A Playground for Families

It might not be an exaggeration to say that the Bahamas is a playground for children—or anyone else who likes building castles in the sand, searching for the perfect seashell, and playing tag with ocean waves.

While water-related activities are the most obvious enticements, these relaxed and friendly islands also offer a variety of indoor options, particularly in Nassau and on adjacent Paradise Island. Nassau is rich in colonial heritage, with historic **Parliament Square** and the **Bahamas Historical Society Museum,** which has a collection of photographs, documents, military uniforms, weapons, and tools, some items dating back to prehistoric days. For tales of the high seas, **Pirates of Nassau** has artifacts and interactive exhibits of the original pirates of the Caribbean.

Let the kids pick out their favorite straw-hat-wearing pony at the **Surrey Horse Pavilion** on Prince George Wharf and take a leisurely clip-clopping ride through the old city of Nassau. For a few extra dollars, most guides will extend your tour beyond the typical route to include other sites. Keep your guidebook handy to verify facts. Guides are trained but often add their own twist on history, which can be entertaining to say the least.

Both Nassau and Freeport, on Grand Bahama Island, offer the chance to have close encounters of the dolphin kind. **Blue Lagoon Island Dolphin Encounter,** off Paradise Island, lets you stand waist deep in a protected pool of water and interact with trained dolphins, or put on snorkeling gear and swim with them. In Freeport, **UNEXSO** (formerly known as the Underwater Exploration Society, one of whose founders was Jacques Cousteau) has a similar program at Sanctuary Bay, a refuge for dolphins. After a performance of back flips and other tricks, these intelligent creatures literally snuggle up to be petted. Older children and adults also can spend a day learning how these remarkable creatures are trained.

For water-sports enthusiasts, snorkeling, parasailing, and boating opportunities abound. In Exuma, rent a powerboat and take the kids to Hog Beach, Big Major Island, to see the famous **swimming pigs.** Rumor has it that about 50 years ago, a farmer brought some pigs to the island to forage in the wild and serve as the food supply for his family. The farmer is long gone, but the pigs remain, swimming into the surf to greet arriving boats and beg for day-old bread.

Much of the most incredible scenery of the Bahamas is underwater. Seasoned scuba enthusiasts could head out every day and have a completely different experience each time. Dive the wall, swim with sharks, or just nose around some of the islands' spectacular coral reefs. Many dive operators offer half-day shallow dives for complete beginners. At Stuart Cove's Dive Bahamas kids from 12 and up can go 15 feet under with a SUB (Scenic Underwater Bubble) and zoom around the reefs. But you don't even have to get wet to get a glimpse of some of the 50,000-odd creatures of the sea. At **Atlantis,** a resort on Paradise Island, purchase a day pass and explore the world's largest open air, salt water aquarium. For a dose of action and adrenaline, hit the waterslides or float in a tube through a shark-filled lagoon.

was later named to honor Queen Victoria's reign. Pick up some souvenirs at the ad-hoc straw market along the narrow road that leads to the site. ⊠ *Top of Elizabeth Ave. hill, south of Shirley St.*

1 Rawson Square. This shady square connects Bay Street to Prince George Wharf. As you enter off Bay Street, note the statue of Sir Milo Butler, the first post-independence (and first native Bahamian) governor general. Horse-drawn surreys wait for passengers along Prince George Wharf (expect to pay about $10 for a half-hour ride through Nassau's streets). Between Rawson Square and Festival Place, check out (or perhaps stop inside) the open-air **hair-braiding pavilion,** where women work their magic at prices ranging from $2 for a single strand to $100 for an elaborate do. An often-overlooked pleasure near the pavilion is Randolph W. Johnston's lovely bronze statue, *Tribute to Bahamian Women.* ⊠ *Bay St.*

> **KEEP LEFT**
>
> Driving on the left is one of the many leftovers from colonial British rule. As history goes, the Brits kept to the left so they could easily draw and use their sword on the right if an enemy approached. These days, most of the cars driven in the Bahamas are imported from the United States and are designed for right hand driving, yet islanders still keep to the other side.

PARADISE ISLAND

The graceful, arched Paradise Island bridges ($1 round-trip toll for cars and motorbikes from Nassau to P.I.; free for bicyclists and pedestrians), 1 mi east of Nassau's Rawson Square, lead to and from the extravagant world of Paradise Island.

Until 1962, Paradise Island was largely undeveloped and known as Hog Island. A&P heir Huntington Hartford changed the name when he built the island's first resort complex. Although several huge high-rise resorts have been erected since then—as have many multimillion-dollar houses—you can still find several quiet getaway spots. The north shore is lined with white-sand beaches, and the protected south shore, lining Nassau Harbour, is a haven for yachts. Aptly renamed, the island *is* a paradise for beach lovers, boaters, and fun lovers. Casinos abound.

SIGHTS TO SEE

★ ☾ **17 Atlantis, Paradise Island.** The unmistakable sight of this peach fantasia comes into view long before you cross the Paradise Island Bridge. The towering sunstruck visage is Royal Towers, the largest wing of the Atlantis resort. With a glitzy shopping mall, the biggest casino in the country, and seemingly unlimited choices for dining and drinks (35 restaurants and bars), Atlantis is as much a tourist attraction as a resort hotel. At Dolphin Cay, opened in 2007, you can interact with 17 dolphins displaced in Gulfport, Mississippi, after Hurricane Katrina, and a few of their babies, since born at the facility. Aquaventure, a 63-acre waterscape, offers thrilling waterslides and high-intensity rapids as well as a lazy river tube ride through the sprawling grounds. Celebrity sightings are frequent at both Nobu restaurant and Aura nightclub. Many of the resort's facilities, including the restaurants and casino, are open to nonguests. For a peek at the rest—including the world's largest man-made marine habitat, consisting of 11 lagoons—take the guided Discover Atlantis tour, which begins near the main lobby at an exhibition called "The Dig." This wonderful series of walk-through aquariums, themed around the lost continent and its

> **GOLDEN COUNTRY**
>
> Even though the Bahamian national anthem isn't heard as often as others, when Olympic medals per capita are tallied, the little island nation with just about 300,000 people tops the charts. In Athens 2004, the Bahamas was first per capita. The United States, 39th, despite its significantly larger medal haul.

re-created ruins, brings you face to face with sharks, manta rays, and innumerable forms of exotic sea life. The rest of the tour tempts you with a walk through the many waterslides and pools inaccessible to nonguests. ⊠ *Casino Dr.* ☎ *888/528–7155 or 242/363–3000* ✉ *Discover Atlantis tour $32 adults, $22 kids 4–11; Aquaventure day pass $105 adults, $75 kids; beach day pass $55 adults, $30 kids; casino admission free* ☉ *Tours daily 9–4:45, casino daily 24 hrs.*

⑱ Cabbage Beach. This stretch of white sand along the north side is one of the prettiest on New Providence. Although resorts and private homes line much of its length, several minutes' stroll to the east will take you to a quiet span of beach overlooking emerald waters, brightly colored parasails, and sailboats.

★ **⑳ Potter's Cay.** Walk the road beneath the Paradise Island Bridge to Potter's Cay to watch sloops bringing in and selling loads of fish and conch—pronounced *konk*. Along the road to the cay are dozens of stands where you can watch the conch, straight from the sea, being extracted from its glistening pink shell. If you don't have the know-how to handle the tasty conch's preparation—getting the diffident creature out of its shell requires boring a hole at the right spot to sever the muscle that keeps it entrenched—you can enjoy a conch salad on the spot, as fresh as it comes, and take notes for future attempts. Empty shells are sold as souvenirs. Many locals and hotel chefs come here to purchase the fresh catches; you can also find vegetables, herbs, and such condiments as fiery Bahamian peppers preserved in lime juice, and locally grown pineapples, papayas, and bananas. Join in on a raucous game of dominoes outside many of the stalls. Some stalls are closed on Sunday. There's also a police station and dockmaster's office, where you can book an inexpensive trip on a mail boat headed to the Out Islands. Be aware that these boats are built for cargo, not passenger comfort, and it's a rough ride even on calm seas.

★ **⑲ Versailles Gardens.** Fountains and statues of luminaries and legends (such as Napoléon and Josephine, Franklin Delano Roosevelt, David Livingstone, Hercules, and Mephistopheles) adorn Versailles Gardens, the terraced lawn at the One & Only Ocean Club, once the private hideaway of Huntington Hartford. At the top of the gardens stand

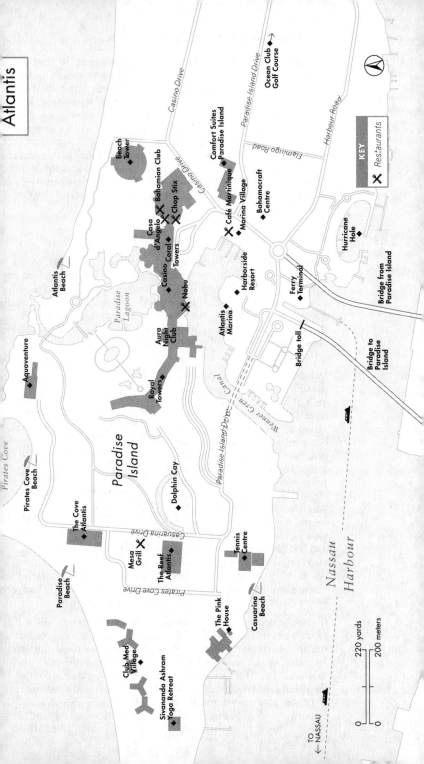

Atlantis

Pirates Cove

Paradise Beach

Pirates Cove Beach

Aquaventure

Atlantis Beach

Beach Tower

Paradise Lagoon

Casa d'Angelo ✕

Bahamian Club

Chop Stix ✕

Casino Drive

Casino Drive

Casino Royale Towers

Nobu ✕

Aura Night Club

Royal Towers

Paradise Island

Club Med Village

Sivananda Ashram Yoga Retreat

The Cove Atlantis

Mesa Grill ✕

The Reef Atlantis

Dolphin Cay

Casuarina Drive

Pirates Cove Drive

The Pink House

Tennis Centre

Casuarina Beach

Werner Gren Canal

Paradise Island Drive

Comfort Suites Paradise Island

Café Martinique ✕

Marina Village

Bahamacraft Centre

Atlantis Marina

Harborside Resort

Ferry Terminal

Bridge toll

Bridge to Paradise Island

Bridge from Paradise Island

Hurricane Hole

Flamingo Road

Harbour Road

Paradise Island Drive

Ocean Club Golf Course →

Nassau Harbour

TO NASSAU ←

0 — 220 yards
0 — 200 meters

the **Cloisters,** the remains of a stone monastery built by Augustinian monks in France in the 13th century. They were imported to the United States in the 1920s by newspaper baron William Randolph Hearst. (The cloister is one of four to have ever been removed from French soil.) Forty years later, Hartford bought the Cloisters and had them rebuilt on their present commanding site. At the center is a graceful, contemporary white marble statue called *Silence,* by U.S. sculptor Dick Reid. Nearly every day, tourists take or renew wedding vows under the delicately wrought gazebo overlooking Nassau Harbour. Although the garden is owned by the One & Only Ocean Club, visitors are welcome so long as they check in at the security gate. ⊠ *One & Only Ocean Club, Paradise Island Dr.* ☎242/363–2501.

EASTERN NEW PROVIDENCE

New Providence Island's eastern end is residential, although there are some interesting historic sites and fortifications here. From East Bay Street, just beyond the Paradise Island bridges, it's a short, scenic drive along Eastern Road, which is lined with gracious homes (and during the early summer months, the red and deep orange blooms of the Royal Poinciana tree), to Eastern Point (also known as East End Point)— about 20 minutes, but a lot longer during rush hour.

SIGHTS TO SEE

Fort Montagu. The oldest of the island's three forts, Montagu was built of local limestone in 1741 to repel Spanish invaders. The only action it saw was when it was occupied for two weeks by rebel American troops—among them a lieutenant named John Paul Jones—seeking arms and ammunition during the Revolutionary War. The small fortification is quite simple, but offers a lovely elevated view of Nassau Harbour. The second level has a number of weathered cannons. A narrow public beach, which disappears at high tide, looks out upon Montagu Bay, where many international yacht regattas and Bahamian sloop races are held annually. ⊠ *East of Bay St. on Eastern Rd.* ☎ *Free.*

> **HERE'S WHERE**
>
> Catch a glimpse of the late Anna Nicole Smith's mansion at water's edge east of Nassau. Fans of the former Playboy model–reality-show star can gather at the wrought-iron gate to the house, which is easily spotted from Eastern Road. Smith died in Florida in February 2007, but was living in the Bahamas before her death, where she was ultimately buried in March 2007.

Fox Hill. Settled by freed slaves who were given land grants, which they paid for either in cash or labor, this residential area was originally four smaller settlements. Today there's not much here of tourist interest— except on the second Tuesday of August, when the community holds its annual Fox Hill Day celebration. It falls a week after the rest of the island celebrates Emancipation Day (some say that's because back in 1834 it took a week for the news of the emancipation to reach the community here). Festivities include music, home-cooked food, arts-

New Providence Island

Western Esplanade

TO
ROSE ISLAND
REEFS

Salt Cay

Athol Island

Lost Ocean Hole

Montagu Bay

Cabbage Beach

Casino Dr.

Fort Montagu

The Retreat

Eastern Point

Prince George Wharf

E. Bay St.

Nassau

Village Rd.

Eastern Rd.

Bernard Rd.

Fox Hill Rd.

Fox Hill

Winton Hwy.

Paradise Beach

Fort Charlotte

East St.

Wulff Rd.

Prince Charles Dr.

Yamacraw Hill Rd.

Arawak Cay

Nassau Botanic Gardens

East St.

South Beach

ATLANTIC OCEAN

Saunders Beach

West Bay St.

Ardastra Gardens, Zoo and Conservation Centre

Harrold Rd.

Blue Hill Rd.

Carmichael Rd.

Crystal Palace Casino

Cable Beach

Deloport Pt.

John F. Kennedy Drive

Lake Cunningham

Gladstone Rd.

Cay Point

Bonefish Pond

Rock Pt.

Caves Beach

The Caves

Lake Nancy

Lake Killarney

Carmichael Rd.

Millars Sound

Love Beach

West Bay St.

Windsor Field Rd.

Nassau International Airport

Blake Rd.

Coral Harbour Rd.

Gambier Deep Reef

Sea Gardens

Northwest Point

Old Fort Bay

Adelaide Rd.

Corry Sound

Adelaide Village

Lyford Cay

Lyford Cay Drop-off

Pleasant Bay

Clifton Point

West Bay St.

Goodfellow Farms

Commonwealth Brewery

Adelaide Beach

South West Bay

KEY	
◪	Dive Sites
◆	Exploring Sights

4 miles

6 km

and-crafts booths, and the annual climbing of the greasy pole. Call the Ministry of Tourism (☎242/322–7500) for more information.

The Retreat. Nearly 200 species of exotic palm trees grace the 11 verdant acres appropriately known as the Retreat, which serves as the headquarters of the Bahamas National Trust. Stroll in blessed silence through the lush grounds, past smiling Buddhas, and under stone arbors overhung with vines. It's a perfect break on a steamy Nassau day. The Retreat hosts the Jollification—the unofficial start to the Christmas season—every third weekend in November. Carols, festive food and drinks, a kids' holiday craft center, and local artisans selling native and Christmas crafts make this a must-do event. ⊠ *Village Rd.* ☎242/393–1317 ≋$2, Jollification $10 ☉ Weekdays 9–5.

WESTERN NEW PROVIDENCE & SOUTH COAST

Starting from downtown Nassau, West Bay Street follows the coast west past the resorts, posh residential neighborhoods, and ever-increasing new developments of Cable Beach, then past popular Love Beach to Northwest Point. Just beyond is Lyford Cay, the island's most exclusive community, whose residents include actor Sean Connery. Old-money pioneers started settling the cay four decades ago, and along with its 200-odd houses there's a private golf course for residents. Your experience of Lyford Cay is likely to be voyeuristic at best—an entrance gate wards off all but residents and friends.

The interior and southwestern coast of New Providence is developing fast, but still offers pristine coastal scenery and long, low stretches of palmetto and pine forest. The loop around the island's west and south coasts can be done in a couple of hours by car or scooter; however, you may wish to take time out for lunch and a swim along the way.

SIGHTS TO SEE

Adelaide Village. The small community on New Providence's southwestern coast sits placidly, like a remnant of another era, between busy Adelaide Road and the ocean. It was first settled during the early 1830s by Africans who had been captured and loaded aboard slave ships bound for the New World. They were rescued on the high seas by the British Royal Navy, and the first group of liberated slaves reached Nassau in 1832. Today, there are two sides to Adelaide—the few dozen families who grow vegetables, raise chickens, and inhabit well-worn, pastel-painted wooden houses, shaded by casuarina, mahogany, and palm trees; and the more upscale beach cottages that are mostly used as weekend getaways. The village has a primary school, some little grocery stores, and the popular **Avery's Restaurant and Bar** (⊠ *Adelaide Rd.* ☎ 242/362–1547), serving delicious native dishes Tuesday–Sunday, 11 AM–11 PM.

Arawak Cay. Known to Nassau residents as "The Fish Fry," Arawak Cay is one of the best places to knock back a Kalik beer (brewed right on New Providence Island), chat with the locals, watch or join in a fast-paced game of dominoes, or sample traditional Bahamian fare. You can get small dishes such as conch fritters or full meals at one of the pastel-color waterside shacks. Order a fried snapper served up with a sweet homemade roll, or fresh conch salad (a spicy mixture of chopped conch—just watching the expert chopping is a show as good as any in town—mixed with diced onions, cucumbers, tomatoes, and hot peppers in a lime marinade). The two-story Twin Brothers and Goldie's Enterprises are two of the most popular places. Try their fried "cracked conch" and Goldie's famous Sky Juice (a sweet but potent gin, coconut-water, and sweet milk concoction sprinkled with nutmeg). There's usually a live band on the outdoor stage Friday and Saturday nights.

> ### SNAKES ALIVE!
>
> The Bahamas has five types of snakes, none poisonous, but the most interesting is the Bahamian boa constrictor, threatened with extinction because Bahamians kill them on sight. The Bahamian boa is extremely unusual in that it has remnants of legs, called spurs. The male uses his spurs to tickle the female. Ask one of the trainers at Ardastra Gardens and Zoo to show you the boa, so you can see the tiny legs.

To reach Arawak Cay, head west along Bay Street, follow the main road around the British Colonial Hilton hotel, and continue west past Western Esplanade, which many locals also call Long Wharf Beach. The cay is on the north side of the T-junction of West Bay and Chippingham Road. It's approximately a five-minute drive or 20-minute walk.

Ardastra Gardens, Zoo, and Conservation Centre. Marching flamingos? These national birds of the Bahamas give a parading performance at Ardastra daily at 10:30, 2:10, and 4:10. The brilliant pink birds are a delight—especially for children, who can walk among the flamingos after the show. The zoo, with more than 5 acres of tropical greenery and ponds, also has an aviary of rare tropical birds including the bright green Bahama parrot, native Bahamian creatures such as rock iguanas and the little (and harmless) Bahamian boa constrictors, and a global collection of small animals. A crowd favorite is the wild boar who has a favorite resting place right in the middle of the walkway. Wander around on your own, or join one of the periodic tours. ⊠ *Chippingham Rd., south of W. Bay St.* ☎ *242/323–5806* ⊕ *www.ardastra.com* 🎫 *$12* ⊙ *Daily 9–5.*

The Caves. These large limestone caverns that the waves sculpted over the aeons are said to have sheltered the early Arawak Indians. An oddity perched right beside the road, they're worth a glance—although in truth, there's not much to see, as the dark interior doesn't lend itself to exploration. Just a short drive beyond the caves, on an island between traffic lanes, is **Conference Corner,** where U.S. president John F. Kennedy, Canadian prime minister John Diefenbaker, and British prime minister Harold Macmillan planted trees on the occasion of their 1962 summit in Nassau. ⊠ *W. Bay St. and Blake Rd.*

Fun Flamingo Facts

Female flamingos lay one egg a year, and both parents take turns sitting on the mud nest for 28 days. Both parents also produce milk in the crop at the base of the neck for the chick, for three months. The feathers of the parents turn white while they feed the chick because of the loss of carotene. The loyal flamingos are monogamous and usually mate for life, but are very social birds that like to live in groups.

Their "knees," which look like they are bent backward, are not knees but ankles. Their knees are tucked under their feathers. What looks like the leg is actually the foot extending from the ankle, so the birds are walking on their toes. And while most humans would tire of it after just a few minutes, standing on one leg is really the most comfortable position for a flamingo.

Inagua, one of the Bahamas' southernmost islands, is home to the world's largest breeding colony of West Indian flamingos. Here you can catch a flock of flamingos taking flight, their pink wings fringed with black, creating a striking contrast against a brilliant blue sky. The majestic birds have a symbiotic relationship with the Inagua-based Morton Salt Company, feeding off the brine shrimp living in the coastal salt pans. It is this diet which gives the mature flamingo its brilliant deep pink plumage.

Short of taking a trip to Inagua, the best place to see the national bird of the Bahamas is Ardastra Zoo and Gardens in Nassau, where you can watch dozens of birds "march" in three daily shows, and after the show you can walk among them in the garden.

Commonwealth Brewery. Kalik, Nassau's very own beer, pale in color but with a full-bodied taste, is brewed here. Try regular Kalik, Kalik Light, or the more potent Kalik Gold, which packs a punch. The local beverage—by far the most popular among Bahamians—is named for the clicking sound of the cowbells used in the Junkanoo Parade. Call about public tours, a new addition planned for 2008. ⊠ *Clifton Pier and Southwest Rd.* ☎ *242/362–4789.*

Crystal Palace Casino. Try your luck at baccarat, blackjack, roulette, craps, and Caribbean stud poker—or simply settle for the slots. There's plenty to keep you entertained in this 2007-remodeled casino, including a sports book for betting on your favorite teams, and games from pai gow poker to Let It Ride and war tables. ⊠ *Nassau Wyndham Resort & Crystal Palace Casino, Cable Beach, Nassau* ☎ *242/327–6200 Ext. 6530* ⊕ *www.bahamar.com* ☉ *Tables weekdays 10 AM–4 AM, weekends 24 hrs; slots daily 24 hrs.*

★ **Fort Charlotte.** Built in 1788, this imposing fort comes complete with a waterless moat, drawbridge, ramparts, and a dungeon, where children love to see the torture device where prisoners were "stretched." Young, local guides bring the fort to life. (Tips are expected.) Lord Dunmore, who built it, named the massive structure in honor of George III's wife. At the time, some called it Dunmore's Folly because of the staggering expense of its construction. It cost eight times more than was originally planned. (Dunmore's superiors in London were less than ecstatic with the high costs, but he managed to survive unscathed.) Ironically, no shots were ever fired in battle from the fort. It's about 1 mi west of central Nassau. Bring a picnic lunch. The fort and its surrounding 100 acres offer a wonderful view of the cricket grounds, the beach, and the ocean beyond. Inquire about Segway tours offered through the grounds by a separate company. ⊠ *W. Bay St., at Chippingham Rd.* 🎟 *$5* ☉ *Tours daily 8–4.*

Love Beach. One of the island's loveliest little beaches is near New Providence's northwestern corner. About 1 mi off Love Beach is 40 acres of coral and sea fan, with forests of fern, known as the Sea Gardens. The clear waters are a favorite with snorkelers.

Nassau Botanic Gardens. Six hundred species of flowering trees and shrubs, a small cactus garden, and two freshwater ponds with lilies, water plants, and tropical fish cover 18 acres. The many trails that wind through the gardens are perfect for leisurely strolls. Various events are held here each year including the Annual Dog Show in March and the International Food Festival the third weekend in October, when the many cultural groups living on the island cook and sell their native dishes and perform traditional songs and dances. The Botanic Gardens are across the street from the **Ardastra Gardens and Conservation Centre,** home of Nassau's zoo. Note that although the gardens have set hours, gates sometimes still remain locked. ⊠ *Chippingham Rd., south of W. Bay St.* ☎ *242/323–5975* 🎟 *$1* ☉ *Weekdays 8–4, weekends 9–4.*

BEACHES

New Providence is blessed with stretches of white sand studded with palm and sea grape trees. Some of the beaches are small and crescent shaped, whereas others stretch for miles. Right in downtown Nassau is the **Western Esplanade.** Also known as Long Wharf Beach, this stretch of white sand sweeps west from the British Colonial Hilton on Bay Street and offers public restrooms. On Paradise Island, **Paradise Beach,** at the island's far western tip, is a nice stretch of sand. Paradise Island's real showpiece is 3-mi-long **Cabbage Beach,** which rims the north coast from the Atlantis lagoon to Snorkeler's Cove. At the east end you can rent Jet Skis and nonmotorized pedal boats, and go parasailing.

Cable Beach is on New Providence's north shore, about 3 mi west of downtown Nassau. Resorts line much of this beautiful, broad swath of white sand, but there is public access. Jet skiers and beach vendors abound, so don't expect quiet isolation. Just west of Cable Beach is a rambling pink house on the Rock Point promontory, where much of the 1965 Bond film *Thunderball* was filmed. Tiny, crescent-shaped **Caves Beach** is beyond Cable Beach on the north shore, about 7 mi from downtown just before the turnoff on Blake Road that leads to the airport. **Love Beach,** a snorkeler's favorite, is on the north shore beyond Caves Beach, about 9 mi from town (about a 20-minute drive). Access technically lies within the domain of Love Beach residents, but they aren't inclined to shoo anyone away. On the south shore, drive down to **Adelaide Beach,** at the end of Adelaide Village, for sand that stretches down to Coral Harbour and is a real shell seeker's treat at low tide. The people who live at New Providence's east end flock to **South Beach,** at the foot of Blue Hill Road on the south shore.

WHERE TO EAT

With the escalation of Bahamian tourism, meal preparation at the better dining spots has become as sophisticated as that in any leading U.S. city. European chefs brought in by the top restaurants have trained young Bahamians in the skills of haute cuisine. Chinese, Indian, Mexican, Creole, and Japanese fare have become available, and celebrity chefs are lending their name and culinary style to some of the trendier offerings.

However, don't neglect the Bahamian food. Several relatively inexpensive spots serve traditional dishes, which now also appear on the ritzier menus: peas 'n' rice, conch (chowder, fritters, and cracked), Bahamian lobster, "stew" or "boil" fish, grouper fingers, fresh local bread, and, for dessert, guava duff, a warm marriage of boiled guava dough and sweet sauce. Because meats and some seafood are mostly imported, local fish is usually the most economical entrée.

Note: Many all-inclusive hotels offer meal plans for nonguests.

AMERICAN

$ ✕**Green Parrot.** Sip a green-colored Parrot Crush while tackling the large Works Burger as you sit and enjoy the cool breeze and lovely Nassau Harbour scenery. This casual all outdoor restaurant and bar is popular with locals. The menu includes burgers, wraps, quesadillas, and other simple but tasty dishes. An extended all-night happy hour on Friday means the huge bar is lively and packed. There are karaoke and the occasional live band on Thursday and Saturday nights. ✉*E. Bay Street, west of the bridge to Paradise Island* ☏*242/322–9248* ⊕ *www.greenparrotbar.com* ▭*MC, V*

BAHAMIAN

★ $$$ ✕**The Poop Deck.** Just east of the bridge from Paradise Island and a quick cab ride from the center of town is this favorite local haunt. There's usually a wait for a table, and it's worth waiting a little longer for one overlooking the marina and Nassau Harbour. The restaurant's popularity has resulted in a second Poop Deck on Cable Beach's west end, but for residents, this is still the place. Expect spicy dishes with names such as Mama Mary's steamed fish and Rosie's chicken; there's also an extensive wine list, and a popular shot list for those looking to get the party started. Start with Paula's Conch Fritters and then select a fresh whole hog snapper for the chef to fry up. It's usually served head to tail, so if you're squeamish, ask your waiter to have the head cut off before it come out on your plate. Save room for guava duff and a calypso coffee spiked with secret ingredients. ✉*E. Bay St., at Nassau Yacht Haven Marina, east of bridge from Paradise Island* ☏*242/393–8175* ⊕*www.thepoopdeckrestaurants.com* ▭*AE, MC, V.*

$ ✕**Double D's.** Don't let the dark-tinted windows and green lighting over the doorway put you off. Inside you'll find a pleasant but simply decorated restaurant offering friendly service and good native food. This is a popular spot with locals for its Bahamian cuisine and 24-hour service in a town where most kitchens are closed at 10 PM. Try boil fish—a peppery lime-based broth filled with chunks of boiled potatoes, onions, and grouper—or be adventurous and order a bowl of pig feet or sheep-tongue souse. All come with a chunk of johnnycake or a bowl of steaming white grits. Although souplike, these Bahamian delicacies are typically served only for breakfast. ✉*E. Bay St, at the foot of the bridge from Paradise Island* ☏*242/393–2771* ▭ *MC, V.*

BRAZILIAN

★ $$$$ ✕**Humidor Churrascaria Restaurant.** The salad bar at this casual restaurant offers everything from simple salad fixings to scrumptious seafood salads and soups. And this is just the start. Each table setting includes a coaster that's red on one side and green on the other. Just

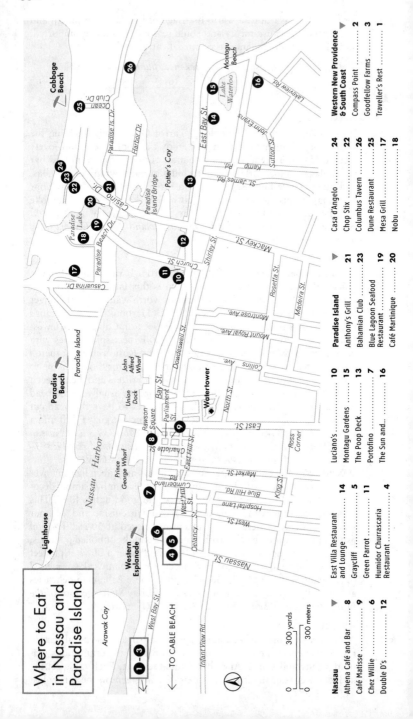

Where to Eat in Nassau and Paradise Island

0 ─── 300 yards
0 ─── 300 meters

← TO CABLE BEACH

Nassau

Athena Café and Bar	8
Café Matisse	9
Chez Willie	6
Double D's	12
East Villa Restaurant and Lounge	14
Graycliff	5
Green Parrot	11
Humidor Churrascaria Restaurant	4
Luciano's	10
Montagu Gardens	15
The Poop Deck	13
Portofino	7
The Sun and...	16

Paradise Island

Anthony's Grill	21
Bahamian Club	23
Blue Lagoon Seafood Restaurant	19
Café Martinique	20
Casa d'Angelo	24
Chop Stix	22
Columbus Tavern	26
Dune Restaurant	25
Mesa Grill	17
Nobu	18

Western New Providence & South Coast

Compass Point	2
Goodfellow Farms	3
Traveller's Rest	1

like a stoplight, green means go and red means stop. Waiters serve a never-ending selection of delicious skewered meats until you turn your coaster to red and declare uncle. When you're done, stop by the smoking lounge to see the cigar rollers in action or stroll along the garden terraces and fountains out back. ⊠ *W. Hill St. off Cumberland Rd., next to Graycliff Hotel* ☎ *242/328–7050* ⊟ *AE, MC, V* ⊗ *No lunch weekends.*

CHINESE

$$$ ✕ **East Villa Restaurant and Lounge.** Set in a converted Bahamian home, this is one of the most popular Chinese restaurants in town. The Chinese-Continental menu includes entrées such as conch with black bean sauce, *hung shew* (walnut chicken), and steak *kew* (cubed prime fillet served with baby corn, snow peas, water chestnuts, and vegetables). The New York strip steak is nirvana. A short taxi ride from Paradise Island or downtown Nassau, this is the perfect spot if you're seeking something a little different from the typical area restaurants. Dress is casual elegance. ⊠ *E. Bay St., near Nassau Yacht Club* ☎ *242/393–3377* ⊟ *AE, MC, V.*

> ### GLAMOROUS GRAYCLIFF
>
> A meandering maze underneath historic Graycliff's sprawling kitchen and dining area houses more than 200,000 bottles of wine and champagne, as well as a humidor once owned by President John F. Kennedy (sitting on a table next to a special edition Marilyn Munroe Napa Valley Magnum). Graycliff's wine cellar is one of the most extensive and impressive in the world. It costs $1,000 to book the elegant private cellar dining room, but tours are free.

CONTINENTAL

$$$$ ✕ **Graycliff.** A meal at this hillside mansion begins in the elegant parlor, where, over live piano music, drinks are served and orders are taken.
odor's Choice
★ It's a rarefied world, where waiters wear tuxedos and Cuban cigars and cognac are served after dinner. While you're waiting, you may get a chance to sample some of the new molecular gastronomical delights. Soups that are solid until they melt in your mouth and become hot and creamy are a specialty. Graycliff's signature dishes include Kobe beef, Kurobuta pork, and lobster wrapped in prosciutto with roasted pepper sauce. The wine cellar contains more than 200,000 bottles that have been handpicked by owner Enrico Garzaroli, some running into the tens of thousands of dollars. You can even buy the world's oldest bottle of wine, a German vintage 1727, for $200,000. ⊠ *W. Hill St. at Cumberland Rd., across from Government House* ☎ *242/322–2796* ⊕ *www.graycliff.com* ⚲ *Reservations essential* ⊟ *AE, MC, V* ⊗ *No lunch weekends.*

★ $$$$ **The Sun and…** If you're hoping to catch sight of international superstars, this is a good place to look. Dine in a series of rooms surrounding an enclosed garden area with a rock pool and fountain—as magical a dining setting as Nassau offers. Feast on such creations as seared medallions of foie gras with a Madeira demi-glace and fricassee of lobster Martinique. End your meal divinely with one of Belgian owner-chef Ronny Deryckere's six soufflés, which range from almond amaretto to guava. Dress is elegant, but jackets are not required. ✉ *Lakeview Rd and E. Shirley St.* ☎ *242/393–1205* ⊕ *www.sun-and.com* ✍ *Reservations essential* ▭ *AE, MC, V* ☉ *Closed Sun. and Mon., Aug., and Sept. No lunch Sat.*

$$$ ✗ **Montagu Gardens.** Angus beef and fresh native seafood—flame-grilled and seasoned with home-mixed spices—are the specialties at this romantic restaurant in an old Bahamian mansion on Lake Waterloo. The dining room opens to a walled courtyard niched with Roman-style statues and gardens that lead to a waterside balustrade. Besides seafood and steak (carnivores should try the filet mignon smothered in mushrooms), menu selections include chicken, lamb, pasta, ribs, and several Bahamian-inspired dishes such as conch fritters and minced crawfish with taco chips. A favorite dessert is Fort Montagu Mud Pie. ✉ *E. Bay St.* ☎ *242/394–6347* ▭ *D, MC, V* ☉ *Closed Sun.*

ECLECTIC

$$$ ✗ **Portofino.** Nassau's movers and shakers meet at the British Colonial Hilton for homemade Italian pasta dishes and pizza as well as Bahamian favorites such as pan-seared snapper with mango sauce, conch chowder, and guava duff. The lavish lunch buffet far surpasses the usual hotel fare. For breakfast, don't miss the Bahamian johnnycake. Ask for a window seat so you can see the cruise ships come and go in the harbor. After dinner, you can walk to the hotel's private beach for a lovely view of the harbor and Paradise Island. ✉ *British Colonial Hilton Nassau, W. Bay St.* ☎ *242/322–3301* ⊕ *www.hiltoncaribbean. com/nassau* ▭ *AE, MC, V.*

$$ ✗ **Café Matisse.** Low-slung settees, stucco arches, and reproductions of the eponymous artist's works set a casually refined tone at this restaurant, owned by a husband-and-wife team—he's Bahamian, she's northern Italian. Sit in the ground-floor garden under large white umbrellas or dine inside the century-old house for lunch or dinner. Start with beef carpaccio, then dive into freshly made pasta such as duck-filled ravioli and shrimp in a spicy red curry sauce, or such delights as pizza frutti di mare (topped with fresh local seafood). ✉ *Bank La. and Bay St., behind Parliament Sq.* ☎ *242/356–7012* ⊕ *www.cafe-matisse.com* ✍ *Reservations recommended* ▭ *AE, D, MC, V* ☉ *Closed Sun., Mon, and Aug.*

Fodor's Choice
★

FRENCH

$$$ ✗ **Chez Willie.** Elegant and romantic, this restaurant specializes in French cuisine with a Bahamian twist. Dine by candlelight in the intimate dining room or alfresco on the patio overlooking the lush gardens. Start with caviar or goose-liver pâté, then try the signature grouper served in a puff pastry with crabmeat and coconut cream sauce. Or go with someone you love and share the chateaubriand for two. ✉ *W. Bay St.* ☎ *242/322–5364 or 242/322–5366* ⊕ *www.chezwillierestaurant.com* ✍ *Reservations essential* ▭ *AE, MC, V.*

GREEK

$ ✗ **Athena Café and Bar.** A mainstay since 1960, this Greek restaurant provides a break from the Nassau culinary routine. Sit on the second floor among Grecian statuary, or on the balcony overlooking the action below. Enjoy souvlaki, moussaka, and spanakopita, among other specialties, along with Greek beer in a relaxed and friendly atmosphere. Gregarious owner Peter Mousis and his family serve tasty fare at moderate prices, including breakfast seven days a week. ⊠ *Bay St., at Charlotte St.* ☎ 242/322–8833 ⊟ *AE, D, MC, V* ⊗ *No dinner Mon.–Thurs. Closed Sun.*

ITALIAN

$$$ ✗ **Luciano's.** Green Roofs, the sprawling former residence of the late Sir Roland Symonette (the country's first premier), houses this harborside restaurant. The mansion's mahogany woodwork, gardens, and terraces create a romantic setting for dining on Tuscan fare, including escarole, white bean, and sausage soup; bistecca fiorentina; grouper al piccata; and homemade pastas—including risotto with stone crab and asparagus. The sweeping view of Paradise Island and the towers of Atlantis is particularly lovely at sunset. Reservations are essential for waterside tables. ⊠ *E. Bay St., 2 blocks west of Paradise Island bridge* ☎ 242/323–7770 ⊟ *AE, D, MC, V.*

.RADISE ISLAND

BAHAMIAN

★ $$$$ ✗ **Dune Restaurant.** Feast on intricately prepared dishes while overlooking Cabbage Beach at the renowned One & Only Ocean Club. Go for breakfast or lunch for the most reasonable prices. For breakfast, try the smoked salmon with potato pancake and chive sour cream or the egg-white omelet with fresh herbs. Dinner entrées include roasted grouper, rack of lamb, and sirloin steak. It's a great place to unwind amid ocean breezes. ⊠ *One & Only Ocean Club, Ocean Club Dr.* ☎ 242/363–3000 Ext. 64739 ⊕ *www.oneandonlyresort.com* ⌲ *Reservations essential* ⊟ *AE, MC, V.*

CARIBBEAN

$$ ✗ **Anthony's Grill.** Color is the standout feature of Anthony's: bright red, yellow, and blue tablecloths spiked with multihued squiggles; yellow-and-green walls with jaunty cloths hanging from the ceilings; booths printed with bright sea themes; and buoyant striped curtains. The lively spirit is reflected in the cheery service you'll receive at breakfast, lunch, or dinner. The extensive menu (68 items to choose from) includes penne pasta, fresh seafood such as herb-crusted red snapper, steaks, burgers, ribs, and salads. ⊠ *Paradise Village Shopping Plaza* ☎ 242/363–3152 ⊕ *www.anthonysgrillparadiseisland.com* ⊟ *AE, MC, V.*

CHINESE

$$$ ✗ **Chop Stix.** Atlantis's Chinese restaurant has been given a new name, an updated decor, and a brand new tantalizing menu. Try the coconut curried chicken with mango or grouper seared in a wok and drizzled with a mouthwatering garlic sauce. For a late night bite, pop in for dim sum Friday and Saturday. The menu includes avocado egg rolls, peanut butter dumplings, and lobster shu mei. ⊠ *Atlantis* ☎ 242/363–3000 ⌲ *Reservations essential* ⊟ *AE, D, DC, MC, V* ⊗ *Closed Mon. No lunch.*

CONTINENTAL

$$$$ ✕**Bahamian Club.** Reminiscent of a British country club, this handsome restaurant has walls lined with dark oak, overstuffed chairs, and leather banquettes. Meat is the house specialty—grilled T-bone steak, veal chop, roast prime rib, and chateaubriand for two—but grilled swordfish steak, Bahamian lobster, salmon fillet, and other fresh seafood dishes are all prepared with finesse. Dinner is accompanied by soft piano music; between courses, couples can waltz on the small dance floor. ⊠*Atlantis* ☎*242/363–3000* ⚠*Reservations essential* ⊟*AE, D, DC, MC, V* ⊗*No lunch*.

ECLECTIC

★ **$$$$** ✕**Mesa Grill.** Bobby Flay is the latest celebrity chef to lend his name and expertise to the restaurant lineup at Atlantis. Located in the Cove hotel, Mesa Grill (his first international outpost) serves up the Southwestern cuisine he is known for, but with a Bahamian twist. The menu features unique dishes such as crispy squid and cracked conch salad with orange-chipotle vinaigrette, and Bahamian lobster tail with red chili coconut sauce. More traditional Flay-inspired dishes like blue corn pancake with barbecued duck, and New Mexican spice-rubbed pork tenderloin are also available. ⊠*The Cove Atlantis* ☎*242/363–3000* ⊕*www.atlantis.com* ⚠*Reservations essential* ⊟*AE, MC, V.*

FRENCH

$$$$ ✕**Café Martinique.** The original restaurant made famous in the 1965

FodorsChoice James Bond film *Thunderball* has long been bulldozed, but with the help
★ of renowned international chef Jean-Georges Vongerichten and New York designer Adam D. Tihany, Atlantis resurrected a classic. Nestled in the center of Marina Village on Paradise Island, Café Martinique is the height of sophistication in design, service, and cuisine. The decor includes a wrought-iron birdcage elevator and a mahogany staircase, and a grand piano helps create the fine dining atmosphere. The classic French gourmet menu offers simple, classic dishes made spectacular thanks to the highest quality ingredients and chef Jean-George's influence. ⊠*Marina Village, Atlantis* ☎*242/363–3000* ⊕*www.atlantis. com* ⚠*Reservations essential* ⊟*AE, MC, V.*

ITALIAN

$$$ ✕**Casa D'Angelo.** Modeled after the wildly popular Casa d'Angelo in South Florida, Chef Angelo Elia brings his famous Tuscan-style cuisine to Paradise. The antipasti display whets the appetite for such dishes as tagliatelle with calamari, free-range chicken flavored with roasted garlic, white wine, cherry tomatoes, and fresh herbs, or the grilled veal chop in a dark Barolo-and-Portobello sauce sprinkled with Gorgonzola. The dessert pastries are delectable. ⊠*Atlantis* ☎*242/363–3000* ⊟*AE, D, DC, MC, V* ⊗*No lunch.*

JAPANESE

★ **$$$$** ✕**Nobu.** The innovative Japanese restaurant conceived and run by chef Nobu Matsuhisa opened December 2005 in Atlantis's Royal Towers adjacent to the casino. The central dining room is surrounded by a Japanese pagoda, and guests seated at a long communal sushi bar can watch the chefs work. Reservations are suggested. ⊠ *Royal Towers, Atlantis* ☎ *242/363–3000 Jacket required* ☰ *AE, D, DC, MC, V* ◷ *No lunch.*

SEAFOOD

$$$ ✕ **Blue Lagoon Seafood Restaurant.** The decor tends toward the nautical, with hurricane lamps and brass rails, in this narrow third-floor dining room looking out to Nassau on one side and Atlantis to the other. Choose from simply prepared dishes such as lobster thermidor or stone crab claws, or fancier

selections such as almond-fried shrimp and stuffed grouper au gratin. ⊠ *Club Land'Or* ☎ *242/363–2400* ⊕ *www.clublandor.com* ⚑ *Reservations essential* ☰ *AE, DC, MC, V* ◷ *No lunch.*

$$$ ✕ **Columbus Tavern.** Watch the boats in Nassau Harbour through this restaurant's enormous open windows as you dine on the fisherman's fiesta—a tasty combination of blackened lobster, shrimp, and scallops with a spicy Creole sauce. Or set aside your seafaring ways and try the steak Diane flambé—it's served flaming, as the name implies. The tavern serves three meals a day, every day. ⊠ *Paradise Island Dr.* ☎ *242/363–2534* ⊕ *www.columbustavernbahamas.com* ☰ *AE, MC, V.*

ᴬBLE BEACH

ASIAN

$$$ ✕ **Indigo.** This eclectic restaurant doubles as an art gallery—walls are lined with Bahamian originals, many of them painted by the owner's late father Brent Malone. There's an extensive sushi menu, as well as Bahamian-influenced Asian cuisine. Fresh salads are a big hit and the coconut conch chowder is not to be missed. Live music, particularly on weekends, ranges from steel-pan bands to classical guitarists. The funky inside bar is a popular local predinner hangout, and reservations are recommended Friday night. ⊠ *W. Bay St., at Sandals roundabout* ☎ *242/327–2524* ☰ *AE, MC, V* ◷ *Closed Sun.*

$$ ✕ **Moso.** Opened in November 2007 as part of the first phase of the billion-dollar transformation of the Cable Beach hotels, Moso has Asian appeal from the moment you walk in. Vibrant red and black furnishings and elegant orchids accent the space; a wall of windows offers pool and ocean-view dining. Try the salmon or lobster, the grilled filet mignon, or the chicken breast cooked either Cantonese-style or flavored with a teriyaki or Szechuan rub. Finish up your meal with a cinnamon-banana spring roll. ⊠ *Wyndham Nassau Resort, W. Bay St.* ☎ *242/327–6200* ⚑ *Reservations essential* ☰ *AE, MC, V* ◷ *Closed Tues. No lunch.*

BAHAMIAN

$$$ ✕**Androsia Bahamian Cuisine Steak & Seafood Restaurant.** New owners have transformed this former international restaurant into one with a decidedly Bahamian appeal. You'll find a wide selection of seafood at this simply decorated, but pleasant restaurant. Try the Pirate Platter, a combo of locally available seafood or the Bimini Snapper, stuffed with sautéed onions, tomatoes, and fresh herbs. ⊠ *W. Bay St., in Shoppers Haven Plaza* ☏242/327–7805 or 242/327–6430 ▭*MC, V*

MEDITERRANEAN

$$$ ✕**Provence.** The chef bills his fare as *cuisine du soleil*—you can see why with the fiery, grilled rib-eye steak in peppercorn sauce, and the oven-roasted Atlantic salmon with citrus butter. At dinner, try the Mediterranean bouillabaisse, braised osso buco, or pan-seared sea bass and black grouper fillets. Or just drop by the tapas bar for tasty appetizers, such as escargots fricassee and pan-seared sea scallops. Provence is popular with the well-to-do and Hollywood set. ⊠*Old Town Sandyport* ☏242/327–0985 ▭*AE, D, MC, V* ⊗*Closed Sun. No lunch Sat.*

SEAFOOD

$$$$ ✕**The Poop Deck at Sandyport.** A more upscale version of the other Poop Deck, this waterside restaurant has soaring ceilings, a cool-pink-and-aqua color scheme, and a dazzling view of Cable Beach. Start with sweet-potato fish cakes or grilled shrimp and Brie before diving into the fresh catch of the day, paired with a selection from the extensive wine list. There's a smattering of choices for the seafood-phobic. ⊠ *W. Bay St.* ☏242/327–3325 ⊕*www.thepoopdeckrestaurants.com* ▭*AE, D, MC, V* ⊗*Closed Mon.*

STEAK

★ $$$ ✕**Black Angus Grill.** This steakhouse offers some of the best certified Angus beef on the island. Bring your appetite if you're going to try the double porterhouse which is carved right in front of you, table-side. It's not all about the beef, though. The shrimp skewer and conch and grouper ceviche are delightful alternatives. Finish up with the Cay lime pie made with Bahamian instead of the traditional Florida citrus. ⊠ *Wyndham Nassau Resort, W. Bay St.* ☏242/327–6200 ▭*AE, MC, V* ⊗*Closed Sun.*

WESTERN NEW PROVIDENCE & SOUTH COAST

AMERICAN

$$$ ✕**Compass Point.** This friendly restaurant and bar boasts one of the best sunsets on the island. Sit indoors or out on the terrace overlooking the ocean and enjoy their signature grouper amandine, French double lamb chops marinated in a rosemary sauce, or lobster-and-crab spinach risotto. Sunday brunch, from 10 to 3 PM, is a special treat. The long outdoor bar stays open until the last guest leaves and there's live music on weekends. ⊠ *W. Bay St., near Gambier Village* ☏242/327–4500 ⊕ *www.compasspointbeachresort.com* ▭*MC, V.*

BAHAMIAN

$ ✕**Traveller's Rest.** A scenic 10-mi drive along the coast from downtown Nassau brings you to this relaxed family restaurant, which has a great ocean view. The food is delicious, but service tends to be slow, so sit and enjoy the view or challenge your tablemate to a game of Connect Four. The fresh seafood dinner served just steps from the beach is a real treat—conch, grouper, and crawfish are the heavy hitters. Try the "smudder fish"—a tasty local fish literally smothered in onions, peppers, and other vegetables. Dine outside or in, and toast the sunset with a fresh-fruit banana daiquiri—a house specialty. ⊠ *W. Bay St., Gambier* ☎242/327–7633 ▤*AE, MC, V.*

ECLECTIC

$ ✕**Goodfellow Farms.** This unique treat is well worth the long drive to the western end of the island. The vegetable farm has a country store and small restaurant with outdoor dining under shady trees. Lunch is simple—cranberry-almond chicken salad wraps, flank steak, or Bahamian crawfish pasta salad served over greens picked from the farm earlier in the day. There is a strict no-tipping policy enforced. Call to see if they've started serving dinner. ⊠ *W. Bay St., Mount Pleasant Village* ⌖*Take left at Lyford Cay roundabout, go over the hill, entrance to farm road is signposted* ☎242/377–5000 ⊕*www.goodfellowfarms.com* ▤*MC, V* ☉*Closed Sun. No dinner.*

ⅣHERE TO STAY

New Providence Island is fortunate to have an extensive range of hotels, from simple, family-owned guesthouses to the megaresorts at Cable Beach and on Paradise Island. Downtown Nassau's beaches are not beautiful; if you want to be beachfront on a gorgeous white strand, stay on Cable Beach or Paradise Island's Cabbage Beach. Reasons to stay in Nassau include proximity to shopping and affordability (although the cost of taxis to and from the better beaches can add up). Nassau's British Colonial Hilton, for instance, is a top-rate hotel, but its man-made beach, although pretty, can't compare to Cabbage Beach or Cable Beach.

The homey, friendly little spots will probably not be on the beach—and you'll have to go out to eat unless you have access to a kitchen (although some inns will prepare meals for you on request). On the flip side, your stay is likely to be relaxing, low-key, and less removed from everyday Bahamian life. The plush resorts are big and beautiful, glittering and splashy, but they can be overwhelming. In any case, these big, top-dollar properties generally have more amenities than you could possibly make use of, a selection of dining choices, and a full roster of sports and entertainment options. The battle for the tourist dollar rages ceaselessly between Cable Beach and Paradise Island. The competition encourages agents to put forth an endless stream of travel deals, with enticements such as free snorkeling gear, free scuba lessons, and free admission to Las Vegas–style revues.

There are still a few peaceful retreats on P.I., but the boisterous megaresort Atlantis has eliminated most of the quiet strolling lanes and brought its own brand of flash to the island. The Baha Mar Resorts Group has started its billion dollar overhaul of the dated Cable Beach strip. The Wyndham and newly re-branded Sheraton resorts have gotten face lifts and soon the entire layout of the strip will be changed. Just opened in July 2008, the 16-room Marley Resort and Spa adds to the Cable Beach mix. Rita Marley, who lived in the home with her husband, the late Bob Marley, Jamaican reggae legend, owns the hotel. Some prefer the lineup of resorts along the Cable Beach strip, others like the look of P.I., which has hotels scattered around every corner (and which is, unlike Cable Beach, walkable from downtown).

A tax ranging from 6% to 12%, representing resort and government levies, is added to your hotel bill. Some hotels also add a gratuity charge of between $2.50 and $4 (or higher) per person, per day, for the housekeeping or pool staff. The prices below are based on high-season (winter) rates, generally in effect from December through March. Expect to pay between 15% and 30% less off-season at most resorts. In general, the best rates are available through packages, which almost every hotel offers. Call the hotel directly or ask your travel agent.

NASSAU

★ $$$$ 🏨 **Graycliff.** The old-world flavor of this Georgian colonial landmark—built in the 1720s by ship captain Howard Graysmith—has made it a perennial favorite with the upscale crowd. Past guests include the Duke and Duchess of Windsor, Winston Churchill, Aristotle Onassis, and the Beatles. Al Capone stayed here when his sweetie, Polly Leach, owned it during the Roaring '20s, and Lord Mountbatten visited when Lord and Lady Dudley were the proprietors. It's easy to forget that you're steps from downtown Nassau when you stay here. Thick foliage envelops a series of garden villas and cottages, amid limestone courtyards with ponds and fountains. Rooms are uniquely styled in a plush old-world upscale decor. They each bear a Bahamian name—Hibiscus, Yellowbird, Baillou (for the name of the road it overlooks). For refined Continental fare, the hotel's namesake restaurant is one of the island's premier places to dine. **Pros:** one of the most luxurious accommodations on the island, lush tropical gardens, beautiful amenities, large rooms. **Cons:** centered around the busy restaurant and bar area, not easily accessible for handicapped, no beach access. ⊠ *W. Hill St.* ☎ *242/322–2796 or 800/688–0076* ⊕ *www.graycliff.com* 🛏 *7 rooms, 13 suites* ♿ *In-hotel: 2 restaurants, bars, pools, gym, spa* ⊟ *AE, MC, V.*

★ $$ 🏨 **British Colonial Hilton Nassau.** The first Colonial Hotel, built by Standard Oil cofounder Henry Flagler in 1899, attracted socialites, royals, and industrialists at the turn of the 20th century and during the boom years of Prohibition. That building was destroyed by fire in 1921, and the present Mediterranean-style British Colonial—an exact replica—opened a year later, featuring a lustrous saffron facade, gleaming marble floors, and soaring arched ceilings. This landmark building is the social heart of Nassau, the setting for political meetings and the city's most important events. Guest rooms have dark mahogany furniture and marble baths; most have ocean views. The resort sits on eight lush acres with spectacular views of Nassau Harbour. It's the best business choice in the Bahamas, and is also a popular spot for weddings. Watch for brides descending the grand staircase in the lobby on Saturday and Sunday afternoons. **Pros:** right on Bay Street, quiet beach and pool area, centrally located. **Cons:** busy with local meetings and events, man-made beach, hard to access at peak traffic times. ⊠*1 Bay St.* ☎*242/322–3301* ⊕*www.hiltoncaribbean.com/nassau* ⇔*288 rooms, 21 suites* ♿*In-room: safe, ethernet. In-hotel: restaurant, room service, bar, pool, gym, beachfront, diving, water sports, laundry service, executive floor, public Internet* ⊟*AE, D, DC, MC, V.*

> ### THE PALM BEACH CONNECTION
>
> Palm Beach, Florida, and Nassau shared America's late-19th-century movers and shakers courtesy of Standard Oil cofounder Henry Flagler. He built the Breakers Hotel in Palm Beach which had ferries that traveled to his other hotel, the luxurious British Colonial in Nassau. Flagler lived in the two-story house on Parliament Street in Nassau that was, for many years after his death, the Green Shutters restaurant, across the street from the legendary Victoria Hotel, one of the world's most luxurious resorts in its day. In the mid-1900s it was torn down, but the name remains on a column at the driveway entrance, which now leads to an empty lot.

$ 🏨**El Greco Hotel.** A pleasant Greek owner and a friendly staff make it a point to get to know their guests and ensure they have a nice stay. Although the decorations are not elaborate, the rooms are large, quiet, and have soothing earth tones. Rooms surround a small pool tucked within a bougainvillea-filled courtyard. El Greco is directly across the street from the public Western Esplanade beach. The hotel appeals primarily to a European crowd, and for those on a budget who want to be in Nassau, it's a pleasant find. Guest are allowed to use the lobby phone to make free (!!!) calls to the United States. **Pros:** close to downtown, friendly staff, free overseas calls. **Cons:** no on-site restaurant, public beach is across busy street. ⊠*W. Bay St.* ☎*242/325–1121* 📠*242/325–1124* ⇔*27 rooms* ♿*In-hotel: bar, pool, public Internet* ⊟*AE, D, MC, V.*

$ 🏨**Quality Inn.** This simple and quiet six-floor hotel is a welcome addition to the New Providence budget lodging market. It's clean and well kept, with pleasantly decorated rooms. Ask for a room with an ocean view, as many rooms have only a partial view or none at all. In fact, the rooms vary wildly in size, with a few just barely bigger than the bed. Front desk staff will generally show you what's available and let you take your pick if you ask. Sliding glass doors open to false balconies, but allow nice cool breezes in. Be aware that each guest must pay a daily service charge of $11.50. **Pros:** walking distance from downtown, relatively inexpensive, Continental breakfast on site. **Cons:** on two busy streets, popular with spring breakers, public beach is across the street. ⊠*W. Bay St. and Nassau St.* ☎*242/322–1515* ⊕*www.qualityinn.com* ⇔*63 rooms* ♿*In-room: dial-up. In-hotel: restaurant, bar* ⊟*AE, D, DC, MC, V.*

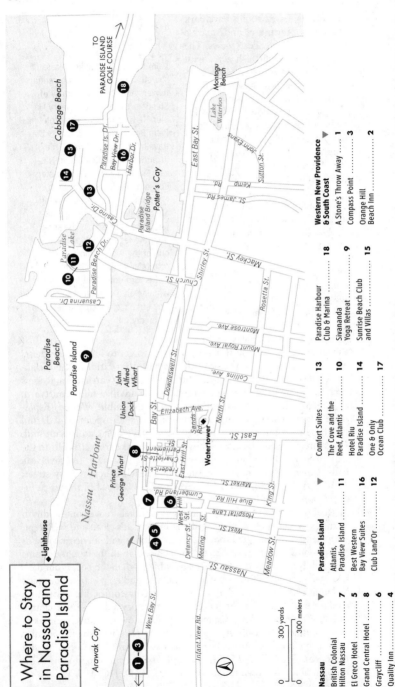

Where to Stay in Nassau and Paradise Island

♦ Lighthouse

Arawak Cay

Nassau Harbour

Prince George Wharf
Union Dock
John Alfred Wharf

Paradise Beach

Paradise Island

Paradise Lake

Casuarina Dr.
Paradise Beach Dr.

Casino Dr.
Paradise Island Bridge
Paradise Is. Dr.
Bay View Dr.
Harbor Dr.

Cabbage Beach

TO PARADISE ISLAND GOLF COURSE

Potter's Cay

Lake Waterloo
Montagu Beach

West Bay St.
Infant View Rd.

Delancy St.
Meeting St.
West St.
Hospital Lane
Blue Hill Rd.
Cumberland Rd.
King St.
Market St.
East Hill St.
Charlotte St.
Parliament St.
Frederick St.
West Hill St.
Nassau St.
Meadow St.
Bay St.
Dowdeswell St.
Elizabeth Ave.
East St.
North St.
Sands Rd.
♦ Watertower

Collins Ave.
Mount Royal Ave.
Montrose Ave.
Church St.
Shirley St.
Mackey St.
Rosetta St.
East Bay St.
St. James Rd.
Kemp Rd.
John Evans
Sutton St.

0   300 yards
0   300 meters

¢   🏨**Grand Central Hotel.** Since the early 1940s when George Constantakis arrived from Greece and opened this hotel, the Grand Central has been an affordable inn with a perfect location, steps away from Bay Street in downtown Nassau. Horse-drawn surreys pass by on the narrow lane of Charlotte Street, making it easy to picture yourself in colonial Nassau. Ask for a room that opens onto a balcony with views of the cruise ships docked at the end of the street. Guest rooms are clean and tidy, with two double beds or one double bed and a single, new pine furniture, and private baths with tubs and showers. Eleven rooms are in a guesthouse next door. Jimmy's take-out restaurant, next door, offers authentic Bahamian breakfasts and lunches, including fried chicken and pan-seared snapper. This hotel is the best deal in Nassau, and room prices include taxes and service. **Pros:** in the heart of downtown Nassau, guesthouse feel. **Cons:** on busy street, no pool or beach. ⊠ *Charlotte St.* ☎ *242/322–8356* ⊕ *www.grand-central-hotel. com* 🛏 *35 rooms* ⊟ *AE, MC, V.*

RADISE ISLAND

$$$$ 🏨**The Cove Atlantis & the Reef Atlantis.** Physically part of Atlantis, but
dor's Choice   worlds apart in terms of overall look, experience, and sophistication,
★   the Cove and the Reef are the newest (and classiest) additions to the megaresort we've all come to love or hate. The 600-suite Cove opened in March 2007 with no little fanfare. From the spectacular open-air lobby to Bobby Flay's new Southwestern/Caribbean Mesa Grill, it's no wonder this beach haven is already "in" with the cool kids. The name of the game at the Cove is exclusivity, from the private poolside cabanas stocked with gourmet treats to en-suite spa treatments from Mandara Spa. Although families are welcome (there's a separate family pool), most would rather stay in one of Atlantis's main towers, so little ones can be closer to the Aquaventure water park. The Reef, brand-spankin' new for December 2007, is a 497-suite beachside condo/hotel right next door to the Cove. Each unit is decked out with a stainless steel kitchen or kitchenette (some have in-suite washers and dryers), which makes this setup perfect for self-sufficient families or those trying to stretch their dollar. **Pros:** the ultimate in luxury, uncrowded pools, incredible ocean and harbor views. **Cons:** quite a hike from the casino/restaurant/club scene that is Atlantis, on-site entertainment and dining are expensive. ⊠ *Casino Dr.* ☎ *242/363–3000 or 800/285–2684* ⊕ *www.atlantis.com* 🛏 *Cove: 600 suites. Reef: 497 suites.* ♨ *In-room at Cove: safe, Wi-Fi. In-room at Reef: safe, kitchen, refrigerator, Wi-Fi. In-hotel at Cove: 2 restaurants, room service, bars, pools, gym, spa, beachfront, water sports, laundry service, public Wi-Fi. In-hotel at Reef: pool, gym, spa, beachfront, water sports, laundry facilities, laundry service, public Wi-Fi* ⊟ *AE, D, DC, MC, V.*

$$$$ 🏨**One & Only Ocean Club.** Once the private hideaway of A&P heir
dor's Choice   Huntington Hartford, this ultraexpensive resort on magnificent Cab-
★   bage Beach's quietest stretch provides the ultimate in understated—and decidedly posh—elegance. Its Versailles Gardens includes 35 acres of terraced serenity and an imported French cloister. Set amid private

CLOSE UP

Bond in the Bahamas

In *Casino Royale*, the 21st James Bond installment, Bond took on the bad guys at an embassy, which was, in reality, the lovely Buena Vista Restaurant and Hotel in Nassau, which closed shortly after filming. The ruggedly handsome new Bond, Daniel Craig, also had the glamorous background of the One & Only Ocean Club resort on Paradise Island, where another Bond, Pierce Brosnan, frequently stays.

Bond and the Bahamas have a long relationship. Six Bond films have used the Bahamas as a backdrop, including *Thunderball*, filmed in 1965 with the original 007, Sean Connery. Connery loved the Bahamas so much he has chosen to live here year-around in the luxury gated community of Lyford Cay.

Thunderball was filmed at the Café Martinique, which, after being closed for more than a decade, reopened at Atlantis resort on Paradise Island in 2006. Scenes were also shot at the Mediterranean Renaissance–style British Colonial, built in the 1920s, and

now a Hilton. The hotel pays tribute to its illustrious Bond history with a Double-O Suite, which is filled with Bond memorabilia including posters, books, and Bond films.

The Rock Point house, better known to 007 fans as Palmyra, the villain Emilio Largo's estate, was another Bond location, and Bay Street where Bond and his beautiful sidekick Domino attended a Junkanoo carnival is still the location of Junkanoo twice a year. The *Thunderball* remake, *Never Say Never Again*, was also shot in the Bahamas, using many of the same locations as the original.

Underwater shots for many of the Bond flicks were filmed in the Bahamas, including Thunderball Grotto, popular with snorkelers, near Staniel Cay in the Exumas, while Nassau's offshore reefs were the underwater locations for the 1983 film *Never Say Never Again*, the 1967 film *You Only Live Twice*, the 1977 film *The Spy Who Loved Me*, and *For Your Eyes Only*, released in 1981.

gardens, the spacious colonial-style rooms have intricately carved furniture and marble bathrooms. The open-air restaurant, Dune, is perched over the beach. **Pros:** ultraexclusive, lovely beach, top-rate amenities. **Cons:** not within walking distance of Atlantis and its myriad restaurant and nightlife choices. ⌂ *Ocean Club Dr.* ☎ *242/363–250 or 800/321–3000* ⊕ *www.oneandonlyresorts.com* ⇥ *114 rooms, 1 suites, 5 cottages* △ *In-hotel: 2 restaurants, room service, bars, tennis courts, pool, gym, spa, beachfront, water sports, bicycles, laundry service* ▤ *AE, D, DC, MC, V.*

★ $$$$ ▦ **Sunrise Beach Club and Villas.** Lushly landscaped with crotons, coco nut palms, bougainvillea, and hibiscus, this low-rise, family-run resort on Cabbage Beach has a tropical wonderland feel. Two pools sustain the ambience with statuary and tropical plantings, and the beach is accessible via a long flight of wooden stairs built right into the cliff. Paths wind through the floral arcadia, past trickling fountains, archways, and terra-cotta tiles with color insets. Choose from one-bedroom town houses with spiral staircases that lead to an upstairs bedroom, two-bedroom apartments, or three-bedroom villas. All have full

1

equipped kitchens, king-size beds, and patios. **Pros:** on one of the best beaches on the island, lively bar on property, great for families. **Cons:** no activities, not within walking distance to other restaurants. ☒ *Casino Dr.* ☎242/363–2234 ⊕*www.sunrisebeachclub.com* ⮑*18 1-, 2-, and 3-bedroom units* ⌂*In-room: kitchen, dial-up. In-hotel: bar, pools, beachfront, laundry facilities, public Internet* ☐*AE, D, MC, V.*

★ ☾   🖼**Atlantis, Paradise Island.** A bustling fantasy world—part water park, $$$–$$$$ entertainment complex, megaresort, and beach oasis—this is by far the biggest and boldest resort in the country. The overriding theme here is water—for swimming, snorkeling, and observing marine life, as well as for mood and effect, in lagoons, caves, waterfalls, and several walk-through aquariums (touted as the largest artificial marine habitat in the world). The public areas are lavish, with fountains, glass sculptures, and gleaming shopping arcades. Numerous sporting activities are available, and there is plenty of nightlife on the premises; the casino, ringed by restaurants, is the largest in the Bahamas and the Caribbean. The most expensive rooms are in the glamorous, high-rise Royal Towers, but the Coral Towers and Beach Towers rooms are nice and still offer access to all the fun and activities. In high season (winter) expect long lines at restaurants. Despite the large number of guests on property, the pool and beach area is so expansive, you'll be sure to find a secluded spot just for you. Be aware, some Fodors.com users have complained about the resort's poor service. **Pros:**never run out of things to do, very kid-friendly, an incredible resort experience. **Cons:** very big so requires lots of walking, thousands of guests, food and drinks are expensive, service is lacking. ☒*Casino Dr.* ☎242/363–3000 or 800/285–2684 ⊕*www.atlantis.com* ⮑*2,097 rooms, 230 suites* ⌂*In-room: safe, dial-up. In-hotel: 17 restaurants, room service, bars, tennis courts, pools, gym, spa, beachfront, water sports, children's programs (ages 4–12), executive floor* ☐*AE, D, DC, MC, V* ⍾*MAP.*

$$$ 🖼**Club Land'Or.** In Atlantis's shadow just over the bridge from Nassau, this friendly time-share property has one-bedroom villas with full kitchens, bathrooms, living rooms, desks, and patios or balconies that overlook the lagoon, the gardens, or the pool. The units are described as accommodating four people, but they seem better suited for couples. The Blue Lagoon Seafood Restaurant is a favorite of locals and guests. Many activities are planned throughout the week. **Pros:** everything you need for an extended vacation, walking distance to Marina Village and Atlantis. **Cons:** surrounded by Atlantis resort, beach is quite a walk away. ☒*Paradise Beach Dr.* ☎242/363–2400 ⊕*www.clublandor.com* ⮑*72 villas* ⌂*In-room: kitchen, dial-up. In-hotel: restaurant, bars, pool, laundry facilities* ☐*AE, D, MC, V* ⍾*EP, MAP.*

$$$ 🖼**Comfort Suites.** This all-suites, three-story pink-and-white hotel has an arrangement with Atlantis that allows guests to use the megaresort's facilities. Kids can also enroll at Atlantis's Kids Camp. For many, that's reason enough to stay here, in the middle of the Paradise Island action. If you'd rather stay on the grounds, try a poolside lunch and a drink at the swim-up bar. Cozy rooms have sitting areas with sofa beds. Cabbage Beach is just a hop, skip, and a jump away. Rates include breakfast. **Pros:** access to Atlantis amenities, near shops and restaurants.

Cons: not located on a beach, in the midst of busy traffic. ✉ *Paradis Island Dr.* ☎ *242/363–3680 or 800/228–5150* ⊕ *www.comfortsuites com* ➪ *229 junior suites* ⌂ *In-room: safe. In-hotel: restaurant, ba pool* ⊟ *AE, D, MC, V* ⏣ *CP.*

$$ ▦ **Best Western Bay View Suites.** This 4-acre condominium resort has lush, intimate feel. Guests socialize around three pools (two for genera use, one reserved for the villas) that are surrounded by tropical plants including several hibiscus and bougainvillea varieties. Choose betwee one- or two-bedroom suites, villas, and town houses, all of which ar spacious, clean, comfortable, and decorated in bright island style. A rooms have private balconies or garden terraces. Cabbage Beach is 10-minute walk away. **Pros:** private "at home" feeling; free wireles throughout, including pool area. **Cons:** long walk from beach, no res taurant on property. ✉ *Bay View Dr.* ☎ *242/363–2555 or 800/757 1357* ⊕ *www.bayviewvillage.com* ➪ *25 suites, 2 villas, 3 town house* ⌂ *In-room: kitchen, Wi-Fi. In-hotel: bar, tennis court, pools, laundr facilities, public Wi-Fi* ⊟ *AE, D, MC, V.*

$$ ▦ **Hotel Riu Paradise Island.** The all-inclusive, high-rise Riu is not a grand as Atlantis next door, but it isn't far from its neighbor's casin and shares a quieter bit of the same lovely beach. The price per pe son includes meals, snacks, drinks, activities, entertainment, taxe and gratuities. **Pros:** all-inclusive, Atlantis amenities right next doo beautiful beach. **Cons:** 14-story hotel casts shade over the beach earl in the afternoon. ✉ *6307 Casino Dr.* ☎ *242/363–3500 or 888/666 1881* ⊕ *www.riu.com* ➪ *379 rooms* ⌂ *In-room: safe. In-hotel: 4 re taurants, tennis court, pool, gym, spa, beachfront, diving* ⊟ *AE, L DC, MC, V* ⏣ *AI.*

$$ ▦ **Paradise Harbour Club & Marina.** With a marina and an enviable loca tion, this collection of oversize, comfortable apartments is a great choic for those who want the freedom of a private residence with the facil ties of a large resort. Full kitchens (complete with refrigerator, miniba and dishwasher) lend a homey feeling to these somewhat characte less but very cushy lodgings. Commodious closet and sink space ar among the extras. If you prefer a view, opt for the top-floor digs. **Pro** quiet location, cooking facilities. **Cons:** need to walk or be shuttle to and from the beach, new condo built nearby towers over the prop erty. ✉ *Paradise Island Dr.* ☎ *242/363–2992* ⊕ *www.phc-bahama com* ➪ *23 units* ⌂ *In-room: kitchen. In-hotel: bar, pool, bicycl* ⊟ *AE, MC, V.*

¢ ▦ **Sivananda Yoga Retreat.** Accessible only by boat, this resort is th antithesis of high-rollers' Atlantis down the road. Guest rooms in th main house and tiny one-room bungalows overlook a gorgeous whit sand beach in a 5-acre compound that stretches from Nassau Harbo to the ocean; air-conditioning is an additional $10 per day. Tent sit are available for $55 per person. This retreat is for those who are ser ous about yoga and good health: two two-hour meditations—the fir one starting at 5 AM—and two two-hour yoga classes are mandato each day. However, during free time from 10 AM to 4 PM the retrea shuttle boat will take guests to Nassau for shopping and sightseein Yoga class platforms are next to the beach and harbor, and there a also meditation rooms, frequent guest lecturers, and special classes for advanced teacher certification. The per-person price includes two vegetarian meals each day. Rooms are austere, and guests are expected to help clean communal bathrooms. Alcohol, coffee, tea, meat, fish, cigarettes, radios, and TVs are not allowed. **Pros:** ideal for peace and quiet, inexpensive accommodations, free shuttle to and from

> ### POINCIANA JUNE
>
> During the early summer months, the Royal Poinciana trees, which go unnoticed most of the year, burst into bloom and their bright orange and red flowers are a sure sign that summer is here. There are a few hybrids with yellow flowers found around the island.

Nassau. **Cons:** strict regulations, very basic accommodations, no road access. ⊠ *Paradise Island* ☎ *242/363–2902 or 800/441–2096* ⊕ *www. my-yoga.net* ⊃ *35 single private rooms, 7 dormitory-style rooms, 12 rooms facing the beach, and tent sites* ⟐ *In-room: no a/c, no phone, no TV* ⊟ *AE, MC, V* ⟐ *AI.*

BLE BEACH

$$$$ 🖫 **Sandals Royal Bahamian Resort & Spa.** Cable Beach's most expensive spot presents elegantly furnished rooms with views of the ocean, pool, or grounds replete with pillars and faux Roman statuary. There's a state-of-the-art fitness club, and a multilingual concierge service that assists foreign guests. Nine restaurants offer cuisines ranging from Caribbean to Japanese (make reservations well in advance), and nightly entertainment takes place in the resort's amphitheater. **Pros:** no children, beautiful setting, private offshore cay. **Cons:** no children, need car or taxi to go into town, convention center popular for local functions. ⊠ *W. Bay St.* ☎ *242/327–6400 or 800/726–3257* ⊕ *www.sandals.com* ⊃ *403 rooms* ⟐ *In-room: Wi-Fi. In-hotel: 9 restaurants, room service, bars, tennis courts, pools, gym, spa, beachfront, diving, water sports* ⊟ *AE, D, MC, V* ⟐ *AI.*

$$$ 🖫 **Guanahani Village.** These substantial, well-furnished time-share and rental accommodations are perfect for young families or groups of friends traveling together. The stucco units are spread across landscaped grounds. Tiled three-bedroom luxury villas, oceanfront or garden-side, sleep six comfortably—up to eight using roll-aways (so the price is really quite reasonable when shared by several people). Each unit has oversize rooms, a delightful secluded patio, a fully equipped kitchen, a washer and dryer, and a dishwasher. The pool overlooks the ocean. **Pros:** spring breakers not allowed, great for families, tennis courts. **Cons:** no major activities, need car to go into town. ⊠ *W. Bay St.* ☎ *242/327–7568 or 242/327–4254* ⊕ *www.bluewaterresortnassau. com* ⊃ *35 units* ⟐ *In-room: kitchen, Wi-Fi. In-hotel: tennis court, pool* ⊟ *AE, D, MC, V.*

$$$ 🖫 **Sheraton Cable Beach Resort.** In 2007, this nine-story property underwent a multi-million dollar renovation. Situated on seven acres of prime beachfront property, the Sheraton has a modern, stylish, grown-up feel. But the hotel caters to kids, too, with three pools, a kids' center complete with computers, and arts and crafts. Almost all of the beautifully decorated rooms have either a pool or beach view, and all include 32-inch flat-screen TVs. Rooms have Internet access and there's Wi-Fi available in the lobby. The hotel is connected by a shopping arcade to the Crystal Palace Casino, and guests can use amenities at the Wyndham next door. **Pros:** live band on weekends, newly renovated, lots to do. **Cons:** area will be undergoing major renovations as part of the Baha Mar complex. ⊠ *W. Bay St.* ☎*242/327–6000* ⊕*www.bahamar.com* ⇥*694 rooms* ⌂*In-room: dial-up, safe. In-hotel: 3 restaurants, room service, bars, tennis courts, pools, gym, beachfront, water sports, bicycles, children's programs (ages 4–12), public Wi-Fi* ⊟*AE, D, DC, MC, V* ⫶○⫶*AI, EP.*

$$$ ▦**SuperClub Breezes Bahamas.** Right on Cable Beach, this property offers couples and singles an all-inclusive rate that covers lodging, entertainment, unlimited food and beverages, land and water sports, airport transfers, taxes, and gratuities. Take advantage of the fitness center, three freshwater pools, swim-up bar, and nightly entertainment, including local bands, toga or pajama parties, and karaoke. A huge fish chandelier and multicolor tile floor decorate the open-air lobby. Large, modern rooms are pleasant, although not striking. **Pros:** no one under 14 allowed, walking distance to Cable Beach casino. **Cons:** no children, need car or taxi to access town, in midst of Baha Mar renovation area. ⊠ *W. Bay St.* ☎*242/327–5356 or 800/859–7873* ⊕*www.breezes bahamas.com* ⇥*400 rooms* ⌂*In-hotel: 5 restaurants, bars, tennis courts, pools, gym, beachfront, water sports, bicycles, no kids under 14* ⊟*AE, MC, V* ⫶○⫶*AI.*

$$ ▦**West Wind II.** Privacy is the lure of these cozy villas on Cable Beach's west end, 6 mi from downtown. Two-bedroom, two-bath condominiums have fully stocked kitchens and balconies or patios overlooking the ocean or pools. The reasonable prices and relaxed atmosphere are ideal for families or groups on a budget, and the pleasant, quiet location—off the road amid manicured lawns and pruned gardens— gives children the freedom to play outdoors. The spectacular sea view somewhat compensates for the tiny and very windy beach. A bus stop and taxi stand are right outside. **Pros:** great for families, condos sleep six, right on Cable Beach. **Cons:** no major activities, need car or taxi to go downtown, basic amenities. ⊠ *W. Bay St.* ☎*242/327–7211 or 242/327–7019* ⊕*www.westwind2.com* ⇥*54 villas* ⌂*In-room: kitchen. In-hotel: tennis courts, pools, beachfront, water sports, laundry service* ⊟*MC, V.*

$$ ▦**Wyndham Nassau Resort & Crystal Palace Casino.** Like the Sheraton next door, this property got the Baha Mar treatment in 2007. It's still flashy, but with a more modern look. The large pool area includes a twisting waterslide and the attached casino goes all night long. There's a fully equipped fitness center with stunning beach views for guests only. High rollers can opt to stay in the Casino Tower with 30 high end executive suites. The Rainforest Theatre hosts headliners of yesterday and today, and a new cabaret show is slated to begin in the near future. **Pros:** casino on site, variety of restaurants, great pool and beach area. **Cons:** sprawling layout means lots of walking, outside looks dated, in the midst of Baha Mar renovation site ⊠ *W. Bay St.* ☎*242/327–6200*

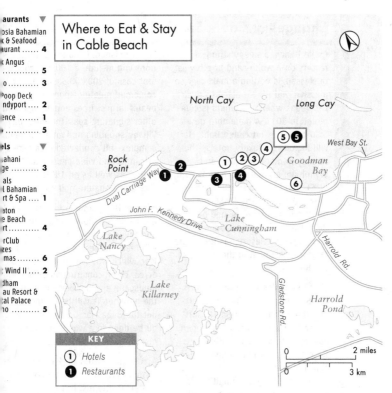

Where to Eat & Stay in Cable Beach

North Cay

Long Cay

West Bay St.

Rock Point

Goodman Bay

Dual Carriage Way

John F. Kennedy Drive

Lake Cunningham

Lake Nancy

Harrold Rd.

Gladstone Rd.

Lake Killarney

Harrold Pond

| KEY |
| Hotels |
| Restaurants |

0   2 miles

0   3 km

or 800/222–7466 ⊕*www.wyndhamnassauresort.com* ↩*820 rooms,
30 suites* ⅏*In-hotel: 6 restaurants, room service, bars, pool, gym,
beachfront, water sports, children's programs (ages 4–12), executive
floor, public Internet* ▤*AE, D, DC, MC, V* ⑩*FAP, MAP.*

ESTERN NEW PROVIDENCE & SOUTH COAST

$$ ⚏**Compass Point.** This whimsical-looking hotel made up of brightly
colored one- and two-story cottages offers a relaxing alternative to
many of the area's major resorts. Built by Island Records founder Chris
Blackwell, oceanfront rooms include a private downstairs deck com-
plete with a kitchenette for entertaining. Windows on all sides of the
rooms open to allow a cool breeze in. There is a double suite, but
it's not ideal for families with young children as the second cottage is
detached. Sit on the dock and enjoy one of the most stunning sunset
views the island has to offer. There's Internet access throughout, but
for those who didn't bring a laptop, a closet has been converted into
Hut.com, complete with a computer and printer for guests. **Pros:** best
view on the island, cool breeze wafts into rooms, access to incredible
private beach. **Cons:** in flight path, not ideal for children, expensive
taxi ride to town. ⊠*W. Bay St., Gambier* ☎*242/327–4500* ⊕*www.*

Changes at Cable Beach

Cable Beach, a sleepy string of resorts on a white-sand beach west of Nassau, is getting a makeover so massive that it's expected to rival Las Vegas when everything is completed in 2011. A mammoth new $1.6-billion resort called Baha Mar will include six luxury hotels—the already in place Sheraton and Wyndham, as well as a new Westin, W, St. Regis, and possible Caesars Resort & Casino. The 3,550-room beachside complex—owned by the Baha Mar Development Company and Starwood Resorts—is the single largest investment in the history of the Bahamas.

Cable Beach's two current resorts—the Sheraton Cable Beach Resort and the Wyndham Nassau Resort & Crystal Palace Casino—are open and operating as Cable Beach Resorts during the building of Baha Mar. The company has already spent more than $150 million renovating these two hotels and casino. The hotels will continue to operate separately until at least 2009 as the rest of Baha Mar goes up. Renovations at the Wyndham include flat-screen TVs and refrigerators in all guest rooms, and two bars are being added to the casino. The Sheraton Cable Beach Resort was completely overhauled, and now features a sophisticated lobby and brand-new room furnishings. Together, the current resorts offer 1,250 guest rooms and suites (most with ocean views), 13 restaurants and lounges, more than a half mile of gorgeous white-sand beach, and a variety of water-sport activities. Headliners continue to perform at the Rainforest Theatre and a new Cabaret Show is in the works.

When finished, Baha Mar's attractions will include a 100,000-square-foot casino, 200,000 square feet of combined meeting space, the Caribbean's largest freestanding spa with other signature spas, the West Bay Village shopping and entertainment complex—all connected by a series of canals and wide pedestrian paths—as well as an 18-hole Jack Nicklaus Signature golf course.

Michael Hong, known for his work on the $1.6 billion Bellagio Resort and Wynn Resort in Las Vegas, will lead the design team for Baha Mar, which will sprawl across 1,000 acres. The reconstruction of the landscape and the development of the new hotels will be extensive, but the Baha Mar Group says it will all be done in a way that does not disturb guest experience.

Across the harbor on Paradise Island, Kerzner International, the owner of Atlantis, has completed its $1 billion-plus phase three of development. The themed destination resort includes a variety of hotel options appealing to different tastes, an outdoor area that is more theme park than typical resort pool, and restaurants from burger joints to luxurious gourmet dining experiences.

For more information on Baha Mar, visit www.bahamar.com or www. crystalpalacevacations.com, or call 800/222–7466. For Atlantis updates, call 888/528–7155 or visit www. atlantis.com.

compasspointbeachresort.com ⇋18 cottages △In-room: kitchen, Wi-Fi. In-hotel: restaurant, bar, pool, public Wi-Fi. ▤D, MC, V.

$$
Fodor's Choice
★

🏨 **A Stone's Throw Away.** Featuring seaside comfort in fashionable surroundings, this "gourmet bed-and-breakfast"—as the French and Belgian owners describe it—is the latest luxury-boutique hideaway for celebrities. The three-story colonial-style inn with wraparound verandas is perched on a limestone cliff overlooking the beach, 13 mi west of Nassau. The public rooms and guest rooms have the atmosphere of a century-old manor house with pickled wood ceilings, pine plank floors, oriental rugs, leather plantation chairs, mahogany antiques, and a dining room that serves breakfast, lunch, and dinner. Guests can read on the porch, walk to the beach, or relax by a small pool and waterfall. **Pros:** serene, secluded public beach access, friendly staff. **Cons:** in flight path, long distance from anything else, hotel access up a steep staircase cut out of the limestone hill. ⊠*Tropical Garden Rd. and W. Bay St., Gambier* ☎*242/327–7030* ⊕*www.astonesthrowaway.com* ⇋*8 rooms, 2 suites* △*In room: dial-up. In-hotel: restaurant, room service, bar, pool, beachfront* ▤*AE, MC, V.*

$

🏨 **Orange Hill Beach Inn.** If you prefer down-home coziness over slick glamour, then this charming inn—on the site of a former orange plantation perched on a hilltop overlooking the ocean—is the place to stay. Guests are treated like family, and the homey feel extends to the comfortably eclectic living room and daytime honor bar. Danny and Judy Lowe—he's Bahamian, she's Irish—have owned the inn for more than 20 years. Orange Hill has a reputation as an inexpensive alternative for honeymooners and scuba divers. It's a half-hour drive from town, 15 minutes from the casino, and 300 feet from a pleasant roadside beach. Rooms and apartments vary considerably in size. Two cottages, including a hexagonal cabin with a pitch-pine ceiling and a sweeping view of the ocean, were added in 2005. **Pros:** across the road from a nice beach, small, family-style service. **Cons:** long distance from town, not much by way of activities. ⊠*W. Bay St.* ☎*242/327–5184* ⊕*www.orangehill.com* ⇋*30 rooms, 2 cottages* △*In-hotel: restaurant, bar, pool, laundry facilities* ▤*D, MC, V.*

NIGHTLIFE & THE ARTS

NIGHTLIFE

Paradise Island resorts have their own flashy clubs where residents and visitors alike come to enjoy late-night entertainment. The attire for attending these soirees is typically as casual as the atmosphere, although some clubs require dressier duds. The casinos are also casual, so leave your black tie at home. You have to be at least 18 years old to gamble; Bahamians and permanent residents are not permitted to indulge by law. Most coffeehouses are open late into the evening, but note that a few close around 6.

CABLE BEACH

CASINO　**Crystal Palace Casino.** Four hundred new slot machines, craps, baccarat, blackjack, roulette, Big Six, and face-up 21 are among the games in this 2007-renovated 35,000-square-foot space. There's a Sportsbook facility equipped with big-screen TVs that air live sporting events. Both VIPs and low-limit bettors have their own areas. Casino gaming lessons are available for beginners. Tables and slots are open 24 hours daily. ⊠*Wyndham Nassau Resort & Crystal Palace Casino, W. Bay St.* ☎*242/327–6200* ⊕*www.wyndhamnassauresort.com.*

NASSAU

COFFEEHOUSE　**Caffè Caribe.** In the Logos Bookstore, this tiny spot has a simple, modern look with high tables and stools. Salads, quiches, and sandwiches supplement the coffee selection; there's a long list of fruity- and nutty-flavored espressos. It closes at 6 PM weekdays, Saturday at 7 PM. ⊠*Harbour Bay Shopping Centre, E. Bay St.* ☎*242/394–7040* ⊗*Closed Sun.*

Flamingo Cigars and Gourmet Café. This simple shop is a refuge from Bay Street's shopping frenzy. The smoker's lounge upstairs is a hidden wood-paneled nook in which to savor the Cohibas and Montecristos for sale. ⊠*1 Bay St., east side of British Colonial Hilton* ☎*242/325–8510.*

NIGHTCLUBS　**Club Waterloo.** Claiming to be Nassau's largest indoor-outdoor nightclub, this club has five bars and nonstop dancing Monday through Saturday until 4 AM, and live bands on the weekend. Try the spring-break-special Waterloo Hurricane, a tropical mixture of rums and punches. ⊠*E. Bay St.* ☎*242/393–7324.*

Fluid Lounge. The hottest nightclub in Nassau is also the hardest to find. Look for the sign on downtown Bay Street in the Kings Court building. You'll walk downstairs to two bars and two dance floors, where a well-dressed crowd moves to Top 40s hits and R&B. Ladies get in free Fridays and Saturdays before 11 PM; club opens at 9. ⊠*W. Bay St., between Market and Frederick, Downtown* ☎*242/356–4691* ⊕*www.clubfluidbahamas.com* ⊠ *Admission $20, with taxi pass $5 (buy one for $5 from any taxi driver)* ⊗*Closed Mon. and Wed.*

PARADISE ISLAND

CASINO　**Paradise Island Casino.** At 50,000 square feet (100,000 if you include the dining and drinking areas), this is the Caribbean–Bahamian area's largest facility. Featuring a spectacularly open and airy design, the casino is ringed with restaurants and offers more than 1,100 slot machines, baccarat, blackjack, roulette, craps tables, and such local specialties as Caribbean stud poker. There's also a high-limit table area, and most of the eateries have additional games. Tables are open from 10 AM to 4 AM daily; slots, 24 hours. ⊠*Atlantis* ☎*242/363–3000.*

NIGHTCLUBS　**Aura.** This is the country's hottest nightclub, located upstairs at the Atlantis Casino. It's the place to see and be seen, though many of the celebrities that frequent the club opt for the ultraexclusive private lounge. Dancing goes on all night and the beautiful bartenders dazzle the crowd with their mixing techniques. Music varies, depending on the

CLOSE UP

Junkanoo

1

It's after midnight, and the streets of Nassau are crowded but hushed; the only sound is a steady buzz of anticipation. Everyone is waiting. Suddenly the streets erupt in a kaleidoscope of sights and sounds—the Junkanoo groups are rushing down Bay Street. Their vibrant costumes sparkle in the light of the street lamps, and the crowd shouts with delight. The revelers bang on goatskin drums, clang cowbells, and blow on conch-shell horns, hammering out a steady beat of celebration. It's Junkanoo time again!

Junkanoo holds an important place in the history of the Bahamas, but the origin of the word *Junkanoo* remains a mystery. Many believe it comes from John Canoe, an African tribal chief who was brought to the West Indies in the slave trade and then fought for the right to celebrate with his people. Others believe the word stems from the French *gens inconnus*, which means "the unknown people"—significant because Junkanoo revelers wear costumes that make them unrecognizable.

The origin of the festival itself is more certain. Though its roots can be traced back to West Africa, it began in the Bahamas during the 16th or 17th century when Bahamian slaves were given a few days off around Christmas to celebrate with their families. They left the plantations and had elaborate costume parties where they danced and played homemade musical instruments. They wore large, often scary-looking masks, which gave them the freedom of anonymity, so they could let loose without fear of being recognized.

Junkanoo is an important part of the Christmas season in the Bahamas. Parades are held in the wee hours of the morning (1 or 2 AM until dawn) on Boxing Day (December 26) and again on New Year's Day. Surprisingly, what appears to be a random, wild expression of joy is actually a very well-organized and planned event. Family and friends gather in large groups (often as many as 500–1,000) and perform together in the parade. Competition is heated among the groups, who choose a different theme each year and keep it a closely guarded secret until Junkanoo day, when their efforts are revealed. Most groups spend months preparing for the big day at what they call their "base camp" or "shack." They choreograph dance steps, choose music, and design intricate costumes. Then it's time to practice, practice, practice. Judges watch the event closely and award prizes for best music, best costumes, and best overall group presentation. With thousands of dollars of prize money up for grabs, people go to extremes to please the crowd and put on the best show.

The grandest Junkanoo celebration is in Nassau, where the best views are upstairs on Bay Street or on the benches that line the streets. Plan ahead and order bleacher seat tickets ($10–$50) online at www.tajiz.com. You can also experience Junkanoo on Grand Bahama Island, Eleuthera, Bimini, and Abaco. If you miss the festivities, be sure to stop by the **Junkanoo Expo** in downtown Nassau to see some of the most memorable costumes and floats from years past.

crowd. ✉ *Atlantis* ☏ *242/363–3000* ⊕ *www.atlantis.com* 💳 *Atlantis guests $20, nonguests $50–$100* ⊘ *Opens at 9* PM.

Oasis Lounge. There's live piano or vocal music here nightly from 7:30 to midnight. ✉ *Club Land'Or* ☏ *242/363–2400*.

THE ARTS

CABLE BEACH

THEATER   **Rainforest Theatre.** The redesigned theater, which now has an atmosphere true to its name, presents lavish shows. Some of the headliners who've performed here include Michael Bolton, Patti LaBelle, Boyz II Men, and the Pointer Sisters. Check with the resort for the latest offerings ✉ *Wyndham Nassau Resort & Crystal Palace Casino* ☏ *242/327–6200 Ext. 6758.*

NASSAU

THEATER   **Dundas Centre for the Performing Arts.** Plays, concerts, ballets, and musicals by local and out-of-town artists are staged here throughout the year. The box office is open from 10 AM to 4 PM. ✉ *Mackey St.* ☏ *242/393–3728.*

SPORTS & THE OUTDOORS

For all of its dining, shopping, and nightlife possibilities, Nassau's draw—as with all of the Bahamas—remains its outdoor life. With flawless weather nearly year-round, few visitors to New Providence fail to experience at least some of the natural delights that remain, even among the frenzied construction. Many of these pleasures revolve around the water, and everyone from experienced boaters and divers to novice snorkelers can enjoy seeing (in the words of one local promotion) "how the other two-thirds live." You can participate in sports activities or lie back and enjoy a cruise, often with snorkeling or other water-based fun involved.

BOATING

From Chub Cay—one of the Berry Islands 35 mi north of New Providence—to Nassau, the sailing route goes across the mile-deep Tongue of the Ocean. The Paradise Island Lighthouse welcomes yachters to Nassau Harbour, which is open at both ends. The harbor can handle the world's largest cruise liners; sometimes as many as eight tie up at one time. Two looming bridges bisect the harbor connecting Paradise Island to Nassau. Sailboats with masts taller than the high-water clearance of 72 feet must enter the harbor from the east end to reach marinas east of the bridges. On the Nassau side of the harbor, **Nassau Yacht Haven** (☏ *242/393–8173* ⊕ *www.nassauyachthaven.com*) is a 150-berth marina—the largest in the Bahamas—that also arranges fishing charters. **Brown's Boat Basin** (☏ *242/393–3331*), on the Nassau side, offers a place to tie up your boat, as well as on-site engine repairs. The marina at **Atlantis, Paradise Island** (☏ *242/363–3000*) has 63 megayacht slips. At the western end of New Providence, **Lyford Cay** (☎ *242/362–4131*), a posh development for the rich and famous, has an excellent marina, but there is limited availability for the humble masses.

A number of outfitters rent Jet Skis in front of Atlantis and the Hotel Riu on Cabbage Beach. If your children would enjoy sitting in a row on a rubber banana and bouncing along behind a motorboat, ride the big banana at **Premier Watersports** (☎ *242/324–1475, 242/427–0939 cellular*), at the beach at the Riu and Atlantis.

SHING

The waters here are generally smooth and alive with many species of game fish, which is one of the reasons why the Bahamas has more than 20 fishing tournaments open to visitors every year. A favorite spot just west of Nassau is the Tongue of the Ocean, so called because it looks like that part of the body when viewed from the air. The channel stretches for 100 mi. For boat rental, parties of two to six will pay $300 or so for a half day, $600 for a full day.

Born Free Charters (☎ *242/393–4144*) has three boats and guarantees a catch on full-day charters—if you don't get a fish, you don't pay. **Brown's Charters** (☎ *242/324–2061*) specializes in 24-hour shark fishing trips, as well as reef and deep-sea fishing. The **Charter Boat Association** (☎ *242/393–3739*) has 15 boats available for fishing charters. **Chubasco Charters** (☎ *242/324–3474* ⊕ *www.chubascocharters.com*) has four boats for sportfishing and shark-fishing charters. **Nassau Yacht Haven** (☎ *242/393–8173* ⊕ *www.nassauyachthaven.com*) runs fishing charters out of its 150-slip marina.

TNESS CLUBS & SPAS

A number of health clubs and gyms are available for those in the mood for an indoor workout or some spa pampering—an energizing alternative to shopping on an overcast day. Most clubs are stocked with the latest high-tech machinery, including stair climbers, treadmills, and exercise bikes, and offer aerobics and other fitness classes. If you plan to stay in the area for a stretch, check to see if package rates are available.

Bally Total Fitness (✉ *One Sandyport Plaza, west of Cable Beach* ☎ *242/327–2685* ⊕ *www.ballybahamas.com*), a full-service gym, offers exercise enthusiasts the standards, but try a fun Bahamian-inspired class, including Junkanoo and Soca fitness routines. Day passes are available for $15.

Located at Atlantis but open to the public, the Indonesian-inspired **Mandara Spa** (⊠*Atlantis, Casino Dr.* ☎*242/363–3000* ∰ *www.mandara spa.com*) has treatments utilizing traditions from around the world.

Windermere Day Spa at Harbour Bay (⊠*E. Bay St.* ☎*242/393–8788*) has a variety of ultramodern spa treatments—such as hydrotherapy and salt glows—as well as top-quality facials, massages, manicures, and pedicures.

GOLF

One & Only Ocean Club Golf Course (6,805 yards, par 72), formerly the Paradise Island Golf Club, had a major face-lift care of Tom Weiskopf. The championship course is surrounded by the ocean on three sides, which means that winds can get stiff. Call to check on current availability and up-to-date prices (those not staying at Atlantis or the One & Only Ocean Club may find themselves shut out completely). ⊠*Paradise Island Dr., next to airport* ☎*242/363–3925, 800/321–3000 in U.S.* ☜*18 holes $225 for nonguests. Clubs $35* ⊙*Daily 7–6.*

HORSEBACK RIDING

Happy Trails Stables gives guided 90-minute trail rides, including basic riding instruction, through remote wooded areas and beaches on New Providence's southwestern coast. Two morning group rides are offered, but private rides can be arranged at any time. Courtesy round-trip bus transportation from hotels is provided (about an hour each way). Tours are limited to eight people. There's a 200-pound weight limit, and children must be at least 12 years old. Reservations are required. ⊠*Coral Harbour* ☎*242/362–1820 or 242/323–5613* ☜*$110 per person* ▤*MC, V* ⊙*Mon.–Sat. by appointment*

PARASAILING

Premier Watersports (☎*242/324–1475, 242/427–0939 cellular*) gives you the chance to be lifted into the skies for five to eight minutes—at $50 a pop. Ask for Captain Tim or his crew on Cabbage Beach in front of the large hotels. You must be at least 8 years old.

SCUBA DIVING & SNORKELING

Most hotels have diving instructors who teach short courses, followed the next day by a reef trip. Many small operations have sprung up in which experienced divers with their own boats run custom dives for one to five people; these are often one-person efforts. In many cases, the custom dive will include a picnic lunch with freshly speared lobster or fish cooked over an open fire on a private island beach.

DIVE SITES

New Providence Island has several popular dive sites and a number of dive operators who offer regular trips. The elusive (and thus exclusive) **Lost Ocean Hole** (east of Nassau, 40–195 feet) is aptly named because it's difficult to find. The rim of the 80-foot opening in 40 feet of water is dotted with coral heads and teeming with small fish—grunts, margate, and jacks—as well as larger pompano, amberjack, and sometimes nurse sharks. Divers will find a thermocline at 80 feet, a large cave at 100 feet, and a sand ledge at 185 feet that slopes down to 195 feet. The series of shallow reefs along the 14 mi of Rose Island is known as **Rose Island Reefs** (Nassau, 5–35 feet). The coral is varied, although the reefs are showing the effects of the heavy traffic. Still, plenty of tropical fish live here, and the wreck of the steel-hulled ship *Mahoney* is just outside the harbor. **Gambier Deep Reef,** off Gambier Village about 15 minutes west of Cable Beach, goes to a depth of 80 feet. **Sea Gardens** is off Love Beach on the northwestern shore beyond Gambier. **Lyford Cay Drop-Off** (west of Nassau, 40–200-plus feet) is a cliff that plummets from a 40-foot plateau almost straight into the inky blue mile-deep Tongue of the Ocean. The wall has endless varieties of sponges, black coral, and wire coral. Along the wall, grunts, grouper, hogfish, snapper, and rockfish abound. Off the wall are pelagic game fish such as tuna, bonito, wahoo, and kingfish. The south-side reefs are great for snorkelers as well as divers because of the reefs' shallowness.

OPERATORS

All dive shops listed below are PADI facilities. Expect to pay about $65–$99 for a two-tank dive or beginner's course. Shark dives run $100–$125, and certification may cost $400 and up.

Bahama Divers Ltd. (☎ *242/393–1466 or 800/398–3483* ⊕ *www.bahamadivers.com*), the largest and most experienced dive operation in the country, offers twice-a-day dive safaris as well as half-day snorkeling trips. PADI certification courses are available for $500 a person, and there's a full line of scuba equipment. Destinations are drop-off sites, wrecks, coral reefs and gardens, and an ocean blue hole. For Paradise Island guests, Bahama Divers has opened a small dive operation (which also carries snorkel equipment for rent) in the Sheraton Grand.

Stuart Cove's Dive South Ocean (☎ *242/362–4171 or 800/879–9832*), on the island's south shore, is considered by aficionados to be the island's leading dive shop. Although they're pros at teaching beginners (scuba instruction and guided snorkel tours are available), experienced thrill-seekers flock to Stuart Cove's for the famous shark dives (Cove is one of the world's leading shark handlers). Also popular are his Out Island "Wilderness Safaris," and "Wall Flying Adventures," in which you ride an underwater scooter across the ocean wall. Check out the collection of celebrity photos. The shop runs dive trips to the south-shore reefs twice a day. The mini-sub adventure, which requires no experience, is $110, snorkeling expeditions cost $55 for adults and $30 for kids 12 and under. The shark dives are $145 for a three-hour dive.

SPECTATOR SPORTS

Among other imperishable traditions, the British handed down to the Bahamians such sports as soccer, rugby, and cricket. The latter, somewhat confusing sport (bring an expert with you, or you'll never know what's going on) is played at Haynes Oval. Baseball games take place at Queen Elizabeth Sports Center, rugby at Winton Estates, and softball at Clifford Park. For information on spectator sports, call the **Ministry of Tourism** (☎ *242/322–7500 or 800/224–2627*), or check the local papers for sports updates and calendars.

> ### GET INTO THE GAME!
>
> If you happen to be in Nassau on a Saturday or Sunday afternoon, you should drop by Haynes Oval cricket field and watch the Bahamas Cricket Club members play the country's national sport. You don't have to follow what the men in white are doing, just enjoy the game from the balcony of the Cricket Club Pub over a dinner of bangers and mash, kidney pie, and a Murphy's or Guinness. The field is wedged between Fort Charlotte and a beach—all the ingredients for a great afternoon.

SHOPPING

For many, shopping is one of Nassau's greatest delights. Bargains abound between Bay Street and the waterfront. For more upscale items, don't forget to look in the hotel arcades. You can return home with a suitcase full of handmade Bahamian goods or splurge at duty-free shops that offer savings so good you simply have to load up. You'll find duty-free prices—generally 25%–50% less than U.S. prices—on imported items such as crystal, linens, watches, cameras, jewelry, leather goods, and perfumes. Prices here rival those in other duty-free destinations.

Most of Nassau's shops are on Bay Street between Rawson Square and the British Colonial Hotel, and on the side streets leading off Bay Street. Some stores, however, are beginning to pop up on the main shopping thoroughfare's eastern end. Although a few shops will be happy to mail bulky or fragile items home for you, most won't deliver purchases to your hotel, plane, or cruise ship. Be aware that prices in shops are fixed, and do observe the local dress customs when you go shopping: shorts are acceptable, but beachwear is not.

MARKETS & ARCADES

The **International Bazaar**, a collection of shops under a huge, spreading bougainvillea, sells linens, souvenirs, and offbeat items. This funky shopping row is on Bay Street at Charlotte Street in Nassau.

The **Nassau Arcade**, on Bay Street between East Street and Elizabeth Avenue, just east of Parliament Square, houses a few small stores, including the Bahamas' Anglo-American bookstore, a tiny storefront with a smattering of interesting reading material.

Prince George Plaza, which leads from Bay Street to Woodes Rogers Walk near the dock, just east of the International Bazaar, has about two dozen shops with varied wares.

ᴘECIALTY SHOPS

ANTIQUES, ARTS & CRAFTS

Bahamacraft Centre (✉ *Paradise Island Dr., across from Hurricane Hole Plaza, Paradise Island*) offers some top-level Bahamian crafts, including a selection of authentic straw work. Dozens of vendors sell everything from baskets to shell collages inside this vibrantly colored building. You can catch a shuttle bus from Atlantis to the center.

Balmain Antiques and Gallery (✉ *Bay St. near Charlotte St., Nassau* ☎242/323–7421) collects Bahamian artwork as well as antique maps, prints, bottles, and small furniture.

BAKED GOODS

Bahamas Rum Cake Factory. Delicious Bahamian rum-soaked cakes made and packaged in tins right on the premises (peek into the bakery) are a great souvenir. Just make sure you take one home for yourself! ✉ *E. Bay St., Nassau* ☎242/328–3750.

The Bread Shop (✉ *Shirley St., east of Mackey St., Nassau* ☎242/393–7973) is, as the sign proclaims, "The home of Rosie's Raisin Bread." Cinnamon rolls, pound and banana cakes, and other sweet delights are also offered in this amiable spot in Nassau's east end.

Model Bakery (✉ *Dowdeswell St., Nassau* ☎242/322–2595), in the east end, is another great local bakery. Be sure to try the cinnamon twists.

CHINA, CRYSTAL, LINENS & SILVER

Linen Shop (✉ *Bay St., Nassau* ☎242/322–4266) sells fine embroidered Irish linens and lace.

CIGARS

Expansive displays of Cuban cigars, imported by Bahamian merchants, lure aficionados to the Bahamas for cigar sprees. Be aware, however, that some merchants on Bay Street and elsewhere in the islands are selling counterfeits—sometimes unwittingly. If the price seems too good to be true, chances are it is. Check the wrappers and feel to ensure that there's a consistent fill before you make your purchase. A number of stores along the main shopping strip stock only the best authentic Cuban stogies.

Graycliff (✉ *W. Hill St., Nassau* ☎242/302–9150 ⊕ *www.graycliff. com*) carries one of Nassau's finest selections of hand-rolled cigars, overseen by the prestigious Avelino Lara, who created some of Cuba's best-known stogies. In fact, Graycliff's operation is so popular that it has expanded the hotel to include an entire cigar factory, which is open to the public for tours and purchases. A dozen Cuban men and women roll the cigars; they live on the lovely premises and work here through a special arrangement with the Cuban government. True cigar buffs will seek out the Graycliff's owner, Enrico Garzaroli.

Havana Humidor (✉ *Crystal Court at Atlantis, Paradise Island* ☎ *242/363–5809*) has the largest selection of authentic Cuban cigars in the Bahamas. Watch cigars being made, or browse through the cigar and pipe accessories.

ECLECTIC

Bahama Handprints (✉ *Island Traders Building Annex, off Mackey St., Nassau* ☎ *242/394–4111* ⊕ *www.bahamahandprints.com* ⊘ *Closed weekends*) features local artists' sophisticated tropical prints in an array of colors. Also look for leather handbags, a wide range of women's clothing, housewares, and bolts of fabric. Ask for a free tour of the factory in back.

The Island Shop and Island Bookstore (✉ *Bay St., Nassau* ☎ *242/322-4183*) has two floors of travel guides, novels, paperbacks, gift books, and international magazines, as well as clothing, swimwear, and souvenirs. Take a peek at the Bahamian section, which has books on everything from history to cookery.

My Ocean (✉ *Charlotte St., south of Bay St., Nassau* ☎ *242/325–3050* ⊘ *Closed Sun.*) sells candles, soaps, salt scrubs, and lotions in island and ocean-inspired scents and colors, all locally made. The store also sells an eclectic mix of international home accents and gifts.

FASHION

Clothing is no great bargain in Nassau, but many stores sell fine imports. Perhaps the best local buy is brightly batiked Androsia fabric—available by the yard or sewn into sarongs, dresses, and blouses.

Brass and Leather (✉ *Charlotte St., off Bay St., Nassau* ☎ *242/394-5676*) sells leather goods for men and women, including bags, shoes, and belts.

Cole's of Nassau (✉ *Parliament St., Nassau* ☎ *242/322-8393* ✉ *Crystal Court at Atlantis, Paradise Island* ☎ *242/363–4161* ✉ *Bay Street, next to John Bull, Nassau* ☎ *242/356–2498*) is a top choice for designer fashions, sportswear, bathing suits, shoes, and accessories.

Fendi (✉ *Bay St., at Charlotte St., Nassau* ☎ *242/322–6300*) occupies a magnificent old building and carries the Italian house's luxury line of handbags, luggage, watches, jewelry, and shoes.

Tempo Paris (✉ *Bay St., Nassau* ☎ *242/323–6112*) offers men's clothing by major designers, including Ralph Lauren, Calvin Klein, and Gianni Versace.

JEWELRY, WATCHES & CLOCKS

Coin of the Realm (✉ *Charlotte St., off Bay St., Nassau* ☎ *242/322–4862 or 242/322–4497*) has Bahamian coins, stamps, native conch pearls, tanzanite, and semiprecious stone jewelry.

Colombian Emeralds International (✉ *Bay St., near Rawson Sq., Nassau* ☎ *242/326–1661* ✉ *Atlantis, Paradise Island* ☎ *242/322–3020*) is the local branch of this well-known jeweler; the stores carry a variety of fine jewelry in addition to their signature gem.

The Jewelry Box (⊠*Bay St., Nassau* ☎*242/322–4098*) specializes in tanzanite jewelry. It's the largest Bahamian supplier of this gem—mined in the foothills of Mt. Kilimanjaro—but it also sells other precious and semiprecious stones and 14-karat gold jewelry.

John Bull (⊠*284 Bay St., Nassau* ☎*242/322–4252* ⊠*Crystal Court at Atlantis, Paradise Island* ☎*242/363–3956*), established in 1929 and magnificently decorated in its Bay Street incarnation behind a Georgian-style facade, fills its complex with wares from Tiffany & Co., Cartier, Mikimoto, Nina Ricci, and Yves Saint Laurent. The company has 15 locations throughout Nassau.

PERFUMES AND COSMETICS
John Bull (⊠*284 Bay St., Nassau* ☎*242/322–4252* ⊠*Crystal Court at Atlantis, Paradise Island* ☎*242/363–3956*) has fragrances by Chanel, Yves Saint Laurent, and Estée Lauder. There are 15 locations throughout Nassau.

Perfume Bar (⊠*Bay St., Nassau* ☎*242/325–1258*) carries the best-selling French fragrance Boucheron and the Clarins line of skin-care products, as well as scents by Givenchy, Fendi, and other well-known designers.

The Perfume Shop & The Beauty Spot (⊠*Bay and Frederick Sts., Nassau* ☎*242/322–2375*) is a landmark perfumery that has the broadest selection of imported perfumes and fragrances in the Bahamas. Experienced makeup artists are on hand to help pick out the perfect foundation or blush from a wide array of lines including Lancôme, Clinique, and Chanel.

EW PROVIDENCE ISLAND ESSENTIALS

To research prices, get advice from other travelers, and book travel arrangements, visit ⊕*www.fodors.com.*

RANSPORTATION

BY AIR
Lynden Pindling International Airport (NAS), 8 mi west of Nassau by Lake Killarney, is served by an increasing number of airlines. American Eagle, an American Airlines subsidiary, flies into Nassau daily from Miami and Fort Lauderdale, and offers regular seasonal flights in and out of Chicago O'Hare. Bahamasair, the national carrier, has daily flights from Miami and Fort Lauderdale, as well as five flights weekly from Orlando. Continental flies in daily from Newark under service operated by Nassau–Paradise Island Express, and daily from West Palm Beach, Fort Lauderdale, and Miami on Gulf Stream International, another Continental partner. Delta is one of the busier carriers, with daily flights from Atlanta, Cincinnati, Charleston, New York City, and Orlando. JetBlue offers service from Boston and New York (JFK). Spirit offers flights out of Fort Lauderdale. US Airways flies in daily from Charlotte, North Carolina, and offers seasonal services from Philadelphia.

Airlines & Contacts **Bahamasair** (☎ *242/377–5505 or 800/222–4262*)
Continental (☎ *242/377–2050 or 800/231–0856*). **Delta** (☎ *800/221–1212*)
Gulf Stream International (☎ *242/377–4314 or 800/992–8532*). **JetBlue**
(☎ *242/377–4314 or 800/588–5388*). **Spirit Airlines** (☎ *800/772–7117*). **US**
Airways (☎ *242/377–8887 or 800/622–1015*).

Airport Information **Lynden Pindling International Airport (NAS)**
(☎ *242/702–1000*).

BY BOAT

Nassau is a port of call for a number of cruise lines, including Carnival
Cruise Lines, Celebrity Cruises, Disney Cruise Line, Imperial Majesty
Cruises, Norwegian Cruise Lines, and Royal Caribbean International.
Ships dock at Prince George Wharf, in downtown Nassau.

Ferries operate during daylight hours (usually 9–5:30) at half-hour
intervals between Prince George Wharf and Paradise Island. The one-
way cost is $3 per person.

BY BUS

No bus service is available from the airport to New Providence hotels,
except for guests on package tours. (Breezes, Sandals, and Atlantis have
promotional booths at the airport.)

For the adventuresome, consider jitney bus service to get around Nassau and its environs. Rides in these buses, which career along with
windows open and music blaring, range from smooth sailing to hair-
raising. If you want to join locals on a jitney, hail one at a bus stop,
hotel, public beach, or in a residential area. Most carry their owner's
name in boldly painted letters, so they're easy to spot, and with downtown's main streets being one way, it's not hard to tell where they're
going. If you're not sure of the jitney's direction, ask your concierge
on which side of the street to stand, or check with the friendly drivers.
The fare is $1; exact change is required. Call out to the driver as your
stop approaches. In downtown Nassau, jitneys wait on Frederick Street
and along the western end of Bay Street. Bus service runs throughout
the day until 7.

BY CAR

For exploring at your leisure, it's best to have a car. Rentals are available at Nassau International Airport, downtown, on Paradise Island,
and at some resorts. Plan to pay $80–$120 per day, depending on the
type of car. Gasoline costs between $4 and $5 a gallon. Remember to
drive on the left.

Avis Rent-A-Car has branches at the Nassau International Airport, on
Paradise Island in the Paradise Village Shopping Centre, and downtown, just west of the British Colonial Hotel. Budget has branches at
the Nassau International Airport and on Paradise Island. Dollar Rent-
a-Car, which often has the lowest rates (there are often $39 rentals
available), can be found at Nassau International Airport and downtown, at the base of the British Colonial Hotel. Hertz has branches at
Nassau International Airport and on East Bay Street, a block east of the
bridge from Paradise Island. Thrifty has a branch at the airport.

Major Agencies **Avis Rent-A-Car** (☎ *242/326–6380 or 800/288–0668*). **Budget** (☎ *242/323–7191 or 242/363–3095*). **Dollar Rent-a-Car** (☎ *242/325–3716*). **Hertz** (☎ *800/654–3131 or 242/377–8684*). **Thrifty** (☎ *242/325–3716*).

BY CARRIAGE

Beautifully painted horse-drawn carriages will take as many as four people around Nassau at a rate of $10 per adult and $5 per child for a 30-minute ride; don't hesitate to bargain. Most drivers give a comprehensive tour of the Bay Street area, including an extensive history lesson. Look for the carriages on Woodes Rogers Walk, in the center of Rawson Square.

BY SCOOTER

Two people can ride around the island on a motor scooter for about $35 for two hours, $40 for three hours, $50 for a full day. Helmets and insurance for both driver and passenger are mandatory and are included in the rental price. Many hotels have scooters on the premises. You can also try any of the scooter rental booths on West Bay Street, in the British Colonial Hilton parking lot, or check out the stands in Rawson Square. Remember to drive on the left.

BY TAXI

Taxis are generally the best and most convenient way to get around New Providence. Fares are determined by zone. The fare is $6 for trips within downtown Nassau and on Paradise Island (which includes the bridge toll), $9 from Paradise Island to downtown, and $18 from Cable Beach to Paradise Island (including toll). Fares are for two passengers; each additional passenger is $3, regardless of the destination. It's customary to tip taxi drivers 15%. You also can hire a car or small van for about $50 per hour.

A taxi ride from the airport to Cable Beach costs $20; to Nassau, $35; and to Paradise Island, $45 (this includes the $1 causeway toll). These are fixed costs for two passengers; each additional passenger is $3 and excess baggage costs $2 a bag.

Bahamas Transport has radio-dispatched taxis. You can call the Taxi Cab Union directly for a cab. There are also stands at major hotels, or the front desk can call you a cab.

Taxi Companies **Bahamas Transport** (☎ *242/323–5111*). **Taxi Cab Union** (☎ *242/323–4555 or 242/323–5818*).

CONTACTS & RESOURCES

BANKS & EXCHANGE SERVICES

Principal banks on New Providence Island are Bank of the Bahamas, Citibank, First Caribbean, Royal Bank of Canada, and Scotiabank. Banks are open on the island Monday through Thursday from 9:30 to 3 and Friday from 9:30 to 5. Banks are closed on the weekend, but most have international ATMs scattered throughout the island.

EMBASSIES

Contacts **U.S. Embassy** (⊠ *Queen St., across from British Colonial Hilton, Nassau* ☎ *242/322–1181* 🖶 *242/328–7838*).

EMERGENCIES

In an emergency dial 911 or 919. Princess Margaret Hospital is government operated, and Doctors Hospital is private.

Contacts **Ambulance** (☎ *911, 919, or 242/322–2881*). **Doctors Hospital** (⊠ *Collins Ave. and Shirley St., Nassau* ☎ *242/322–8411*). **Police** (☎ *911, 919, or 242/322–4444*). **Princess Margaret Hospital** (⊠ *Shirley St., Nassau* ☎ *242/322–2861*).

TOUR OPTIONS

Island tours include sightseeing tours of Nassau and the island, glass bottom boat tours to Sea Gardens, and cruises to offshore cays, all starting at $12. A full day of ocean sailing will cost around $60. In the evening, there are sunset and moonlight cruises with dinner and drinks ($35–$50) and nightlife tours to casino cabaret shows and nightclubs ($28–$45). Tours may be booked at hotel desks or directly through tour operators, which have knowledgeable guides and a selection of tours in air-conditioned cars, vans, or buses.

CRUISE TRIPS One of the best ways to enjoy Nassau's seafaring pleasures is to sign up with one of the many day or evening cruise operators, typically on a catamaran or similar sailboat. These offerings range from three-hour snorkeling trips to romantic sunset cruises or full-day excursions. Prices are fairly standard among the operators: A half-day snorkeling cruise will run about $45, and a full day $60, usually including a drink and snacks; prices for a sunset sail, with drinks and hors d'oeuvres are around the same. Full-day or dinner cruises, both with meals, cost around $50. Hotel transportation is generally included.

Barefoot Sailing Cruises transports you to a secluded Rose Island beach for snorkeling and sunbathing on a half-day sail or snorkel cruise; other options include an all-day island barbecue and champagne sunset cruise. Feeling luxurious? Arrange a private dinner cruise.

Flying Cloud runs half-day catamaran cruises at 9:30 and 2, as well as sunset "sail-and-a-dinner" cruises on which you can enjoy a candlelight meal in a secluded cove. A five-hour Sunday cruise departs at 10 AM.

Island Tours offers a half-day catamaran excursion to Rose Island beach for beach volleyball and snorkeling. Snacks and an open bar are included, as are bus transfers to and from your hotel.

Sea Island Adventures runs full-day trips to Blackbeard Cay for snorkeling and a tropical lunch, as well as sunset cruises. Private charters can also be arranged.

Cruise Lines **Barefoot Sailing Cruises** (☎ *242/393–0820* ⊕ *www.barefootsailingcruises.com*). **Flying Cloud** (☎ *242/363–4430* ⊕ *www.flyingcloud.info*). **Island Tours** (☎ *242/327–8653*). **Sea Island Adventures** (☎ *242/327–8459* ⊕ *www.bahamasvacationguide.com/seaislandadventures.html*).

OUT ISLANDS TRIPS Several options exist for getaways to the less-frequented Out Islands. Expect to pay from $115 for no-frills ferry service to several hundred dollars for full-day excursions with meals, snorkeling, and sightseeing.

Bahamas Fast Ferries provides a wonderful way to escape to Harbour Island—possibly the most charming island in the Bahamas—Spanish Wells, or unspoiled Eleuthera; the high-speed, colorful, and extremely safe *Bo Hengy* catamaran whisks you from Nassau to Out Island getaways in two hours. Book just transport or, better yet, the Bo Hengy Harbour Island package ($174 for adults, $114 for children), which includes a historic walking tour of Harbour Island, a great lunch, and beach time at the famous pink sands—Fast Ferries has its own fully equipped cabana on the beach with complimentary refreshments. You'll return to Nassau by nightfall.

Exuma Powerboat Adventures offers full-day excursions to the Exuma Cays on their three speedboats. You can feed iguanas at Allan's Cay, participate in a nature walk, and do some snorkeling in the Exumas' Land and Sea Park. There are also shallow-water shark feeds. It's a great way to experience some of the beauty of the less-developed islands outside Nassau. Lunch is included.

Island World Adventures offers full-day excursions to Saddleback Cay in the Exumas on a high-speed powerboat. You can take a guided trek and learn about Bahamian flora and fauna, or just snorkel and sunbathe the day away. The all-inclusive trip is $190, which includes lunch, soft drinks, beer, and rum punch.

Seaplane Safaris utilizes low-flying craft for the Exuma Cays trip, allowing you to glide over the water's surface. You can swim right off the seaplane into Thunderball Grotto, an eerie natural formation (scenes from the James Bond movie bearing its name were filmed here), and enjoy some snorkeling, explore nature trails, or simply loll on the beach on Warderick Wells, the headquarters of the Land and Sea Park. Lunch is included, and the trip takes a full day.

Contacts Bahamas Fast Ferries (☎ 242/323–2166 ⊕ www.bahamasferries.com). **Exuma Powerboat Adventures** (☎ 242/63–1466 ⊕ www.powerboatadventures.com). **Island World Adventures** (☎ 242/363–3333 ⊕ www.islandworldadventures.com). **Seaplane Safaris** (☎ 242/393–2522 or 242/393–1179).

SPECIAL-INTEREST TOURS During the Close Encounter ($85 per person) arranged by Dolphin Encounters on Blue Lagoon Island (Salt Cay), just east of Paradise Island, you stand in waist-deep water while dolphins play around you. The two-hour program consists of an educational session as well as the encounter. Trainers are available to answer questions. Swim-with-the-Dolphins ($165 per person) actually allows you to swim with these friendly creatures for about 30 minutes. Programs are available daily 8–5:30, and there's a nominal cost for transfer from your hotel. Make reservations as early as possible.

Bahamas Outdoors Ecoventures is a unique, half-day ecotourism adventure that combines all-terrain bicycle rides through forests and along coastlines and birding and nature tours by car ($59 per person).

Seaworld Explorer is a "semi-submarine" that cruises through the harbor as it makes its way to Sea Gardens Marine Park; you can sit above water on the deck or descend to view the ocean life firsthand through undersea windows. It costs $45 per person for a 1½-hour trip.

Contacts **Bahamas Outdoors Ecoventures** (☎ *242/362–1574* ⊕ *www.bahamas outdoors.com).* **Dolphin Encounters** (☎ *242/363–1003* ⊕ *www.dolphinencounters. com).* **Seaworld Explorer** (☎ *242/356–2548).*

WALKING **TOURS** A one-hour walking tour around Historic Nassau, arranged by the Tourist Information Office at Rawson Square, is offered daily from 10 am to 2 PM. The cost is $10. Call ahead for information and reservations.

Contact **Historic Nassau** (☎ *242/395–8382).*

VISITOR INFORMATION

The Ministry of Tourism's Help Line is an information source that operates from 8 AM to midnight daily. The ministry also operates tourist information booths at Nassau International Airport, open daily from 8:30 AM to 11:30 PM, and at the Welcome Center (Festival Place) adjacent to Prince George Wharf, open daily from 9 AM to 5 PM. The numbers are 242/323–3182 and 242/323–3183. Ask about Bahamahosts, trained tour guides who will tell you about island history and culture and pass on their individual knowledge of Bahamian folklore.

The Ministry of Tourism's People-to-People Program sets you up with a Bahamian family with similar interests to show you local culture firsthand. It's best if you make arrangements—through your travel agent or by calling direct—prior to your trip. People-to-People also holds teas at Government House and sponsors activities for spouses of conference attendees, student exchanges, and pen-pal programs.

Visitor information **Ministry of Tourism** (☎ *242/322–7500 or 242/302–2000* ⊕ *www.bahamas.com* **People-to-People Program** (☎ *242/324–9772 o 242/356–0435* ⊕ *www.peopletopeople.bahamas.com).*

WEDDINGS Fallen in love? The Ministry of Tourism's Wedding Division arranges weddings for visiting couples. Ministry staff will take care of all the paperwork and set up ceremonies ranging from a simple seaside "I do" to more outrageous nuptials. Underwater vows, anyone?

Contact **Wedding Division** (☎ *242/356–0435).*

Grand Bahama Island

WORD OF MOUTH

"Across the street from the (Westin), there's a marketplace with lots of little restaurants and stores. I'd recommend eating most of your meals over there. Much cheaper but still very good. The area felt very safe."

-caribtraveler

"Rent a scooter and head out to Gold Rock Beach, a really fun day trip, and the beach is superb. There are many beaches along the way that were totally empty of people, really nice."

—soboyle

Updated by
Chelle Koster
Walton

GRAND BAHAMA, ONCE A MECCA for gamblers and golfers in th
'60s and '70s, is again coming into its own as modern vacatione
discover its miles of gorgeous, largely underutilized beaches; its cle
turquoise waters and teeming coral reefs; and its vast acreage of und
veloped backcountry and fishing settlements. The fourth-largest islar
in the Bahamas after Andros, Eleuthera, and Great Abaco, it lies on
52 mi off Palm Beach, Florida. The Gulf Stream's ever-warm waters la
its western tip, and the Little Bahama Bank protects it from the nort
east. On average, about 14% of the more than 5 million people wh
come to the Bahamas each year visit Grand Bahama Island.

In 1492, when Columbus set foot on the Bahamian island of San Sa
vador, Grand Bahama was already populated. Skulls found in cav
here attest to the existence of the peaceable Lucayans, who were co
stantly fleeing the more bellicose Caribs. The skulls show that th
parents flattened their babies' foreheads with boards to strengthe
them, making them less vulnerable to the cudgels of the Caribs, wh
were reputedly cannibalistic.

Spanish conquistadors visited the island briefly in the early 16th ce
tury. They used it as a watering hole but dismissed it as having n
commercial value and went on their way. In the 18th century, Loyalis
settled on Grand Bahama to escape the wrath of American revolutio
aries who had just won the War of Independence. The 150-year-old S
Peter's Anglican Church in the settlement of Eight Mile Rock, just we
of Freeport Harbour, survives from the era of colonial exodus. Whe
Britain abolished the slave trade early in the 19th century, many of t
Loyalists' former slaves settled here as farmers and fishermen.

Grand Bahama took on new prominence in the Roaring '20s, whe
the island's western end became a convenient jumping-off point f
rumrunners ferrying booze to Florida during Prohibition. In the 195(
when the harvesting of Caribbean yellow pine trees (now protected l
Bahamian environmental law) was the island's major industry, Ame
can financier Wallace Groves envisioned Grand Bahama's grandic
future. In 1955, largely due to Groves's efforts and those of Briti
industrialist Sir Charles Hayward, the Bahamian government signed a
agreement that set in motion the development of a planned city, a po
an airport, roads, waterways, and utilities. City builders also promot
a brand of exotic tourism and industrial development free of corpora
property, excise, or income taxes and custom duties. From that agre
ment, the city of Freeport and later Lucaya evolved. They are separat
by a 4-mi stretch of East Sunrise Highway (aka Churches Row, for
the houses of worship that line it), although few can tell you where o
community ends and the other begins.

Most of Grand Bahama's commercial activity is concentrated in Fre
port, the Bahamas' second-largest city. Despite hurricane setbac
the city's restaurants, clubs, and International Bazaar shopping cen
bustle with activity.Cruise-ship passengers arrive at Lucayan Harbo
mostly from the Fort Lauderdale and Cape Canaveral Florida por
The harbor sports a clever Bahamian-style look, and an entertainme

GRAND BAHAMA'S TOP 5

The Dolphin Experience. Choose your level of involvement, from merely petting dolphins to diving with them.

Fish Fry. Head to Smith's Point every Wednesday night to feast and party with the locals on the beach. On Thursday night, the festivities move to Eight Mile Rock's Sunset Village.

Lucayan National Park. Take in a variety of habitats at this natural beauty—from secluded beaches to bat caves.

Port Lucaya Marketplace. The most lively spot on the island, this charming Bahamian-style cluster of shops, cafés, and bars also encompasses a harbor from where fishing and boating charters of all sorts depart.

Snorkel or Dive. There's only one way to truly see the beautiful fish and dolphins that populate the incredible reefs and caves around Grand Bahama Island—so grab a snorkel or regulator and hop on in.

and-shopping village. The airport, updated in 2005, also has a welcoming, modern feel.

Lucaya, with its grand and sprawling Westin and Sheraton Grand Bahama Island Resort (formerly Our Lucaya), claims the role of island tourism capital. With its modern shopping complex, as well as a 38,000-square-foot casino, it has raised the bar for the island. In West End, Westin-Sheraton's challenge was met with the groundbreaking for the future Ginn Sur Mer luxury residential-resort marina and golf development, which has folded the existing deluxe Old Bahama Bay resort into its total 2,200 acres. The development will roll out during the next 10 years, with some resort facilities—a golf course and more than 100 new bungalows—to open by the end of 2009.

Despite the bustle of commerce and the influx of tourists, 96-mi-long Grand Bahama offers many opportunities to enjoy solitude and nature. For the past few decades, tourism forces have shifted the emphasis away from Freeport greater Grand Bahama Island, raising awareness of what lies beyond shopping and gambling. Nature-lovers should not miss two spots on the island: the Bahamas National Trust's (BNT) Lucayan National Park and the BNT Rand Nature Centre. Ecosensitivity has spawned stimulating ecotourism adventures, including kayak trips through the national park, bird-watching excursions to spot species not found elsewhere in North America, scuba and snorkeling tours of coral reefs, and horseback rides through pine forests and along ocean beaches.

Grand Bahama Island also affords a plenitude of opportunities for heritage tourism. The friendly local population is accessible in daily interaction and through the People-to-People Program (☎ *242/352–8044* ⊕ *www.peopletopeople.bahamas.com*), which can hook you and your family up with hospitable locals who share like interests. Most restaurants outside the large resorts serve Bahamian cuisine, and many attractions and tours explore the island's history and culture. For a

GREAT ITINERARIES

Numbers in the text correspond to numbers in the margins and on the Freeport-Lucaya map.

IF YOU HAVE 3 DAYS

Begin in the morning with a shopping binge at **Port Lucaya Marketplace** ❹. Stop at UNEXSO ❺ next door to make reservations for tomorrow's swim with dolphins, resort dive course, or excursion. Have lunch at the marketplace before heading to the beach across the street for an afternoon of sunning and water sports. Hit the restaurants and bars at the marketplace for the evening's entertainment. The next day, after your dolphin experience, explore the **Freeport** area, beginning at **International Bazaar** ❶ for more shopping. Get a quick taste of Bahamian nature at **Bahamas National Trust Rand Nature Centre** ❸. Catch a fish fry or beach bonfire for your evening's entertainment. On Day 3, head west to **Taíno Beach** for great beach action, lunch, and sunning. Catch an evening dinner cruise and show with **Bahama Mama Cruises.**

IF YOU HAVE 5 DAYS

With an extra two days, follow the three-day itinerary above and spend Day 4 on an all-day eco- or heritage tour or snorkel excursion. The next day, catch a tour bus to **West End** for an eyeful of local culture. Have dinner in Freeport and prowl the nightclubs around International Bazaar for after-dark fun.

IF YOU HAVE 7 DAYS

A week allows you to explore in greater depth the island's environmental treasures. For the first five days use the itinerary above, and on Day 6 visit **Lucayan National Park** and its beach—either on your own or with a tour group. In the afternoon, do a snorkel or fishing excursion and have dinner at one of the restaurants of Westin and Sheraton Grand Bahama Island Resort. Spend your last morning horseback riding down the beach. In the afternoon, go on a semisubmarine or glass-bottom boat tour. Have dinner at Taíno Beach or Smith's Point.

potent taste of island tradition, plan your visit during Junkanoo celebrations at Christmastime and in summer. A throwback to slaver days, Junkanoo colorfully showcases the song, dance, and spirit of Grand Bahama Island with bright and extravagant costumes, horns, bells, drums, and whistles.

EXPLORING GRAND BAHAMA

Shopping, golfing, and gambling initially drew many of Grand Bahama's first tourists, but today, beach-going, kayaking, and exploring the island's old fishing settlements are also popular on visitors' to-do lists

Freeport, once the hub of the gambling and commercial scenes, await the new owner for its Royal Oasis resort complex of hotels, casino and golf courses to renovate and reopen. Hurricanes in 2004 and 200 shut down the former exotic playground for high-rollers and shop pers. Today, Lucaya sees most of the tourism action, but long before either resort town was invented, settlements clustered around coasta areas where islanders made their living from the sea. That way of life remains intact in the island's far-reaching areas on the West End and East End. Driving to these far-flung areas is a cinch, as traffic is practically nonexistent, especially out toward East End.

The best way to taste local culture is in the restaurants and natural areas. Even in the middle of town, environmental attractions introduce visitors to the curly tailed lizards, Bahama parrots, and "flutterbys" (the Bahamian word for butterflies) that make their home in the islands. Of course, shops, greens, and the casino scene remain prominent to round out the Grand Bahama experience.

IT'S PARTY TIME!

Derived from African masked rituals and, according to legend, a slave named John Canoe who led liberation efforts, Junkanoo is the quintessential form of Bahamian festival. At early Junkanoo parades, revelers wore "scrap" costumes, made from strips of cloth and other bright bits of material. Today, the costumes have grown into elaborate, expensive human floats made of cardboard and brightly colored crepe paper fringes. Freeport's festivities happen New Year's Day; West End's on Boxing Day (Dec. 26).

ABOUT THE RESTAURANTS

For a true Bahamian dining experience, look for restaurants named after the owner or cook—such as Becky's, Geneva's Place, and Georgie's. Conch, grouper, and Bahamian lobster are the specialties, fresh from the local waters. Go to the colorful conch beach shacks at Taíno Beach and at Lucaya, just west of Westin and Sheraton Grand Bahama Island Resort. Equally colorful are the owners of such places, such as Billy Joe and radio personality Tony Macaroni, famous for their conch specialties.

The Grand Bahama dining scene stretches far beyond traditional Bahamian cuisine. The resorts and shopping centers have eateries that rate with Nassau's finest, serving up everything from Italian and English fare to fine Continental and creative Pacific Rim specialties. Most restaurants conveniently display their menus outside.

ABOUT THE HOTELS

Accommodations took a step up when Westin and Sheraton Grand Bahama Island Resort (formerly Our Lucaya) opened its doors in 2000. It had a rejuvenating effect on an island whose resorts had grown dated and faded, and other smaller hotels around the island took the cue to spruce up. With the 2005 groundbreaking of megaresort–residential property Ginn Sur Mer, boasting its own private airport and two golf courses outside of West End, the old capital area promises to rise again to its former bustling status in the days when Jack Tar Village hosted the sterling yacht crowd. Old Bahama Bay was purchased in early 2007 by the Ginn Sur Mer developers.

In Freeport, the Royal Oasis, devastated by hurricane blows in 2004 and 2005, awaits resurrection. At this writing, the resort has been purchased but no projected opening dates or plans are known.

IF YOU LIKE

HITTING THE SAND

What Bahamas vacation is complete without a beach? And Grand Bahama Island has more than its share fringing its 96-mi length. All dusted with platinum sands, some are bustling with water-sports activity—while others lie so far off the beaten path it takes a four-wheel-drive vehicle and local knowledge to find them. Lucaya and Taíno beaches are the most accessible to the general public. Restaurants and bars provide visitors an anchor and offer water-sports rentals and tours. Many resorts off the beach provide free shuttles, and some beach bars have vans that will pick you up at your hotel.

GOLF

Golf was a big deal on the island long before it became fashionable in the late 1990s. This means that many of the golf courses have a classic design, though most have been renovated in recent years. With plenty of room to build, early designers made the fairways long and scenic, while challenging golfers with lots of water. Today's courses retain those characteristics, but have been renovated and improved upon, one notable addition being the golf school at Lucayan Country Club's Lucayan Course.

SHOPPING CLOSE TO HOME

Savvy shoppers head directly to the duty-free shops for great buys on liquor, jewelry, china, perfume, and other luxury items. If you're an experienced Caribbean duty-free buyer, however, you'll quickly realize that these aren't the best deals to be had in the islands—but they are the closest to the United States. At the other end of the scale, the straw markets are fun, colorful, and sell cheap souvenirs that make good gifts. Do realize that most of the items are made in Taiwan or Japan. Look in the galleries and at the row of local arts-and-crafts shops at the Port Lucaya Marketplace for more authentic island craftsmanship.

SNORKELING & SCUBA DIVING

Between the shipwrecks, caves, and coral reefs, Grand Bahama Island offers some of the Bahamas' most varied and vivid underwater scenery. Snorkeling can be anything but tame with blue holes and marine life to discover. Most resorts have snorkeling and scuba facilities. A pioneer in diving, Underwater Explorers Society (UNEXSO) has set a high standard for scuba charters. It's particularly famous for its shark and dolphin dives.

EXPLORING NATURE

Rare birds and stretches of undisturbed wilderness attract nature-lovers to the island's "bush," as natives call it. Explore by foot, bike, kayak, or jeep safari to discover not only the island's natural wonders but also its intriguing past. Geological features range from gorgeous sandy beaches to limestone caves and pine forests. With the right guide, you'll learn how social and natural history intertwine on the island, where bush medicine and fishing are only two of the ways man still depends on nature.

Grand Bahama Island accommodations remain some of the Bahamas' most affordable, especially those away from the beach. The majority of these are located near the two major shopping centers and provide free shuttle service to the nearest stretch of sand.

WHAT IT COSTS IN U.S. DOLLARS					
	¢	$	$$	$$$	$$$$
AURANTS	under $10	$10–$20	$20–$30	$30–$40	over $40
ELS	under $100	$100–$200	$200–$300	$300–$400	over $400

Restaurant prices are for a main course at dinner, excluding gratuity, typically 15%, which is often automatically added to the bill. Hotel prices are for two people in a standard double room in high season, excluding service charges and 6%–12% tax.

TIMING

Anytime is a good time to take advantage of Grand Bahama Island's sunny skies and Gulf Stream–warmed waters. Summers can get oppressively hot (into the mid- and high 90s) and muggy, however; unless you're planning on doing a lot of snorkeling, diving, and other water sports, you may want to schedule your trip for cooler months. After-noon thunderstorms and occasional tropical storms and hurricanes also make summer less attractive weatherwise. The island averages around 20 days of rain per month from June to September, but it usually falls briefly in the afternoon. The good news is that hotel rates plummet and diving and fishing conditions are great.

As one of the northernmost Bahama Islands, Grand Bahama experiences temperatures dipping into the 60s with highs in the mid-70s in January and February, so you may need a jacket and wet suit. On the upside, the migrant bird population swells and diversifies during that time of year. The other timing considerations are seasonal crowds and the subsequent increase in room rates. High tourist season runs from Christmas to Easter, peaking during spring break (late February to mid-April), when the weather is the most agreeable. To avoid the crowds, high prices, heat, and cold, visit from October through mid-December.

OUND THE ISLAND

Grand Bahama's appeal lies in its combination of commercial vitality and natural beauty. In the two main towns, Freeport and Lucaya, visitors can find much of what bustling Nassau has to offer: resort hotels, fine restaurants, golfing, duty-free shopping complexes, and gambling. But on Grand Bahama, unlike New Providence, the touristy spots take up only a small portion of an island that, on the whole,

> **DID YOU KNOW?**
>
> The term "Lucayan" is derived from the Arawak Indian word Lukka-Cairi, or "Island People." The early tribespeople gave the Bahama Islands its first name, the Lucayas.

consists of uninhabited stretches of sand and forest.

Just steps from the action, outdoor opportunities abound, particularly water-related ones. The island is a mecca for scuba divers and is home to the world-famous Underwater Explorers Society (UNEXSO), plus a plethora of other dive centers. Surrounding waters lure anglers from around the world to compete in big-game and bonefishing tournaments, such as the Bahamas Waho Championship, part of which is held in Grand Bahama each winte For many landlubbers, the island's golf courses—known for their lor fairways and water challenges—guarantee year-round entertainment. surge in ecosensitivity has generated an increase in nature-based tou ism opportunities, both on land and in the water. And then there swimming and snorkeling, perhaps two of the most popular vacatic activities in the Bahamas.

> ### FOLLOW THE SIGNS
>
> Roads in Grand Bahama Island are good, and the billboards are entertaining, if instructive: UNDERTAKERS LOVE OVERTAKERS (i.e., people who pass), and LITTERING IS STUPID; DON'T DO IT. How's that for straightforward?

FREEPORT

Freeport, once an attractive, planned city of modern shopping center resorts, and other convenient tourist facilities, took a bad hit from t hurricanes of 2004 and 2005. It struggles to get back in the game, b still offers attractions and facilities for visitors. The airport is just a fe minutes from downtown, and the harbor is about the same distance

SIGHTS TO SEE

★ ❸ **Bahamas National Trust Rand Nature Centre.** On 100 acres just minut from downtown Freeport, ½ mi of self-guided botanical trails sho off 130 types of native plants, including many orchid species. The ce ter is the island's birding hot spot, where you might spy a red-tail hawk or a Cuban emerald hummingbird sipping hibiscus nectar. T new visitor center hosts changing local art exhibits and some reside animals, including a Bahama boa. Outside you can visit the caged on eyed Bahama parrot the center has adopted. On Tuesday and Thursd free guided tours focusing on the use of plants in Bahamian bush me cine depart at 10:30 AM. The reserve is named for philanthropist Jam H. Rand, the former president of Remington Rand, who donated hospital and library to the island. ⊠ *E. Settlers Way* ☎ *242/352–54.* 🖃 *$5* ⏰ *Weekdays 9–4; guided nature walk by advance reservation*

❶ **International Bazaar.** Though the 2004 post-hurricane closure of t Royal Oasis Resort and Casino has given this once-vibrant shoppi area a down-at-the-heels look, some restaurants and shops, along wi the straw market, remain open, especially along the perimeter and International Arcade at the south end. At the entrance stands a 35-fc torii arch, a red-lacquered gate that is a traditional symbol of w come in Japan. ⊠ *W. Sunrise Hwy. and Mall Dr.* ☎ *No phone* 🖃 *Fr* ⏰ *Mon.–Sat. 10–6.*

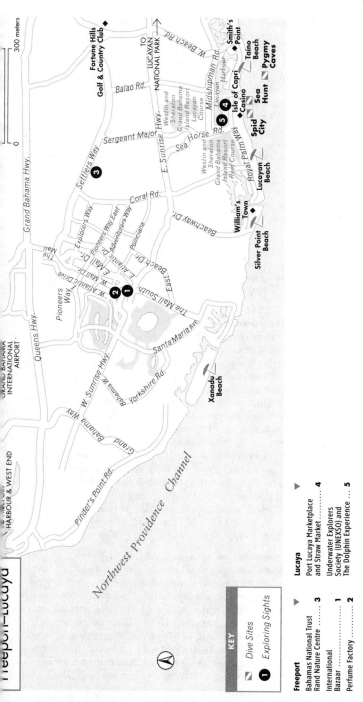

Freeport-Lucaya

300 meters

TO LUCAYAN NATIONAL PARK →

GRAND BAHAMA INTERNATIONAL AIRPORT

HARBOUR & WEST END

Northwest Providence Channel

Grand Bahama Hwy.

Queens Hwy.

Pinder's Point Rd.

W. Sunrise Hwy.

Grand Bahama Way

Bahama W. Sunrise Hwy.

Yorkshire Rd.

Santa Maria Ave.

Pioneers Way

The Mall

Explorer's Way

E. Mall Dr.

W. Mall Dr.

Adventurers Way

Pioneers Dr.

Atlantic Dr.

Poinciana

E. Atlantic Dr.

Beach Dr.

East

The Mall South

Beachway Dr.

Coral Rd.

Settler's Way

Sergeant Major

Balao Rd.

E. Sunrise Hwy.

Sea Horse Hwy.

Westin and Sheraton Grand Bahama Island Resort Lucayan Course

Westin and Sheraton Grand Bahama Island Resort Reef Course

Midshipman Rd.

W. Beach Rd.

Lucayan Harbour

Royal Palm Way

Fortune Hills Golf & Country Club

Xanadu Beach

Silver Point Beach

William's Town

Lucayan Beach

Spid City

Isle of Capri Casino

Sea Hunt

Taino Beach

Smith's Point

Pygmy Caves

KEY

◪ Dive Sites

❶ Exploring Sights

Freeport

Bahamas National Trust
Rand Nature Centre **3**

International
Bazaar **1**

Perfume Factory **2**

Lucaya

Port Lucaya Marketplace
and Straw Market **4**

Underwater Explorers
Society (UNEXSO) and
The Dolphin Experience ... **5**

2

★ ❷ **Perfume Factory.** The quiet and elegant Perfume Factory occupies a replica 19th-century Bahamian mansion—the kind built by Loyalists who settled in the Bahamas after the American Revolution. The interior resembles a tasteful drawing room. This is the home of Fragrance of the Bahamas, a company that produces perfumes, colognes, and lotions using the scents of jasmine, cinnamon, gardenia, spice, and ginger. Take a free five-minute tour of the mixology laboratory and get a free sample. For $30 an ounce, you can blend your own perfume using any of the 35 scents ($15 for 1½ ounces of blend-it-yourself body lotion). Sniff mixtures until they hit the right combination, then bottle, name, and take home the personalized potion. ⊠ *Behind International Bazaar, on access road* ☎ 242/352–9391 ⊕ *www.perfumefactory.com* ⊠ *Free* ⊙ *Weekdays 9:30–5, Sat. 11–3.*

LUCAYA

Lucaya, on Grand Bahama's southern coast and just east of Freeport, was developed as the island's resort center. These days, it's booming with a megaresort complex, a fine sandy beach, duty-free shopping, championship golf courses, a first-class dive operation, Port Lucaya's marina facilities, and a casino.

SIGHTS TO SEE

⟲ ❺ **The Dolphin Experience.** Encounter Atlantic bottlenose dolphins in Sanc-
Fodor's Choice tuary Bay at one of the world's first and largest dolphin facilities, about
★ 2 mi east of Port Lucaya. A ferry takes you from Port Lucaya to the bay to observe and photograph the animals. If you don't mind getting wet, you can sit on a partially submerged dock or stand waist deep in the water, and one of these friendly creatures will swim up and touch you. You can also engage in one of two swim-with-the-dolphins programs, but participants must be 55 inches or taller. The Dolphin Experience began in 1987, when it trained five dolphins to interact with people. Later, the animals learned to head out to sea and swim with scuba divers on the open reef. A two-hour dive program is available. You can buy tickets for the Dolphin Experience at the Underwater Explorers Society (UNEXSO) in Port Lucaya, but be sure to make reservations as early as possible. ⊠ *Port Lucaya* ☎ 242/373–1244 or 800/992–3483 ⊕ *www.unexso.com* ⊠ *2-hr interaction program $75, 2-hr swim program $169, dolphin dive $199, open-ocean experience $199* ⊙ *Daily 9–5.*

★ ❹ **Port Lucaya Marketplace.** Lucaya's capacious and lively shopping complex—a dozen low-rise, pastel-painted colonial buildings whose style was influenced by traditional island homes—is on the waterfront 4 mi east of Freeport and across the street from a massive resort complex. The shopping center, whose walkways are lined with hibiscus, bougainvillea, and croton, has about 100 well-kept establishments, among them waterfront restaurants and bars, and shops that sell clothes, crystal and china, watches, jewelry, perfumes, and local arts and crafts. The marketplace's centerpiece is **Count Basie Square**, where live bands often perform Bahamian music, jazz, and gospel in the gazebo bandstand.

Lively outdoor watering holes line the square, which is also *the* place to celebrate the holidays: a tree-lighting ceremony takes place in the festively decorated spot and fireworks highlight the New Year's Eve party. ⊠ *Sea Horse Rd.* ☎ *242/373–8446* ⊕ *www.portlucayamarketplace. com* ☉ *Mon.–Sat. 10–6.*

> ### RUN DOGGIE RUN
>
> Island dogs, known as "potcakes"—a reference to the bottom of the rice pans they clean up—run wild, so be careful when driving. Efforts in recent years has raised awareness of the need for neutering and spaying.

5 **Underwater Explorers Society (UNEXSO).** One of the world's most Fodors Choice respected diving facilities, UNEXSO welcomes more than 50,000 ★ individuals each year and trains hundreds of them in scuba diving. Facilities include a 17-foot-deep training pool with windows that look out on the harbor, changing rooms and showers, docks, equipment rental, a snack bar, and an air-tank filling station. ⊠ *On wharf at Port Lucaya Marketplace* ☎ *242/373–1244 or 800/992–3483* ⊕ *www. unexso.com* ✉ *Beginner reef dives $60, dives from $49, night dives $70, dolphin dives $199, shark dives $89* ☉ *Daily 8–5.*

BEYOND FREEPORT-LUCAYA

Grand Bahama Island narrows at picturesque West End, Grand Bahama's capital and home to descendants of the island's early settlers.

Little seaside villages, with concrete-block houses painted in bright blue and pastel yellow, fill in the landscape between Freeport and West End. Many of these settlements are more than 100 years old. Their names derive from geographical features or the original homesteaders' surnames, and most residents are descendants of these founders. On your way west, veer left at the Eight Mile Rock settlement intersection to drive past the town's historic St. Peter's Church and cemetery and Sunset Village cook shacks. The seaside backroad eventually returns you to the main road at James Town.

The East End is Grand Bahama's "back-to-nature" side. The road east from Lucaya is long, flat, and mostly straight. It cuts through vast pine forest to reach McLean's Town, the end of the road. Curly tailed lizards, raccoons, pelicans, and other native creatures populate this part of the island.

SIGHTS TO SEE

Fodors Choice **Lucayan National Park.** In this 40-acre seaside land preserve, trails and ★ elevated walkways wind through a natural forest of wild tamarind and gumbo-limbo trees, past an observation platform, a mangrove swamp, sheltered pools containing rare marine species, and what is believed to be the largest explored underwater cave system in the world (7 mi long). You can enter the caves at two access points; one is closed in June and July, the bat nursing season. Twenty miles east of Lucaya, the park contains examples of the island's five ecosystems: beach, sandy or whiteland coppice (hardwood forest), mangroves, rocky coppice, and

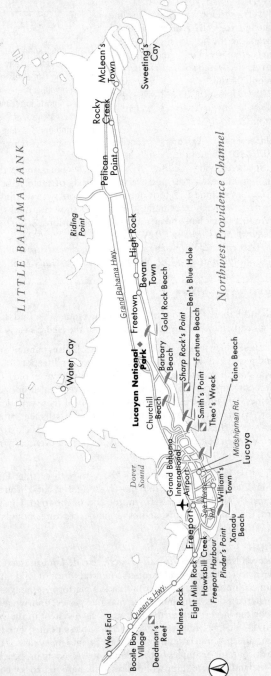

Grand Bahama Island

LITTLE BAHAMA BANK

Water Cay

Dover Sound

Riding Point

Pelican Point

Rocky Creek

McLean's Town

Sweeting's Cay

Grand Bahama Hwy.

Freetown

Bevan Town

High Rock

Ben's Blue Hole

Gold Rock Beach

Barbary Beach

Sharp Rock's Point

Lucayan National Park

Churchill Beach

Smith's Point

Fortune Beach

Theo's Wreck

Northwest Providence Channel

Grand Bahama International Airport

Seal horse Rd.

William's Town

Midshipman Rd.

Taino Beach

Lucaya

Freeport

Eight Mile Rock

Hawksbill Creek

Freeport Harbour

Pinder's Point

Xanadu Beach

West End

Bootle Bay Village

Deadman's Reef

Holmes Rock

Queen's Hwy.

KEY

Dive Sites

Exploring Sights

10 miles

0

pine forest. Across the road from the caves, trails and rickety, warped boardwalks lead through pine forest and mangrove swamp to Gold Rock Beach, a beautiful, lightly populated strand of white sand edged by some of the island's highest dunes, aquamarine sea, and coral reef. Signs along the trail detail the park's distinctive features. Tickets can be purchased in advance at Rand Nature Centre or on-site. ⊠ *Grand Bahama Hwy.* ☎ *242/352–5438* 💰 *$3* ⏱ *Daily 8:30–4:30.*

EACHES

Some 60 mi of magnificent, pristine stretches of sand extend between Freeport-Lucaya and McLean's Town, the island's isolated eastern end. Most are used only by people who live in adjacent settlements along the way. The outlying beaches have no public facilities, so beachgoers often headquarter at one of the local beach bars. The Westin-Sheraton complex in Lucaya has its own beaches and water-sports activities, and guests at Freeport hotels are shuttled free to nearby sandy shores. **Xanadu** is a mile-long strip of white sand with an outdoor bar, water-sports concessions, and resort. Its Tuesday night Fish Fry & Bonfire is popular with visitors. **Taíno** appeals to families, water-sports enthusiasts, and partiers alike. Its powdery white sands stretch long and wide, and a restaurant and popular conch shack replenish beachgoers. Tony Macaroni's hosts volleyball Saturdays and Sundays and a jazz jam on Sunday evenings.

FodorsChoice ★

Local residents prefer the sandy solitude of **William's Town,** south of Freeport (off East Sunrise Highway and down Beachway Drive) and east of Xanadu Beach, where seclusion is broken only by the occasional passing of horseback riders.

★ East of Port Lucaya, several delightful beaches run along the **South Shore—Smith's Point, Churchill Beach, Fortune Beach,** and lesser-known, very secluded and lovely **Barbary Beach.** Farther east, at the end of the trail from the Lucayan National Park, you'll find **Gold Rock Beach,** which is a 20-mi drive from the Lucaya hotels. A second access road to Gold Rock Beach lies up the road a couple of miles and takes you past the filming location of *Pirates of the Caribbean.* On the West End, snorkeling beachgoers escape by tour to **Paradise Cove.**

WHERE TO EAT

Grand Bahama Island's restaurants afford rich opportunities for sampling native cuisine. Practically every restaurant has something made with conch on the menu—the mollusk is both a Bahamian icon and a staple. In the culinary hierarchy of the Bahamian islands, Grand Bahama ranks slightly below Nassau in both sophistication and price, but above many of the Out Islands in variety and creativity.

You'll find many options in Lucaya and some also in Freeport, from elegant hotel dining rooms and charming waterside cafés to local hangouts and familiar fast-food chains. Menus often combine Continental,

Moving Toward Ecotourism

Beyond the 6-mi strip that comprises Grand Bahama Island's metropolis lies another 90 mi of unadulterated wilderness. The balance of the island is given to natural and uncrowded beaches, old-island settlements, and untamed "bush," as locals call the wilds.

The emphasis on the island's natural attributes begins below the water line with **UNEXSO** diving and the **Dolphin Experience.** UNEXSO's preoccupation with extreme diving led to the exploration of the island's unique cave system and the opening of **Lucayan National Park,** a portal to the underground labyrinth accessible to the public. One of the caves holds a cemetery of the island's aboriginals, the Lucayans. The park also gives intrepid visitors a taste of the beauty and seclusion of out-of-town beaches.

Kayaking, biking, snorkeling, boating, jeeping, and cultural safaris provide ways for visitors to take in Grand Bahama Island's most precious treasures.

Grand Bahama Nature Tours, a top-notch operation, follows backwater kayaking trails to Lucayan National Park and other off-the-beaten-path destinations. Knowledgeable native guides give lessons on island ecology en route.

Right in downtown Freeport, the **Bahamas National Trust Rand Nature Centre** was one of the precursors to ecotourism on Grand Bahama Island. It still provides an oasis for rare birds as well as residents and visitors. On the island's other extreme, close to West End, **Paradise Cove** takes you below the waves. Here you can rent snorkeling equipment or kayaks to experience the island's best swim-to reef—Deadman's Reef.

Ecotourism promises to be a fixture on Grand Bahama Island, attracting a new brand of island vacationer, one more adventurous and ready to experience the less-touted and richer offerings of Grand Bahama's great outback. For more information, contact the **Ecotourism Association of Grand Bahama** (☎ *242/352–8044, 800/448–3386 in the U.S.*).

American, and Bahamian fare. A native fish fry takes place on Wednesday evening at Smith's Point, east of Lucaya (taxi drivers know the way). Here you can sample fresh fish, sweet-potato bread, conch salad, and all the fixings cooked outdoors at the beach. It's a great opportunity to meet local residents and taste real Bahamian cuisine—and there's no better setting than seaside under the pines and palms. Other local parties take place on Thursday night at Sunset Village, a cluster of home-style Bahamian restaurants across from the beach at the west edge of Eight Mile Rock. Tony Macaroni is a local personality known for his roast conch and his Sunday-evening jams starting around 7 PM on Taíno Beach. An automatic 15% gratuity is added to most dining tabs.

REEPORT

BAHAMIAN

$ ✕ **Becky's Restaurant & Lounge.** This popular eatery opens at 7 AM and may be the best place in the Freeport tourism area to fuel up before a full day of beaching or shopping. Its diner-style booths provide a comfortable backdrop for the inexpensive menu of traditional Bahamian and American food, from conch salad and curried mutton to seafood or a BLT. Pancakes, eggs, and special Bahamian breakfasts—stew fish, boil fish, or chicken souse (the latter two are soups flavored with lime), with johnnycake or grits—are served all day. ⊠ *E. Beach Dr. and E. Sunrise Hwy.* ☎ *242/352–5247* ▤ *D, MC, V.*

★ $ ✕ **Geneva's Place.** Geneva's sets the standard for home-cooked Bahamian food. Cook and owner Geneva Munroe will prepare your grouper or pork chops broiled, steamed, or fried; your conch cracked (fried light and flaky), or, for breakfast, stewed. Everything comes with a choice of comfort side dishes such as peas 'n' rice and yummy baked macaroni and cheese. For lunch, salads and sandwiches provide lighter options. The simple dining room oozes cheerfulness in shades of yellow. ⊠ *E. Mall Dr. and Kipling La., across from Wendy's* ☎ *242/352–5085* ▤ *AE, D, MC, V.*

CONTINENTAL

$$ ✕ **Ruby Swiss European Restaurant.** The extensive Continental menu offers options for every budget with burgers, inexpensive dishes such as fried chicken, and fine seafood, steak, and veal. Specialties include steak Diana (flamed with cognac), Wiener schnitzel, lobster thermidor, and desserts flambéed table-side. The wine list's 70-odd varieties represent five countries. Dinnertime guitar music adds a romantic touch to the bustling dining-hall scene. Snacks are served into the wee hours (4 AM weekdays, 5 AM weekends). ⊠ *W. Sunrise Hwy., across from the old Crowne Plaza Tower at Royal Oasis* ☎ *242/352–8507* ▤ *AE, D, DC, MC, V* ⊘ *No lunch weekends.*

ENGLISH

$ ✕ **Prince of Wales Lounge.** Still a lively option in the International Bazaar area, this local favorite is an authentic English-style pub that serves fish-and-chips, sandwiches, steaks, sweet-and-sour baby back ribs, and draft ale in a medieval setting. The adjacent sports bar specializes in pizza. ⊠ *Ranfurly Circus, opposite International Bazaar* ☎ *242/352–2700* 🖃 *AE, D, MC, V.*

ITALIAN

★ **$$**　✕ **Silvano's.** In a bright, circular, sunshine-yellow dining room, Silvano's serves a wide selection of Italian-style fish, pasta, and meat. Specialties here include table-flamed filet mignon, veal scallopine, vegetable lasagna, and linguine al pesto. The best dining option in the downtown area, it's located across the street from International Bazaar in a compound of eateries known as Ranfurly Circus. ⊠ *Ranfurly Circus, opposite International Bazaar* ☎ *242/352–5111* 🖃 *AE, D, MC, V* ⊗ *Closed Sun. May–Dec.*

LUCAYA

AMERICAN

$$$　✕ **Churchill's Chophouse.** Unwind in the handsome wood piano bar before enjoying a top-quality meal in the dining room, surrounded by white wainscoting and French windows. The atrium ceiling over the circular room illuminates Bahamian life with mural scenes and heavy chandeliers, and the atmosphere evokes the plantation era. In this elegant setting, the menu focuses on beef, but escapes single-mindedness with braised lamb, grilled wild king salmon with grilled figs, lobster-and-asparagus risotto, lobster surf-and-turf, and other dishes of equal sophistication. ⊠ *Westin and Sheraton Grand Bahama Island Resort* ☎ *242/373–1333* 🖃 *AE, D, DC, MC, V* ⊗ *Days of operation vary according to season. No lunch.*

🔄 **$**　✕ **Prop Club.** Spare bits of recovered aircraft wreckage and brightly painted chairs accent this casual resort hangout, which becomes a lively dance floor by night. Giant glass-paned garage doors open to make this an indoor-outdoor place where young and old come to dine and party on the beach. The menu is casual, with offerings like pizza, jerk burgers, blackened grouper, and baby back ribs. ⊠ *Westin and Sheraton Grand Bahama Island Resort* ☎ *242/373–1333* 🖃 *AE, D, DC, MC, V.*

BAHAMIAN

$　✕ **Billy Joe's on the Beach.** Eating fresh conch salad and drinking Kalik beer with your toes in the sand: it doesn't get any better or more Bahamian. Billy Joe was such a fixture on the beach, selling his freshly made-on-the-spot (watch it being prepared!) conch salad, cracked conch, and grilled conch, that when the Westin and Sheraton was built, they allowed him to stay on the property. This is where resort guests go "slumming" without having to travel farther than the edge of the property's beach. Fish and fries, fried lobster, cheeseburgers, and

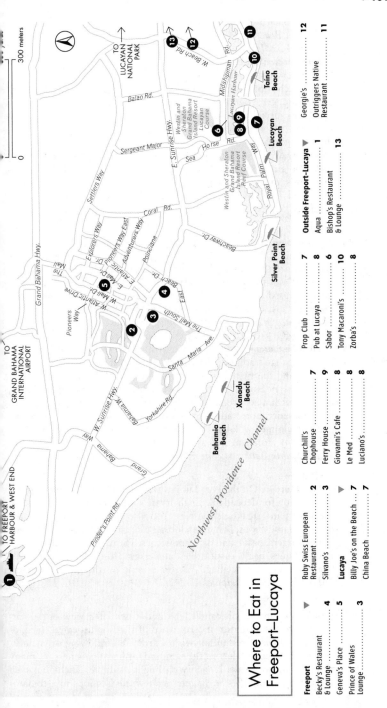

Where to Eat in Freeport-Lucaya

Freeport ▶

cracked conch are other specialties. ⊠ *Lucaya Beach* ☎ *242/373–1333 Ext. 5803* ▭ *No credit cards.*

$ ✕ **Tony Macaroni's.** For a taste of the local beach scene, find this weathered, thatch-roofed shack at Taino Beach and get your fill of roast conch, the specialty of the "house." Operated by a local personality,

the popular eatery also sells conch salad, roast lobster and shrimp, and Gully Wash cocktails (green coconut water, sweetened condensed milk, and gin) for noshing plein-air on a stilted deck overlooking pristine sands and sea. Sunday evenings, Tony hosts a jazz jam starting at around 7 PM. ⊠ *Taino Beach* ☎ *242/441–1862* ▭ *No credit cards* ⊗ *Closed Mon.*

ECLECTIC

★ $$$ ✕ **Ferry House.** If you're looking for creative gourmet on Grand Bahama Island, this is the place. Its changing menu—always well executed—leans toward the experimental, with dishes like roasted duck and spinach salad, sushi rolls, mango-glazed pork tenderloin, and lemon and thyme-infused grilled lobster. The windowed dining room hangs over the water just outside the Port Lucaya Marketplace. ⊠ *Port Lucaya Marketplace* ☎ *242/373–1595* ⊕ *www.ferryhousebahamas.com* ▭ *AE, D, DC, MC, V* ⊗ *No dinner Mon. No lunch weekends.*

$$ ✕ **Sabor Restaurant & Bar.** If you want your fresh seafood prepared with
FodorsChoice more dare than tradition, pick a dockside table at this new culinary star.
★ Opened and run by the talent team from Iceland that originally operated the Ferry House, Sabor draws the local yachtie crowd for lunch, dinner, and Sunday brunch. Saffron mussels, tiger shrimp wonton with jalapeño sauce, horseradish-and-ginger-crusted salmon, crispy snapper, and a lunchtime "wok bar" keep things mixed up on the waterfront. ⊠ *Pelican Bay Hotel, Sea Horse Way at Port Lucaya* ☎ *242/373—5588* ⊕ *www.sabor-bahamas.com* ▭ *MC, V.*

ENGLISH

$ ✕ **Pub at Lucaya.** On the Port Lucaya waterfront, this amiable pub has a reputation for dependable English fare such as bangers 'n' mash and shepherd's and steak-and-ale pies. You also can't go wrong with the frenched lamb chops, Bahamian lobster tail, or strip sirloin. Lunchtime brings burgers, pasta, and deli sandwiches. The nautical decor incorporates antiques, heavy rustic tables, and ersatz Tiffany lamps suspended from a wood-beam ceiling. Ask for a table on the outside terrace. ⊠ *Port Lucaya Marketplace* ☎ *242/373–8450* ▭ *AE, DC, MC, V.*

FRENCH

$$$ ✕ **Luciano's.** Linens, soft candlelight, and a twinkling view of the har
FodorsChoice bor add to the glamour and romance of this sophisticated, second-
★ story Port Lucaya restaurant with a dedicated following of yachters and locals. Luciano's has set the standard for fine dining here for many years. Its menu speaks French with English subtitles, including such specialties as *coquilles St. Jacques provencale* (scallops in a tomato-

based wine sauce), *filet au poivre vert* (tenderloin fillet with green peppercorn sauce), scampi flambé, Dover sole, stuffed quail, and chateaubriand for two, served in the formal, subdued dining room or on the veranda overlooking the marina. For a big finish, order the flambéed crêpes suzette for two. ⊠*Port Lucaya Marketplace* ☎*242/373–9100* ⊕*www.thebahamasguide.com/lucianos* ▭*AE, D, MC, V* ⊙*Closed Sun.*

> **CONCHING OUT**
>
> Conch harvesting is illegal in the United States and closely regulated in other tropical locations to guard against overfishing. Currently, conch harvesting is limited to 10 per person in the Bahamas, but populations, while still plentiful, are slowly becoming depleted.

GREEK

$ ✕**Zorba's Greek Cuisine.** Besides Greek favorites, this longtime Port Lucaya tenant serves Bahamian dishes, too. Join the port's yacht-in clientele and shoppers for breakfast, lunch, or dinner on the white-and-blue trimmed sidewalk porch for gyros, moussaka, Greek salad, pizza, conch fritters, fried snapper, and roasted leg of lamb. ⊠*Port Lucaya Marketplace* ☎*242/373–6137* ▭*MC, V.*

ITALIAN

$ ✕**Giovanni's Cafe.** Tucked away under the bougainvillea at Port Lucaya Marketplace, this corner café evokes a bit of Italy. As you relax on the patio or study the giant mural of an Italian waterway inside the café, treat yourself to local seafood such as lobster in white wine cream sauce and panfried grouper in lemon-wine sauce. Full-flavored, classic Italian dishes include spaghetti carbonara and chicken marsala. If you're on a budget, come between 4 and 6 for $10 early-bird pasta dinners. ⊠*Port Lucaya Marketplace* ☎*242/373–9107* ▭*AE, MC, V* ⊙*No lunch.*

$ ✕**"Le Med" Mediterranean.** Enjoy a taste of Europe while gazing upon yachts bobbing in harbor. Outdoors is the best spot for breakfast, lunch, or dinner, but there's also spacious indoor dining around a European-style bakery. Under the same management as Luciano's, it goes a more casual route with tapas, crepes, pasta, seafood, sandwiches, and homemade French pastries. ⊠*Port Lucaya Marketplace* ☎*242/374–2804* ▭*AE, MC, V.*

PAN-ASIAN

★ $$ ✕**China Beach.** For fine Pacific Rim dining with a view of the ocean, make a reservation here, the island's top option for Asian eats. Vegetarians will find plenty to choose from on the changing menu; sample sushi rolls, Japanese dumplings, stir-fried conch, Szechuan prawns, and other Asian specialties. ⊠*Westin and Sheraton Grand Bahama Island Resort* ☎*242/373–1333* ▭*AE, D, DC, MC, V* ⊙ *Days of operation vary according to season. No lunch.*

OUTSIDE FREEPORT-LUCAYA

Get out of town for a taste of true Bahamian cooking. Some of the island's far-flung restaurants provide courtesy shuttles from hotels.

BAHAMIAN

★ $ ✕**Bishop's Restaurant & Lounge.** A longtime favorite of locals and visitors who venture out into the East End's settlements, Bishop's serves all the Bahamian favorites with homemade goodness and a view of the sea. The cracked conch is light and crunchy, the peas 'n' rice full-flavored. There are also barbecued ribs, broiled lobster, burgers, and sandwiches. A $30 minimum for charge card use applies. ✉*High Rock* ☎242/353–4515 ▤*MC, V.*

$ ✕**Georgie's on the Beach.** Repeat Grand Bahama Island visitors who recognize this name, formerly from Port Lucaya Marketplace, know to go here for cracked conch, lobster, peas 'n' rice, and all the trademarks of authentic Bahamian cuisine. Only now they can enjoy it on the beach: Georgie has taken over Club Caribe and totally renovated and rebuilt it to make it viable after the 2004 and 2005 hurricanes. Sit outdoors on the beach for lunch or dinner; it's also open weekends for breakfast. ✉*Mather Town, off Doubloon Rd. on Spanish Main Dr.* ☎242/373–8513 ▤*AE, D, MC, V* ☉*Closed Wed. year-round and Tues. in the fall.*

$ ✕**Outriggers Native Restaurant.** For Bahamian food fixed by Bahamians, head east to the generational property of an old island family, just beyond Taíno Beach. When you stop at Gretchen Wilson's place for cracked conch, lobster tail, fried grouper, and barbecue chicken downhome style, you'll feel as though you're dining in someone's spotlessly clean home. On Wednesday nights the quiet little settlement comes to life when Outriggers throws its famous weekly fish fry. Tuesday and Thursday nights, there are beach bonfires. In winter the Outriggers Beach Club, across the street, serves light lunch. ✉*Smith's Point* ☎242/373–4811 ▤*No credit cards* ☉ *No lunch.*

ECLECTIC

★ $$ ✕**Aqua.** Aqua gives Bahamian food an upgrade in a style it calls Bahamian fusion. Intimate and elegant, overlooking megamillion-dollar yachts in the harbor, the windowed dining room sets the stage for finely prepared seafood and grilled meats, including lobster stuffed with almonds, mushrooms, and corn bread; grouper simmered Bahamian style with tomatoes; and quail with raisins served in a pineapple shell. ✉*Old Bahama Bay, West End* ☎242/350–6500 or 800/444–9469 ⏴*Reservations essential* ▤*AE, D, MC, V.*

WHERE TO STAY

Once a leader in exotic, glamorous resort-casinos, Grand Bahama is again setting the standard, with resort complexes in Lucaya and the West End. You can choose from among Grand Bahama's approximately 2,500 rooms and suites, ranging from attractive one- and two-bedroom units in sprawling resort complexes to fishing lodges to comfortable rooms in economy-oriented establishments. The island's more extravagant hotels include the sprawling, three-pronged Westin and Sheraton Grand Bahama Island Resort; nearby Pelican Bay; Viva Wyndham Fortuna Beach, an

2

all-inclusive east of Lucaya; and the West End's elegant Old Bahama Bay. The latter, like many Grand Bahama resorts, caters to the boating crowd. As it rolls out over the next 10 years, Ginn Sur Mer, a 2,200-acre residence-and-resort complex that has absorbed Old Bahama Bay, will add to West End's reputation as a high-end destination with 5,000 vacation rental condos and homes, a full-service marina, a private airport with customs facilities, two golf courses, a casino, a water park, and a spa. Back in the Lucaya area, Grand Bahama Yacht Club broke ground in 2006 on the 200-room Condo Hotel & Golf Suites with a beach club and golf amenities center; however, progress has stalled indefinitely, and there is no estimated opening date at this writing.

Small apartment complexes and time-share rentals are economical alternatives, especially if you're planning to stay for more than a few days. If you value proximity to the beach, stay at Old Bahama Bay, Xanadu, Westin and Sheraton Grand Bahama Island, Island Seas, or Viva Wyndham Fortuna Beach, which are right on the beach. UNEXSO, Grand Bahama Island's scuba central, and Port Lucaya Marketplace are within easy walking distance of Lucaya's hotels. In 2005, Hurricane Wilma closed down Freeport's largest resort, the Royal Oasis, as well as a few other smaller properties. At this writing, there is no news about the future of the Royal Oasis.

Families will find that many hotels offer babysitting services and children's programs. Some establishments allow children under 12 to stay in your room for free and may not charge you for a crib or roll-away bed.

Resort and government taxes of 6%–12% are added to your hotel bill. Rates from April 15 through December 14 tend to be 25%–30% lower than those charged during the rest of the year.

REEPORT

$$ ⊞ **Island Seas Resort.** This time-share property accommodates non-members looking for fun on the beach away from urban and tourism bustle. Balconies overlook the flowery courtyard, where thatch-roofed CoCoNuts Grog & Grub and a free-form pool with waterfalls and a swim-up bar are the centerpiece. The beach, used by guests from other non-beachside resorts, is busy with water-sports activity. One- and two-bedroom rooms are done in bright, modern, island style. The property has 195 rooms, but not all are available for rental. The resort provides guests with a courtesy shuttle to Port Lucaya. A small, basic gym and massage room were added in 2007. **Pros:** fun pool and bar area, great beach, above-average rooms, shopping shuttle. **Cons:** fitness center is below par, other resort guests use property, not convenient to restaurants. ✉ *123 Silver Point Dr., William's Town* ☎*401/324–6864 or 888/874–5360* ⊕*www.islandseas.com* 🛏*90 rooms* ☝*In-hotel: restaurant, bar, pool, gym, spa, beachfront, bicycles, no elevator, laundry facilities, public Internet, public Wi-Fi* ▤*AE, D, MC, V.*

★ $ ▦**Best Western Castaways.** Near the action in Freeport, this property is one of the nicer budget options in the area. The coral rock–accented lobby introduces four stories of rooms in rattan and earth and floral tones. Family friendliness is underscored by a playground next to the pool, and a beach shuttle is provided. In 2007, the hotel added a tour desk and small fitness center. The restaurant is open for dinner and its famous breakfast, plus there's a selection of other dining options within easy walking distance. **Pros:** close to International Bazaar, reputable restaurant, nice array of services and facilities. **Cons:** the neighborhood is currently in a slump, lacking atmosphere. ✉ *E. Mall Dr.* ☎*242/352–6682 or 800/937–8376* ⊕*www.castaways-resort.com* 🛏*97 rooms, 21 suites* ☝*In-room: safe, refrigerator, Wi-Fi. In-hotel: restaurant, bars, pool, laundry facilities, public Internet, public Wi-Fi* ▤*AE, D, MC, V.*

$ ▦**Royal Islander.** All the amenities without the sticker shock: this two-story, tin-roof, motel-style property near the International Bazaar provides free scheduled shuttle service to Xanadu Beach. The rooms have light-wood and rattan furnishings, lively tropical fabrics, framed pastel prints, and tile floors on the lower level. You'll find carpeted floors upstairs, where no-smoking rooms are available. An inviting white-and-floral lobby faces the spacious pool area. **Pros:** affordable, convenient to Freeport and airport, free beach shuttle. **Cons:** Freeport area is losing vitality, no beach on property, low on character. ✉ *E. Mall Dr.* ☎*242/351–6000* ⊕*www.royalislanderhotel.com* 🛏*100 rooms* ☝*In-hotel: restaurant, bar, pool, no elevator, public Internet, public Wi-Fi, no-smoking rooms* ▤*AE, MC, V.*

$ ▦**Xanadu Beach Resort & Marina.** Boat-in guests, divers, and beach-lovers who wish to avoid the upscale Lucaya scene choose landmark Xanadu. Howard Hughes spent the last few years of his life in the penthouse suite of this hotel, which he owned in the 1970s. The resort recently completed a valiant and dramatic comeback after being devastated by fire and hurricanes. The trademark pink exterior has been repainted yellow, and goldenrod tones with arched brick accents and a fireplace now warm the lobby. Located only a few minutes from town, the property's tower (still known as the Howard Hughes Tower), pool wing, and villas overlook the oval pool and fountain, marina, parking lot, or beach. Rooms show their age but have been spruced up with a new designer look. Coconut palms sway at the wide, gorgeous beach, complete with a bar and grill. **Pros:** affordable, great beach, solid diving operation, planned guest activities. **Cons:** hard to find, other resort guests use beach, somewhat dated. ✉*Sunken Treasure Dr., turn off E. Mall at Pinta Ave.* ☎*242/352–6782 or 888/790–5264* ⊕*www.xanadu beachhotel.com* 🛏*137 rooms, 49 suites* ☝*In-room: safes. In-hotel: 2*

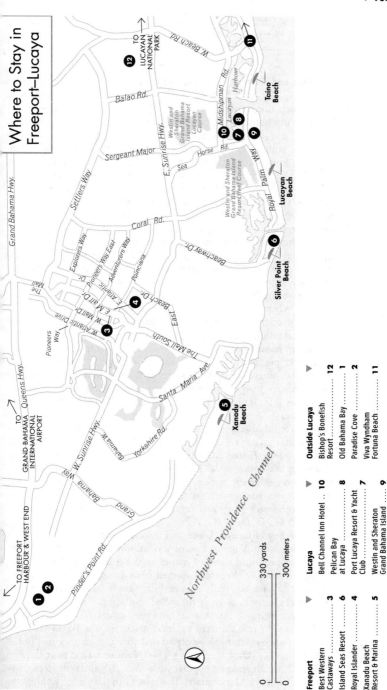

Where to Stay in Freeport–Lucaya

Freeport

Best Western Castaways	**3**
Island Seas Resort	**6**
Royal Islander	**4**
Xanadu Beach Resort & Marina	**5**

Lucaya

Bell Channel Inn Hotel	**10**
Pelican Bay at Lucaya	**8**
Port Lucaya Resort & Yacht Club	**7**
Westin and Sheraton Grand Bahama Island	**9**

Outside Lucaya

Bishop's Bonefish Resort	**12**
Old Bahama Bay	**1**
Paradise Cove	**2**
Viva Wyndham Fortuna Beach	**11**

restaurants, bars, pool, beachfront, diving, bicycles, laundry facilities, public Wi-Fi ☰*AE, D, MC, V.*

LUCAYA

☾ $$–$$$
Fodor'sChoice
★

Westin and Sheraton Grand Bahama Island Resort. Formerly known as Our Lucaya Beach & Golf Resort, here's where it's always happening, from beach fun to nightlife and gambling. Lucaya's grandest resort spreads three hotels along 7½ acres of soft-sand beach (the entire resort covers 372 acres). The focus here is on dramatic play-area water features and golf. The property has a 38,000-square-foot casino, 11 restaurants, lounges, a children's camp, a first-rate spa, and a shopping complex. Westin is a 100% smoke-free resort and guests are fined $200 if evidence of smoking in a guest room is found.

Sheraton. Geared toward family vacationers, this resort has a water park with a sugar-mill ruins theme, complete with a zero-depth-entry pool and waterslide. The headquarters for children's programs is nearby: a bright, circular building with peekaboo windows for undetected parental spying. The resort's public areas and 511 rooms have a tropical Miami Beach flair. Sheraton offers an all-inclusive plan including alcoholic beverages year-round.

Westin Breakers Cay. This 10-floor high-rise resort curves like a wavy cruise ship between the other two, with oversize rooms and suites done with art deco interpretation, restaurants, a long lap pool, and a small half-moon infinity pool encasing a swim-up bar on the beach.

Westin Lighthouse Pointe. Two-story structures built to replicate Caribbean-style plantation manors house this property's all-water-view rooms and suites. The 21 lanai suites each come with a butler. A half-moon infinity pool clasps the property and visually blends into the ocean beyond. Stay here if you want to be farther from the hustle and bustle.

Pros: beautiful beach, great water features, wide variety of accommodations, casino, and restaurants. **Cons:** big!, expensive restaurants, lots of kids. ⊠*Sea Horse La.* ☎*242/373–1333, 877/687–5822 in U.S.* ⊕*www.ourlucaya.com* ⇆*1,151 rooms, 68 suites* ⚷*In-room: safe, refrigerator, ethernet, dial-up. In-hotel: 11 restaurants, room service, bars, golf courses, tennis courts, pools, gym, spa, beachfront, water sports, children's programs (ages 3–12), public W-Fi, no-smoking rooms* ☰*AE, D, DC, MC, V.*

$$
Fodor'sChoice
★

Pelican Bay at Lucaya. Close to the beach and a clear step above typical small-inn Bahamian accommodations, Pelican Bay has a tidy, modern appeal, and some of its newer suites overflow with character and decorative elements collected from around the world. Building exteriors are fancifully trimmed in West Indian latticework and red barrel-tile roofs. Smartly furnished rooms and suites overlook the pool and whirlpool, the channel, and the marina. The newest suites have extras like rain showers, espresso machines, and boxes built into the doors into which fresh pastries are delivered each morning (a full Continental breakfast is also available). Pelican Bay is next door to UNEXSO, which makes it popular with divers. It's also only steps away from Port Lucaya Marketplace. The resort provides a ferry shuttle to

Taíno Beach. Lucaya Beach access is a 15-minute walk away. **Pros:** stylish, comfortable, water views, great restaurants, convenient to Port Lucaya and UNEXSO. **Cons:** no beach, no water sports, expensive. ⊠ *Sea Horse Way at Port Lucaya* ☎242/373–9550 or 800/600–9192 ⊕*www.pelicanbayhotel.com* ♺89 *rooms, 94 suites* ♿*In-room: safe, refrigerator, Wi-Fi. In-hotel: 2 restaurants, bar, pools, laundry facilities, public Internet, no-smoking rooms* ▭*AE, D, MC, V* ⑩*CP.*

$ ▦**Port Lucaya Resort & Yacht Club.** Members can dock at the 50-slip marina; others pull in next door at Port Lucaya Marina, but the property is also conducive to shoppers and those who don't mind a walk to the beach to save on lodging rates. Golf carts transport guests to 10 brightly painted buildings around the Olympic-size swimming pool and hot tub. The rooms have garden, pool, or marina views, punctuated sparingly with rattan furniture, tile floors, large wall mirrors, and tropical floral patterns. The walk to the beach takes less than 10 minutes. At night, Port Lucaya Marketplace's celebratory sounds spill into buildings 7, 8, 9, and 10, and guests can enjoy the festivities from their balconies. **Pros:** near Port Lucaya Marketplace, boat docking, affordable. **Cons:** can be noisy, plain rooms, limited services. ⊠ *Bell Channel Bay Rd.* ☎242/373–6618 or 800/582–2921 ⊕*www.portlucayaresort. com* ♺157 *rooms, 3 suites* ♿*In-hotel: pool, no elevator, laundry service, no-smoking rooms* ▭*AE, D, MC, V.*

¢ ▦ **Bell Channel Inn Hotel.** Right on the water near Port Lucaya with easy access to the island's best down-under sites, this hotel is perfect for scuba-oriented and budget travelers. The inn has its own dive shop and lodging-dive packages. The dive boat conveniently leaves from behind the hotel, and the shop is full service with equipment rentals and certification courses. All but two of the simply furnished rooms are equipped with a small refrigerator; all have a view of the channel and Port Lucaya. The hotel's convivial restaurant-bar serves seafood and good spirit come happy hour each day. A small pool sits on a wood deck along the water, and the hotel provides free shuttle service to the beach at Island Seas. **Pros:** diver-friendly, affordable, on the water. **Cons:** no beach, away from shopping and restaurant scene, small rooms. ⊠*Kings Rd.* ☎242/373–1053 ⊕*www.bellchannelinn. com* ♺32 *rooms* ♿*In-room: refrigerator (some), Wi-Fi. In-hotel: restaurant, bar, pool, diving, no elevator, laundry facilities, public Wi-Fi* ▭*AE, D, MC, V.*

UTSIDE FREEPORT-LUCAYA

☾ $$$ ▦ **Old Bahama Bay at Ginn Sur Mer.** Relax and luxuriate in relative seclusion at this hotel designed for boating vacationers as well as fly-in odor'sChoice guests looking to get away from it all. Waterfront suites, one and ★ two bedrooms, have heavy wood furnishings and restful views of the beach through French doors. All suites contain wet bars, bathrobes, cooking utensils, and DVD/CD players (with a complimentary on-site library). Premium suites include jetted bathtubs and in-room laundry facilities. Bike, kayak, and snorkel equipment use is complimentary. Although endearingly intimate and individual, Old Bahama Bay has all the amenities of a full-grown, self-contained resort, including a casual and a fine restaurant and a customs office, making it one of the Bahamas' top small marina properties. This property will become part of the developing 2,200-acre Ginn Sur Mer, complete with a spa, expanded marina, water park, two golf courses, and 5,000 rental condos and homes, which are expected to open by 2010. A private airstrip is already open. **Pros:** peace and serenity, top-shelf marina, close to local color. **Cons:** limited dining choices, far from airport and shopping, currently in the midst of a construction site. ☒ *West End* ☎ 242/350–6500 or 800/444–9469 ⊕ *www.oldbahamabay.com* ☞ *67 rooms, 6 2-bedroom suites* ⌂ *In-room: safe, kitchen. In-hotel: 2 restaurants, bar, pool, gym, spa, beachfront, water sports, bicycles, no elevator, children's program (ages 4–12)* ▤ *AE, D, MC, V.*

> ### LEGEND OF THE SEA
>
> Old Bahama Bay named its newest restaurant, Bonefish Folley's Bar & Grille, for a well-loved West End fishing legend who has taken celebrities, presidents, and regular folk out on his charters for more than 60 years. After recent hurricanes, the American ambassador rebuilt his home on West End. You'll see the "Bonefish Folley & Sons" sign out front.

★ ☾   ✕▦ **Viva Wyndham Fortuna Beach.** Popular with couples and families,
$$–$$$ this secluded resort provides a casual, low-stress, all-inclusive getaway. One price covers meals, drinks, tips, nonmotorized water sports, and nightly entertainment. A 1,200-foot private beach bustles with activity. Meals are served buffet style in the huge, gazebo-like dining pavilion named Junkanoo or table-side at guest-only Italian La Trattoria and Asian Bambu. A massive renovation in 2007 redecorated and expanded amenities for many of the simple rooms, featuring light-wood furniture, tile floors, and balconies or porches. In December 2007, the resort added Viva Circus – an opportunity to learn everything from juggling to trapeze-flying. Guest and professional circus performances also have been added to Viva's entertainment menu. Kids under age 12 stay free with adults and can take advantage of the kids' club, family shows, and children's pool. **Pros:** family friendly, dining variety, secluded beach, lots of activities. **Cons:** sequestered feel, rooms are small, resort bustles. ☒ *Churchill Dr. and Doubloon Rd.* ☎ 242/373–4000, 800/996–3426 *in U.S.* ⊕ *www.vivaresorts.com* ☞ *276 rooms* ⌂ *In-room: safe, refrigerator. In-hotel: 3 restaurants, bar, tennis courts, pool, gym, beachfront, diving, water sports, bicycles, no elevator, children's programs (ages 4–12), laundry service, public Internet* ▤ *AE, D, MC, V* ▯⌖*AI.*

$$ ▦ **Paradise Cove.** Devoted snorkelers and peace-lovers seek out this offbeat location. Owned by a local family, Paradise Cove has begun rebuilding after 2005's hurricane demise. At press time, two brand new two-bedroom stilted cottages were in place. (Lower rates are available for those wanting only to rent the units as a one-bedroom with the other room locked off). More units and possibly a clubhouse with a dining room are in the planning stages. The small property is the only lodging on Deadman's Reef, quiet and far removed from the resort world. By day, activity mounts as snorkelers arrive by bus.

The comfortable, nicely decorated accommodations have full kitchens. There's a protected stretch of beach, and snorkeling gear is available for a fee. Kayaks are available for guests' use. Staff can arrange spear fishing and other fishing excursions. **Pros:** superb snorkeling, quiet in the off-hours, run by local family. **Cons:** far from restaurants and shopping, swarmed with bussed-in visitors during the day. ⊠*Deadman's Reef* ☎*242/349–2677* ⊕*www.deadmansreef.com* ⇨*2 apartments, 3 cottages* ⌂*In-room: kitchen, VCR. In-hotel: bar, beachfront, water sports, no elevator* ⊟*AE, D, MC, V.*

> ### "FLYING TEETH"
>
> Known in some parts as no-see-ums, what the Bahamians call the practically invisible sand flies are a force to be reckoned with, especially at the West End. At and after sunset they come out in force on still nights, and their bites can result in itchy, red welts. Dress in long sleeves and pants or apply a repellent. Avon's Skin-So-Soft lotion is the generally accepted deterrent, and Old Bahama Bay resort considerately stocks its rooms with a bottle.

★ $ ✕▦ **Bishop's Bonefish Resort.** Stay on the beach in a small community east of Lucaya, without the hefty price tags and bustle of Lucaya. Owned by Bahamian Ruben "Bishop" Roberts, the property comprises seven white-tile, spacious rooms. Bishop will arrange bonefishing excursions to the East End, feed you at his landmark restaurant, and talk politics with you at the new beach bar. ⊠ *High Rock* ☎*242/353–4515* ⇨*7 rooms* ⌂*In-room: refrigerator. In-hotel: restaurant, bar, beachfront* ⊟*AE, MC.*

ME-SHARING

Contact any of the following for information about rentals. For information about other time-share houses, apartments, and condominiums, check with the Grand Bahama Ministry of Tourism (☎*242/352–8044, 800/448–3386 in U.S.* ⊕*www.grandbahama.bahamas.com*).

Freeport Resort & Club (⊠ *Near International Bazaar Rum Cay Dr.* ☎*242/352–5371* ⊕*www.freeportresort.com*) has 52 suites in a garden setting.

Mayfield Beach and Tennis Club (⊠ *Port-of-Call Dr. at Xanadu Beach, Freeport* ☎*242/352–9776*) has 10 town houses that share a pool, small beach, and tennis court.

Ocean Reef Yacht Club & Resort (⊠*Bahama Reef Blvd., Freeport* ☎*242/373–4661* ⊕*www.oryc.com*) has 64 one- to three-bedroom apartments midway between the International Bazaar and Port Lucaya. The resort has a marina, restaurant, tennis courts, and pools.

NIGHTLIFE & THE ARTS

NIGHTLIFE

The casino at Westin and Sheraton Grand Bahama Island Resort and the shopping-dining complex across the street at Port Lucaya are among the island's top attractions. At Isle of Capri Casino, you can try your luck with state-of-the-art slot machines, craps and blackjack tables, roulette, and baccarat. There's no specific dress code, although bathing suits and bare feet are not permitted. You must be at least 18 years old to go into the casino, and residents of the Bahamas are not permitted to gamble. Photography is prohibited.

For noncasino evening and late-night entertainment, Port Lucaya is filled with restaurants and bars, and there's often live entertainment in the middle square. Other options include finding a bonfire beach party or fish fry or taking a cruise on a sunset party boat. On Sunday nights, the party takes to the main drag in West End and the bar-crawling lasts into the wee hours. You can also find nightclubs near International Bazaar; they're generally open from 8 or 9 until 3. You may even be able to find some excitement without leaving your resort—many hotels organize their own nighttime entertainment.

CASINO

★ **Isle of Capri Casino** (⊠ *Westin and Sheraton Grand Bahama Island Resort* ☎ *242/350–2000, 888/687–4753 in U.S.* ⊕ *www.isleofcapricasino.com/lucaya*), a 38,000-square-foot, bright, tropically decorated play land, has more than 350 slot machines and 33 game tables consisting of mini-baccarat, Caribbean stud and three-card poker, craps, blackjack, and roulette. There's also a special Jewel of the Isle room, featuring high-limit table games and track and Sportsbook betting. The Cove restaurant serves salads and sandwiches. The casino is open from 10 AM until 3 AM (or at the manager's discretion) daily; slot machines are open 24 hours on weekends.

NIGHTCLUBS

★ **Bahama Mama Cruises** (⊠ *Superior Watersports at Port Lucaya* ☎ *242/373–7863* ⊕ *www.superiorwatersports.com*) has some of the best nightlife in Grand Bahama. In addition to sunset "booze cruises," Bahama Mama offers a surf-and-turf dinner with a colorful "native" show (a local term used to indicate entertainment with a traditional cultural flair); it's $79 for adults, $45 for children (ages 2–12). The Sunset Cruise and Show is $45. Reservations are essential. The dinner cruise is offered Monday, Tuesday, Friday, and Saturday 6–9 (April–September) or 6:30–9:30 (October–March); the Sunset Cruise and Show runs Monday, Wednesday, and Friday on the same time schedule.

Club Amnesia (⊠ *Across from International Bazaar on E. Mall Dr.* ☎ *242/351–2582*) is one of the hot spots around International Bazaar; it rocks weekend nights with live entertainment, a huge dance floor, and a youthful crowd.

2

Corner Bar (⊠*Port Lucaya Marketplace* ☎*242/373–2414*) is one of four bars that ring Port Lucaya Marketplace's Count Basie Square. This one appeals to a slightly more sophisticated crowd, with its menu of shots and daiquiris, cigars, long colorful tile-faced bar, and next-door bistro.

Daiquiri Bar (⊠*Port Lucaya Marketplace* ☎*No phone*) is where the spring break set hangs, and there's even a Spring Breaker rum tipple in their honor. The crowd perches on stools around the window bar ordering $1 or $2 shots and grooving to recorded music.

Prop Club Sports Bar & Dance Club (⊠*Westin and Sheraton Grand Bahama Island Resort* ☎*242/373–1333*) hosts live music that propels guests out to the giant dance floor, plus karaoke on certain evenings, and sports-TV Sundays. Seating is indoors as well as outdoors on the beach. Open daily for lunch and dinner and nightly entertainment.

Rumrunners (⊠*Port Lucaya Marketplace* ☎*242/373–7233*) is another of the Count Basie Square big four. It specializes in keeping young bar-hoppers supplied with sexy tropical frozen drinks and punches, Kalik beers at two for $5, burgers, and conch fritters.

E ARTS

THEATER

Freeport Players' Guild (☎*242/352–5533*), a nonprofit repertory company, produces American comedies, musicals, and dramas in the 450-seat Regency Theatre during its September–June season.

Grand Bahama Players (☎*242/373–2299*) perform at Regency Theatre, staging cultural productions by Bahamian, West Indian, and North American playwrights.

Port Lucaya Marketplace (⊠*Sea Horse Rd.* ☎*242/373–8446*), which opens daily at 10, has a stage that becomes lively after dark, with calypso music and other performances at Count Basie Square (ringed by four popular hangouts: the Corner Bar, the Daiquiri Bar, Rumrunners, and the Pub at Port Lucaya.

PORTS & THE OUTDOORS

CYCLING

By virtue of its flat terrain, broad avenues, and long, straight stretches of highway, Grand Bahama is perfect for bicycling. In November, the island hosts the annual Conchman Triathlon, comprising a 1K swim, 25K bike ride, and a 5K run. When biking, wear sunblock, carry a bottle of water, and look left. Inexpensive bicycle rentals (about $20 a day plus deposit) are available from some resorts, and the Viva Wyndham Fortuna Beach allows guests free use of bicycles.

Shaking & Scraping to the Sounds of Bahamian Music

The radio crackles, the DJ puts the needle to the vinyl, or the band begins to play. The upbeat pulse of Bahamian music circulates through the room. Suddenly you find yourself moving in place, and then across the floor.

Caribbean music seems to create an undeniably contagious urge to dance. Perhaps it's the strong underlying rhythm common to most island music of this region, including the immensely popular **calypso,** originally from Trinidad, and **reggae,** which spread to nearby islands from Jamaica. Both have roots in the drum beats of Africa, which were brought by slaves and spiked with French, British, Spanish, and Portuguese flavors from shipmasters and plantation owners. In the Bahamas, though, the dominant sound is homegrown **soca.**

The fundamental component of soca, calypso, and reggae is the 4/4 beat, the base upon which the melody is built. Whereas calypso emphasizes the downbeat and reggae the backbeat, soca music accentuates all four beats evenly—creating tunes that are catchy and easy to dance to. A good Bahamian band can play all three rhythms, often combining them to create a hybrid effect. It's not uncommon to hear a cover of a Bob Marley reggae song in soca style, or a soca-inspired rendition of Harry Belafonte's well-known calypso tune "Marianne."

Soca music has many faces. In some cases its closest relative is calypso, other times it's reggae, dub, ragga, or even hip-hop. A single keyboard—or a full symphony orchestra—can create soca. The formula for most contemporary soca songs is a simple melodic line played on a keyboard or an electric guitar, aggressively rapped lyrics, and that characteristic driving rhythm, played on either a beat machine or a drum.

The drums that are so crucial to Bahamian and Caribbean music come in a myriad of forms. Popular with Caribbean bands are the steel pan, originally constructed out of 55-gallon oil drums, and the conga, often associated with Latin music but played throughout the world. The traditional Bahamian drum is a handmade goatskin-covered instrument. It's the mainstay of another well-known Bahamian sound, **rake and scrape** music.

Rake and scrape is typically made using recycled objects. An ordinary saw held in a musician's lap, then bent and scraped, becomes an instrument. Plastic juice bottles are filled with pigeon peas, painted in bright colors, and turned into maracas. Add a goatskin drum, and you have all you need for a rake and scrape ensemble, although many bands now add a guitar, saxophone, or both.

There's a **Rake 'N' Scrape Festival** each June on Cat Island, in which dozens of bands from all over the Caribbean perform. Some people view the festival as an extremely important event, given that rake and scrape is often seen as a dying art. To counter this trend, many of the old-time players teach at local schools to keep the tradition alive for the next generation of Bahamians.

For a biking tour that takes you from beach to shopping contact **Grand Bahama Nature Tours** (⊠ *Queen's Cove* ☎866/440–4542 or 242/373–2485 ⊕*www.gbntours.com*). The five-hour tour includes beachside lunch for $79 per person.

⟩ATING & FISHING

CHARTERS

Private boat charters for up to four people cost $300 and up for a half day and $350 and up for a full day. Bahamian law limits the catching of game fish to 18 dolphinfish, kingfish, or wahoo per vessel.

★ **Bonefish Folley & Sons** (⊠ *West End* ☎242/346–6500) can take you deep-sea fishing or flats fishing. "Bonefish," now almost 90-years-old and a legend in these parts, makes fewer trips than his two sons. Rates are negotiable.

★ **Capt. Phil & Mel's Bonefishing Guide Services** (⊠*McLean's Town* ☎242/353–3960 or 877/613–2454) provides a colorful and expert foray into the specialized world of bonefishing. A whole day (eight hours) for up to two people will run you $400, transportation included; a half day costs $300.

Reef Tours Ltd. (⊠*Port Lucaya Marketplace* ☎242/373–5880 ⊕*www.bahamasvacationguide.com/reeftours*) offers sportfishing for four to six people on custom boats. Equipment and bait are provided free. All vessels are licensed, inspected, and insured. Trips run from 8:30 to 12:15 and from 1 to 4:45, weather permitting ($110 per angler, $50 per spectator). Full-day trips are also available, as are bottom fishing excursions, glass-bottom boat tours, snorkeling trips, and sailing-snorkeling cruises. Reservations are essential.

MARINAS

★ **Grand Bahama Yacht Club at Lucayan Marina Village** (⊠*Midshipman Rd., Port Lucaya* ☎242/373–8888 ⊕*www.lucayanmarina.com*) offers complimentary ferry service to Port Lucaya; the marina has 150 slips accommodating boats up to 175 feet long, a fuel dock, customs and immigrations clearing, swimming pools, a bar and grill, and a clubhouse under construction.

★ **Old Bahama Bay** (⊠ *West End* ☎242/350–6500) has 72 slips to accommodate yachts up to 120 feet long. Facilities include a customs and immigration office, fuel, showers, laundry, and electric, cable, and water hookups.

Port Lucaya Marina (⊠*Port Lucaya Marketplace* ☎242/373–9090 ⊕*www.portlucayamarina.com*) also owned by Grand Bahama Yacht Club, offers a broad range of water sports, free wireless Internet access, a pump-out station, and has 106 slips for vessels no longer than 190 feet. Customs and immigrations officials are on-site full-time.

Xanadu Beach Resort and Marina (⊠*Sunken Treasure Dr., Freeport* ☎242/352–6783 Ext. 1333) has 400 feet of dockage and 77 slips; it's an official port of entry.

CRICKET

For a taste of true Bahamian sports, visit the **Lucaya Cricket Club** (⊠ *Baloa Rd., Lucaya* ☎ *242/373–1460*). If you feel like joining in, go to training sessions on Tuesday, Thursday, or Sunday. Visitors can use equipment free of charge. The clubhouse has a bar, gym, and changing rooms. Tournaments take place at Easter and Thanksgiving times.

FITNESS CENTERS

Grand Bahama Fitness Centre (⊠ *E. Atlantic Dr. off E. Sunrise Hwy., Freeport* ☎ *242/352–7867*) offers weight and cardio machines, aerobic, dance, self-defense and yoga classes, and a free nursery. Fees are $8 per day, $20 per week; it's closed Sunday.

Olympic Fitness Center (⊠ *Coral Beach Hotel, Lucaya* ☎ *242/373–8181*) has Universal machines, weights, and aerobics classes overlooking the hotel's pool. Costs are $7 per day, $20 per week.

★ **Senses Spa** (⊠ *Westin and Sheraton Grand Bahama Island Resort, Lucaya* ☎ *242/350–5281*) has state-of-the-art cardio and exercise equipment, including free weights, a spinning studio, and fitness classes. The fee is $25 for nonguests per day, which includes use of the sauna facilities.

GOLF

Because Grand Bahama is such a large island, it can afford long fairways puddled with lots of water and fraught with challenge. Two championship golf courses at the Westin and Sheraton Grand Bahama Island Resort and one 9-hole course constitute a major attraction on the island. The Lucayan Course operates a golf school and hosts the Breitling Pro-Am in December. Note that green fees tend to be lower in the off-season (mid-May–mid-December). Currently, two courses at the former Royal Oasis resort remain closed.

Fortune Hills Golf & Country Club is a 3,453-yard, 9-hole, par-36 course—a Dick Wilson and Joe Lee design—with a restaurant, bar, and pro shop. ⊠ *E. Sunrise Hwy., Lucaya* ☎ *242/373–4500* 🖾 *$53 for 9 holes, $70 for 18 holes, cart included. Club rental $14 for 9 holes, $18 for 18 holes* ⊙ *Closed Mon.*

Fodor's Choice   **Westin and Sheraton Grand Bahama Island Resort Lucayan Course,** designed
★ by Dick Wilson, is a dramatic 6,824-yard, par-72, 18-hole course featuring a balanced six straight holes, six classic left-turning doglegs, and six right-turning holds. The 18th hole has a double lake, and a new clubhouse is being built nearby. Its state-of-the-art instruction facilities include a practice putting green with bunker and chipping areas, covered teaching bays, and a teaching seminar area. A shared electric cart is included in green fees. ⊠ *The Westin and Sheraton Grand Bahama Island Resort, Lucaya* ☎ *242/373–2002* 🖾 *Resort guests $120, nonguests $140.*

Westin and Sheraton Grand Bahama Island Resort Reef Course is a par-72, 6,930-yard course designed by Robert Trent Jones Jr., with lots of water, wide fairways flanked by strategically placed bunkers, and a tricky dogleg left on the 18th hole. ⊠ *The Westin and Sheraton Grand Bahama Island Resort, Lucaya* ☎ *242/373–2002* ⊑ *Resort guests $120, nonguests $140.*

RSEBACK RIDING

★ **Pinetree Stables** runs trail and beach rides twice a day. All two-hour trail rides are accompanied by a guide—no previous riding experience is necessary, but riders must be at least 8 years old. Reservations are essential. ⊠ *Beachway Dr., Freeport* ☎ *242/373–3600* ⊕ *www.bahamas vacationguide.com/pinetree.html* ⊑ *$85 for a 2-hr beach ride.*

YAKING

Many resorts rent kayaks for playing in the waves; for more serious adventures, your hotel can hook you up with an outfitter.

★ **Grand Bahama Nature Tours** (⊠ *Queen's Cove, Freeport* ☎ *242/373–2485 or 866/440–4542* ⊕ *www.gbntours.com*) leads group kayaking tours of Lucayan National Park and other custom tours. ⇨ *For more information,* ⇨ *see the Ecotours section in Grand Bahama Island Essentials.*

Ocean Motion Watersports (⊠ *Westin and Sheraton Grand Bahama Island Resort, Freeport* ☎ *242/374–2425 or 242/373–2139* ⊕ *www. oceanmotionbahamas.com*) rents one- and two-person sea kayaks for $20–$25 per hour.

RASAILING

Ocean Motion Watersports (⊠ *Westin and Sheraton Grand Bahama Island Resort, Freeport* ☎ *242/374–2425 or 242/373–2139*) charges $60 for its flights from Lucaya Beach. It also has Hobie Cat and WaveRunner rentals, waterskiing and banana boat rides, and a water trampoline.

Paradise Watersports (⊠ *Island Seas Resort, Freeport* ☎ *242/373–4001*) has parasailing tow boats and offers five-minute flights for $60.

RSONAL WATERCRAFT

Ocean Motion Watersports (⊠ *Westin and Sheraton Grand Bahama Island Resort, Freeport* ☎ *242/374–2425 or 242/373–2139* ⊕ *www.oceanmotionbahamas.com*) rents WaveRunners for $60 per half hour and conducts one-hour guided tours for $120 per one- to two-person craft.

SCUBA DIVING

An extensive reef system runs along Little Bahama Bank's edge; sea gardens, caves, and colorful reefs rim the bank all the way from the West End to Freeport–Lucaya and beyond. The variety of dive sites suits everyone from the novice to the advanced diver. The island is home to UNEXSO, considered one of the finest diving schools and marine research facilities in the world. It also made shark diving synonymous with Grand Bahama Island. Most dive operators offer a "discover" or "resort" course where first-timers can try out open-water scuba diving with a short pool course and an instructor at their side.

Grand Bahama Island offers dive sites from 10 to 100-plus feet deep. **Ben's Blue Hole** is a horseshoe-shaped ledge overlooking a blue hole in 40 to 60 feet of water. **Pygmy Caves,** for moderately experienced divers, provides a formation of overgrown ledges that cut into the reef. **Sea Hunt** site is a shallow dive and is named for the *Sea Hunt* television show, portions of which were filmed here. One of Grand Bahama Island's signature dive sites, made famous by the UNEXSO dive operation, **Shark Junction** is a 45-foot dive where 4- to 6-foot reef sharks hang out, along with moray eels, stingrays, nurse sharks, and grouper. UNEXSO provides orientation and a shark feeding with its dives here. **Spid City** has an aircraft wreck, dramatic coral formations, blue parrot fish, and an occasional shark. You'll dive about 40 to 60 feet down. For divers with some experience, **Theo's Wreck,** a 228-foot cement hauler, was sunk in 1982 in 100 feet of water.

Caribbean Divers (⊠ *Bell Channel Inn, opposite Port Lucaya* ☎ *242/373–9111* ⊕ *www.bellchannelinn.com*) offers guided tours; NAUI, PADI, and SSI instruction; and equipment rental. A resort course allows you to use equipment in a pool and then in a closely supervised open dive for $89. A one-tank dive costs $35. Shark-feeding (two-tank) dives are $25 extra.

Fodor's Choice ★ **UNEXSO (Underwater Explorers Society)** (⊠ *Port Lucaya Marketplace* ☎ *242/373–1244 or 800/992–3483* ⊕ *www.unexso.com*), a world-renowned scuba-diving facility with its own 17-foot dive pool, provides rental equipment, guides, and boats. A wide variety of dives available for beginners and experienced divers, starting at $109 for Discover Scuba Reef Diving resort course. Its escorted Mini-B Reef Adventure requires no training and costs $60. UNEXSO and its sister company, the Dolphin Experience, are known for their work with Atlantic bottlenose dolphins.

Xanadu Undersea Adventures (⊠ *Xanadu Beach Resort, Freeport* ☎ *242/352–3811 or 800/327–8150* ⊕ *www.xanadudive.com*) offers a resort course for $99, single dives for $40, shark dives for $80, and night dives for $60. It provides free pickup from other resorts.

SNORKELING

Old Bahama Bay (⊠ *West End* ☎ *242/350–6500*) rents snorkel equipment and conducts 90-minute snorkeling tours for $40–$60.

★ ◔ **Paradise Cove** (✉ *Deadman's Reef* ☎ *242/349–2677* ⊕ *www.deadmansreef.com*) allows you to snorkel right offshore at Deadman's Reef, a two-system reef with water ranging from very shallow to 35 feet deep. It's considered the island's best spot for snorkeling off the beach— you're likely to see lots of angelfish, barracudas, rays, and the occasional sea turtle. Bus tours deliver you to the spot or you can stay at one of the cottages. Its Red Bar is a popular gathering place for watersports enthusiasts. There is an access fee of $3 per person; snorkel equipment rentals are available for $10 a day, $5 an hour extra for wet suits or $3 for ski belts. Try the battery-operated Seascooters, which pull you through the water, for $15 an hour. For $39, a snorkel tour includes a briefing, narrated transportation, equipment, and lunch ($35 without lunch). It's a great deal, especially if you go early and stay late.

> **HERE'S WHERE**
>
> The last time locals spotted pirates on Grand Bahama Island was in 2005 when Johnny Depp and his crew were filming the second and third movies in the *Pirates of the Caribbean* series. They used a special device in Golf Rock Creek at one of the world's largest open-water filming tanks to give the illusion that the pirate ship was pitching and yawing. You can view the set through a chain-link fence at the new Gold Rock Beach access about a mile past Lucayan National Park.

Paradise Watersports (✉ *Island Seas Resort, Freeport* ☎ *242/373–4001*) offers a 90-minute reef snorkeling cruise for $35.

★ ◔ **Pat & Diane Fantasia Tours** (✉ *Port Lucaya Resort* ☎ *242/373–8681 or 888/275–3603* ⊕ *www.snorkelingbahamas.com*) takes snorkelers to a shallow reef two times a day on cruises aboard a fun-boat catamaran with a 30-foot rock-climbing wall and slide into the water. The fee is $40 each for the two-hour trip.

NNIS

★ **Westin and Sheraton Grand Bahama Island Tennis Center** has four lighted courts: grass, rebound, French red clay, and deco-turf. Wimbledon-white tennis attire is required on the grass court. Racquet rental and stringing, lessons, and clinics are available. ✉ *Westin and Sheraton Grand Bahama Island Resort* ☎ *242/373–1333* ✇ *$25–$100 per hr.*

HOPPING

In the stores, shops, and boutiques in Freeport's International Bazaar and at the Port Lucaya Marketplace, you can find duty-free goods costing up to 40% less than what you might pay back home. At the numerous perfume shops, fragrances are often sold at a sweet-smelling 25% below U.S. prices. Be sure to limit your haggling to the straw markets.

Shops in Freeport and Lucaya are open Monday–Saturday from 9 or 10 to 6. Stores may stay open later in Port Lucaya. Straw markets, grocery stores, and drugstores are open on Sunday.

MARKETS & ARCADES

International Arcade (⊠*Adjacent to International Bazaar* ☎*No phone*) has a varied collection of shops, currently the best in the Freeport area.

International Bazaar (⊠*W. Sunrise Hwy. and E. Mall Dr.* ☎*242/352–2828*) carries imported goods, exotic items, and duty-free merchandise. Heavily impacted by regional hurricane damage in 2004, this once-attractive landmark is in a slump. A small straw market gathers on one side.

> **GET TWISTED**
>
> One of tourists' favorite Bahamian souvenirs is braided hair. Licensed braiders, found where ever visitors shop, generally charge $2 per braid up to 15 and $120 for a full head. For the best of the best, head to Port Lucaya Marketplace.

★ **Port Lucaya Marketplace** (⊠*Sea Horse Dr.* ☎*242/373–8446* ⊕*www.port lucayamarketplace.com*) has more than 100 boutiques and restaurants in 13 pastel-color buildings in a harborside setting. Local musicians often perform at the bandstand in the afternoons and evenings.

★ **Port Lucaya Straw Market** (⊠*Sea Horse Dr.* ☎*No phone*) is a collection of wooden stalls at the Port Lucaya complex's east and west ends. Vendors will expect you to bargain for straw goods, T-shirts, and souvenirs.

SPECIALTY SHOPS

ART

★ **Bahamian Tings** (⊠*15B Poplar Crescent St., Freeport* ☎*242/352–9550*) carries well-made Bahamian crafts.

The Glassblower Shop (⊠*International Arcade* ☎*242/352–8585*) features the work of Sidney Pratt, who demonstrates his craft in the shop's front window.

Hoyte's Art & Nature (⊠*Port Lucaya Marketplace* ☎*242/373–8326*) sells a higher quality of handicrafts than the straw markets and souvenir shops. Look for painted canvases and handbags, and quality wood carvings.

Leo's Art Gallery (⊠*Port Lucaya Marketplace* ☎*242/373–1758*) showcases the expressive Haitian-style paintings of local artist Leo Brown.

CHINA & CRYSTAL

Island Galleria (✉ *International Arcade and Port Lucaya Marketplace* ☎ *242/352–8194 or 242/373–8404*) carries china and crystal by Waterford, Wedgwood, Aynsley, Swarovski, and Coalport, as well as Lladró figurines.

CIGARS

Note: it's illegal to bring Cuban cigars into the United States.

Havana Trading Company (✉ *Westin and Sheraton Grand Bahama Island Resort* ☎ *242/351–5685*) has Cuban cigar rollers at work. The shop also sells Cuban and other liquor.

Smoker's World (✉ *International Bazaar* ☎ *242/351–6899*) sells Cuban and Dominican cigars and paraphernalia.

FASHION

Animale (✉ *Port Lucaya Marketplace* ☎ *242/374–2066*) is known for the wild appeal of its fine ladies clothing and jewelry.

Bandolera (✉ *Port Lucaya Marketplace* ☎ *242/373–7691* ⊕ *www.bandolera.com*) sells European-style women's fashions, bags, and jewelry for the young and flirty.

JEWELRY & WATCHES

The Colombian (✉ *Port Lucaya Marketplace* ☎ *242/373–2973*) purveys a line of Colombia's famed emeralds plus other jewelry and crystal.

Colombian Emeralds International (✉ *Port Lucaya Marketplace, and Westin and Sheraton Grand Bahama Island Resort* ☎ *242/352–8400, 242/373–4215, or 800/666–3889* ⊕ *www.dutyfree.com*) is *the* place to find emeralds, diamonds, rubies, sapphires, and gold jewelry. The best brands in watches, including Tag Heuer, Breitling, and Omega, are also available here.

Freeport Jewellers (✉ *International Bazaar and Port Lucaya Marketplace* ☎ *242/352—2004 or 242/372–2776*) caters to locals and visitors with watches, heavy gold and silver chains, gemstones, and sea charms. Its larger Port Lucaya store also sells cigars, crystal, and Fossil brand watches.

LEATHER GOODS

Unusual Center (✉ *Port Lucaya Marketplace* ☎ *242/373–7333*) carries eel-skin leather, peacock-feather goods, and jewelry.

MISCELLANEOUS

Photo Specialist (✉ *Port Lucaya Marketplace* ☎ *242/373–7858*) repairs cameras and carries photo and video equipment.

★ **Sun & Sea Outfitters** (✉ *UNEXSO, Port Lucaya Marketplace* ☎ *242/373–1244*) sells everything water-related, from snorkel equipment and marine animal T-shirts to dolphin jewelry and swimsuits.

MUSIC

Da Muzik Box (✉ *Port Lucaya Marketplace* ☎ *242/374–5113*) carries a full selection of Caribbean and American pop music.

PERFUMES

Parfum de Paris (⊠ *International Arcade, Port Lucaya Marketplace, an* *Westin and Sheraton Grand Bahama Island Resort* ☎ *242/352–816* *or 242/373–8403*) offers the most comprehensive range of fragrance on the island.

★ **Perfume Factory** (⊠ *International Bazaar* ☎ *242/352–9391*) sells a larg variety of perfumes, lotions, and colognes by Fragrance of the Baha mas, all under $21. Its biggest-selling Pink Pearl cologne actually con tains conch pearls, and Sand cologne for men has a little sterilize island sand in each bottle. You can also create your own scent an brand name and register it.

GRAND BAHAMA ISLAND ESSENTIALS

To research prices, get advice from other travelers, and book trav arrangements, visit ⊕www.fodors.com.

TRANSPORTATION

BY AIR

Grand Bahama International Airport is just off Grand Bahama High way, about six minutes from downtown Freeport and about 10 minute from Port Lucaya.

Several U.S. airlines fly to Grand Bahama International Airport fro cities on the east coast, including Atlanta, New York City, Miami, an Fort Lauderdale. Interisland flights to and from Nassau and other de tinations are also available.

AirTran flies from Atlanta nonstop daily, with connections to maj U.S. cities. American Eagle serves Freeport from Miami four tim daily, with American Airlines connections from many U.S. citie Bahamasair serves Grand Bahama International Airport with fligh from Fort Lauderdale, as well as via Nassau, daily. Continental/Co tinental Connection (Gulfstream) travels daily from Fort Lauderda on weekdays. Delta flies from Atlanta, Fort Lauderdale, Orland Miami, Tampa, West Palm Beach, Charlotte, Philadelphia, and Ne York (LaGuardia). Spirit Airlines flies daily from Fort Lauderdale. U Airways flies direct from Charlotte, North Carolina, and New Yor (LaGuardia) daily, and from Philadelphia on Saturday.

Airlines & Contacts **AirTran** (☎ *800/247–8726*). **American Eagle** (☎ *800/43 7300*). **Bahamasair** (☎ *242/352–8341 or 800/222–4262*). **Continental Co nection** (☎ *242/352–6447 or 800/231–0856*). **Delta** (☎ *242/351–4814 800/221–1212*). **Spirit** (☎ *242/352–8881 or 800/622–1015*). **US Airways** (*800/428–4322*).

Airport Information **Grand Bahama International Airport** (☎ *242/352–602*

BY BOAT

Grand Bahama Island is the port of call for Carnival Cruise Line, Discovery Cruises, and Norwegian Cruise Lines (⇨ see *Cruises in Essentials, at the back of the book*). Discovery Cruises provides daily ferry service from Fort Lauderdale, a five-hour trip each way.

A free government ferry runs between McLean's Town, at the East End, to Sweeting's Cay. It departs from Sweeting's Cay at 7:10 AM and 4 PM; and from McLean's Town at 8:30 AM and 5 PM. Pinder's Ferry Service travels twice daily from McLean's Town to Crown Haven in the Abacos at 8:30 AM and 4:30 PM; the trip takes an hour. The cost is $65 one way.

BY BUS

Buses are an inexpensive way to travel the 4 mi between downtown Freeport and Port Lucaya Marketplace daily until about 10 PM. The fare is $1. Buses from Freeport to the West End cost $5 each way; to the East End, $15. Exact change is required. Some resorts provide free shuttle service to shopping and beaches. No bus service is available between the airport and hotels.

BY CAR

If you plan to drive around the island, it's cheaper to rent a car than to hire a taxi. You can rent automobiles, jeeps, and vans at the Grand Bahama International Airport. Cars start at $80 per day for a daily rate, jeeps $85, plus an insurance fee of up to $17 is often levied. You can decline the insurance, but consequences can be dire if there's the least little scratch. Some agencies provide free pickup and delivery service to Freeport and Lucaya resorts.

Major Agencies Avis Rent-A-Car (☎242/352–7666, 888/897–8448 in U.S.). **Dollar Rent-A-Car** (☎242/352–9325, 800/800–4000 in U.S.). **Hertz** (☎242/352–9277, 800/654–3131 in U.S.). **Thrifty** (☎242/352–9308, 800/367–2277 in U.S.).

Local Agencies Bahama Buggies (☎242/352–8750 ⊕ www.bahamabuggies.com). **Cartwright's Rent-A-Car** (☎242/351–3002 ⊕ www.cartwrightsrentacar.com). **Island Jeep & Car Rental** (☎242/373–4002 ⊕ www.the-bahamas-car-rentals.com). **KSR Car Rental** (☎242/351–5737 ⊕ www.ksrrentacar.com).

BY SCOOTER

Grand Bahama's flat, well-paved roads make for good, safe scooter riding. Rentals run about $35 a day with a $200 deposit (about $25 for two hours). Helmets are required and provided. Look for rentals at Port Lucaya Marketplace and many resorts.

BY TAXI

Taxi fares are fixed by the government (but generally you're charged a flat fee for routine trips, and these rates can vary slightly) at $3 for the first ¼ mi and 40¢ for each additional ¼ mi, regardless of whether the taxi is a regular-size cab, a van, or a stretch limo. Additional passengers over two are $3 each. Grand Bahama Taxi Union can provide service for visitors arriving by air. There's a taxi waiting area outside the Westin and Sheraton Grand Bahama Island Resort.

Taxis meet all cruise ships. Passengers (two) are charged $16 f
trips to Freeport and $24 to Lucaya. The price per person dro
with larger groups.

Metered taxis also meet all incoming flights. Rides cost about $11 f
two to Freeport, $19 to Lucaya.

Taxi Companies **Grand Bahama Taxi Union** (⊠ *Grand Bahama Internation*
Airport ☎ *242/352–7101*).

CONTACTS & RESOURCES

BANKS & EXCHANGE SERVICES
Banks are generally open Monday–Thursday 9:30–3 and Friday 9:3(
4:30. Some of the major banks on the island include Bank of the Bah
mas, Scotiabank, First Caribbean Bank, Fidelity Financial Service
FINCO, and British American Bank.

EMERGENCIES
Dial 911 to reach the police in case of an emergency. Ambulance servi
and the fire department have separate numbers.

Contacts **Ambulance** (☎ 242/352–2689). **Bahamas Air Sea Rescue** (☎ 242/32
2628). **Fire Department** (☎ 242/352–8888 or 911). **Police** (☎ 911). **Rand Mem
rial Hospital** (⊠ E. Atlantic Dr., Freeport ☎ 242/352–5101).

TOUR OPTIONS
Tours can be booked through the tour desk in your hotel lobby,
tourist information booths, or by calling one of the tour operato
listed below.

A three-hour sightseeing tour of the Freeport–Lucaya area costs $35.
tour of Lucayan National Park runs about $40. Grand Bahama Natu
Tours' Bahamas Jeep Safari lets you drive your own open-top vehic
on a convoy through pine forests and along the coast. The cost of t
five-hour trip is $79 per person.

A host of tour operators on Grand Bahama offer a combination
the tours described above. Executive Tours and H. Forbes Char
& Tours have sightseeing land tours that can be booked through t
major resorts. For on-the-water fun, contact Reef Tours Ltd.

Information **Executive Tours** (☎ 242/373–7863 ⊕ www.executiveto
bahamas.com). **Grand Bahama Nature Tours** (☎ 866/440–4542 or 242/373–24
⊕ www.gbntours.com). **H. Forbes Charter & Tours** (☎ 242/352–9311 ⊕ ww
forbescharter.com).

BOAT TOUR   If you don't want to go too far underwater, try an excursion on the Se
world Explorer semisubmarine, which never fully submerges. Desce
into the hull of the boat and observe sea life in air-conditioned comf
from a vantage point 5 feet below the surface. The vessel departs fr
Port Lucaya and travels to Treasure Reef daily at 9:30, 11:30, a
1:30. The two-hour voyage with transportation and snorkeling co
$45, $25 for children.

2

A glass-bottom boat tour to offshore reefs with Reef Tours Ltd. costs $25; sailing tours are $35. For a speedy airboat excursion through the island's estuaries and other undiscovered spots, hook up with Bahamas EcoVentures Airboat Nature Venture. The $79 price tag includes lunch, beverage, and transportation.

For evening entertainment, a dinner cruise will cost around $80, with a show. Sunset "booze cruises" run about $45 each with a show, transportation included.

Contact **Bahamas EcoVentures** (☎ *242/352-9323* ⊕ *www.bahamaseco ventures.com*). **Reef Tours Ltd.** (☎ *242/373-5880* ⊕ *www.bahamasvacationguide. com/reeftours*). **Seaworld Explorer** (✉ *Port Lucaya Marina* ☎ *242/373-7863* ⊕ *www.superiorwatersports.com*).

BREWERY TOUR Pre-arranged tours through the Grand Bahama Brewing Company, the island's only microbrewery, end with a sampling of its four all-natural Lucayan and Hammerhead label products. The $5 tour price can be credited toward a purchase.

Contact **Grand Bahama Brewing Company** (☎ *242/351-5191*).

ECOTOURS Grand Bahama Nature Tours' eco-excursions explore pristine wilderness by kayak, van, snorkel, and foot. The six-hour tour includes 1½ hours of kayaking through Grand Bahama's mangrove environment for a look at bird and marine habitats, a guided nature hike through Lucayan National Park and its caves, swimming on Gold Rock Beach, and lunch. A five-hour excursion combines kayaking and snorkeling at Peterson Cay, a small island off Golf Rock Beach. The guides are extremely knowledgeable, particularly about flora and fauna. Air-conditioned transport is provided to and from your hotel, all for $79.

Contact **Grand Bahama Nature Tours** (✉ *Queen's Cove, Freeport* ☎ *242/373-2485 or 866/440-4542* ⊕ *www.gbntours.com*).

VISITOR INFORMATION

The Ministry of Tourism has a tourist information center at International Bazaar in Freeport. Branch offices are at the Grand Bahama International Airport, Lucayan Harbour, and at the southeast entrance to the Port Lucaya Marketplace. Tourist information centers are open daily 9–5.

Tourist Information **Ministry of Tourism Grand Bahama Office** ☎ *242/352-8044, 800/448-3386 in U.S.* ⊕ *www.grandbahama.bahamas.com*).

The Abacos

WORD OF MOUTH

"The thing that brings me back again and again to Abaco is being able to rent a boat and go on adventures every day on your own, safely and easily—great memories."

—ishkribbl

"The Abaco cays are like a string of pearls off the coast of larger Great Abaco island, and between them is a beautiful sheltered sea. The beaches are marvelous, and each of the major cays has a charming settlement where there are a handful of shops, restaurants, bars. Hopetown is probably the most famous, with its red-striped lighthouse, candy colored cottages, and nearly landlocked harbour."

—Callaloo

Updated by
Stephen F.
Vletas

THE ATTITUDE OF THE ABACOS might best be expressed by the sig posted in the window of a Hope Town shop: IF YOU'RE LOOKING FO WAL-MART—IT'S 200 MILES TO THE RIGHT. In other words, the residents o this chain of more than 100 islands know that there's another world ou there, but don't necessarily care to abandon theirs, which is a little mor traditional, slow-paced, and out of the way than most alternatives.

Here you'll feel content in an uncrowded environment, yet still hav access to whatever levels of accommodation and services you desir Ecotourism is the "in" thing, and aficionados have revitalized explora tion of Abaco's Caribbean Pine Forests, which are home to wild boa wild horses, the rare Bahamas Parrot, and a myriad of other bird an plant life. Hiking and biking through these forests, and along abar doned beaches at the forest's edges are popular activities. Sea kayakin in pristine protected areas provides a rewarding sense of adventu also, and more conventional activities include golf, tennis, and beac volleyball. But if you don't feel like doing anything at all, that's a high rated activity, too.

The Abacos' calm, naturally protected waters, long admired for the beauty, have also helped the area become the Bahamas' sailing cap tal. Man-O-War Cay remains the Bahamas' boatbuilding center; i residents turn out traditionally crafted wood dinghies as well as hig tech fiberglass craft. The Abacos play host annually to international famous regattas and to a half dozen game-fish tournaments. Outsic the resorts, the ocean-side villages of Hope Town and New Plymou also appeal to tourists for their charming New England ambience.

The 10 or so inhabited cays of the Abacos were first settled more tha 200 years ago by New England Loyalists, who in 1783 began fleeir the upstart United States to what they perceived as a safe haven fe those loyal to the crown. Joined by plantation owners and their slav from Virginia and the Carolinas, the newcomers found it hard goir on the rocky, infertile land, and soon turned to the sea. Some starte fishing and boatbuilding, others took advantage of the occasional shi wreck. The "wreckers" of the Abacos worked at night, luring unsu pecting ships onto rocks and shoals by shining misleading lights, the plundering the cargo. Of course, not all of these wrecks were caused I unscrupulous islanders. Some ships were lost in storms and foundere on hidden reefs, reefs that still pose dangers that keep 21st-centu boaters on the lookout.

Today the legacy of the British settlers remains intact. Many of the Ab cos' 13,000 residents have accents reminiscent of their ancestors— charming combination of an island cadence with a vaguely Scottish English lilt. Seafaring is still a major source of income, especially boa building, fishing, and guided fishing trips. Because the Abacos are or of the Out Islands' most visited destinations, an increasing number residents work in the tourist industry.

PLORING THE ABACOS

The Abacos, 200 mi east of Palm Beach, Florida, are a short boat ride from Grand Bahama. Little Abaco Island, Great Abaco Island, and many smaller offshore cays comprise the mini-archipelago, which stretches in a languid crescent for more than 120 mi from Walker's Cay in the north to Hole-in-the-Wall in the south. The dazzling cays lie in the Atlantic, mostly east or north of Great Abaco. Larger populated cays include Green Turtle, Great Guana, Man-O-War, and Elbow, all of which offer full services for boaters and just the right sprinkling of small resorts and enchanting settlements. The majority of the other cays are uninhabited, and together they provide a 100-mi-long sheltered cruising area that beckons to explorers in search of aqua-green bays, coral reefs, hidden coves, and white strands of beach.

Indulge in the complete package: Immaculate deserted beaches, deluxe full-service marinas, Out Island tranquility combined with easy travel, and top-quality accommodations. Plus, you can hit the links at world-class golf courses at Treasure Cay and Winding Bay, go bonefishing in the Marls, play tennis, or go diving or snorkeling. To *really* get away from it all, drive into Little Harbour, an artists' community, and completely disappear for a week. If you're an angler, abandon your cell phone and hole up in Sandy Point.

On Great Abaco proper you'll find rugged stretches of white limestone bluffs, miles of kelp-strewn beaches devoid of footprints, landlocked lakes, pine forests where wild horses and boar roam, and the Bahamas' third-largest community: the thriving commercial center of Marsh Harbour. The town has a variety of accommodation options, rental cars and boats, groceries, a plethora of restaurants and shops, and the Bahamas' largest marina. The drugstores are decently stocked, and one of the best medical clinics in the islands is here. Up north on Little Abaco, tourism is less prominent, and locals live as they have for the last hundred years—farming, fishing, and spending time with family and friends. This is a good area to explore by car—but be sure to save some time to relax on the stunning beaches around Fox Town.

Convenient commercial air service from Florida or Nassau to the Marsh Harbour and Treasure Cay airports makes reaching the Abacos fairly easy. Scheduled ferry service from Marsh Harbour and Treasure Cay to the offshore cays is convenient and reliable, and most ferry boats are covered, so you'll stay dry during rough-weather crossings. Mail boats from Nassau also visit ports up and down the island on a weekly basis. You should always be prepared for inclement weather; seasoned travelers always take rain jackets with hoods. Wear either sandals or tennis shoes with good support and traction, since the gunwales of the ferries and the docks are usually slippery.

ABOUT THE RESTAURANTS

Fish, conch, land crabs, and rock lobster—called crawfish by the locals—have long been the bedrock of local cuisine. Although a few menus, mostly in upscale resorts, feature dishes with Italian, Asian, or

THE ABACOS' TOP 5

Bonefishing in the Marls. One of the most spectacular wilderness flats regions anywhere, with an endless maze of lush mangrove creeks, hidden bays, and sandy cays. Hire a professional guide to show you the best spots.

Cay hopping. Rent your own boat and spend a day or more skipping from Green Turtle to No Name, Great Guana, Elbow, Snake, Tilloo—or wherever you please. Settle onto your own private strip of beach and enjoy.

Green Turtle Cay nightlife. When the Gully Roosters play, the island

rocks. Any local will be able to tell you when and where you can catch their next show. (And be sure to stop in at Miss Emily's Blue Bee Bar for a mind-altering rum, pineapple juice, and apricot brandy Goombay Smash.)

Little Harbour. Drop out and kick back; spend a day—or a week—in this serene bay-side artists' colony pursuing life's simple island pleasures.

Nippers Beach Bar & Grill on Great Guana Cay. Their Sunday pig roast is the best beach party of the year—and they have it every week, so there's no excuse for missing it.

Continental influences, most restaurants in the Abacos still serve simple Bahamian fare, with a few nods to American tastes.

The Abacos are not particularly dieter-friendly. Breakfasts tend toward the hearty eggs-bacon-and-pancakes variety. At lunch, even in the trendiest spots, you'll likely find variations on a few standards: fresh grouper "burgers," or breaded, fried fish fillets served on slightly sweet Bahamian buns; cracked conch, which is tenderized, deep-fried conch meat; and hamburgers and sandwiches, all usually sided with french fries, coleslaw, or local favorites like peas 'n' rice and macaroni and cheese. Dinner provides more options. You might eat local favorites like pork chops, fried chicken, or minced lobster cooked with tomatoes, garlic, and onions at a bare-bones diner; or head for a fancier restaurant and choose from an ever-changing array of seafood dishes with international flair, such as lobster risotto, sesame-crusted ahi tuna with wasabi sauce, or monkfish wrapped in pancetta.

Remember that almost nothing is grown locally, so high-quality fruits and vegetables are a rarity, especially right before the weekly boat bearing provisions arrive. (By the same token, don't be surprised if all dishes on the menu aren't available every day.) The remoteness also means meals aren't cheap, even in the humblest spot. Lunch usually costs at least $10 per person, and you can easily spend upward of $30 apiece at dinner, even without drinks.

ABOUT THE HOTELS

Small, intimate hotels and cottage-style resorts are the rule in the Abacos. There are, however, a few full-scale resorts, like Treasure Cay Hotel Resort and Marina, and Abaco Beach Resort & Boat Harbour, with multiple restaurants, bars, pools, and features like tennis courts, but most accommodations are beachside condos, houses, or cottages, or

IF YOU LIKE

SNORKELING & DIVING

With clear, shallow waters and a series of colorful coral reefs extending for miles, the Abacos provide both the novice and the experienced underwater explorer plenty of visual stimulation. The reefs, often within swimming distance of shore, are teeming with triggerfish, grouper, parrot fish, green moray eels, angelfish, jacks, damselfish, sergeant majors, stingrays, sea turtles, dolphins, and even the occasional reef or nurse shark. Dive operators are available at most marinas, but you can also venture out on your own, especially with a rented boat. Good places to start include the reefs near Guana Cay; Fowl Cay National Reserve between Man-O-War and Scotland cays; Pelican Cays National Park, just south of Marsh Harbour; and the reefs around Green Turtle Cay, where a Key West organization called Reef Relief has helped islanders install a series of 18 mooring buoys where you can safely anchor your boat without fear of damaging the fragile reef.

Maps of the buoys, which stretch from uninhabited Nun Jack Cay in the north to No Name Cay in the south, can be picked up at many Green Turtle Cay businesses. Visibility is generally high year-round, but the clear water turns cloudy after heavy storms and high seas. The relatively northern location of the Abacos means you may need a wet suit from December through March. But no matter what the time of year, the sheer number of good sites and relatively low visitor traffic translate to a fantastic view of life under the sea that you rarely have to share.

A LIVING HISTORY

Though the Abacos may be most famous for beaches, sailing, and fishing, you'd be missing the boat, so to speak, if you didn't explore the area's rich history. And that doesn't mean spending all those sunny days inside a museum, although there are fine, small museums in Hope Town and New Plymouth, each worth a visit to learn about the boatbuilding and seafaring traditions of the Loyalists who settled these islands.

Because the original settlements have been so well preserved, it's possible to absorb history just by wandering through them. In Hope Town, look for the gingerbread cottages with white picket fences, built 100 or more years ago but still lived in today. In New Plymouth, check out the sculpture garden depicting the accomplishments of famous Bahamians. While you're there, observe the architecture: the neat clapboard homes, shops, and churches, many with carefully tended flower boxes and airy front porches, have survived hurricanes and tropical storms and still look much like they did when they were built a century ago. On Man-O-War Cay, witness boatbuilding as it's been done for generations, or see women carefully crafting modern bags out of the same cloth their ancestors used for sails. And everywhere in the Abacos, simply try engaging the local residents in conversation. Nearly all of them, but especially those over 60, have some great tales to tell of what it's like to live on an island where many grew up without cars, TVs, telephones, or daily mail service.

3

hotels with just a handful of rooms and a single small restaurant. What you may give up in modern amenities and bells and whistles like spas or 24-hour room service, you'll gain in privacy and beauty. Many hotels have water views, and with a cottage or private house you may even get your own stretch of beach. Although accommodations tend to be simple, air-conditioning has become a standard feature, and more places are adding previously unheard-of luxuries like satellite TV, in-room phones, DVD players, and wireless Internet access. Again, small and remote doesn't equate with inexpensive; it's just about impossible to find lodging for less than $100 a night, and not uncommon to pay more than $250 a night for beachside accommodations with all the conveniences.

WHAT IT COSTS IN U.S. DOLLARS					
	¢	$	$$	$$$	$$$$
RESTAURANTS	under $10	$10–$20	$20–$30	$30–$40	over $40
HOTELS	under $100	$100–$200	$200–$300	$300–$400	over $400

Restaurant prices are for a main course at dinner, excluding gratuity, typically 15%, which is often automatically added to the bill. Hotel prices are for two people in a standard double room in high season, excluding service charges and 6%–12% tax.

TIMING

June, July, and early August are the best months for sailing, boating, and swimming; the season of the most popular regatta and fishing tournaments; and the time you're likely to pay a premium for hotels, boats, and cars—if you can book them at all. December through May is a pleasant time to visit, though most locals refuse to get in the water during those months. With average high temperatures in the 70s and low 80s, you might disagree, although in January and February, those highs can sometimes dip as low as 50°F when a norther blows through. January is a prime month for wahoo fishing (and wahoo eating—it's a succulent, textured, white-meat delicacy) with tournaments at Treasure Cay and Boat Harbour marinas. This is also the middle of lobster fishing season, which runs from August through March. If you enjoy fresh lobster, this is the best time to indulge.

In September and October, typically the peak of hurricane season, the number of visitors drops to a trickle, and many hotels and restaurants shut down for two weeks to two months. If you're willing to take a chance on getting hit by a storm, this can still be a great time to explore, with discounts of as much as 50% at the hotels that remain open.

GREAT ABACO ISLAND

Most visitors to the Abacos make their first stop on Great Abaco Island's east coast at **Marsh Harbour,** the Bahamas' third-largest city and the Abacos' commercial center. Besides having the biggest international airport in the Abacos, Marsh Harbour is considered by boaters to be one of the easiest harbors to enter. It has several full-service marinas, including the 190-slip Boat Harbour Marina and the 80-slip Conch Inn Marina.

Stock up on groceries and supplies here on the way to other islands. The downtown area has several supermarkets with a better selection than the sometimes limited supplies on the smaller islands, as well as a few department and hardware stores. Most of the gift shops are on the main street, which has the island's only traffic lights. If you need cash, this is the place to get it as well; the banks here are open every day and have ATMs, neither of which you will find on the

> **DID YOU KNOW?**
>
> Bahamian currency includes a $3 bill. There's also a half-dollar bill and a 15-cent piece, which is square and decorated with a hibiscus. All of the banknotes feature a Spanish galleon watermark and a see-through sand dollar. Banknotes are printed in England, while all coins are minted in Canada.

smaller, more remote cays. There are also gas stations, doctors, government offices, and a number of good, moderately priced restaurants.

Drive 25 minutes south of Marsh Harbour to get to the **Abaco Club on Winding Bay,** a glamorous private golf and sporting club set on 534 acres of stunning oceanfront property. The clubhouse, restaurant, and pool, which sit on 65-foot high white limestone bluffs, offer guests and members a mesmerizing view of the purple-blue Atlantic Ocean, and the bay has more than 2 mi of sugar-sand beaches. Amenities and activities at the club include an 18-hole tropical links golf course, a luxurious European-style spa and fitness center, scuba diving, snorkeling, horseback riding, tennis, bonefishing, and offshore fishing. Real estate for sale includes 70 exquisite two- and three-bedroom turnkey cottages and 60 estate homesites. The Ritz-Carlton group manages the property, and they have plans to build a fishing village in Cherokee Sound and a small private marina in Little Harbour. Nonmembers can stay in the hotel-style cabanas and cottages and use all facilities one time while evaluating the membership and real estate options. The hotel portion of the club could open to the general public by the end of 2008. ⊠*South of MarshHarbour* ☎*242/367–0077 or 888/303–2765* ⊕*www.theabacoclub.com*

The small, eclectic artist's colony of **Little Harbour** was settled by the Johnston family more than 50 years ago. **Pete Johnston's Foundry** (☎*242/477–5487*), the only bronze foundry in the Bahamas, is the centerpiece, and sculptor Johnston and his sons and acolytes cast magnificent lifelike bronze figures using the age-old lost-wax method. In **Pete's Pub and Gallery** (☎*242/366–3503 or 954/840–3698* ⊕*www. petespubandgallery.com*), you can view the fine bronzes, unique gold jewelry, and other original island art for sale. The work is astounding in quality and originality, and much of it is well-priced. Next door in the outdoor tiki-hut restaurant and bar you can wiggle your toes in the sand while you chow down on fresh seafood, burgers, and cold tropical drinks. Try the mango-glazed grouper, lemon-pepper mahimahi, or coconut cracked conch while you kick back and enjoy the view of the harbor. And if you want to be part of the local scene, don't miss the

GREAT ITINERARIES

IF YOU HAVE 3 DAYS

Make your base in **Marsh Harbour**, the biggest city in the Abacos, and spend the first day getting settled in your hotel, exploring the city or a nearby beach, and having a leisurely dinner on Restaurant Row, overlooking the busy marina. Restaurant options range from fine dining to munching conch fritters and sipping Goombay Smashes at a local hangout. If you arrive on a weekend, you can probably find a swinging nightspot where you can shake it to the rhythms of live island music. On Day 2, get up early and take the ferry to **Hope Town**, the **Elbow Cay** settlement often considered the most picturesque in the Abacos, with its candy-stripe lighthouse, rows of neat clapboard cottages painted in pastel hues, and plenty of restaurants, shops, and historic sites. Day 3 brings a choice: for another dose of Loyalist history, take the ferry again, this time to **Man-O-War Cay**, the boatbuilding capital of the region; or stay put and book a diving or fishing trip out of one of the Marsh Harbour marinas.

IF YOU HAVE 5 DAYS

Follow the suggested three-day itinerary, and on Day 4 go to **Treasure Cay** and catch the first ferry to **Green Turtle Cay**, your base for the next two days. Stroll through **New Plymouth** for the remainder of your morning, stopping to wander through the sculpture garden, which memorializes accomplished Bahamians, and the **Albert Lowe Museum**, getting a dose of island history, as well as learning about shipbuilding and hurricane survival. After a lunch of locally caught conch or grouper, spend the afternoon at **Ocean Beach** or on calmer **Gillam**

Bay, then dress up for a fancy dinner at one of the two fine resorts on **White Sound.** On your last day, if you're a golfer, you'll want to hit the links at nearby Treasure Cay, where the 18-hole course is considered one of the finest in the Caribbean, yet is so blissfully uncrowded that tee times aren't necessary. And if you're an angler, book a day of bonefishing or offshore fishing with a local guide. Otherwise, rent a small boat and visit some of the uninhabited nearby cays, such as **Nun Jack, No Name,** and **Crab,** where the snorkeling and deserted white-sand beaches are sublime.

IF YOU HAVE 7 DAYS

Add two days to the **Marsh Harbour** portion of the five-day itinerary above. On the first additional day, take a ferry to **Great Guana Cay**, which has some of the most beautiful beaches in the Abacos and one of the best party-scene restaurants, **Nippers.** On the second day, rent a car and explore the southern reaches of **Great Abaco Island,** perhaps searching for the endangered Bahama parrot at the **Bahamas National Trust Sanctuary**, or checking out the bronze sculptures at **Pete Johnson's Foundry** in **Little Harbour**. Another alternative, if you're a boater, is to rent a boat your first day in Marsh Harbour and spend the week island-hopping. If all that sounds like too much work, consider experiencing life like a local: bring some books, sunblock, and a few swimsuits; rent a cottage, a dinghy, and a golf cart, perhaps on **Elbow Cay** or **Great Guana Cay**; and learn to practice the fine art of relaxation.

Saturday wild pig roasts (April through July). By car, Little Harbour is about 30 minutes south of Marsh Harbour.

About 30 mi south of Marsh Harbour is the seaside settlement of **Cherokee Sound,** home to fewer than 100 families. Most of the residents make their living catching crawfish or working in the growing tourism industry; many lead offshore fishing and bonefishing expeditions. The deserted Atlantic beaches and serene salt marshes in this area are breathtaking, and though development at Winding Bay and Little Harbour are progressing, the slow-paced, tranquil feel of daily life here hasn't changed. Take, for example, the no-name bay just north of the settlement, where **The Sand Bar,** a magnificent wooden pier, juts out into glass-clear waters that are home to schools of bonefish. The pier is more than a football field in length, with an open-air restaurant and bar that serves cold Kaliks, grilled burgers, grouper, conch salad, and fries, along with other Bahamian specialties. This place is easy to miss if you're not paying attention, as the road to Cherokee Sound is a winding, curvy strip of cement that skirts the edges of mangrove-lined creeks and bays cut into the coral. About a mile before the settlement, you'll see a sign on your left. Follow the narrow road, park in one of the areas just before a locked gate, and walk over to the Sand Bar. It's a nice choice for lunch or afternoon drinks—when it's open. Often it's not—you just have to go and take your chances. The more things change, the more they stay the same.

Sandy Point, a "takin' it easy, mon" fishing village with miles of beckoning beaches and a couple of bonefishing lodges, is slightly more than 50 mi southwest of Marsh Harbour. The Great Abaco Highway leg, which runs into the settlement, ends at **Rickmon Bonefish Lodge.** You can park your car here, have a cold drink in the lodge bar, and enjoy the beach or fish the flats on your own when the tide is low. There are no communities to visit south of Sandy Point, but a major navigational lighthouse stands at **Hole-in-the-Wall,** on Great Abaco's southern tip. The lighthouse was constructed in 1838 against local opposition from islanders who depended on salvaging shipwrecks for their livelihood. Over the years the lighthouse has survived sabotage and hurricanes, and was automated in 1995 to continue serving maritime interests. The Bahamas Marine Mammal Research Organization has leased the site to monitor whale movements and conduct other ocean studies. A rugged, winding single lane dirt road leads to the lighthouse. Access this dirt track off the Great Abaco Highway, about 40 mi south of Marsh Harbour near the dogleg to Sandy Point.

The dirt track passes through the dense pine woodlands of the 20,500-acre **Abaco National Park** (☎ 242/393–1317), established by the **Bahamas National Trust** in 1994 as a sanctuary for the endangered Bahama parrot; your best chance to see the bird is at dawn. More than 100 other species have been sighted in this area. The 15-mi dirt track ends at the Hole-in-the-Wall lighthouse complex, which is a starkly beautiful and desolate location overlooking the blue-green ocean. The drive from the paved highway takes about one and a half hours, and can only be done in a 4X4 vehicle. Most rental companies don't allow their vehicles

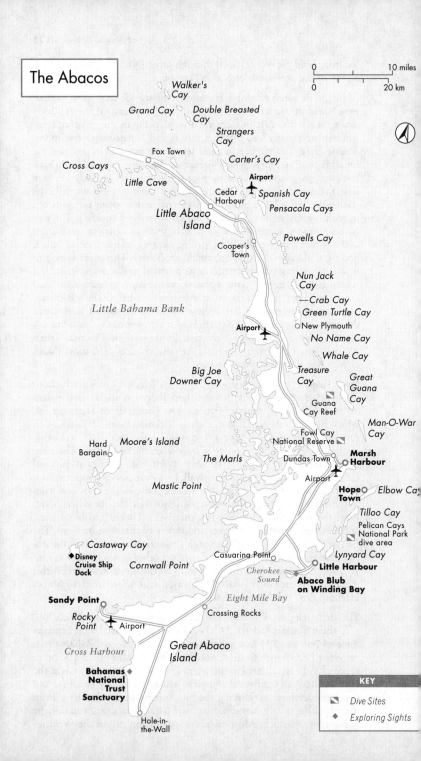

The Abacos

0 _____ 10 miles

0 _____ 20 km

Walker's Cay

Grand Cay

Double Breasted Cay

Strangers Cay

Cross Cays

Fox Town

Carter's Cay

Little Cave

Cedar Harbour

✈ Airport

Spanish Cay

Pensacola Cays

Little Abaco Island

Cooper's Town

Powells Cay

Little Bahama Bank

Nun Jack Cay

Crab Cay

Green Turtle Cay

✈ Airport

New Plymouth

No Name Cay

Whale Cay

Big Joe Downer Cay

Treasure Cay

Great Guana Cay

Guana Cay Reef

Man-O-War Cay

Hard Bargain

Moore's Island

Fowl Cay National Reserve

Dundas Town

Marsh Harbour

The Marls

Mastic Point

✈ Airport

Hope Town

Elbow Cay

Tilloo Cay

Pelican Cays National Park dive area

Castaway Cay

◆ Disney Cruise Ship Dock

Cornwall Point

Casuarina Point

Lynyard Cay

Little Harbour

Cherokee Sound

Abaco Blub on Winding Bay

Sandy Point

Eight Mile Bay

Rocky Point

✈ Airport

Crossing Rocks

Great Abaco Island

Cross Harbour

Bahamas National Trust Sanctuary ◆

Hole-in-the-Wall

KEY	
🔲	Dive Sites
◆	Exploring Sights

on roads like this, so proceed at your own risk. The lighthouse is not technically open to visitors, though visiting the area around the point is OK, and people still do climb the rickety stairs to the top of the lighthouse where views of the island and the sea are mesmerizing.

WHERE TO EAT

BAHAMIAN

★ $$$ ✕**Angler's Restaurant.** Dine on roasted rack of lamb with garlic mashed potatoes or a broiled lobster tail while overlooking gleaming rows of yachts moored in the Boat Harbour Marina at the Abaco Beach Resort. White tablecloths with fresh orchid arrangements and sea-blue napkins folded like seashells create an ambience a step up from typical island dining. It's not uncommon to see guests dressed in sports coats and cocktail dresses fresh off a stunning mega-yacht alongside other guests in shorts and T-shirts with kids in tow. Everyone can equally enjoy fresh grilled catch of the day—don't pass up the grilled wahoo—seafood pastas, Bahamian chicken, or charbroiled steaks. For dessert try the calorie-drenched guava duff. ⊠*Abaco Beach Resort, off Bay St., Marsh Harbour* ☎*242/367–2158* ⊕*www.abacoresort. com* ⊟*AE, D, MC, V.*

★ $$$ ✕**Wally's.** This two-story, pink, colonial villa sits across Bay Street from the marina, fronted by green lawns, hibiscus, and white-railed verandas. This is the Abacos' most popular restaurant—*the* place to go for good food, potent rum cocktails, and serious people-watching. Lunch is a scene, especially if you sit outside, where you'll find a mix of locals, tourists, and boat people munching on Greek or Caesar salads, spicy grouper, tarragon chicken, and mahimahi burgers. Inside is a stylish bar, a boutique, and three dining rooms, all adorned with Haitian-style paintings. Dinner is served Friday and Saturday only, and the menu includes wild boar, turtle sautéed in onions and mushrooms, grilled wahoo, and tender lamb chops. Save room for the irresistible key lime pie. ⊠*E. Bay St., Marsh Harbour* ☎*242/367–2074* ⊟*AE, D, MC, V* ⚑*Reservations essential* ☉*Closed Sun. and Sept.–Oct. No dinner Mon.–Thurs.*

$$ ✕**Curly Tails Restaurant and Bar.** Enjoy kick-back harborside dining for breakfast, lunch, and dinner at the Conch Inn Hotel and Marina. Enjoy your breakfast outside on the open air deck and go for the cheese omelet or sweet pancakes. At lunch, salads, burgers, cracked conch, and grouper fillets go great with a cold Kalik. Try dinner in the air-conditioned dining room. Fresh grilled snapper and mahimahi can be prepared with an Asian flare, while broiled lobster and tomato-smothered chicken are traditional favorites. If you're into sunsets, don't miss the daily happy hour. Sample a frozen Tail Curler or a Curlytini to go with your conch fritters. There's also live music every week. ⊠ *Conch Inn Hotel and Marina, Bay St., Marsh Harbour* ☎*242/367–4000* ⊕*www. conchinn.com* ⊟*MC, V.*

$$ ✕**Hummingbird Restaurant and Bar.** At this unassuming diner tucked inside Memorial Plaza Mall, locals trade gossip over heaping plates of pancakes and cheese-stuffed omelets at breakfast, then move on to hearty lunches of cracked conch, burgers, and salads. At dinner, the dress code and the vibe remain casual, but the food presentation gets

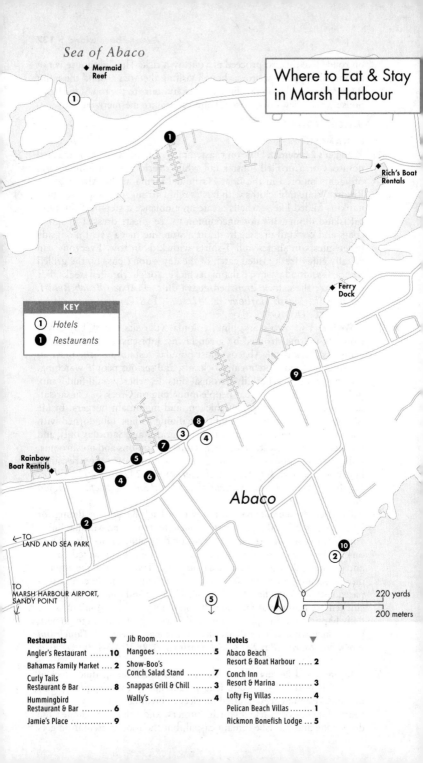

Where to Eat & Stay in Marsh Harbour

Sea of Abaco

◆ Mermaid Reef

◆ Rich's Boat Rentals

◆ Ferry Dock

KEY
① Hotels
❶ Restaurants

Rainbow Boat Rentals ◆

Abaco

← TO LAND AND SEA PARK

TO MARSH HARBOUR AIRPORT, SANDY POINT

0			220 yards
0			200 meters

Restaurants ▼

Angler's Restaurant **10**

Bahamas Family Market **2**

Curly Tails Restaurant & Bar **8**

Hummingbird Restaurant & Bar **6**

Jamie's Place **9**

Jib Room **1**

Mangoes **5**

Show-Boo's Conch Salad Stand **7**

Snappas Grill & Chill **3**

Wally's **4**

Hotels ▼

Abaco Beach Resort & Boat Harbour **2**

Conch Inn Resort & Marina **3**

Lofty Fig Villas **4**

Pelican Beach Villas **1**

Rickmon Bonefish Lodge ... **5**

kicked up a notch; try the stuffed pork chops or go Bahamian with a grilled turtle steak. If you want to look like you're in the know, ask for a booth when you make your reservation. ⊠ *Memorial Plaza, Marsh Harbour* ☎ *242/367–2922* ▤ *MC, V.*

$$ ✕ **Jib Room.** Expect casual lunches of hot wings, conch burgers, fish nuggets, and nachos in this harbor-view restaurant and bar, located inside the Marsh Harbour Marina. Dinner is served twice a week, and these "barbecue nights" are especially popular; on Wednesday it's baby back ribs, fish, chicken, potato salad, slaw, and baked beans. On Saturday it's grilled steak, featuring New York strip, with fish and chicken as options along with baked potatoes and salad. If you're dying for a steak after a steady fish diet, these are the best in the Abacos. ⊠ *Pelican Shores, Marsh Harbour* ☎ *242/367–2700* ⊕ *www. jibroom.com* ▤ *MC, V* ⚷ *Reservations essential* ⊗ *Closed Sun.–Tues. No dinner Thurs. and Fri.*

$$ ✕ **Snappas Grill and Chill.** Savvy boat people and in-the-know locals hang out here in the Harbour View Marina. The polished wood bar is the center of gravity around which the dining room sprawls outward toward the open-air waterside deck. Killer appetizers include grilled shrimp, chicken kabobs, and sizzling onion rings. For lunch the grilled fish Caesar salad and the Snappa Filly are hard to beat. Fresh grilled catch of the day and grilled conch are crossover items that always hit the spot. When the sun goes down—the sunsets are dazzling—order a NY steak or grilled lobster with a garden salad. Want more? Party on with live music Friday and Saturday nights. ⊠ *Harbour View Marina, Bay St., Marsh Harbour* ☎ *242/367–2278* ⊕ *www.snappasbar.com* ▤ *MC, V.*

$ ✕ **Jamie's Place.** There's nothing fancy about this clean, bright, diner-style eatery, but the welcome is warm, the Bahamian dishes well executed, and the prices are right, with most meals clocking in at $14 or less. Choose fried chicken, cracked conch, or fresh-caught dolphin (also called mahimahi), with a side of mashed or roasted potatoes, peas 'n' rice, macaroni and cheese, or coleslaw. Jamie's is also an ice-cream parlor, with a dozen flavors. Locals love this place, and it's stayed one of Great Abaco Island's best-kept secrets. ⊠ *Queen Elizabeth Dr., Marsh Harbour* ☎ *242/367–2880* ▤ *No credit cards* ⊗ *Closed Sun.*

¢ ✕ **Show-Boo's Conch Salad Stand.** JUST BE NICE implores the hand-lettered sign on this ramshackle stand, between Harbour View and Conch Inn marinas. Follow the instructions and you'll be rewarded with what the proprietor claims to be "the world's best conch salad," often diced and mixed while you watch. Hours are erratic, especially during the September–November off-season. To find out if Show-Boo showed up for business, just swing by around lunchtime and see if there's a line forming in front of his stand. ⊠ *Queen Elizabeth Dr., Marsh Harbour* ☎ *No phone* ▤ *No credit cards* ⊗ *No dinner.*

DELI

¢ ✕ **Bahamas Family Market.** At lunchtime, the best bargains in town are at the lunch counter inside this small grocery. Jamaican meat pies stuffed with curried beef or chicken go for $4. A sub sandwich full of Italian salami and cheese, plus chips and a soft drink, is just $8. At breakfast, snag a fresh-baked pastry and coffee for $3. There's no eating area, but they'll heat up your order if you'd like. It's also the perfect spot to pack your boat or car cooler for a picnic. ⊠ *Queen Elizabeth Dr., at stoplight, Marsh Harbour* ☎ *242/367–3714* ⊟ *No credit cards.*

ECLECTIC

★ $$ ✕ **Mangoes.** An open-air deck makes Mangoes a great place for water-side dining. Enjoy cracked conch, grouper tacos, and zesty salads at lunch; at dinner try house specialties like smudder grouper, fried and seasoned with tomato, thyme, and pepper sauce; baked grouper with mango and cilantro salsa; grilled rack of lamb; or the catch of the day grilled, fried, or blackened. If it's wahoo, order it grilled with lots of extra key limes. The bread pudding is an after-dinner highlight, made with bananas, coconut, and sweet, doughy Bahamian bread. The restaurant is housed in a complex that contains a boutique selling resort wear and fine jewelry from South America, and a 29-slip marina—which means you can sail in from the offshore cays, tie up in front, enjoy a meal, and do some shopping. ⊠ *Queen Elizabeth Dr., Marsh Harbour* ☎ *242/367–2366* ⊟ *AE, D, MC, V* ⊙ *Closed Oct.*

WHERE TO STAY

$$$$ ⊡ **Rickmon Bonefish Lodge.** Well-regarded fishing guide Ricardo Burrows operates this comfortable waterside lodge at the end of the road in Sandy Point. The whitewashed, plantation-style building has 11 modern rooms, each with air-conditioning and satellite TV; five overlook the ocean through sliding French doors. Fishing packages—which include top private guides, all meals, and accommodations—are the most popular option here, but nonfishing guests can fill their time beachcombing, bird-watching, snorkeling, and boating. The location is ideal for accessing the flats around Castaway Cay, Moore's Island, and the southern Marls. **Pros:** perfect location for bonefishing, some of the best professional fly fishing guides in the Abacos. **Cons:** average restaurant, no high-speed Internet. ⊠ *Sandy Point* ☎ *242/366–4477 or 800/211–8530* ⊕ *www.anglingdestinations.com* ⇨ *11 rooms* ⬡ *In-room: no phone. In-hotel: restaurant, bar, beachfront, no elevator, laundry service* ⊟ *No credit cards* ⦿ *AI.*

⟳ $$ ⊡ **Abaco Beach Resort & Boat Harbour.** One of the liveliest party spots Fodor'sChoice   on the island, this place rocks during the half-dozen fishing tourna-
★   ments it hosts every year. The boating crowd keeps the place hopping the rest of the year as well, with a slight slowdown in August and September. The resort is set on 52 manicured acres overlooking the Sea of Abaco, just five minutes from the Marsh Harbour airport or a short ferry ride away from Hope Town on Elbow Cay. The spacious ocean-view rooms have natural-stone floors, white wicker furnishings, marble wet bars, built-in hair dryers, and in-room satellite TVs. Dine on roasted rack of lamb with garlic mashed potatoes or a broiled lobster tail at Angler's Restaurant, which overlooks gleaming rows of yachts moored in the marina. The resort's dive shop will arrange fishing charters and boat rentals; use of small sailboats and kayaks is complimentary. Lounge poolside and enjoy fruity rum drinks at the swim-up bar while your kids explore the beach playground. **Pros:** ideal location

for all water-related activities, easy access to town shops and restaurants, one of the best marinas in the Abacos. **Cons:** can be crowded and noisy during fishing tournaments, check-in can be a process. ⊠*East of Conch Sound Marina, Marsh Harbour* ☎*242/367–2158 or 800/468–4799* ⊕*www.abacoresort.com* ⇱*72 rooms, 10 suites* ��*In-room: safe, refrigerator. In-hotel: 2 restaurants, bars, tennis courts, pools, gym, beachfront, diving, water sports, bicycles, no elevator, laundry facilities, public Wi-Fi* ☰*AE, D, MC, V* ⅤⓄⅠ*FAP, MAP.*

$$ ▦**Pelican Beach Villas.** On a quiet, private peninsula opposite the main settlement of Marsh Harbour sit seven waterfront clapboard cottages, cheerily painted in pale pink, yellow, blue, and green. Inside the air-conditioned rooms are rattan furnishings with pastel cushions and porcelain tile floors. A small sand beach is out front, and the cottages are near Mermaid Reef, a primo snorkeling spot. There's no restaurant on-site, but there's food within walking distance at the Marsh Harbour Marina; for other options, you'll need to rent a car or, better yet, a small runabout, which you can tie up for free at the 100-foot dock. **Pros:** tranquil beach location, near some of the best snorkeling in the Abacos, many repeat guests. **Cons:** no restaurant, need to rent a car or boat, on the expensive side for less than full-service accommodations. ⊠*Northwest of Marsh Harbour Marina* ☎*877/326–3180 or 242/367–3600* ⊕*www.pelicanbeachvillas.com* ⇱*7 cottages* ⅍*In-room: kitchen. In-hotel: beachfront, laundry facilities* ☰*AE, D, MC, V.*

$ ✕▦**Conch Inn Resort & Marina.** This low-key, one-level marina hotel is a good choice for budget travelers, but make reservations well in advance. Each simple room has two double beds, white-tile floors, white rattan furniture, and color-splashed bedspreads. Curly Tails restaurant serves delicious breakfasts, including cheesy omelets and thick, sweet pancakes, plus lunch and dinner daily. The 80-slip marina, one of Marsh Harbour's busiest, is the Bahamas' headquarters for the Moorings sailboat charter service and Nautic Blue Power Yacht Vacations. Top restaurants, shopping, and small beaches are within easy walking distance. **Pros:** smack dab in the middle of everything in Marsh Habour—marina, shops, and restaurants; easy to arrange boat rentals and diving; good value for comfortable rooms. **Cons:** far from beaches, small pool area. ⊠*E. Bay St.,Marsh Harbour* ☎*242/367–4000* ⊕*www.conchinn.com* ⇱*10 rooms* ⅍*In-room: no phone, refrigerator. In-hotel: restaurant, bar, pool, diving, bicycles, laundry facilities* ☰*AE, MC, V.*

$ ▦**Lofty Fig Villas.** The longtime owners envelope guests with exceptional hospitality, as does the super-friendly staff. The intimate compound has six spacious villas with pool or harbor views. Kitchens are fully equipped, and the supermarket is about a 10-minute walk away. Restaurants, marinas, bars, and a dive shop are even closer—basically right out the front door. For families or groups on a budget, this is a super option. **Pros:** location, location, location; good pool area for hanging out; excellent value with warm and friendly service. **Cons:** room furnishings are dated, no place to tie up a rental boat. ⊠*Across from Mangoes Restaurant and Conch Inn Resort, Marsh Harbour*

☎242/367–2681 ⊕www.loftyfig.
com ⇨6 villas ⌂In-room: no
phone, kitchen. In-hotel: pool,
public Internet ⊟D, MC, V.

SPORTS & THE OUTDOORS

BICYCLING **Rental Wheels of Abaco** (⊠E. Bay
St. ☎242/367–4643) rents bicycles
for $10 a day; they also have Suzuki
and Yamaha mopeds. They are
located on the main strip between
Conch Inn Marina and the turn-off
to Boat Harbour Marina.

BOATING You can get around Marsh Harbour, Great Abaco Island, and most of
the nearby settled cays by car or ferry, but it's more fun to have your
own boat. Marsh Harbour has the biggest selection of rental boats
and the largest marinas in the Abacos, so even if you're staying on
another cay, you may want to reserve your boat here. You can rent
anything from a small dinghy to a 46-foot yacht or catamaran that will
sleep six or more. Most rentals are available on a daily, three-day, or
weekly basis. Count on spending at least $100 a day for a small boat
and $180 for a larger one; the sky's the limit for a deluxe yacht with
crew. Reserving your boat in advance is recommended, and remember
that rates don't include fuel, which can cost nearly $4 per gallon in
the Bahamas. Sailboats can be chartered by the week or longer, with
or without crew.

In Marsh Harbour, **Boat Harbour Marina** (☎242/367–2158 ⊕www.
abacobeachresort.com) has 190 fully protected slips and a slew of amenities, including accommodations at the Abaco Beach Resort. **Conch Inn
Marina** (☎242/367–4000 ⊕www.conchinn.com) is one of the busiest
in Marsh Harbour and has 80 slips, with accommodations available at
the Conch Inn. **Habour View Marina** (☎242/367–3910 ⊕www.harbour
viewmarina.com), the first marina on the west end of Bay Street, and
across from Wally's Restaurant, has extra-wide slips and 100-foot piers
to accommodate boats with unlimited beam size, private pool, wireless
Internet, and Snappas Restaurant. **Mangoes Marina** (☎242/367–4255)
has 29 slips and a full range of amenities, including on-shore showers, a
pool, and a popular restaurant of the same name. **Marsh Harbour Marina**
(☎242/367–2700 ⊕www.jibroom.com) has 68 slips and is the only
full-service marina on the left side of the harbor, near Pelican Shores. It
is a 10-minute drive from most shops and restaurants.

The Moorings (☎242/367–4000 or 888/952–8420 ⊕www.moorings.
com) rents 36- to 47-foot sailboats from its base at the Conch Inn
Resort & Marina in Marsh Harbour. **Nautic Blue Power Yacht Vacations**
(☎242/367–4000 or 800/416–0224 ⊕www.nauticblue.com) has 34-
to 46-foot powerboats, and is the sister operation to the Moorings.
Rainbow Rentals (☎242/367–4602 ⊕www.go-abacos.com/rainbow)
has custom-built 22-foot catamarans complete with freshwater showers, as well as powerboats, on the Marsh Harbour waterfront west of

Union Jack Dock. **Rich's Rentals** (☎242/367–2742 ⊕*www.richsrentals. com*) is the best place for 21- to 26-foot Paramount powerboats, all fully equipped for diving and fishing. It's located just past the turn-off to Abaco Beach Resort, just follow the signs. Twenty-four-hour emergency service is available. **Sea Horse Boat Rentals** (☎242/367–2513 ⊕*www.seahorseboatrentals.com*) has a variety of boats, from 26-foot Paramounts to 18-foot Boston Whalers. They're on the east side of Marsh Harbour in the Boat Harbour Marina, a convenient location for people staying on Lubbers Quarters and Elbow Cay. They also have an office in Hope Town.

EVENTS   Several sporting events are held annually in the Abacos. You can catch the **Boat Harbour Billfish Championship** (⊕*www.bahamasbillfish.com*) in June. Each July, **Regatta Time in Abaco**, a series of five sailboat races, takes place in five cays, with the party scene attracting even more par-ticipants than the races. In September there's a spectator event titled the **All Abaco Regatta,** with native Bahamian sloops competing in races, plus nightly festivals with food stands and live music. For informa-tion about Abacos events, call Marsh Harbour's **Abaco Tourist Office** (☎242/367–3067). The **Out Island Promotion Board** (☎954/475–8315 ⊕*www.myoutislands.com*) has information on everything from special events to art galleries.

FISHING   You can find bonefish on the flats, yellowtail and grouper on the reefs, or marlin and tuna in the deeps of the Abacos. Premier fly-fishing guide **Justin Sands** (☎242/367–3526 *or* 242/359–689✗*www.bahamas-vacationguide.com/justfish.html*) works out of a state-of-the-art Hell's Bay flats skiff that will put you on tailing bones in the skinniest water. Justin was the Abacos bonefish champ in two years running, and he will guide you in the Marls or around Snake Cay, Little Harbour, and Cherokee Sound. Advance reservations are a must. Brothers Buddy and Christopher Pinder have a combined 30 years' experience in the local waters, and their **Pinder's Bone Fishing** (☎242/366–2163) offers year-round excursions in the Marls, a maze of mangroves and flats on the western side of Abaco. Advance reservations are essential. **Strike And Fight, Capt. Ray Thurston** (☎242/375–9910) will put you on marlin, dorado, tuna, wahoo, and other offshore species in season. Full- or half-day blue-water fishing must be booked in advance.

SCUBA DIVING   There's excellent diving throughout the Abacos. Many sites are clus-
& SNORKELING   tered around Marsh Harbour, including the reef behind **Guana Cay,** which is filled with little cavelike catacombs, and **Fowl Cay National Reserve**, which contains wide tunnels and a variety of fish. **Pelican Cays National Park** is a popular dive and snorkeling area south of Marsh Harbour. This shallow, 25-foot dive is filled with sea life; turtles are often sighted, as are spotted eagle rays and tarpon. The park is a 2,000-acre land and marine park protected and maintained by the Bahamas National Trust. Hook up your own boat to one of the moorings, or check with the local dive shops to see when trips to the park are sched-uled. Snorkelers will want to visit Mermaid Beach, just off Pelican Shores Road in Marsh Harbour, where live reefs and green moray eels make for some of the Abacos' best snorkeling.

Dive Abaco (☎242/367–2787 or 800/247–5338 ⊕www.diveabaco.com), at the Conch Inn in Marsh Harbour, offers scuba and snorkeling trips on their custom dive boats. Sites explored include reefs, tunnels, caverns, and wreck dives. Dive Abaco also maintains a boat and office at Abaco Beach Resort. **Rainbow Rentals** (☎242/367–4602) rents catamarans and snorkeling gear. **Sea Horse Boat Rentals** (☎242/367–2513) rents snorkeling gear.

TENNIS **Abaco Beach Resort** (☎242/367–2158) opens its two lighted courts to visitors. A tennis pro is on hand for clinics and private lessons for adults and children, and there are round-robin tournaments for guests.

WINDSURFING Windsurfing equipment and sea kayaks are available free of charge to hotel and marina guests at the **Abaco Beach Resort** (☎242/367–2158).

SHOPPING

At Marsh Harbour's traffic light, look for the turquoise-and-white stripe awnings of **Abaco Treasures** (☎242/367–3460), purveyors of fine china, crystal, perfumes, and gifts.

Iggy Biggy (✉E. Bay St., Marsh Harbour ☎242/367–3596), inside a couple of bright-pink cottages, is your best bet for hats, sandals, tropical jewelry, sportswear, and souvenirs. If you are looking for gifts to take back home, you should be able to find something cool here.

Nassau straw hats and baskets, shell-encrusted coasters and candlesticks, and pillows and linens made in the Abacos are the best choices at **Island-Style Gifts** (✉Royal Harbour Village ☎242/367–5861).

Sip an iced latte or a strong mug of joe while perusing the ceramics, quilts, pillows, carved wooden boats, and other locally produced artwork at **Java in Abaco** (✉Royal Harbour Village ☎242/367–5523). There's also a book exchange where you can replenish your supply of paperbacks.

John Bull (✉E. Bay St., Marsh Harbour ☎242/367–2473 ⊕www.johnbull.com), on the water across from the entrance to the Abaco Beach Resort, sells Rolex and other brand-name watches, fine jewelry by designers such as David Yurman and Yvel, and makeup and perfume from Chanel, Christian Dior, Clinique, and Lancôme. Fine leather goods, silk ties and scarves, and cool sunglasses are also on hand, along with a well-stocked humidor filled with Cuban cigars.

Johnston Studios Art Gallery (⊠ *Little Harbour* ☎242/367–2720), 30 minutes south of Marsh Harbor, displays original bronzes by the Johnston's, as well as unique gold jewelry, prints, and gifts.

Sand Dollar Shoppe (⊠ *Royal Harbour Village* ☎242/367–4405) sells resort wear, including a decent children's selection, and jewelry, featuring locally made Abaco Gold necklaces and earrings.

BOW CAY

★ In the charming village of **Hope Town,** most of the families of the 300-odd residents have lived here for at least several generations, in some cases as many as 10. Hope Town lies southeast of Marsh Harbour on Elbow Cay. Scheduled ferry service from Marsh Harbour is available several times a day.

You'll find few cars here, and although modern conveniences like high-speed Internet and satellite TV are becoming more common, they are a relatively new development. In fact, most residents remember the day the island first got telephone service—back in 1988. Before that, everyone called each other the way many still do here and in the other Out Islands: by VHF, the party line for boaters. If you are boating, want to communicate with the locals, or would like to make a dinner reservation on one of the cays, you should carry a VHF radio and have it tuned to channel 16.

This laid-back community enthusiastically welcomes visitors. Upon arrival you'll first see a much-photographed Bahamas landmark, a 120-foot-tall, peppermint-striped lighthouse built in 1838. The light's construction was delayed for several years by acts of vandalism; then-residents feared it would end their profitable wrecking practice. Today, the **Hope Town Lighthouse** is one of the Bahamas' last three hand-turned, kerosene-fueled beacons. Weekdays 10–4 the lighthouse keeper will welcome you at the top for a superb view of the sea and the nearby cays. There's no road between the lighthouse and the town proper. You can take your own boat here or use the ferry, but if you take a ferry it probably won't be back for at least an hour.

For an interesting walking or bicycle tour of Hope Town, follow the two narrow lanes that circle the village and harbor. (Most of the village is closed to cars and golf carts.) The saltbox cottages—painted in brilliant blues, purples, pinks, and yellows—with their white picket fences, flowering gardens, and porches and sills decorated with conch shells, will remind you of a New England seaside community—Bahamian style. Some have fanciful names, like Summer Magic or Valentines, while others are charmingly practical. Your walk will take you past **Hope Town School,** the original 110-year-old, one-room schoolhouse, painted red and white. The hand-carved corners made by Loyalist shipwrights are still in evidence.

You may want to stop at the **Wyannie Malone Historical Museum** (☎242/366–0293) on Queen's Highway, the main street. It contains Hope Town memorabilia and photographs. Admission is $3, but because the museum is staffed by volunteers, hours vary, and the museum closes completely in September and October. Many descendants of Mrs. Malone, who settled here with her children in 1875, still live on Elbow Cay.

Smack in the town's center stands an old, turquoise municipal building with offices clearly labeled commissioner, post office, and visitor information. Forget about the first two—they've long since relocated—but Hope Town's Visitor Information "office" is a cement room with a few well-papered bulletin boards on which everything from current happenings to restaurant menus is posted.

> ### HAVE IT ALL
>
> Renting a beach house for a week or longer? Maybe you can't take everything with you, but **GPS Bahamas** (☎ 242/367–0400 or 954/689–6761 ⊕ www.gpsbahamas.com) offers air-freight service for everything from perishable foods to electronics and computers. It beats the mail boat. They also offer catalog shopping and delivery, so if you're tired of the CDs and DVDs you have, just order some new ones.

There are several churches in this tiny town. On Sunday morning, you'll hear sermons floating through open windows. Don't be surprised if you come upon an alfresco Catholic service in the dockside park. Residents joke that the priest has to stand in the hot sun while the congregation enjoys the shade of sprawling trees "so he won't talk so long."

WHERE TO EAT

BAHAMIAN

★ $$ ✕ **Abaco Inn Restaurant.** Set in the country-club-style main lodge splashed with lively Bahamian colors, the restaurant serves breakfast, lunch, and dinner to guests and visitors in classic island style. Attentive friendly service and expansive ocean views are appetite enhancers. Fresh baked bread, fruit, and egg dishes are breakfast highlights. But where the restaurant really shines is in its well-deserved reputation for serving the freshest seafood on the island. At lunch sample the grilled grouper or spicy cracked conch. For dinner, grilled wahoo, hog snapper, or mahimahi can be prepared to your liking. When you make your reservation, ask for a table on the enclosed patio overlooking the ocean. ✉ 2 mi south of Hope Town ☎ 242/366–0133 ⚑ Reservations essential ▤ AE, D, MC, V.

★ $$ ✕ **Harbour's Edge.** Hope Town's happening hangout for locals and tourists, this bar and restaurant's deck is the best place to watch the goings-on in the busy harbor; you can tie your boat up right in front. Kick back and have an icy Kalik, or for extra punch, try a Kalik Gold—just make sure someone else drives your golf cart or boat afterward. Live bands occasionally play on weekends, and this is a great spot for an after-dinner drink. For lunch, try the tender conch burgers, white caps, or lobster salad. For dinner, the fresh grilled seafood and pasta dishes are some of the best in the islands. Authentic Bahamian breakfasts are served on Sunday, and you can also rent bikes here for $8 a day. ✉ Lower Rd., Hope Town ☎ 242/366–0292 or 242/366–0087 ▤ MC, V ☾ Closed Tues.

$ ✕**Cap'n Jack's.** There are a handful of booths and a small rowdy bar, but most of this casual eatery's seating is out on the pink-and-white-striped dock-patio. Locals, boat people, and land-based tourists gather here every day for value-priced eats and drinks. The menu is nothing fancy, but provides reliable grouper burgers, pork chops, fresh fish catch-of-the-day, and cracked conch. When it's in season, there's sometimes a lobster special. Cap'n Jack's serves three meals a day, offers a full bar, and has live music Wednesday and a DJ Friday nights mid-December through August. ⊠*Hope Town* ☎*242/366–0247* ▤*MC, V.*

$ ✕**On the Beach Bar and Grill.** Burgers, fries, conch, fish, and icy rum drinks are served up with a terrific Atlantic view at this open-air bar and grill perched high on the beach dunes across the road from the small Turtle Hill resort. It closes at sunset because all seating is open to the elements, and a gully washer of a storm can shut the place down. Go in your bathing suit and enjoy the beach and snorkeling right out front. ⊠*Queens Hwy., between Hope Town and White Sound* ☎*242/366–0557* ⌕*Reservations not accepted* ▤*AE, MC, V* ⊙*Closed Mon.*

WHERE TO STAY

$$–$$$ ⊞**Elbow Cay Properties.** Besides being the most cost-efficient way to stay on Elbow Cay, a private house or villa is also likely to be the most comfortable. This longstanding rental agency handles a variety of properties, from cozy two-bedroom, one-bath cottages to a six-bedroom, six-bath villa better described as a mansion. Many of the rental homes are on the water, with a dock or a sandy beach right out front. The owners are set on finding you a place to match your wishes and budget. They can also arrange boat rentals. There are no Sunday check-ins, as the agency is closed. **Pros:** variety of accommodation options in all price ranges, style choices from beachy casual to ultra luxury, close to town but still remote and private. **Cons:** check-in process can take a while, no Sunday check-in, do-it-yourself vacation. ⊠*Western Harborfront, Hope Town* ⊕*www.elbowcayrentals.com* ⊅*50 units* ▤*MC, V.*

★ $$–$$$ ⊞**Hope Town Hideaways.** Choose one of the comfy island homes scattered on 11 acres of gardens, with access to the harbor and the beach, or go more upscale with a West Indies–style Flamingo Villa, perfectly situated across from the lighthouse at the entrance to the harbor. The spacious two-bedroom, two-bath villas have large kitchens, satellite TV, and Internet access, deluxe bedrooms with balconies, and wrap-around decks with pools and barbecues. Owners Peggy and Chris Thompson also run a property-management company that rents more than 75 private cottages and houses, including spectacular beachfront retreats at Tahiti Beach on the south end of the cay. Most of these units sleep four or more, and some of the more upscale properties can accurately be described as mansions. Peggy and Chris can also arrange for everything from boat and golf-cart rentals to island excursions and fishing guides. **Pros:** variety of accommodation and style options in all price ranges, convenient locations. **Cons:** check-in can take a while for first-time guest, do-it-yourself vacation. ⊠*1 Purple Porpoise Pl., Hope Town* ☎*242/366–0224* ⊕*www.hopetown.com* ⊅*75 units* ▤*AE, D, MC, V.*

$$ 🏠 **Turtle Hill Vacation Villas.** Bougain-villea- and hibiscus-lined walkways encircle the central swimming pool of this cluster of six villas, each with its own private patio. Inside, villas have central air-condition-ing, full kitchens that open into the spacious dining–living room, light-wood paneling, tile floors, and rattan furnishings, as well as

> **SURF'S UP, DUDE!**
>
> Though it's not well-known, there is good surfing off Elbow Cay. If you want to wake up to the waves, stay at the Abaco Inn or at the Sea Spray Resort, or rent a house at Tahiti Beach.

sleeper sofas. A mile long crescent beach is steps away, as is the On the Beach Bar and Grill. Each villa comes with a golf cart for jaunts into town. Choose an upper villa for views of the ocean. **Pros:** comfortable accommodations for families and small groups, steps away the beach. **Cons:** you have to golf cart out to restaurants for dinner if you don't want to cook in, extra charge for daily maid service. ⊠ *Off Queens Hwy. between Hope Town and White Sound* 🕾 *508/540–2519 or 800/339–2124* ⊕ *www.turtlehill.com* 🛏 *4 2-bedroom villas, 2 3-bedroom villas* ⌂ *In-room: no phone, kitchen, VCR. In-hotel: pool, no elevator* 🖃 *AE, D, MC, V.*

★ $ ✕🏠 **Abaco Inn.** The motto here is "Barefoot elegance," making this beachfront resort the ideal place for a couples getaway. The cozy rooms—seven with Atlantic Ocean views and seven overlooking the harbor and the Sea of Abaco—have simple, comfortable furnishings and individual hammocks. Luxury villas have kitchenettes, small living areas, and sunrise and sunset water views. After your complimentary pickup in Hope Town, rent your own boat so you can zoom into town or to the smaller neighboring cays. Excellent reefs for surfing, snor-keling, and diving are nearby. The bar is a lively spot for guests and locals to mingle, and for couples to watch the magenta sunsets. The restaurant, which serves some of the freshest seafood on the island, is outstanding. Ask for a table on the enclosed patio overlooking the ocean. The lounge has satellite TV and live music on occasion. **Pros:** self-contained resort with the best restaurant on the island; easy access to beaches, surfing, and fishing; hypnotic ocean views. **Cons:** 10-min-ute golf cart or boat ride to Hope Town. ⊠ *2 mi south of Hope Town* 🕾 *242/366–0133* ⊕ *www.abacoinn.com* 🛏 *14 rooms, 8 villas* ⌂ *In-room: no phone, kitchen (some), no TV. In-hotel: restaurant, bar, pool, beachfront, bicycles, no elevator, laundry facilities, airport shuttle* 🖃 *AE, D, MC, V.*

$ ✕🏠 **Hope Town Harbour Lodge.** You can have it all at this casually classy resort—spectacular views of the Atlantic Ocean and the beach, quality amenities, and a location steps away from the town and harbor. Pleas-ant rooms are decorated island style, but for a splurge, treat yourself to one of the ocean-view or oceanfront cottages, with light pine paneling, terra-cotta tile floors, full kitchenettes, and French doors opening onto private decks. Lunch is poolside, with views of the ocean. At dinner in the Upper Terrace, warm up with a key-lime martini rimmed with graham-cracker crumbs before tackling a steak or grilled wahoo with creamy butter and lime. Book early, reservations are essential for both

Fodor's Choice
★

3

the restaurant and the lodge. Discounted rates are available September 2 to December 15. **Pros:** best lodging location on Elbow Cay for views, beach, and access to town; casual patio restaurant for lunch overlooking the ocean; romantic. **Cons:** breakfast buffet gets hit hard so late risers are often left with few choices; Internet access can be sporadic. ⊠ *Upper Rd., Hope Town* ☎ *242/366–0095 or 866/611–9791* ⊕ *www.hopetownlodge.com* ⊷ *12 rooms, 6 cabanas, 6 cottages, 1 private house* ⬥ *In-room: no phone, kitchen (some), refrigerator (some), no TV. In-hotel: 2 restaurants, bars, pool, beachfront, no elevator, laundry service, public Internet* ⊟ *D, MC, V.*

$ 🏠 **Sea Spray Resort and Marina.** Consider this resort if you're planning to catch any waves, or you just want to get away from it all. The accommodations are just off Garbanzo Beach, which is popular with surfers. One-, two-, and three-bedroom villas have full kitchens, satellite TVs, air-conditioning, and large decks with outdoor grills. You can rent motorboats, bikes, and snorkeling gear. The on-site store sells everything from charcoal to surfboard wax. There's also a 60-slip full-service marina, swimming pool with ample deck chairs for catching rays, and a swinging tiki bar that rocks at happy hour and after dinner. The bar also has a wide-screen TV for taking in sporting events, and a restaurant where you can enjoy the ocean view while feasting on steamed lobster or grilled, freshly caught grouper. Free shuttle service is available to Hope Town, about a 10-minute drive. **Pros:** the Atlantic beach is on one side of the resort, and the leeward side marina on the other; self-contained relaxing retreat near the Abaco Inn; full-service marina for boaters and guests. **Cons:** restaurant food is just OK, 10-minute golf cart or boat ride to Hope Town. ⊠ *South end of White Sound* ☎ *242/366–0065* ⊕ *www.seasprayresort.com* ⊷ *7 villas* ⬥ *In-room: no phone, kitchen. In-hotel: restaurant, bar, pool, diving, water sports, bicycles, public Internet* ⊟ *D, MC, V* ⊗ *Closed Sept. and Oct.*

SPORTS & THE OUTDOORS

BOATING **Hope Town Hideaways** (☎ 242/366–0224) has 12 slips, mostly used for guests staying in their rental cottages and houses. Call well in advance to reserve yours. **Island Marine** (☎ 242/366–0282) has 17- to 23-foot boats available for rent from $90 to $135 a day. **Sea Horse Boat Rentals** (☎ 242/367–2513) has Bimini-top boats ranging in length from 18 to 26 feet. They're located in Hope Town. **Sea Spray Resort and Marina** (☎ 242/366–0065) has a full-service marina with 60 slips and boat rentals.

FISHING Former Abaco bonefish champ **Justin Sands** (☎ 242/367–3526 or 242/359–6890 ⊕ www.bahamasvacationguide.com/justfish.html) will guide you in the Marls or around Snake Cay, Little Harbour, or Cherokee Sound, but you need to book him well in advance. **Buddy Pinder** (☎ 242/366–2163) is another top-level bonefishing guide for the Marls and Cherokee Sound, and sometimes works with Justin. Booking in advance is essential. Fly- and spin-fishing guides **Donny and Jimmy Lowe** (☎ 242/366–2275) will take you to the waters surrounding Cherokee Sound, including the Bight of Old Robinson and Little Harbour. **Day's Catch** (☎ 242/366–0059) books charter fishing excursions on the nearby reefs with Captain Will Key, who will even clean your fish afterwar Key is especially patient with children, who will enjoy learning about th fish as much as they'll enjoy landing one. **Seagull Charters** (☎242/366 0266) sets up guided deep-sea excursions with Captain Robert Low who has more than 35 years' experience in local waters.

SCUBA DIVING **Day's Catch** (☎242/366–0059) takes out small groups (up to six peopl
& SNORKELING of snorkelers and divers in a 21-foot offshore center console boat.

★ **Froggies Out Island Adventures** (☎242/366–0431 or 888/774–932 ⊕*www.froggiesabaco.com*) has snorkel and dive trips, scuba an resort courses, full-day adventure tours, island excursions, and dolphi encounters. You can also rent snorkeling and diving gear to ventu out on your own. Professional and friendly service has earned Froggi a lot of repeat customers. You need to book your excursions as far advance as possible.

WINDSURFING **Sea Spray Resort** (☎242/366–0065) attracts windsurfers to the choi waters just off Garbanzo Beach.

SHOPPING

Ebbtide (☎242/366–0088) is on the upper path road in a renovate Loyalist home. Come here for such Bahamian gifts as batik clothe original driftwood carvings and prints, and nautical jewelry. Brow through the extensive Bahamian book collection or pick up a mag zine. **Fantasy Boutique** (⊠*Queen's Hwy.* ☎242/366–0537) has a ni selection of souvenirs, beach wraps, T-shirts, arts and crafts, an Cuban cigars.

★ **Iggy Biggy** (⊠*Queen's Hwy.* ☎242/366–0354) is the only shop Hope Town that carries the lovely Abaco Ceramics handmade in Tre sure Cay. They also sell home decorations, handmade dishware an glasses, wind chimes, sandals, resort wear, jewelry, and island music

MAN-O-WAR CAY

Fewer than 300 people live on skinny, 2½-mi-long **Man-O-War Ca** many of them descendants of early Loyalist settlers named Albury, wh started the tradition of handcrafting boats more than two centuri ago. These residents remain proud of their heritage and continue build their famous fiberglass boats today. This shipwrighting center the Abacos lies south of Green Turtle and Great Guana cays, an ea 45-minute ride from Marsh Harbour by water taxi or aboard a sma rented outboard runabout. Man-O-War Cay also has a 28-slip marin three churches, a one-room schoolhouse, several shops, grocery store and restaurants that cater largely to visitors.

A mile north of the island, you can dive to the wreck of the USS *Adiro dack,* which sank after hitting a reef in 1862. It lies among a host cannons in 20 feet of water. The cay is also a marvelous place to wa or to take a rented golf cart for a spin—no cars are allowed on th island. Two main roads, Queen's Highway and Sea Road, are shade with arching sea grape trees interspersed with palms and pines. Th island is secluded, but it has kept up-to-date with satellite television an full phone and Internet service. Still, the old-fashioned, family-oriented roots show in the local policy toward liquor: it isn't sold anywhere on the island. (But most folks won't mind if you bring your own.)

WHERE TO EAT & STAY

BAHAMIAN

$ ✕**Hibiscus Cafe.** This local favorite isn't fancy, but it turns out dependable Bahamian dishes. Lunchtime is casual, with burgers, grouper, and conch. Dinner, served Thursday through Saturday, is slightly more formal, with grilled seafood and rack of lamb among the specialties. ✉*Waterfront* ☎242/365–6380 ⊟*No credit cards* ⊘*Closed Sun. Closed at times in Sept. and Oct. No dinner Mon.–Wed.*

$ ✕**The Pavilion.** Locals and tourists alike come here for Friday- and Saturday-night steak, chicken, ribs, or lamb dinners, served with the expected Bahamian sides of baked macaroni and cheese and peas 'n' rice. For lunch, chow down on grouper fingers, cracked conch, and coleslaw while you enjoy a view of the Man-O-War Marina. ✉*Waterfront* ☎242/365–6185 *or* 242/365–6008 ⊟*No credit cards* ⊘*Closed Sun. Closed mid-Aug.–Sept.*

$$ ▦**Schooner's Landing.** Perched on a rocky promontory overlooking a long, isolated beach, this small, Mediterranean-style resort has three two-bedroom town-house condos with ocean views; two of these units include lofts for children or extra friends. Rooms are airy, with wicker furniture and ceramic tile floors, and include fully equipped kitchens, ceiling fans, TVs, and stereos with CD players. Gaze out to sea from the freshwater swimming pool's wraparound deck, or lounge in the gazebo, which has a barbecue and wet bar. There's no restaurant, but you can easily walk to almost every establishment, eating or otherwise, on the cay. The resort also has golf carts for rent, and the nearby grocery store delivers. **Pros:** spectacular setting on a bluff overlooking the Atlantic Ocean, easy access to deserted beaches, stress-melting atmosphere. **Cons:** not much to do, island restaurants are just OK, groceries can be scarce at times. ✉*Man-O-War Cay* ☎242/365–6072 *or* 242/367–4469 ⊕*www.schoonerslanding.com* ➥*3 condominiums* ⌂*In-room: kitchen, VCR. In-hotel: pool, beachfront, no elevator, laundry service* ⊟*AE, MC, V.*

SPORTS & THE OUTDOORS

BOATING **Man-O-War Marina** (☎242/365–6008) has 28 slips and rents 26-foot boats (and for landlubbers, golf carts). For people coming from Marsh Harbour or other cays, the Albury Ferry dock is adjacent.

BA DIVING **Man-O-War Dive Shop** (✉*Man-O-War Marina* ☎242/365–6013 *or* 242/365–6008) rents tanks and snorkeling equipment. Fowl Cay Undersea Park, located just north of Man-O-War Cay, is a good place for snorkeling.

SHOPPING

★ **Albury's Sail Shop** (☎242/365–6014) is popular with boaters, who stock up on duffel bags, briefcases, jackets, hats, and purses, all made from duck, a colorful, sturdy canvas fabric traditionally used for sails. **Island Treasures** (☎242/365–6072) has a wide selection of T-shirts, souvenirs, resort wear, candles, and ceramics. **Joe's Studio** (☎ *242/365–6082*) sell paintings by local artists, books, clothing, and other nautically ori ented gifts, but the most interesting souvenirs are the half models o sailing dinghies. These mahogany models, which are cut in half an mounted on boards, are meant to be displayed as wall hangings. Artis Joe Albury, one of the store's owners, also crafts full, 3-D boat models which go for as much as $1,800.

GREAT GUANA CAY

Fodor'sChoice   The essence of **Great Guana Cay** can be summed up by its unofficia
★   motto, painted on a hand-lettered sign: IT'S BETTER IN THE BAHAMAS, BU ... IT'S GOODER IN GUANA. This sliver of an islet just off Great Abaco accessible by ferry from Marsh Harbour or by private boat, is the kin of place people picture when they dream of running off to disappea on an exotic island, complete with alluring deserted beaches and grass dunes. Only 100 full-time residents live on 7-mi-long Great Guana Cay where you're more likely to run into a rooster than a car during you stroll around the tranquil village. Still, there are just enough luxurie here to make your stay comfortable, including a couple of small, laid back resorts, and a restaurant–bar with one of the best party scenes i the Abacos. The island also offers easy access to bonefishing flats yo can explore on your own.

How long this serene relaxed way of life will last is now open to debate as **Baker's Bay Golf & Ocean Club**, being developed by the **Discovery Lan Company** (☎ *242/367–0612* ⊕ *www.discoverylandco.com*), will cove 588 acres of the pristine northwestern section of the cay. The devel opment received the green light from the Bahamas Supreme Court i October 2006, against the wishes of some community members. I December 2007, Prime Minister Hubert A. Ingraham personally visite the project and gave it his unconditional approval, saying the develop ment was in "the national interest." The developers plan to be sel contained and eco-friendly.

So far, general traffic has increased on the island, but the tranquil life style has stayed the same. People staying at Dolphin Beach Resort, fo example, will find it better and more relaxing than ever. The Baker Bay resort has more than 6 mi of shoreline that will include mor than 300 beachfront homes and a 158-slip marina with surround ing commercial village. The resort's private, members only Ocea Club will have a sprawling clubhouse with fine and casual dining spa and gym facilities, and a Tom Fazio–designed golf course. Ther will also be numerous commercial shops and a variety of restaurant to go along with the full services marina. The marina and villag with approximately 110 luxury rental cottages is expected to ope in November 2008. The Tom Fazio golf course is projected to ope in November 2009.

WHERE TO EAT & STAY

★ $$$ ✕**Docksiders Seafood and Steak House.** Casual colonial elegance and personalized service greet guests at this bayside restaurant at Fisher's Bay, part of the Dolphin Beach Resort. Crab cakes, buffalo shrimp, simmering conch chowder, and orange almond salads are tasty lunch fare. The full-service bar is the perfect spot to sip a cocktail and watch the sunset. At dinner surf and turf reigns supreme along with a nice wine list. For serious carnivores, porterhouse and ribeye steaks, rack of lamb, and filet mignon are specialties. If you still have room, the Macadamia tart and key lime pie are simple sublime. ⊠ *Dolphin Beach Resort, Fisher's Bay* ☎*800/222–2646 or 242/365–5137* ⚑*Reservations essential* ⊟*MC, V* ⊗*Closed Sun. and Mon. Closed Sept.–mid-Oct.*

> ### CELEBRATE GOOD TIMES!
>
> All-day pig roasts are a common weekend event, from Nippers on Great Guana Cay to Pete's Pub in Little Harbour. These events are a fun and inexpensive way to enjoy a day on the beach with lots of tasty Bahamian chow, live music, dancing, and island camaraderie. Ask at your hotel for a schedule of events.

★ $$ ✕**Nippers Beach Bar & Grill.** With awesome ocean views and a snorkeling reef just 10 yards off its perfect beach, this cool bar and restaurant is a must-visit hangout. Linger over a lunch of burgers and sandwiches or a dinner of steak and lobster, then chill out in the solar-heated double pool, one for children and one with a swim-up bar for adults. Nurse a "Nipper Tripper"—a frozen concoction of five rums and two juices. If you down more than one or two of these, you'll be happy to take advantage of the Nippermobile, which provides free transport to and from the cay's public dock. And on Sunday, everybody who is anybody, or not, revels in the all day party disguised as a pig roast. ⊠*Great Guana Cay* ☎*242/365–5143* ⊕*www.nippersbar.com* ⊟*AE, D, MC, V.*

$$$ 🛏**Flip Flops on the Beach.** Reserve one of the four one- or two-bedroom beachside bungalows at this casually elegant boutique and you can melt into the island lifestyle of sun, sand, serenity, and ocean breezes on arrival. Bungalows are bright, fresh, and furnished with white wicker, mahogany four-poster beds with 1,000-thread-count sheets, and an array of modern kitchen appliances. Additional amenities are satellite flat-screen TV, patio furnishings, charcoal grill, beach chairs and umbrellas, and Bath & Body Works toiletries. A private beach pavilion is ideal for picnicking or enjoying a sunset cocktail. Guests may use the pool, tennis court, and other facilities at the adjacent Dolphin Beach Resort. Restaurants and shops are a short walk or golf-cart ride away. **Pros:** beachfront location, the essence of tranquility, quality accommodations and in-room amenities. **Cons:** remote location means there is no nightlife, shopping, or larger resort style activities; no Internet service. ⊠*Great Guana Cay* ☎*800/222–2646 or 242/365–5137* ⊕*www.flipflopsonthebeach.com* ⏂*4 bungalows* ⚐*In-room: no phone, kitchen. In-hotel: beachfront* ⊟*MC, V* ⊗*Closed Sept.–mid-Oct.*

$$ 🛏**Dolphin Beach Resort.** You'll be tempted to stay forever at this upscale island haven. Spacious, uniquely designed rooms and larger cottages—handcrafted of Abaco pine by Guana Cay shipwrights—are all painted

dor's Choice
★

in bright Junkanoo colors. Each island-style cottage is individually furnished and includes a private deck or terrace. Two cottages are se away from the resort, ideal for honeymooners. Outside, secluded show ers are surrounded by bougainvillea and sea grape trees. Boardwal nature trails winding through the carefully tended 15-acre propert lead to miles of secluded beach. Prime fishing, diving, and snorkelin are nearby, and guided tours can be arranged by the accommodatin resort staff. **Pros:** beachfront location with casually luxurious accom modations; excellent on-site restaurant; personalized service. **Cons:** you are looking for nightlife, shopping, lots of people, this is not th place for you; no Internet service. ⊠*Fisher's Bay* ☎*800/222–264 or 242/365–5137* ⊕*www.dolphinbeachresort.com* ⌦*9 cottages, rooms* ⌖*In-room: no phone, kitchen, VCR. In-hotel: restaurant, ba tennis court, pool, beachfront, diving, water sports, bicycles* ⊟*MC,* ⊗*Closed Sept.–mid-Oct.*

SPORTS & THE OUTDOORS

BOATING **Orchid Bay Yacht Club and Marina** (☎*242/365–5175* ⊕*www.orchidba net*) has 32 deep-water slips and full services for boaters at the entranc to the main settlement bay, across from the public docks. The clu office rents luxury apartments, cottages, and homes, and prime re: estate is for sale. There's also a swimming pool and a restaurant tha serves fresh seafood, steaks, and healthy salads on an outdoor dec overlooking the marina. A poolside menu of burgers and casual fa is also available.

SCUBA DIVING **Dive Guana** (☎*242/365–5178* ⊕*www.diveguana.com*), on the groun of Dolphin Beach Resort, organizes scuba and snorkeling trips an island tours. The shop also rents boats, kayaks, and bicycles. Rentir a boat, at least for a day, is the best way to get around and enjoy oth nearby cays.

TREASURE CAY

Running through large pine forests that are still home to wild hors and boars, the wide, paved Sherben A. Boothe Highway leads nort

Fodor'sChoice from Marsh Harbour for 20 mi to **Treasure Cay,** which is technical
★ not an island but a large peninsula connected to Great Abaco by a na row spit of land. Here you'll find a small community of mostly wint residents, a 3,000-acre farm that grows winter vegetables and fruit f export, and a spectacular 3½-mi-long beach, often called the best the Abacos.

While Treasure Cay is a large-scale real-estate development project, i also a wonderful small community where expatriate residents share th laid-back, sun-and-sea atmosphere with longtime locals. The develo] ment's centerpiece is the Treasure Cay Hotel Resort & Marina, with Dick Wilson–designed golf course and a 150-slip marina that has bo rentals, a dive shop, pool, restaurant, and lively bar. Despite its nam there is no hotel at the resort, only a large grouping of condominiun and villas around the marina that are rented by the night, week, month. Treasure Cay's central location makes it a great base for explo ing and enjoying the Abacos. Historic Elbow Cay, Man-O-War Cay, and Green Turtle Cay are all easily accessible by boat, and car rentals are available to travel north to Fox Town or south to Sandy Point.

Treasure Cay's commercial center consists of two rows of shops near the resort as well as a post office, Laundromat, ice-cream parlor, a couple of well-stocked grocery stores, and BaTelCo, the Bahamian telephone company. You'll also find car-, scooter-, and bicycle-rental offices here.

> ### LOOKING FOR FUN?
>
> Something is happening almost every night of the week (well, maybe not Sunday night). From pizza night at the Tipsy Seagull in Treasure Cay to barbecue night at the Jib Room in Marsh Harbour, to live bands on Fridays. Check with your hotel for a schedule of events.

3

WHERE TO EAT

BAHAMIAN

★ $$$ ✕**Spinnaker Restaurant and Lounge.** Ceramic tiled floors, rattan furniture, and floral print tablecloths accent this large resort restaurant—250 guests fit in the air-conditioned main dining area and the adjacent screened-in outdoor patio—and bar at the Treasure Cay Marina. Locals and tourists mix in an often rowdy atmosphere, though things quiet down in the off-season. Conch fritters, salads, burgers, and grilled grouper are the usual lunch fare. Dinner boasts an international flare with grilled steaks and lamb chops, along with seafood pasta, grilled mahimahi, broiled lobster, and a salad bar. Even with reservations you often have to wait, but you can relax in the lounge and enjoy an array of cocktails and frozen rum drinks. ⊠ *Treasure Cay Marina* ☎*242/365–8801* ⌂*Reservations essential* ▤*AE, D, MC, V.*

$$ ✕**Coconuts.** Tourists and locals flock to this popular spot, located at the intersection of Treasure Cay Road and the main highway. The well-appointed dining room's white tablecloths and classy dishware lend a bit of elegance to the island-casual mood. A wide selection of American and Bahamian dishes includes fresh grilled grouper and hog snapper, broiled lobster, rack of lamb, seafood pasta, and baked chicken smothered in tomatoes and onions. The separate bar is a cool place to enjoy a cocktail or relax while waiting for a table. Reservations are a must, especially on the weekends. Free shuttle service is available from the parking lot in front of the Treasure Cay Marina. ⊠*Queen's Hwy. at Treasure Cay Rd.* ☎*242/365–8885* ⌂*Reservations essential* ▤*MC, V* ⊗*Closed part of Sept. and Oct.*

$ ✕**Touch of Class.** Ten minutes north of Treasure Cay, this locals'-favorite, no-frills restaurant serves traditional Bahamian dishes such as grilled freshly caught grouper and minced local lobster stewed with tomatoes, onions, and spices. Reasonably priced appetizers, such as conch chowder and conch fritters, and a full bar make this a nice option for a night out. Free shuttle service is available from the parking lot in front of the Treasure Cay Marina. ⊠*Queen's Hwy., at Treasure Cay Rd.* ☎*242/365–8195* ▤*MC, V* ⊗*Closed Sun. Closed part of Sept. and Oct.*

★ ¢   ✕**Café La Florence.** Stop off at this bakery-café in the Treasure Ca
resort's main shopping strip for just-made muffins and the best cin
namon rolls in the universe. Or go for a light lunch of lobster quich
conch chowder, or a spicy, Jamaican-style meat patty. Anglers can orde
picnic lunches to go. You can also arrange for the chef to cater priva
dinners of lobster, steak, and the like in your rented condo. Florence
ice-cream parlor next door is your answer for treats à la mode. ⊠*Trea
sure Cay* ☎*242/365–8354* ▤*No credit cards* ☉*Sometimes closed fo
part of Sept. and Oct.*

WHERE TO STAY

★ $$$ ▦**Bahama Beach Club.** Ideal for families and small groups, these two
to four-bedroom condos are right off the famous Treasure Cay beac
Decor varies, but each unit has ceramic-tile floors and stylish ratta
furniture with colorful accents, as well as a fully equipped kitche
and a large living room. All also have a patio or balcony overlookin
the water and the grounds, which are landscaped with tropical palm
These are some of the nicest condos in the Abacos, and they are with
a few minutes' walk of the Treasure Cay Hotel Resort & Marina. Pro
luxury accommodations on one of the most beautiful beaches in th
world; large pool area with Jacuzzi; walking distance to the marin
restaurants, and shops. **Cons:** check-in can be slow; if something
your condo needs fixing, maintenance can take a while. ⊠*Treasu
Cay* ☎*800/284–0382 or 242/365–8500* ⊕*www.bahamabeachclu
com* ⇗*44 condos* ⟐*In-room: kitchen, Wi-Fi. In-hotel: pool, beac
front, laundry facilities, public Wi-Fi* ▤*AE, MC, V.*

☾ $ ▦**Treasure Cay Hotel Resort & Marina.** Treasure Cay is best known for
FodorśChoice   18-hole golf course, which *Golf Digest* frequently rates as the Bahama
★   best, and its first-class 150-slip marina. The property has suites an
town house–style accommodations set along the marina's boardwal
Suites have mini-refrigerators, toaster ovens, and small dining counte
town houses have vaulted ceilings, spacious living–dining areas, mo
ern kitchens, full and loft bedrooms, and balconies. The indoor–ou
door Spinnaker restaurant serves Bahamian and Continental cuisin
A more casual, kid-friendly option is Thursday night pizza at the Tip
Seagull poolside bar and grill, also a popular happy hour destinatio
and there's live music and dancing twice a week. The resort can arran
fishing, diving, and island excursions. **Pros:** most convenient locatio
in Treasure Cay, good on-site restaurants and bar, Dick Wilson cha
pionship golf course. **Cons:** if you forget to make a dinner reservati
in the main season you could be out of luck at the restaurant, po
area can get crowded with boat people and happy hour patrons
the Tipsy Seagull Bar. ⊠*Treasure Cay Marina* ☎*242/365–8801
800/327–1584* ⊕*www.treasurecay.com* ⇗*54 suites, 33 townhous
⟐In-room: kitchen. In-hotel: 2 restaurants, bars, golf course, tenn
courts, pool, beachfront, diving, water sports, no elevator, laundry s
vice* ▤*AE, D, MC, V* ℔*EP, FAP, MAP.*

SPORTS & THE OUTDOORS

BICYCLING   **Wendell's Bicycle Rentals** (☎*242/365–8687*) rents mountain bikes by th
half day, day, or week.

BOATING Located at the Treasure Cay Marina, **J.I.C. Boat Rentals** (☎*242/365–8582* ⊕*www.jicboatrentals.com*) rents center-console boats for fishing and cruising the nearby cays; one-, three-, and seven-day rates are available. Try to reserve your boat at least two to three weeks in advance. Golf cart, snorkeling gear, and fishing equipment rentals are also available; book ahead for these as well. Alternatively, **Rich's Rentals** (☎*242/367–2742* ⊕*www.richsrentals.com*) in Marsh Harbour rents boats by the day, three-day block, or week. Daily rentals range from $140 to $225 for 21- to 26-foot Bimini-top fishing boats, perfect for island-hopping. Advance reservations are a must.

EVENTS A popular sportfishing destination, Treasure Cay hosts several fishing tournaments annually, including a leg of the **Bahamas Billfish Championship** in May. June brings the annual **Treasure Cay International Billfish Tournament.** Call Treasure Cay Services (☎*954/525–7711 or 800/327–1584*) for information about fishing and golf tournaments, regattas, and other special events.

FISHING Advanced reservations are a must to fish with **Justin Sands** (☎*242/367–3526 or 242/359–6890* ⊕*www.bahamasvacationguide.com/justfish.html*), the Abaco's two-time bonefish champ.

★ Top professional bonefish guide **O'Donald Macintosh** (☎*242/365–0126 or 242/477–5037*) meets clients each day at Café La Florence in Treasure Cay for full or half days of guided bonefishing in the northern Marls or outside Coopers Town. In more than 20 years of guiding, O'D has built up a large, loyal base of repeat clients, so you'll need to book him well in advance—especially in the prime months of April, May, and June. Arrange for local deep-sea fishing or bonefishing guides through **Treasure Cay Hotel Resort & Marina** (☎*242/365–8250*).

GOLF A half mile from the **Treasure Cay Hotel Resort & Marina** (☎*800/327–1584*
★ *or 954/525–7711* ⊕*www.golfbahamas.com*) is the property's par-72, Dick Wilson–designed course, with carts available. There's no need to reserve tee times, and the course is usually delightfully uncrowded—ideal for a leisurely round. A driving range, putting green, and small pro shop are also on-site.

BA DIVING No Name Cay, Whale Cay, and the Fowl Cay Preserve are popular
ORKELING marine-life sites. The 1865 wreck of the steamship freighter *San Jacinto* also affords scenic diving and a chance to feed the resident green moray eel. **Treasure Divers** (☎*242/357–6796* ⊕*www.treasure-divers.com*), in the Treasure Cay Marina, rents equipment and takes divers and snorkelers out to a variety of sites.

TENNIS **Treasure Cay Hotel Resort & Marina** (☎*800/327–1584 or 242/365–8801*) has six of the best courts in the Abacos, four of which are lighted for night play.

DSURFING Windsurfers and a complete line of nonmotorized watercraft are available for rent at the **Treasure Cay Hotel Resort & Marina** (☎*242/365–8250*).

CLOSE UP

Boating in the Abacos

The Abacos provide superb recreational cruising grounds. If you tune your VHF radio to channel 16, you'll be able to communicate with just about everyone in the area.

In the northern portion of the archipelago, Grand Cay is a laid-back settlement of about 200 people and four times that many Bahamian potcakes (mixed-breed dogs). Most yachters will find the anchorage off the community dock adequate, and the docks at Rosie's Place can take boats up to 80 feet, depending on traffic. Double anchors are advised to handle the harbor's tidal current.

Heading south from Grand Cay, you'll pass a clutch of tiny cays and islets, such as Double Breasted Cays, Roder Rocks, Barracuda Rocks, Miss Romer Cay, Little Sale Cay, and Great Sale Cay. Great Sale Harbour provides excellent shelter. Other small islands in the area are Carter Cay, Moraine Cay, Umbrella Cay, Guineaman Cay, Pensacola and Allen's cays (which are now virtually one island since a hurricane filled in the gap between them), and the Hawksbill Cays. Most offer varying degrees of lee anchorage. Fox Town, due south of Hawksbill Cay on Little Abaco's western tip, is the first refueling stop for powerboats traveling east from West End.

A narrow causeway joins Little Abaco to Great Abaco, where the largest community at the north end is Coopers Town. Stock up here on provisions. You'll also find a coin laundry, a telephone station, a few restaurants, bakeries, and a resident doctor here. Just northeast of Coopers Town is the private island 81-slip marina at Spanish Cay.

Cruising south, you'll pass Powell Cay, Nun Jack Cay, and Crab Cay on the way to Green Turtle Cay, which has excellent yachting facilities at White Sound to the north and Black Sound to the south. The Green Turtle Club dominates White Sound's northern end, whereas Bluff House, halfway up the sound, has docks on the inside and a dinghy dock below the club on the Sea of Abaco side.

South of New Plymouth on Great Abaco's mainland is the Treasure Cay Hotel Resort & Marina, with one of the area's longest and finest beaches. Complete facilities for boaters are available here; you can also stop over to play a round of golf.

Straight back out in the Sea of Abaco is Great Guana Cay and its famous 7-mi strip of pristine beaches. Just south is a New England–style charmer: Man O-War Cay, a boatbuilding settlement with more deserted beaches and the 28-slip Man-O-War Marina.

Continuing south, the Bahamas' most photographed lighthouse sits atop Elbow Cay, signaling the harbor opening to Hope Town, an idyllic small resort community.

Back on Great Abaco, you'll find the Abacos' most populous settlement at Marsh Harbour, which has plenty of facilities for boaters. These include the modern 190-slip Boat Harbour Marina, a full-service operation on the island's east side. The other side of town has additional marinas, including the 80-slip Conch Inn Marina, Marsh Harbour Marina and its 68 slips, and a couple of smaller facilities.

SHOPPING

Near Treasure Cay resort is **Abaco Ceramics** (☎242/365–8489 ☉ *Closed weekends*), which offers its signature white-clay pottery with blue fish designs.

REEN TURTLE CAY

A 10-minute ferry ride from a Treasure Cay dock will take you to **Green Turtle Cay.** The tiny island is steeped in Loyalist history; some residents can trace their heritage back to their ancestors' arrival from the U.S. colonies more than 200 years ago. The cay is surrounded by several deep bays, sounds, bonefish flats, and irresistible beaches.

New Plymouth, first settled in 1783, is Green Turtle's main community. Many of its approximately 550 residents earn a living by diving for conch or selling lobster and fish to the Abaco Seafood Company, but an increasing number depend on businesses catering to tourists and vacation-home owners. On some summer days during the height of Green Turtle's tourist season, the visitors on the island can outnumber the residents.

There are a few grocery and hardware stores, several gift shops, a post office, a bank, a handful of restaurants, and several offices—not to mention the homes that have been owned, in some cases, by the same families for generations. Narrow streets flanked by wild-growing flora (such as amaryllis, hibiscus, and poinciana) wind between rows of New England–style white-clapboard cottages with brightly colored shutters. During the Civil War, New Plymouth provided a safe haven for Confederate blockade runners. One Union ship, the USS *Adirondack,* was pursuing a gunrunner and wrecked on a reef in 1862 at nearby Man-O-War Cay. One of the ship's cannons now sits at the town harbor.

If your accommodations aren't in New Plymouth proper, you'll need transportation into town. Many hotels provide an occasional shuttle, and there are a couple of taxis on the island, but most people travel via golf cart or boat. Your hotel can help arrange a boat rental through one of several rental companies on the island. Don't worry, you won't miss having a car; even in the slowest golf cart, you can get from one end of the island to the other in 20 minutes or less.

New Plymouth's most frequently visited attraction is the **Albert Lowe Museum,** on the main thoroughfare, Parliament Street. The Bahamas' oldest historical museum, it's dedicated to a model-ship builder and direct descendant of the island's original European-American settlers. You can learn island history through local memorabilia from the 1700s, Lowe's model schooners, and old photographs, including one of the aftermath of the 1932 hurricane that nearly flattened New Plymouth. One of the galleries displays paintings of typical Out Island scenes by acclaimed artist Alton Lowe, Albert's son. Mrs. Ivy Roberts, the museum's director, enjoys showing visitors around and sharing stories of life in the Out Islands before the days of high-speed Internet and daily airline flights. ⊠*Parliament St.* ☎*242/365–4094* ⊡*$5 adults* *$3 children* ⊙*Mon.–Sat. 9–11:45 and 1–4.*

Just a few blocks from the Albert Lowe Museum, on Victoria Street is **Miss Emily's Blue Bee Bar** (☎*242/365–4181*), which stands next to the old gaol (jail), a tiny stone building thought to be more than 100 years old and, happily, no longer in use. Mrs. Emily Cooper, creator of the popular Goombay Smash drink, passed away in 1997, but her daughter Violet continues to serve up the famous rum, pineapple juice and apricot brandy concoction. The actual recipe is top secret, and in spite of many imitators throughout the islands, you'll never taste Goombay this good anywhere else. It's worth a special trip to try one. Mementos left by customers—business cards, expired credit cards, T-shirts, and autographed dollar bills—and Junkanoo masks cover the walls and ceiling.

The past is present in the **Memorial Sculpture Garden,** across the street from the New Plymouth Inn. (Note that it's laid out in the pattern of the British flag.) Immortalized in busts perched on pedestals are local residents who have made important contributions to the Bahamas. Plaques detail the accomplishments of British Loyalists, their descendants, and the descendants of those brought as slaves, such as Jeanne I. Thompson, a contemporary playwright and the country's second woman to practice law.

WHERE TO EAT

AMERICAN

$ ✕ **Jolly Roger Bar and Bistro.** This casual eatery on the water in the Bluff House Marina offers tasty lunches and, in the evening, a less formal alternative to the reservations-only fine dining in the Clubhouse restaurant. Sitting under a canvas umbrella on the deck is the best way to enjoy the view of the sailboat-filled harbor, but you can also eat in the air-conditioned pub-style dining room. Menu choices range from standard Bahamian (conch fritters and burgers) to new American (roasted pork tenderloin with salsa, salads with goat cheese and roasted vegetables, and even, on occasion, sushi). Another fun option is to enjoy a rum drink from the bar while catching some rays at the pool. ⊠*Between Abaco Sea and White Sound, at Bluff House Beach Hotel marina* ☎*242/365–4247* ⊟*AE, MC, V.*

BAHAMIAN

$$ ✕ **Captain's Table.** Reopened in November 2007, the colonial-style dining room serves memorable Bahamian-style dinners with a Continental touch. The menu changes nightly, though there is always a choice of seafood, meat, or chicken. When it's available, don't pass up the hog snapper. The nightly fresh fish is always well-prepared, meat lovers can enjoy roasts, steaks, and chops. For dessert, don't miss the key lime pie. Call for reservations and to see if they are open. During low season many restaurants and businesses close without notice. ⊠*New Plymouth Inn, Parliament St.* ☎*242/365–4161* ⊟*D, MC, V.*

$ ✕ **McIntosh Restaurant and Bakery.** At this simple, diner-style restaurant, lunch means excellent renditions of local favorites, such as fried grouper and cracked conch, and sandwiches made with thick slices of slightly sweet Bahamian bread. At dinner, large portions of pork chops, lobster, fish, and shrimp are served with rib-sticking sides like baked macaroni and cheese, peas 'n' rice, and coleslaw. Save room for a piece of pound cake or coconut cream pie, baked fresh daily and displayed in the glass case up front. ⊠*Parliament St.* ☎*242/365–4625* ▤*MC, V* ☾*Closed Sun.*

$ ✕**Pineapples Bar & Grill.** Hang out, take a dip in the freshwater pool, and enjoy Bahamian fare with a flair. In Black Sound, at the entrance to the Other Shore Club and Marina, you'll find this simple open-air restaurant with a canopy-shaded bar and picnic tables next to the pool. Some of the best conch fritters in the islands are served from noon on. At lunch try a fresh salad or spicy jerk chicken; for dinner, grilled daily caught fish. The jerk-spiced grouper is sensational. Specialty drinks include a Pineapple Smash and a Yellowbird, both capable of mellowing your mood. ⊠*Black Sound* ☎*242/365–4039* ⊕*www.pineapples bar.com* ▤*No credit cards* ☾*Closed Sun.*

$ ✕**The Wrecking Tree.** The wooden deck at this casual restaurant was built around the wrecking tree, a place where 19th-century wrecking vessels brought their salvage. Today it's a cool place to linger over a cold Kalik and a hearty lunch of cracked conch, fish-and-chips, or zesty conch salad. Dinners may include turtle steak or grilled lobster—if you order by 5 PM. Otherwise, choose from dishes like fresh-caught grouper and fried chicken. They have great pastries, too—take some back to your hotel or rental cottage. And ask for Phil Stubb's CD if you like island music. ⊠*Bay St.* ☎*242/365–4263* ▤*No credit cards* ☾*Closed Sun.*

CONTINENTAL

★ $$$ ✕**Green Turtle Club Dining.** Breakfast and lunch are served harbor-side; on a covered screened-in patio. At lunch treat yourself to a lobster salad, lobster corn chowder, cheeseburger, or a grilled grouper sandwich. Dinner is where the club really shines, transporting you back to the 1920s with elegant dining beneath antique chandeliers. Reservations must be made by 5 PM each day, and there is one seating at 7:30 PM. For those who prefer a casual setting, you can eat outside on the enclosed patio. Shrimp cocktail, raspberry-glazed Cornish game hens, medallions of lobster in ginger beurre blanc, seared tuna Mediterranean, and grilled NY strip steaks are just a few of the temptations. For dessert, guava crème brûlée will finish you off. ⊠ *Green Turtle Club* ☎*242/365–4271* ◬*Reservations essential* ▤*AE, D, MC, V* ☾*Closed Sept.*

WHERE TO STAY

$$ ✕▥**Bluff House Beach Hotel.** From its perch on a rocky bluff overlooking White Sound, this romantic hilltop hideaway provides sweeping views of the sheltered harbor or the Sea of Abaco. The split-level suites have tropical-style wicker furniture, parquet-inlay floors, and double doors opening onto balconies with sensational ocean vistas. Even more spacious are the two- and three-bedroom villas, with huge screened-in verandas overlooking the marina. Or go for the ultimate decadence with the three-bedroom Yachtsman's Cottage, which is ideal for fami-

odor'sChoice

lies or couples traveling together. Formal dinners are still served by reservation only in the dining room, although hours are irregular. The open-air, natural pine cocktail lounge and library is a tranquil spot for an afternoon or predinner cocktail. **Pros:** inspiring views, spacious luxury accommodations, tranquil and romantic. **Cons:** 20-minute golf cart ride or 10-minute boat ride to New Plymouth, no reliable Internet service. ⊠ *Between Abaco Sea and White Sound* ☎ *242/365–4247 or 800/745–4911* ⊕ *www.bluffhouse. com* ⇆ *4 rooms, 8 suites, 9 villas, 1 cottage.* ⌂ *In-room: no phone,*

> ## GETTING HITCHED IN THE ABACOS
>
> What could be more memorable than a beachfront wedding, barefoot, dressed in a tuxedo or full-length wedding gown? Many hotels and resorts offer wedding packages, but Hope Town Harbour Lodge on Elbow Cay and Bluff House on Green Turtle Cay are two obvious stand-outs that can accommodate the entire wedding party. These are romantic spots for a honeymoon, too.

kitchen (some), refrigerator, no TV. In-hotel: 2 restaurants, bars, tennis court, pools, beachfront, water sports, no elevator, laundry service ⊟ *AE, D, MC, V* ⍾ *EP, MAP.*

$$ 🏨 **Coco Bay Cottages.** Sandwiched between one beach on the Atlantic and another calmer, sandy stretch on the bay are five spacious cottages—including two three-bedroom cottages added in 2006—that all have views of the water. Each has attractive rattan furniture and a modern kitchen with utensils. Conch Shell and Conch Pearl, the three-bedroom cottages, each have a master suite with king bed and walk-in closet, washer and dryer, and DVD player. Snorkeling and diving are excellent around the reef that protects the Atlantic beach. The bay where sunset views are fabulous, is prime territory for shell collecting and bonefishing. A separate building holds a library with games and books, satellite TV, and exercise equipment. If you rent a boat—it's recommended—you can tie up at the property's bay-side dock. **Pros:** spacious well-located do-it-yourself accommodations, awesome beaches, Wi-Fi for those who can't totally get away. **Cons:** renting a boat and/or golf cart is essential; if you don't like silence, the peace and quiet will kill you. ⊠ *Coco Bay, North of Green Turtle Club* ☎ *242/365–5464 or 800/752–0166* ⊕ *www.cocobaycottages.com* ⇆ *5 cottages* ⌂ *In-room: kitchen, DVD (some), Wi-Fi. In-hotel: gym, beachfront, water sports, public Wi-Fi* ⊟ *D, MC, V.*

★ $$ 🏨 **Green Turtle Club.** The longstanding colonial tradition and ambience of casual refinement continues at this well-known resort. Cheerful yellow cottages are scattered up a hillside amid lush trees and shrubs. Villa accommodations have decks overlooking the water and docks for rental boats; poolside rooms are more formal, furnished with mahogany Queen Anne–style furniture, gleaming hardwood floors, and Oriental rugs. Breakfasts and lunches are served on a screened, terra-cotta-tile patio, but it's dinner under the harbor-view dining room's chandeliers that makes the club shine. Choose from an ever-changing menu that might include fresh grilled lobster, sautéed lemon grouper, or rack of lamb, accompanied by the best selection of wines in the Abacos. The modern 40-slip marina makes it easy to dock your boat out front, and the ferry to New Plymouth stops here several times a day. In a 10-minute walk you can be bonefishing in Coco Bay or laying on the secluded Atlantic Ocean beach. If you need anything else, the accommodating hotel staff can arrange it. **Pros:** excellent on-site restaurants for casual or fine dining, easy access to great beaches, personalized service. **Cons:** if you're looking for Bahamian casual, this isn't it; no reliable public Internet. ⊠*North end of White Sound* ☎*242/365–4271 or 866/528–0539* ⊕*www.greenturtleclub.com* ⇩*24 rooms, 2 suites, 8 villas* ⚒*In-room: no phone, refrigerator, VCR (some), no TV (some). In-hotel: 2 restaurants, bar, pool, beachfront, water sports, no elevator, laundry facilities* ⊟*AE, D, MC, V* ⊙*Closed Sept.* ⦿*EP, MAP.*

$$ 🏠 **Island Property Management.** A five-bedroom, oceanfront mansion with wraparound veranda, full-time staff, and a marble fireplace could be yours. Or rent a two-bedroom cottage in the heart of New Plymouth. This agency has more than 50 cottages and houses for rent to meet different budgets and needs. They can also help arrange excursions and boat and golf-cart rentals. Most homes have water views, and some have docks for your rental boat. Their offices in New Plymouth are in a blue two-story building along with Coldwell Banker, just down from the ferry dock. **Pros:** do-it-yourself flexibility in spacious accommodations, prime beachfront locations, good value for families and small groups. **Cons:** you pay extra for daily maid service; not all units have Internet; if something is not working in the unit, maintenance can be slow. ⊠*Various Green Turtle Cay locations* ☎*242/365–4047 or 561/202–8333* ⊕*www.abacoislandrentals.com* ⇩*50 units* ⊟*D.*

$$ 🏠 **Linton's Beach and Harbour Cottages.** These three classic Bahamian-style cottages are ideally placed between Long Bay and Black Sound. Two beachside cottages are on a rise overlooking Pelican Cay and the Atlantic. Each has two comfortable bedrooms, a screened-in porch, a combination living–dining room with built-in settees, a well-stocked library, and a fully equipped kitchen. The Harbour Cottage, with one air-conditioned bedroom, is on Black Sound, steps away from the dock. If you're renting a boat, you can tie it up right out front. Families, groups of friends, and couples looking for an escape will enjoy this location. **Pros:** well-located do-it-yourself cottages, value priced for families and groups. **Cons:** gathering groceries and supplies can be an adventure, beach cottages don't have phones or TV. ⊠*S. Loyalist Rd , Black Sound* ☎*772/538–4680* ⊕*www.lintoncottages.com* ⇩*3 cottages* ⚒*In-room: no a/c (some), no phone (some), kitchen, no TV (some). In-hotel: beachfront, bicycles, laundry service, public Internet* ⊟*No credit cards.*

$ 🏠 **New Plymouth Inn.** This charming, two-story historic hotel with white balconies and a turn-of-the-20th-century style lobby and drawing room bar is conveniently located in New Plymouth's center. Originally built in 1830, the hotel reopened in November 2007 with fresh paint, linens, and upgrades to some furniture. A patio pool is nestled in well-manicured tropical gardens, and the cozy rooms have comfortable beds with hand-made quilts and terra-cotta-tile baths. The rates are among the most affordable options on the cay and include breakfast. **Pros:** central

New Plymouth location, good value for Green Turtle Cay, excellent restaurant for dinner. **Cons:** rooms are small so don't bring a lot of luggage, no public Internet service. ✉*Parliament St.* ☎*242/365–4161* ⊕*www.newplymouthinn.com* ⇥*9 rooms* ♿*In-room: no phone, no TV. In-hotel: restaurant, bar, pool, no elevator* ▱*D, MC, V* ☉*Closed Sept. and part of Oct.*

NIGHTLIFE

At night, Green Turtle can be deader than dead or surprisingly lively. Bet on the latter if the local favorites, the **Gully Roosters,** are playing anywhere on the island. Known locally as just the Roosters, this reggae-calypso band is the most popular in the Abacos. Its mix of original tunes and covers can coax even the most reluctant reveler onto the dance floor. The band's home base is **Rooster's Rest** (☎242/365–4066), a pub and restaurant in a bright blue building at the entrance to New Plymouth. The band's schedule there is erratic; ask at your hotel or just drive by one of their haunts on a Friday or Saturday night to see what's happening. In addition to Rooster's Rest, try **Bluff House Beach Resort** (☎242/365–4247) and **Green Turtle Club** (☎242/365–4271), both of which also sell Rooster CDs, a good souvenir of your visit.

★ Other nighttime options include a visit to **Miss Emily's Blue Bee Bar** (☎242/365–4181), where you might find a singing, carousing crowd knocking back the world-famous Goombay Smash. (Or not—many Goombay novices underestimate the drink's potency, and end up making it an early night.) **Pineapples Bar & Grill** (☎242/365–4039 ⊕*www.pineapplesbar.com*), on the water in front of the Other Shore Club and Marina, has a hopping happy hour and live music every Friday. Locals hang out at **Sundowner's** (☎242/365–4060), a waterside bar and grill where attractions include a pool table and, on weekend nights, a DJ spinning dance music on the deck under the stars.

SPORTS & THE OUTDOORS

BICYCLING The flat roads of Green Turtle Cay are perfect for getting around by bicycle. **D&P Rentals** (☎242/365–4655) rents mountain bikes for $10 a day.

BOATING It's highly recommended that you reserve your boat rental at the same time you book your hotel or cottage. If you're unable to rent a boat on Green Turtle Cay, try nearby Treasure Cay or Marsh Harbour.

Bluff House Beach Hotel (☎242/365–4247) has a marina with 40 slips, and a full range of services, everything from Texaco fuel to laundry facilities. **Green Turtle Club** (☎242/365–4271) has 40 slips and is home to Green Turtle Divers dive shop. **The Other Shore Club Marina and Cottages** (☎242/365–4226 *or* 242/365–4338 ⊕*www.othershoreclub.com*), tucked into quiet and protected Black Sound, is an ideal place to keep your small cay-hopping boat if you are staying in one of Green Turtle's many rental houses and cottages. The club has its own rental cottages and can arrange fishing, diving, and snorkeling trips.

Donny's Boat Rentals (☎242/365–4119) rents boats ranging from 14-foot Whalers to 23-foot Makos. **Paradise Boat Rentals** (☎242/365–4359

3

⊕*www.abacoboatrentals.com*) has custom-built Albury's Brothers 20-foot runabouts crafted on Man-O-War Cay. The Bimini tops are retractable, and boats include ice chests, anchors, paddles, first-aid kits, life vests, compasses, VHF radios, rod holders, and large dry storage. **Reef Rentals** (☎*242/365–4145*) has fishing boats and pleasure crafts ranging from 19 to 21 feet.

EVENTS The **Bluff House Fishing Tournament** is held in May. In the beginning of July, the **Bahamas Cup** boat race, part of **Regatta Time in Abaco,** circumnavigates Green Turtle Cay. **All Abaco Regatta,** the work-boat race between Green Turtle and Treasure Cay, is held at the end of October. For information on special events, call the **Abaco Tourist Office** (☎*242/367–3067*). The **Out Island Promotion Board** (☎*954/475–8315*) has details on island tournaments and other seasonal events.

FISHING **Captain Rick Sawyer** (☎*242/365–4261* ⊕*www.abacoflyfish.com*) is one of Abaco's best guides, and the top recommendation on Green Turtle Cay. Rick's company, **Abaco Flyfish Connection and Charters,** offers bonefishing on 17-foot Maverick flats skiffs, and reef and offshore fishing aboard his 33-foot Tiara sportfisher. Book as far in advance as you can. **Ronnie Sawyer** (☎*242/365–4070*) works with Rick and on his own. Call **Joe Sawyer** (☎*242/365–4173*) for a morning of reef fishing in his 29-foot boat.

UBA DIVING **Brendal's Dive Center** (☎*242/365–4411* ⊕*www.brendal.com*) leads
NORKELING snorkeling and scuba trips, plus wild dolphin encounters, glass-bot-
★ tom boat cruises, and more. Personable owner Brendal Stevens has been featured on the Discovery Channel and CNN, and he knows the surrounding reefs so well that he's named some of the groupers, stingrays, and moray eels that you'll have a chance to hand-feed. Trips can include a seafood lunch, grilled on the beach, and complimentary rum punch. Kayak and canoe rentals are available.

Rent some snorkel gear or bring your own, and call **Lincoln Jones** (☎*242/365–4223*), known affectionately as "the Daniel Boone of the Bahamas," for an unforgettable snorkeling adventure. Lincoln will dive for conch and lobster (in season) or catch fish, then grill a sumptuous lunch on a deserted beach.

TENNIS **Bluff House Beach Hotel** (☎*242/365–4247*) has one hard-surface court; rackets and balls are provided.

SHOPPING

Golden Reef (✉*Parliament St.* ☎*242/365–4511*) sells jewelry, including Abaco Gold jewelry made in Marsh Harbour, plus resort wear, kids' clothing, swimwear, and gifts.

Colorful Abaco Ceramics, handmade in Treasure Cay, are the best bet at **Native Creations** (✉*Parliament St.* ☎*242/365–4206*). The shop also sells beaded jewelry, picture frames, candles, postcards, and books.

Annexed to Plymouth Rock Liquors and Café, **Ocean Blue Gallery** (✉*Parliament St.* ☎*242/365–4234*) is a small gallery with framed and unframed paintings, sculptures, and other works by more than 50 local artists. The adjoining liquor store sells Cuban cigars and more than 60 kinds of rum.

Sid's Grocery (☎242/365–4055) has the most complete line of groceries on the island, plus a gift section that includes books on local Bahamian subjects—great for souvenirs or for replenishing your stock of reading material.

Vert's Model Ship Shop (✉ *Corner of Bay St. and Gully Alley* ☎242/365–4170) has Vert Lowe's handcrafted two-mast schooners and sloops. Model prices range anywhere from $100 to $1,200. If Vert's shop door is locked—and it often is—knock at the white house with bright pink shutters next door. If you're still unsuccessful, inquire at the Green Turtle Club, where Vert has worked for more than 30 years.

SPANISH CAY

Only 3 mi long, this privately owned island was once the exclusive retreat of millionaires, and many visitors still arrive by yacht or private plane. Although several private upscale homes dot the coast, a small resort also rents rooms and condos. A well-equipped marina, great fishing, and some fine beaches are among the attractions here.

WHERE TO EAT & STAY

$$ ✕▥ **Spanish Cay Resort and Marina.** Take your pick here—either a beachfront room or a two-room hotel suite tucked away on a hill overlooking the marina and the Sea of Abaco. Decisions, decisions. Regardless of location, all rooms have tile floors, pastel draperies and bedspreads, private porches, king or double beds, and desks. Two- to four-bedroom condos and luxury villas are also available. The Pointe House restaurant ($$) serves three meals daily; locally caught fish is your best bet for dinner. The adjacent bar has a game room and outdoor deck for enjoying a sunset cocktail. The 81-slip marina can handle yachts up to 250 feet, and boat rentals are available. **Pros:** totally off-the-beaten path location, lots of privacy on remote beaches, full-service marina. **Cons:** for entertainment you need to rely on yourself, no dependable Internet service, accommodations are dated. ✉ *Spanish Cay* ☎242/365–0083 *or 954/689–9248* ⊕*www.spanishcay.com* ⇆*18 rooms, 5 condos, 12 villas* ⚷*In-room: no phone, refrigerator. In-hotel: restaurant, bar, tennis courts, pool, beachfront, no elevator, laundry service* ☰*MC, V* ☉*Sometimes closed in Sept. and Oct.*

THE ABACOS ESSENTIALS

BY AIR

Most flights land at the international airports in Marsh Harbour or Treasure Cay. Some private planes and charter carriers use the airstrip at Spanish Cay. There's also a small public airstrip in Sandy Cay.

Many carriers operate seasonal schedules to the Abacos. Some routes are flown daily from December through August, and three times a week from September through November. In addition, many airlines serving the Abacos are very small and change schedules frequently, even in season.

Air Sunshine flies from Fort Lauderdale to Marsh Harbour and Treasure Cay. American Eagle has a daily flight to Marsh Harbour from Miami. Bahamasair flies daily from Nassau to Marsh Harbour and Treasure Cay. Cherokee Air is the charter-plane service of choice for island-hopping to or from the Abacos. Continental Connection flies into both Marsh Harbour and Treasure Cay from Miami and Fort Lauderdale. Vintage Props and Jets flies into Marsh Harbour and Treasure Cay from four airports in Florida: Daytona Beach, Melbourne, Orlando, and New Smyrna Beach. Yellow Air Taxi has scheduled charters into Marsh Harbour and Treasure Cay from Fort Lauderdale and West Palm Beach.

Airlines & Contacts Air Sunshine (☎ 954/434–8900 or 800/327–8900). **American Eagle** (☎ 242/367–2231 or 800/433–7300). **Bahamasair** (☎ 242/367–2095 in Marsh Harbour, 242/365–8601 in Treasure Cay). **Cherokee Air** (☎ 242/367–2089). **Continental Connection** (☎ 242/367–3415 in Marsh Harbour, 242/365–8615 in Treasure Cay, 800/231–0856). **Vintage Props and Jets** (☎ 800/852–0275). **Yellow Air Taxi** (☎ 888/935–5694).

BY BOAT

Boats are a key method of transportation among the many islands of the Abacos. A good system of public ferries and boat rental agencies allows you to reach even the most remote cays. Assuming you have plenty of time and a sense of adventure, you can even arrive in the Abacos by mail boat.

BOAT RENTAL If you don't want to be bound by the somewhat limited schedule of the ferries, rent a small boat. Most hotels and many rental cottages have docking facilities that allow you to keep your boat within easy reach. Boats can be rented on most islands with tourist facilities, but the best selections are at the main visitor destinations, including Marsh Harbour, Treasure Cay, Hope Town, and Green Turtle Cay.

Boat Rental Information Donny's Boat Rentals (☎ 242/365–4119). **J. I. C. Boat Rentals** (☎ 242/365–8582). **Paradise Boat Rentals** (☎ 242/365–4359). **Rainbow Rentals** (☎ 242/367–4602). **Reef Rentals** (☎ 242/365–4145). **Rich's Rentals** (☎ 242/367–2742). **Sea Horse Boat Rentals** (☎ 242/367–2513).

FERRIES In contrast to the mail boats, the two major ferry services serving the Abacos are very punctual. Every day except Sunday and holidays, Albury's Ferry Service leaves Marsh Harbour for the 20-minute ride to Hope Town at 7:15, 9, 10:30, 12:15, 2, 4, and 5:30; ferries make the return trip at 8, 9:45, 11:30, 1:30, 3, 4, and 5. A same-day round-trip costs $22. One-way tickets cost $16. Albury's also provides service between Marsh Harbour and Man-O-War Cay or Guana Cay. Charter excursions can also be booked.

The Green Turtle Cay Ferry leaves the Treasure Cay airport dock at 8:30, 10:30, 11:30, 1:30, 2:30, 3:30, 4:30, and 5 (except Sunday) and returns from Green Turtle Cay at 8, 9, 11, 12:15, 1:30, 3, and 4:30. One-way fares are $8, and a same-day round-trip fare is $13. The ferry makes several stops in Green Turtle, including New Plymouth the Green Turtle Club, and the Bluff House Beach Hotel.

Ferry Information Albury's Ferry Service (☎ *242/367–0290 or 242/359–686.* ⊕ *www.alburysferry.com*). **Green Turtle Cay Ferry** (☎ *242/365–4166*).

MAIL BOATS A mail boat is scheduled to depart every Tuesday from Potter's Cay Nassau, for Marsh Harbour and Green Turtle Cay, returning to Nassau on Thursday. Another boat is supposed to depart Nassau each Friday for Sandy Point, at the southern tip of Great Abaco, and return to Nassau on Friday. However, the schedule is often affected by wind rain, tides, mechanical problems, and other issues. Each one-way journey takes about six hours. For details, call the Dockmaster's Office at Potter's Cay.

Contact Dockmaster's Office (☎ *242/393–1064*).

BY CAR

Cars are not necessary on most of the smaller cays in the Abacos in fact, rental cars aren't even available in most locations. On Great Abaco, however, you'll need a car if you want to venture beyond Marsh Harbour or Treasure Cay. Rentals are $75 a day and up, and gasoline costs about $4 per gallon. You might negotiate a better rate if you rent for a week or longer.

Local Agencies A & P Rentals (☎ *242/367–2655*). **Cornish Car Rentals** (☎ *242/365–8623*). **H & L Car Rentals** (☎ *242/367–2854*). **Rental Wheels of Abaco** (☎ *242/367–4643*).

BY GOLF CART

Golf carts are the vehicle of choice on the majority of the smaller cays including Elbow Cay, Green Turtle Cay, Great Guana Cay, and Man-O-War Cay. Each can carry four adults comfortably, if slowly. The standard rates are $45 to $50 per day for a gas cart, or $240 per week Electric-powered carts, which usually must be recharged nightly, are slightly cheaper. Big-wheel carts, which provide a smoother ride on the bumpy, pothole-filled roads common in the islands, cost a little more and are not available at all locations. Reservations are always recommended, but are essential from April–July.

In Hope Town, try Hope Town Cart Rentals, Island Cart Rentals, or T&N Cart Rentals. In Treasure Cay, rent from Blue Marlin Rentals. On Green Turtle, Bay Street Rentals is on the grounds of the Bluff House Beach Hotel. D & P Rentals rents carts from an office at the Green Turtle Club. In New Plymouth, try Island Roadrunner or Seaside Carts. On Man-O-War, the Man-O-War Marina has golf carts.

Contacts Bay Street Rentals (☎ *242/365–4070*). **Blue Marlin Rentals** (☎ *242/365–8687*). **D & P Rentals** (☎ *242/365–4655*). **Hope Town Cart Rentals** (☎ *242/366–0064*). **Island Cart Rentals** (☎ *242/366–0448*). **Island Roadrunner** (☎ *242/365–4610*). **Man-O-War Marina** (☎ *242/365–6008*). **Seaside Carts** (☎ *242/477–5497*). **T&N Cart Rentals** (☎ *242/366–0069*).

BY TAXI

Taxi service is available on Great Abaco, Green Turtle Cay, Elbow Cay, Treasure Cay, and Marsh Harbour. Taxis meet arriving planes at the airports and will take you to your hotel or to a ferry dock, where you can catch a water taxi to neighboring islands such as Green Turtle Cay, Great Guana, or Elbow Cay. Hotels will arrange for taxis to take you on short trips and back to the airport. Fares are generally $1.50 per mi. A 15% tip is customary.

3

NTACTS & RESOURCES

BANKS & EXCHANGE SERVICES

Banks are generally open Monday–Thursday 9:30–3 pm and Friday until 4:30. They are sometimes closed on Wednesday.

Contacts **Royal Bank of Canada** (☏ *242/367–2420 Marsh Harbour, 242/365–8119 Treasure Cay*).

EMERGENCIES

The Marsh Harbour Clinic has a resident doctor and a nurse. There are also small government clinics staffed by nurses in Hope Town and New Plymouth, but hours are limited and change frequently. There are several private doctors in Marsh Harbour, and hotels will contact medical personnel upon request. Serious medical emergencies will require evacuation by plane to Nassau or Florida. It's a good idea to buy travel insurance that includes medical evacuation coverage.

Contacts **Abaco Medical Clinic** (☏ *242/367–4240*). **Marsh Harbour Clinic** (☏ *242/366–4010*). **Police or Fire Emergencies** (☏ *919*).

TOUR OPTIONS

From Green Turtle Cay, Brendal's Dive Center offers fully catered and captained sunset "booze cruises," and glass-bottom boat excursions where dolphin sightings are often a highlight. Froggies Out Island Adventures is the choice on Elbow Cay for sunset cruises and tours of the nearby cays.

Contacts **Brendal's Dive Center** (☏ *242/365–4411 or 800/780–9941* ⊕ *www. brendal.com*). **Froggies Out Island Adventures** (☏ *242/366–0431* ⊕ *www. froggiesabaco.com*).

VISITOR INFORMATION

Marsh Harbour's **Abaco Tourist Office** is open weekdays 9 to 5:30 (☏ *242/367–3067* ⊕ *www. bahamas.com*).

Eleuthera & the Exumas

WORD OF MOUTH

"Spend your days finding the next pink sand beach and snorkeling off those beaches. Eleuthera also has just offshore Harbour Island, the hot new destination small enough to explore on foot, with several resorts. The kids would love the golf cart transportation on this island; it is becoming more 'upscale' by the minute though."

—joan

"Exuma is beautiful, especially if you rent a car and travel south of George Town, and see miles of empty white sand beaches."

—Robert59

Updated
by Cheryl
Blackerby and
Kevin Kwan

ELEUTHERA AND THE EXUMAS ARE known for their undeveloped beaches, secluded sandy coves, turquoise water, and piney woods with thickets of shady casuarina, sea grapes, mahogany, and coco plums. These islands are among the prettiest in the Bahamas, with gentle hills, unspoiled "bush" (backwoods), and gardens of tumbling purple lantana and sky-blue plumbago corralled by white picket fences covered with cobalt morning glories and red bougainvillea. Hotels and inns are painted in the shades of a Bahamian sunset, which, by the way, are best watched from the comfort of inviting verandas and seaside decks. The laid-back, easygoing pace of the islands guarantees a restful respite. Residents welcome visitors warmly; most will be happy to let you know where to find the best beach for surfing or a placid cove for children. And of course they will recommend the best restaurant for conch chowder. People here are serious about fishing, and can show you the choice spots, which might be on the shore behind your little inn. While some of the other Out Islands attract deep-sea fishermen seeking marlin and tarpon, the lure here is bonefish, the feisty breed that prefers the shallow, sandy flats that surround these islands.

Eleuthera was founded in 1648 by a British group fleeing religious persecution; the name is taken from the Greek word for freedom. These settlers, who called themselves the Eleutheran Adventurers, gave the Bahamas its first written constitution. In the late 1800s, Eleuthera dominated the world's pineapple market, and these small, intensely sweet fruits are still grown on tiny family farms dotting the island. You'll also find powdery pink and starch white beaches, charming guest houses, and a handful of luxurious resorts, some with the best seafood you'll ever eat. If you're looking for all of this and a bit more "action," ferry over to Harbour Island, Eleuthera's chic neighbor. With its uninterrupted three-mile pink sand beach, world-class dining, and sumptuous inns, the island has long been a favorite hideaway for jet-setters and celebrities.

On the Exumas, you'll find wild cotton left over from plantations established by Loyalists after the Revolutionary War. Breadfruit trees, which a local preacher bought from Captain William Bligh in the late 18th century, are in abundance as well. Today, the Exumas are known as the Bahamas' onion capital, although many of the 3,600-odd residents earn a living by fishing and farming. However, the tourism industry has been the islands' top employer since the mammoth Four Seasons Resort opened in 2003.

Your first impression of the people of the Exumas may be that almost all of them have the surname Rolle. The late American actress Esther Rolle's parents were from Exuma. Dennis Rolle imported the first cotton seeds to these islands and his son, Lord John, had more than 300 slaves, to whom he bequeathed not only his name but also the 2,300 acres of land that were bestowed on him by the British government in the late 18th century. Today Rolle's descendants are still entitled to land for building homes and farms.

ELEUTHERA & THE EXUMAS' TOP 5

Dunmore Town. Harbour Island's New England–style village begs to be explored on foot or by golf cart.

George Town. Here's where it's all happening on Great Exuma; the best parties are late Friday afternoon.

Stocking Island. Gnarly waves, a beautiful beach, boisterous open-air bars and cafés, an eco-cottage complex, and volleyball on the beach make the island (a mile from George Town) popular for yachties and other visitors.

Surfer's Beach, Eleuthera. Gidget and Moondoggie would have loved the waves and the funky, junky beach shack here.

Williams Town. History runs deep in this quiet settlement, where the oldest building in the Exumas, the Cotton House, built in the 1780s, still stands.

4

XPLORING ELEUTHERA & THE EXUMAS

Eleuthera is shaped like a fishhook, 110 mi long and 2 mi wide, with just a little more than 11,000 residents. It lies 200 mi southeast of Florida and 60 mi east of Nassau. The mainland is charmingly undeveloped, which contrasts nicely with Harbour Island, a chic enclave of pastel 18th- and 19th-century clapboard houses, often called the St. Barths of the Bahamas. It's reachable by a 10-minute ferry ride from North Eleuthera. Harbour Island is famous worldwide for its 3-mi stretch of powdery pink-sand beach, usually included in lists of the most beautiful beaches on the planet.

The Exumas begin less than 35 mi southeast of Nassau and stretch south for about 60 mi, flanked by the Great Bahama Bank and Exuma Sound, and have 3,500 residents. They are made up largely of some 365 fragmented little cays, mostly uninhabited. The two main islands, Great Exuma and Little Exuma, lie in the south, connected by a bridge; together they are about 50 mi long. The islands' capital, George Town, on Great Exuma, is the site of one of the Bahamas' most prestigious and popular sailing events, the Family Islands Regatta, in which locally built wooden work boats compete. In winter, George Town's Elizabeth Harbour is a haven for yachts. The surrounding waters are legendary for their desolate islands, coves, bays, and harbors.

Eleuthera and the Exumas are a quick flight from Miami, Fort Lauderdale, or Nassau. You can also take a fast ferry from Nassau; the trip takes just a few scenic hours. It's easy to explore the islands by rented car, bicycle, or golf cart, although you'll need to rent a motorboat to reach some of the smaller uninhabited islands. Be warned: Eleuthera is known for reckless drivers, so be extremely alert if you're on a bike.

IF YOU LIKE

CONCH SALAD

This Bahamian staple is akin to ceviche. Fresh-caught conch is removed from its shell, diced, and mixed with chopped onions and red or green bell peppers. The mix is drizzled with fresh lime and sour orange juices, and spiced with either homemade hot sauce or finely minced local hot peppers, or both. Often the best places to try conch salad are one-room shacks at the water's edge, such as the cluster of shacks called **Fish Fry** just north of George Town in Exuma, or at **Queen Conch** on Harbour Island, Eleuthera, where the salad is made right in front of you. In restaurants, conch salad can be an appetizer or a main course. Conch also is chopped and fried in fritters, stewed with potatoes as chowder, and fried up as cracked conch.

PINK SANDS & SECLUDED HAVENS

Go to Eleuthera or the Exumas to sink your toes into soft sand and be lulled into a happy stupor by the sounds of gentle waves. The slightly curved 3-mi pink-sand beach on Harbour Island, Eleuthera, usually rates in the world's top 10 beaches, and deservedly so. Its sand is of such a fine consistency that it's almost as soft as talcum powder, and the gentle slope of the shore makes small waves break hundreds of yards offshore; you have to walk out quite a distance to get past your waist. On moonlit nights, the waves seem lighted from underneath, and the beach becomes your private planetarium for stargazing. On Exuma, head a few miles north or south from George Town, the island's main city, to find isolated spots of wide sand.

SNORKELERS' PARADISE

The 176-square-mi Exuma Cays Land and Sea Park is a favorite of divers and snorkelers attracted by rare pillar coral and huge schools of multicolor fish, and sightseers who just want to enjoy the isolated and pristine ecosystem that flourishes here under the watchful eye of park rangers. They patrol in motorized boats to ensure that nobody damages the precious coral reefs, poaches fish, or bothers the dolphins and porpoises. Stretching some 22 mi between Compass Cay and Norman's Cay along the string of islands at the far northern end of the Exumas, this park is reachable only by seaplane or boat. That's part of its charm. The nearest "civilization" is an hour or more away in Staniel Cay, where there's a marina, restaurant, and tiny airport.

A WARM BAHAMIAN WELCOME

Most of the people you'll meet on Exuma and Eleuthera have lived here for their entire lives, except maybe for a few years of college or work, or a brief visit to the United States to buy school clothes, a car, or visit medical specialists. Their ties to their homeland and extended families tend to be strong and secure—perhaps this is why the local residents seem to be exceptionally friendly and have an openness about them. Everybody says "good morning" or "good afternoon" with a smile when they see you. Express the smallest interest in the history, food, or culture of the islands, and you'll probably be rewarded with convivial conversation. Good manners are important here, and making guests feel welcome is at the top of the list.

ABOUT THE RESTAURANTS

Although the ambience is usually casual, food is taken seriously here, especially island specialties like conch salad and fritters, the succulent Bahamian lobster most locals call crawfish, and barbecued pork or chicken. Fresh fish and seafood, usually pulled that morning from the waters just beyond the restaurant kitchen, is the highlight of most menus. If you've never had fresh conch, these islands are the place to indulge, especially at one of the conch shacks favored by island residents. The conch is often so fresh that it may be sitting in a tank outside until you place your order. It is then diced, mixed with chopped red and green bell peppers and tomatoes, seasoned with each chef's own secret recipe of lemon, lime, and sour orange juices, and topped with a tangy dash of hot pepper sauce or minced chili pepper.

> **DID YOU KNOW?**
>
> Folks are friendly in Eleuthera and the Exumas and will readily hail you on the street to chat. Understand that when a man greets a woman as "baby," it doesn't have a derogatory context; it's a term of endearment that women also use when addressing other women.

Most restaurants serve Bahamian food, with a few lamb dishes and steak thrown in. Italian, Continental, and Asian dishes may show up on the menu, too, offering alternatives for those who want a change in taste. Newer restaurants, particularly in Eleuthera, feature experimental and fusion cuisine, a trend that is becoming increasingly popular. Many dining establishments are closed two days a week, including Sunday, which is family day on these deeply religious and family-oriented islands.

ABOUT THE HOTELS

There's an undeniable appeal to staying at a place that treats you like family, and this type of establishment is not hard to come by in these parts. Most hotels have their own restaurants and offer several different meal plans. Many of the hotels have remodeled and are offering more lavish features in response to the opening of the luxurious Four Seasons Resort Great Exuma at Emerald Bay in 2003, the largest and most upscale resort on the two islands. It has the only full-service spa and golf course on either island. The development of the February Point Resort Estates community has also raised the stakes for lodging options in Exuma.

On Eleuthera, the new Powell Pointe Resort at Cape Eleuthera offers guests an upscale resort/marina experience, while older favorites, such as the Cove Eleuthera and Pineapple Fields, add a touch of simple elegance amongst the island's low key lodging options. Ten miles south of Rock Sound, the original Cotton Bay Club hotel is being rebuilt as part of a new resort, managed by Starwood Hotels & Resorts. The clubhouse and 73-room guesthouse are expected to open in late 2009; a residential development and a new Starwood Luxury Collection golf course designed by Robert Trent Jones Jr., which will replace the old Robert Trent Jones Sr. course, are in the works for phase two. Cotton Bay was once an exclusive club, the domain of Pan Am's founder, Juan

Trippe, who would fly his friends to the island on a 727 Yankee Clipper for a weekend of golf.

	¢	$	$$	$$$	$$$$
WHAT IT COSTS IN U.S. DOLLARS					
RESTAURANTS	under $10	$10–$20	$20–$30	$30–$40	over $40
HOTELS	under $100	$100–$200	$200–$300	$300–$400	over $400

Restaurant prices are for a main course at dinner, excluding gratuity, typically 15%, which is often automatically added to the bill. Hotel prices are for two people in a standard double room in high season, excluding service charges and 6%–12% tax.

TIMING

High season for tourism in Eleuthera and the Exumas is late November through April, when residents of cold-weather climates head to the Bahamas to defrost and soak up some rays. For the cheapest hotel rates and some of the best deals on water-sports packages, visit in summer or fall. For those who want to catch some action and don't mind crowds, the liveliest times to visit Eleuthera and the Exumas are around Christmas and New Year's during the annual Junkanoo celebration of music and dance, in March during spring break and the Bahamian Music and Heritage Festival (which takes place the second weekend of the month), and during the annual Family Islands Regatta in April, when the harbor of George Town, Exuma, is filled with hundreds of multimillion-dollar yachts. Late-summer hurricane season from August to November can be steamy and in wintertime from December to March, low temperatures might dip into the 60s.

ELEUTHERA ISLAND

SPANISH WELLS

Off Eleuthera's northern tip lies St. George's Cay, the site of **Spanish Wells.** The Spaniards used this as a safe harbor during the 17th century while they transferred their riches from the New World to the Old. Supposedly they dug wells from which they drew water during their frequent visits. Today, water comes from the mainland. Residents—the few surnames go back generations—live on the island's eastern end in clapboard houses that look as if they've been transported from a New England fishing village. Descendants of the Eleutheran Adventurers continue to sail these waters and bring back to shore fish and lobster (most of the Bahamas' langoustes are caught here), which are prepared and boxed for export in a factory at the dock. So lucrative is the trade in crawfish, the local term for Bahamian lobsters, that the 700 inhabitants may be the most prosperous Out Islanders in the Bahamas. Those who don't fish here grow tomatoes, onions, and pineapples. You can reach Spanish Wells by taking a five-minute ferry ride ($7) from the Gene's Bay dock at North Eleuthera.

GREAT ITINERARIES

IF YOU HAVE 3 DAYS

Fly into **North Eleuthera** and make your way to a hotel near the famous 3-mi pink-sand beach on **Harbour Island**, a taxi and boat ride from the airport. Leave your windows open so you can hear the free-roaming roosters wake you up in time to see the incredible pink and mauve sunrise. Take a morning walk on the beach, then veg out with a good book, interrupted only by lunch at an ocean-side restaurant. Stroll through **Dunmore Town** in the afternoon, stopping at the crafts stands, admiring the quaint clapboard houses along Bay Street, and visiting the centuries-old churches. The next day, go scuba diving or snorkeling, or hire a guide and try to snag at least one of the swift, canny bonefish for which Eleuthera is famous. End the day with dinner in Dunmore Town. Take the ferry to **Spanish Wells** on your last day. Rent a golf cart and enjoy this prosperous lobster-fishing island, with its neat, upscale homes and tiny alcove beaches. Be sure to try some fresh lobster before leaving.

IF YOU HAVE 5 DAYS

Follow the suggested three-day itinerary, and on Day 4 take the ferry to "the mainland," what Harbour Island's residents call the main island of **Eleuthera**. Rent a car and drive south past **Glass Window**, where you can stand in one spot and see the brilliant blue and often fierce Atlantic Ocean to the west and the placid Bahama Sound to the east. Check out the cathedral-like cavern called **The Cave** to prowl the stalagmites and hunt for bats and pirates' booty. In the afternoon, drive to **Hidden Beach** off **James Point** for some private sunbathing or snorkeling. Continue south to **Governor's Harbour**, the island's largest town, and grab dinner at Tippy's, the upscale, laid-back beach bistro overlooking the Atlantic Ocean. The next morning, drive to **Rock Sound** and then head either to **Ocean Hole**, a large inland saltwater lake, or to the windswept **Bannerman Town** and visit the lighthouse and beautiful pink-sand beach.

IF YOU HAVE 7 DAYS

Add a hop to the Exumas to the three-day agenda above. The best way to fly between Eleuthera and the Exumas is through Fort Lauderdale on Continental Connection, which involves a three-hour layover with an evening arrival. You can also connect through Nassau on Bahamasair. After your flights, you'll be ready to relax at the closest beach or bar to your hotel room. The next day, camp out on the beach, go golfing, or treat yourself to a massage. On Day 5, go diving at **Angel Fish Blue Hole** or snorkeling at **Stocking Island Mystery Cave,** a blue-hole grotto filled with Technicolor fish, accessible via a short ferry ride from **George Town**. Watch the sunset over dinner at an ocean-side restaurant. Finish the week at one of the beachfront hotels in **George Town**, preferably including a Saturday night so you can join in the festivities at **Palm Bay Beach Club,** where an outdoor barbecue and bonfire attract most of the island's inhabitants for a friendly evening of dancing.

4

WHERE TO STAY

☾ **$$** ▦ **Abner's Rentals.** Abner Pinder's wife, Ruth, keeps these two attached two-bedroom houses as spotless as her own. A tiny, private sand beach overlooking the ocean is just steps from the patio. A house rental includes the discounted use of a golf cart so you can explore the island and pick up groceries at one of the local shops. There's a three-night minimum stay; it's $1,400 per house per week. ⊠ *Between 12th and 13th Sts.* ☎ *242/333–4890* ➹ *2 houses* ☾ *In-room: kitchen* ▭ *No credit cards.*

HARBOUR ISLAND

Fodor'sChoice **Harbour Island** has often been called the Nantucket of the Caribbean
★ and the prettiest of the Out Islands because of its powdery pink-sand beaches (3 mi worth!) and its pastel-color clapboard houses with dormer windows, set among white picket fences, narrow lanes, quaint shops, and tropical flowers. The frequent parade of the fashionable and famous, and the chic small inns that accommodate them, has earned the island another name: the St. Barths of the Bahamas. But residents have long called it Briland, their faster way of pronouncing "Harbour Island." These inhabitants include families who go back generations to the island's early settlement, as well as a growing number of celebrities, supermodels, and tycoons who feel that Briland is the perfect haven to bask in small town charm against a stunning oceanscape.

The best way to get around is to rent a golf cart or bike; or hire a taxi, since climbing the island's hills can be quite strenuous in the midday heat. Some of the Bahamas' most attractive small hotels, each strikingly distinct, are tucked within the island's 2 square mi. At several perched on a bluff above the shore, you can fall asleep with the windows open and listen to the waves lapping the beach. Harbour Island is reached via a 10-minute ferry ride from the North Eleuthera dock. Fares are $5 per person in a boat of two or more, plus an extra dollar to be dropped off at the private Romora Bay Club docks and for nighttime rides.

Old trees line the narrow streets of **Dunmore Town,** named after the 18th-century royal governor of the Bahamas, Lord Dunmore, who built a summer home here and laid out the town, which served as the first capital of the Bahamas. The community was once second in the country to Nassau in terms of its prosperity. It's the only town on Harbour Island, and you can take in all its attractions during a 20-minute stroll. Stop first at the **Harbour Island Tourist Office** (☎ *242/333–2621*) on Dunmore Street to get a map and ask about current events. Nearby on the same street, visit the Bahamas' oldest Anglican church, **St. John's,** built in 1768, and the distinguished 1848 **Wesley Methodist Church.** Both hold services.

On Bay Street, **Loyalist Cottage,** one of the original settlers' homes (circa 1797), has also survived. Many other old houses in the area, with gingerbread trim and picket fences, have such amusing names as Beside the Point, Up Yonder, and The Royal Termite. Across the street is a row of straw-work stands, including Dorothea's, Pat's, and Sarah's, where you'll find straw bags, hats, and T-shirts. Food stands sell conch salad, Kalik beer, coconut water, and fruit juices.

If you stroll to the end of Bay Street and follow the curve to the western edge of the island, you'll find the **Lone Tree,** one of the most photographed icons of Harbour Island. This enormous piece of driftwood is said to have washed up on shore after a bad storm and anchored itself on the shallow sandbar in a picturesque upright position, providing the perfect photo op for

> ### HEAVENLY MUSIC
>
> The best live music on Harbour Island is at the little yellow Church of God in Dunmore Town on Sunday mornings. Mick Jagger and Lenny Kravitz have dropped by to hear Pastor Samuel Higgs, drummer and bass player, and guitarist Rocky Sanders, both of whom played Europe's clubs for years before settling down on the island.

countless tourists. Off the eastern Atlantic shore lies a long coral reef, which protects the beach and has excellent snorkeling. You can see multicolor fish and a few old wrecks.

WHERE TO EAT

Note that most Harbour Island hotels and restaurants are closed from September through mid- to late October.

AMERICAN

$ ✕ **Dunmore Deli.** Patrick Tully's exceptional deli satisfies the epicurean demands of Briland's more finicky residents and visitors, while its shaded wooden porch, filled with hanging plants and bougainvillea, makes this the perfect spot for a lazy breakfast or lunch. Treat yourself to the Briland Bread Toast, their amazingly fluffy take on French toast, or pick up one of their inventive deli sandwiches for a picnic on the beach. While here, you can also stock up on a variety of international coffee, imported cheese, produce, and other gourmet items you won't find anywhere else on the island. ⌧*King St., Dunmore Town* ☎*242/333–2644* ▤*MC, V* ☙*Closed Sun. No dinner.*

BAHAMIAN

★ $$$ ✕ **Sunsets on the Bay.** This waterfront pavilion at the Romora Bay Club perfectly frames sunsets over Harbour Island, so be sure to get there in time to snag a good seat for the show. Popular with locals, the restaurant serves mid-priced Bahamian specialties such as conch fritters for a casual lunch or dinner. The bartender is always happy to create new drinks just to suit your vibe, and be sure to greet Goldie the parrot, who has held court over the bar for more than 50 years. ⌧*Romora Bay Club, south end of Dunmore St., Dunmore Town* ☎*242/333–2325* ⌦*Reservations essential* ▤*AE, D, MC, V* ☙*Closed Sun.*

★ $ ✕ **Ma Ruby's.** Although you can sample local Bahamian fare at this famous eatery, the star of the menu is the cheeseburger, purportedly the inspiration for Jimmy Buffet's "Cheeseburger in Paradise" song. Maybe it's the rustic charm of the breezy patio, or the secret seasonings on the melt-in-your-mouth patty, but this burger served between thick slices of homemade Bahamian bread is definitely otherworldly. Be sure

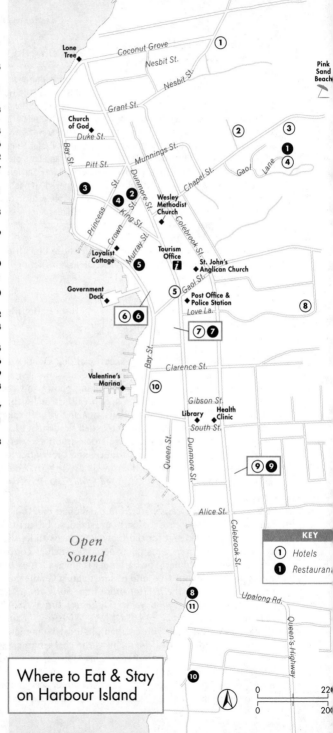

Hotels ▼

Bahama
House Inn **5**

Baretta's
Seashell Inn **1**

Coral Sands
Hotel **3**

Dunmore
Beach Club **4**

The Landing **6**

Pink Sands **2**

Rock House **7**

Romora Bay
Club **11**

Runaway Hill
Inn **8**

Tingum Village
Hotel **9**

Valentine's
Resort &
Marina **10**

Restaurants ▼

Acquapazza **10**

Arthur's Bakery
& Cafe **2**

Dunmore Deli **4**

Harbour
Lounge **5**

The Landing **6**

Ma Ruby's **9**

Queen Conch **3**

Rock
House **7**

Sip Sip **1**

Sunsets
on the Bay **8**

Where to Eat & Stay
on Harbour Island

to save room for Ma's coconut tart or key lime pie. ⊠ *Tingum Village Hotel,Colebrooke St., Dunmore Town* ☎242/333–2161 ▭*MC, V.*

¢ ╳**Queen Conch.** Four blocks from the ferry dock on Bay Street, Lavaughn Percentie reigns over her colorful snack stand, renowned for its freshly caught conch salad ($8), which is diced in front of you, mixed with fresh vegetables, and ready to eat right at the counter. On weekends, get there early to put in your order, as visitors from the world over place large orders to take home. ⊠*Bay St., Dunmore Town* ☎242/456–1383 ▭*No credit cards* ◷*Closed Sun.*

CAFE

¢ ╳**Arthur's Bakery and Cafe.** Bread and pastries are baked every morning by *White Shadow* screenwriter Robert Arthur and his Trinidadian wife Anna. The friendly café has a quiet garden nook where you can savor your morning brew with an apple turnover, banana pancakes, or any of their daily breakfast offerings. Computers with Internet access are also available for a fee. ⊠*Crown St. and Dunmore St., Dunmore Town* ☎242/333–2285 ▭*No credit cards* ◷*Closed Sun. No dinner.*

CONTINENTAL

$$$ ╳**Harbour Lounge.** Owners of the Bubble Room restaurant—a long-time Captiva Island, Florida, favorite—now own this pink building with green shutters across from the government dock. The front deck is a prime spot for people watching, as well as for sunsets over cocktails. The lunch and dinner fare might include smoked dolphin-fish dip with garlic pita chips, grouper cake salad, cracked conch, and tequila shrimp. ⊠*Bay St., Dunmore Town* ☎242/333–2031 ▭*MC, V* ◷*Closed Mon.*

ECLECTIC

$$$$ ╳ **The Landing.** You never know which billionaire or rock star you'll
dor's Choice rub elbows with at the Hemingway-esque bar, but none of it matters
★ once you've moved on to the dining room and are under the spell of Sydney-trained chef Ken Gomes, whose dishes soar with a South East Asian flair. Standouts include the surprisingly ingenious pairing of goat cheese ravioli with shrimp, pan-fried grouper with red Thai curry, and a vanilla cheesecake with mango syrup. One of the Caribbean's top dining destinations, the Landing also offers an impressive wine selection. If the weather is nice, request a romantic table on the porch. ⊠ *The Landing, Bay St., Dunmore Town* ☎242/333–2707 ⌕*Reservations essential* ▭*AE, MC, V* ◷*Closed Tues. and Wed.*

$$ ╳**Sip Sip.** Locals and travelers alike seek out this popular snow-cone-
dor's Choice green house overlooking the beach for a little "sip sip" (Bahamian for
★ gossip) and delicious inspired food. Chef and owner Julie Lightbourn uses whatever is fresh, local, and in season to create "Bahamian with a twist" dishes, so check what daily specials are on the blackboard. Conch chili is one of her signatures, consider yourself lucky if the lobster quesadillas are available, and don't miss the decadent carrot cake with ginger-caramel. Sip Sip only serves lunch, from 11:30 to 4. ⊠*Court Rd., Dunmore Town* ☎242/333–3316 ▭*MC, V* ◷*Closed Tues. No dinner.*

ITALIAN

$$ ✕**Acquapazza.** Briland's only Italian restaurant offers a change o
pace from the island's standard fare, and a change of scenery, too
It's located on the island's south end at the Harbour Island Marina
with a dockside terrace where you can take in the sunset while sippin
one of their exclusively imported Italian wines. Chefs and co-owner
Haymo Elzenbaumer and Manfredi Mancini's hearty portions of frie
calamari and pasta e fagioli don't disappoint, and their seafood entrée
are always a good choice. ⊠*Harbour Island Marina, South end o
island off Queens Hwy.* ☎*242/333–3240* ⚓*Reservations essentia
*☐*AE, MC, V.*

NEW AMERICAN

★ $$$$ ✕**The Rock House.** Splendid harbor views and a transporting Mediter
ranean loggia vibe create the perfect atmosphere for chef Jennifer Lear
month's California Continental menu, infused with tropical accents
Imaginative dishes include curried Colorado lamb chops and Thai-styl
stone crab and lobster spring rolls. The Rock House also takes it
drinks seriously, with an extensive list showcasing California boutiqu
wines. Dining here is refined and serene thanks to the flawless service
so linger over coffee and one of their decadent desserts, like rum cak
with butter sauce or homemade Pilon espresso ice cream. ⊠ *The Roc
House Hotel, Bay St., Dunmore Town* ☎*242/333–2053* ⚓*Reserva
tions essential* ☐*AE, MC, V.*

WHERE TO STAY

$$$$ 🏨**Dunmore Beach Club.** This classic Old Bahamian–style hotel evoke
a 1940s private club in the tropics. With its colorfully painted ba
white Chippendale-chaired dining room, and faded paperbacks in th
clubhouse library, it's a favorite with the New England yachting se
A guest-to-staff ratio of almost one-to-one services the eight privat
cottages scattered throughout the grounds, which are done in tradi
tional wicker and floral chintz, with spacious marble bathrooms tha
have separate sink-vanity areas and stand-alone showers. **Pros:** on th
beach, oceanside bar service, spacious bathrooms, private terraces an
lawn chairs for every cottage. **Cons:** cottages too close for real privac
small clubhouse, slightly stuffy atmosphere. ⊠*Gaol La., Dunmor
Town* ☎*242/333–2200 or 877/891–3100* ⊕*www.dunmorebeach
com* ⇆*16 1-bed to 4-bed units in 8 cottages* ⌂*In-room: refrigera
tor. In-hotel: restaurant, bar, tennis court, beachfront, laundry servic
public Wi-Fi* ☐*D, MC, V* ⊚*FAP.*

$$$$ 🏨**Pink Sands.** Harbour Island's famed beach-front resort has long bee
praised by celebrities and honeymooners alike for its 25 private cot
tages scattered over 20 secluded acres. Biba designer Barbara Hulanick
updated the resort in 2007 with her eclectic touches, including a cas
cading mother of pearl chandelier that dominates the lounge. The ren
ovations have infused the main house with a sexy, retro 1970s vibe
Yet with all the creature comforts in the way of luxurious bedding
plasma screen TVs, and imposing native wood furniture, the gues
cottages feel surprisingly non-descript. But with three tennis courts
a secluded pool, and the legendary namesake beach just steps awa

will you really care? The Blue Bar serves Bahamian-infused European cuisine all day long and has a prime vantage point overlooking the beach. **Pros:** truly private cottages, state-of-the-art media room, discreet and well-trained staff. **Cons:** uninspired decor in guest cottages, some cottages quite a walk from the main house, resort is next to a cemetery. ⊠ *Chapel St., Dunmore Town* ☎ *242/333–2030* ⊕ *www.islandoutpost.com* ⇔ *25 1- and 2-bedroom cottages* ♿ *In-room: safe, VCR. In-hotel: 2 restaurants, bars, tennis courts, pool, gym, beachfront, water sports, laundry service, public Wi-Fi* ▭ *AE, D, MC, V* ⦿ *MAP* ⊗ *Closed 2 wks in mid-Oct.*

LOCAL FLAVOR

If you're wondering where the real action is on the weekends, head for Brian's, where barbecue ribs and jerk chicken are expertly grilled on a Dunmore Street front patio every Friday and Saturday night. The barbecue party really heats up after 10 PM and stays packed till the wee hours, because it's where everyone eventually ends up after a night of work or partying.

$$$–$$$$
odor's Choice
★

⌗ **Rock House.** With a drawing room straight out of a villa on the Amalfi coast, the Rock House is Harbour Island's most luxurious boutique hotel. Originally a complex of historic harborside buildings, the hotel was decadently renovated and re-imagined in 2002 by owners Wallace Tutt (the builder of Gianni Versace's mansion in Miami) and Don Purdy, who attentively orchestrate a pampering, intimate haven for their discriminating international clientele. Fresh orchids fill every room, private cabanas line the heated courtyard pool, and the congenial staff cater to your every need. Guest rooms are a sophisticated mix of contemporary and island furnishings; outfitted with thoughtful amenities like a picnic basket for beach forays and custom-designed extra-padded mattresses. After feasting at the Rock House's celebrated restaurant, you'll want to take advantage of the island's only fully outfitted gym (exclusively for guest use). **Pros:** heavenly beds, stellar service, best gym on the island. **Cons:** not on the beach, lack of views from rooms. ⊠ *Bay St.* ☎ *242/333–2053* ⊕ *www.rockhousebahamas.com* ⇔ *7 rooms, 3 suites* ♿ *In-room: safe, VCR. In-hotel: restaurant, bar, public Wi-Fi, no kids under 18, no-smoking rooms* ▭ *AE, MC, V* ⦿ *CP.*

$$$–$$$$

⌗ **Runaway Hill Inn.** Set on beautiful rolling grounds, this quiet seaside inn feels far removed from the rest of the island, which is precisely the point. This is not a place you'll be waited on hand and foot. Rather, longtime guests appreciate the lived-in feel of this rambling 1938 New England style beach house, where you have the run of the place and can be left alone to mix a drink at the honor bar, relax poolside, or head down the steps to the beach. At dinnertime, chef Kent MacDonald offers French cuisine with modern fusion touches. Guest rooms are simply furnished in a comfortable contemporary style, and bathrooms feature colorful tilework and Fresh bath products. Request Room No. 2, where you can savor the breathtaking view of the ocean while lying in your bed. **Pros:** oceanfront location with direct beach access, well-stocked library, intimate atmosphere. **Cons:** main house showing wear and tear, limited service. ⊠*Colebrooke St., Dunmore Town* ☎*242/333–2150* ⊕*www.runawayhill.com* 📞*10 rooms* ⌂*In-hotel: restaurant, bar, pool, beachfront, airport shuttle, no kids under 18* ▤*AE, D, MC, V* �𝍫*EP, MAP.*

DON'T FORGET TO WAVE

When cruising along in your golf cart, follow the polite Briland custom and remember to hail everyone that passes by, whether they're in another golf cart, a car, or just walking on the street. Locals know how to spot all the first-time tourists—they're the ones who don't wave a friendly hello!

☾ **$$$**   🏨**Coral Sands Hotel.** An elegant yet energetic flair accents this 9-acre oceanfront resort, right on the pink sand beach. The main lobby is a study in British Colonial style, while the billiard room off the bar attracts a younger, hipper crowd. Guest rooms are spread out over three buildings, and rooms in the Lucaya building are the largest with balconies and ocean views. All are decorated in a modern tropical style with neutral tones, streamlined wood furniture and flat-screen TVs. Worth the extra splurge is the Beach House, a two-bedroom cottage right on the sand that's closer to the water than any other rental property on the island. At night, the lights are dimmed, candles flicker, and chef Ludovic Jarland serves up Caribbean cuisine with a French flair in the Terrace restaurant, where open arches frame views of the lush gardens and the sea beyond. **Pros:** direct ocean access, trendy beach resort feel, billiard room. **Cons:** rooms vary in quality and style, some rooms feel cramped, only one private cottage. ⊠*Chapel St.* ☎*242/333–2350 or 800/468–2799* ⊕*www.coralsands.com* 📞*32 rooms, 4 suites, 1 2-bedroom beach house* ⌂*In-room: no TV. In-hotel: restaurant, bars, tennis court, pool, beachfront, water sports, laundry service, public Wi-Fi* ▤*AE, D, MC, V* �𝍫*EP, MAP.*

☾ **$$$**   🏨**Romora Bay Club.** Three pink Adirondack chairs on the dock welcome you to this colorful and casual resort situated on the bay side of the island. Guest rooms are in cottages with private terraces or balconies, built on sloping grounds, each idiosyncratically decorated (one room might feature a French armoire and Salvador Dali prints, while another has a four-poster bed and African tribal masks). Fans of this older property don't mind a little wear and tear, preferring its laid back atmosphere and exceedingly friendly staff. The resort also boasts what is perhaps the island's best sunset view, which you can enjoy while you're splashing around in the infinity pool, lounging in one of the cabanas on the small private beach, or sipping a frosty cocktail at their restaurant Sunsets on the Bay. **Pros:** friendly staff, water views from every room, private bayside beach. **Cons:** rooms need updating, sloping steps from dock to cottages are a hassle for luggage, main house is being converted into a resort showroom. ⊠*South End of Dunmore St., Dunmore Town* ☎*242/333–2325* ⊕*www.romorabay.com* 📞*14 rooms, 4 suites* ⌂*In-room: VCR. In-hotel: 2 restaurants, bars, tennis court, pool, gym, public Wi-Fi* ▤*AE, D, MC, V* ⟠*MAP.*

$$$ 🏨**Valentine's Resort and Marina.** With the largest marina on Harbour Island, equipped with 51 slips capable of accommodating yachts up to 170 feet, this resort is ideal if you are a self-sufficient traveler or family that doesn't require many amenities but enjoys spacious condo-style rooms and water-focused activities. Valentine's draws a serious boating crowd with its dockside bar and complete dive shop. Each junior suite or one and two bedroom unit is well-appointed in a modern colonial style, with rich dark woods and plush beige sofas sharing space with sepia-toned photographs and plasma screen TVs. Luxurious bathrooms come with soaking tubs, glass shower stalls, and L'Occitane bath products. For the best marina views, request a room in the Andros building. **Pros:** very comfortable, modern rooms, state-of-the-art marina, large swimming pool. **Cons:** not oceanfront, impersonal condo-style atmosphere, lack of service. ⊠ *Bay St., Dunmore Town* ☎ *242/333–2142* ⊕ *www.valentinesresort.com* ⇆ *41 rooms* ⚘ *In-hotel: restaurant, bar, tennis court, pool, diving, bicycles, public Wi-Fi* ⊟ *AE, D, MC, V* ⦿| *EP, MAP.*

★ **$$–$$$** 🏨 **The Landing.** Spare white walls and crisp white linens evoke a timeless, understated chic at the Landing, which is acclaimed as much for its singular style as for its superb cuisine. Each of its seven intimate guest rooms are simply decorated in a Colonial plantation style. Want a memorable harbour view? An antique telescope peers out of a lookout nook from the Attic Room, which also boasts a gleaming white bathroom complete with a sumptuous white chaise lounge. Soothe yourself in the garden's tranquil pool when you're beached out—and don't miss the sybaritic outdoor shower, cleverly designed around the roots of an ancient fig tree. **Pros:** chic and comfortable rooms, glorious outdoor shower, acclaimed dining. **Cons:** 10 AM check-out time, limited hotel services, not on the beach. ⊠ *Bay St.* ☎ *242/333–2707 or 242/333–2740* ⊕ *www.harbourislandlanding.com* ⇆ *5 rooms* ⚘ *In-room: no phone, no TV. In-hotel: restaurant, bar, public Wi-Fi* ⊟ *D, MC, V* ⊗ *Closed Sept. 10–Nov. 1* ⦿| *BP.*

★ **$** 🏨 **Bahama House Inn.** Originally deeded in 1796 and built by Thomas W. Johnson, Briland's first doctor and justice of the peace, this handsome seven-bedroom bed-and-breakfast set in a garden filled with bougainvillea, royal poincianas, and hibiscus thrives, thanks to the loving preservation work of genial innkeeper John Hersh. Each guest room is quaintly furnished with a distinctive array of antiques and local artwork, and overlooks either the harbour or garden. A favorite is the Harry Potter Room, tucked under the stairs but much more spacious than you'd imagine with its vaulted ceiling. Enjoy an alfresco full breakfast every morning on the verdant deck. **Pros:** central location in the middle of Dunmore Town, historical house, peaceful garden. **Cons:** not on the beach, limited hotel services. ⊠ *Dunmore St.* ☎ *242/333–2201* ⊕ *www.bahamahouseinn.com* ⇆ *7 rooms* ⚘ *In-room: no TV. In-hotel: no kids under 12* ⊟ *MC, V* ⊗ *Closed July–Oct. 15* ⦿| *CP.*

$ 🏨 **Baretta's Seashell Inn.** If all you need is a clean affordable room that's close to the beach, Baretta's is the place for you. This family-run inn is right next door to the famed Pink Sands Resort and a three-minute walk down a path to the quieter north end of the beach. While the property itself might not impress at first glance with its slightly overgrown yard, its 12 rooms are spotless, surprisingly spacious, and cheerfully decorated with bright pastel bedspreads and comfortable furniture. Two mini-suites even have king-sized beds and Jacuzzi tubs in the bathrooms. The inn's restaurant is a local haunt that serves authentic Bahamian cuisine. **Pros:** well-maintained rooms, close to the beach, locally-owned business. **Cons:** no views, slightly off the beaten path, limited services. ⊠*Nesbitt St., Dunmore Town* ☏*242/333–2361* ⊕*www.barettasseashellinn.com* ▭*12 rooms* ⌂*In-hotel: restaurant bar, laundry service, public Internet* ▭*MC, V.*

☻ $ ⊡**Tingum Village Hotel.** Each of the rustic cottages on this property owned by the Percentie family, are named after different islands of the Bahamas. The native theme continues inside the lodgings, where rooms are individually decorated with simple beach furniture and tropical prints. Larger cottages are ideal for families, with king-size beds, kitchenettes, and two-person whirlpool tubs. There's no lobby to speak of since the room where you check in also doubles as the famous Ma Ruby's restaurant, but the place is full of local charm and just a short walk from the pink-sand beach. Juanita Percentie, "Ma" Ruby's enterprising daughter, also rents a luxurious and tricked-out five-bedroom beach villa nearby, complete with a romantic rooftop bedroom, gourmet kitchen, and waterfall pool with swim-up bar. **Pros:** family friendly, local flavor, Ma Ruby's restaurant. **Cons:** no frills decor and furnishings, some rooms need refurbishing, rustic grounds. ⊠*Colebrook St.* ☏*242/333–2161* ▭*12 rooms, 5 1-bedroom and 2 2-bedroom suites, 1 3-bedroom cottage* ⌂*In-hotel: restaurant, bar, public Wi-Fi* ▭*MC, V* ⍩*EP, MAP.*

NIGHTLIFE

Enjoy a brew on the wraparound patio of **Gusty's** (⊠*Coconut Grove Ave.* ☏*242/333–2165*), on Harbour Island's northern point. This lively hot spot has sand floors, a few tables, and patrons shooting pool or watching sports on satellite TV. On weekends, holidays, and in high season, it's a very crowded and happening dance spot with a DJ, especially after 10 PM.

Enter through the marine life–muraled hallway at **Seagrapes** (⊠*Colebrook and Gibson Sts.* ☏*242/333–2389*) to a large nightclub with a raised stage that's home to the local Funk Gang band. Seagrapes is usually the last stop in the local club crawl which begins at Gusty's and moves on to the Vic-Hum, before ending up here.

Vic-Hum Club (⊠*Barrack St.* ☏*242/333–2161*), owned by "Ma" Ruby Percentie's son Humphrey, occasionally hosts live Bahamian bands in a room decorated with classic record album covers; otherwise, you'll find locals playing Ping-Pong and listening and dancing to loud recorded music, from calypso to American pop and R&B. Mick Jagger and other rock stars have dropped by. Look for the largest coconut ever grown in the Bahamas—33 inches in diameter—on the bar's top shelf.

SPORTS & THE OUTDOORS

BICYCLING   Bicycles are a popular way to explore Harbour Island; rent one—or golf carts, motorboats, scooters, Jet Skis, and kayaks—at **Michael's Cycles** (⊠*Colebrooke St.* ☏*242/333–2384 or 242/464–0994*).

BOATING & FISHING There's great bonefishing right off Dunmore Town at Girl Bay. Charters cost about $150 for a half day. The Harbour Island Tourist Office can help organize bone- and bottom-fishing excursions, as can all of the major hotels.

SCUBA DIVING & SNORKELING **Current Cut,** the narrow passage between North Eleuthera and Current Island, is loaded with marine life and provides a roller-coaster ride on the currents. **Devil's Backbone,** in North Eleuthera, offers a tricky reef area with a nearly infinite number of dive sites and a large number of wrecks. **Ocean Fox Diving and Deep-sea Fishing Center** (☎242/333–2323) rents scuba equipment and offers instruction, certification, dive packages, and daily dive trips. **alentine's Dive Center** (☎242/333–2080 ⊕www.valentinesdive.com) rents and sells equipment and provides all levels of instruction, certification, dive packages, and daily group and custom dives.

> **DID YOU KNOW?**
>
> Eleuthera, and particularly Harbour Island, are famous for their pink-sand beaches, which, contrary to popular opinion, come primarily from tiny pink insects, not coral. The fine crystals, as rosy as the first blush of a ripe mango, are the crushed pink and red shells of microscopic insects, foraminifera. One of the most abundant single-cell organisms in the ocean, foraminifer live on the underside of reefs and the sea floor. After the insects die, the waves smash the shells, which wash ashore along with sand and bits of pink coral.

SHOPPING

Most small businesses on Harbour Island close for a lunch break between 1 and 3.

Bahamian Shells and Tings (✉Coconut Grove Ave., Dunmore Town ☎242/333–2839 ⊙Closed Sun.) sells islandwear, souvenirs, and crafts, many handmade on Harbour Island.

Blue Rooster (✉Dunmore St. ☎242/333–2240 ⊙Closed Sun.) is the place to go for festive party dresses, sexy swimwear, fun accessories, and exotic gifts.

Briland's Androsia (✉Bay St. ☎242/333–2342 ⊙Closed Sun.) has a unique selection of clothing, beachwear, bags, and home items handmade from the colorful batik fabric created on the island of Andros.

Dilly Dally (✉Dunmore St. ☎242/333–3109) sells Bahamian-made jewelry, maps, T-shirts, CDs, decorations, and other fun island souvenirs.

John Bull (✉Bay St. ☎242/333–2950 ⊙Closed Sun.), a duty-free shop that's part of a Nassau-based chain, sells watches, fine jewelry, perfume, cigars, and sunglasses from international brands.

Miss Mae's (✉Dunmore St., Dunmore Town ☎242/333–2002 ⊙Closed Sun.) offers an exquisite and discerningly curated collection of fashion forward clothing, accessories, and gifts from international designers and artisans.

Patricia's Fruits and Vegetables (⊠ *Pitt St., Dunmore Town* ☎ *242/333-2289* ⊗ *Closed Sun.*) is where locals go for homemade candies, jams and other Bahamian condiments. Her famous hot sauce and native thyme (sold in recycled Bacardi bottles) make memorable gifts.

Pink Sands Gift Shop (⊠ *Pink Sands Resort* ☎ *242/333–2030*) offers trendy selection of swimwear, accessories, casual clothing, and trinkets.

Princess Street Gallery (⊠ *Princess St.* ☎ *242/333–2788* ⊗ *Closed Sun.*) displays original art by local and internationally renowned artists, as well as a diverse selection of illustrated books, home accessories, and locally made crafts.

The Shop at Sip Sip (⊠ *Court Rd., Dunmore Town* ☎ *242/333–331* ⊗ *Closed Tues.*) sells its own line of T-shirts and a small but stylish selection of handmade jewelry, custom-designed totes, Bahamian straw work, and gifts found by owner Julie Lightbourn on her far-flung travels.

Sugar Mill (⊠ *Bay St.* ☎ *242/333–2173* ⊗ *Closed Sun.*) features glamorous selection of resortwear, accessories, and gifts from designers around the world.

GREGORY TOWN & ENVIRONS

The tiny pastel homes of **Gregory Town** dot a hillside that slides down to the sea. The town's annual Pineapple Festival begins on the Thursday evening of the Bahamian Labor Day weekend, at the beginning of June. With live music, juicy ripe pineapple (served every possible way), and settlement-wide merriment continuing into the wee hours, this is Gregory Town's liveliest happening, and a great time to plan your visit.

At a narrow point of the island a few miles north of Gregory Town, the ★ **Glass Window Bridge**, a slender concrete structure, links the two sea-battered bluffs that separate the Governor's Harbour and North Eleuthera districts. Sailors going south in the waters between New Providence and Eleuthera supposedly named this area the Glass Window because they could see through the narrow cavity to the Atlantic on the other side. Stop to watch the northeasterly deep-azure Atlantic swirl together under the bridge with the southwesterly turquoise Bahama Sound, producing a brilliant aquamarine froth. Artist Winslow Homer found the site stunning, and painted *Glass Window* in 1885. It's thought that the bridge was a natural span until the early 1900s, when rough current finally washed it away.

If you're too lulled by the ebb and flow of lapping waves and prefer your shores crashing with dramatic white sprays, a visit to Eleuthera's **Grottoes and Hot Tubs** will revive you. The sun warms these tidal pools—which the locals call "moon pools"—making them a markedly more temperate soak than the sometimes-chilly ocean. On most days refreshing sprays and rivulets tumble into the tubs, but on some it can turn dangerous; if the waves are crashing over the top of the cove

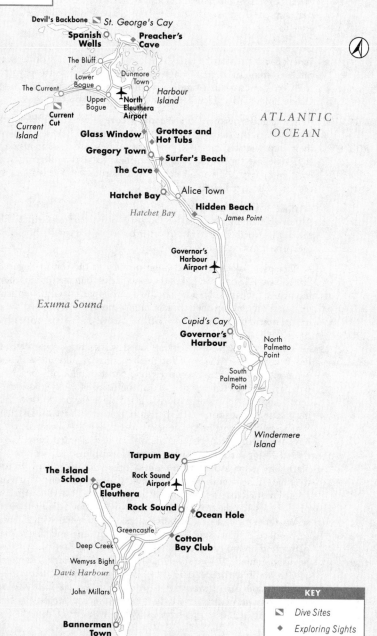

eutheria

Devil's Backbone ◿ St. George's Cay
Spanish ○   ◆ **Preacher's**
Wells   **Cave**

The Bluff ○

Lower   Dunmore
Bogue ○   Town ○
The Current ○   *Harbour*
        Upper   ✈ **North**   *Island*
        Bogue **Eleuthera**
Current □   **Airport**
Island **Current**
          Cut

Glass Window ◆   **Grottoes and**
                        Hot Tubs
Gregory Town ○ ◆ **Surfer's Beach**
    The Cave ◆
                 Alice Town
Hatchet Bay ○   ○
              Hidden Beach
Hatchet Bay   *James Point*

                Governor's
                Harbour
                Airport ✈

Exuma Sound

        Cupid's Cay
        Governor's ○
        Harbour   North
                           Palmetto
                           Point
                    South
                    Palmetto
                    Point

                        Windermere
                        Island

Tarpum Bay ○

The Island   Rock Sound
School ◆   Airport ✈
    ○ **Cape**
    Eleuthera
        Rock Sound ○ ◆ **Ocean Hole**
    Greencastle
              ◆ **Cotton**
Deep Creek ○   **Bay Club**
Wemyss Bight ○
Davis Harbour
John Millars ○

Bannerman
Town

KEY
◿ *Dive Sites*
◆ *Exploring Sights*

ATLANTIC
OCEAN

0 _____ 10 miles
0 _____ 15 km

centerpiece mesa, pick another day to stop here. If you're driving from Gregory Town, the entrance is approximately 5 mi north on the right (Atlantic) side of the Queen's Highway, across the road from two thin tree stumps. If you reach the one-lane Glass Window Bridge, you've gone too far.

Gregory Town's claim to fame lies about 2½ mi south of town, where ★ **Surfer's Beach,** the site of a funky shack from the 1960s, still draws wave catchers from December through May. If you don't have a jeep, you can walk the ¾ mi to this Atlantic-side beach—follow rough-and-bumpy Ocean Boulevard at Eleuthera Island Shores just south of town.

EN ROUTE At the island's northern tip, **Preacher's Cave** is where the Eleutheran Adventurers (the island's founders) took refuge and held services when their ship wrecked in 1648. Note the original stone altar inside the cave. The last 2 mi of the road to Preacher's Cave is a hilly, rocky, dirt road, but passable if you go slowly. Across from the cave is a long succession of deserted pink-sand beaches.

WHERE TO EAT & STAY

Although Bahamians consider Gregory Town part of Central Eleuthera, the North Eleuthera airport is closer to the town's hotels than the airport in Governor's Harbour.

¢ ✕ **Thompson Bakery.** Located appropriately at the top of Sugar Hill Street, Daisy Thompson bakes the island's best banana muffins, cinnamon rolls, pineapple bread, pizza, and pineapple, coconut, and lemon tarts in a tiny hilltop enclave. Her family reputedly developed the recipe for pineapple rum. ⊠ *Sugar Hill St.* ☎ *242/335–5053* ▭ *No credit cards* ⊘ *Closed Sun.*

♻ $$ ✕▦ **The Cove Eleuthera.** Thirty secluded acres dotted with charming
Fodor's Choice beach cottages set the tone for this relaxing island escape. A rocky
★ promontory separates two coves: one has a small sandy beach with palapas, lounge chairs, and kayaks, the other is rocky and ideal for snorkeling. The poolside patio is a good place for breakfast or relaxing cocktails, but sitting at the bar and chatting with resident bartender Wallace will become one of your favorite activities. Clustered cottages have ocean or garden views, tile floors, high slanted ceilings, 600 thread-count sheets, and white rattan furnishings. MP3 players and alarm clocks are available on request (otherwise the point is to forget the time). Take in both the sunrise and the sunset from one of two suites in the Point House; it's built on the promontory with a 180-degree view of the coves and the sea. The spacious, window-lined dining room ($$) serves three meals a day, blending classic Continental with Bahamian to produce delights such as lobster tail with lime and thyme beurre blanc, and potato-crusted sea bass. Order the key lime pie, you won't be disappointed. ⊠ *3 mi south of Glass Window Bridge, 1½ mi north of Gregory Town* ☎ *242/335–5142 or 800/552–5960* ⊕ *www.thecove eleuthera.com* ⇆ *12 rooms, 8 1-bedroom suites, 2 2-bedroom suites* ♿ *In-room: no phone, no TV. In-hotel: restaurant, bar, tennis court, pool, diving, water sports, bicycles, public Wi-Fi* ▭ *D, MC, V.*

NIGHTLIFE

★ **Elvina's Bar and Restaurant** (✉ *Queens Hwy.* ☎ *242/335–5032*) is a favorite with locals and tourists alike. Walls are covered with license plates and bumper stickers, there's a pool table for friendly competition, and the surfboards hanging from the ceiling have been stowed there by surfer regulars. Elvina's husband, known around these parts as "Chicken Ed," is from Louisiana, and the jambalaya here is the real thing, so come hungry. There's karaoke on Tuesday and Friday nights (which are the big party nights at this establishment), where the place really gets hopping after 9 PM. Lenny Kravitz, who owns a home nearby, may show up with friends such as Denzel Washington in tow.

SPORTS & THE OUTDOORS

SURFING In Gregory Town, stop by **Rebecca's** (☎ *242/335–5436*), a general store and crafts shop, where local surf guru "Ponytail Pete" stocks a few supplies and sometimes posts a chalkboard listing surf conditions and tidal reports.

Snorkelers and divers will want to spend some time at **Goulding's Cay** beach, 3 mi north of Gregory Town. Swim out to the tiny offshore island to witness a concentration of sea anemones so spectacular it dazzled even Jacques Cousteau's biologists (it's as if someone laid down a carpet). Goulding's Cay is also a nice 1,500-foot shelling stretch for beachcombers.

SHOPPING

Island Made Shop (✉ *Queen's Hwy.* ☎ *242/335–5369*), run by Pam and Greg Thompson, is a good place to shop for Bahamian arts and crafts, including Androsia batik (made on Andros Island), driftwood paintings, Abaco ceramics, and prints. Look for the old foam buoys which have been carved and painted into fun faces.

TCHET BAY & ENVIRONS

Hatchet Bay has mid-Eleuthera's only marina. Be sure to notice the names of the town's side roads, which have such colorful designations as Lazy Road, Happy Hill Road, and Smile Lane. Just south of town, the Rainbow Inn and Restaurant is the hub of activity for this stretch of the island.

North of Hatchet Bay lies **The Cave,** a subterranean, bat-populated tunnel complete with stalagmites and stalactites. Pirates supposedly once used it to hide their loot. An underground path leads for more than a mile to the sea, ending in a lofty, cathedral-like cavern. Within its depths, fish swim in total darkness. The adventurous may wish to explore this area with a flashlight (follow the length of guide string along the cavern's floor), but it's best to inquire first at one of the local stores or the Rainbow Inn for a guide. To find the cave, drive north from Hatchet Bay and watch for the vine-covered silo on Queen's Highway's north side. Take the left turn soon thereafter, marked by a white stripe down the center of Queen's Highway. En route to the Cave is Sweeting's Pond, the focus of all sorts of local myths. Some claim there are Loch Ness–like creatures living in it. Others believe that wrecked plane lies on the bottom.

WHERE TO EAT & STAY

★ $ ✕🏠 **Rainbow Inn.** Immaculate, generously sized cabins—all with larg private porches—have sweeping views of the water and passing fer ries. The restaurant is one of the island's best, with a classy but no-fus atmosphere and exhibition windows that face gorgeous sunsets. Island ers drive great distances for a meal here, especially when the fame Dr. Seabreeze strums away and sings island tunes on rib night (Tues day) and steak night (Thursday). The Nautical Bar, hung with authen tic ships' wheels salvaged from wrecks, attracts British and America expats as well as locals. Nurse Goombay Smashes as long as you like American co-owner "Krabby" Ken won't be bashful about letting yo know when it's time to leave. A beautiful beach is a long walk dow the paved road; better rent a car for your stay. ⊠ 2½ mi south o Hatchet Bay ☎242/335–0294 or 800/688–0047 ⊕ www.rainbowinn com ⇆4 apartments, 2 2-bedroom villas, 1 3-bedroom villa ⌕ In room: no phone, kitchen. In-hotel: restaurant, bar, tennis court, po ☐ MC, V ☺ Closed Sept.–Nov. 15 ⦿ EP, MAP.

NIGHTLIFE

The debonair **Dr. Seabreeze**—a friend of Lenny Kravitz—strums h acoustic guitar while singing island songs Tuesday and Thursday nigh at the Rainbow Inn and Wednesday and Friday nights at Unique Vi lage. To be sure you don't miss him, check with the resorts beforehar to confirm his schedule.

GOVERNOR'S HARBOUR

Governor's Harbour is Eleuthera's largest settlement. But don't let th fool you, the pace is still slow here, with two banks, a few groce stores, and a handful of small restaurants and lodging options. Son of the island's wealthiest residents live in this pretty Victorian tow looped around the harbor. If you're here when the mail boats M/ *Bahamas Daybreak III* and M/V *Eleuthera Express* chug in, you witness the sight of residents unloading cars, mattresses, lumber, ma stacks of vegetables, and other household necessities. You might al see the same Eleutherans loading their own vegetables for export Nassau. While they're here, they'll stop in at their mailboxes at t small post office in the town's pink government building.

If you're cooking during your stay, note that the Governor's Harbo waterfront is a great place to buy fresh fish and conch.

WHERE TO EAT

$$ ✕ **Mate & Jenny's Restaurant & Bar.** A few miles south of Governor's Ha bour, this casual neighborhood restaurant specializes in pizza. Try o topped with conch. Sandwiches, Bahamian specialties, and ice-crea sundaes are also served. The walls are painted with tropical suns scenes and decorated with photos and random memorabilia, and t jukebox and pool table add to the joint's local color. Pizza pie pric

range from $10 to $25, depending on the toppings. ⊠*S. Palmetto Point* ☎*242/332–1504* ▭*MC, V* ⊗*Closed Tues.*

$ ✕ **Buccaneer Club.** On a hillside overlooking the town and the harbor, this mid-19th-century farmhouse is now an atmospheric restaurant serving breakfast and lunch, with an outdoor dining area surrounded by a garden of bougainvillea, hibiscus, and coconut palm. The beach is a leisurely five-minute stroll away, and the harbor, where you can also swim, is within shouting distance. Sample such native specialties as grouper, conch, and crawfish. ⊠*Haynes Ave.* ☎*242/332–2000* ▭*D, MC, V* ⊗*Closed Sun. No dinner.*

$ ✕ **Tippy's.** Despite its barefoot-casual atmosphere (old window shutters used as tabletops, sand in the floor's crevices), the menu at this open-air beach bistro is a sophisticated mix of Bahamian and European, with a menu that changes daily based on the fresh local products available. Expect things like lobster salad, specialty pizzas, and fresh fish prepared with some sort of delectable twist. This place may look like a beach shack, but everything has been well planned—they even imported an Italian chef to satisfy discriminating palates. Try to grab a table on the outdoor deck, which has a fantastic view of the beach. Locals and visitors keep this place hoping year-round. ⊠*S. Palmetto Pt.* ☎*242/332–3331* ▭*No credit cards* ⊗*Closed Mon. Closed Oct.*

Fodor'sChoice ★

WHERE TO STAY

★ $$ 🏨 **Pineapple Fields.** Set back on 80 acres of manicured wilderness, and across the street from a pink-sand Atlantic beach, Pineapple Fields is the perfect base for a disappearing act. Hole up in one of 32 condo units, each with front and back verandas, a full kitchen, and a living room with pull out queen sofa. Washers and dryers in each unit are especially handy for families and visitors who aren't planning to leave any time soon. Guests love Tippy's, the beach bistro across the street that serves a changing menu of sophisticated European-influenced fare. A 30-acre, multi-million dollar botanical garden is being planned on site in conjunction with the Bahamas National Trust. The first phase is set to open in January 2009. When you've had enough seclusion, Governor's Harbour, Eleuthera's largest town, is just a couple of miles down the road. ⊠*Banks Road* ☎*242/332–2221 or 877/677–9539* ⊕*www.pineapplefields.com* ⌁*32 condo units* ☖*In-room: safe, kitchen, refrigerator, DVD, VCR, Wi-Fi. In-hotel: 2 restaurants, bar, tennis court, pool, beachfront, diving, water sports, bicycles, children's programs (ages 6–18), laundry facilities, public Wi-Fi, parking (no fee), some pets allowed, no-smoking rooms* ▭*MC, V.*

$ 🏨 **Duck Inn and Orchid Gardens.** Facing west into the sunset, overlooking beautiful Governor's Harbour, two colonial cottages and a two-story home built in the 1850s are surrounded by a tropical garden with a world-class orchid collection. John and Kay Duckworth bought the compound from a Canadian timber baron and restyled the houses. With one bedroom each, the cottages are perfect for couples, whereas the four-bedroom, two-bath house can sleep eight. Each dwelling has a full kitchen (there are grocery stores just a block away) and a veranda. A full-time gardener tends to tropical fruit trees including plums, papayas, figs, dates, and carambolas; guests are welcome to pick and eat.

⊠*Queen's Hwy.* ☎*242/332–2608* ⊕*www.theduckinn.com* ⇨*2 cottages, 1 house* ⑃*In-room: kitchen* ⊟*MC, V.*

$ ▦**Laughing Bird Apartments.** Jean Davies and her son Pierre own these four tidy apartments on an acre of land at the water's edge. Linens and crockery (including an English teapot and china cups) are furnished. You can stock your kitchen with produce from local stores or dine at any of the four restaurants within walking distance. This is a quiet, on-your-own kind of place, where relaxing and fishing are the name of the game. ⊠*Off Queen's Hwy.* ☎*242/332–2012* 🖷*242/332–2358* ⇨*4 apartments* ⑃*In-room: kitchen. In-hotel: beachfront* ⊟*D, MC, V.*

$ ▦**Quality Cigatoo Inn.** Surrounded by a white picket fence, this resort sits high on a hill next to other gracious 19th-century mansions overlooking Governor's Harbour. It has crisp white buildings trimmed in vibrant hues with indoor and outdoor tropical gardens. Rooms are decorated in an island theme and have private patios or balconies. The resort is a 15-minute walk from a pink-sand beach. The Cigatoo Room restaurant is popular and specializes in Bahamian and Chinese cuisine. The guest services department arranges bonefishing or deep-sea fishing trips, day trips to other islands, and car or bike rentals. ⊠*Queen's Hwy.* ☎*242/332–3060* ⊕*www.choicehotels.com* ⇨*22 rooms* ⑃*In-hotel: restaurant, bar, tennis courts, pool, public Wi-Fi* ⊟*MC, V.*

$ ▦**Unique Village.** Just south of Governor's Harbour near North Palmetto Point, this resort has large, tile-floor rooms. The round restaurant, with its pagoda-style natural-wood ceiling, wraparound covered deck, and panoramic view of the beach, makes this restaurant-bar a popular spot for locals and visitors. Try the Caesar salad or any of the seafood specialties, especially the substantial lobster salad. The small bar has satellite TV and high captain's chairs. The resort also organizes deep-sea fishing trips. ⊠*Resorts Drive, off of Queen's Hwy.* ☎*242/332–1830* ⊕*www.uniquevillage.com* ⇨ *10 rooms, 2 2-bedroom villas, 2 1-bedroom villas* ⑃*In-room: kitchen (some). In-hotel: restaurant, bar, beachfront, water sports, public Wi-Fi* ⊟*MC, V.*

SPORTS & THE OUTDOORS

SNORKELING If you have a four-wheel-drive vehicle, take the road east at the settlement of James Cistern to reach James Point, a beautiful beach with snorkeling and 3- to 10-foot waves for surfers. About 4 mi north of James Cistern on the Atlantic side, take the rough-hewn steps down to **Hidden Beach**, a sandy little hideaway sheltered by a rock-formation canopy, affording maximum privacy. It's also a great spot for novice snorkelers.

EN ROUTE About halfway between Rock Sound and Governor's Harbour, distinguished **Windermere Island** is the site of vacation homes of the rich and famous, including members of the British royal family. Don't plan on any drive-by ogling of these million-dollar homes, though; the security gate prevents sightseers from passing.

ROCK SOUND

One of Eleuthera's largest settlements, the village of **Rock Sound** has a small airport serving the island's southern part. **Front Street,** the main thoroughfare, runs along the seashore, where fishing boats are tied up. If you walk down the street, you'll eventually come to the pretty, whitewashed **St. Luke's Anglican Church,** a contrast to the deep blue and green houses nearby, with their colorful gardens full of poinsettia, hibiscus, and marigolds. If you pass the church on a Sunday, you'll surely hear fervent hymn singing through the open windows. Rock Sound has the island's largest supermarket shopping center, where locals stock up on groceries

> **LEARNING IN PARADISE**
>
> Tucked away at the tip of Cape Eleuthera is the Island School, a pioneering high school that's a model of sustainability—students and teachers work together to run a campus where rainwater is captured for use, solar and wind energy is harnessed, food comes from their own small farm and waste water is filtered and re-used to irrigate landscaping. This "mind, body, and spirit experience" aims to inspire students to be responsible, caring global citizens. Powell Pointe Resort offers special school tours to their guests.

and supplies. The extravagant Cotton Bay Club, complete with golf course and restaurants, will add some glitz to the area. At this writing, the resort is slated to open in late 2009.

Ocean Hole, a large inland saltwater lake a mile southeast of Rock Sound, is connected by tunnels to the sea. Steps have been cut into the coral on the shore so visitors can climb down to the lake's edge. Bring a piece of bread or some fries and watch the fish emerge for their hors d'oeuvres, swimming their way in from the sea. The hole had been estimated to be more than 100 fathoms (600 feet) deep, but, in fact, its depth was measured by a local diver at about 75 feet. He reports that there are a couple of cars at the bottom, too.

CAPE ELEUTHERA

Home to the new megaresort/marina Powell Pointe, **Cape Eleuthera** is the ultimate secluded resort getaway, with not much to do besides embark in aqua adventures and relax.

WHERE TO STAY

$$$$
Fodor'sChoice
★

Powell Pointe Resort at Cape Eleuthera. How many times can you say wow in one vacation? Let us count the ways at Powell Pointe Resort at Cape Eleuthera, opened in May 2007. Nestled between the aquamarine and emerald waters of Rock and Exuma Sounds, gigantic town homes feature two bright bedrooms, each with full bath, and a stainless-steel kitchen. Watch breathtaking sunsets painted over the full service marina from your second-floor balcony, or from the Starbucks-inspired coffee shop's veranda, which turns into a wine bar at night. By day, explore the resort's 18-mi-long shoreline, which is home to more than 20 beaches. For a unique experience, have the staff take you by boat to one of the five nearby, footprint-free islands for the day. Pack a picnic and your seashell bucket and get ready for complete solitude. ⊠ *Cape Eleuthera* ☎ *242/422–9977* ⊕ *www.capeeleuthera. com* ⇨ *19 townhomes* ⟂ *In-room: kitchen, refrigerator, DVD, Wi-Fi. In-hotel: 2 restaurants, diving, water sports, bicycles, children's pro-grams, laundry facilities, public Wi-Fi, parking (no fee), no-smoking rooms* ⊟ *AE, MC, V.*

BANNERMAN TOWN

The tiny settlement of **Banner-man Town** (population 40) is at the island's southern tip, which is punctuated by an old cliff-top light-house. From Eleuthera's north end (near Preacher's Cave), it's about a three-hour drive down the Queen's Highway. The pink-sand beach here is gorgeous, and on a clear day you can see the Bahamas' highest point, Mt. Alvernia (elevation 206 feet), on distant Cat Island. The town lies about 30 mi from the **Cotton Bay Club,** past the quiet little fishing villages of **Wemyss Bight** (named after Lord Gordon Wemyss, a 17th-century Scottish slave owner) and **John Millars** (population 15), barely touched over the years.

> ### A SWINGING TIME
>
> In Eleuthera, the game that brings the crowds is fast-pitch softball. The Eleuthera Twin City Destroyers were the men's champions of the 2006 Bahamas Softball Federa-tion tournament. On most any weekend afternoon from March to November, you can find the team playing at Rock Sound or Palmetto baseball parks on the island, known as the Softball Capital of the Bahamas. Eleuthera pitchers and brothers Edney and Edmond Bethel are both players for the Bahamas National Team, which has been consistently in the top 10 in the world.

WHERE TO EAT

$ ✕ **Sammy's Place.** This spotless stop is owned by Sammy Culmer and managed by his friendly daughter Margarita. It serves conch fritters, fried chicken and fish, and peas 'n' rice. When it's available in season, don't miss the guava duff, sweet bread with swirls of creamy guava, for dessert. It's open 7:30 AM–10 PM daily, even on Sunday, when many other restaurants are closed. ⊠ *Albury La.* ☎ *242/334–2121* ⊟ *D.*

SHOPPING

Island Made at the Almond Tree (⊠ *Queen's Hwy.* ☎ *242/334–2385* ⊙ *Closed Sun.*) is a blue house with yellow trim. Inside, the quaint gift shop has a collection of handmade gifts, jewelry, and straw baskets. The landscape paintings on driftwood are big sellers.

ELEUTHERA ESSENTIALS

To research prices, get advice from other travelers, and book travel arrangements, visit ⊕ *www.fodors.com.*

RANSPORTATION

BY AIR

Eleuthera has three airports: North Eleuthera; Governor's Harbour, near the center of the island; and Rock Sound, in the southern part of the island. Head for the one closest to your hotel. Fly into Governor's Harbour if you're staying south of Gregory Town, and into North Eleuthera if you're staying in Gregory Town or to the north. Several North American carriers and national airlines fly to each of the airports.

Bahamasair has daily service from Nassau to all three airports. Cherokee Air offers chartered flights from Marsh Harbour in the Abacos to North Eleuthera. Lynx Air flies direct from Fort Lauderdale to Governor's Harbour Friday through Monday, and to North Eleuthera Thursday through Sunday. Southern Air flies charters three times daily from Nassau to North Eleuthera and Governor's Harbour. Continental Connection through United Airlines have daily flights to North Eleuthera from Miami and Fort Lauderdale. Continental also flies nonstop from Fort Lauderdale to Governor's Harbour. Twin Air flies daily from Fort Lauderdale to Governor's Harbour, Rock Sound, and North Eleuthera. Yellow Air Taxi flies on demand from Fort Lauderdale to North Eleuthera and Governor's Harbour.

Airlines & Contacts **Bahamasair** (☎ 800/222–4262). **Cherokee Air** (☎ 242/367–3450). **Continental Connection** (☎ 800/231–0856). **Lynx Air** (☎ 888/596–9247). **Southern Air** (☎ 242/323–6833, 242/335–1720 Governor's Harbour, 242/354–2035 North Eleuthera). **Twin Air** (☎ 954/359–8266). **Yellow Air Taxi** (☎ 888/935–5694).

Airport Information **Governor's Harbour** (☎ 242/332–2321). **North Eleuthera** (☎ 242/335–1242). **Rock Sound** (☎ 242/334–2177).

BY BOAT

Mail boats leave from Nassau at Potter's Cay; for schedules, contact the Dockmaster's Office at Potter's Cay, Nassau.

M/V *Current Pride* sails to the Current, Lower Bogue, Upper Bogue, and Hatchet Bay on Thursday, returning Tuesday. M/V *Bahamas Daybreak III* leaves on Monday for South Eleuthera, stopping at Rock Sound, and returns on Tuesday. It then leaves Thursday from Nassau for the Bluff and Harbour Island, returning on Sunday. The *Eleuthera Express* sails for Governor's Harbour and Spanish Wells on Monday and Thursday, returning to Nassau on Tuesday and Sunday, respectively. The fare is $30 for all Eleutheran destinations, and travel time is 5 hours each way.

Bahamas Ferries connects Nassau to Harbour Island, Governor's Harbour, and Spanish Wells daily. A round-trip fare costs $110; excursion rates (including a tour, refreshments, and a trip to the beach) are somewhat higher. The trip from Bahamas Ferries terminal on Potter's Cay, Nassau to Harbour Island, with a stop on Spanish Wells, takes two hours. Ferries leave Nassau at 8 AM and return at 3:55 (2 on Sunday). Call to confirm departure times and rates; on busy days, an extra trip is sometimes added. Make reservations well in advance for trips around Columbus Day, the weekend of the annual North Eleuthera Regatta.

Boat & Ferry Information **Bahamas Ferries** (☎ *242/323–2166* ⊕ *www.bahamasferries.com*). **Dockmaster's Office** (☎ *242/393–1064*).

BY CAR

Visiting Eleuthera's main sights will require renting a car. North to south is about a three-hour drive. Governor's Harbour, which lies approximately at Eleuthera's midpoint, is a 40-minute drive from Glass Window in the north, and a 35-minute drive from Rock Sound in the south. You can also rent a bike or scooter to explore the island. On Harbour Island and Spanish Wells, you're better off renting a golf cart.

Arranging a car rental through your hotel will most likely be your least complicated option. You can usually have a vehicle delivered to you at the airport. Daily rentals run about $70. Request a four-wheel-drive if you plan to visit Preacher's Cave or Surfer's Beach.

Local Agencies **Baretta's** (✉ *Harbour Island* ☎ *242/333–2361*). **Dingle Motor Service on Eleuthera** (✉ *Rock Sound* ☎ *242/334–2031*). **Gardiner's Automobile Rentals on Eleuthera** (✉ *Governor's Harbour* ☎ *242/332–2665*). **Hilton's Car Rentals on Eleuthera** (✉ *Governor's Harbour* ☎ *242/335–6241*). **Stanton Cooper on Eleuthera** (✉ *Governor's Harbour* ☎ *242/359–7007 or 242/332–1620*).

BY GOLF CART

Even if you're a big walker, you'll want a golf cart if you spend more than a couple of days on Harbour Island; there are several golf-cart rental companies there. Cart rates start at $50 a day for a four-seater and go up according to size (a six-seater is the largest); definitely negotiate if you'll be renting for longer. You can rent a cart directly at the dock.

Contacts **Abner's Rentals** (☎ *242/333–4890*). **Baretta's** (☎ *242/333–2361*). **Dunmore Rentals** (☎ *242/333–2372*). **Johnson's Rentals** (☎ *242/333–2376*). **Ross's Garage** (☎ *242/333–2122*). **Reggie's Golf Carts** (☎ *242/333–2116*). **Sunshine Carts** (☎ *242/333–2509*).

BY TAXI

Taxis are available through your hotel. On Eleuthera, have your hotel call for a taxi about a half hour before you need it. On Harbour Island, taxis generally arrive a few minutes after being called. Taxis are almost always waiting at the North Eleuthera and Harbour Island water taxi docks.

Taxis also wait for incoming flights at all three airports. If you land at North Eleuthera and need to get to Harbour Island, off Eleuthera's north coast, take a taxi ($5 per passenge) to the Three Island ferry dock, a water taxi ($5 per passenger) to Harbour Island, and, on the other side, another taxi. Follow a similar procedure to get to Spanish Wells, also off Eleuthera's north shore, at Gene's Bay ($7 round trip). Taxi service from Governor's Harbour Airport to the Cove Eleuthera is $42 for two people, though the taxi fare from North Eleuthera to the Cove is only $27 for two people. The fare from Governor's Harbour to Pineapple Fields is $26.50, and from Rock Sound airport to Powell Pointe resort in Cape Eleuthera, the fare is $48.75.

⟩NTACTS & RESOURCES

BANKS & EXCHANGE SERVICES

Banks on Eleuthera and its islands are open Monday through Thursday from 9:30 to 3, Friday from 9:30 to 4:30. First Caribbean International Bank has a branch in Governor's Harbour. Royal Bank of Canada runs Harbour Island's only bank, in addition to branches in Governor's Harbour and Spanish Wells. Scotiabank has branches in North Eleuthera and Rock Sound.

Contacts **First Caribbean International Bank** (☎ *242/332–2300*). **Royal Bank of Canada** (☎ *242/333–2250 Harbour Island, 242/332–2856 Governor's Harbour, 242/333–4131 Spanish Wells*). **Scotiabank** (☎ *242/335–1400 North Eleuthera, 242/334–2620 Rock Sound*).

EMERGENCIES

Governor's Harbour, Harbour Island, Rock Sound, and Spanish Wells each have their own police and medical emergency numbers.

Contacts **Medical Clinics** (☎ *242/332–2774 Governor's Harbour, 242/333–2227 Harbour Island, 242/334–2226 Rock Sound, 242/333–4064 Spanish Wells*). **Police** (☎ *242/332–2111 Governor's Harbour, 242/335–5322 Gregory Town, 242/333–2111 Harbour Island, 242/334–2244 Rock Sound*).

SIGHTSEEING GUIDES

Arthur Nixon is probably the most knowledgeable authority on Eleuthera. His presentation will make you want to stand up and applaud. Tell him how much time you have and where you want to go, and he'll take you there, telling stories en route.

Contact **Arthur Nixon** (☎ *242/332–2052 or 242/359–7879*).

VISITOR INFORMATION

Contact the Eleuthera Tourist Office in Governor's Harbour or the Harbour Island Tourist Office on Dunmore Street for brochures and information about the islands. Both are open weekdays 9–5. Visit the Bahamas Ministry of Tourism Web site and the Out-Islands Promotion Board's site for additional information.

Tourist Information **Bahamas Ministry of Tourism** (☎ *242/302–2000 or 800/224–2627* ⊕ *www.bahamas.com*). **Eleuthera Tourist Office** (✉ *Governor's Harbour* ☎ *242/332–2142* 🖷 *242/332–2480*). **Harbour Island Tourist Office** (✉ *Dunmore St.* ☎ *242/333–2621* 🖷 *242/333–2622*). **Out-Islands Promotion Board** (☎ *800/688–4752* ⊕ *www.myoutislands.com*).

THE EXUMAS

LITTLE EXUMA & GREAT EXUMA

★ The old village of **Williams Town** lies at Little Exuma Island's southern tip. Out here, you can see salt raking at certain times of the year, and wild cotton still grows along the way to the picturesque hilltop ruins of the **Hermitage,** a former plantation house. Ask for directions to Pelican's Bay, down an unmarked gravel road north of town. Besides finding a romantic, secluded beach, you can step across a line marking the Tropic of Cancer.

★ At the juncture of Great and Little Exuma, a one-lane bridge crosses the short pass to **The Ferry,** Little Exuma's earliest settlement. The town holds the island's smallest church—St. Christopher's Anglican, built for one family's use—pretty gardens, and the home of the "Shark Lady," Gloria Patience, the now-deceased legendary shark hunter of Exuma. On the Great Exuma side, you can see the remains of the historic ferry landing. The bridge replaced the ferry in 1966 and is a great fishing spot.

Rolle Town, a typical Exuma village devoid of tourist trappings, sits atop a hill overlooking the ocean, 5 mi south of George Town. Some of the buildings are 100 years old, and three tombs off the main road date back to the Loyalists.

Although **George Town** is the island's hive of activity, it's still on the no-need-for-a-traffic-light scale. The most imposing structure here is in the town center—the white-pillared, sandy pink, colonial-style **Government Administration Building,** modeled on Nassau's Government House and containing the commissioner's office, police headquarters, courts, and a jail. Atop a hill across from the government building is the whitewashed **St. Andrew's Anglican Church,** originally built around 1802 and renovated in 1991. Behind the church is the small, sea-fed Lake Victoria. A leisurely stroll around town will take you past a straw market and a few shops. You can buy fruit and vegetables and bargain with fishermen for some of the day's catch at the **Government Dock,** where the mail boat comes in. The wharf is close to **Regatta Point** (☎242/336–2206), an attractive guesthouse named after the annual Family Islands Regatta that curls around Kidd Cove, where the 18th-century pirate Captain Kidd supposedly tied up.

★ **Fish Fry** is the name given to a jumble of one-room beachside structures about 2 mi north of George Town, favored by locals for made-to-order fish and barbecue; there's even a sports bar with TVs in each corner. Some shacks are open weekends only, but most are open nightly until 11 PM or midnight.

★ Slightly more than a mile off George Town's shore lies **Stocking Island.** The 4-mi-long island has only 10 inhabitants, a gorgeous white beach rich in seashells and popular with surfers, and plenty of good snorkeling sites. Jacques Cousteau's team is said to have traveled some 1,700 feet into **Mystery Cave,** a blue-hole grotto 70 feet beneath the island.

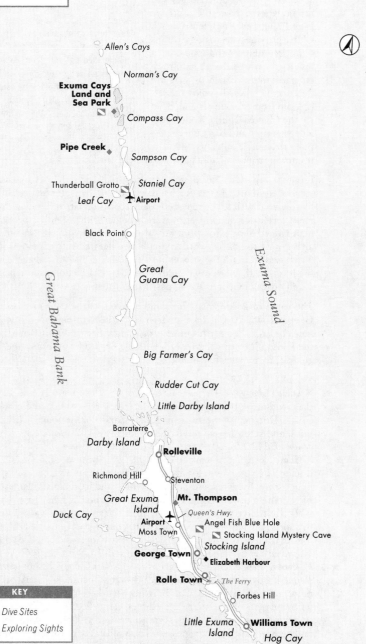

The Exumas

0   20 miles

0   30 km

Allen's Cays

Norman's Cay

**Exuma Cays
Land and
Sea Park**

Compass Cay

Pipe Creek

Sampson Cay

Thunderball Grotto   *Staniel Cay*

Leaf Cay   ✈ **Airport**

Black Point

*Great
Guana Cay*

Exuma Sound

Great Bahama Bank

Big Farmer's Cay

Rudder Cut Cay

Little Darby Island

Barraterre

Darby Island   **Rolleville**

Richmond Hill   Steventon

*Great Exuma
Island*   **Mt. Thompson**

Duck Cay   *Queen's Hwy.*

Airport   Angel Fish Blue Hole

Moss Town   Stocking Island Mystery Cave

George Town   *Stocking Island*

◆ **Elizabeth Harbour**

Rolle Town   *The Ferry*

Forbes Hill

*Little Exuma
Island*   **Williams Town**

Hog Cay

KEY

Dive Sites

Exploring Sights

Club Peace & Plenty's ferry runs over to Stocking Island twice daily at 10 AM and 1 PM and charges $10 for nonguests. Near the Stocking Island pier, **Peace & Plenty Beach Club** provides changing rooms (with plumbing) and operates a lunch spot where Dora's hamburgers and famous conch burgers are the eats of choice. To enjoy the setting sun from Stocking Island, head for the **Chat & Chill,** a lively open-air restaurant and bar right on the point (reachable only by boat). The restaurant picks up guests at Government Dock.

> **DID YOU KNOW?**
>
> Legend has it that Mt. Thompson's Three Sisters Rocks were formed when three sisters, all unwittingly in love with the same English sailor, waded out into deep water upon his departure, drowned, and turned into stone. If you look carefully next to each "sister," you'll see smaller boulders—the children the fickle sailor left them with.

From the top of **Mt. Thompson,** rising from the beach, there is a pleasing view of the **Three Sisters Rocks** jutting above the water just offshore. During your walks, you may glimpse peacocks on Great Exuma. Originally, a peacock and a peahen were brought to the island as pets by a man named Shorty Johnson, but when he left to work in Nassau, he abandoned the birds, who gradually proliferated into a colony. The birds used to roam the streets but development has forced them into the bush, so they are rarer sights these days. Mt. Thompson is about 12 mi north of George Town, past Moss Town.

The town of **Rolleville** sits on a hill above a harbor, 20 mi north of George Town. Its old slave quarters have been transformed into livable cottages. The town's most prominent citizen, Kermit Rolle, runs the **Hilltop Tavern** (☎242/345–6006), a seafood restaurant and bar guarded by an ancient cannon.

WHERE TO EAT

$$ ✕ **Eddie's Edgewater.** The specialty at this popular spot is turtle steak, but the menu also offers fried chicken, lobster, T-bone steak, and cracked conch. Don't miss the rake 'n' scrape band on Monday; washtubs, saws, and screwdrivers serve as instruments. ⊠*Charlotte St., George Town* ☎*242/336–2050* ▭*AE, MC, V* ⊙*Closed Sun.*

★ $$ ✕ **Sam's Place.** If you want to dine where the locals do, hit Sam's. Proprietor Sam Gray owns a complex of businesses in town, including the liquor store. Breakfast is especially favored and Exumians call ahead to see whether the day's menu includes stew fish, boil fish, or souse. Those who don't have time to sit down at the clean, modern café—which overlooks the bay—line up for takeout. Dinner selections are typical—lobster (called "crawfish" here), steak, lamb chops, and cracked conch. ⊠*Queen's Hwy., George Town* ☎*242/336–2579* ▭*AE, MC, V.*

★ $ ✕ **Chat & Chill.** Yacht folks, locals, and visitors alike rub shoulders at Kenneth Bowe's very hip and upscale—yet still casual—eatery on the point at Stocking Island. You may hear locals refer to it as KB's, for its owner. All of the incredible edibles are grilled over an open fire. Awesome conch burgers with secret spices and grilled fish with onions and potatoes are not to be missed. The Sunday pig roasts are fabulous.

You can get here only by boat, but transportation is provided from the Government Dock. Since there's no phone, contact Chat & Chill via VHF 16. ⊠ *Stocking Island, George Town* ☎ *No phone* ▭ *No credit cards.*

HERE'S WHERE

Ask anyone where to find the best conch fritters in the Exumas, and invariably you'll hear Santana's Grill, a little stand on the water in Williams Town.

$ ✕ **Iva Bowe's Central Highway Inn.** About 10 mi from George Town, close to the airport, this casual lunch and dinner spot has an island-wide reputation for having the best native food. Try one of the delectable shrimp dishes—coconut beer shrimp, spicy Cajun shrimp, or scampi, all for around $15. ⊠ *Queen's Hwy., Ramsey 9* ☎ *242/345–7014* ▭ *No credit cards* ⊙ *Closed Sun.*

★ ¢ ✕ **Arlean's Meal on Wheel.** A bright-yellow former school bus is now a tiny, spotless kitchen on wheels. Noted for its 'dogs, divine lobster burger, and the "MacJean," a hearty breakfast sandwich with sausage or bacon and sometimes cheese on homemade Bahama bread, the dishes are all cooked in a unique "dry-fry" method (no oil). The minibus is parked every weekday from 7 to around 3 at the bottom of schoolhouse hill (a well-known landmark). ⊠ *Queen's Hwy., George Town* ☎ *No phone* ▭ *No credit cards* ⊙ *Closed weekends.*

¢ ✕ **Big D's Conch Shack.** For the freshest conch salad and the coldest beer, look for the splatter-painted seaside shack a stone's throw from the Four Seasons Emerald Bay resort, where Big D does the fishing every day. ⊠ *Queen's Hwy., Steventon* ☎ *242/358–0059* ▭ *No credit cards* ⊙ *Closed Mon.*

¢ ✕ **Towne Café.** George Town's bakery serves breakfast (especially popular on Saturday)—consider trying the "stew" fish or chicken souse—and lunches of grilled fish or seafood sandwiches with three sides. It's open until 5 PM. ⊠ *Marshall Complex, George Town* ☎ *242/336–2194* ▭ *No credit cards* ⊙ *Closed Sun. No dinner.*

WHERE TO STAY

$$$$ ▦ **February Point Resort Estates.** This gated residential community and resort has 52 villas, including privately owned homes, and 12 villas available as guest accommodations. The two-story villas painted in pastel colors have magnificent harbor views of Elizabeth Harbour, and range from two to six bedrooms. Luxuriously decorated, the villas are serviced by housekeepers every other day. Guests may use the community's fitness center, tennis courts, and infinity pool. The waterfront restaurant serves Bahamian and international cuisine. ⊠ *Queen's Hwy., George Town* ☎ *242/336–2693 or 800/726–2988* ⊕ *www.februarypoint.com* ☜ *6 homes* △ *In-room: kitchen, DVD. In-hotel: restaurant, bar, tennis courts, pool, gym, water sports, laundry facilities* ▭ *MC, V.*

♻ $$$$ ▦ **Four Seasons Resort Great Exuma at Emerald Bay.** The luxurious Four Seasons is the only full-service resort on Great Exuma Island. When it opened in 2003, it changed the island's guesthouse demeanor, causing an upswing in the upscale. The 470 acres of pristine grounds lie adjacent to a quarter mile–long strip of beach. There's an elaborate

Fodor'sChoice
★

spa with two-person treatment rooms for couples, and a casino, as well as water sports, tennis courts, the island's only golf course, and a children's area with its own pool. Guests stay in lemon-yellow colonial-style villas clustered on landscaped grounds. Rooms are decorated in rich, dark woods and rattan offset by pastel walls and sunny artwork. Each room has its own patio or balcony facing the bay. The emphasis is on service, with custom-stocked bars in each room and a 24-hour beach butler. The resort's three restaurants have Bahamian and Continental dishes,

> ### IN THE KNOW
>
> To get to know Exuma island-ers better, hook up with the **People-to-People Program** (☎242/336–2430 or 242/336–2457 ⊕www.peopletopeople.bahamas.com). The group hosts a tea the first Friday of each month where visitors can learn about bush medicine and other aspects of local life. The location changes monthly; for more information, check with your hotel or at the airport.

heavy on the seafood. The signature restaurant, Il Cielo, looks out onto the resorts grounds through gaping windows and serves fine pastas, risottos, and seafood. The newest restaurant, Ting'm, sits outdoors at the edge of one of Exuma's most gorgeous beaches. ⊠*Queen's Hwy., Farmer's Hill* ☎*242/336–6800* ⊕*www.fourseasons.com* ⬧*183 rooms, 43 suites* ⌂*In-room: safe, kitchen (some), DVD, dial-up. In-hotel: 3 restaurants, room service, bars, golf course, pools, water sports, children's programs (ages 5–12), laundry service, public Wi-Fi* ▭*AE, D, MC, V.*

★ $$$$ **Hotel Higgins Landing.** Laid out on undeveloped Stocking Island is this award-winning eco-hotel that is 100% solar powered—though everything still works when the weather's overcast. Wood cottages have louvered jalousie windows with dark-green shutters and private, spacious decks with ocean views. Interiors have antiques, queen-size beds, tile floors, and folksy Americana decor. By day, the bar is an alfresco living room where you can play checkers or darts, or read books from the hotel's library. Colorful blossoms and tropical birds abound. Rates include gourmet dinners, though be aware that it is a fixed menu, and guests with special dietary requests should enquire ahead before booking. ⊠*Stocking Island* ☎*242/357–0008* ⊕*www.higginslanding. com* ⬧*4 cottages* ⌂*In-room: kitchen. In-hotel: restaurant, bar, gym, beachfront, water sports, public Wi-Fi, no kids under 12, no-smoking rooms* ▭*MC, V* ⦿*MAP.*

$$$–$$$$ **Exuma Beach Inn.** This 16-room resort on 300 feet of narrow beach is a mile west of George Town. Under new ownership, rooms were redone in 2008with luxurious new beddings, stone-tiled floors, and newly-tiled showers with double or single vanity sinks. French doors opening onto private patios or balconies that overlook the pool and a beautiful white sand beach. Marvel at the lodge's tiered, stained-pine cathedral ceiling. ⊠*Queen's Hwy., George Town* ☎*242/336–2250 or 800/525–2210* ⊕*www.exumabeachinn.com* ⬧*16 rooms* ⌂*In-hotel: bar, pool, beachfront* ▭*AE, MC, V.*

★ ☾ ⌂ **Palm Bay Beach Club.** Palm Bay, one of George Town's most mod-
$$$–$$$$ ern accommodations, is all about light and color. The bungalows
have brightly painted, gingerbread-trim exteriors (like turquoise
with hibiscus pink) and cheerfully sunny interiors with one or two
bedrooms. There are five two-bedroom oceanfront villas, renting for
$625 per night, for those wanting to splurge. Clustered on olean-
der-lined boardwalk paths along a pretty sand beach, the indulgence
can definitely be justified. Each unit has a patio and a kitchenette or
kitchen. Kayaks and paddleboats are available at no charge to guests.
The huge circular poolside bar and patio attracts what seems like
everybody on the island for Saturday night parties with live music.
The restaurant serves coconut shrimp, conch burgers, barbecue ribs,
and a Bahamian special of the day. ⊠ *Queen's Hwy., George Town*
☎ *888/396–0606 or 242/336–2787* ⊕ *www.palmbaybeachclub.com*
⇥ *71 bungalows, 5 villas* ⌂ *In-room: safe, kitchen (some), DVD
(some). In-hotel: restaurant, bar, pool, water sports, laundry service,
public Wi-Fi* ⊟ *AE, MC, V.*

★ $$$ ⌂ **Peace & Plenty Bonefish Lodge.** The Out Islands' swankiest bonefish-
ing lodge is on a peninsula 10 mi south of George Town. Dark wood
and handsome hunter-green accents lend a gentleman's-club feel to the
bar and dining room, where photos of anglers and their catches grace
the walls; there's also a fly-tying station. The large rooms have white
rattan furnishings, louvered wooden doors, and private balconies overlooking the water. Guests will find contemplative, restful spots on the
large deck, upstairs veranda, or in a hammock on the sandy point
that juts out beyond the lodge's fish pond. The dining room is open to
outside guests for lunch and dinner six days a week (closed Tuesday);
lodge guests can opt for an all-inclusive plan or dine à la carte. Most
guests buy room-fishing packages with a three-night minimum. The
lodge has a popular new pool table, poker table, and fly-tying table.
⊠ *Queen's Hwy., Ferry* ☎ *242/345–5555* ⊕ *www.ppbonefishlodge.net*
⇥ *8 rooms* ⌂ *In-hotel: restaurant, bars, water sports, bicycles, public
Wi-Fi* ⊟ *MC, V* ☾ *Closed late June–Oct.* ℐℴ| *AI, BP.*

★ $ ⌂ **Club Peace & Plenty.** The first of Exuma's hotels and granddaddy of
the island's omnipresent Peace & Plenty empire, this pink, two-story
hotel is in the heart of the action in George Town. Rooms have private
balconies—most overlooking the pool with ocean views to the side,
although some have full ocean vistas. It doesn't have a true on-property beach, but its Beach Club on Stocking Island is a five-minute ferry
shuttle away (free for guests). In high season the hotel is known for
its Friday-night parties on the pool patio, where Lermon "Doc" Rolle
has held court at the bar since the '70s. The indoor bar, which was
once a slave kitchen, attracts locals and a yachting crowd, especially
during the Family Islands Regatta. At dinner, the hotel's restaurant
goes the standard Out-Island route with huge portions of its two specialties: French rack of lamb and a 12-ounce New York strip steak.
Breakfast and dinner plans are available. ⊠ *Queen's Hwy., George
Town* ☎ *242/336–2551 or 800/525–2210* ⊕ *www.peaceandplenty.
com* ⇥ *32 rooms* ⌂ *In-room: refrigerator. In-hotel: restaurant, bars,
pool, diving, public Wi-Fi* ⊟ *AE, MC, V* ℐℴ| *EP, MAP.*

4

$ ⛅**Coconut Cove Hotel.** The Paradise Suite at this intimate hotel has its own private terrace, a king-size bed, walk-in closet, and an immense bathroom with a black-marble Jacuzzi. Other rooms have queen-size beds, tile floors, and scenic views from private terraces. Bathrobes and fresh-daily floral arrangements add an elegant touch. The restaurant menu includes Continental and Italian cuisine, with gourmet pizzas served at the bar or by the fireplace. ⊠*Queen's Hwy., George Town* ☎*242/336–2659* ⊕*www.exumabahamas.com/coconutcove.html* ⬎*11 rooms, 1 cottage* ⟁*In-room: refrigerator. In-hotel: restaurant, bar, pool, diving, laundry service* ▭*AE, MC, V.*

$ ⛅**Regatta Point.** Soft pink with hunter green shutters, this handsome two-story guesthouse overlooks Kidd Cove from its own petite island. Connected to George Town by a short causeway, the property is only a five-minute walk from town but far enough from the fray to have a secret hideaway's charm. Rooms have picturesque views of Elizabeth Harbour, large vaulted ceilings, and porches. Leave the louvered windows open to be lulled to sleep by the waves. The hotel has no restaurant, but units come with modern full-size kitchens, and maid service is included. Dock usage is free to guests, and rental boats are available. ⊠*Kidd Cove, George Town* ☎*242/336–2206 or 800/688–0309* ⊕*www.regattapointbahamas.com* ⬎*6 suites* ⟁*In-room: kitchen. In-hotel: beachfront, laundry service* ▭ *No credit cards.*

NIGHTLIFE

In season, the poolside bashes at **Club Peace & Plenty** (☎*242/336–2551*) fuelled by live bands, keep Bahamians and vacationers on the dance floor Friday nights. On Monday, head to **Eddie's Edgewater** (☎*242/336–2050*) for rousing rake 'n' scrape music. The front porch and the game room behind the restaurant are popular spots where locals hang out all week long, especially come Friday afternoon. On Saturday, the bonfire and barbecue combination pack 'em in at **Palm Bay Beach Club** (☎*242/336—2787*).

SPORTS & THE OUTDOORS

BOATING Because of its wealth of safe harbors and regatta events, the Exumas is a favorite spot for yachtsmen. Renting a boat allows you to explore the cays near George Town and beyond, and a number of area hotels allow guests to tie up rental boats at their docks. For those who want to take a water jaunt through Stocking Island's hurricane holes, sailboats are ideal.

To sail the Exumas without the hassle of owning or captaining, book a day charter on the **Flying Fish** (☎*242/357–0441*). Snacks and meals are provided, plus there's extra fun to be had sliding into the water and snorkeling. **Minns Water Sports** (☎*242/336–3483* ⊕*www.mwsboats. com*) rents Boston Whalers ranging from 15 to 22 feet. You can reserve a full-day (8 to 5) rental; half-day (four-hour) rentals are available on a first-come, first-served basis. Rates start at $90 for a half day.

★ **Starfish**(☎*877/398–6222 or 242/336–3033* ⊕*www.kayakbahamas. com*) rents Hobie Cat and Sea Pearl sailboats with gear starting at $50 for a half day.

EVENTS The **Annual New Year's Day Cruising Regatta** is held at the Staniel Cay Yacht Club, with international yachts taking part in a series of races. At the beginning of March, the **Cruiser's Regatta** hosts visiting boats for a week of races, cookouts, and partying in George Town. The **Family Islands Regatta** is the Bahamas most important yachting event of the year. It takes place in April. Starting the race in Elizabeth Harbour in George Town, island-made wooden sailboats compete for trophies. Onshore, the town is a three-day riot of Junkanoo parades, Goombay music, arts-and-crafts fairs, and continuous merriment.

> ## BONEFISH ARE THE LURE
>
> In the shallow flats off Exuma's windward coast, the elusive bonefish, the "ghosts of the sea," roam. Patient fishermen put feather-weight thumbnail-sized flies on the lines, calculate the tides and currents, and cast out about 50 feet in hopes of catching one. For sure success, avid fishermen pay guides about $300 a day to help them outsmart the skinny gray fish that streak through crystal water.

The **Music & Heritage Festival** is held each March in Regatta Park.

FISHING Exuma is a fishing haven, a great place to hunt the elusive bonefish (in season year-round and highly prized among fly fishermen). Most hotels can arrange for local guides, and a list is available from the **Exuma Tourist Office** (☎ *242/336–2430*). **Fish Rowe Charters** (☎ *242/357–0870* ⊕ *www.fishrowecharters.com*) has a 40-foot Hatteras that holds up to four fishermen. Deep-water charters run $800 for a half day, $1,600 for a full day. **Cely Smith** (☎ *242/345–2341 or 242/551–8501*) is both a bonefishing and fly-fishing guide. Fisherman and boat owner **Gus Thompson** (☎ *242/345–5214*) will help you hook big game as well as feisty bonefish.

GOLF Golf legend Greg Norman designed the 18-hole, par-72 championship course, featuring six ocean-side holes, at **Four Seasons Resort Great Exuma at Emerald Bay** (☎ *242/336–6882*), the island's only golf course. There are preferred tee times for hotel guests, who pay $145, including golf cart; the fee for nonguests is $175.

KAYAKING **Starfish** (☎ *877/398–6222 or 242/336–3033* ⊕ *www.kayakbahamas. com*) has guided half-day kayak trips to Crab Cay and Moriah Cay ★ National Park in sturdy, flat-bottom, oceangoing kayaks. Adults pay $85, children pay $68 for four-hour excursions. Kayak lessons are free with rentals, which start at $35 for a half day in a single. Deliveries are available on rentals of three days or longer.

SCUBA DIVING **Angel Fish Blue Hole,** minutes from George Town, is a popular dive site filled with angelfish, spotted rays, snapper, and the occasional reef shark. **Dive Exuma** (☎ *242/336–2893* ⊕ *www.dive-exuma.com*) offers dive instruction, certification courses, and scuba trips. Two-tank dives are $150; blue-hole one-tank dives are $100. **Stocking Island Mystery Cave** is full of mesmerizing schools of colorful fish but is for experienced divers only.

SNORKELING   **Starfish** (☎877/398–6222 or 242/336–3033 ⊕www.kayakbahamas. com) rents snorkel equipment by the half day, day, or week.

TENNIS   Nonguests can use the two Laycold cushion-surfaced courts at **February Point** (☎242/336–2693 or 877/839–4253) for $35 a day; use of the adjacent fitness center is $20. Four Har-Tru tennis courts, which are lighted for night play, are available to nonguests at **Four Seasons Resort Great Exuma at Emerald Bay** (☎242/336–6800), depending on availability, for $25 per hour.

SHOPPING

In the Exumas, George Town is the place to shop, but expect mostly local goods and crafts. **Exuma Markets** (⊠*Across from Scotia Bank, George Town* ☎*242/336–2033*) was the island's largest grocery until Emerald Island opened in 2005 at Emerald Bay, near the Four Seasons. Yachties tie up at the skiff docks in the rear, on Lake Victoria. FedEx, emergency e-mail, and faxes for visitors are accepted here as well. **Exuma Master Tailor Shop** (⊠*Across street from Exuma Markets, George Town* ☎*242/554–2050*), with one- to two-day service at very reasonable prices, will duplicate a favorite designer dress or suit while you are out sunning. Bring your own material, buttons, and zippers. **Sandpiper Arts & Crafts** (⊠*Queen's Hwy., George Town* ☎*242/336–2084*) has upscale souvenirs, from high-quality cards and books to batik clothing and art.

CAYS OF THE EXUMAS

A band of cays—with names like Rudder Cut, Big Farmer's, Great Guana, and Leaf—stretches north from Great Exuma.

Boaters will want to explore the waterways known as **Pipe Creek** (☎242/355–2034), a winding passage through the tiny islands between Staniel and Compass cays. There are great spots for shelling, snorkeling, diving, and bonefishing. The **Samson Cay Yacht Club**, at the creek's halfway point, is a good place for lunch or dinner.

Fodor'sChoice   **Staniel Cay** is a favorite destination of yachters and makes the perfect
★   home base for visiting the Exuma Cays Land and Sea Park. The island has an airstrip, two hotels, and one paved road. Virtually everything is within walking distance. Oddly enough, as you stroll past brightly painted houses and sandy shores, you are as likely to see a satellite dish as a woman pulling a bucket of water from a roadside well. At one of three grocery stores, boat owners can replenish their supplies. The friendly village also has a small red-roof church, a post office, and a straw vendor.

Just across the water from the Staniel Cay Yacht Club is one of the Bahamas' most unforgettable attractions: **Thunderball Grotto,** a beautiful marine cave that snorkelers (at low tide) and experienced scuba divers can explore. In the central cavern, shimmering shafts of sunlight pour through holes in the soaring ceiling and illuminate the glass-clear water. You'll see right away why this cave was chosen as an exotic setting for such movies as 007's *Thunderball* and *Never Say Never Again,* and the mermaid tale *Splash.*

Above Staniel Cay, near the Exumas' northern end, lies the 176-square-mi **Exuma Cays Land and Sea Park,** which spans 22 mi between Conch Cut and Wax Cay Cut. You must charter a small boat or seaplane to reach the park, which has more than 20 mi of petite cays. Hawksbill Cay and Warderick Wells (both with remains of 18th-century Loyalist settlements) have marked hiking trails, as does Hall's Pond. At Shroud Cay, jump into "Camp Driftwood," where the strong current creates a natural whirlpool that whips you around a rocky outcropping to a powdery beach. Part of the Bahamas National Trust, the park appeals to divers, who appreciate the vast underworld of limestone, reefs, drop-offs, blue holes of freshwater springs, caves, and a multitude of exotic marine life, including one of the Bahamas' most impressive stands of rare pillar coral. Strict laws prohibit fishing and removing coral, plants, or even shells as souvenirs.

North of the park is **Norman's Cay,** an island with 10 mi of rarely trod white beaches, which attracts an occasional yachter. It was once the private domain of Colombian drug smuggler Carlos Lehder. It's now owned by the Bahamian government. **Allen's Cays** are at the Exumas' northernmost tip and are home to the rare Bahamian iguana.

WHERE TO STAY

$ 🏨 **Staniel Cay Yacht Club.** The club once drew such luminaries as Malcolm Forbes and Robert Mitchum. It's now a low-key getaway for yachties and escapists. The cottages, perched on stilts along a rocky bank, have broad ocean vistas and dramatic sunsets, which you can treasure from a chaise longue on your spacious private balcony. Take a tour of the cay in one of the club's golf carts. Meal plans for breakfast and dinner cost an extra $35 per person per day. All-inclusive packages are also available. ⊠ *Staniel Cay* ☎ *242/355–2024 or 954/467–8920* ⊕ *www. stanielcay.com* ⚲ *5 1-bedroom cottages, 3 2-bedroom cottages, 1 3-bedroom cottage* ⚭ *In-room: no phone, refrigerator, no TV. In-hotel: restaurant, bar, public Wi-Fi* ⊟ *AE, MC, V* ⅋ *AI, EP, MAP.*

NIGHTLIFE

Club Thunderball (⊠ *East of Thunderball Grotto* ☎ *242/355–2125*) is a sports bar–dance club built on a bluff overlooking the water. Run by a local pilot, it serves lunch every day except Monday and has Friday evening barbecues.

SPORTS & THE OUTDOORS

BICYCLING Contact **Chamberlain Rentals** (☎ *242/355–2043*) if you want to pedal around Staniel Cay.

BOATING & **Staniel Cay Yacht Club** (☎ *242/355–2024*) rents 13-foot Whalers and
FISHING arranges fishing guides.

UBA DIVING **Exuma Cays Land and Sea Park** and **Thunderball Grotto** are excellent snor-
NORKELING keling and dive sites. **Staniel Cay Yacht Club** (☎ *242/355–2024*) rents masks and fins for snorkeling and fills tanks from its compressor.

Islands of the Stars

The Bahamas have served as a source of inspiration for countless artists, writers, and directors. The country's movie legacy dates back to the era of silent films, including the now-legendary original black-and-white version of Jules Verne's *20,000 Leagues Under the Sea*, which was filmed here in 1907. Since the birth of color film, the draw has only increased—directors are lured by the possibility of using the islands' characteristic white sands and luminous turquoise waters as a backdrop. Among the more famous movies shot in the Bahamas are *Jaws*, the cult favorite whose killer shark has terrified viewers for two decades; *Flipper*, the family classic about a boy and a porpoise; *Splash*, whose main character is a mermaid who becomes human; and *Cocoon*, about a group of elderly friends who discover an extraterrestrial secret to immortality. Most recently, parts of the two sequels to *Pirates of the Caribbean, Dead Man's Chest* and *At World's End*, were shot on location in the Exumas. *Thunderball* and *Never Say Never Again* were both shot on location in Staniel Cay, one of the northernmost islands of the Exumas chain.

You can swim and snorkel in **Thunderball Cave**, site of the pivotal chase scene in the 1965 Sean Connery film. The ceiling of this huge, dome-shaped cave is about 30 feet above the water, which is filled with yellowtails, parrots, blue chromes, and yellow and black striped sergeant majors. Swimming into the cave is the easy part—the tide draws you in—but paddling back out can be strenuous, especially because if you stop moving, the tide will pull you back.

Well before Connery gave the cave its name, Ian Fleming, the creator of 007,

set his book *Dr. No* on Great Inagua. **Ernest Hemingway** wrote about the Bahamas as well. He visited Bimini regularly in the 1930s, dubbing it the "Sportsfishing Capital of the World." His hangout was the Compleat Angler, a bar that housed a small Hemingway museum until it burned down in January 2006. Among the items the museum displayed were Hemingway's drawings for *The Old Man and the Sea*—rumor has it that the protagonist looks suspiciously like one of the Angler's former bartenders.

The Bahamas not only seem to spark the imaginations of artists, but have also become a playground for the rich and famous in recent years. **Lenny Kravitz** and **Patti LaBelle** own homes in Eleuthera, while the stars of *Cocoon*, the late **Hume Cronyn** and **Jessica Tandy**, were regular visitors to Goat Cay, a private island just offshore from George Town, Exuma. **Johnny Depp** purchased a cay in the Exumas after filming on location for *Pirates*, and **Nicholas Cage** and **Faith Hill** and **Tim MacGraw** own private islands in the area as well. Many world-famous celebrities and athletes hide out at **Musha Cay**, an exclusive retreat in the northern part of the Exumas, where a week's stay sets you back $24,750 for the entire island. **David Copperfield** bought Musha and its five houses in July 2006 for $50 million, renaming it Copperfield Cay. Although the cay won't name its guests, the all-knowing taxi drivers at the George Town airport mention **Oprah Winfrey** and **Michael Jordan** as a couple of the esteemed visitors.

HE EXUMAS ESSENTIALS

To research prices, get advice from other travelers, and book travel arrangements, visit ⊕www.fodors.com.

BY AIR

You can fly from Fort Lauderdale, St. Petersburg, Sarasota, or Miami to the Exuma International Airport, located 9 mi from George Town. You can also fly into Staniel Cay, near the top of the chain, which has a 3,000-foot airstrip that accepts charter flights and private planes—but you must clear customs at the Andros, Nassau, or Exuma airport first.

Air Sunshine flies on demand from Fort Lauderdale to George Town. American Eagle has daily service from Miami; call for summer scheduling. Bahamasair has daily flights from Nassau to George Town. Continental Connection/Gulfstream flies twice daily between Fort Lauderdale and George Town. Watermakers Air offers two daily flights from Fort Lauderdale to Staniel Cay. Lynx Air International flies from Fort Lauderdale to George Town on Thursday, Friday, and Saturday.

Airlines & Contacts Air Sunshine (☎954/435-8900 or 800/327-8900). **American Eagle** (☎800/433-7300). **Bahamasair** (☎800/222-4262). **Continental/ Gulfstream** (☎800/231-0856). **Lynx Air International** (☎888/596-9247). **Watermakers Air** (☎954/771-0330).

BY BOAT

M/V *Grand Master* travels from Nassau to George Town on Tuesday and returns to Nassau on Friday. Travel time is 12 hours, and the fare is $45 each way. M/V *Captain Sea* leaves Nassau on Tuesday for Staniel Cay, Big Farmer's Cay, Black Point, and Barraterre, returning to Nassau on Saturday. The trip takes 14 hours each way, with one-way fares ranging from $50 if you are only going to one cay, or $70 if you are going to all the islands. Call the Dockmaster's Office at Potter's Cay, Nassau, for fares to specific destinations.

Bahama Ferries' air-conditioned *Seawind* and *Sealink* carry passengers and vehicles from Nassau to George Town Monday through Wednesday, returning to Nassau Tuesday through Thursday. To reach Stocking Island from George Town, the Club Peace & Plenty Ferry leaves from the hotel's dock twice daily at 10 and 1. The ferry departs from the Stocking Island dock at 10:30 and 1:30. The fare is $10 round-trip for non–Peace & Plenty guests.

Boat & Ferry Information Bahamas Ferries (☎242/323-2166). **Club Peace & Plenty Ferry** (☎242/336-2551). **Dockmaster's Office** (☎242/393-1064).

BY CAR

Most of the car rental agencies in the Exumas are located in George Town, and if you call to make a reservation, many of them will also deliver the cars to you at a convenient location. Hotels can also arrange car rentals.

Local Agencies Airport Rent a Car (✉ *George Town Airport* ☎242/345-0090). **Exuma Transport** (✉ *Queens Hwy below Ministry of Tourism* ☎242/336-2101).

Thompson's Rentals (✉ *George Town, across from the Palm Bay Resor* ☎ *242/336–2442*).

BY GOLF CART
Staniel Cay Yacht Club (☎*242/355–2024*) rents golf carts for exploring Staniel Cay.

BY SCOOTER
In George Town, Prestige Scooter Rental (☎*242/524–0066*) rents motor scooters for $60 a day.

BY TAXI
Taxis wait at the airport for incoming flights. The cost of a ride from the airport to George Town is about $25 for two people, each additional passenger is charged $3. Your George Town hotel will arrange for a taxi if you wish to go exploring or need to return to the airport.

Contacts **Exuma Transit Services** (☎ *242/345–0232*). **Kermit Rolle** (☎ *242/345–0002*). **Luther Rolle Taxi Service** (☎ *242/345–5003*).

CONTACTS & RESOURCES

BANKS & EXCHANGE SERVICES
The Scotiabank in George Town is open Monday–Thursday 9:30–3 and Friday until 4:30. There's also a Royal Bank of Canada and a Bank of the Bahamas.

EMERGENCIES
Contacts **Health Clinic** (☎ *242/336–2088*). **Police** (☎ *911, 242/336–2666 in George Town, 242/355–2042 in Staniel Cay*).

TOUR OPTIONS
From George Town, Captain Cole arranges overnight trips up to the Exuma Cays Land and Sea Park. Exuma Glass Bottom Boat keeps you dry as you explore local reefs and blue holes. Luther Rolle will take you on an informative tour of Little and Great Exuma, or contact Christine's Island Tours, which does bush medicine tours, or Exuma Transit Services, whose island tours include lunch at a native restaurant or dinner with rake 'n' scrape music.

Contacts **Captain Cole** (☎ *242/345–0359* ⊕ *www.offislandadventures. com*). **Christine's Island Tours** (☎ *242/358–4016*). **Exuma Transit Services** (☎ *242/334–0232*). **Exuma Glass Bottom Boat** (☎ *242/357–0570*). **Luther Rolle** (☎ *242/345–5003 or 242/357–0662*).

VISITOR INFORMATION
The Exuma Tourist Office is in George Town, across the street from the Exuma Markets, one block from the Government Administration Building.

Tourist Information **Exuma Tourist Office** (☎ *242/336–2430* ⊕ *www.exuma-bahamas.com*). **Out-Islands Promotion Board** (☎ *800/688–4752* ⊕*www.out-islands.bahamas.com*).

The Other Out Islands

WORD OF MOUTH

"What you will find in the Out Islands is peace and quiet, and a lively bar or two (depending on the night). You'll find spectacular beaches with nary a soul in sight, a handful of like-minded travelers, and charming—but oftentimes bare bones—accommodations. The luxury comes from the quiet and the closeness to nature, not from marble baths and spa pedicures."

—Callaloo

Updated by
Stephen F.
Vletas

THE QUIET, SIMPLER WAY OF life on the Bahamas Out Islands, some
times referred to as the Family Islands, is startlingly different from
Nassau's and Freeport's fast-paced glitz and glitter. Outside New Provi
dence and Grand Bahama, on the dozen or so islands that are equippe
to handle tourists, you'll leave the sophisticated resorts, nightclubs
casinos, and shopping malls behind. Instead, you'll be rewarded wit
a peaceful, relaxing vacation that will melt away your stress faster tha
a stick of butter evaporates in a frying pan. Sports abound here, too
virtually all the Out Islands have good to excellent fishing, boating, an
diving, and you'll often have endless stretches of beach all to yoursel:

Along with the utter lack of stress of an Out Islands holiday, you'll fin
largely unspoiled environments. Roughing it in Inagua, for example
is a small price to pay for the glorious spectacle of thousands of pin
flamingos lifting off from a mangrove-ringed lake to fill the azure sk
And a day of sightseeing can mean little more than a stroll down nar
row, sand-strewn streets in a fishing village, past small, pastel home
where orange, pink, and bright-red bougainvillea spill over the wall
Meals, even those served in hotels, almost always incorporate loca
specialties, from conch and fresh-caught fish to chicken with peas 'r
rice. Island taverns are small and usually noisy with chatter. You ca
make friends with locals over a beer and a game of pool or darts muc
more quickly than you would in the average stateside cocktail loung
Nightlife may involve listening to a piano player or a small village rak
'n' scrape combo in a clubhouse bar, or joining the crowds at a loca
disco playing everything from R&B to calypso.

For the most part, you won't find hotels that provide the costly com
forts that are taken for granted in Nassau and Freeport, with the excep
tion of Kamalame Cay on Andros, Bimini Bay Resort on North Bimin
and Club Med–Columbus Isle on San Salvador. Out Islands accommo
dations are generally modest lodges, rustic cottages, and small inns–
many without telephones and TVs (inquire when making reservation
if these are important to you). Making a phone call, or receiving on
will sometimes require a trip to the local BaTelCo (Bahamas Telecom
munications Corporation) telephone station.

The Out Islands were once mostly the purview of private plane an
yacht owners. The tourist who discovered a hideaway on Andros, Eleu
thera, or in the Exumas would cherish it and return year after yea
to find the same faces as before. But some islands are now becomin
more and more popular, largely because of increased airline activit
Most islands are served from Nassau or Florida daily. Others may onl
have a couple of incoming and outgoing flights a week. If you want t
partake in simple island life without feeling completely cut off, choos
a slightly busier spot that is closer to the mainland United States, suc
as Bimini. If you go farther away from the mainland, to places like Ca
Island or San Salvador, you'll feel much more like you're getting awa
from it all.

OUT ISLANDS' TOP 5

Charter a boat. Explore the necklace of islands that comprise the Biminis and the Berries. Start in Bimini, and end up in Chub Cay. It's quite possible that you may choose not to come back.

Dive and bonefish on Andros Island. Go with the diving experts at Small Hope Bay and drop "over the wall." Then cruise the West Side flats with top professional guides in pursuit of the elusive "gray ghost."

Explore Long Island. Possibly the most alluring of all the Out Islands, Long Island is an absolute jewel. Base yourself at Stella Maris Resort, rent a car, and head out. Don't forget your snorkeling gear, fishing rods, and a cooler of goodies.

Go deep-sea fishing at Pittstown Point Landing. This is wild bluewater fishing the way it used to be: marlin, tuna, dorado, wahoo, and more, with no other boats in sight. Eat, drink, fish, sleep ... eat, drink, fish, sleep ... you get the idea. The bonefishing isn't bad either.

Hide on Cat Island. If you're looking for romance, hole up with that special person at Fernandez Bay Village or Hawk's Nest Resort. There's sun, sea, and sand—what more do you need?

5

EXPLORING THE OUT ISLANDS

The Out Islands span a sweeping area of shallow seas and deep ocean—from the Biminis, just off southern Florida, to Great Inagua, northeast of Cuba. The northern islands of the Biminis, the Berries, and Andros are quick and easy to reach from Florida via scheduled and chartered flight service. Dominated by the Great Bahama Bank, these islands are tailor-made for sportfishing, diving, snorkeling, swimming, and boating. Bimini receives more boaters than any other island in the Bahamas and is a weekend party spot. Great Harbour, the largest of the Berry Islands, is sedate, self-contained, and oriented toward family beach and water-sport vacationing. Andros is vast, an ultimate retreat for bonefishing and diving. The northern islands are mostly flat, lush with mangroves, rimmed with white-sand beaches, and laced with miles of creeks and lakes. People walk between settlements, or ride bikes or golf carts. Exploring is best done by boat, not car, though taxis are available to cover longer distances.

The southern islands are more remote, exposed to the open Atlantic, and ruggedly dramatic. They're usually reached by air from Nassau. Good roads on Cat and Long islands allow for convenient exploration by car. Here you'll find miles of pink-sand beaches, bonefish flats, and aquamarine bays. Settlements are spread out, and services, including gas stations, are not always available. The weather is a few degrees warmer and more consistent south of the Tropic of Cancer, which slices through the center of Long Island. Club Med on San Salvador, designed for pampered relaxation, is the essence of quiet luxury. Crooked and Acklins islands, with populations of about 400 people each, are outposts for the self-sufficient adventurer. The same is true for Great Inagua, where the best way to explore is with a local guide.

ABOUT THE RESTAURANTS

Dining is a casual "get together" experience, and rarely involves anything fancy. Restaurants, lodges, and inns serve traditional Bahamian fare—fresh seafood, grilled chicken, johnnycakes, and barbecued pork with all the fixings (potato salad, coleslaw, peas 'n' rice, and baked macaroni and cheese). Most islands have restaurants that are open during normal mealtime hours, but there are exceptions. Call ahead whenever possible, especially on Crooked, Acklins, and Great Inagua islands. Beachside restaurants are often small, with simple wooden tables and casual dress. Sunset cocktails are one of the pleasures of daily life; thatched conch stands and colorful roadside bars are a treat—and a cool way to mingle with local residents. During regatta season (June and July), life on the Out Islands gets merrily crazy, and pig roasts with live music are not-to-be-missed events.

WHAT IT COSTS IN U.S. DOLLARS					
	¢	$	$$	$$$	$$$$
RESTAURANTS	under $10	$10–$20	$20–$30	$30–$40	over $40
HOTELS	under $100	$100–$200	$200–$300	$300–$400	over $400

Restaurant prices are for a main course at dinner, excluding gratuity, typically 15%, which is often automatically added to the bill. Hotel prices are for two people in a standard double room in high season, excluding service charges and 6%–12% tax.

ABOUT THE HOTELS

The Out Islands have accommodations to suit most tastes, from a handful of luxury properties on private cays and remote beaches to simple fishing lodges and funky hotels with swinging nightlife on the weekends. Figure out what you want—the overall experience, service, amenities, activities—then do your homework. A number of lodges cater specifically to anglers and divers and are not well suited to overall vacationing or for families with small children. Many resorts and lodges don't have air-conditioning, in-room telephones, or Internet. Most do have a phone for guest use on the property and some will have a computer with Internet in the lobby area. If these things are important to you, check with the hotel before you book. And remember, even locations that say they have Internet service may not have it all the time, as connections can go on the blink without warning.

Comfortable motel-style accommodations are most common, and these lodges usually have a restaurant and bar. Places located on the water are better cooled by ocean breezes, which are a huge help in keeping down the bugs—mosquitoes, sand flies, and doctor flies. Family-owned and -operated properties tend to be exceptionally warm and friendly, though you can expect a welcoming reception wherever you go. Off-season rates usually begin in May, with some of the best discounted package deals available in October, November, and early December.

IF YOU LIKE

OUT ISLANDS CUISINE

Out Islands restaurants are often family-run and focus on home-style dishes. They typically serve a combination of Bahamian, Continental, and American fare. Instead of the menu, it's the ingredients and individual flare of the chef that set one place apart from the next. While fried food, especially seafood, is a staple, more chefs are experimenting with alternate cooking methods, especially baking and grilling. If you see grilled or blackened hog snapper on a menu, give it a try, as this is one of the most popular island dishes. Lobster chunks marinated in wine and sautéed is another specialty.

To get a sense of what the locals eat at home, try ordering any fish prepared "Bahamian style," meaning baked and smothered in tomatoes and spices. For a true taste of Out Islands food, don't go home without sampling conch salad with lemon and hot peppers. If you're on the hunt for the freshest conch salad, look for one of the out-of-the-way stands where the commercial fishermen clean their catch. Another worthy culinary challenge is the quest for the best key lime pie, a local dessert favorite.

YOUR OWN PRIVATE PARADISE

Aside from the large resorts, most hotels on the Out Islands are small and owner-operated, which ensures a personal touch. Some accommodations use an honor-bar system—mix your own and sign for it—so you really feel at home. These are the places that people return to year after year to visit the locals who have become their friends. Although such hotels may not be any cheaper than the big, plush resorts, many visitors feel that it's hard to put a price on the total escape that the more low-key accommodations have to offer. What would you pay for a powdery pink beach that stretches for miles with no footprints but your own? Or water so clear that snorkeling makes you feel like you're flying?

THE AGE-OLD SPORT OF FISHING

Fishing is believed to have been an integral part of Bahamian culture for as long as people have inhabited the islands. The majority of settlements in the Out Islands were established for subsistence fishing and sponging. Commercial fishing, focused on lobster, grouper, and snapper, is what drives the economies of many of these communities today. Sportfishing began with an emphasis on offshore angling—trolling an assortment of lures, rigged baits, and teasers on conventional tackle rods and reels to entice deepwater game fish into striking distance—for marlin, tuna, wahoo, and dolphin. Bonefishing—stalking bonefish on foot or in a poled boat across clear shallow-water flats, and then sight-casting your bait, jig, lure, or fly to specific fish that you spot—entered the mix in the 1920s and 1930s. Now, big-game blue-water fishing and fly-fishing the flats are ingrained in the local fabric. Fishing guides are often second- or third-generation professionals with a contagious enthusiasm for their sport and an encyclopedic knowledge of the best spots.

5

Club Med–Columbus Isle offers early-bird booking bonuses and runs pricing promotions year-round.

TIMING

The peak tourist season is mid-December through April for visitors in the sun-sea-and-sand vacation mode. From the beginning of May, and on through the fall, room rates tend to drop by as much as a third. May, June, July, October, and November are good months for diving, snorkeling, boating, and beach activities at discount prices. Hurricane season technically runs from June through November; August and September (the most likely months for hurricanes) can be hot and steamy and many resorts and restaurants are closed.

Off-season discount rates often won't include lodges focused on fishing as April through June are prime months for flats and offshore anglers. This is also the perfect time to combine fishing with diving, snorkeling, and beach exploring. October and November are excellent fishing months as well, and the winter period of December through March is good when the weather cooperates. Winter cold fronts—a relative term, with temperatures dropping into the high 60s to low 70s—move down from Florida and can bring wind and clouds for several days, which makes swimming, sunning, and fishing less appealing. To play the weather odds, your best bet is to go to the southern islands (Long Island, San Salvador, Crooked, Acklins, and Great Inagua) December through March. Cold fronts often stall out before reaching these southern islands, and daily temperatures average about five degrees warmer than on the northern islands.

You'll rarely have to worry about crowds in the Out Islands. However, sailing regattas on Andros, Long, and Cat islands (April through July) and fishing tournaments in the Biminis and Berries (November through May) are popular events that bring out the partying spirit in locals and visitors alike.

ANDROS

The Bahamas' largest island (100 mi long and 40 mi wide) and one of the least explored, Andros's land mass is carved up by myriad channels, creeks, lakes, and mangrove-covered cays. The North, Middle, and South Bights cut through the width of the island, creating boating access to both coasts. Andros is best known for its bonefishing and diving, and is also a glorious ecotourism spot with snorkeling, blue hole exploration, sea kayaking, and nature hikes. More than a dozen small lodges on the eastern shore cater to sun and sea revelers.

The Spaniards who came here in the 16th century called it *La Isla de Espíritu Santo*—the Island of the Holy Spirit—and it has retained its eerie mystique to this day. In fact, the descendants of a group of Seminole Indians and runaway slaves who left the Florida Everglades in the mid-19th century settled in Andros and remained hidden until a few decades ago. They continue to live as a tribal society. Their village, near the island's northern tip, is called Red Bay, and they make a living by

GREAT ITINERARIES

IF YOU HAVE 3 DAYS

If you've decided to sample the natural treasures of the Out Islands, the **South Bight** of **Andros** is a clearcut Fodor's choice. Fly to Congo Town airport, then take your first day to relax on the beach; or jump right in with a kayaking tour of the nearby cays and **Lisbon Creek.**

On your second day, sign up for a guided snorkeling exploration of the area's vivid blue holes and the blackcoral barrier reef swarming with sea life. In the afternoon go on a nature hike in a pine forest in search of wild orchids and exotic birds. Enjoy sunset cocktails on the beach. For your last day, set out on a boating adventure to the secluded **West Side** for fishing, exploring, and picnicking. Here, the aquamarine water melds with the sky in a dreamy purple haze that creates a dazzling portrait of tranquility.

If you're a bonefishing enthusiast, spend your three days in **Cargill Creek.** Fish for the elusive gray ghost with top professional guides in the **North and Middle Bights** and along the white-sand beaches of **Big Wood Cay.** The lodges in the area can also arrange diving and snorkeling excursions and island sightseeing tours.

IF YOU HAVE 5 DAYS

Follow the suggested three-day itinerary, then transfer to **Fresh Creek.** On the way you can stop at the **Androsia Batik Works Factory** in **Andros Town**, and shop for colorful island-made fabrics and other gifts at the **Androsia Outlet Store.** After settling in, get your adrenaline flowing with an "over-the-wall" dive in the **Tongue of the Ocean.** If you're not certified, you can take the **Small**

Hope Bay Lodge resort course, and begin diving around the nearby reef in the afternoon. Or lounge on the beach, swim, and snorkel over shallow-water coral heads. Sip sunset cocktails and relax in the evening. Your last day can be filled with other water sports and activities—windsurfing, snorkeling, fishing, or exploring from Fresh Creek to **Captain Bill's Blue Hole,** where you can enjoy a leisurely picnic and a cooling swim. If you're looking for some serious exercise, make this trip on a bicycle, about 6 mi one way from **Fresh Creek.**

Dedicated anglers don't need to move anywhere else. A continued stay at **Cargill Creek** will mean fishing more of the countless flats throughout the Bights. Venture back to the **West Side,** where you can pursue tarpon and permit along with bonefish.

IF YOU HAVE 7 DAYS

Add on to the five-day itinerary above by flying to **Bimini** for your last two days. Charter a deep-sea fishing boat or dive over the famous **Atlantis** lost city site. On your final day, hop the ferry to South Bimini to wander the white-sand beaches, snorkel and swim, shop in the **Native Straw and Craft Market,** or visit the **Bimini Museum.** Top it all off with a romantic beachside dinner at **Casa Lyon,** Bimini's best restaurant, followed by dancing to live music at **Big John's Conch Shell Bar.**

weaving straw goods. The Seminoles are credited with originating th myth of the island's legendary (and elusive) chickcharnies—red-eyed bearded, green-feathered creatures with three fingers and three toe that hang upside down by their tails from pine trees. These mythic characters supposedly wait deep in the forests to wish good luck to th friendly passerby and vent their mischief on the hostile trespasser.

Andros's undeveloped West Side adjoins the Great Bahama Bank, vast shallow-water haven for lobster and game fish, including tarpo Shifting shoals and sandbars, and flats that go dry during low tide create hazards for boaters. Immense bays, tiny sloughs, and mangro swamps snake in and out of the chalk-color shoreline. The island's lu green interior is covered with wild orchids and dense pine and maho any forests. The forests provide nesting grounds for parrots, partridge quail, white-crowned pigeons, and whistling ducks, and hunters con to Andros from September through March in search of game.

The island's roughly 8,000 residents live in about a dozen settlemen on the eastern shore from Morgan's Bluff in the north to Mars Bay the south. Farming and commercial fishing are the mainstays of th economy, and the island is the country's largest source of fresh wate

The Andros Barrier Reef—the world's third-largest reef—is within mile of the east shore and runs for 140 mi. It has an enchanting varie of marine life and is easily accessible to divers. Sheltered waters with the reef average 6–15 feet, but on the other side of the reef ("ov the wall") lie the depths (more than 6,000 feet) of the Tongue of t Ocean, where the U.S. and British navies test submarines and underw ter weapons. Operating under the acronym AUTEC (Atlantic Und water Test and Evaluation Center), their base is near Andros Town.

NICHOLL'S TOWN

Nicholl's Town, at Andros's northeastern corner, is the island's larg village, with a population of about 600. This friendly community h stores for supplies and groceries, a few motels, a public medical clin a telephone station, and small restaurants. A few miles north of Nic oll's Town is a crescent beach and a headland known as **Morga Bluff,** named after the 17th-century pirate Henry Morgan, who alle edly dropped off some of his stolen loot in the area. Morgan's Bl is the site of the All Andros Crabfest in June, an annual party w a crafts fair, sailboat races, live music, and plenty of Bahamian fo and drink.

Several miles south of Nicholl's Town, **Conch Sound** is a wide protect bay with long strands of white sand and tranquil waters. Swimm and bonefishers can wade on their own on the easily accessible flats

WHERE TO EAT & STAY

$ ✕ **Conch Sound Inn Restaurant and Bar.** This diner-style restaurant ser hearty Bahamian and traditional dishes on the pool terrace. Scramb eggs, bacon, grits, home fries, and pancakes will fill you up at brea fast. For lunch, conch ceviche, burgers, fried conch, and grouper w

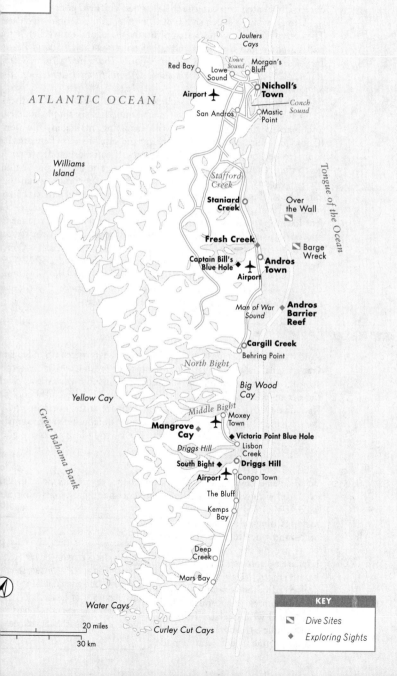

Andros

Joulters
Cays

ATLANTIC OCEAN

Red Bay   Lowe   Morgan's
           Sound   Bluff
Lowe
Sound   **Nicholl's**
           Airport   **Town**
                              Conch
                              Sound
           San Andros   Mastic
                         Point

Williams
Island
                    Stafford
                    Creek   *Tongue of the Ocean*
           Staniard
           Creek   Over
                                  the Wall

           Fresh Creek
                                        Barge
                              Andros   Wreck
           Captain Bill's **Town**
           Blue Hole
                    Airport

                    Man of War   ◆ **Andros**
                    Sound   **Barrier**
                                      Reef

                              Cargill Creek
                              Behring Point
           North Bight

                              Big Wood
                              Cay
Yellow Cay
           Middle Bight
                    Moxey
           Mangrove Town
           Cay   ◆ **Victoria Point Blue Hole**
           Driggs Hill   Lisbon
                              Creek
           South Bight ◆ **Driggs Hill**
                    Airport
Great Bahama Bank   Congo Town

                              The Bluff

                              Kemps
                              Bay

                              Deep
                              Creek

                              Mars Bay

Water Cays

20 miles

30 km
                    Curley Cut Cays

KEY	
◥	*Dive Sites*
◆	*Exploring Sights*

slaw are menu mainstays. Fresh fish, usually fried (though you can request grilled or pan-sautéed), and broiled lobster dominate the dinner choices, but often you can order Bahamian chicken, pork chops, or a steak to go with a garden salad, peas 'n' rice, or macaroni and cheese. The convivial staff creates a snappy atmosphere, and on weekends the bar is a party spot for locals and guests alike. ⊠ *Conch Sound Resort Inn, Conch Sound Hwy. between Nichols Town and Conch Sound* ☎*242/329–2060* ▭*No credit cards* ⊘*Sometimes closed Aug. and Sept.; call ahead.*

$ 🍽 **Conch Sound Resort Inn.** This secluded inn several kilometers northeast of Nichols Town on the road to Conch Sound has six simple but clean and spacious motel-style rooms with carpeting, mahogany furniture, handmade quilts, soft-cushioned chairs, and satellite TV. There are also four two-bedroom suites with kitchenettes. If you'd prefer not to cook, go to the restaurant for basic Bahamian fare. The beach is a 10-minute walk away, but the hotel will provide transportation when they can. The staff is extremely welcoming and friendly, and will make you feel like family. Bonefishing and diving can be arranged. **Pros:** excellent location for anglers to fish the north end of the island, restaurant and bar on-site, friendly people. **Cons:** you need to rent a car to stay here or use taxis which are expensive, no Internet service. ⊠ *Conch Sound Hwy, between Nichols Town and Conch Sound* ☎*242/329–2060* ▤*242/329–2338* ☎*6 rooms, 4 suites* ⌂*In-room: no phone, kitchen. In-hotel: restaurant, bar, pool, laundry service* ▭*No credit cards* ⊘*Sometimes closed Aug. and Sept.; call ahead.*

STANIARD CREEK

Sand banks that turn gold at low tide lie off the northern tip of **Staniard Creek**, a small island settlement 9 mi north of Fresh Creek, accessed by a bridge off the main highway. Coconut palms and casuarinas shade the ocean-side beaches, and offshore breezes are pleasantly cooling. **Kamalame Cove** and its nearby private cay are at the northern end of the settlement. Three creeks snake into the mainland, forming extensive mangrove-lined back bays and flats. The surrounding areas are good for wading and bonefishing.

WHERE TO STAY

★ $$$$ 🍽 **Kamalame Cay.** This 96-acre all-inclusive resort sits on a private cay laced with white-sand beaches and coconut palms. Gleaming, airy accommodations have plush furnishings, linens, and towels. Cottages and one- to three-bedroom villas are on the beach, with sitting areas, soaking tubs, and private terraces. Meals and cocktails are served in the veranda-wrapped plantation-style great house, which is adorned with oversize furniture and antiques. Guests feast on fresh fruits, prime beef, homemade

> **BEST OF THE BEST**
>
> Looking for a carefree, romantic honeymoon spot? With sun, sand, delicious food and drink ... and lots of privacy, of course. Try Kamalame Cay on north Andros, and ask for a beachfront cottage or villa.

breads and soups, and innovative seafood dishes. You can fish, dive, snorkel, lounge by the pool, or head to the deluxe spa facility. Rates include meals, house wines, liquor, use of pool, tennis court, snorkeling gear and sea kayaks, and airport transfers. **Pros:** discreet pampering; delicious, innovative food; many daily activities, including outstanding bonefishing. **Cons:** no nightlife or shopping, you'll need insect repellent when the breeze is down. ⊠ *At the north end of Staniard Creek* ☎242/368–6281 or 800/790—7971 ⊕*www.kamalame. com* ⇨*4 marina rooms, 2 beach rooms, 5 cottages, 5 villas* �‑*In-room: no phone, kitchen (some), refrigerator, no TV. In-hotel: restaurant, room service, bar, tennis court, pool, spa, beachfront, diving, water sports, bicycles, laundry service, public Wi-Fi, airport shuttle* ⊟*MC, V* ⍩*AI.*

¢ ⌂**Love at First Sight.** At the mouth of Stafford Creek, self-sufficient anglers and do-it-yourself vacationers can sit on the sundeck, sip a cold Kalik, and contemplate the vast bonefish flats of North Andros (or take a wilderness hike through the pine forests to a remote landlocked lake). Bright motel-style rooms are comfortable, with double beds and private bath. The restaurant serves traditional Bahamian seafood, steaks, chicken, and pork, and at the bar you can enjoy an array of fruity rum drinks. Bonefishing and diving excursions can be arranged. Most guests arrive at Andros Town airport, but San Andros is an equal distance away. **Pros:** on-site restaurant and bar, economical location to explore northern Andros. **Cons:** if you want to explore, you'll need to rent a car; office is only open three days a week for Internet service. ⊠ *On the main highway, at the mouth of Stafford Creek* ☎242/368–6082 ⊕*www.loveatfirstsights.com* ⇨*10 rooms* ⚑*In-room: no phone, refrigerator, no TV. In-hotel: restaurant, bar, pool, laundry service, public Internet* ⊟*No credit cards* ⍩*Sometimes closed part of Aug. and Sept.; call ahead.*

SH CREEK–ANDROS TOWN

Batik fabric called Androsia is made in **Andros Town,** a small community in central Andros on the south side of Fresh Creek. This brilliantly colored fabric is designed and dyed at the **Androsia Batik Works Factory,** a 3-mi drive from Andros Town airport. You can visit the factory and see how the material is made, plus take lessons in the art of batik. It's open weekdays 8–4 and Saturday 9–5. Batik fabric is turned into wall hangings and clothing for men and women, which are sold throughout the Bahamas and the Caribbean, and are very popular with the locals. Adjacent to the factory is the **Androsia Outlet Store** (☎242/368–2080 ⊕*www.androsia.com*), where you can buy original fabrics, clothing, Bahamian carvings and straw baskets, maps, CDs, and books. It's open 9–5 every day except Sunday.

About 30 mi south of Nicholl's Town on the east coast, and on the north side of a creek that shares the same name, is the small hamlet of **Fresh Creek.** A few restaurants, including **Hank's Place,** line the waterfront, along with several boat docks and a small hotel with a convenience store. A few blocks in from the creek are a couple of markets, shops, and offices. The creek itself cuts over 16 mi into the island creating tranquil bonefishing flats and welcoming mangrove-lined bay that can be explored by boaters and sea kayakers.

Andros lures fishing enthusiasts to its fabulous bonefishing flats, an divers can't get enough of the sprawling **Andros Barrier Reef**, just of Fresh Creek–Andros Town. Snorkelers can explore such reefs as th Three Sisters, where visibility is clear 15 feet to the sandy floor an jungles of elkhorn coral snake up to the surface. Divers can delve int the 60-foot-deep coral caves of the Petrified Forest, beyond which th wall slopes down to depths of 6,000 feet. Anglers can charter boa to fish offshore or over the reef, and bonefishers can wade the flats o their own in Fresh Creek.

WHERE TO EAT & STAY

★ $ ✕ **Hank's Place Restaurant and Bar.** On the north side of Fresh Creek a block or so east of the bridge, this restaurant and bar is shaded b coconut palms and graced with clear views of the water. Bahamia specialties—panfried grouper, baked hog snapper, fresh conch sala ribs, chicken, and pork chops—make it a favorite hangout for loca and visitors. Fresh lobster, prepared to your liking, is available in sea son (August–March). Hank's signature cocktail, aptly named "Hank Panky," is a dynamite frozen rum and fruit juice concoction. If you' looking for a cheap stay, Hank has four air-conditioned guest room for rent. He also rents flats boats and he can arrange fishing guide ⊠*Fresh Creek* ☎242/368–2447 ⊕*www.hanks-place.com* ⚠*Reserv tions not accepted* ▭*MC, V.*

★ ☾ $–$$ ▥ **Small Hope Bay Lodge.** This casual, palm-shaded oceanfront proper has a devoted following of divers, snorkelers, eco-adventurers, angler and families. Rooms with Androsia batik prints and straw work a in beachside cottages made of coral rock and Andros pine. The home main lodge—with a dining room, bar-lounge, game room, and readir area—is the center of activity. Tasty Bahamian meals include lavis seafood buffets and pig roasts. For an additional charge you can sele bonefishing and specialty diving packages, such as guided exploratio of blue holes, diving instruction and certification, and "over-the-wal dives. Rates include meals, taxes, service charges, and airport tran fers. **Pros:** best dive operation on Andros, laid-back natural ambianc warm and welcoming service. **Cons:** limited nightlife, you'll need inse repellent when the wind dies down. ⊠*Small Hope Bay, Fresh Cre ☎242/368–2014 or 800/223–6961* ⊕*www.smallhope.com* ⚲*20 co tages* ⚡*In-room: no a/c; no phone, no TV. In-hotel: restaurant, ba beachfront, diving, water sports, bicycles, laundry service, public Inte net, some pets allowed* ▭*AE, D, MC, V* ⭕*AI.*

$ ▥ **Andros Lighthouse Yacht Club and Marina.** This is the best place Andros to park your boat, though if you have a full-time captain the are a number of anchorages around the island. You're sure to me an ever-changing parade of people in the cocktail lounge and resta rant (there's a Bahamian buffet lunch on Sundays), and the bar h its lively moments on the weekends. The spacious rooms and vill are comfortable, but in need of renovation. Boat rentals and fishi guides can be arranged. It's a five-minute walk across the bridge to Hank's Place Restaurant and Bar and the convenience stores of the main settlement area. The 31-space full-service marina can take boats up to 85 feet in length. Fishing guides and diving can be arranged. **Pros:** best location on Andros to safely park your boat; easy access to town, shops, restaurants. **Cons:** facility is in need of renovation, service at check-in and in the restaurant is often slow. ⊠*Andros Town* ☎*242/368–2305* ⊕*www.androslighthouse.com* ⌨*12 rooms, 8 villas* ⌕*In-room: refrigerator. In-hotel: restaurant, bar, pool, water sports, bicycles, no elevator, laundry service* ▤*AE, D, MC, V.*

> **DID YOU KNOW?**
>
> In the Bahamas, mail is still delivered by mail boats, as it has been for decades. Mail boats leave Nassau's Potter's Cay carrying mail, cars, produce, consumer goods, and passengers on trips to more than 30 Bahamian islands. The voyages range from the four-hour cruise to Andros to the overnight trip to Inagua in the south.

SPORTS & THE OUTDOORS

BICYCLING In Andros Town, bicycles are available at **Andros Lighthouse Yacht Club and Marina** (☎*242/368–2305*). Cruise around Fresh Creek after renting a bike from **Small Hope Bay Lodge** (☎*242/368–2014*).

BOATING & FISHING **Small Hope Bay Lodge** (☎*242/368–2014 or 800/223–6961*) has bone-, deep-sea, fly-, reef, and seasonal tarpon fishing, as well as a "west side overnight"—a two-night camping and bone- and tarpon-fishing trip to the island's uninhabited western end. Rates run $250–$300 for a half day and $375–$500 for a full day (full-day trips include all gear and lunch).

ARGILL CREEK

Fishing—bonefishing in particular—is this tranquil area's principal appeal, with wadable flats winding along the shoreline all the way to Behring Point. Cargill Creek is approximately 20 mi south of Andros Town (30 minutes by taxi). Taxi fare is about $40 one way for two passengers. Bonefishing packages run $350 to $600 per person per day at the half dozen lodges in the area.

WHERE TO STAY

$$$$ 🏨 **Andros Island Bonefishing Club.** If you're a hard-core bonefisher, and want to do some diving as well, AIBC is a good choice. Guests have access to 100 square mi of lightly fished flats, including wadable flats right out front. Owner Captain Rupert Leadon is a gregarious, attention-grabbing presence with many a story of the elusive bonefish, and his team of professional guides are highly regarded. The 20-acre waterfront property is laced with palm trees and well-tended gardens and lawns. Rooms are comfortable, with queen-size beds, mini-refrigerators, and ceiling fans. The dining room–lounges have satellite TV and fly-tying tables. Meals are hearty, with Bahamian fare such as fresh grilled seafood and peas 'n' rice served up family style. Package rates include room, meals, guided fishing, laundry service, and airport trans-

Undersea Adventures in Andros

Andros probably has the largest number of dive sites in the country. With the third-longest barrier reef in the world (behind those of Australia and Belize), the island offers about 100 mi of drop-off diving into the Tongue of the Ocean.

Uncounted numbers of **blue holes** are forming in the area. In some places, these constitute vast submarine networks that can extend more than 200 feet down into the coral (Fresh Creek, 40–100 feet; North Andros, 40–200-plus feet; South Bight, 40–200 feet). Blue holes are named for their inky-blue aura when viewed from above and for the light-blue filtered sunlight that is visible from many feet below. Some of the holes have vast cathedral-like interior chambers with stalactites and stalagmites, offshoot tunnels, and seemingly endless corridors. Others have distinct thermoclines (temperature changes) between layers of water or are subject to tidal flow.

The dramatic Fresh Creek site provides an insight into the complex Andros cave system. There isn't much coral growth, but there are plenty of midnight parrot fish, big southern stingrays, and some blacktip sharks. Similar blue holes are found all along the barrier reef, including several at Mastic Point in the north and the ones explored and filmed off South Bight.

Undersea adventurers also have the opportunity to investigate wrecks such as the *Potomac,* a steel-hulled freighter that sank in 1952 and lies in 40 feet of water off Nicholl's Town. And off the waters of Fresh Creek, at 70 feet, lies the 56-foot-long World War II LCM (landing craft mechanized) known only as the **Barge Wreck,**

which was sunk in 1963 to create an artificial reef. Now encrusted with coral, it's home to a school of groupers and a blizzard of tiny silverfish. There is a fish-cleaning station where miniature cleaning shrimp and yellow gobies clean grouper and rockfish by swimming into their mouths and out their gills, picking up food particles. It's an excellent subject matter for close-up photography.

The split-level **Over the Wall** dive at Fresh Creek takes novices to the 80-foot ledge and experienced divers to a pre–Ice Age beach at 185 feet. The wall is covered with black coral and all kinds of tube sponges. **Small Hope Bay Lodge** is the most respected dive resort on Andros. It's a friendly, informal place where the only thing taken seriously is diving. There's a fully equipped dive center with a wide variety of specialty dives, including customized family-dive trips with a private dive boat and dive master. If you're not certified, check out the lodge's morning "resort course" and be ready to explore the depths by afternoon. If you are certified, don't forget to bring your C card.

If you are leery of diving but want to view the spectacular undersea world, try a snorkeling excursion. Shallow reefs, beginning in six feet of water, and extending down to sixty feet or more, are ideal locations for spotting myriad brightly colored fish, sea urchins, and starfish. Don't forget your underwater camera!

Winter water temperatures average about 74°F, 23°C. In the summer, water temperatures average about 84°F, 28°C.

fers. **Pros:** one of the best bonefishing lodges in the Bahamas, prime location on Cargill Creek. **Cons:** not much for nonanglers other than diving and relaxing. ⊠*Cargill Creek* ☎*242/368–5167* ⊕*www.andros bonefishing.com* ↻*30 rooms* ⚘*In-room: no phone, refrigerator, no TV. In-hotel: 2 restaurants, bars, pool, diving, water sports, laundry service, public Internet* ⊟*MC, V* ⎟⊚*AI.*

SPORTS & THE OUTDOORS

FISHING **Andy Smith** (☎*242/368–4261 or 242/368–4044*) is highly recom-
★ mended for guiding anglers through the Bights and on the West Side.
★ **Charlie Neymour** is another respected bonefishing and tarpon guide. Con-
tact Nottages Cottages (☎*242/368–4297* ⊕*www.bigcharlieandros.com*) to hire him. Call **Tranquility Hill Fishing Lodge** (☎☎*242/368–4132*) at Behring Point to book Barry Neymour, Frankie Neymour, Deon Neymour, Ivan Neymour, Dwain Neymour, Ray Mackey, and Ricardo Mackey, all recommended guides. Rooms and all-inclusive fishing pack-ages are available at Tranquility Hill.

5

ANGROVE CAY

Remote **Mangrove Cay** is sandwiched between two sea-green bights, separating it from north and south Andros and creating an island of black coral shorelines, gleaming deserted beaches, and dense pine for-ests. **Moxey Town,** known locally as Little Harbour, rests on the north-east corner in a coconut grove. Pink piles of conch shells and mounds of porous sponges dot the small harbor of this commercial fishing and sponging community. Anglers come on a mission, in search of giant bonefish on flats called "the promised land" and "land of the giants." A five-minute boat ride takes fly-fishers to Gibson Cay to wade hard sand flats sprinkled with starfish.

The **Victoria Point Blue Hole** is good for snorkeling and diving, and there are a number of pristine spots sure to please naturalists looking for birds or wild orchids. The cay's main road runs south from Moxey Town, past the airport, then along coconut-tree-shaded beaches to the settlement of Lisbon Creek. From here, a free government ferry (☎*242/369–0331*) makes trips twice daily (usually at 8 and 4) across the South Bight to Driggs Hill, South Andros.

WHERE TO EAT & STAY

★ $$ ✕**Barefoot Bar and Grill.** Every table has a perfect ocean view at this warm and friendly beachfront restaurant and bar at the Seascape Inn. Owners Mickey and Joan McGowan do the baking and cooking them-selves. Enjoy the sunrise over coffee with steaming scones, cinnamon buns, orange-walnut break, and fresh fruit. Chicken salad, burgers, sandwiches on kaiser rolls, and at times, quesadillas, are ample lunch temptations. Lunch items can also be prepared to take along as picnics on a daily outing. Chicken in white wine lime sauce, roast pork loin, grilled steaks, and fresh fish of the day are a few dinner sensations. Even if you're are full, the passion cake, mango cheesecake, and homemade ice creams should not be missed. ⊠*Seascape Inn* ☎*242/369–0342* ⊟*AE, MC, V* ⊙*Might be closed in July and Aug.; call ahead.*

$ ⊡ **Mangrove Cay Inn.** Set in a coconut grove with wild orchid and hibiscus gardens, the inn caters to island aficionados and anglers alike. The rooms are decorated in peach and green with light Andros pine walls. Enjoy your favorite fresh seafood dish or a cold Kalik while relaxing in the restaurant and bar. Rent a bicycle to explore the cay, roam miles of nearby beach, or hire a fishing guide. Two cottages are also available for rent—a one-bedroom and a two-bedroom, with full kitchens and satellite TV, overlooking a saltwater lake filled with baby tarpon and snappers. Rates include taxes and gratuity. **Pros:** on-site restaurant and bar, quiet location near the beach, friendly staff. **Cons:** this isn't for you if you are not an angler or are high maintenance, you need insect repellent on calm humid days. ⊠ *5 minutes south of the Mangrove Cay Airport on the island's main road* ☎*242/369–0069* ⊕*www. mangrovecayinn.net* ↩*12 rooms, 2 cottages* ⊘*In-room: no phone, kitchen (some), no TV (some), ethernet (some). In-hotel: restaurant, bar, bicycles, laundry service* ▤*No credit cards.*

★ $ ⊡ **Seascape Inn.** Five individual impeccably-maintained cottages with private decks overlook the glass-clear ocean. Many repeat guests say this is the most relaxing place in the world, and they take advantage of it by vacationing here two or three times a year. The elevated restaurant and beachfront bar is *the* place to relax, swap stories, and enjoy cocktails with the locals. Breakfasts, included in the room rate, consist of homemade banana bread, cinnamon buns, assorted muffins, and fresh fruit. On-site owners Mickey and Joan McGowan make guest feel like family. Mickey leads the diving program and can arrange for a fishing guide, or point you in the right direction to explore land and sea on your own. **Pros:** perfect beachfront location for a do-it-yourself vacation, outstanding food, guests are treated like family. **Cons:** no air-conditioning or TV, you need insect repellent when the wind is down. ⊠*About 5 minutes south of the Mangrove Cay Airport on the island's main road* ☎ *242/369–0342* ⊕*www.seascapeinn.com* ↩*4 1-bedroom cottages, 1 cottage suite* ⊘*In-room: no a/c, no phone, no TV. In-hotel: restaurant, bar, beachfront, diving, water sports, bicycles, laundry service, public Internet* ▤*AE, MC, V* ⵔ*BP.*

SPORTS & THE OUTDOORS

BICYCLING   Rent a bicycle from **Seascape Inn** (☎*242/369–0342*) and pedal around the island.

DIVING &   The dive shop at **Seascape Inn** (☎*242/369–0342*) has snorkeling and
SNORKELING   diving excursions, and rents dive equipment and kayaks. A minimum of four people is required per group. You need to call a day in advance.

SOUTH ANDROS–DRIGGS HILL

Driggs Hill, on South Andros, is a small settlement of pastel houses, a tiny church, a grocery store, the government dock, and the Emerald Palms Resort of South Andros. A mile south is the Congo Town airport. Eight miles farther south, the Bluff settlement sprawls atop a hill overlooking miles of golden beaches, lush cays, and the Tongue of the Ocean. Here skeletons of Arawak natives were found huddled together.

A local resident attests that another skeleton was found—this one of a 4-foot-tall, one-eyed owl, which may have given rise to the legend of the mythical, elflike chickcharnie.

WHERE TO EAT & STAY

$$ ✕ **Emerald Palms Clubhouse Restaurant.** The breakfast buffet in the Clubhouse Restaurant at the Emerald Palms Resort is a pleasant way to energize your day. You can choose from fresh fruits and cereals or scrambled eggs and bacon. The brightly colored dining room overlooks the resort's pool and beach. At lunch, burgers, conch salad, pan fried grouper, and club sandwiches can be served on the terrace by the pool. The adjacent bar is a relaxing spot for a predinner cocktail. Nightly dining specialties are broiled lobster, grilled fresh mahimahi, steaks, chops, and chicken prepared Bahamian style. A children's menu is available. ⊠ *Emerald Palms Resort, Driggs Hill* ☎*242/369–2713* ▱*AE, D, DC, MC, V.*

$$$–$$$$ ▥ **Tiamo Resorts.** You arrive at this low-key yet sophisticated South Bight eco-resort via private ferry. Over-the-top service awaits, along with a cold drink in the lodge—a stress-free gathering place with wood-beam ceilings that naturally combines bar, lounge, library, and dining room. Individual bungalows with wraparound porches are strung out along the powdery beach, shaded by coconut palms.

Fodor's Choice ★

> **BEST OF THE BEST**
>
> Want some low-key pampering and eco-adventure? There's no better spot than Tiamo Resort on South Andros. You can explore the island and ocean wilds on foot or in a sea kayak. But don't try to lose weight here because the food is just too good!

Commodious bedrooms with soft linens are positioned to receive the cooling ocean breeze. Leisurely meals, exquisitely prepared with the freshest ingredients, include seafood delights, homemade breads, and luscious desserts. All meals and snacks are included in the room rate. To explore the wilds of sea and land, guided snorkeling, sea kayaking, nature hikes, and fishing excursions can be arranged at your whim. **Pros:** 1.5-to-1 staff-to-guest ratio, spectacular private beachfront location, best meals in the Bahamas. **Cons:** you'll need insect repellent on calm humid days. ⊠ *South Bight, accessible only by boat* ☎*242/357–2489* ⊕*www.tiamoresorts.com* ▭*11 bungalows* ⌂*In-room: no a/c, no phone, no TV. In-hotel: restaurant, bar, beachfront, diving, water sports, laundry service, no kids under 12* ▱*AE, D, DC, MC, V* ❐*AI.*

$ ▥ **Emerald Palms Resort of South Andros.** This boutique oceanside property has 18 one- and two-bedroom villas with marble floors, mahogany furniture, king-size or twin beds, individual gardens, and private decks surrounded by palm trees. The spacious clubhouse rooms run along the blue-tile pool and out to the glimmering beach. Ask for one of the beachfront rooms or villas. Hearty Bahamian breakfasts, light zesty lunches, and theme-night four-course dinners are served in the poolside restaurant. A cabana bar overlooks the gin-clear sea. The resort is family-friendly, and island excursions and guided fishing can be arranged. **Pros:** spacious villa accommodations are ideal for families and small groups, pristine beachfront location, good access to prime diving and fishing. **Cons:** need to create your own nightlife, service can be slow in the restaurant. ⊠*Driggs Hill* ☎*242/369–2713* ⊕*www.emerald-palms. com* ➷*18 rooms, 18 villas* ♿*In-room: no phone (some), kitchen (some). In-hotel: restaurant, bars, pool, beachfront, water sports, bicycles, laundry service, public Internet* ▤*AE, D, DC, MC, V.*

SPORTS & THE OUTDOORS

FISHING   **Emerald Palms Resort of South Andros** (☎*242/369–2711*) can arrange boat rentals and schedule guides for bonefishing, reef fishing, or deep-sea fishing.

ANDROS ESSENTIALS

TRANSPORTATION

BY AIR

There are four airports on Andros. The San Andros airport is in North Andros; the Andros Town airport is in Central Andros; the South Andros airport is in Congo Town; and the Mangrove Cay airport is on Mangrove Cay. Check with your hotel for the closest airport. Several small airlines and charter companies have flights from Nassau. Daily charter service is also available from Fort Lauderdale and Freeport.

Bahamasair does not offer consistent service to Andros. Western Air has two flights per day from Nassau to each of the four Andros airports; it offers the best and cheapest service to Andros. Lynx Air International flies from Fort Lauderdale to Congo Town three days a week, and is a good choice for travelers going to Tiamo or Emerald Palms. Gulfstream International flies from Fort Lauderdale to Andros Town four days a week. Major Air has charter service from Freeport to all four airports, and regular service Friday and Sunday. Small Hope Bay Lodge offers flights from Fort Lauderdale to Andros Town for a minimum of two passengers and can arrange charter flights for island-hopping.

Airlines & Contacts **Bahamasair** (☎*242/339–4415 or 800/222–4262*). **Gulfstream International** (☎*800/231–0856*). **Lynx Air International** (☎*888/596–9247*). **Major Air** (☎*242/352–5778*). **Small Hope Bay Lodge** (☎*242/368–2014 or 800/223–6961*). **Western Air** (☎*242/377–2222 Nassau, 242/329–4000 San Andros, 242/368–2759 Andros Town, 242/369–0003 Mangrove Cay, 242/369–2222 Congo Town*).

Airport Information **Andros Town** (☎*242/368–2030*). **Congo Town** (☎*242/369–2640*). **Mangrove Cay** (☎*242/369–0083*). **San Andros** (☎*242/329–4224*).

BY BOAT

A free government ferry makes the half-hour trip between Mangrove Cay and South Andros twice daily. It departs South Andros at 8 AM and 4 PM and departs Mangrove Cay at 8:30 AM and 4:30 PM, but schedules are subject to change. Call the Commissioner's Office for more information.

From Potter's Cay Dock in Nassau, the M/V *Lisa J III* sails to Morgan's Bluff and Nicholl's Town in the north of the island every Wednesday, returning to Nassau the following Tuesday. The trip takes six hours and costs $30. The M/V *Lady D* leaves Nassau on Tuesday for Fresh Creek (with stops at Stafford Creek, Blanket Sound, and Behring Point) and returns to Nassau on Sunday. The trip takes 5½ hours, and the fare is $35. The M/V *Mangrove Cay Express* leaves Nassau on Thursday evening for Driggs Hill, Mangrove Cay, and Cargill Creek and returns on Tuesday afternoon. The trip takes 5½ hours and costs $30. The M/V *Captain Moxey* leaves Nassau on Monday and calls at Kemp's Bay, Long Bay Cays, and the Bluff on South Andros. It returns to Nassau on Wednesday. The trip takes 7½ hours; the fare is $35. Schedules are subject to change due to weather conditions or occasional dry-docking. For more information, contact the Dockmaster's Office at Potter's Cay.

Boat & Ferry Information Commissioner's Office (☎ 242/369–0331). **Dockmaster's Office** (☎ 242/393–1064).

5

BY CAR
The main roads are generally in good shape, but watch out for potholes and remember to drive on the left. Many visitors opt to get around by bicycle. If you need a rental car, your best bet is to have your hotel make arrangements. It's smart to book a month or more in advance during high season (March–May), as the number of vehicles is limited.

BY TAXI
Taxis meet incoming planes at the airports, but they can also be arranged ahead of time through hotels. Rates are around $1.50 a mile, though most fares are set from one location to another. You should always agree on a fare before your ride begins. Cab drivers will charge $80–$120 for a half-day tour of the island.

ONTACTS & RESOURCES

BANKS & EXCHANGE SERVICES
The Canadian Imperial Bank of Commerce in San Andros is open Wednesday 10:30–2:30. There are also banks in Fresh Creek, Kemps Bay, and on Mangrove Cay that are open two to three days a week, usually Monday and Wednesday, and sometimes Friday.

Bank Information Canadian Imperial Bank of Commerce (☎ 242/329–2382).

EMERGENCIES
Telephone service is available only through the front desk at most Andros hotels, so emergencies should be reported to the management. Medical clinics are in Mastic Point, Nicholl's Town, Lowe Sound, Fresh Creek, and Kemps Bay.

Contacts Medical Clinics (☎ 242/329–2055 *Nicholl's Town/North Andros, 242/368–2038 Fresh Creek, 242/369–0089 Mangrove Cay, 242/369–4849 Kemp's Bay/South Andros*). **Police** (☎ 919 *North Andros, 242/368–2626 Fresh Creek/Central Andros, 242/369–4733 Kemp's Bay/South Andros*).

THE BERRY ISLANDS

The Berry Islands consist of more than two dozen small islands and almost a hundred tiny cays stretching in a sliver moon–like curve north of Andros and New Providence Island. Although a few of the islands are privately owned, most of them are uninhabited—except by rare birds using the territory as their nesting grounds or by visiting yachters dropping anchor in secluded havens. The Berry Islands start in the north at Great Stirrup Cay, where a lighthouse guides passing ships, and they end in the south at Chub Cay, only 35 mi north of Nassau.

Most of the islands' 700 residents live on Great Harbour Cay, which is 10 mi long and 1½ mi wide. Its main settlement, Bullock's Harbour, has a couple good restaurants near the marina, plus a grocery store and some small shops. The Great Harbour Cay resort and beach area, a few miles away from Bullock's Harbour, was developed in the early 1970s. In 2007, more than 15 new homes were built, and many of the older beach villas and cottages were remodeled. Some owners rent their properties through **Air Charter Bahamas** (☎ *305/885–6665 or 866/359–4752 ⊕www.aircharterbahamas.com*). Although the area has long been geared toward offshore fishing, in recent years family vacations and bonefishing have become more popular. Both Chub and Great Harbour cays are close to the Tongue of the Ocean, where big-game fish roam. Remote flats south of Great Harbour, from Anderson Cay to Money Cay, are excellent bonefish habitats, as are the flats around Chub Cay. Deeper water flats hold permit and tarpon.

The Berry Islands appear just north of Andros Island on the Bahamas map at the front of the book.

CHUB CAY

WHERE TO EAT & STAY

$ ✕⚏ **Chub Cay Marina & Resort.** This is one of the best sportfishing locations anywhere, with the Tongue of the Ocean at its doorstep and the Great Bahama Bank bending around to the Joulters Cays. The full-service luxury yacht marina reopened in June 2006, along with 16 renovated hotel rooms in the Harbour House hotel. The hotel restaurant serves three meals a day, with wonderful fresh seafood nightly. Boaters have 110 slips, and the resort has a beachfront infinity swimming pool and a bar. The 22,000-square-foot, three-level clubhouse and restaurant is scheduled to open in late 2008. More than 20 five-bedroom villas are going up; eight of these opulently furnished units, in varying configurations with ultramodern kitchens, are available for rental. The five-year plan for the resort includes 65 villa homes, 55 marina town houses, three restaurants, bars, and a shopping village. A 5,000-foot paved airstrip is open for private and charter aircraft. Flats fishing guides can be arranged. **Pros:** the full-service marina is one of the best hurricane holes in the Bahamas, excellent location for flats and offshore fishing, good on-site restaurant and bar. **Cons:** noisy and congested with construction, check-in and other service are often slow. ⊠ *Chub Cay, Berry Islands* ☎242/325–1490 *or* 877/234–2482 ⊕www.chub-

cay.com ⇋*16 rooms; 8 villas* ⚓ *In-room: no phone, kitchen (some), refrigerator (some), DVD (some). In-hotel: restaurant, bars, tennis court, pool, beachfront, bicycles, no elevator, laundry facilities, public Wi-Fi* ☰*AE, MC, V.*

SPORTS & THE OUTDOORS

BOATING The clarity of Bahamian waters is particularly evident when you cross the Great Bahama Bank from the Bimini area, then cruise along the Berry Islands on the way to Nassau. The water's depth is seldom more than 20 feet here. Grass patches and an occasional coral head or flat coral patch dot the light-sand bottom. Starfish abound, and you can often catch a glimpse of a gliding stingray or eagle ray. You might spot the odd turtle, and if you care to jump over the boat's side with a mask, you might also pick up a conch or two in the grass. Especially good snorkeling and bonefishing, and peaceful anchorages, can be found on the lee shores of the Hoffmans and Little Harbour cays. When it's open, **Flo's Conch Bar,** at the southern end of Little Harbour Cay, serves fresh conch prepared every way you can imagine.

> ### EARLY BIRD DINNERS
>
> Dinner is commonly served in most restaurants starting at 6 PM, and can be over by 8:30. It is always best to call ahead for reservations, and to let the restaurant know you are coming for sure, as hours can be irregular, or restaurants can just decide to close if they think they aren't going to be busy.

REAT HARBOUR CAY

WHERE TO EAT

★ $$ ✕**Coolie Mae's.** Expats, locals, and visitors rate Mae's food as the best on the island. Her bright sign makes the casual 60 seat restaurant in the Village, on the north side of the marina entrance, easy to find. Mae's secret is simple: she uses the best and freshest ingredients available each day to serve up wonderful home-style chow. Midday try the conch salad, panfried grouper, or a tasty burger. Broiled lobster, steaks, pork chops, and fried conch along with peas 'n' rice and macaroni and cheese are dinner specialties. The menu changes daily. Conch fritters and cocktails are often served at sunset, and island art exhibits are on display throughout the year. ⊠*The Village* ☎*242/367—8730* ☰*No credit cards* ☉*Call ahead for daily hours, can be closed in hurricane season.*

$$ ✕**Tamboo Dinner Club.** A tradition at the Great Harbour Marina, this supper club is open Wednesday and Saturday, and other nights with reservations depending on the season. There is usually a lively crowd enjoying grilled seafood and Bahamian specialties like smothered chicken with macaroni and cheese. The bar has satellite TV and backgammon. ⊠*Great Harbour Marina* ☎*242/367–8203* ☰*No credit cards* ☉*Sometimes closed in Aug. and Sept.; call ahead.*

$ ✕**The Beach Club.** This is the island's cool locale for breakfast and lunch, across the road from the airport, overlooking the beach and turquoise water. At breakfast go for the eggs and ham with home grits. At lunch they grill a nice cheeseburger, and whatever fresh fish they have at the time. Takeout is available, including fishing lunches. Dinner is available on request, but if you eat at the open-air tables, be sure to have insect repellent, especially if the wind is down. Hours and days are irregular, so talk to the locals or go by to see if it's open. ⊠*Across from Great Harbour Airport* ☎*No phone* ▤*No credit cards.*

WHERE TO STAY

$$–$$$$ 🏠**Tat's Rental.** Located in the Beach Villas, just northeast of the airport, this property management company rents spacious marina town houses, beach villas, and beach homes. The 1,600-square-foot town houses, for couples or groups of up to eight guests, include a private dock on the marina for boats up to 30 feet. Beach villas range in size from studios to three bedrooms, and are situated on the 8-mi-long crescent beach just to the east of the airport. Custom homes on this same beach, some brand new, range in size from three to five bedrooms and can include satellite TV. Tat's also rents cars and jeeps. **Pros:** best selection of beachfront rentals on the island, airport greeting and check-in service, other activities and rentals can be arranged. **Cons:** no phones or Internet service, most units don't have TV. ⊠*Beach Villas, Great Harbour Cay* ☎*242/367–8123 or 242/464–4361* ⊕*www.tatsrental. com* ⤳*Rentals vary* ⌂*In-room: no phone, kitchen, no TV (some). In-hotel: no elevator, laundry facilities* ▤*AE, MC, V.*

★ $–$$$ 🏠**Berry Islands Vacation Rental.** There are two convenient marina location options—the Anglers Roost one-bedroom apartment, and the Seaside Cottage, a lovely three-bedroom house with huge decks, a freshwater pool and outside bar, and a dock that can take boats up to 50 feet long. Both rentals were repainted in late 2007 and refurnished with comfortable bamboo couches and other touches, plus they have satellite TV and VHF radio. The apartment is ideal for one couple, or two guys on a fishing trip. The house works for families and groups of friends. Or rent both to create a four-bedroom setup. The minimum rental on the Seaside Cottage is one week. Four sea kayaks are included; ideal for exploring and flats fishing. You must book well in advance for these prime rentals. **Pros:** ideal off-the-beaten-path location for couples or families, easy access to beaches and bonefish flats, economical. **Cons:** you need to rent a golf cart to get around and gather supplies. ⊠ *Located on a private peninsula about 5 minutes by boat, 10 minutes by golf cart, from Great Harbour Marina* ☎*561/313–4760 or 242/367–8155* ⊕*www.berryislands.com* ⤳*2 villas* ⌂*In-room: kitchen, VCR. In-hotel: pool, bicycles, no elevator, laundry facilities.*

¢ 🏠**Great Harbour Inn.** Perched at the water's edge on the marina in Great Harbour, this inn has convenient access to the area's restaurants, shops, and activities. The suites, clean and neat but in need of renovation, range in size from 450 to 900 square feet, and have private baths, mini-kitchens, and laundry facilities. The larger water-view suites have decks and porches. To make a reservation you must be persistent, as the owners don't always answer the phone. But hey, this laid-back style is a main reason people go to Great Harbour, and of course there are the fabulous beaches and fishing. **Pros:** good choice for a no-frills economical getaway, easy access to nearby beaches and fishing. **Cons:** no TV or Internet service, can be hot and buggy when the wind is down.

✉*On the waterfront at Great Harbour Marina* ☎*242/367–8370 or 242/451–8370* ⊕*www.greatharbourinn.itgo.com* ➪*5 suites* ♿*In-room: no phone, kitchen, no TV. In-hotel: no elevator, laundry service* ▭*No credit cards.*

SPORTS & THE OUTDOORS

BOATING   In the upper Berry Islands, the full-service **Great Harbour Cay Marina** (☎*242/367–8005*) has 80 slips that can handle boats up to 150 feet. Accessible through an 80-foot-wide channel from the bank side, the marina has one of the Bahamas' most pristine beaches running along its east side. The marina is also one of the best hurricane holes in the Bahamas. **Happy People's** (☎*242/367–8117*) has boats available for exploring the island. They also rent bikes, golf carts, and jeeps.

FISHING   **Percy Darville** (☎*242/464–4149 or 242/367–8005*) knows the flats of the Berries better than anyone, and two of his sons are now guiding with him. Call him as far in advance as possible to book a guide or rent a boat.

> **STOCK UP**
>
> Planning to rent a private house? Be sure to take all essentials with you, including food, toiletries, insect repellent, and medicine, and check with local island providers in advance to see when the supply boats arrive. Then dash down to the local store the minute the supply boat docks to be sure food, drink, and other items are available. Fresh produce, eggs, milk, meat, and cheese are the most commonly out-of-stock food items.

5

HE BERRY ISLANDS ESSENTIALS

RANSPORTATION

BY AIR
Air Charter Bahamas flies to Great Harbour Cay and Chub Cay from South Florida. Private flights are chartered to fit your schedule, although the company, with advance notice and flexibility on your part, can attempt to group you with other passengers to provide you with a better fare. They also can arrange beach villas for rental for their air-charter clients. A number of other air-charter companies fly to Great Harbour and Chub Cay from Nassau.

Airlines & Contacts Air Charter Bahamas (☎*305/885–6665 or 866/359–4752*).

BY BOAT
Captain Gurth Dean leaves Potter's Cay, Nassau, Friday evening for Bullock Harbour, with stops in Sandy Point and Moore's Island, Abaco. The trip takes about seven hours and costs $40 one way. Return is Sunday morning. *Bimini Mack* leaves Potter's Cay, Nassau, Thursday afternoon for Chub Cay, with stops in Bimini and Cat Cay, which is just south of Bimini. The trip takes about 12 hours and costs $45 one

way. Return is Monday morning. For schedules and specific destinations, call the Dockmaster's Office at Potter's Cay.

Boat & Ferry Information Dockmaster's Office (☎ 242/393–1064).

CONTACTS & RESOURCES

EMERGENCIES
Contacts **Great Harbour Cay Medical Clinic** (☎ 242/367–8400). **Police** (☎ 242/367–8344).

THE BIMINIS

The Biminis have long been known as the Bahamas' big-game-fishing capital. The nearest of the Bahamian islands to the U.S. mainland, they consist of a handful of islands and cays just 50 mi east of Miami, across the Gulf Stream that sweeps the area's western shores. Most visitors spend their time on North Bimini. Marinas such as Weech's Bimini Dock, the Bimini Big Game Marina, and Blue Water Marina—all on skinny North Bimini's eastern side—provide more than 150 slips for oceangoing craft, many of them belonging to weekend visitors who make the short trip from Florida ports. The Biminis also have a notorious history as a jumping-off place for illicit dealings; first during the Civil War, when it was a refuge for profiteers bringing in war supplies from Europe, and then during Prohibition, when it was a haven for rumrunners. Today things are pretty quiet—rumrunners have been replaced by anglers and Floridians. And since 2006, with the opening of Bimini Bay Resort's deluxe 136-slip marina, there is now almost twice the space for boaters to park and party. South Bimini has a 53-slip marina complete with a customs and immigration center at the Bimini Sands resort complex. Just looking for a beach? North Bimini's western side, along Queen's Highway, is one long stretch of inviting white sand divided into three sections: Radio Beach, Blister Beach, and Spook Hill. All three sections are ideal for swimming, snorkeling, or just catching rays.

Most of the hotels, restaurants, churches, and stores in the Biminis are along North Bimini's King's and Queen's highways, which run parallel to each other. Everything on North Bimini, where most of the islands' 1,600 inhabitants reside, is so close that you do not need a car to get around. Sparsely populated South Bimini, separated from its big brother by a narrow ocean passage, is where Juan Ponce de León allegedly looked for the Fountain of Youth in 1513. Tourists have easy access to the Fountain of Youth site by way of a very good road, close to South Bimini's little airstrip.

Ernest Hemingway did battle with his share of game fish around North Bimini, which he visited for the first time in 1935 from his home in Key West. He made frequent visits, and wrote much of *To Have and Have Not* and *Islands in the Stream* here. He is remembered in the area as a picaresque hero, not only for his graphic descriptions of fishing

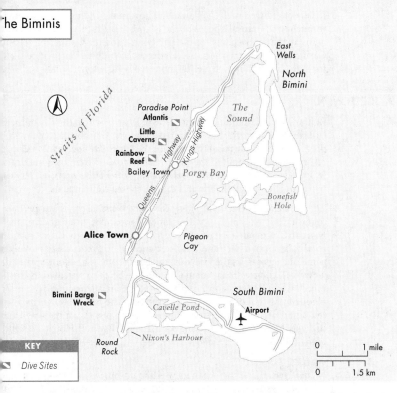

exploits, but for his drinking and brawling, including a fistfight he had with his brother Leicester on the Bimini dock. Other notables lured to the island include Howard Hughes and Richard Nixon. The American with the strongest ties to the Biminis was entrepreneur Michael Lerner. He discovered Bimini years before Hemingway and is the man credited with teaching the writer how to catch giant tuna. Lerner was a great friend to the Biminis and established, among other things, the Lerner Marine Research Laboratory, which conducted research on dolphins and sharks from 1947 to 1974.

Now, spring break brings hordes of students who cruise over from Fort Lauderdale for wild nights. Unlike the rest of the Out Islands, Bimini experiences its busy season in the summer, owing to the invasion of vacationing boaters from Florida. In 2006, the landscape and atmosphere of North Bimini changed considerably with the opening of the Bimini Bay Resort. The efficient design and layout of this tropical-hued luxury resort complex includes the 136-slip Fisherman's Village Marina, the 96-slip Nautica Yacht Club Marina designed specifically for megayachts, oceanfront homesites, marina condominiums and town houses, private island homesites, and restaurants, with more to come—namely, a Robert Trent Jones Jr. golf course and a Conrad Hotel and Casino, scheduled for completion in 2010. So far the developers have worked well with the Bahamian government to preserve the environment and natural appeal of the island, though there are detractors who say the future plans for the golf course and the Conrad Hotel and Casino are more than the natural habitat can endure. Time will tell, but for sure, North Bimini is no longer a sleepy little Out Island.

ALICE TOWN

Bimini's main community, Alice Town, is at North Bimini's southern end. It's neat and tidy, and painted in happy Caribbean pastels. In a prominent location stand the ruins of the **Bimini Bay Rod and Gun Club,** a resort and casino built in the early 1920s and destroyed by a hurricane in 1926. A short walk away is the **Bimini Native Straw and Craft Market,** which bustles on weekends and during fishing tournaments.

The back door of the small, noisy **End of the World Saloon** is always open to the harbor. This place—with a sandy floor and visitors' graffiti, business cards, and other surprises on every surface—is a good spot to meet local folks over a beer and a lobster and conch pizza, while playing a game of ring toss. In the late '60s, the bar became a hangout of the late New York congressman Adam Clayton Powell, who retreated to North Bimini while Congress investigated his alleged misdemeanors. A marble plaque in his honor is displayed in the bar. The bar is 100 yards from the Bimini Bay Rod and Gun Club ruins, and just down the way from Brown's Marina and Big John's Conch Shell Bar and Hotel. ⊠*King's Hwy.* ☎*No phone* ☉*Daily 9* AM–3 AM.

WHERE TO EAT

★ **$$$** ✕**Casa Lyon.** Enjoy the ocean view while noshing on artistic yet simple island dishes from the freshest of ingredients. Breakfast includes hot baked breads, eggs any style, fresh fruit, and juices. Dinner—the most formal on the island—includes starters of stir-fried seafood infusion, crisp salads, and cracked conch or crab. For your entrée, try the country-style roast beef with gold mashed potatoes, or a grilled grouper or wahoo with sesame seed and pineapple glaze. For dessert, the homemade apple pie is even better à la mode. The restaurant is in the Bimini Bay Resort, within walking distance of their marina. ⊠*Bimini Bay Resort, King's Hwy.* ☎*242/347–2900* ▭*AE, MC, V* ☉ *No lunch.*

$$ ✕**Tackle Box Bar & Grill.** Part of the Bimini Big Game Resort & Yacht Club, this is a popular anglers' and boaters' hangout. The restaurant serves American breakfasts of eggs, bacon, and French toast; lunches of burgers, fries, fritters, salads, and sandwiches; and at dinner try the grilled fresh fish or conch pizza. For the party crowd, late-night snacks are available. The bar overlooks the marina, and has live music once a week, usually on Friday night, and definitely during fishing tournaments. ⊠*King's Hwy.* ☎*242/347–3391* ▭*AE, MC, V.*

$ ✕**Captain Bob's.** Across from the Sea Crest Marina, centrally located in Alice Town, this casual joint starts serving rib-sticking American and Bahamian breakfasts at 6:30 AM seven days a week. This is an ideal place for anglers to start their day before heading out to the flats or the blue water. Lunches of burgers, conch, soups, salads, and fresh

Running for Rum

Following Britain's defeat in the American Revolutionary War, Southern loyalists brought their slaves to the Bahamas. They grew cotton under the Crown's protection, maintaining the "cotton connection" through the Civil War, when Bahamians got rich running Confederate cotton to English mills and sending military equipment to Southern rebels.

A century later, Bahamians grew wealthy once again, this time smuggling a precious liquid from Britain—liquor. After the Civil War, temperance took hold in America, and soon made its way across the water. Although many Bahamians "took the pledge" not to drink, their government did not follow the U.S. path to **Prohibition.** With alcohol legal and certain islands less than 60 mi from American shores, the Bahamas once again became an important trans-shipping point for contraband.

British and Scottish whiskey, rum, and gin distillers began transporting large quantities of liquor to the Bahamas. Their ships were too large to dock at Nassau harbor, so they anchored offshore, out of view of the American Consul and revenue agents. The goods were off-loaded onto smaller vessels and stored in a network of warehouses on shore, which became known as "**rum row.**" Some supplies were taken to the Out Islands for further transport. U.S. ships, often sailing under another flag to avoid detection, smuggled the bootleg booze to thirsty Americans, carrying the cargo through international waters, and ending up at drop-off points from Florida to New Jersey. But first, smugglers had to avoid U.S. Coast Guard ships that were prowling close to the Bahamas—this may have been the origin of the term "**rumrunning.**"

After Prohibition was repealed, the Bahamas lapsed into economic stagnation, but the United States maintained its interest in the islands due to their proximity. During World War II, the U.S. military set up camp, establishing an air and sea station in the Bahamas. Though the station is no longer in use, the islands still house military communications facilities, plus drug enforcement agents who guard against today's generation of smugglers.

In 1962 **Bacardi & Company,** the world's largest rum producer, opened a distillery in Nassau, which is set to close in 2009. Although there's also a Bahamian brewery, which produces the ever-popular **Kalik** beer, rum is the alcoholic beverage of choice in the Bahamas. The basic cocktail formula is simple: one or more types of rum plus fruit juice. You can order these drinks at every bar. This trio is the most popular:

Bahama Mama—light rum, coconut rum, Nassau Royale (vanilla-flavored rum), orange and pineapple juices.

Rum Punch—dark rum, orange and pineapple juices, grenadine, a dash of bitters.

Goombay Smash—light rum, coconut rum, pineapple juice, a dash of Galliano, and grenadine.

5

fish are served until 2 PM Monday through Saturday and until 1 PM on Sunday. If you call ahead, they can prepare fishing lunches to take out on your boat. ⊠ *Queen's Hwy.* ☎ *242/347–3260* ▭ *No credit cards* ⊘ *No dinner.*

$ ✕ **Red Lion Pub.** Venture through twin doors emblazoned with the red Tudor lions and treat yourself to fresh seafood, steaks, and Bahamian dishes in this casual, no-smoking restaurant. ⊠ *King's Hwy.* ☎ *242/347–3259* ▭ *No credit cards* ⊘ *Closed Mon. No lunch.*

WHERE TO STAY

★ $$$$ **Bimini Bay Resort.** You can choose an ocean view, a bay view, or both at this luxury resort that includes radiant condominiums and townhouses with island art, hardwood and rattan furnishings, lavish bedrooms and baths, and ultramodern kitchens. There are also larger single-family beach houses that make it hard for some guests to return to their own permanent homes. Why leave such posh digs in paradise? The pastel painted wooden structures, landscaping, fountains, and road systems blend with the natural terrain of beaches, palms, and the two bay-side marinas with infinity swimming pools to wow visitors. Spa Chakra opened in August 2008, offering an array of body and facial treatments. The Casa Lyon restaurant serves island delights; enjoy your lunch at the infinity pool grill. **Pros:** luxury accommodations and amenities on the beach, top quality marinas with all services. **Cons:** additional construction is still in progress, many staff members are still in training. ⊠ *King's Hwy., north of Bailey Town* ☎ *242/347–2900 or 305/513–0506* ⊕ *www.biminibayresort.com* ⇨ *20 studios, 29 1-bedroom condos, 113 2-bedroom condos, 12 3-bedroom condos, 3 3-bedroom estate homes, 6 4-bedroom estate homes* ♿ *In-room: kitchen, DVD (some), Wi-Fi (some). In-hotel: 3 restaurants, bars, pools, spa, beachfront, water sports, bicycles, no elevator, laundry service, public Internet, public Wi-Fi* ▭ *AE, MC, V.*

★ $$ **Bimini Big Game Resort & Yacht Club.** This resort is a favorite among the fishing and yachting crowd who take advantage of the full-service 103-slip marina. Anglers often prefer the spacious cottages, each with a built-in wet bar, refrigerator, and outdoor grill. First-floor rooms have views of the lush gardens or pool, while second-floor rooms have superb bay-front views. The beach is only a five-minute walk away. The Gulfstream Restaurant boasts upscale dining, inside or out, with cuisine ranging from grilled wahoo with lime sauce to T-bone steaks. If you plan to stay during one of the major fishing tournaments, reserve well in advance. **Pros:** camaraderie and clubhouse atmosphere, well-trained friendly staff, excellent marina for fishing boats. **Cons:** can be wild and noisy during fishing tournaments (though this might be a pro for some), some of the rooms could use renovation. ⊠ *King's Hwy., at pink wall* ☎ *242/347–3391 or 800/737–1007* ⊕ *www.biminibiggame.com* ⇨ *35 rooms,*

> **BEST OF THE BEST**
>
> Looking for a little more action in your Out Island vacation? Try the Bimini Bay Resort on North Bimini. Excellent restaurants, live music, and a generally bustling vibe have swept over this famous and infamous isle.

12 cottages, 4 penthouses &In-room: *kitchen (some), refrigerator (some). In-hotel: 2 restaurants, bars, pool, no elevator, laundry service, public Internet* =AE, D, MC, V.

★ $$ 🏨**Bimini Sands Resort & Marina.** Overlooking the Straits of Florida, this luxury property rents one- or two-bedroom condominiums with direct beach access. The bright, high-ceiling condos have balconies and patios with views of the tropical surroundings, the marina, or the beach. The Petite Conch restaurant serves three meals a day, blending Bahamian staples with American favorites. There's a 53-slip Texaco Starport marina, ship's store, and a convenient customs office, so guests with boats can tie up and clear their paperwork without venturing to North Bimini. An all-night water taxi shuttles you to North Bimini to shop, dine, and party. Boat and golf-cart rentals are available. **Pros:** two good restaurants (including a sushi bar), water and other excursions are happily arranged, full-service marina with customs clearance. **Cons:** South Bimini location is away from the "action" on North Bimini. ✉*Bimini Sands* ☎242/347–3500 ⊕*www.biminisands.com* 🛏*21 1- or 2-bedroom condominiums* &In-room: *kitchen. In-hotel: 2 restaurants, bars, tennis court, pools, beachfront, water sports, bicycles, no elevator, laundry facilities, public Wi-Fi* =AE, MC, V.

$ 🏨**Big John's Conch Shell Bar and Hotel.** Seven deluxe hotel rooms, remodeled in 2006, five with ocean views, two with town views, are perfect for the traveler who wants to get away from the megaresort scene, but still stay in style. Amenities include flat-screen TVs, antique nautical furniture, high-thread-count sheets, soft oversize towels, and boutique soaps. Downstairs, the casual island lounge serves up icy rum drinks along with a full array of international cocktails. Much of the staff used to work at the now-closed Compleat Angler. A large flat-screen satellite TV is available to watch your favorite sporting events. The Hypnotics, Bimini's favorite band for 20 years, plays live music Thursday through Saturday. **Pros:** central Alice Town location, great value for very pleasant accommodations on the bay, can park your boat at Brown's Marina, located in front of the hotel. **Cons:** lively bar can make getting to sleep a challenge if you turn in early, no pool but the beach is in walking distance. ✉*King's Hwy., across from Gateway Gallery* ☎242/347–3117 ⊕*www.bigjohnshotel.com* 🛏*7 rooms* &In-room: *no phone. In-hotel: bar, no elevator, laundry service* =No credit cards.

$ 🏨**Sea Crest Hotel and Marina.** Tucked between the beach and the marina, this three-story hotel has comfortable, simply furnished rooms with tile floors, cable TV, balconies, and one of the island's friendliest owner-management teams. Pick a room or suite on the third floor; they have lofty, open-beam ceilings and lovely sea or marina views. The marina is across the street (King's Highway). Diving, snorkeling, and fishing charters can be arranged. There's a 5% surcharge for credit cards. **Pros:** economical and comfortable, central location, welcoming service. **Cons:** rooms could use renovation, no Internet service, credit-card fee. ✉*King's Hwy.* ☎242/347–3071 ⊕*www.seacrestbimini.com* 🛏*25 rooms, 1 2-bedroom suite, 1 3-bedroom suite* &In-room: *no phone, refrigerator. In-hotel: no elevator* =MC, V.

SPORTS & THE OUTDOORS

BICYCLING   **Bill and Nowdla Keefe's Bimini Undersea** (☏ *242/347–3089*) rents bikes for $7 per hour, $15 for a half day, or $25 per day.

BOATING &   **Bimini Big Game Resort & Marina** (☏ *242/347–3391 or 800/737–1007*
FISHING   ⊕ *www.biminibiggame.com*), a 103-slip marina, charges $800–$900 for a day ($475–$500 for a half day) of deep-sea fishing. **Bimini Sands Marina** (☏ *242/347–3500* ⊕ *www.biminisands.com*), on South Bimini, is a top-notch 53-slip marina capable of accommodating vessels up to 100 feet. Convenient customs clearance for guests is at the marina. Rent a 15-foot Whaler for $140 per day or a Wave Runner for $50 per half hour. Rental fishing gear (flats and blue water) is also available. **Blue Water Marina** (☏ *242/347–3166*), with 32 modern slips, charges from $750 a day, and from $450 a half day for deep-sea fishing, with captain, mate, and gear included. **Fisherman's Village Marina** (☏ *242/347—2900* ⊕ *www.biminibayresort.com*, a 136-slip full service marina, has bluewater boats for charter fishing, a liquor store, ice cream shop, gourmet pizza restaurant, and customs and immigration offices. **Weech's Bimini Dock** (☏ *242/347–3028*), with 20 slips, has four Boston Whalers, which it rents for $135 a day or $75 a half day.

The following are highly recommended bonefish guides, and they must be booked in advance: **Bonefish Ansil** (☏ *242/347–2178 or 242/347–3098*), **Bonefish Ebbie** (☏ *242/347–2053 or 242/359–8273*), **Bonefish Ray** (☏ *242/347–2269*), and **Bonefish Tommy** (☏ *242/347–3234*).

EVENTS   The Biminis host a series of fishing tournaments and boating events throughout the year, including the **Bahamas Wahoo Challenge** (November and February), the **Bimini Break and Blue Marlin Tournament** (May), the **Bimini Festival of Champions** (May), the **Annual Bimini Native Tournament** (August), the **Bimini Family Fishing Tournament** (August), and the **Small BOAT—Bimini Open Angling Tournament** (September). The island also hosts an annual **Bimini Regatta**, which takes place in the spring. For information on dates, tournament regulations, and recommended guides, call the **Bahamas Tourist Office** (☏ *800/327–7678*) in Florida and ask for the sportfishing section.

SCUBA DIVING   The Biminis offer excellent diving opportunities, particularly for
& SNORKELING   watching marine life. The **Bimini Barge Wreck** (a World War II landing craft) rests in 100 feet of water. **Little Caverns** is a medium-depth dive with scattered coral heads, small tunnels, and swim-throughs. **Rainbow Reef** is a shallow dive popular for fish gazing. And, of course, there's **Atlantis,** thought to be the famous "lost city." Dive packages are available through most Bimini hotels. You can also check out the best diving options through the **Bahamas Diving Association** (☏ *954/236–9292* ⊕ *www.bahamasdiving.com*).

Bill & Nowdla Keefe's Bimini Undersea (☏ *242/347–3089 or 800/348–4644* ⊕ *www.biminiundersea.com*), headquartered at Bimini Big Game Resort & Yacht Club, lets you snorkel near a delightful pod of Atlantic spotted dolphins for $119 per person. You can also rent or buy snorkel and diving gear. One-, two-, and three-tank dives cost $49, $89, and $119 per person, respectively. Dive packages with accommodations at Bimini Big Game Resort are available.

SHOPPING

Bimini Native Straw and Craft Market (⊠*Next door to Bahamas Customs Bldg.* ☎*No phone*) has about 20 vendors, including Nathalie's Native Bread stand. Upstairs in the Burns House Building, the **Gateway Gallery** (⊠*King's Hwy.* ☎*242/347-3131*) sells top-quality

PLAN AHEAD

Even though you're going to the laid-back islands, you need to reserve your guides, boats, cars, and golf carts in advance. And if you ask, these friendly islanders might include an airport greeting and transfer to your hotel.

Bahamian arts and crafts, original artwork by Biminites, hand-sculpted figures depicting daily Bahamian life, and Bahamian music. **Pritchard's Grocery** (⊠*Queen's Hwy., next to Baptist church* ☎*No phone*) is known as the home of the sweet Bimini native bread. Consider placing an order to take home.

ELSEWHERE ON NORTH BIMINI

Toward King's Highway's north end, you'll see bars, grocery shops, clothing stores, the pink medical center, and a group of colorful fruit stalls. This part of the island, from Bailey Town to the new Bimini Bay Resort, is clean, fresh, and colorful.

Atlantis, a curious rock formation under about 20 feet of water, 500 yards offshore at Bimini Bay, is shaped like a backward letter J, some 600 feet long at the longest end. It's the shorter 300-foot extension that piques the interest of scientists and visitors. The precision patchwork of large, curved-edge stones form a perfect rectangle measuring about 30 feet across. A few of the stones are 16 feet square. It's purported to be the "lost city" whose discovery was predicted by Edgar Cayce (1877–1945), a psychic with an interest in prehistoric civilizations. Archaeologists estimate the formation to be between 5,000 and 10,000 years old. Carvings in the rock appear to some scientists to resemble a network of highways. Skeptics have pooh-poohed the theory, conjecturing that they are merely turtle pens built considerably more recently.

Most of the island's residents live in **Bailey Town** in small, pastel-color concrete houses, repainted in 2006. Bailey Town lies on King's Highway, north of the Bimini Big Game Resort & Yacht Club and before the Bimini Bay Resort. This part of the island has changed dramatically due to new development, which has created many jobs for the people in Bailey Town.

The **Bimini Museum,** sheltered in the restored (1920) two-story original post office and jail—a three-minute walk from the old seaplane ramp—showcases varied artifacts, including Adam Clayton Powell's domino set, Prohibition photos, rum kegs, Martin Luther King Jr.'s immigration card from 1964, and a fishing log and rare fishing films of Papa Hemingway. The exhibit includes film shot on the island as early as 1922. ⊠*King's Hwy.* ☎*242/347-3038* 🎫*$2* ⊙*Mon.–Sat. 9–9, Sun. noon–9.*

OFF THE
BEATEN
PATH

Healing Hole. Locals recommend a trip here for curing what ails you—gout and rheumatism are among the supposedly treatable afflictions Ask your hotel to arrange a trip out to this natural clearing in North Bimini's mangrove flats. You can take a leap of faith into the water and if nothing else, enjoy a refreshing dip.

THE BIMINIS ESSENTIALS

BY AIR

Gulfstream International, Continental's commuter, has two flights a day from Fort Lauderdale Airport in high season, and one flight per day in low season. They offer SunPac Vacation packages in conjunction with Bimini Bay Resort. Island Air Charters offers schedule flights four days a week, and charter flights at your convenience, from For Lauderdale's Jet Center to South Bimini. Chalk's International Airlines flies four times a week, Monday, Thursday, Friday, and Saturday from Ft. Lauderdale to South Bimini. Western Air flies to Bimini from Nassau's domestic air terminal.

Airlines & Contacts Chalk's International Airlines (☎877/924–2557). **Gulfstream International** (☎800/231–0856). **Island Air Charters** (☎954/359–994. or 800/444–9904). **Western Air** (☎242/347–4100 or 242/377–2222).

BY BOAT

M/V *Bimini Mack* sails from Potter's Cay, Nassau, to Bimini, Cat Cay and Chub Cay on Thursday afternoon. The return is Monday morning The trip takes 12 hours and costs $45 one way. For information, call the Dockmaster's Office at Potter's Cay.

Boaters often travel from Florida to Bimini, mostly from West Palm Beach, Fort Lauderdale, and Miami. Crossing the Gulf Stream, however, should only be done by skippers who can plot a course using charts for that purpose. There are a half dozen or so routes that are most commonly used to cross the Stream from Florida to the Bahamas with the route from Fort Lauderdale to Bimini being the most popular for sailboats and power craft. The distance is 48 nautical mi. The time to make the crossing depends on the type of craft and the boat's speed. Sailors often like to make an evening departure, and arrive in the morning. Speedboaters sometimes zip over to Bimini for lunch or dinner and then return home. It's important for boaters to consult official government charts for obstructions, sands banks, and other impediments, and to be familiar with harbor entrances and procedures. I using proper safety, the crossing is a delight, and the fishing to and from can be sensational.

Boat & Ferry Information Dockmaster's Office (☎242/393–1064).

BY BUS

Taxi 1 & 2, operated by Sam Brown, has minibuses available for a tour of the island. Arrangements can be made through your hotel.

BY CAR
Visitors do not need a car on North Bimini and there are no car-rental agencies.

BY GOLF CART
Rental golf carts are available at the Sea Crest Hotel Marina and Bimini Blue Water Marina from Capt. Pat's (☎ *242/347–3477*) for $60 a day or $20 for the first hour and $10 for each additional hour. Most hotels will arrange golf-cart rentals for you. It's best to make arrangements in advance of your arrival.

BY TAXI
Sam Brown's Taxi service meets arriving visitors at the South Bimini Airport, then transfers incoming passengers to the ferry dock for the short ride to Alice Town. From there, visitors can walk or take a taxi to their accommodations. The entire process costs $5. Ferries cannot take you directly to your hotel or marina—to Bimini Bay Resort for example—because government regulations protect the taxi union.

5

CONTACTS & RESOURCES

BANKS & EXCHANGE SERVICES
The Royal Bank of Canada is open Monday, Wednesday, and Friday from 9:30 to 3. Cash advances are given on MasterCard and Visa only.

Bank Information **Royal Bank of Canada** (☎ *242/347–3030*).

EMERGENCIES
North Bimini Medical Clinic has a resident doctor and a nurse.

Contact **North Bimini Medical Clinic** (☎ *242/347–2210*). **Police** (☎ *919*).

VISITOR INFORMATION
The Biminis Tourist Office is open weekdays from 9 to 5:30 and also has a booth at the straw market.

Tourist Information **Biminis Tourist Office** (✉ *Government Bldg., Alice Town* ☎ *242/347–3529*).

CAT ISLAND

Cat Island is 130 mi southeast of Nassau and is a close neighbor of San Salvador, the reputed landing place of Christopher Columbus. Many Cat Islanders maintain, however, that Columbus landed here instead and that Cat Island was once known as San Salvador. Sir Sidney Poitier is a famous local; he left as a youth before becoming a famed movie actor and director. His daughter Ann lives here and spearheads the annual Rake 'N' Scrape Festival held in June.

The island was named after a frequent notorious visitor, Arthur Catt, a piratical contemporary of Edward "Blackbeard" Teach. Slender Cat Island is about 50 mi long and boot shaped, with high cliffs and dense forest. The Cat, as it's often called, is filled with living history, including semi-ruined, vine-covered mansions and crumbling remnants of slave villages that are perfect for exploring.

Good roads, including Queen's Highway, stretch from Orange Creek in the north to Port Howe and Hawk's Nest in the south. You'll rarely see another car, but watch out for local kids using the highway as a basketball court. The Cat's shores are ringed with mile upon mile of exquisite beaches edged with casuarina trees. Most of these beaches are on the "north shore," or windward side of the island, and can be reached via rough and rugged dirt and rock roads cut through the heavy vegetation.

Some of the original inhabitants' descendants, who migrated long ago to the United States, are slowly returning here. Large new homes have started to appear throughout the island, whose population is about 2,000. Residents fish, farm, and live a peaceful day-to-day existence guided by the philosophy, "What nature and the Lord will provide." The biggest event of the year is the Annual Cat Island Regatta in August.

ARTHUR'S TOWN & BENNETT'S HARBOUR

The claim to fame of **Arthur's Town** is that it was the boyhood home of actor Sidney Poitier, who wrote about growing up here in his autobiography. His parents and relatives were farmers. The village has a BaTelCo station, a few stores, and Pat Rolle's **Cookie House Bakery** (☎242/354–2027)—a lunch and dinner spot and an island institution. During slower times of the year, lunch and dinner are not always served, or hours can be irregular. Call ahead, or just stop by to say hello as Pat is a wealth of island knowledge and more than happy to bend your ear. Also, with advance notice, you can request fresh baked goods. When you drive south from Arthur's Town, which is nearly at the island's northernmost tip, you'll wind along a road that passes through small villages and past bays where fishing boats are tied up.

One of the island's oldest settlements of small, weather-beaten houses, **Bennett's Harbour** is some 15 mi south of Arthur's Town. At times, fresh baked breads and fruit are available at makeshift stands at the government dock, and there is good bonefishing in the creek. Be aware, however, that Hurricane Noel, in late October 2007, caused water damage in Arthur's Town and Bennet's Harbour, and modified sandbars and creeks. In early 2008 most of the damage had been cleaned up, but some docks and facilities were still not repaired or replaced. Visitors should call ahead to check on any damage caused to locations they plan to stay.

WHERE TO EAT & STAY

★ $ ✕**Sammy T's Restaurant and Bar.** Overlooking the pool and the beach, eat inside the well-appointed dining room or out on the wooden deck under thatched umbrellas. At breakfast try one of the huge omelets with cheese, tomatoes, and peppers. At lunch the salads are fresh and served with Sammy T's secret dressing, or savor the grilled conch or pan-fried grouper. Want a burger? They're big and tasty. Afternoon snacks of a

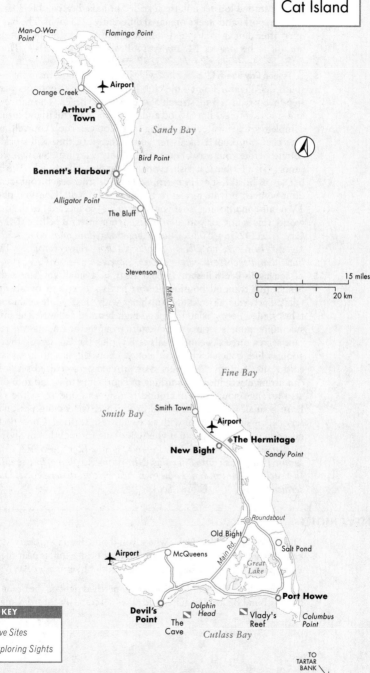

Cat Island

Man-O-War Point
Flamingo Point
Airport
Orange Creek
Arthur's Town
Sandy Bay
Bird Point
Bennett's Harbour
Alligator Point
The Bluff
Stevenson
Main Rd.
15 miles
20 km
Fine Bay
Smith Town
Smith Bay
Airport
The Hermitage
New Bight
Sandy Point
Roundabout
Old Bight
Salt Pond
Airport
McQueens
Main Rd.
Great Lake
Port Howe
Devil's Point
Dolphin Head
Vlady's Reef
Columbus Point
The Cave
Cutlass Bay

KEY
▮ *Dive Sites*
♦ *Exploring Sights*

TO TARTAR BANK

things conch are served in the bar and on the deck. The evening delights include stuffed lobster tail, fresh grilled or baked catch of the day, plus chicken, pork, and steaks prepared differently each night. The bar stays open after dinner as demand indicates, and the fresh-fruit rum drinks are not to be missed. ⊠*Sammy T's Beach Resort, Bennet's Harbour* ☎*242/354–6009 or 242/427–5897* ▭*MC, V* ☉*Closed Sept.*

$ ▦**Pigeon Cay Beach Club.** Set in a wide bay a mile off the main road—just south of Alligator Point—the club has seven deluxe cottages perched steps away from a 3-mi stretch of sugary white beach. The native stone and stucco cottages have wood and tile floors, colorful island furniture, complete kitchenware, and ceiling fans. You can cook yourself, or the club chef can prepare meals for you. Either way, they will stock your cottage before your arrival (just send your grocery list). Snorkel, kayak, canoe, sail a Hobie Cat, fish, swim, or just lie on the beach. The beach bar serves breakfast every morning. **Pros:** pristine beachfront location, do-it-yourself private retreat to get away from it all. **Cons:** no phones, TV or air-conditioning, so if you need to be "connected" to the outside world, this is not for you; don't forget your insect repellent. ⊠*Pigeon Cay* ☎☎*242/354–5084* ⊕*www.pigeoncay-bahamas.com* ⟿*7 cottages* ⌂*In-room: no a/c, no phone, kitchen, refrigerator, no TV. In-hotel: bar, beachfront, water sports, bicycles* ▭*AE, MC, V.*

★ $ ▦**Sammy T's Beach Resort.** Tucked away in a small cove on a dream beach, this tranquil boutique resort has six one- and two-bedroom villas. Each villa has rattan furnishings with plush white cushions and fabrics, tiled floors, island art, and high-beamed ceilings. The inviting swimming pool is set back a few steps from the beach, and the restaurant serves three delicious meals a day, plus the bar serves afternoon goodies like conch fritters and conch chowder that go great with a cold Kalik. Sammy T and his staff provide personalized service and can arrange activities from fishing to snorkeling to island tours. They also arrange your airport ground transfers to and from the resort. **Pros:** a small private Out Island experience, welcoming personalized service, on-site restaurant with excellent fresh seafood. **Cons:** no Internet service, stay in Nassau if you're looking for nightlife or shopping. ⊠*Bennet's Harbour* ☎*242/354–6009 or 242/427—5897* ⊕*www.sammytbahamas.com* ⟿*6 villas* ⌂*In-room: no phone, kitchen, DVD. In-hotel: restaurant, bar, pool, gym, beachfront, water sports, laundry service* ▭*MC, V* ☉*Closed Sept.*

NEW BIGHT

The settlement of **New Bight,** where you'll find a small grocery store, a bakery, a gas station that rents cars, and the Bridge Inn, is near the New Bight (also called "The Bight") airport, south of Fernandez Bay Village.

At **Twin Palms** (☎*242/342–3108*), a bar perched right on the ocean, hear famous Blind Blake play guitar and rake 'n' scrape on Saturday nights.

At the top of 206-foot Mt. Alvernia, **The Hermitage** is the final resting place of Father Jerome. Above the tomb's entrance, carved in stone, is the epitaph BLESSED ARE THE DEAD WHO DIE IN THE LORD, and inside, past the wooden gate that hangs on its hinges, his body lies interred. He died in 1956 at the age of 80 and was supposedly buried with his arms outstretched, in a pose resembling that of the crucified Christ.

Father Jerome, born John Hawes, traveled the world and eventually settled in the Bahamas. An Anglican who converted to Roman Catholicism, he built two churches, St. Paul's and St. Peter's, in Clarence Town, Long Island, as well as the St. Augustine Monastery in Nassau. He retired to Cat Island to live out his last dozen years as a hermit, and his final, supreme act of religious dedication was to carve the steps up to the top of Mt. Alvernia. Along the way, he also carved the 12 Stations of the Cross. At the summit, he built a child-size abbey with a small chapel, a conical bell tower, and living quarters comprising three closet-size rooms.

> ### ISLAND SPECIALTIES
>
> You can't go to the islands and skip conch salad and key lime pie. The best conch salads are usually found at out-of-the-way or little-known stands run by a single person who makes the salads fresh daily, and when it's gone it's gone. The best key lime pies are made with graham cracker crust. Go in search of the best of the best, it's a fun game.

The pilgrimage to the Hermitage begins next to the commissioner's office at New Bight, at a dirt path that leads to the foot of Mt. Alvernia. Try not to miss the slightly laborious experience of climbing to the top. The Hermitage provides a perfect, inspired place to pause for quiet contemplation. It also has glorious views of the ocean on both sides of the island. A caretaker clears the weeds around the tomb—which islanders regard as a shrine—and lights a candle in Father Jerome's memory.

WHERE TO EAT & STAY

$$$$ ✕ **Fernandez Bay Village Restaurant.** Meals are served in the Clubhouse at Fernandez Bay Village, and outside on the beach terrace. The breakfast buffet is loaded; you can pile on sweet rolls, croissants, bacon, sausage, grits, and fruit, or order the daily specials of French toast, omelets, or eggs Benedict. Grilled cheese, tuna, turkey, and ham sandwiches, conch chowder, and conch burgers are just a sampling of lunch options. The sumptuous dinner buffet can include conch fritter, filet mignon, lobster tail, grilled catch of the day along with scalloped potatoes, salads, and fresh baked breads. Spice apple cake goes great with an after dinner drink from the bar. ⊠ *Fernandez Bay Village, 1 mi west of New Bight airport* ☎ 242/342–2018 ▤ *AE, MC, V* ☉ *Closed Sept., but call to confirm.*

$$ ✕ **Island HoppInn Tiki Bar and Restaurant.** New for 2008 is this authentic island style open air Tiki Hut restaurant and bar right on the beach, just steps away from the tranquil lapping waters of Fernandez Bay. The 24-seat eatery has a barbecue grill for cooking up fresh fish of the day, shrimp, lobster, steaks, and ribs. Owner chef Cathy Bencin is

renowned for her conch chowder, fish and vegetable stews, fresh baked breads, and killer desserts. Guests staying at the Inn, which has a B&B casualness, mix in by cooking their own dinners at times. The service is good, the crowd, when there is one, a lot of fun, and the tropical rum drinks are a mellowing delight. ⊠ *Island HoppInn, Fernandez Bay* ☎ *242/342–2100* ⊟*MC, V* ☉*Closed Sept. and part of Oct., but call ahead to confirm.*

★ $$ 🏨 **Fernandez Bay Village.** This is one of the best kick-back retreats in the islands. Brick-and-stone villas and cottages are spread along a dazzling, horseshoe-shaped white-sand beach shaded by casuarina pines and hibiscus. Villas have kitchens, terraces facing the sea, private gardens, and accommodations for four to six people. Cottages are for two people, and have private patios and garden baths. Canoes, Sunfish sailboats, and kayaks are free to use. Boats and guides can be hired for fishing or snorkeling expeditions. Savory native dishes, including lobster, conch, and prime steaks, are served in the lodge dining room and on the beachside patio, and can be part of an all-inclusive package. **Pros:** a "wow" beachfront location, private spacious accommodations, friendly staff can arrange all water sport activities. **Cons:** not all units have air-conditioning, so be sure to ask for it if you want it; no TVs; you need insect repellent for outside evening dining. ⊠*1 mi west of New Bight airport* ☎*242/342–2018 or 800/940–1905* ⊕*www.fernandez bayvillage.com* 🛏*6 villas, 10 cottages* ⚒*In-room: no a/c (some), no phone, refrigerator (some), kitchen (some), no TV. In-hotel: restaurant, bar, beachfront, water sports, bicycles, laundry service, public Internet* ⊟*AE, MC, V.*

★ $$ 🏨 **Island HoppInn.** The resort's four suites—one and two bedroom— are perched ocean side overlooking magical Fernandez Bay. Step off your private porch and you're on the beach. The roomy yet cozy suites have rattan furnishings, tropical decor, modern kitchens, and outdoor garden showers. In the Inn's Great Room, or on the adjoining beach deck, meals, and cocktails are served family style; everything from fresh baked breads, to conch fritters, grilled fish, and delectable desserts. The owners emphasize personal service for each guest, and can arrange activities from fishing to snorkeling and diving, car rental or a romantic dinner served in your suite. **Pros:** small private resort on the perfect white sand beach, you can cook on the outside grill or have meals included in your package, on-site owner/ managers go the extra mile to provide exceptional service. **Cons:** don't forget your insect repellent for evenings outside. ⊠*Fernandez Bay* ☎*216/978–8800 or 242/342–2100* ⊕*www.islandhoppinn.com* 🛏*4 suites* ⚒*In-room: kitchen, DVD (some), Wi-Fi. In-hotel: restaurant, room service, bar, beachfront, water sports, laundry service, public Wi-Fi* ⊟*MC, V.*

$ 🏨 **Bridge Inn.** Use this friendly, family-run motel and apartment property as a base for exploring the island on your own—including the nearby beach. The wood-paneled rooms have high ceilings, private baths, and cable TV. The snappy apartment has 2 bedrooms, 1 baths, cable TV, and a full kitchen. The dining room serves tasty local fare for breakfast. They can pack you a picnic lunch, and there's fresh seafood for dinner, along with live entertainment most Friday and Saturday nights. Complimentary shuttle service is available from the New Bight airport. **Pros:** economical accommodations in a central location for exploring the island, short walk to the beach, friendly people. **Cons:** five other apartments are rented long-term so lots of family activity going on. ⊠*New Bight* ☎*242/342–3013* ⊕*www.catisland-bridgeinn.com* ⮐*12 rooms, 1 2-bedroom apartment* ⌂*In-room: no phone, kitchen (some). In-hotel: restaurant, bar, no elevator, laundry service* ▤*MC, V.*

> THINK LIKE A CAT

Cat Island is often overlooked by travelers, but it has some of the most dramatically beautiful pink-sand beaches in the islands, and the north shore is completely deserted. You'll need a 4X4 to drive there, or go on a bike and take a picnic.

5

RT HOWE

At the conch shell–lined traffic roundabout, head east out toward **Port Howe,** believed by many to be Cat Island's oldest settlement. Nearby lie the ruins of the **Deveaux Mansion,** a stark two-story, whitewashed building overrun with vegetation. Once it was a grand house on a cotton plantation, owned by Captain Andrew Deveaux of the British Navy, who was given thousands of acres of Cat Island property as a reward for his daring raid that recaptured Nassau from the Spaniards in 1783. Just beyond the mansion ruin is the entrance road to the Greenwood Beach Resort, which sits on an 8-mi stretch of unblemished velvet-sand beach.

WHERE TO STAY

$ ▦ **Greenwood Beach Resort.** Set on an 8-mi stretch of pink shell-strewn sand, this remote resort is about 35 minutes from the New Bight airport. The large clubhouse, with its yellow-and-white walls and vivid tropical paintings, is the center of activity. You can relax at the attractive stonework bar or on the stone veranda, which has open vistas of the violet-blue Atlantic; or catch some rays at the pool or beach. Rooms are bright and cheerfully decorated with colorful fish stencils and rattan furnishings. Breakfast and dinner are served family style. Picnic lunches are prepared for day excursions. This is an ideal location for vacationers looking for beachfront tranquility. **Pros:** private Atlantic beach location, great snorkeling on coral heads in front of resort, good on-site restaurant. **Cons:** long drive to explore other parts of the island, if you want an air-conditioned room you need to reserve it in advance. ⊠*Port Howe* ☎*242/342–3053* ⊕*www.greenwoodbeachresort.com* ⮐*16 rooms* ⌂*In-room: no a/c (some), no phone, no TV. In-hotel: restaurant, bar, pool, beachfront, diving, water sports, bicycles, no elevator, laundry service, public Internet, public Wi-Fi* ▤*MC, V.*

DEVIL'S POINT

The small village of **Devil's Point,** with its pastel-color, thatch-roo
houses, lies about 10 mi west of Columbus Point. Beachcombers wi
find great shelling on the pristine beach. You'll also come across th
ruins of the **Richman Hill–Newfield Plantation.**

WHERE TO EAT & STAY

★ $$ ✕ **Hawk's Nest Resort Restaurant and Bar.** High beamed ceilings, tile
floors, and blue ceramic-topped tables create a cheerful ambience t
go with the dazzling array of menu choices. Start your day with fres
juices and croissants, smoked salmon, cheese-and-ham crepes, or egg
Benedict. Creamy white conch chowder, lobster salad, burgers wit
fries, and grouper sandwiches lead the lunch selections. Poached sca
lops or grilled Thai tuna are tasty starters for dinner, followed by mai
dishes that include Szechuan chicken, lamb tenderloin, stuffed lobste
tail, or grilled fresh fish of the day (if it's wahoo, don't miss it). Still hav
room? Try the ice-cream-filled crepes with chocolate sauce. ⊠ *Hawk*
Nest Resort & Marina ☎*242/342–7050* ▭*MC, V* ⊘*Closed Sep*
15–Nov. 1.

★ $$ 🏠 **Hawk's Nest Resort & Marina.** At Cat Island's southwestern tip, th
waterfront resort, just yards from a long sandy beach, has its ow
3,100-foot runway and a 28-slip full-service marina with PADI div
center. The patios of the guest rooms, the dining room, and the loung
overlook the pool and the aquamarine Exuma Sound. With cheerf
pastel-colored walls and bright bedspreads, rooms have either or
king-size or two queen-size beds with baths that have both tubs an
showers. A hearty breakfast is included in the daily rate, or you ca
choose a full meal plan. The personal service is outstanding, and sta
can arrange island excursions, refer you to bonefishing guides, or se
up diving adventures. **Pros:** best marina in this area of the Baham
for bluewater fishing, quality accommodations and food, best loca
tion for diving southern Cat Island. **Cons:** if you want to explore th
rest of Cat Island, it's a long drive. ⊠*Devil's Point* ☎*242/342–705*
⊕*www.hawks-nest.com* ⇘*10 rooms, 1 2-bedroom house* ⊘*In-room*
no phone, VCR. In-hotel: restaurant, bars, pool, beachfront, divin
water sports, bicycles, no elevator, laundry service ▭*MC, V* ⥾*B*
⊘*Closed Sept. 15–Nov. 1.*

SPORTS & THE OUTDOORS

FISHING   Bluewater angling boat owners make a point of using **Hawk's Ne**
Marina (☎*242/342–7050*) to access the dynamite offshore fishin
Look for wahoo, yellowfin tuna, dolphin, and white and blue ma
lin along the Exuma Sound drop-offs, Devil's Point, Tartar Bank, an
Columbus Point. March through July is prime time, though wint
fishing, December through February, is also prime for wahoo. You ca
arrange bonefishing through the marina with top guide Nathaniel G
bert; just call him Top Cat.

SCUBA DIVING   **The Cave** has a big channel with several exits to deeper ocean. Re
sharks, barracudas, and other tropical fish are frequently seen her
Tartar Bank is an offshore site known for its abundant sea life, inclu

ing sharks, triggerfish, turtles, eagle rays, and barracuda. **Vlady's Reef,** also known as "The Chimney," is near the Guana Cays. Coral heads have created numerous canyons, chimneys, and swim-throughs. You're likely to catch a glimpse of large stingrays.

Dive Cat Island (☎242/342–7050) at Hawk's Nest Marina is PADI certified and conducts daily guided diving adventures, rents diving and snorkeling gear, and has equipment and sundries for sale. The running time to dive sites off the southern tip of the island is 15 to 30 minutes in the shop's 27-foot Panga, outfitted with VHF and GPS.

T ISLAND ESSENTIALS

ANSPORTATION

BY AIR

5

Cat Island Air flies daily to New Bight from Nassau and is the best and cheapest service to the southern part of the island. Southern Air flies from Nassau to Arthur's Town and is the best service for the northern portion of the island. Bahamasair flies from Nassau to Arthur's Town or New Bight three times a week. Lynx Air and Gulfstream (Continental's commuter) fly into New Bight from Fort Lauderdale.

If you are going to Fernandez Bay Village, Island HoppInn, Greenwood Beach Resort, or Hawk's Nest Resort, fly into New Bight. If you are going to Pigeon Cay or Sammy T's, fly to Arthur's Town.

Airlines & Contacts **Bahamasair** (☎800/222–4262). **Cat Island Air** (☎242/377–3318). **Gulfstream/Continental** (☎800/523–3273). **Lynx Air** (☎954/772–9808 or 888/596–9247). **Southern Air** (☎242/377–2014).

BY BOAT

The *Lady Rosalind* leaves Potter's Cay, Nassau, every Thursday for Bennett's Harbour and Orange Creek, returning on Saturday. The trip takes 14 hours and costs $40 one way. *Sea Hauler* leaves Potter's Cay on Tuesday for Smith Bay, and Old and New Bight, returning on Monday. The trip is 12 hours, and the fare is $40 one way. For information, call the Dockmaster's Office at Potter's Cay.

Boat & Ferry Information **Dockmaster's Office** (☎242/393–1064).

BY CAR

The New Bight Service Station rents cars and can pick you up from New Bight airport. You can rent a car from Gilbert's Food Market (ask for Candy), which also picks up from the airport. Greenwood Beach Resort, Sammy T's Beach Resort, Fernandez Bay Village, Island HoppInn, and Hawk's Nest Resort will all arrange car rentals for guests. Rates depend on the number of days you're renting, but $75 per day is average. The best way to enjoy the overall Cat Island experience is to rent a car, at least for one day, and do some exploring on your own.

Contacts **Gilbert's Food Market** (☎242/342–3011). **New Bight Service Station** (☎242/342–3014).

BY TAXI

Fernandez Bay Village meets guests at New Bight airport, and the transfer is complimentary. If you miss your ride or no taxis are available, just ask around the parking lot for a lift. Anyone going in your direction (there's only one road) will be happy to drop you off.

CONTACTS & RESOURCES

EMERGENCIES

Cat Island has three medical clinics—at Smith Town, Old Bight, and Arthur's Town. There are few telephones on the island, but your hotel's front desk will be able to contact the nearest clinic in case of an emergency.

CROOKED & ACKLINS ISLANDS

Bahamas historians tell us that as Columbus sailed down the lee of Crooked Island and its southern neighbor, Acklins Island (the two are separated by a short water passage), he was riveted by the aroma of native herbs wafting out to his ship. Soon after, Crooked Island, which lies 225 mi southeast of Nassau, became known as one of the "Fragrant Islands." The first known settlers didn't arrive until the late 18th century, when Loyalists brought their slaves from the United States and established cotton plantations. It was a doomed venture because of the island's poor soil, and those who stayed made a living of sorts by farming and fishing. A salt and sponge industry flourished for a while on Fortune Island, now called Long Cay. The cay, across the cut from French Well off the southwestern corner of Crooked Island, is the proposed home of a large new marina and resort development near the mostly abandoned settlement of Albert Town. The cay is also home to a flock of over 500 flamingos.

Today, Crooked and Acklins islands inhabitants, about 400 people on each island, continue to survive by farming and fishing. The islands are best known for splendid diving and bone-, tarpon, and offshore fishing—and not much else. They're about as remote as populated islands in the Bahamas get. A number of residents rely on generators for electricity. Phone service, where available, can often go out for days at a time.

Although the plantations have long since crumbled, two relics of that era are preserved by the Bahamas National Trust on Crooked Island's northern part, which overlooks the Crooked Island Passage separating the cay from Long Island. Spanish guns have been discovered at one ruin, **Marine Farm**, which may have been used as a fortification. An old structure, **Hope Great House**, has orchards and gardens that are still tended by the Bahamas National Trust.

Crooked Island is 30 mi long and surrounded by 45 mi of barrier reef that are ideal for diving. They slope from 4 feet to 50 feet, then plunge to 3,600 feet in the Crooked Island Passage, once one of the most important sea roads for ships following the southerly route from the West Indies to the Old World. The one-room airport is in **Colonel Hill**, across the main road from a wide bay and white-sand bonefish flat. If you drive up to the settlement, you get an uninterrupted view of the region all the way to the narrow passage at Lovely Bay between Crooked Island and Acklins Island. There are two lighthouses.

The sparkling white **Bird Rock Lighthouse** (built in 1872) in the north once guarded the Crooked Island Passage. The rotating flash from its 115-foot tower still welcomes pilots and sailors to the Pittstown Point Landings resort, currently the islands' best lodging facility.

> ### PLAY THE TIDES
>
> If you're going bonefishing, tide pooling, or snorkeling, you'll want up-to-date tide information for the best results. A low incoming tide is usually best for bonefishing, though the last of the falling is good, too. Low tides are best for beachcombing and tide pools, while higher tides can give better coverage to your favorite reef. Ask your hotel, fishing guide, or local dive shop for current tide information.

The **Castle Island Lighthouse** (built in 1867), at Acklins Island's southern tip, formerly served as a beacon for pirates who used to retreat there after attacking ships.

Crooked and Acklins islands appear southeast of Long Island on the Bahamas map at the front of this guide.

WHERE TO STAY

$$ ▦ **Pittstown Point Landings.** A true anglers paradise, this is one of the best flats, inshore, and offshore fishing destinations in the Caribbean. Shaded by coconut palms, the remote property on Crooked Island's northwestern tip has miles of open beach at its doorstep and unobstructed views of the emerald water surrounding Bird Rock Lighthouse. Rooms are motel-style units with double beds. Ask for an ocean view and air-conditioning. The main lodge—which has a restaurant, bar, and library—once housed the Bahamas' first post office. Captain Robbie Gibson leads snorkeling, diving, reef, and offshore fishing adventures. All-inclusive bonefishing packages are available with top guides. **Pros:** mind-bending ocean and beachfront location, good on-site restaurant and bar, private airstrip on the property for easy access. **Cons:** take a lot of insect repellent and have it on when you step out of the plane; don't go unless you want remote, private, and nothing to do but fish and relax. ⊠*Portland Harbour, Pittstown Point Landings, Crooked Island* ☎242/344–2507 ⊕*www.pittstownpoint.com* ⇆*12 rooms* ⌂*In-room: no a/c (some), no phone, no TV, Wi-Fi. In-hotel: restaurant, bar, beachfront, water sports, bicycles, laundry service, public Wi-Fi* ☰*AE, MC, V.*

$ ▦ **Casuarina Villas.** Five modern one- and two-bedroom cottages sit on a ½-mi stretch of white-sand beach between Landrail Point and Pittstown Point Landings. Each has a full kitchen, satellite TV, and a western-facing deck to watch the magnificent sunsets. A local market, gas station, and two restaurants are 2 mi away in Landrail Point, and transportation can be provided. The management will treat you like family. They can arrange meals in your cottage with advance notice, find you a rental car, or set up a diving excursion. They can also book you with the top fly-fishing guides on the island including Mike Carroll, Jeff Moss, and Clinton Scavela. **Pros:** beachfront location; spacious, economical accommodations; great place to hang out, fish, and relax. **Cons:** you need to arrange your transportation to eat, get supplies, etc.; take plenty of insect repellent. ⊠ *Landrail Point, Crooked Island* ☎ *242/344–2197, 242/344–2036, or 242/636–4056* ⌨ *5 cottages* ♨ *In-room: no phone, kitchen. In-hotel: beachfront, water sports, laundry facilities* ▭ *No credit cards.*

SPORTS & THE OUTDOORS

FISHING   Crooked Island has a number of highly regarded bonefishing guides with quality boats and fly-fishing tackle. Most can be booked through Pittstown Point Landings, but the guides also take direct bookings. Be aware that telephone service to and from Crooked and Acklins island is not always operational.

Michael Carroll (☎ *242/636–7020*), **Derrick Ingraham** (☎ *242/556–8769*) **Elton "Bonefish Shakey" McKinney** (☎ *242/344–2507*), **Randy McKinney** (☎ *242/422–3276*), **Jeff Moss** (☎ *242/457–0621*), and **Clinton Scaval** (☎ *242/422–3596 or 242/344–2197*) are all knowledgeable professional guides. **Captain Robbie Gibson** (☎ *242/344–2507*) is the most experienced reef and offshore fishing captain on Crooked Island, where astounding fishing in virgin waters is the rule. Many wahoo weighing more than 100 pounds are landed each season with his assistance. Robbie's personal best wahoo is a whopping 180 pounds. He's also a skilled guide for anglers pursuing tuna, marlin, sharks, barracuda, jacks, snapper, and grouper.

SCUBA DIVING   **The Wall** starts at around 45 feet deep and goes down thousands more. It's about 50 yards off Crooked Island's coast and follows the shoreline for many miles. For more information, contact the Pittstown Point Landings hotel.

CROOKED & ACKLINS ISLANDS ESSENTIALS

TRANSPORTATION

BY AIR
Bahamasair flies from Nassau to Crooked and Acklins islands twice a week. Airports are in Colonel Hill on Crooked Island and at Spring Point on Acklins Island. Pittstown Point Landings can pick up its guests flying into Colonel Hill by prior arrangement. The private airstrip at Pittstown Point Landings is complimentary for hotel guests. Nonguests pay landing and parking fees. This airstrip is most convenient for private and charter flights if you're staying in the area of Pittstown and Landrail Point.

Airlines & Contacts Bahamasair (☎ *800/222–4262*)

BY BOAT

M/V *United Star* sails from Potter's Cay in Nassau to Acklins Island, Crooked Island, and Long Cay once a week on a varying schedule. Call the Dockmaster's Office in Potter's Cay for schedule information. The fare is $70 one way, and the trip takes 18 hours. Ferry service between Cove Landing, Crooked Island, and Lovely Bay, Acklins Island, usually operates twice daily on varying schedules between 9 and 4.

Boat & Ferry Information Dockmaster's Office (☎ *242/393–1064*)

BY CAR

You should reserve a car prior to your arrival with your hotel, but even with a reservation, be prepared for the possibility of not having one. Gas is also not always available on the island, as it's delivered by mail boats, which are sometimes delayed. Fortunately, it's easy to get a ride to most places with locals.

)NTACTS & RESOURCES

EMERGENCIES

The police and commissioner are on Crooked Island. The two government medical clinics on Acklins Island are at Spring Point and Chesters Bay. Crooked Island's clinic is at Landrail Point. The resident doctor and nurse for the area live in Spring Point. Nurses are also available at Colonel Hill on Crooked Island, and Masons Bay on Acklins. You can contact these medical professionals through your hotel.

Contacts Commissioner (☎ *242/344–2197*). **Police** (☎ *242/344–2599*).

IAGUA

Great Inagua, the Bahamas' third-largest island, is 25 mi wide and 45 mi long. The terrain is mostly flat and covered with scrub. An unusual climate of little rainfall and continual trade winds created rich salt ponds, which have brought prosperity to the island over the years. The Morton Salt Company harvests a million tons of salt annually at its Matthew Town factory. About a quarter of the Inaguan population earns its living by working for the company. Inagua is best known for the huge flocks of shy pink flamingos that reside in the island's vast national park and on the property belonging to the salt company. In addition to the famous flamingos, the island is home to one of the largest populations of the rare Bahama parrot, as well as herons, egrets, owls, cormorants, and more than a hundred other species of birds.

Although the birds have moved in wholeheartedly, the island remains virtually undiscovered by outsiders. Avid bird-watchers make up the majority of the tourists who undertake the long trip to this most southerly of the Out Islands, about 300 mi southeast of Nassau and 50 mi off the coast of Cuba. The local people are friendly and curious about each new face in town, so you won't feel like just another tourist. And

since crowds and traffic are nonexistent, there's nothing to bother yo
but the rather persistent mosquito population (be sure to bring stron
insect repellent). On the other hand, tourist facilities are very few an
far between. There's no official visitor information office on the islane
The only inhabited settlement on Inagua is Matthew Town, a small, b
clean network of workers' homes and essential services. The "hotels
are more like guesthouses or B&Bs, and are often difficult to contac
so be persistent.

If you're a beach lover, Inagua is not for you. Although there are
couple of small swimming areas near Matthew Town and a few longe
stretches farther north, no perfect combination of hotel and beach ha
been built here. However, the virgin reefs off the island have caused
stir among intrepid divers who bring in their own equipment. The buz
is that Inagua could become a hot dive destination. Adventurous sel
sufficient bonefishers have also discovered untouched flats with larg
bones on the northwest and southwest shorelines. There are permit an
tarpon, too, but that's a secret.

Great Inagua Island appears in the southeast corner of the Baham
map at the front of this guide.

MATTHEW TOWN

About 1,000 people live on Inagua, whose capital, Matthew Tow
is on the west coast. The "town" is about a block long. The larg
pink, run-down government building (with the commissioner's offic
post office, and customs office) is the dominant structure, along wit
a power plant and several Morton Salt Company machine shop
There are a grocery and liquor store, a bank, a clinic with a reside
doctor, a small cinema, several guesthouses, a few restaurants an
bars that keep irregular hours, and the small Kiwanis park that ha
a bench for sunset-gazing. Huge, no longer functional satellite dish
are prominently displayed in the yards of many houses, attesting t
the money that flowed through the island in the heady drug-smu
gling days of the 1980s. With smuggling on the rise again, the Roy
Bahamas Defense Force (in cooperation with the United States DE/
has established a southern satellite base here as part of a beefed u
drug interdiction program.

The **Erickson Museum and Library** is a welcome part of the communit
particularly the surprisingly well-stocked, well-equipped library. Th
Morton Company built the complex in the former home of the Ericksc
family, who came to Inagua in 1934 to run the salt giant. The museu
displays the island's history, to which the company is inextricably tie
The posted hours are not always that regular. ⊠ *Gregory St., on th*
northern edge of town across from the police station ☎ *242/339–18€*
🖾 *Free* ☉ *Weekdays 9–1 and 3–6, Sat. 9–1.*

The desire to marvel at the salt process lures few visitors to Inagu
but the **Morton Salt Company** (☎ *242/339–1300*) is omnipresent c
the island: it has more than 2,000 acres of crystallizing ponds an

more than 34,000 acres of reservoirs. More than a million tons of salt are produced every year for such industrial uses as salting icy streets. (More is produced when the Northeastern United States has a bad winter.) Even if you decide not to tour the facility, you can see the mountains of salt glistening in the sun from the plane. In an unusual case of industry assisting its environment, the crystallizers provide a feeding ground for the

> **HOW TO GET THERE**
>
> If the commercial air schedules don't work well with your vacation plans, it is a good idea to charter a flight. You can fly commercial to George Town, Exuma, then charter to Long, Cat, Crooked or Inagua for a lot less money than if you chartered all the way from Nassau or Ft. Lauderdale.

flamingos. As the water evaporates, the concentration of brine shrimp in the ponds increases, and the flamingos feed on these animals. Tours are available.

WHERE TO EAT & STAY

¢ ✗**Cozy Corner.** Cheerful and loud, this lunch spot—locals just call it Cozy's—is the best on the island. It has a pool table and a large seating area with a bar. Stop in for a chat with locals over a Kalik and a Bahamian conch burger. Cozy's also serves excellent island-style dinners on request—steamed crawfish, grilled snapper, baked chicken and fries, homemade slaw, macaroni and cheese, and fresh johnnycake. If they're not open when you stop by, they may still fix you food and a drink if you ask. ⊠*Matthew Town* ☎*242/339–1440* ⊟*No credit cards.*

$ ▦**Sunset Apartments.** A good bet for accommodations on Inagua, these apartments sit right along the water on Matthew Town's southern side. The cement units all have modern Caribbean-style terra-cotta tile floors, rattan furniture, small terraces, a picnic area, and a gas grill. About a five-minute walk away is a small, secluded beach called the Swimming Hole. Ezzard Cartwright, the owner, is the only fly-fishing guide on the island, and he offers all-inclusive bonefishing packages. He's usually out working, so calling after 7 PM Bahamas time is the best chance to reach him. **Pros:** great place for bonefishing, Ezzard is a wonderful host and a top fly-fishing guide. **Cons:** no Internet service, nothing to do but fish and bird watch, you need to pay in cash. ⊠*Matthew Town* ☎*242/339–1362* ⊅*2 apartments* ♿*In-room: no phone, kitchen. In-hotel: no elevator* ⊟*No credit cards.*

¢ ▦**The Main House.** The Morton Salt Company operates this small, affordable guesthouse. On the second of two floors, air-conditioned rooms share a sitting area with couches and a telephone. Rooms are spotless and spacious with dark-wood furnishings, Masonite-paneled walls, and floral-print drapes and spreads. The green-and-white hotel is right in Matthew Town, behind the grocery store and directly across the street from the island's power plant. **Pros:** inexpensive and clean, good spot to stay if you are visiting the National Park. **Cons:** no Internet service, nothing to do at night, power plant can be noisy. ⊠*Matthew Town* ☎*242/339–1266 or 242/339–1267* ⊅*5 rooms* ♿*In-room: no phone, refrigerator. In-hotel: no elevator* ⊟*No credit cards.*

5

¢ 🖵 **Walkine's Guest House.** On the main drag and in the mix of the residential community, this cinder-block duplex has five motel-style air-conditioned rooms with cable TV. All rooms are bright and comfortable, with two twin beds. Three rooms have private baths, and two share a bath. The owner, Eleanor Walkine, lives in the duplex next door, and will prepare meals on request. **Pros:** inexpensive and clean, good spot to stay if you are visiting the National Park. **Cons:** often hard to reach by phone, no Internet service, nothing to do at night. ✉ *Matthew Town* ☎ *242/339–1612* 🛏 *5 rooms* ⚐ *In-room: no phone* ▭ *No credit cards.*

SPORTS & THE OUTDOORS

BICYCLING The **Pour More Bar** (☎ *242/339–1232*) rents bikes for exploring the island.

ELSEWHERE ON THE ISLAND

Although you'll spot them in salt ponds throughout the island, birds and other wildlife also reside in the **Inagua National Park,** managed by **The Bahamas National Trust** (BNT), which spreads over 287 square mi and occupies most of the island's western half. Nature lovers, ornithologists, and photographers are drawn to the area and to Lake Windsor (a 12-mi-long brackish body of water in the island's center) to view the spectacle of more than 60,000 flamingos feeding, mating, or flying (although you will rarely see all those birds together in the same place). When planning your trip, keep in mind that November through June is the best time to see the birds, and the breeding season is March through May. Flamingos live on Inagua year-round, but the greatest concentrations come at these times. If you visit right after hatching, the scrambling flocks of fuzzy, gray baby flamingos—they can't fly until they're older—are quite entertaining. On the northwest side of the park is the **Union Creek Reserve,** where BNT is working with the Caribbean Conservation Corporation on marine turtle research. To tour any part of the park or reserve, you must be accompanied by a BNT warden. Contact the **Bahamas National Trust's Nassau office** (☎ *242/393–1317* ⊕ *www.thebahamasnationaltrust.org*) to make reservations for your visit. E-mail is your best bet for getting a response. BNT will send a visitor reservation form that you must fill out and return with your flight information, length of stay, and number of people in your party. You must also pay for your tour before arrival on Inagua.

From **Southwest Point,** a mile or so south of the capital, you can see Cuba's coast—slightly more than 50 mi west—on a clear day from atop the lighthouse (built in 1870 in response to a huge number of shipwrecks on offshore reefs). This is one of the last four hand-operated kerosene lighthouses in the Bahamas. Be sure to sign the guest book after your climb.

NAGUA ESSENTIALS

RANSPORTATION

BY AIR

Bahamasair has flights on Monday, Wednesday, and Friday from Nassau to the Matthew Town Airport.

Airlines & Contacts **Bahamasair** (☎ 242/339–4415 or 800/222–4262).

BY BOAT

M/V *Trans Cargo II* makes weekly trips from Nassau to Matthew Town, also stopping at Abraham's Bay, Mayaguana. The cost is $70 one way, and the trip takes approximately 24 hours. For information on specific schedules contact the Dockmaster's Office at Potter's Cay, Nassau.

Boat & Ferry Information **Dockmaster's Office** (☎ 242/393–1064).

BY CAR

Inagua Trading Ltd. has several cars for rent by the day. BNT Warden Henry Nixon can also arrange for vehicle rentals. Both are often difficult to contact by phone, so be persistent.

Local Agency **Inagua Trading Ltd.** (☎ 242/339–1330). **Warden Henry Nixon** (☎ 242/339–1616).

BY TAXI

Taxis sometimes meet incoming flights, though taxi service is not always reliable. It's best to make prior arrangements with your hotel.

Airport Information **Matthew Town Airport** (☎ 242/339–1254).

ONTACTS & RESOURCES

BANKS & EXCHANGE SERVICES

The Bank of the Bahamas in Matthew Town is open Monday through Thursday 9:30–2 and Friday 9:30–5:30.

Contact **Bank of the Bahamas** (☎ 242/339–1815).

EMERGENCIES

There's no general emergency number in Inagua—call the police or hospital directly in case of an emergency.

Contacts **Hospital** (☎ 242/339–1249). **Police** (☎ 242/339–1263).

TOUR OPTIONS

Warden Henry Nixon leads most tours into Inagua National Park and to Union Creek Reserve. Mr. Nixon is also a certified birding tour guide. He can arrange for rental vehicles and generally point you in the right direction for all activities on Inagua. He's difficult to reach by phone, so you have to be persistent. You have the best chance of reaching him in the early evening.

Contact **Warden Henry Nixon** (☎ 242/339–1616).

LONG ISLAND

Never more than 4 mi wide but close to 80 mi long, Long Island truly lives up to its name. The Queen's Highway traverses its length, through the Tropic of Cancer and some 35 settlements and farming towns. The island is known for its astonishing contrasts in geography, with chalk-white limestone cliffs, forested hillsides, mangrove swamps, and stark flatlands where salt is produced. Exposed to the open Atlantic, the east coast consists of black iridescent reefs, protected coves, long strands of shelling beaches, and craggy bluffs that drop precipitously into the deep blue sea. The tranquil west coast is composed of powdery-white beaches, wide-open sandy flats, and calm turquoise bays.

Long Island was one of Columbus's early stopping-off places. In 1790 American Loyalists from the Carolinas brought their slaves to the island, where they built plantations and planted more than 4,000 acres of cotton. The rich soil made crop growing more successful here than on any other Out Island, but with the abolition of slavery, the plantations failed. Agriculture, however, remains a thriving part of the local economy, and pothole farming is the favored method of growing corn, peas, squash, pineapples, bananas, and other fruits.

The island has blossomed into an Out Island jewel, with the full-time population settling in around 4,000 residents. Resort, diving, and snorkeling services have been enhanced in recent years, and vast, unexplored bonefish flats are drawing anglers who enjoy remote fishing. Sailing enthusiasts will find Joe's Sound—sandwiched between Cape Santa Maria beach and Glenton Sound—to be a protected haven that rivals any in the Bahamas. A sheltered deep-water marina with fuel and other services in Clarence Town has created more convenient boating access to the southern islands.

CAPE SANTA MARIA & STELLA MARIS

★ Columbus originally named the island's northern tip **Cape Santa Maria** in honor of one of his ships. He called the entire island Fernandina, out of respect for his Spanish sponsor. Cape Santa Maria is known for its irresistibly dazzling beaches, which are considered among the best in the country.

Take a side trip on the unpaved road out to **Columbus Cove,** 1½ mi north of the Cape Santa Maria resort. The monument and plaque that commemorate Columbus's landing are here, as well as tremendous views of the protected harbor he sailed into. Divers can explore the wreck of a ship, the M/V *Comberbach,* which lies just off the headland. The Stella Maris Resort sunk the leaky 103-foot freighter in 1985 to create an artificial reef and an excellent dive site nearly 100 feet under. The road to the cove is too rough for most vehicles, but it happens to be a fine walk. An easier way to reach the cove is by boat. Anglers can fish for bonefish and tarpon at the lower tidal stages, and the beach is perfect for a lazy picnic.

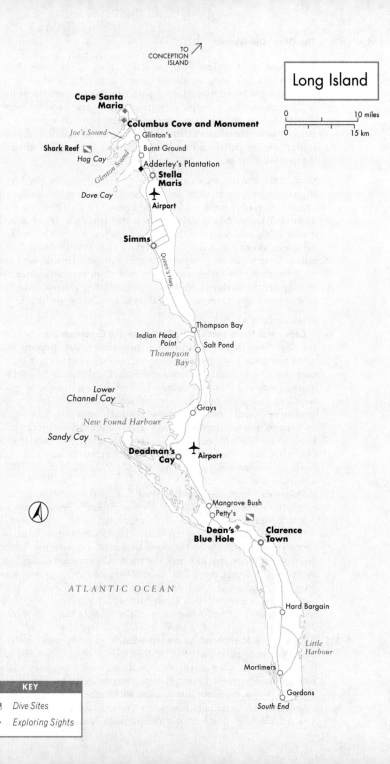

TO
CONCEPTION
ISLAND

Long Island

0		10 miles
0		15 km

**Cape Santa
Maria**

Columbus Cove and Monument

Joe's Sound   Glinton's

Shark Reef

Hog Cay   Burnt Ground

Glenton Sound   Adderley's Plantation

**Stella
Maris**

Dove Cay

✈
Airport

Simms

Queen's Hwy.

Thompson Bay

*Indian Head
Point*   Salt Pond

*Thompson
Bay*

*Lower
Channel Cay*

New Found Harbour   Grays

Sandy Cay

**Deadman's
Cay**   ✈ **Airport**

Mangrove Bush
Petty's

**Dean's
Blue Hole**   **Clarence
Town**

ATLANTIC OCEAN

Hard Bargain

*Little
Harbour*

Mortimers

Gordons

South End

KEY
◢ *Dive Sites*
◆ *Exploring Sights*

Stella Maris, meaning Star of the Sea, lies about 12 mi south of Cape Santa Maria. It's home to the all-encompassing Stella Maris Resort Club, along with an airport. In a world of its own, the resort has a full-service marina, a couple of restaurants, several bars, the island's only fly-fishing shop, a simple shopping complex with a bank, a post office, and a general store. If you're interested in aquatic adventures, contact the resort, which runs numerous daily outings, including diving and fishing trips.

Shark Reef, about 4 mi west of Hog Cay, is easily reached by boaters from Cape Santa Maria and Joe's Sound. The water is startlingly clear, and the drop-off from the white-sand bottom to deep blue is a visual wonder. You can take a guided diving excursion and watch a scuba master safely feed dozens of sharks at a time. Just north of Stella Maris, off Queen's Highway, are the ruins of the 19th-century **Adderley's Plantation.** Long Island was another Bahamian island where fleeing Loyalists attempted, with little success, to grow cotton. You can still see parts of the plantation's three buildings up to roof level. The remains of two other plantations, **Dunmore's** and **Gray's,** are also on the island.

WHERE TO EAT & STAY

$$ ✕ **Cape Santa Maria Beach House Restaurant and Oceanside Bar.** Upstairs in the Cape Santa Maria Beach House, guests can enjoy sweeping vistas of the turquoise bay during the day, and bobbing boat lights in the evening along with the gentle sounds of the sea. Breakfast can be light with toast, cereal, and fruit, or splurge with French toast or a cheese omelet with bacon. Lunch favorites are cheeseburgers, conch fritters, club sandwiches, salads, and soups. Fresh broiled lobster (in season), grilled mahimahi, panfried grouper, steaks, and chops are dinner staples. The key lime pie is a sure bet for dessert. Full bar service is available in the Oceanside Bar, on the beachfront deck, and in the restaurant. ⊠ *Cape Santa Maria Beach Resort and Villas* ☏*242/338–5273* ▤*AE, MC, V* ◷*Closed Sept. and Oct.*

$$ ✕ **Stella Maris Restaurant and Bar.** Fresh fruit and home-baked muffins highlight the breakfast buffet, though you can order French toast, eggs any style, or omelets. Though you can eat lunch in the dining room, it's delightful to enjoy your burgers, club and tuna sandwiches, salads, and conch chowder outside on the stone terrace overlooking the Atlantic. Need an afternoon snack? Check out the sandwiches and conch fritters in the bar. For dinner, the grilled lamb chops, fried conch, and pan-seared grouper or hog snapper are top choices, though baked chicken, chops, and pastas are tasty as well. Fresh fruit with ice cream is a great hot weather dessert. ⊠ *Stella Maris Resort Club, Stella Maris* ☏*242/338–2051* ▤*AE, D, MC, V* ◷*Sometimes closed in Sept.; call ahead.*

★ $$$ ▦ **Cape Santa Maria Beach Resort and Villas.** This cushy resort has colonial-style cottages spread along a 4-mi stretch of velvety white-sand beach. Spacious one- or two-bedroom units have their own large, fully furnished screened porches steps away from the turquoise water. Twelve 1,500-square-foot luxury villas with high-speed Internet, entertainment centers, and full kitchens are also available for nightly rental. The marble-floor Beach House reception building contains a small gym, gift shop, and TV room, and upstairs there is a restaurant that overlooks the bay. Magenta sunsets are the trademark of the beachside bar. The water-sports activities office arranges Hobie Cat sailing, snorkeling, and deep-sea, reef, or bonefishing excursions. **Pros:** on one of the most spectacular stretches of sand on earth, tranquil waters is great for swimming, luxury villas. **Cons:** restaurant service is slow, be sure to have insect repellent for outdoor evening activities or dining. ⊠ *Cape Santa Maria Beach* ☎ *242/338–5273 or 800/663–7090* ⊕ *www.cape santamaria.com* ⇨ *21 1- to 2-bedroom bungalows, 12 luxury villas* ⌂ *In-room: no phone, safe, kitchen (some), refrigerator, no TV, ethernet (some). In-hotel: restaurant, bar, gym, beachfront, water sports, bicycles, no elevator, laundry facilities, public Wi-Fi* ▭ *AE, MC, V* ☉ *Closed Sept. and Oct.*

★ $ 🏨 **Stella Maris Resort Club.** Sitting atop a hilly east-coast ridge overlooking the Atlantic, this sprawling resort's range of daily activities makes it a Bahamian classic. You can swim in three freshwater pools, lounge on a series of private beaches, or explore sandy coves with excellent snorkeling. Dive, fish, sail, sea kayak, hike, or take advantage of free morning and afternoon activity programs. The resort has colorful, spacious hillside rooms and cottages, and sprawling oceanfront houses, a few with private pools. Fresh seafood is the highlight of the restaurant's rotating menus. There is a weekly rum punch pool party, a cave party, weekly beach barbecues, and other lively events. As for service, you won't find a better trained or more friendly staff anywhere in the Bahamas. **Pros:** perfect location to relax and enjoy sun, sea, and sand; top-quality scuba diving and bonefishing; friendliest people you will meet in the islands. **Cons:** expect somewhat dated room decor, you will need insect repellent for evening activities and outdoor dining. ⊠ *Stella Maris* ☎ *242/338–2051 or 800/426–0466* ⊕ *www.stella marisresort.com* ⇨ *20 rooms, 12 1-bedroom cottages, 7 2-bedroom cottages, 4 beach houses* ⌂ *In-room: no phone, refrigerator, no TV, Wi-Fi (some). In-hotel: restaurant, bars, tennis courts, pools, beachfront, diving, water sports, bicycles, no elevator, laundry service, public Internet, public Wi-Fi* ▭ *AE, D, MC, V.*

5

SIMMS & SOUTH

Simms is one of Long Island's oldest settlements, 8 mi south of Stella Maris past little pastel-color houses. Some of these homes display emblems to ward off evil spirits, an indication of the presence of Obeah, the voodoolike culture found on many of the Bahamian islands. There are a few quirky roadside eats to be had on this stretch of Queen's Highway. On the road's east side, look for a small conch-salad stand that's intermittently open and prepares the snack right before your eyes. Immediately south of Simms, you may see rising smoke and tables out in the front yard of **Jeraldine's Jerk Pit.** The barbecued chicken and pork are delectable, though they are only open occasionally.

The annual **Long Island Regatta,** featuring Bahamian-made boats, is held in Salt Pond every June. The regatta is the island's biggest event, attracting contestants from all over the islands. Three days of partying and pig roasts are sparked at night by lively local bands. Salt Pond is 10 mi south of Simms.

The town of **Deadman's Cay** is the island's largest settlement. Here you'll find a few shops, churches, and schools. Just east of Deadman's Cay, **Cartwright's Cave** has stalactites and stalagmites and eventually leads to the sea. The cave has apparently never been completely explored, although Arawak drawings were found on one wall. For guided cave tours, contact **Leonard Cartwright** (☎242/337–0235). Leonard will customize a tour to your needs, though he is often difficult to reach by phone, so be persistent in calling him. There are several other caves, supposedly pirate-haunted, around Simms, Millers, and Salt Pond; a local should be able to point you in the right direction.

> **IN THE KNOW**
>
> There are new restaurants, small shops, and fruit and conch stands opening (and closing) all the time. When you arrive, ask your taxi driver what's new on the island. Cabbies usually know everything as they travel around more than hotel staff.

Between Deadman's Cay and Clarence Town, just past the settlement of Petty's, watch for the pink-and-white pillars that line the turnoff for **Dean's Blue Hole.** At 660 feet, it's thought to be the world's second-deepest blue hole. Curious divers will want to contact the **Dive shop at Stella Maris** (☎242/338–2050).

Clarence Town has Long Island's most celebrated landmarks, **St. Paul's Church** (Anglican) and **St. Peter's Church** (Catholic). They were both built by Father Jerome, a priest who is buried in a tomb in the Hermitage atop Cat Island's Mt. Alvernia. As an Anglican named John Hawes, he constructed St. Paul's. Later, after converting to Catholicism, he built St. Peter's. The architecture of the two churches is similar to that of the missions established by the Spaniards in California in the late 18th century. Clarence Town is simply gorgeous, fringed by white-sand beaches, and fronted by a stunning oval-shaped bay of clear aqua-blue water dotted with coral heads, sand bars, and small green cays. The harbor is also home to the local government headquarters and dock.

WHERE TO EAT & STAY

$ ✕**The Forest.** Just south of Clarence Town on the west side of the highway, this popular laid-back restaurant serves spicy wings, potato skins, cracked conch, barbecued chicken, and grouper fingers in a large open room furnished with simple tables and chairs. Some people say their conch salad is even better than Max's, so you should try both and see for yourself. Enjoy a drink at the bar—which is made of seashells embedded in glossy resin—and a game of pool. Every other weekend there's live music and dancing. For dinner, you need to call ahead for reservations. ⊠*Queen's Hwy.* ☎*242/337–3287* ▬*MC, V.*

¢ ✕**Max's Conch Grill and Bar.** If you sit all day on a stool at this pink-, green-, and yellow-stripe roadside gazebo, nursing beers and nibbling on conch, you'll become a veritable expert on Long Island and the life of its residents. Such is the draw of this laid-back watering hole, open 9 to 9 Monday through Saturday—sometimes later when the bar is hopping. Have a chat with Max while sampling his conch salad ($3.50 or $6), conch dumplings (six for $1), or daily specials like baked ham and steamed pork. ⊠*Deadman's Cay* ☎*242/337–0056* ▤*MC, V.*

<table>
<tr><td>BEST OF THE BEST</td></tr>
<tr><td>Like to hang out and do things on your own? At Chez Pierre you can play it by ear, go bonefishing, snorkeling, exploring, or just lie around and do nothing at all.</td></tr>
</table>

★ $ 🏨**Chez Pierre Bahamas.** Six elevated cottages with generous bedrooms, bath, and airy screened porches line this remote Millers Bay beach location, halfway between Stella Maris and Deadman's Cay. Owners Pierre and Anne deliver exceptional personalized service; however, guests here should be self-sufficient and adventurous. Chef Pierre whips up fresh innovative dishes with homegrown ingredients and daily caught seafood in the relaxing oceanfront restaurant. The room rate includes two meals daily. Explore nearby cays in sea kayaks, wade the adjacent flats for bonefish, or schedule a diving adventure through the Stella Maris marina. Fishing guides, car rentals, and airport transfers can be arranged. **Pros:** private beachfront location, easy access to fishing and water sports you can do on your own, personalized service. **Cons:** you need to rent a car to better enjoy your stay here and to explore the island, take plenty of bug spray for the evenings. ⊠*Millers Bay* ☎*418/210–3605, 242/338–8809, or 242/357–1374* ⊕*www.chezpierre bahamas.com* ⇋*6 cottages* ₷*In-room: no a/c, no phone, no TV. In-hotel: restaurant, bar, beachfront, water sports, bicycles, laundry service, public Internet* ▤*AE, MC, V.*

$ 🏨**Gems at Paradise.** On 16 hillside acres overlooking the magnificent beach and bay of Clarence Town Harbour, this resort has one- and two-bedroom condos with upscale island furniture and artwork, Italian tile trimming, and full kitchens. The regular hotel suites have a similar look and mesmerizing balcony views. The resort also has a bar, meeting rooms, sailboats and sea kayaks for rent, and barbecue grills on its private beach. Several good restaurants are within a mile of the resort. We recommend that you rent a car if you stay here. **Pros:** drop-dead gorgeous location and views, easy access to fishing and water sports you can do on your own, car rentals can be arranged. **Cons:** if you don't like walking up stairs, most of the rooms here won't suit you; no on-site restaurant; no reliable Internet service. ⊠*Clarence Town* ☎*242/337–3016 or 242/337–3019* ⊕*www.gemsatparadise.com* ⇋*11 suites, 3 1-bedroom condos, 1 2-bedroom condo* ₷*In-room: no phone, kitchen (some), no TV. In-hotel: bar, beachfront, water sports, no elevator, laundry service* ▤*AE, D, MC, V.*

$ 🏨**Lochabar Beach Lodge.** Mellow and remote, the brightly painted two-story lodge consists of two thoughtfully constructed 600-square-foot guest studios downstairs that overlook a pristine beach and dramatic blue hole. Rooms have dinette islands with stools, although you can also eat alfresco on your deck. The larger upstairs suite includes a full kitchen and private bedroom. At low tide, you can stroll the cove's entire beach and round the point into Clarence Town. You'll need to rent a car to stay here. Bonefishing guides and car rentals can be arranged by the manager, Nancy Knowles. **Pros:** a stunning beachfront location on a mysterious blue hole, you can relax and disappear from civilization, easy access to great fishing. **Cons:** remote location means you are on your own, so make sure this is what you want; if something needs fixing in the lodge, it may take a while; bring plenty of bug spray. ⊠ *1 mi south of Clarence Town* ☎ *242/337–3123* ⊕ *www.bahamasvacationguide.com/lochabarbeachlodge* ⌫ *2 studios, 1 suite* ⌂ *In-room: no a/c (some), kitchen. In-hotel: water sports* ▭ *No credit cards.*

NIGHTLIFE

Just south of Clarence Town, **The Forest** (⊠ *Queen's Hwy., Miley's* ☎ *242/337–3287*) has dancing and partying to live bands playing rock, calypso, and reggae music every other weekend, though schedules vary so you should stop by and check out the current happenings.

SHOPPING

Bonafide Tackle Shop and Cafe (⊠ *Queen's Hwy., Stella Maris* ☎ *242/338–2025*) sells fly-fishing tackle and accessories, clothing, souvenirs, and snacks. You can book a fishing trip here, and arrange for fishing gear rental. Internet access is available. **Wild Tamarind** (⊠ *About ½ mi east of Queen's Hwy., Petty's* ☎ *242/337–0262*) is Denis Knight's ceramics studio. Stop in for a lovely bowl, vase, or sculpture, but call first in case he's out fishing.

SPORTS & THE OUTDOORS

FISHING **Bonafide Bonefishing** (☎ *242/338–2025* ⊕ *www.bonafidebonefishing. com*) is run by guide James "Docky" Smith and his wife, Jill. Highly regarded as one of the best guides in the Bahamas, Docky conducts full- and half-day guided trips in his state-of-the-art 2007 model 17-foot Maverick Mirage flats skiff. Docky also runs reef fishing trips, and he is an expert fly-casting instructor. If you need work on your casting—and who doesn't—you should sign up for a casting lesson with Docky. The operation is based out of Bonafide Tackle Shop and Cafe at Stella Maris, which rents conventional and fly-fishing gear, prepares snacks and box lunches, and sells a range of tackle, clothing, and flies. To fish with Docky, you need to book well in advance.

The 15-slip **Flying Fish Marina** (☎ *242/337–3430* ⊕ *www.flyingfishmarina.net*) in the northern corner of Clarence Town Harbour has fuel and can take boats up to 130 feet. The marina's Outer Edge Bar and Grill serves burgers, fries, fritters, and grilled fish. Full dinners can be arranged with advance notice. Bathrooms, showers, and laundry facilities are available to marina guests. Bonefishing, reef, and offshore guides can be arranged by the management with advance notice. From March through July, you should call a month in advance to reserve a slip. **Silver Strike Fishing** (☎ *242/337–1555 or 242/337–0329*) is operated by guide Cecil Knowles and his wife, Judy. You can book guides by the day, or a complete bonefishing package with accommodations at Lochabar Beach Lodge.

SCUBA DIVING **Conception Island Wall** is an excellent wall dive, with hard and soft coral, plus interesting sponge formations. **Dean's Blue Hole** is lauded by locals as one of the world's deepest ocean holes. It's surrounded by a powder-beach cove. **Shark Reef** is the site of the Bahamas' first shark dive. The Stella Maris Resort has been running trips there for more than 25 years; call them to arrange a dive.

ᗡNG ISLAND ESSENTIALS

ANSPORTATION

BY AIR

Bahamasair flies most days from Nassau to Deadman's Cay, and from Nassau and George Town to Stella Maris Airport. The airport at Stella Maris has a resurfaced runway (2006) and full customs services. American Eagle flies to George Town, Exuma, from Florida, and from there it is an easy and inexpensive charter flight to hop over to Stella Maris. Stella Maris Resort has charter flights from George Town, Exuma, and from Nassau to Stella Maris Airport. If you're a pilot, the island is a great base for exploring other islands. Stella Maris rents well-maintained planes—a four-seat Piper Seneca and a six-seat Piper Navajo—for about $90 an hour. Island Wings, an air charter company owned by Captain Marty Fox, has charter flight service to and from any Bahamian island with a legal airstrip, and to and from Stella Maris or Deadman's Cay.

If you're a guest at Cape Santa Maria or Stella Maris, it's best to fly into the Stella Maris Airport. Use the Deadman's Cay Airport if you're staying in Clarence Town. If you fly into Deadman's Cay Airport and have to take a taxi to Stella Maria Resort or Cape Santa Maria, it will be 45 minutes to one hour driving time and the fare can be $100 or more.

Airlines & Contacts Bahamasair (☎ 242/339–4415 or 800/222–4262). **Deadman's Cay** (☎ 242/337–0536). **Island Wings** (☎ 242/338–2022 or 242/357–1021). **Stella Maris** (☎ 800/426–0466, 954/359–8236, or 242/338–2051 ⊕ www.stellamarisresortairservice.com).

BY BOAT

M/V *Mia Dean* makes a 12-hour weekly trip from Nassau to Clarence Town, on the island's south end. The boat leaves Nassau on Tuesday and returns on Thursday; the fare is $45 one way. The M/V *Sherice M* leaves Nassau on Tuesday with stops in Salt Pond, Deadman's Cay, and Seymour's. The return trip is on Friday. Travel time is 15 hours; the fare is $45 one way. For more information, contact the Dockmaster's Office at Potter's Cay, Nassau.

Boat & Ferry Information Dockmaster's Office (☎ 242/393–1064).

BY CAR

Taylor's Rentals rents high-quality cars for the most reasonable rates on the island. Hotels and lodges will also arrange for guests' automobile rentals.

Local Agency Taylor's Rentals (☎ 242/338–7001).

BY TAXI

Taxis meet incoming flights at both airports. From the Stella Maris Airport, the fare to Stella Maris Resort is $4; to Cape Santa Maria, it's $40. Check with your hotel to see which airport you should use—landing at the wrong airport could mean a $120 cab ride—in which case renting a car will save you money. Guests staying at Chez Pierre pay $25 one way for the taxi from Stella Maris, and $45 one way for the taxi from Deadman's Cay.

CONTACTS & RESOURCES

BANKS & EXCHANGE SERVICES

At Stella Maris Resort Club, Scotiabank is open Tuesday and Thursday 9:30–2 and Friday 9:30–5. Farther south, the Deadman's Cay branch is open Monday–Thursday 9–1 and Friday 9–5. Royal Bank of Canada has a branch on Deadman's Cay; hours are Monday–Thursday 9–1 and Friday 9–5.

Contacts **Scotiabank** (☎ 242/338–2057 Stella Maris, 242/338–2002 Deadman's Cay). **Royal Bank of Canada** (☎ 242/337–1044).

EMERGENCIES

Contacts **Police** (☎ 242/337–0999 Clarence Town, 242/337–0444 Deadman's Cay, 242/338–8555 Simms).

SAN SALVADOR

On October 12, 1492, Christopher Columbus disrupted the lives of the peaceful Lucayan Indians by landing on the island of Guanahani, which he named San Salvador. Apparently he knelt on the beach and claimed the land for Spain. (Skeptics of this story point to a study published in a 1986 *National Geographic* article in which Samana Cay, 60 mi southeast, is identified as the exact point of the weary explorer's landing.) Three monuments on the island commemorate Columbus's arrival, and the 500th anniversary of the event was officially celebrated here.

A 17th-century pirate named George Watling, who frequently sought shelter on the island, changed San Salvador's name to Watling's Island. The Bahamian government switched the name back to San Salvador in 1926.

The island is 12 mi long—roughly the length of Manhattan—and about 5 mi wide along the lake-filled portion of its interior. The Queen's Highway forms an oval that skirts the coastline alongside some of the most dazzling deserted beaches in the Caribbean. Most visitors come for the peaceful isolation and the diving; there are about 950 residents and over 50 dive sites. There's also world-renowned offshore fishing and good bonefishing.

RNANDEZ BAY TO RIDING ROCK POINT

In 1492 the inspiring sight that greeted Christopher Columbus by moonlight at 2 AM was a terrain of gleaming beaches and far-reaching forest. The peripatetic traveler and his crews—"men from Heaven," the locals called them—steered the *Niña, Pinta,* and *Santa María* warily among the coral reefs and anchored, so it's recorded, in **Fernandez Bay.** A **cross** erected in 1956 by Columbus scholar Ruth C. Durlacher Wolper Malvin stands at his approximate landing spot. Ms. Malvin's **New World Museum** (☎ No phone), near North Victoria Hill on the east coast, contains artifacts from the era of the Lucayans. Admission to the museum is free; it's open by appointment only (your hotel can make arrangements). An underwater monument marks the place where the *Santa María* anchored. Nearby, another monument commemorates the Olympic flame's passage on its journey from Greece to Mexico City in 1968.

Fernandez Bay is just south of what is now the main community of **Cockburn Town,** mid-island on the western shore. Queen's Highway encircles the island from Cockburn Town, where the weekly mail boat docks. This small village's narrow streets contain two churches, a commissioner's office, a police station, a courthouse, a library, a clinic, a drugstore, and a telephone station.

Columbus first spotted and made a record of **Riding Rock Point.** The area now serves as the home for the Riding Rock Resort and Marina, a popular resort for divers and boaters. Just north of the point is the island's other resort, the Club Med–Columbus Isle, at the foot of a gorgeous 2-mi-long beach. Riding Rock Point is about a mile north of Cockburn Town.

WHERE TO EAT & STAY

$$ ✕**Riding Rock Seafront Restaurant and Bar.** Eat inside the freshly renovated 75-seat restaurant, or take a table on the patio by the pool. Androsia print table clothes and curtains create a colorful tropical feel. Fruit, fresh baked breads, pancakes, and eggs any style with bacon and grits are daily starters. Burgers, sandwiches, conch chowder, and fried conch are lunch favorites. The just-off-the-boat catch of the day—wahoo, mahimahi, tuna, grouper, snapper—grilled with lemon and butter, or baked with tomatoes and spices, is the dinner specialty each evening. Broiled or stuffed lobster (in season), barbecue shrimp, steaks, and chicken round out the choices, though all are not available each evening as the menu changes based on availability. ⊠ *Riding Rock Resort and Marina* ☎ *242/331–2631* ▭ *D, MC, V* ☉ *Closed at times in Sept.; call ahead.*

★$$$ ⊡**Club Med–Columbus Isle.** The 80-acre oceanfront village is one of Club Med's most luxurious resorts, with state-of-the-art dive facilities, including three custom-made 45-foot catamarans and a decompression chamber. All rooms have patios or balconies and handcrafted furniture. Guided bike tours introduce vacationers to island life. This resort caters primarily to upscale couples, and the atmosphere is more low-key than at most Club Meds. It's one of the most recommended by Club Med

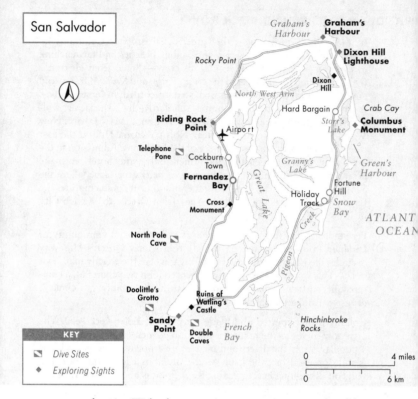

San Salvador

Graham's Harbour
Graham's Harbour
Dixon Hill Lighthouse
Rocky Point
Dixon Hill
North West Arm
Hard Bargain
Crab Cay
Riding Rock Point
Airport
Starr's Lake
Columbus Monument
Telephone Pone
Cockburn Town
Granny's Lake
Green's Harbour
Fernandez Bay
Great Lake
Fortune Hill
Cross Monument
Holiday Track
Snow Bay
ATLANTI OCEAN
North Pole Cave
Pigeon Creek
Doolittle's Grotto
Ruins of Watling's Castle
Sandy Point
Double Caves
French Bay
Hinchinbroke Rocks

KEY

⬔ Dive Sites

◆ Exploring Sights

0   4 miles
0   6 km

fanatics. With advance notice, nonguests can partake of the sumptuous lunches and dinners. **Pros:** beachfront location, activities galore from spectacular diving to bonefishing. **Cons:** change-over days can be hectic (weekends) with full charter flights arriving and departing from Canada and Paris; be aware that many members of the customer service staff are French, and they speak only passable English. ⊠*3 mi north of Riding Rock Point* ☎*888/932–2582 or 242/331–2000* ⊕*www.clubmed. com* ➴*235 rooms* ⌂*In-room: refrigerator, Wi-Fi (some). In-hotel: 3 restaurants, bars, tennis courts, pool, gym, beachfront, diving, bicycles, no elevator, laundry service, concierge, public Internet, public Wi-Fi, airport shuttle* ⊟*AE, D, MC, V* ⊜*AI.*

$ ⌸**Riding Rock Resort and Marina.** A diver's dream, this motel-style resort offers three dives per day to pristine offshore reefs and a drop-off wall teeming with life. It's also the only place to stay on San Salvador if you want to manage your own activities. Remodeled in late 2007, the resort's three buildings house rooms facing either the ocean or the freshwater pool. All rooms have fresh paint, new Androsia curtains and bedspreads, washed-oak furniture, and a sitting area with a table and chairs; ocean-side rooms have refrigerators and queen-size beds. The restaurant serves grilled wahoo and tuna right off the boat as well as hearty pancake breakfasts. There's good bonefishing you can do on your own north of Club Med, and in Pigeon Creek. You should rent a car or a bike at least one day and explore the island. **Pros:** some of the best diving in the world; San Salvador gives you the feeling that you are on your own private island; the marina is in a unique location for boaters to access the virgin offshore fishing for marlin, wahoo, tuna and dolphin. **Cons:** food and fuel supplies can run low at times, the resort is still being remodeled so it's a work in progress. ⊠*Riding Rock Point* ☎*954/359–8353, 800/272–1492, or 242/331–2631* ⊕*www. ridingrock.com* ⌁*42 rooms, 2 villas* ⌂*In-room: refrigerator (some). In-hotel: restaurant, bar, pool, diving, bicycles, no elevator, laundry service, public Wi-Fi* ⊟*D, MC, V.*

SPORTS & THE OUTDOORS

BICYCLING **Riding Rock Resort and Marina** (☎*800/272–1492 or 242/331–2631*) rents bicycles for $8 a day.

UBA DIVING **Club Med** (☎*242/331–2000*) has dive boats and a decompression chamber. There's also tennis, sailing, and windsurfing, among other sports. **Riding Rock Divers**(☎*800/272–1492 or 800/311–8328*), which is part of the Riding Rock Resort and Marina, uses mostly buoyed sites to avoid damaging the marine environment by dropping anchor. The 42- and 46-foot dive boats are spacious and comfortable. Resort and certification courses are offered, and a modern underwater photographic facility is available to guests. All new computerized dive gear and camera gear are on-site for guest rental. Complete dive packages, including meals and accommodations, are available through Riding Rock Resort and Marina. Riding Rock also rents bicycles and snorkeling gear and can arrange reef, inshore, and offshore fishing trips ($500 for a half day and $800 for a full day). The offshore waters hold tuna, blue marlin, dorado, and, in the winter, wahoo.

ROUND SAN SALVADOR

Columbus describes **Graham's Harbour** in his diaries as large enough "to hold all the ships of Christendom." A complex of buildings near the harbor houses the **Bahamian Field Station,** a biological and geological research institution that attracts scientists and students from all over the world.

A couple of miles south of Graham's Harbour stands **Dixon Hill Lighthouse.** Built around 1856, it's still hand-operated. The lighthouse keeper must wind the apparatus that projects the light, which beams out to sea every 15 seconds to a maximum distance of 19 mi, depending on visibility. A climb to the top of the 160-foot landmark offers a fabulous view of the island, which includes a series of inland lakes. The keeper is present 24 hours a day. Knock on his door, and he'll take you up to the top and explain the machinery. Drop $1 in the box when you sign the guest book on the way out.

No road leads to the **Columbus Monument** on Crab Cay; you have to make your way along a bushy path. This initial tribute to the explorer was erected by the *Chicago Herald* newspaper in 1892, far from the presumed site of Columbus's landing. A series of little villages—Polly

Hill, Hard Bargain, Fortune Hill, Holiday Track—winds south of here for several miles along Storr's Lake. You can still see the ruins of several plantations, and the deserted white-sand beaches on this eastern shore are some of the most spectacular in the islands. A little farther along is Pigeon Creek, which is a prime spot for bonefishing.

Sandy Point anchors the island's southwestern end, overlooking French Bay. Here, on a hill, you'll find the **ruins of Watling's Castle,** named after the 17th-century pirate. The ruins are more likely the remains of a Loyalist plantation house than a castle from buccaneering days. A 5- to 10-minute walk from Queen's Highway will take you to see what's left of the ruins, which are now engulfed in vegetation.

SPORTS & THE OUTDOORS

SCUBA DIVING   For more information about these and other sites, contact the Riding Rock Resort and Marina.

Doolittle's Grotto is a popular site featuring a sandy slope down to 140 feet. There are lots of tunnels and crevices for exploring, and usually a large school of horse-eye jacks to keep you company. **Double Caves,** as the name implies, has two parallel caves leading out to a wall at 115 feet. There's typically quite a lot of fish activity along the top of the wall. **North Pole Cave** has a wall that drops sharply from 40 feet to more than 150 feet. Coral growth is extensive, and you might see a hammer-head or two. **Telephone Pole** is a stimulating wall dive where you can watch stingrays, grouper, snapper, and turtles in action.

SAN SALVADOR ESSENTIALS

TRANSPORTATION

BY AIR

Air Sunshine flies from Fort Lauderdale into Cockburn Town on demand. American Eagle flies from Miami on the weekends. Bahamasair flies into Cockburn Town from Nassau daily and also offers direct service from Miami three days a week, though this is subject to change. Spirit Airlines flies from Fort Lauderdale on Saturday only. Club Med has packages that include air charters. Riding Rock Resort and Marina can arrange charters.

Airlines & Contacts **Air Sunshine** (☎ 954/434–8900 or 800/327–8900). **American Eagle** (☎ 800/433–7300). **Bahamasair** (☎ 242/339–4415 or 800/222–4262). **Spirit Airlines** (☎ 800/772–7117 or 586/791–7300).

BY BOAT

M/V *Lady Francis,* out of Nassau, leaves Tuesday for San Salvador and Rum Cay. The trip takes 12 hours, and the fare is $40 one way. The return trip is on Sunday. For information on specific schedules and fares, contact the Dockmaster's Office at Potter's Cay, Nassau.

Boat & Ferry Information **Dockmaster's Office** (☎ 242/393–1064).

BY CAR

Riding Rock Resort and Marina (☎ *800/272–1492 or 954/359–8353*) rents cars for $85 a day.

BY TAXI

Taxis meet arriving planes at Cockburn Town Airport. Club Med meets all guests at the airport (your account is charged $10 for the three-minute transfer). Riding Rock provides complimentary transportation for guests.

⊃NTACTS & RESOURCES

EMERGENCIES

Contacts **Medical Clinic** (☎ *207*). **Police** (☎ *218*).

⊃UT ISLANDS ESSENTIALS

5

To research prices, get advice from other travelers, and book travel arrangements, visit ⊕www.fodors.com.

⊃NTACTS & RESOURCES

EMERGENCIES

There are health centers and clinics scattered throughout the islands, but in the event of emergency, illness, or accident requiring fast transportation to the United States, AAPI Air Ambulance Services provides aero-medical services out of Fort Lauderdale Executive Airport. Its three jet aircraft are equipped with sophisticated medical equipment and a trained staff of nurses and flight medics.

Contact **AAPI Air Ambulance Services** (☎ *954/491–0555 or 800/752–4195*).

TOUR OPTIONS

Florida Yacht Charters, at the high-tech Boat Harbour Marina in Marsh Harbour, offers an endless supply of boats (trawlers, sailboats, and catamarans with inflatable dinghies) and amenities, such as air-conditioning, refrigeration, and GPS. Licensed captains, instruction, and provisioning are also available. For captained yacht charters, contact the Moorings in Marsh Harbour. This is the Bahamas division of one of the largest yacht-charter agencies in the world, which provides many services needed for yachties, from provisions to professional captains. Swift Yacht Charters also has yacht charters. If you're looking for a guided kayak tour, call Ibis Tours.

Tour-Operator Recommendations **In the Bahamas: The Moorings** (☎ *242/367–4000 or 800/535–7289 ⊕www.go-abacos.com/conchinn/moorings*). **In the U.S.: Changes in L'Attitudes** (☎ *727/573–3536 or 800/330–8272 ⊕www.changes. com*). **Florida Yacht Charters** (☎ *305/532–8600 or 800/537–0050 ⊕www.flori-dayacht.com*). **Future Vacations** (☎ *954/522–1440 or 800/456–2323 ⊟954/357–4687*). **Ibis Tours** (☎ *800/525–9411 ⊕www.ibistours.com*). **Swift Yacht Charters** (☎ *800/866–8340 or 508/647–1554 ⊕www.swiftyachts.com*).

VISITOR INFORMATION

The Bahama Out Islands Promotion Board has a fantastic staff that provides information about lodging, travel, and activities in the islands and can book reservations at many of the hotels. On request, the board will send color brochures about island resorts. The Bahamas Ministry of Tourism's Bahamas Tourist Office can assist with travel plans and information.

Tourist Information **Bahama Out Islands Promotion Board** (☎ *305/931-6612* or *800/688-4752* ⊕ *www.myoutislands.com*). **Bahamas Tourist Office** (☎ *242/322-7500* ⊕ *www.bahamas.com*). **Bahama Vacation Guide** (⊕ *www.bahamavacationguide.com*).

Turks & Caicos Islands

WORD OF MOUTH

"Grace Bay beach in Turks & Caicos was by far the most beautiful beach that I have seen. We stayed close to the middle of the beach and took a long walk down each side of the beach from our hotel. It was gorgeous. The different colors of blue in the water was an amazing site."

—travelenthusiast

WELCOME TO TURKS & CAICOS ISLANDS

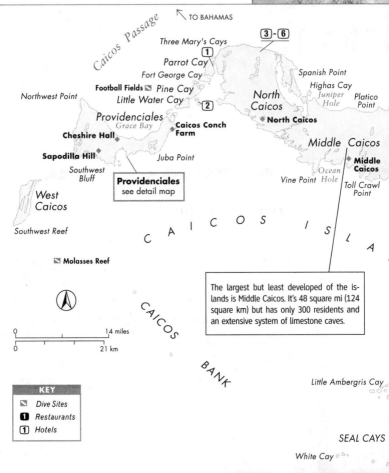

TO BAHAMAS

Caicos Passage

Three Mary's Cays

3 - 6

1

Parrot Cay

Fort George Cay

Spanish Point

Football Fields ⬎ Pine Cay

Higbas Cay

Northwest Point

Little Water Cay

2

Juniper Hole

Platico Point

Providenciales

Grace Bay

Caicos Conch Farm

North Caicos

North Caicos

Cheshire Hall

Sapodilla Hill

Southwest Bluff

Juba Point

Providenciales
see detail map

Middle Caicos

Middle Caicos

Ocean Hole

Vine Point

Toll Crawl Point

West Caicos

C A I C O S   I S L A

Southwest Reef

⬎ **Molasses Reef**

CAICOS

The largest but least developed of the islands is Middle Caicos. It's 48 square mi (124 square km) but has only 300 residents and an extensive system of limestone caves.

0 ――――― 14 miles

0 ――――― 21 km

BANK

Little Ambergris Cay

KEY	
⬎	*Dive Sites*
1	*Restaurants*
1	*Hotels*

SEAL CAYS

White Cay

Only 10 of these 40 islands between the Bahamas and Haiti are inhabited. Divers and snorkelers can explore one of the world's longest coral reefs. Land-based pursuits don't get much more taxing than teeing off at Provo's Provo Golf Club, or sunset-watching from the seaside terrace of a laid-back resort.

GRAPHICAL INFO

gh Providenciales is a major offshore bank-
enter, sea creatures far outnumber humans
s archipelago of 40 islands, where the total
ation is a mere 25,000. From developed
to sleepy Grand Turk to sleepier South
s, the islands offer miles of undeveloped
es, crystal-clear water, and laid-back lux-
sorts.

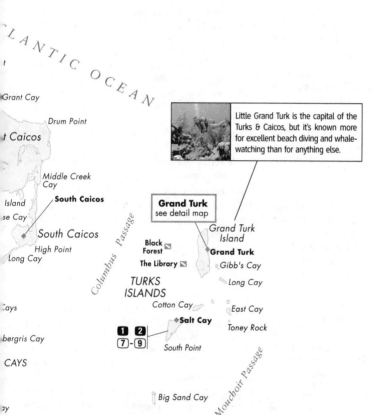

LANTIC OCEAN

Grant Cay

Drum Point

t Caicos

Middle Creek
Cay

Island

se Cay

South Caicos

South Caicos

High Point

long Cay

Black
Forest 🪸

The Library 🪸

TURKS
ISLANDS

Cotton Cay

Columbus Passage

Grand Turk
see detail map

Grand Turk
Island

Grand Turk

Gibb's Cay

Long Cay

Little Grand Turk is the capital of the
Turks & Caicos, but it's known more
for excellent beach diving and whale-
watching than for anything else.

6

Cays

bergris Cay

CAYS

❶ ❷
⑦-⑨

Salt Cay

South Point

East Cay

Toney Rock

Big Sand Cay

Mouchoir Passage

y

P 4 REASONS TO VISIT THE TURKS & CAICOS ISLANDS

Even on well-developed Provo,
there are still miles of deserted
beaches without any footprints or
beach umbrellas in sight.

The third-largest coral reef system
in the world is among the world's
top dive sites.

■ Island-hopping beyond the beaten
path will give you a feel of the
past in the present.

■ Destination spas, penthouse
suites, and exclusive villas and
resorts make celebrity spotting a
popular sport.

TURKS & CAICOS ISLANDS PLANNER

Island Activities

The vast majority of people come to the Turks & Caicos to relax and enjoy the clear, **turquoise water**.

The Turks & Caicos Islands are known for **luxurious hotels**, whether on a private island or on Provo itself.

The smaller islands provide a more-**relaxed environment** and substantially less development.

Provo has excellent **beaches**, particularly the long, soft beach along Grace Bay, where most of the island's hotel development has taken place. If you can believe it, some of the smaller, more-isolated islands in the chain have even better beaches.

Reefs are plentiful and are often close to shore, making **snorkeling** excellent. The **reef and wall diving** are among the best in the Caribbean.

The same reefs that draw colorful tropical fish draw big-game fish, so **deep-sea fishing** is also very good.

If you play **golf**, Provo has one of the Caribbean's finest courses.

Logistics

Getting to the Turks & Caicos: Several major airlines fly nonstop to Providenciales from the U.S.; you can also get connecting service via San Juan. If you are going to one of the smaller islands, you'll usually need to make a connection in Provo. All international flights arrive at Providenciales International Airport (PLS). There are smaller airports on Grand Turk (GDT), North Caicos (NCS), Middle Caicos (MDS), South Caicos (XSC), and Salt Cay (SLX). All have paved runways in good condition. Providenciales International Airport has modern, secure arrival and check-in services.

Hassle Factor: Low–High, depending on the island and your home airport.

Nonstops: Atlanta (Delta), Boston (American), Charlotte (USAirways), Dallas (American), Ft. Lauderdale (Spirit), Miami (American), New York–JFK (American), Philadelphia (USAirways).

On the Ground

You can find taxis at the airports, and most resorts provide pickup service as well. A trip between Provo's airport and most major hotels runs about $10 per person. On Grand Turk a trip from the airport to Cockburn Town is about $8; it's $8 to $15 to hotels outside town on Grand Turk. Transfers can cost more on the smaller islands, where gas is much more expensive.

Renting a Car: If you are staying on Provo, you may find it useful to have a car since the island is so large and the resorts so far-flung, if only for a few days of exploring or to get away from your hotel for dinner. On Grand Turk, you can rent a car, but you probably won't need to. Car- and jeep-rental rates average $35 to $80 per day on Provo, plus a $15 surcharge per rental as a government tax. Reserve well ahead of time during the peak winter season. Most agencies offer free mileage and airport pickup service. Several agencies—both locally owned and larger chains—operate on Provo.

Where to Stay

he Turks & Caicos can be a fairly expensive destination. Most hotels on Providenciales are fairly expensive, but ere are some moderately priced options; most accom- odations are condo-style, but not all resorts are family- iendly. You'll find several upscale properties on the outer lands—including the famous Parrot Cay—but the majority f places are smaller inns. What you give up in luxury, owever, you gain back tenfold in island charm. Though e smaller islands are fairly isolated, that's arguably what akes them so attractive in the first place.

esorts: Most of the resorts on Provo are upscale; many re condo-style, so at least you will have a well-furnished tchen for breakfast and a few quick lunches. There are vo all-inclusive resorts on Provo. A handful of other luxury sorts are on the smaller islands.

nall Inns: Aside from the exclusive, luxury resorts, most of e places on the outlying islands are smaller, modest inns ith relatively few amenities. Some are devoted to diving.

illas & Condos: Villas and condos are plentiful, particu- rly on Provo and usually represent a good value for fami- es. However, you need to plan a few months in advance get one of the better choices, less if you want to stay in a ore-developed condo complex.

Hotel & Restaurant Prices

WHAT IT COSTS IN U.S. DOLLARS

\$\$	\$\$\$	\$\$	\$	¢
staurants				
er \$30	\$20–\$30	\$12–\$20	\$8–\$12	under \$8
tels*				
er \$350	\$250–\$350	\$150–\$250	\$80–\$150	under \$80
tels**				
er \$450	\$350–\$450	\$250–\$350	\$125–\$250	under \$125

, BP, CP **AI, FAP, MAP Restaurant prices are for a main course at din- and include any taxes or service charges. Hotel prices are per night a double room in high season, excluding taxes, service charges, and al plans (except at all-inclusives).

When to Go

High season in Turks & Caicos runs roughly from January through March, with the usual extra-high rates during the Christmas and New Year's holi- day period. Several hotels on Provo offer shoulder season rates in April and May. Dur- ing the off-season, rates are reduced substantially, as much as 40%.

There are three major festivals in the Turks & Caicos. In sum- mer, big names play at the annual **Turks & Caicos Music and Cultural Festival** usually held in August.

In October, Provo is overrun with celebrities for the **Turks & Caicos International Film Festival**, with the movies shown on giant projection screens by the beach.

At the end of November, the **Turks & Caicos Conch Fes- tival** offers native boat races, live music, and conch recipe competitions.

6

By Ramona
Settle

WITH WATER SO TURQUOISE THAT it glows, you may find it difficult t
stray far from the beach. You may find no need for museums, no desi
to see ruins, or even read books. You may find yourself hypnotized b
the many neon hues of blues. The Turks & Caicos have some of th
most beautiful water in the world, so you can expect almost all of you
activities here to be water-based. And the beaches are among the mo
incredible you will ever see. Don't be surprised if you wake up on you
last morning and realize that you have never strayed far from the beac
or those mesmerizing views.

A much-disputed legend has it that Columbus first discovered the
islands in 1492. Despite being on the map for longer than most oth
island groups, the Turks & Caicos Islands (pronounced *kay*-kos) st
remain part of the less-discovered Caribbean. More than 40 islands—
only 8 inhabited—make up this self-governing British overseas territo
that lies just 575 mi (862 km) southeast of Miami on the third-large
coral reef system in the world.

Although ivory-white, soft sandy beaches and breathtaking turquoi
waters are shared among all the islands, the landscapes are a series
contrasts; from the dry, arid bush and scrub on the flat, coral islands
Grand Turk, Salt Cay, South Caicos, and Providenciales to the green
foliage-rich undulating landscapes of Middle Caicos, North Caico
Parrot Cay, and Pine Cay.

The political and historical capital island of the country is Grand Tur
but most of the tourism development, which consists primarily of bo
tique hotels and condo resorts, has occurred in Providenciales, than
to the 12-mi (18-km) stretch of ivory sand that is Grace Bay. On
home to a population of around 500 people plus a few donkey cart
Provo has become a hub of activity, resorts, spas, restaurants, ar
water sports with a population of around 15,000. It's the tempora
home for the majority of visitors who come to the Turks & Caicos.

Despite the fact that most visitors land and stay in Provo, the Tur
& Caicos National Museum—predictably a stickler for tradition—
in Grand Turk. The museum tells the history of the islands that ha
all, at one time or another, been claimed by the French, Spanish, a
British as well as many pirates, long before the predominately Nor
American visitors discovered its shores.

Marks of the country's colonial past can be found in the wooden a
stone, Bermudian-style clapboard houses—often wrapped in deep-r
bougainvillea—that line the streets on the quiet islands of Grand Tur
Salt Cay, and South Caicos. Donkeys roam free in and around the sa
ponds, which are a legacy from a time when residents of these isla
communities worked hard as both slaves and then laborers to rake sa
(then known as "white gold") bound for the United States and Canad
In Salt Cay the remains of wooden windmills are now home to lar
osprey nests. In Grand Turk and South Caicos, the crystal-edge tid
ponds are regularly visited by flocks of rose-pink flamingos hungry f
the shrimp to be found in the shallow, briny waters.

Sea Island cotton, believed to be the highest quality, was produced on the Loyalist plantations in the Caicos Islands from the 1700s. The native cotton plants can still be seen dotted among the stone remains of former plantation houses in the more-fertile soils of Middle Caicos and North Caicos. Here communities in tiny settlements have retained age-old skills using fanner grasses, silver palms, and sisal to create exceptional straw baskets, bags, mats, and hats.

> **WHERE WHEN HOW**
>
> Check out ⊕ *www.wherewhenhow.com*, a terrific source with links to every place to stay, all the restaurants, excursions, and transportation. You can pick up the printed version of the magazine all around the island, or subscribe before you go so you know what do while in the Turks & Caicos.

In all, only 25,000 people live in the Turks & Caicos Islands; more than half are "Belongers," the term for the native population, mainly descended from African and Bermudian slaves who settled here beginning in the 1600s. The majority of residents work in tourism, fishing, and offshore finance, as the country is a haven for the overtaxed. Indeed, for residents and visitors, life in "TCI" is anything but taxing. But while most visitors come to do nothing—a specialty in the islands—this does not mean there's nothing to do.

6

E CAICOS

OVIDENCIALES

Passengers typically become oddly silent when their plane starts its descent, mesmerized by the shallow, crystal-clear turquoise waters of Chalk Sound National Park. This island, nicknamed Provo, was once called Blue Hills after the name of its first settlement. Just south of the airport and downtown area, Blue Hills still remains the closest thing you can get to a more-typical Caicos Island settlement on this, the most developed of the island chain. Most of the modern resorts, exquisite spas, water-sports operators, shops, business plazas, restaurants, bars, cafés, and the championship golf course are on or close by the 12-mi (18-km) stretch of Grace Bay beach. In spite of the ever-increasing number of taller and grander condominium resorts—either completed or under construction—it's still possible to find deserted stretches on this priceless, ivory-white shoreline. For guaranteed seclusion, rent a car and go explore the southern shores and western tip of the island, or set sail for a private island getaway on one of the many deserted cays nearby.

Progress and beauty come at a price: there is considerable construction on the island. No worry—it does not take away from the gorgeous beaches and wonderful dinners. Although you may start to believe that every road leads to a construction site (or is under construction itself), there are, happily, plenty of sections of beach where you can escap the din.

While you may be kept quite content enjoying the beachscape an top-notch amenities of Provo itself, it's also a great starting point fo island-hopping tours by sea or by air as well as fishing and diving trip Resurfaced roads should help you get around and make the most of th main tourism and sightseeing spots.

WHERE TO STAY

For approximate costs, see the dining and lodging price chart in th Turks & Caicos Planner, at the beginning of this chapter.

VILLA RENTALS A popular option on Provo is renting a self-catering villa or privat home. For the best villa selection, plan to make your reservations thre to six months in advance.

Prestigious Properties (*Prestige Pl., Grace Bay* ☎649/946–5355 ⊕*www prestigiousproperties.com*) offers a wide selection of modest to mag nificent villas in the Leeward, Grace Bay, and Turtle Cove areas c Providenciales. **T. C. Safari** (☎649/941–5043 ⊕*www.tcsafari.tc*) ha exclusive oceanfront properties in the beautiful and tranquil Sapodil Bay–Chalk Sound neighborhood on Provo's southwest shores.

HOTELS & RESORTS

$$$$

🔳 **Amanyara.** If you need seclusion, peace, and tranquillity with zenlike atmosphere, this is your place. All accommodations are pavilions, which are simply furnished with an Asian minimalist fla yet have such luxuries as TVs, DVD players, and surround-sour systems. A movie room and well-stocked library are among the fe entertainment options, but small touches, such as a shoe rack at th beach and huggies to keep your bottled water cool, are welcom No need to sign for anything here—the staff will always rememb you by name. When it comes to dining, expect an Asian-influence menu and very high prices; reports on the quality of food have been mixed. One thing is for certain; it's a long, pricey ride to other restau-rants, not to mention excursions. This is a place to come if you are looking for peace and quiet in a remote location on a stunning beach. There is construction on-site, but you can't see it from the beach. A unique feature is that rates include the minibar (except spirits) and all long-distance phone calls. **Pros:** On one of the best beaches on Provo, resort is quiet and secluded. **Cons:** Isolated; far from restaurants, excursions, and other beaches. ✉*Northwest Point* ☎649/941–8133 ⊕*www.aman resorts.com* ⇶*40 pavilions* ⌂*In-*

REQUESTING ROOMS

Most of the resorts on Provo are composed of privately owned condos placed into the resort's rental pool when the owners are not present. Unlike at chain hotels and resorts, you cannot request a particular building, floor, or room unless you are a repeat visitor. If you fall in love with the condo, you can probably purchase it, or one that's similar. There are no taxes in T&C except for a onetime Stamp Duty tax—no property tax and no rental tax—which makes owning your own piece of para-dise even more tempting.

room: safe, refrigerator, DVD. In-hotel: 2 restaurants, room service, bar, tennis courts, pool, gym, spa, beachfront, diving, water sports, no elevator, airport shuttle ⊟*AE, MC, V* ⏐○⏐*EP.*

$$$$ 🖽 **Beaches Turks & Caicos Resort & Spa.** The largest resort in the Turks
☾ & Caicos Islands can satisfy families as eager to spend time apart as
★ together. Younger children and teenagers will appreciate a children's park, complete with video-game center, waterslides, a swim-up soda bar, and even a teen disco. Parents may prefer the extensive spa, pretty beach, and complimentary scuba diving. Rooms, suites, and cottage villas are decorated in standard tropical themes, but the resort's major draw is found outside the rooms, where there are numerous activities and a choice of dining options, from a 1950s-style diner to a Japanese restaurant. This is one of the company's top resorts, with a generally helpful staff and excellent amenities. Butler service is included for the presidential and penthouse suites. In early 2009, look for the new Italian Village and one of the biggest water parks in the Caribbean to open. **Pros:** Great place for families, all-inclusive. **Cons:** With an all-inclusive plan you miss out on great restaurants, construction on the east side of the property. ⊠*Lower Bight Rd., Grace Bay* ☎*649/946–8000 or 800/726–3257* ⊕*www.beaches.com* ⇝*359 rooms, 103 suites* ☾*In-room: safe, dial-up. In-hotel: 9 restaurants, bars, tennis courts, pools, gym, spa, beachfront, diving, water sports, bicycles, no elevator (some buildings), concierge, children's programs (ages newborn–12), public Internet* ⊟*AE, MC, V* ⏐○⏐*AI.*

$$$$ 🖽 **Grace Bay Club & Villas at Grace Bay Club.** This small and stylish resort
☾ retains a loyal following because of its helpful, attentive staff and aura
★ of unpretentious elegance. The architecture is reminiscent of Florence, with terra-cotta rooftops and a shaded courtyard, complete with fountain. Suites, all with sweeping sea views, have earthy tiles, luxurious white Egyptian cotton–covered beds, and Elemis toiletries. The ground-floor suites, fronted by large arched patios and lush azaleas, have a palatial feel and turquoise water views. New, ultraluxurious villas offer families a Grace Bay experience with a large pool, a bar and grill, and an impressive range of children's activities, including a bouncy castle in Kids Town, as well as kayaking trips and all sorts of "edutainment" to keep even teenagers well occupied. There are also cookies, of course. There is construction ongoing at Grace Bay Club Estates, so ask for a room on the Villas side of the property. **Pros:** Gorgeous pool and restaurant lounge areas with outdoor couches, daybeds, and fire pits. **Cons:** No children allowed at Anacaona restaurant, construction on two sides. ⌂*Box 128, Grace Bay* ☎*649/946–5050 or 800/946–5757* ⊕*www.gracebayclub.com* ⇝*59 suites* ☾*In-room: safe, kitchen, VCR (some), ethernet, Wi-Fi. In-hotel: 2 restaurants, room service, bar, tennis courts, pools, spa, beachfront, water sports, bicycles, concierge, laundry facilities, laundry service, public Internet, public Wi-Fi, no children under 12 in some rooms* ⊟*AE, D, MC, V* ⏐○⏐*CP.*

$$$$ 🖽 **Point Grace.** Provo's answer to Parrot Cay has attracted celebrity guests, including Donatella Versace. Asian-influenced rooftop domes blend with Romanesque stone pillars and wide stairways in this plush resort, which offers spacious beachfront suites and romantic cottages

6

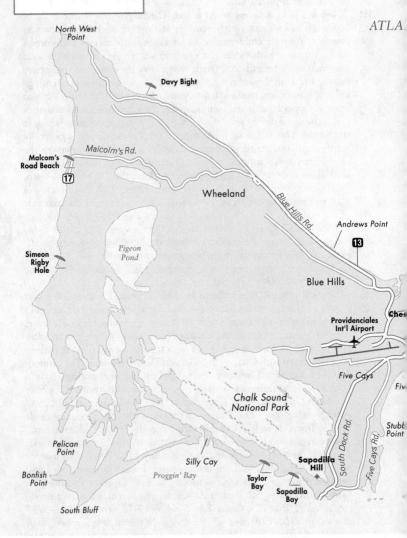

Providenciales

North West
Point

ATLA

Davy Bight

Malcom's
Road Beach   Malcolm's Rd.

17

Wheeland

Blue Hills Rd.

Andrews Point

Simeon
Rigby
Hole

Pigeon
Pond

13

Blue Hills

Providenciales
Int'l Airport

Che

Five Cays

Fiv

Chalk Sound
National Park

Pelican
Point

South Dock Rd.

Five Cays Rd.

Stubb
Point

Bonfish
Point

Silly Cay

Proggin' Bay

Taylor
Bay

Sapodilla
Hill

Sapodilla
Bay

South Bluff

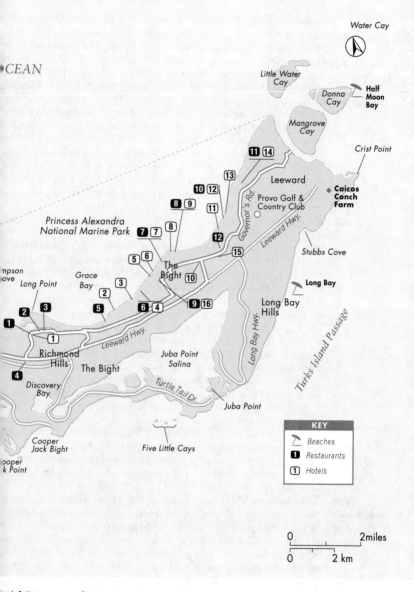

Water Cay

OCEAN

Little Water Cay

Donna Cay

Half Moon Bay

Mangrove Cay

Crist Point

11 **14**

13

Leeward

Caicos Conch Farm

10 **12**

Governor's Rd.

Provo Golf & Country Club

11

Princess Alexandra National Marine Park

8 **9**

7 **7**

8

12

Leeward Hwy.

Stubbs Cove

15

5 **6**

The Bight

10

Long Bay

mpson ove

Long Point

Grace Bay

3

10

2

5

9 **16**

Long Bay Hills

2 **3**

6 **4**

Turks Island Passage

1

1

Leeward Hwy.

Richmond Hills

The Bight

Juba Point Salina

Long Bay Hwy.

4

Discovery Bay

Turtle Tail Dr.

Juba Point

Cooper Jack Bight

Five Little Cays

KEY

Beaches

1 Restaurants

1 Hotels

Cooper k Point

0   2 miles

0   2 km

surrounding the centerpiece: a turquoise infinity pool with perfec
views of the beach. Antique furnishings, four-poster beds, and ar
reproductions give a classic style to the rooms. The second-story cot
tage suites are especially romantic. Bleached-wood cottages, on the
sand dune, house a thalassotherapy spa presided over by elegant French
spa manager Edmonde Sidibé. Other highlights include the restaurants
particularly the beautiful Grace's Cottage. Honeymooners can arrange
a transfer in an authentic London taxi. **Pros:** Relaxing environment
beautiful pool. **Cons:** Can be stuffy (signs around the pool remind you
to be quiet).   *Box 700, Grace Bay* ☎649/946–5096 or 888/924-
7223 *www.pointgrace.com* *23 suites, 9 cottage suites, 2 villa
*In-room: safe, kitchen, VCR (some). In-hotel: 2 restaurants, room
service, bars, pool, spa, beachfront, water sports, bicycles, no elevato
(some buildings), concierge, laundry service, public Internet, no-smok
ing rooms* ☐AE, D, MC, V ☺*Closed Sept.* ⦿*CP.*

$$$$
☺   **Regent Palms.** High on luxury and glitz, this is a place to see and b
seen. The infinity pool, one of the chicest in the Caribbean, has su
pods (round, white cushioned loungers), a swim-up bar, and iPods t
borrow. Suites, which have colonial-style furnishings and luxuriou
bedding and appointments, have two or three bedrooms but can b
subdivided to create one-bedroom suites and regular rooms (whic
will have only a kitchenette); all bedrooms have a separate terrace. On
big plus for families is the washer and dryer in all but regular rooms
The Regent Hotels Group has taken over management and has greatl
improved the service. The spa is stunningly beautiful, offering ever
treatment imaginable; it certainly ranks among the best in the Carib
bean. A new unique feature in the rooms is access to every radio stati
in the world, so you can hear reports from back home while you'r
in paradise. **Pros:** Great people-watching, lively atmosphere, one c
the best spas in the Caribbean. **Cons:** Some would say busy not lively
a little formal and stuffy (cover-ups are required when you go to th
pool). ⊠*Grace Bay* ☎649/946–8666 *www.regenthotels.com* *7
suites* *In-room: safe, kitchen (some), DVD, Wi-Fi. In-hotel: 2 restau
rants, room service, bar, tennis court, pool, gym, spa, beachfront, wate
sports, concierge, children's programs (ages 4–12), laundry facilitie
public Wi-Fi, airport shuttle* ☐AE, D, MC, V ⦿*BP.*

$$$$
Fodor's Choice
★   **The Somerset.** This luxury resort has the "wow" factor, starting wit
the architecture, followed by the service, and ending in your luxur
ously appointed suite. What sets the Somerset apart is that it is also
comfortable place to stay that is more focused on your comfort an
enjoyment than in attracting a celebrity clientele. A laid-back unpr
tentiousness means you don't have to dress up to go to the poo
Unmatched service makes you feel at home. A modern pool deck
equipped with a resistance pool and underwater speakers. The ove
size suites are equipped with such extras as a plasma TV, an XBo
system, a wine chiller, and Viking appliances, including a washer an
dryer, so you don't need to pack heavily. It doesn't get better than thi
Pros: The most beautiful architecture on Provo. **Cons:** Having to leav
⊠*Princess Dr., Grace Bay* ☎649/946–5900 *www.thesomerset.co*
53 suites *In-room: safe, kitchen, DVD, Wi-Fi. In-hotel: restau*

CLOSE UP

From Salt Glows to Thalassotherapy

A Turks Island Salt Glow, where the island's sea salt is mixed with gentle oils to exfoliate, smooth, and moisturize the skin, is just one of the treatments you can enjoy in one of the island spas. Being pampered spa-style has become as much a part of a Turks & Caicos vacation as sunning on the beach. Marine-based ingredients fit well with the Grace Bay backdrop at the Thalasso Spa at **Point Grace**, where massages take place in two simple, bleached-white cottages standing on the dune line, which means you have a spectacular view of the sea-blue hues if you manage to keep your eyes open. The Regent Spa at the **Regent Palms** offers individual treatments with a water feature by day, a fire feature at night. Their signature body scrub uses hand-crushed local

conch shells to smooth the skin. But the widest choice of Asian-inspired treatments (and the most-unforgettable scenery) can be found at the 6,000-square-foot Como Shambhala Spa at the **Parrot Cay Resort,** which has outdoor whirlpools and a central beech-wood lounge overlooking the shallow turquoise waters and mangroves. Provo also has a noteworthy day spa that's not in one of the Grace Bay resorts. Manager Terri Tapper of **Spa Tropique** (⊠ *Ports of Call, Grace Bay Rd., Grace Bay* ☎ 649/941–5720 ⊕ *www.spatropique.com*) blends Swedish, therapeutic, and reflexology massage techniques using oils made from natural plants and products produced locally and within the Caribbean region. The Turks Island Salt Glow has become one of her most popular treatments.

rant, room service, bar, pool, gym, beachfront, water sports, bicycles, children's programs (3–16), public Wi-Fi, concierge, laundry facilities ⊟AE, MC, V ⧖CP.

$$$$ ⊡ **Turks & Caicos Club.** On the quieter, western end of Grace Bay, this
★   intimate all-suites hotel is one of a handful with a gated entrance. The buildings are in a colonial style with lovely gingerbread trim. Though the resort aims for an aura of exclusivity, the staff is warm and friendly. Safari-themed suites, complete with raised four-poster beds and spacious balconies, are a definite plus to this quiet retreat. The rates include a full American breakfast. Check the Web site for unique packages, including one with a professional photographer. **Pros:** Incredible lush grounds, on one of the best stretches of Grace Bay beach, great snorkeling from the beach. **Cons:** Small bathrooms. ⊠ *West Grace Bay beach, Box 687, West Grace Bay* ☎ 649/946–5800 *or* 888/482–2582 ⊕ *www.turksandcaicosclub.com* ♥ 21 suites ⚭In-room: safe, DVD, Wi-Fi, kitchen, dial-up. In-hotel: restaurant, room service, bar, pool, gym, beachfront, water sports, bicycles, no elevator, laundry facilities, public Wi-Fi, airport shuttle ⊟AE, MC, V ⊗Closed Sept. ⧖BP.

$$$$ ⊡ **The Tuscany.** This luxury, gated condo complex at the end of Grace Bay beach is gorgeous. All the condos have three bedrooms with designer furnishings and spacious balconies with oceanfront views; each condo also has three baths and a laundry room, which makes sharing a breeze even if you're not family. Lined by palm trees, the pool has a Tuscan feel and is one of the most beautiful on Provo. One unique feature is

guests have use of their own cell phones, along with preset numbers for restaurants and excursions, for use wherever they go during their stay. **Pros:** Luxurious, all condos with ocean views, beautiful pool. **Cons:** No restaurant and far from the best restaurants, very expensive for self-catering. ⌂ *Box 623, Grace Bay* ☎*649/941–4667* ⊕*www.th tuscanyresort.com* ⇥*30 condos* ⚬*In-room: kitchen. In-hotel: tenni court, pool, gym, beachfront, public Wi-Fi* ▤*AE, MC, V* ⦿*EP.*

$$$$ ▦**Villa Renaissance.** This is luxury for the self-catering tourist. Although it's not a full-service resort, guests do get daily maid service, afternoon tea or coffee at the Pavillion Bar, and a weekly manager's cocktail recep tion. There is no restaurant on-site, but the location puts you in walk ing distance to some of the island's best restaurants. The front desk is always willing to help with concierge service. There is a lighted tenni court, a fitness center, and bicycles for the active. The gorgeous suite have stunning balconies or patios facing the ocean. Resembling a smal Tuscan village square, it is one of the most beautiful buildings on Provo. **Pros:** Luxury for less, one of the prettiest courtyards in Provo. **Cons:** No restaurant, not full-service resort. ⌂ *Box 592, Grace Bay* ☎*649/941– 5300 or 877/285–8764* ⊕*www.villarenaissance.com* ⇥*20 suites* ⚬*In room: safe, kitchen, DVD, dial-up. In-hotel: bar, pool, spa, beachfront bicycles, laundry facilities* ▤*AE, MC, V* ⦿*EP.*

$$$–$$$$ ▦**The Alexandra.** All the comfortable, spacious rooms at this beach ℭ front condo resort have some type of ocean or pool view—no look ing at parking lots here. Amenities and appointments are decidedly upscale: granite countertops, stainless-steel appliances, a washer and dryer, and feather-top pillows on the beds. With the friendliest service on the island, the staff will make you feel like family. At this writ ing, there is some construction at the back of the property, which has prompted the management to offer specials, and these can be some of the best deals on Provo. **Pros:** Luxury for less, all rooms have ocean views. **Cons:** Lots of construction in the vicinity, temporary reception gives a bad first impression. ✉*Princess Dr., Grace Bay* ☎*649/946– 5807 or 800/704–9424* ⊕*www.alexandraresort.com* ⇥*88 room. ⚬In-room: safe, kitchen (some), DVD, Wi-Fi. In-hotel: restaurant bar, tennis courts, pool, gym, beachfront, water sports, laundry facili ties.* ▤*AE, D, MC, V* ⦿*EP.*

$$$–$$$$ **Ocean Club Resorts.** Enormous locally painted pictures of hibiscus make ℭ a striking first impression as you enter the reception area at one of the ★ island's most well-established condominium resorts. Regular shuttles run along the 0.5-mi (1-km) stretch of Grace Bay beach between two artfully landscaped properties, Ocean Club and Ocean Club West. Both resorts claim some of Provo's best amenities. Ocean Club has the advantage of a quieter location away from most of the development and is just a short walk from Provo Golf & Country Club. Ocean Club West has a larger pool with a swim-up bar. Management and ser vice are superb, as are the special value packages offered throughout most of the year. Plenty of beach and pool toys make Ocean Club a good family option. **Pros:** Family-friendly resort with shuttles between the two shared properties. **Cons:** Both resorts are showing their age ⌂ *Box 240, Grace Bay* ☎*649/946–5880 or 800/457–8787* ⊕*www.*

CLOSE UP

What Is a Potcake?

Potcakes are indigenous dogs of the Bahamas and Turks & Caicos Islands. Traditionally, the stray dogs would be fed from the leftover scraps of food that formed at the bottom of the pot; this is how they got their name. Much is being done these days to control the stray dog population. The TCSPCA and Potcake Place are two agencies working to adopt out the puppies. You can "travel with a cause" by adopting one of these gorgeous pups; they come with all the shots and all the papers required to bring them back home to the United States. Even if you don't adopt, you can help by volunteering as a carrier—bringing one back to its adopted family. Customs in the States is actually easier when you are bringing back a potcake! For more information on how you can help, check out the Web site for Potcake Place (⊕ www.potcakeplace.com).

oceanclubresorts.com ⌁*174 suites: 86 at Ocean Club, 88 at Ocean Club West ♿ In-room: safe, kitchen (some), VCR (some), dial-up. In-hotel: 2 restaurants, bars, tennis court, pools, gym, spa, beachfront, diving, water sports, no elevator, concierge, laundry facilities, public Internet, public Wi-Fi* ▤*AE, D, MC, V* ⦿*EP.*

$$$–$$$$
★
🏨 **Royal West Indies Resort.** With a contemporary take on colonial architecture and the outdoor feel of a botanical garden, this unpretentious resort has plenty of garden-view and beachfront studios and suites for moderate self-catering budgets. Room 135 on the western corner has the most dramatic ocean views. Right on Grace Bay beach, the property has a small restaurant and bar for poolside cocktails and dining. Ask at the reception desk for help and advice on where to go explore. Special packages and free-night offers are available during the low season. **Pros:** The best bang for the buck on Provo, on one of the widest stretches of Grace Bay beach. **Cons:** Club Med next door can be noisy, construction on the other side. ✏ *Box 482, Grace Bay* ☎ *649/946–5004 or 800/332–4203* ⊕ *www.royalwestindies.com* ⌁ *99 suites ♿ In-room: safe, kitchen, VCR (some), ethernet, dial-up. In-hotel: restaurant, bar, pools, beachfront, water sports, bicycles, no elevator, concierge, laundry facilities, laundry service, no-smoking rooms* ▤ *AE, MC, V* ⦿ *EP.*

$$$–$$$$
☽
🏨 **Sands at Grace Bay.** Spacious gardens and two pools are surrounded by six rather impersonal three-story buildings at this otherwise well-appointed resort. Guests can expect friendly and helpful staff and excellent amenities, including a spa, good-size fitness room, and a beachside cabana restaurant called Hemingway's. Sparkling ocean views from huge screened patios and floor-to-ceiling windows are best in the oceanfront suites in Blocks 3 and 4, which are also closest to the beach, restaurant, and pool. A complete renovation begun in 2007 has added a beautiful new lobby and made the rooms more luxurious. **Pros:** One of the best places for families, central location to shops and numerous restaurants. **Cons:** Renovation incomplete at this writing, so not all rooms are updated yet. ✏ *Box 681, Grace Bay* ☎ *649/941–5199 or 877/777–2637* ⊕ *www.thesandsresort.com* ⌁ *118 suites*

6

⌂ *In-room: safe, kitchen (some), dial-up, Wi-Fi. In-hotel: restaurant, bar, tennis court, pools, gym, spa, beachfront, water sports, bicycles, no elevator (some buildings), concierge, laundry facilities, laundry service, public Internet, no-smoking rooms, some pets allowed* ▭ *AE, MC, V* ⦿ *EP.*

$$$ ⊞ **Club Med Turkoise.** Guests still fly in from the United States, Europe, and Canada to enjoy the scuba diving, windsurfing, and waterskiing on the turquoise waters at the doorsteps of the area's first major resort. Rooms in the village are basic and set in small, colorful bungalows that were renovated in 2007. In contrast to the otherwise tranquil Grace Bay resorts, this energetic property has a vibrant party atmosphere, nightly entertainment, and even a flying trapeze, catering primarily to fun-loving singles and couples. **Pros:** All-inclusive, active. **Cons:** Although the rooms have been updated, the grounds are showing their age. ✉ *Grace Bay* ☎ *649/946–5500 or 888/932–2582* ⊕ *www.clubmed.com* ⟿ *293 rooms* ⌂ *In-hotel: 2 restaurants, bars, tennis courts, pool, gym, beachfront, diving, water sports, bicycles, no elevator, laundry service, public Internet, no kids under 18* ▭ *AE, D, MC, V* ⦿ *AI.*

$$ ⊞ **Caribbean Paradise Inn.** Not far from Grace Bay beach—but tucked away inland about a 10-minute walk from the beach—this two-story bed-and-breakfast has terra-cotta walls and cobalt-blue trimmings. If you get to know manager Jean-Luc Bohic, you can sometimes persuade him to prepare a barbecue. Rooms are smaller than the usual Provo offerings and are simply decorated with balconies overlooking the palm-fringed pool. **Pros:** Pay less by staying a block from the beach. **Cons:** Front desk not always manned. ⌂ *Box 673, Grace Bay* ☎ *649/946–5020* ⊕ *www.paradise.tc* ⟿ *16 rooms* ⌂ *In-room: safe, Wi-Fi, kitchen (some). In-hotel: bar, pool, no elevator, public Internet, no-smoking rooms* ▭ *AE, MC, V* ⦿ *CP.*

$–$$ ⊞ **Sibonné.** Dwarfed by most of the nearby resorts, the smallest hotel on Grace Bay beach has snug (by Provo's spacious standards) but pleasant rooms with Bermuda-style balconies and a completely circular but tiny pool. Of course, the pool is hardly used because the property is right on the beach. Rooms on the second floor have airy, vaulted ceilings; downstairs rooms have views of and access to the attractively planted courtyard garden, replete with palms, yellow elder, and exotic birdlife. The popular beachfront Bay Bistro serves breakfast, lunch, and dinner. Book early to get one of the two simple value rooms or the beachfront apartment, complete with four-poster bed, which is four steps from the beach; all three are usually reserved months in advance. **Pros:** Closest property to the beach, the island's best bargain on the beach. **Cons:** Pool is small and dated. ✉ *Princess Dr., Box 144, Grace Bay* ☎ *649/946–5547 or 800/528–1905* ⊕ *www.sibonne.com* ⟿ *29 rooms, 1 apartment* ⌂ *In-room: safe, dial-up. In-hotel: restaurant, bar, pool, beachfront, water sports, bicycles, laundry service* ▭ *AE, MC, V* ⦿ *CP.*

$–$$ ⊞ **Turtle Cove Inn.** This pleasant two-story inn offers affordable and comfortable lodging in Turtle Cove Marina. All rooms have either a private balcony or patio overlooking the lush tropical gardens and pool or the marina. Besides the dockside Aqua Bar and Terrace, there's also a souvenir shop and liquor store. The inn is ideally situated for divers looking to roll from their beds into the ocean. **Pros:** Very reasonable prices for Provo, nice marina views, popular and inexpensive restaurant. **Cons:** Not on the beach, requires a car to get around. ⊠ *Turtle Cove Marina, Box 131, Turtle Cove* ☎ *649/946–4203 or 800/887–0477* ⊕ *www.turtlecoveinn.com* ⇆ *28 rooms, 2 suites* ⌂ *In-room: safe, dial-up, refrigerator. In-hotel: restaurant, bar, pool, bicycles, no elevator, no-smoking rooms* ⊟ *AE, D, MC, V* ¶○|*EP.*

WHERE TO EAT

There are more than 50 restaurants on Provo, from casual to elegant, with cuisine from Asian to European (and everything in between). You can spot the islands' own Caribbean influence no matter where you go, exhibited in fresh seafood specials, colorful presentations, and a tangy dose of spice. Pick up a free copy of *Where When How's Dinning Guide* magazine, which you will find all over the island; it contains menus, Web sites, and pictures of all the restaurants.

For approximate costs, see the dining and lodging price chart in the Turks & Caicos Planner, at the beginning of this chapter.

CARIBBEAN ✕ **Simba.** Fishbowl-size glassware is all part of the charm at this larger-
$$–$$$ than-life, safari-themed poolside restaurant at the quieter end of Grace
ᕀ Bay. For the price, presentation of the Caribbean-inspired dishes with fruity twists like the grouper with curry and mango sauce is above expectations. A plus: this is one of just a few places with indoor, air-conditioned seating, but you need a car to get here (unless staying at theTurks & Caicos Club). ⊠ *Turks & Caicos Club, West Grace Bay* ☎ *649/946–5888* ⌂ *Reservations essential* ⊟ *AE, D, MC, V* ⊗ *No dinner Wed.*

$–$$$ ✕ **Da Conch Shack.** An institution in Provo for many years, this brightly colored beach shack is justifiably famous for its conch and seafood. The legendary specialty, conch, is fished freshly out of the shallows and either cooked, spiced, cracked, or fried to absolute perfection. On Friday nights, you can dance in the sand after dinner. This is freshest conch anywhere on the island, as the staff dive for it only after you've placed your order, but if you don't like seafood, there are not many other choices. ⊠ *Blue Hills* ⊟ *No credit cards* ⊗ *No lunch.*

DELI ✕ **Angela's Top o' the Cove New York Style Delicatessen.** Order deli sand-
¢–$ wiches, salads, and enticingly rich desserts and freshly baked pastries at this island institution on Leeward Highway, just south of Turtle Cove. From the deli case you can buy the fixings for a picnic; the shelves are stocked with an eclectic selection of fancy foodstuffs, as well as beer and wine. It's open at 6:30 AM for a busy trade in coffees, cappuccinos, and frappaccinos. This is the best cheesesteak you'll ever have outside Philly, but the location isn't in the heart of where most tourists are staying (it's worth the drive, though). ⊠ *Leeward Hwy., Turtle Cove* ☎ *649/946–4694* ⊟ *AE, MC, V* ⊗ *No dinner.*

ECLECTIC ✕ **Coyaba Restaurant.** Located behind Grace Bay Club and next to
$$$$ Caribbean Paradise Inn, this posh eatery serves nostalgic favorites with
odor's Choice tempting twists in conversation-piece crockery and in a palm-fringed
★ setting. Chef Paul Newman uses his culinary expertise for the daily-

changing main courses, which include exquisitely presented dishes such as crispy whole yellow snapper fried in Thai spices. To minimize any possible pretension, he keeps the resident expat crowd happy with traditional favorites like lemon meringue pie, albeit with his own tropical twist. Don't skip dessert; Paul makes the most incredible chocolate fondant you will ever have. The service is seamless. ⊠ *Off Grace Bay Rd., beside Caribbean Paradise Inn, Grace Bay* 🕾 *649/946–5186* ⚔ *Reservations essential* ⊟ *AE, MC, V* ⊗ *Closed Tues. No lunch.*

$$$$ ✕ **Grace's Cottage.** At one of the prettiest dining settings on Provo, tables
★   are artfully set under wrought-iron cottage-style gazebos and around the wraparound veranda, which skirts the gingerbread-covered main building. In addition to such tangy and exciting entrées as panfried red snapper served with roasted pepper sauce or melt-in-your-mouth grilled beef tenderloin served with truffle-scented mashed potatoes, the soufflés are well worth the 15-minute wait and the top-tier price tag. Portions are small, but the quality is amazing. Service is impeccable (ladies are provided a small stool so that their purse is not on the ground. ⊠ *Point Grace, Grace Bay* 🕾 *649/946–5096* ⚔ *Reservations essential* ⊟ *D, MC, V* ⊗ *No lunch.*

$$$–$$$$ ✕ **Anacaona.** At the Grace Bay Club, this palapa-shaded restaurant has
★   become a favorite of the country's chief minister. But despite the regular presence of government bigwigs, the restaurant continues to offer a memorable dining experience minus the tie, the air-conditioning, and the attitude. Start with a bottle of fine wine; then enjoy the light and healthy Mediterranean-influenced cuisine. The kitchen utilizes the island's bountiful seafood and fresh produce. Oil lamps on the tables, gently revolving ceiling fans, and the murmur of the trade winds add to the Eden-like environment. The entrancing ocean view and the careful service make it an ideal choice when you want to be pampered. Just added: the world's first Infinity Bar, which seems to spill right into the ocean. Children under 12 are not allowed. Long pants and collared shirts are required. ⊠ *Grace Bay Club, Grace Bay* 🕾 *649/946–5050* ⚔ *Reservations essential* ⊟ *AE, D, MC, V.*

$$$–$$$$ ✕ **Bay Bistro.** You simply can't eat any closer to the beach than here,
☾   the only restaurant in all of Provo that is built directly on the sand. Although service can be slow, the food and setting are excellent. You dine on a covered porch surrounded by palm trees and will be able to hear the waves lapping even after dark. The oven-roasted chicken is the best on the island. Junior, the best bartender on the island, can bring your drink balanced on the top of his head if he's not too busy. Brunch on weekends is very popular. Lines can be long if you don't have a reservation. ⊠ *Sibonné, Princess Dr., Grace Bay* 🕾 *649/946–5396* ⊟ *AE, MC, V* ⊗ *No dinner Mon.*

$$$–$$$$ ✕ **O'Soleil.** At the Somerset, this is one of the few indoor restaurants on Provo. White-on-white decor under vaulted ceilings give it a Miami-chic ambience. The executive chef uses mixed international influences, everything from Caribbean to Asian to European in his dishes. Ask for simpler off-the-menu options for the children. Sunday brunch, when they have it, is the best anywhere, but it's not offered every weekend

(call to confirm). ⊠*The Somerset, Princess Dr., Grace Bay* ☎649/946–5900 ▤*AE, D, MC, V.*

$$–$$$$ ✕**Gecko Grille.** You can eat indoors surrounded by giant, painted ♻ banana-leaf murals of camouflaged geckos or out on the garden patio, where the trees are interwoven with tiny twinkling lights. Creative "Floribbean" fare combines native specialties with exotic fruits and zesty island spices and includes Black Angus steaks grilled to perfection. Pecan-encrusted grouper is a longtime menu favorite. Service is among the friendliest on Provo. Wear bug spray at night if sitting outdoors. ⊠*Ocean Club, Grace Bay* ☎649/946–5885 ▤*AE, D, MC, V* ☉*Closed Mon.*

$$$ ✕**Caicos Café.** There's a pervasive air of celebration on the tree-shaded terrace of this popular eatery. Choose from grilled seafood, steak, lamb, or chicken served hot off the outdoor barbecue. Owner-chef Pierrik Marziou adds a French accent to his appetizers, salads, and homemade desserts, along with an outstanding collection of fine French wines. Wear bug spray at night. ⊠*Grace Bay* ☎649/946–5278 ▤*AE, D, MC, V* ☉*Closed Sun.*

$$$ ✕**Magnolia Wine Bar & Restaurant.** Restaurateurs since the early 1990s, ★ hands-on owners Gianni and Tracey Caporuscio make success seem simple. Expect well-prepared, uncomplicated choices that range from European to Asian to Caribbean. The atmosphere is romantic, the presentations attractive, and the service careful. It's easy to see why the Caporuscios have a loyal following. The adjoining wine bar includes a handpicked list of specialty wines, which can be ordered by the glass. The marine setting is a great place to watch the sunset. ⊠*Miramar Resort, Turtle Cove* ☎649/941–5108 ▤*AE, D, MC, V* ☉*Closed Mon. No lunch.*

ITALIAN ✕**Baci Ristorante.** Aromas redolent of the Mediterranean waft from the **$$–$$$** open kitchen as you enter this intimate eatery east of Turtle Cove. Outdoor seating is on a romantic canal-front patio, one of the lovelier settings on Provo. The menu offers a small but varied selection of Italian dishes. Veal is prominent on the menu, but main courses also include pasta, chicken, fish, and brick-oven pizzas. House wines are personally selected by the owners and complement the tasteful wine list. Try the tiramisu for dessert with a flavored coffee drink. Wear bug spray at night. ⊠*Harbour Town, Turtle Cove* ☎649/941–3044 ▤*AE, MC, V.*

SEAFOOD ✕**Aqua Bar & Terrace.** This popular restaurant on the grounds of the Tur- **$$–$$$$** tle Cove Inn has an inviting waterfront dining deck, and it just keeps ♻ getting better. Leaning heavily in the direction of locally caught seafood and farm-raised conch, the menu includes longtime favorites like wahoo sushi, pecan-encrusted conch fillets, and grilled fish served with flavorful sauces. A selection of more-casual entrées, including salads and burgers, appeals to the budget-conscious. There are plenty of child-friendly menu options. Bring bug spray, as you're close to the water. ⊠*Turtle Cove Inn, Turtle Cove Marina, Turtle Cove* ☎649/946–4763 ▤*AE, MC, V.*

BEACHES

★ **Grace Bay** (⊠*Grace Bay, on north shore*), a 12-mi (18-km) sweeping stretch of ivory-white, powder-soft sand on Provo's north coast i simply breathtaking and home to migrating starfish as well as shallow snorkeling trails. The majority of Provo's beachfront resorts are along

★ this shore. **Half Moon Bay** (⊠*15 mins from Leeward Marina, between Pine Cay and Water Cay, accessible only by boat*) is a natural ribbon o sand linking two uninhabited cays; it's only inches above the sparkling turquoise waters and one of the most gorgeous beaches on the island It's only a short boat ride away from Provo, and most of the island' tour companies run excursions there or simply offer a beach drop-off including Silverdeep, J&B Tours, and Caicos Dream Tours (⇨*Boat ing & Sailing, below*). **Malcolm's Beach** (⊠*Malcolm's Beach Rd., keep*

Fodor$Choice
★ *straight after passing Amanyara turn-off*) is one of the most stunning beaches you'll ever see, but you'll need a high-clearance vehicle to reach it. Bring your own food and drinks since there are no facilities or food service unless you have made an arrangement with Amanyara to eat a the resort. The best of the many secluded beaches and pristine sand around Provo can be found at **Sapodilla Bay** (⊠*North of South Dock at end of South Dock Rd.*), a peaceful 0.25-mi (0.5-km) cove protected by Sapodilla Hill, where calm waves lap against the soft sand, and yachts and small boats move with the gentle tide.

SPORTS & THE OUTDOORS

BICYCLING Most hotels have bicycles available, or it's possible to rent one from an independent company. You can rent mountain bikes at **Scooter Bob'** (⊠*Turtle Cove Marina, Turtle Cove* ☎649/946–4684 ⊕*www.provo net/scooter*) for $15 a day.

BOATING & Provo's calm, reef-protected seas combine with constant easterly trad
SAILING winds for excellent sailing conditions. Several multihull vessels offe charters with snorkeling stops, food and beverage service, and sunse vistas. Prices range from $39 for group trips to $600 or more for pri vate charters.

☽ **Caicos Dream Tours** (☎649/243–3560 ⊕*www.caicosdreamtours.com* offers several different snorkeling trips, including one that has yo diving for conch before lunch on a gorgeous beach. The company als offers private charters. For sightseeing below the waves, try the semi submarine operated by **Caicos Tours** (⊠*Turtle Cove Marina, Turtle Cov* ☎649/231–0006 ⊕*www.caicostours.com*). You can stay dry withi the small, lower observatory as it glides along on a one-hour tour of th reef, with large viewing windows on either side. The trip costs $39. **J&** **Tours** (☎649/946–5047 ⊕*www.jbtours.com*) offers half- and full-da excursions to other islands that make for a great day on the beach an in the water. **Sail Provo** (☎649/946–4783 ⊕*www.sailprovo.com*) run 52-foot and 48-foot catamarans on scheduled half-day, full-day, sunset and kid-friendly glowworm cruises, where underwater creatures ligh up the sea's surface for several days after each full moon. **Silverdee** (☎649/946–5612 ⊕*www.silverdeep.com*) sailing trips include tim for snorkeling and beachcombing at a secluded beach. The *Atabeyra* run by **Sun Charters** (☎649/941–5363 ⊕*www.suncharters.tc*), is a retired rumrunner and the choice of residents for special events.

DIVING
odor'sChoice
★

The island's many shallow reefs offer excellent and exciting snorkeling relatively close to shore. Try **Smith's Reef,** over Bridge Road east of Turtle Cove.

Scuba diving in the crystalline waters surrounding the islands ranks among the best in the Caribbean. The reef and wall drop-offs thrive with bright, unbroken coral formations and lavish numbers of fish and marine life. Mimicking the idyllic climate, waters are warm all year, averaging 76°F to 78°F in winter and 82°F to 84°F in summer. With minimal rainfall and soil runoff, visibility is usually good and frequently superb, ranging from 60 feet to more than 150 feet. An extensive system of marine national parks and boat moorings, combined with an ecoconscious mind-set among dive operators, contributes to an uncommonly pristine underwater environment.

Dive operators in Provo regularly visit sites at **Grace Bay** and **Pine Cay** for spur-and-groove coral formations and bustling reef diving. They make the longer journey to the dramatic walls at **North West Point** and **West Caicos** depending on weather conditions. Instruction from the major diving agencies is available for all levels and certifications, even technical diving. An average one-tank dive costs $45; a two-tank dive, $90. There are also two live-aboard dive boats available for charter working out of Provo.

Ⓒ With a certified marine biologist on staff, **Big Blue Unlimited** (✉*Leeward Marina, Leeward* ☎649/946–5034 ⊕*www.bigblue.tc*) specializes in ecofriendly diving adventures, including special trips for kids involving kayaking through the mangroves or walking along nature trails. It also offers Nitrox and Trimix. **Caicos Adventures** (✉*La Petite Pl., Grace Bay* ☎649/941–3346 ⊕*www.tcidiving.com*), run by friendly Frenchman Fifi Kuntz, offers daily trips to West Caicos, French Cay, and Molasses Reef. **Dive Provo** (✉*Ports of Call, Grace Bay* ☎649/946–5040 or 800/234–7768 ⊕*www.diveprovo.com*) is a PADI five-star operation that runs daily one- and two-tank dives to popular Grace Bay sites. **Provo Turtle Divers** (✉*Turtle Cove Marina, Turtle Cove* ☎649/946–4232 or 800/833–1341 ⊕*www.provoturtledivers.com*), which also operates satellite locations at the Ocean Club and Ocean Club West, has been on Provo since the 1970s. The staff is friendly, knowledgeable, and unpretentious. The *Turks & Caicos Aggressor II* (☎800/348–2628 ⊕*www.turksandcaicosaggressor.com*), a live-aboard dive boat, plies the islands' pristine sites with weekly charters from Turtle Cove Marina.

FISHING

The islands' fertile waters are great for angling—anything from bottom- and reef-fishing (most likely to produce plenty of bites and a large catch) to bonefishing and deep-sea fishing (among the finest in the Caribbean). Each July the Caicos Classic Catch & Release Tournament attracts anglers from across the islands and the United States who compete to catch the biggest Atlantic blue marlin, tuna, or wahoo. For any fishing activity, you are required to purchase a $15 visitor's fishing license; oper-

CLOSE UP

Diving the Turks & Caicos Islands

Scuba diving was the original water sport to draw visitors to the Turks & Caicos Islands in the 1970s. Aficionados are still drawn by the abundant marine life, including humpback whales in winter, sparkling clean waters, warm and calm seas, and the coral walls and reefs around the islands. Diving in the Turks & Caicos—especially off Grand Turk, South Caicos, and Salt Cay—is still considered among the best in the world.

Off Providenciales, dive sites are along the north shore's barrier reef. Most sites can be reached in anywhere from 10 minutes to 1½ hours. Dive sites feature spur-and-groove coral formations atop a coral-covered slope. Popular stops like **Aquarium, Pinnacles,** and **Grouper Hole** have large schools of fish, turtles, nurse sharks,

and gray reef sharks. From the south side dive boats go to **French Cay, West Caicos, South West Reef,** and **Northwest Point.** Known for typically calm conditions and clear water, the West Caicos Marine National Park is a favorite stop. The area has dramatic walls and marine life, including sharks, eagle rays, and octopus, with large stands of pillar coral and huge barrel sponges.

Off Grand Turk, the 7,000-foot coral wall **drop-off** is actually within swimming distance of the beach. Buoyed sites along the wall have swim-through tunnels, cascading sand chutes, imposing coral pinnacles, dizzying vertical drops, and undercuts where the wall goes beyond the vertical and fades beneath the reef.

ators generally furnish all equipment, drinks, and snacks. Prices range from $100 to $375, depending on the length of trip and size of boat. For deep-sea fishing trips in search of marlin, sailfish, wahoo, tuna, barracuda, and shark, look up **Gwendolyn Fishing Charters** (⊠ *Turtle Cove Marina, Turtle Cove* ☎ *649/946–5321* ⊕ *www.fishtci.com*). You can rent a boat with a captain for a half- or full-day of bottom- or bonefishing through **J&B Tours** (⊠ *Leeward Marina, Leeward* ☎ *649/946–5047* ⊕ *www.jbtours.com*). Capt. Arthur Dean at **Silverdeep** (⊠ *Leeward Marina, Leeward* ☎ *649/946–5612* ⊕ *www.silverdeep.com*) is said to be among the Caribbean's finest bonefishing guides.

GOLF   The par-72, 18-hole championship course at **Provo Golf & Country Club**
Fodor'sChoice   (⊠ *Governor's Rd., Grace Bay* ☎ *649/946–5991* ⊕ *www.provogolf.*
★   *club.com*) is a combination of lush greens and fairways, rugged limestone outcroppings, and freshwater lakes and is ranked among the Caribbean's top courses. Fees are $160 for 18 holes with shared cart. Premium golf clubs are available. **Turks & Caicos Miniature Golf** (⊠ *Long Bay Rd., Leeward* ☎ *649/231–4653*) is open every day and even offers a free shuttle service to most Grace Bay hotels. A round costs $15, and there is an onsite bar and grill where you can eat after your golf game.

HORSEBACK   Provo's long beaches and secluded lanes are ideal for trail rides on
RIDING   horseback. **Provo Ponies** (☎ *649/946–5252* ⊕ *www.provo.net/provoponies*) offers morning and afternoon rides for all levels of experience. A 45-minute ride costs $45; an 80-minute ride is $65. The rates include transportation from all major hotels.

PARASAILING A 15-minute parasailing flight over Grace Bay is available for $70 (single) or $120 (tandem) from **Captain Marvin's Watersports** (☎649/231–0643), who will pick you up at your hotel for your flight. The views as you soar over the bite-shaped Grace Bay area, with spectacular views of the barrier reef, are truly unforgettable.

TENNIS You can rent equipment at **Provo Golf & Country Club** (✉*Grace Bay* ☎649/946–5991 ⊕*www.provogolfclub.com*) and play on the two lighted courts, which are among the island's best courts. Nonmembers can play until 5 PM for $10 per hour (reservation required).

WINDSURFING Windsurfers find the calm, turquoise water of Grace Bay ideal. **Windsurfing Provo** (✉*Ocean Club, Grace Bay* ☎649/946–5649 ✉*Ocean Club West, Grace Bay* ☎649/231–1687 ⊕*www.windsurfingprovo. tc*) rents kayaks, motorboats, Windsurfers, and Hobie Cats and offers windsurfing instruction.

SHOPPING

There are several main shopping areas in Provo: Grace Bay has the newer Saltmills complex and La Petite Place retail plaza, the new Regent Village, as well as the original Ports of Call shopping village. Two markets on the beach near the Ocean Club and the Beaches Turks & Caicos Resort & Spa allow for barefooted shopping. Handwoven straw baskets and hats, polished conch-shell crafts, paintings, wood carvings, model sailboats, handmade dolls, and metalwork are crafts native to the islands and nearby Haiti. The natural surroundings have inspired local and international artists to paint, sculpt, print, craft, and photograph; most of their creations are on sale in Providenciales.

★ **Anna's Art Gallery & Studio** (✉*The Saltmills, Grace Bay* ☎449/231–3293) sells original artworks, silk-screen paintings, sculptures, and handmade sea-glass jewelry. **ArtProvo** (✉*Regent Village, Grace Bay* ☎649/941–4545) is the island's largest gallery of designer wall art; also shown are native crafts, jewelry, handblown glass, candles, and
★ other gift items. **Bamboo Gallery** (✉*Leeward Hwy., The Market Place* ☎649/946–4748) sells Caribbean art, from vivid Haitian paintings to wood carvings and local metal sculptures, with the added benefit that artists are usually on hand to describe their works. **Caicos Wear Boutique** (✉*La Petite Pl., Grace Bay Rd., Grace Bay* ☎649/941–3346) is filled with casual resort wear, including Caribbean-print shirts, swimsuits from Brazil, sandals, beach jewelry, and gifts. **Greensleeves** (✉*Central Sq., Leeward Hwy., Turtle Cove* ☎649/946–4147) offers paintings and pottery by local artists, baskets, jewelry, and sisal mats and bags. **Royal Jewels** (✉*Providenciales International Airport* ☎649/941–4513 ✉*Arch Plaza* ☎649/946–4699 ✉*Beaches Turks & Caicos Resort & Spa, Grace Bay* ☎649/946–8285 ✉*Club Med Turkoise, Grace Bay* ☎649/946–5602) sells gold and other jewelry, designer watches, perfumes, fine leather goods, and cameras—all duty-free—at several outlets. If you need to supplement your beach-reading stock or are looking
☾ for island-specific materials, visit the **Unicorn Bookstore** (✉*In front of*
★ *Graceway IGA Mall, Leeward Hwy., Grace Bay* ☎649/941–5458) for a wide assortment of books and magazines, lots of information

and guides about the Turks & Caicos Islands and the Caribbean, and a large children's section with crafts, games, and art supplies.

For a large selection of duty-free liquor, visit **Discount Liquors** (⊠ *Leeward Hwy., east of Suzie Turn Rd.* ☎ *649/946–4536*). Including a large fresh-produce section, bakery, gourmet deli, and extensive meat counter, **Graceway IGA Supermarket** (⊠ *Leeward Hwy., Grace Bay* ☎ *649/941–5000*), Provo's largest, is likely to have what you're looking for. Be prepared for sticker shock, as prices are much higher than you would expect at home. Besides having a licensed pharmacist on duty, **Lockland Trading Co.** (⊠ *Neptune Plaza, Grace Bay* ☎ *649/946–8242*) sells flavored coffees, snacks, ice cream, and a selection of souvenirs.

NIGHTLIFE

While Provo is not known for its nightlife, there's still some fun to be found after dark. On Friday nights you can start off by dancing in the sand at Da Conch Shack *(⇨ Where to Eat, above)* followed by live bands at Calico Jack's. Thursday-night and Saturday-night hot spots include Danny Buoy's. On Saturday nights at Turks & Caicos Miniature Golf you can play a round, sing karaoke, and dance the night away, all in one night *(⇨ Golf, above)*. Keep abreast of events and specials by checking **TCI eNews** (⊕ *www.tcienews.com*).

Residents and tourists alike flock to the **BET Soundstage & Gaming Lounge** (⊠ *Leeward Hwy., Grace Bay* ☎ *649/941–4318*) for video lottery games, live music and other entertainment, a casino, and a late-night disco almost every night. **Bonnie's** (⊠ *Lower Bight Rd., Grace Bay* ☎ *649/941–8452*) is a favorite local spot for sports events, movie nights, and endless happy-hour specials. On Friday nights you can find a local band and lively crowd at **Calico Jack's Restaurant & Bar** (⊠ *Port of Call, Grace Bay* ☎ *649/946–5129*). The new **Casablanca Casino** (⊠ *Grace Bay Rd., Grace Bay* ☎ *649/941–3737*) has brought slots, blackjack, American roulette, poker, craps, and baccarat back to Provo. Open from 7 PM until 5 AM, this is the last stop for the night. Grace Bay Club has introduced the new Infinity Bar, the only one of its kind in the world, which gives the impression it goes directly into the ocean. A popular gathering spot for locals to shoot pool, play darts, slam dominoes, and catch up on gossip is **Club Sodax Sports Bar** (⊠ *Leeward Hwy., Grace Bay* ☎ *649/941–4540*). You won't go hungry with snacks such as conch and fish fingers, jerk pork, and typical native dishes. **Danny Buoy's** (⊠ *Grace Bay Rd., Grace Bay* ✛ *Across from Carpe Diem Residences* ☎ *649/946–5921*) is a popular Irish pub.

EXPLORING PROVIDENCIALES

♺ **Caicos Conch Farm.** On the northeast tip of Provo, this is a major mariculture operation, where the mollusks are farmed commercially (more than 3 million conch are here). Guided tours are available; call to confirm times. The small gift shop sells conch-related souvenirs, and the world's only pet conchs, Sally and Jerry, seem more than happy to come out of their shells. ⊠ *Leeward-Going-Through, Leeward* ☎ *649/946–5330* ⊕ *www.caicosconchfarm.com* ⊠ *$6* ☉ *Mon.–Sat. 9–4.*

Cheshire Hall. Standing eerily just west of downtown Provo are the remains of a circa-1700 cotton plantation owned by Loyalist Thomas Stubbs. A trail weaves through the ruins, where interpretive signs tell the story of the island's doomed cotton industry. A variety of local plants are also identified. To visit, you must arrange for a tour through the Turks & Caicos National Trust. The lack of context can be disappointing for history buffs; a visit to North Caicos Wades Green Plantation or the Turks & Caicos National Museum could well prove a better fit. ⊠*Near downtown Providenciales* ☎*649/941–5710 for National Trust* ⊕*www.turksandcaicos.tc/nationaltrust* ⊠*$5* ☉*Daily, by appointment.*

☾ **Sapodilla Hill.** On this cliff overlooking the secluded Sapodilla Bay, you can discover rocks carved with the names of shipwrecked sailors and dignitaries from TCI maritime and colonial past. The less adventurous can see molds of the carvings at Provo's International Airport. ⊠*Off South Dock Rd., west of South Dock.*

TLE WATER CAY

☾
★ This small, uninhabited cay is a protected area under the Turks & Caicos National Trust. On these 150 acres are two trails, small lakes, red mangroves, and an abundance of native plants. Boardwalks protect the ground, and interpretive signs explain the habitat. The cay is home to about 2,000 rare, endangered rock iguanas. Experts say the iguanas are shy, but these creatures actually seem rather curious. They waddle right up to you, as if posing for a picture. Several water-sports operators from Provo and North Caicos include a stop on the island as a part of their snorkel or sailing excursions (it's usually called "Iguana Island"). There's a $5 fee for a permit to visit the cay, and the proceeds go toward conservation in the islands.

RROT CAY

Once said to be a hideout for pirate Calico Jack Rackham and his lady cohorts Mary Read and Anne Bonny, the 1,000-acre cay, between Fort George Cay and North Caicos, is now the site of an ultraexclusive hideaway resort.

For approximate costs, see the dining and lodging price chart in the Turks & Caicos Planner, at the beginning of this chapter.

$$$$
dor$Choice
★ **Parrot Cay Resort.** This private paradise—a favorite for celebrities and aspiring ones—comes with all the trimmings you'd expect for the substantial price. Elaborate oceanfront villas border the island, and their wooden, Far Eastern feel contrasts with the rather bland hillside terracotta and stucco building that houses the spacious suites. Suite and villa interiors are a minimalist and sumptuous mix of cool-white interiors, Indonesian furnishings, and four-poster beds. The villas are the ultimate indulgence, with heated lap pools, hot tubs, and butler service. The resort's main pool is surrounded by a round, thatched bar and the Asian-inspired Lotus restaurant. The giant Como Shambhala Spa takes

destination spas to a whole new level with Indonesian and Balinese therapists. **Pros:** Impeccable service, gorgeous secluded beach, the spa is considered one of the best in the world. **Cons:** Only two restaurants on the entire island, can be difficult to get back to Provo for excursions. ⊠*Parrot Cay* ✆*Box 164, Providenciales* ☎*649/946–7788* ⊕*www. parrotcay.como.bz* ➘*42 rooms, 4 suites, 14 villas* ⌂*In-room: safe, kitchen (some), refrigerator, VCR (some), dial-up, Wi-Fi. In-hotel: 2 restaurants, room service, bars, tennis courts, pool, gym, spa, beachfront, water sports, no elevator, laundry service, public Internet, public Wi-Fi, airport shuttle* ▭*AE, MC, V* ⏅*BP.*

PINE CAY

Pine Cay's 2.5-mi-long (4-km-long) beach is among the most beautiful in the archipelago. The 800-acre private island is home to a secluded resort and around 37 private residences.

For approximate costs, see the dining and lodging price chart in the Turks & Caicos Planner, at the beginning of this chapter.

$$$$ 🏨**Meridian Club.** You might feel unplugged when you step onto Pine
Fodor'sChoice Cay, since there is no TV, telephone, or traffic to be found on the tiny
★ private island. The charm of this resort, which was built in the 1970s, is that it never changes, it prides itself on simplicity rather than celebrity. The simple beachfront cottages, most of the staff, and what is perhaps the world's smallest airport (in truth, a gazebo) have all stayed pretty much the same for years. On some nights, you can drive your golf cart to the runway for Drive-In Movie night. The 2.5-mi (4-km) stretch of beach is deserted, and instead of roads you can find nature trails and sun-dappled paths that crisscross the island, which can be explored by bike or on foot. Cuisine is excellent, with fresh seafood and delicious cakes and tarts served at lunch, dinner, and afternoon tea. Far from being an ivory-tower experience, the club enables you to become part of a small community. Guests are mostly overstressed executives, mature couples, and honeymooners; a large percentage of guests are repeats. Children are welcome only in June and July. **Pros:** The finest beach in T&C, rates are inclusive of some of the best food in the T&C as well as snorkel trips. **Cons:** No TVs, no phones. ⊠*Pine Cay* ☎*649/946–7758 or 866/746–3229* ⊕*www.meridianclub.com* ➘*13 rooms, 1 cottage, 7 private homes* ⌂*In-room: no a/c, no phone, no TV, room service. In-hotel: restaurant, bar, tennis court, pool, beachfront, water sports, bicycles, no elevator, laundry service, public Internet, no kids under 12* ▭*AE, D, MC, V* ⏅*Closed Aug.–Oct.* ⏅*AI.*

NORTH CAICOS

Thanks to abundant rainfall, this 41-square-mi (106-square-km) island is the lushest of the Turks & Caicos. Bird lovers can see a large flock of flamingos here, anglers can find shallow creeks full of bonefish, and history buffs can visit the ruins of a Loyalist plantation. Although there is no traffic, almost all the roads are paved, so bicycling is an excellent

Coming Attractions

The buzz about Turks & Caicos has increased steadily over the last five years, a fact that hasn't missed the ears of developers. Grace Bay, a 12-mi (18-km) stretch of ivory sand on Providenciales, is still a favored location for new properties, including the stunning **Regent Grand,** a grander version of its sister property, Villa Renaissance. **Seven Stars,** a seven-story condominium resort, will be taking the destination to new heights, quite literally; because of its height, Seven Stars will have views like no other resort on Grace Bay. **Windsong** will add some new features to Provo, with a beach bar that appears to be under the water of the pool; it will even have outdoor air conditioning. At this writing, all three of these new resorts are expected to open by summer 2008. Given the volume of construction, it is worth asking your hotel about nearby construction projects to avoid the noise, dust, and obstructed views that can sometimes result.

way to sightsee. The island is predicted to become one of the next tourism hot spots, and foundations have been laid for condo resorts on Horse Stable Beach and Sandy Point. Even though it's a quiet place, you can find some small eateries around the airport and in Whitby, giving you a chance to try local and seafood specialties, sometimes served with homegrown okra or corn.

You can now reach North Caicos from Provo with a daily ferry from Walkin Marina in Leeward; the trip takes about 30 minutes *(⇨ By Boat & Ferry in Turks & Caicos Essentials).* If you rent a car on North Caicos, you can even drive on the new causeway to Middle Caicos, a great day trip from Provo.

WHERE TO STAY

For approximate costs, see the dining and lodging price chart in the Turks & Caicos Planner, at the beginning of this chapter.

$$ 🏨 **Bottle Creek Lodge.** Colorful, self-contained bungalows are scattered
🕘 close to the water, providing a get-away-from-it-all feeling. Although this small resort is not close to the best beaches of North Caicos, it's the perfect place for fishing and relaxing. Bonefishing is right outside your door; the owners also have motorboats available for deep-sea fishing. You'll be welcomed as if you are coming home, and the restaurant has some of the best food on the island. It's possible to use Paypal if you don't have a credit card for payment. **Pros:** Very colorful and peaceful, great fishing. **Cons:** Not close to the best beaches in North Caicos, requires a car. ⊠ *Belmont* ☎ *649/946–7080* ⊕ *www. bottlecreeklodge.com* ⇝ *3 rooms* ⚲ *In-room: kitchen, no phone, no TV, Wi-Fi. In-hotel: restaurant, room service, bar, water sports, bicycles, laundry service, public Internet, some pets allowed, no-smoking rooms* ⊟ *MC, V* ⊚| *EP.*

$–$$ 🏨 **Ocean Beach Hotel & Condominiums.** On Whitby Beach, this horseshoe-shaped two-story, solar-paneled resort offers ocean views, comfortable and neatly furnished apartments, and a freshwater pool at quite reasonable rates. The Silver Palm restaurant is a welcome addition to the on-site amenities, which also include a dive and water-sports operation called Beach Cruiser. Unit 5 has the best views over the beach—especially for honeymooners, who automatically receive a 10% discount. You pay extra for air-conditioning, however. **Pros:** On the best beach of North Caicos. **Cons:** You need a car to get anywhere on North Caicos. ⊠ *Whitby* ☎*649/946–7113, 800/710–5204, 905/690–3817 in Canada* ⊕*www.turksandcaicos.tc/oceanbeach* ⊲*10 suites* ⌂*In-room: kitchen (some), no TV (some). In-hotel: restaurant, bar, pool, beachfront, diving, water sports, bicycles, laundry service, public Internet* ⊟*AE, D, MC, V* ⊘*Closed June 15–Oct. 15* ⦿*EP.*

$ 🏨 **Pelican Beach Hotel.** North Caicos islanders Susan and Clifford Gardiner built this small palmetto-fringed hotel in the 1980s on the quiet, mostly deserted Whitby Beach. The couple's friendliness and insights into island life, not to mention Susan's home-baked bread and island dishes (Cliff's favorite is her cracked conch and island lobster), are the best features. Over the years upkeep of the property has been somewhat inconsistent, but rooms are nevertheless comfortable. Best is the line of cottage-style rooms (numbered 1 through 6), which is exactly five steps from the windswept beach. **Pros:** The beach is just outside your room. **Cons:** At this writing, rooms are still in the very slow process of being renovated and updated. ⊠ *Whitby* ☎*649/946–7112* ⊕*www.pelican beach.tc* ⊲*14 rooms, 2 suites* ⌂*In-room: no phone, no TV. In-hotel: restaurant, bar, beachfront, bicycles, water sports, no elevator* ⊟*MC, V* ⊘*Closed Aug. 15–Sept. 15* ⦿*MAP.*

BEACHES

The beaches of North Caicos are superb for shallow snorkeling and sunset strolls, and the waters offshore have excellent scuba diving. Horse Stable Beach is the main beach for annual events and beach parties. Whitby Beach usually has a gentle tide, and its thin strip of sand is bordered by palmetto plants and taller trees.

EXPLORING NORTH CAICOS

Flamingo Pond. This is a regular nesting place for the beautiful pink birds. They tend to wander out in the middle of the pond, so bring binoculars.

Kew. This settlement has a small post office, a school, a church, and ruins of old plantations—all set among lush tropical trees bearing limes, papayas, and custard apples. Visiting Kew will give you a better understanding of the daily life of many islanders.

☾ **Wades Green.** Visitors can view well-preserved ruins of the greathouse, overseer's house, and surrounding walls of one of the most successful plantations of the Loyalist era. A lookout tower provides views for miles. Contact the National Trust for tour details. ⊠*Kew* ☎*649/941-5710 for National Trust* 🎫*$5* ⊘*Daily, by appointment only.*

DDLE CAICOS

At 48 square mi (124 square km) and with fewer than 300 residents, this is the largest and least developed of the inhabited islands in the Turks & Caicos chain. A limestone ridge runs to about 125 feet above sea level, creating dramatic cliffs on the north shore and a cave system farther inland. Middle Caicos has rambling trails along the coast; the **Crossing Place Trail,** maintained by the National Trust, follows the path used by the early settlers to go between the islands. Inland are quiet settlements with friendly residents. North Caicos and Middle Caicos are now linked by a new causeway; since they are now linked by a road, it's possible to take a ferry from Provo to North Caicos, rent a car, and explore both North Caicos and Middle Caicos.

WHERE TO STAY

For approximate costs, see the dining and lodging price chart in the Turks & Caicos Planner, at the beginning of this chapter.

$$ **Blue Horizon Resort.** At this resort, undulating cliffs skirt one of the most dramatic beaches in the Turks & Caicos. Blue-tin roofs mark the small self-contained open-plan cottages. Screened-in porches and careful positioning ensure that all of the cottages have unobstructed views along the cliffs and out to sea. The lack of amenities and development is actually what makes this spot so special. Tropical Cottage has large, attractive murals; Dragon View cottage has spectacular views of Dragon Cay and is closest to the Crossing Place trail that winds along the cliff tops. **Pros:** Breathtaking views of Mudjin Harbor from the rooms, lack of amenities and development make you feel like you're away from it all. **Cons:** Lack of amenities and development may be too isolated for some. ✉ *Mudjin Harbor, Conch Bar* ☎ *649/946–6141* ⊕ *www.bhresort.com* ➷ *5 cottages, 2 villas* ♿ *In-room: no a/c (some), no phone (some), kitchen (some), no TV (some). In-hotel: beachfront, water sports, bicycles, no elevator, laundry service* ☰ *AE, MC, V* ⁺⊙⁺ *EP.*

EXPLORING MIDDLE CAICOS

☾ **Conch Bar Caves.** These limestone caves have eerie underground lakes and milky-white stalactites and stalagmites. Archaeologists have discovered Lucayan Indian artifacts in the caves and the surrounding area. The caves are inhabited by some harmless bats. If you visit, don't worry—they don't bother visitors. It's best to get a guide. If you tour the caves, be sure to wear sturdy shoes, not sandals.

AVE TOURS Taxi driver and fisherman **Cardinal Arthur** (☎ *649/946–6107*) can give you a good cave tour.

Local cave specialist and taxi driver **Ernest Forbes** (☎ *649/946–6140*) is also happy to oblige with a cave tour and may even arrange a fixed-fee lunch at his house afterward if you ask nicely.

SOUTH CAICOS

This 8.5-square-mi (21-square-km) island was once an important salt producer; today it's the heart of the fishing industry. Nature prevails, with long, white beaches, jagged bluffs, quiet backwater bays, and salt flats. Diving and snorkeling on the pristine wall and reefs are a treat enjoyed by only a few.

BEACHES

The beaches at **Belle Sound** on South Caicos will take your breath away, with lagoonlike waters. On the opposite side of the ridge from Belle Sound, **Long Bay** is an endless stretch of beach, but it can be susceptible to rough surf; however, on calmer days this stretch makes you feel you're on a deserted island. Due south of South Caicos is **Big Ambergris Cay**, an uninhabited cay about 14 mi (23 km) beyond the Fish Cays, with a magnificent beach at Long Bay. To the north of South Caicos, uninhabited **East Caicos** has a beautiful 17-mi (27-km) beach on its north coast. The island was once a cattle range and the site of a major sisal-growing industry. Both places are accessible only by boat.

EXPLORING SOUTH CAICOS

At the northern end of the island are fine white-sand beaches; the south coast is great for scuba diving along the drop-off; and there's excellent snorkeling off the windward (east) coast, where large stands of elkhorn and staghorn coral shelter several varieties of small tropical fish. Spiny lobster and queen conch are found in the shallow Caicos Bank to the west and are harvested for export by local processing plants. The bone-fishing here is some of the best in the West Indies.

Beyond the Blue (✉ *Cockburn Town* ☎ *649/231–1703* ⊕ *www.beyond theblue.com*) offers bonefishing charters on a specialized airboat, which can operate in less than a foot of water. Lodging packages are available.

Boiling Hole. Abandoned salinas make up the center of this island—the largest, across from the downtown ballpark, receives its water directly from an underground source connected to the ocean through this boiling hole.

Cockburn Harbour. The best natural harbor in the Caicos chain hosts the South Caicos Regatta, held each year in May.

THE TURKS

GRAND TURK

Just 7 mi (11 km) long and a little over 1 mi (2.5 km) wide, this island, the capital and seat of the Turks & Caicos government, has been a longtime favorite destination for divers eager to explore the 7,000-foot-deep pristine coral walls that drop down only 300 yards out to sea. On shore, the tiny, quiet island is home to white-sand beaches, the National Museum, and a small population of wild horses and donkeys, which

All in the Family

Belongers, from the taxi driver meeting you to the chef feeding you, are often connected. "Oh, him?" you will hear. "He my cousin!" As development has been mercifully slow, such family connections, as well as crafts, bush medicine, ripsaw music, storytelling, and even recipes, have remained constant. But where do such traditions come from? Recently, researchers came closer to finding out. Many Belongers had claimed that their great-great-grandparents had told them their forebears had come directly from Africa. For decades their stories were ignored. Indeed, most experts believed that Belongers were descendants of mostly second-generation Bermudian and Caribbean slaves.

In 2005, museum researchers continued their search for a lost slave ship called *Trouvadore*. The ship, which wrecked off East Caicos in 1841, carried a cargo of 193 Africans, captured to be sold into slavery, almost all of whom miraculously survived the wreck. As slavery had been abolished in this British territory at the time, all the Africans were found and freed in the Turks & Caicos Islands. Since there were only a few thousand inhabitants in the islands at the time, these first-generation African survivors were a measurable minority (about 7% of the population then). Researchers have concluded that all the existing Belongers may be linked by blood or marriage to this one incident.

During one expedition, divers found a wrecked ship of the right time period. If these remains are *Trouvadore*, the Belongers may finally have a physical link to their past, to go with their more-intangible cultural traditions. So while you're in the islands, look closely at the intricately woven baskets, listen carefully to the African rhythms in the ripsaw music, and savor the stories you hear. They may very well be the legacy of *Trouvadore* speaking to you from the past. For more information, check out ⊕ *www.slaveshiptrouvadore.com.*

leisurely meander past the white-walled courtyards, pretty churches, and bougainvillea-covered colonial inns on their daily commute into town. A cruise-ship complex that opened at the southern end of the island in 2006 brings about 300,000 visitors per year. Despite the dramatic changes this could make to this peaceful tourist spot, the dock is self-contained and is about 3 mi (5 km) from the tranquil, small hotels of Cockburn Town, Pillory Beach, and the Ridge and far from most of the western-shore dive sites. And the influx has also pushed Grand Turk to open up a few new historic sites, including Grand Turk's Old Prison, and the Lighthouse.

WHERE TO STAY

Accommodations include original Bermudian inns, more-modern but small beachfront hotels, and very basic to well-equipped self-catering suites and apartments. Almost all hotels offer dive packages, which are an excellent value.

$$ ⌂ **Arches of Grand Turk.** Upstairs and downstairs, east- and west-facing balconies from these four ridgetop town houses ensure nicely framed views of both sunrise and sunset. Canadian husband-and-wife team

Wally and Cecile Wennick left Florida in the 1990s after more than a decade in the hospitality industry to create this hillside home away from home, less than a five-minute walk from the deserted east beach. The well-equipped town houses are peppered with Cecile's handicrafts, including painted glass bottles, embroidery, and wall hangings that combine to give the airy houses a homespun feel. Weekly housekeeping is included in the rate, but daily maid service costs extra. **Pros:** Quiet getaway, feels like home. **Cons:** Not on the beach, requires a car. ⌧*Lighthouse Rd., Box 226* ☎649/946–2941 ⊕*www.grandturk-arches.com* ✍*4 town houses* ⌂*In-room: kitchen, dial-up, Wi-Fi. In-hotel: pool, bicycles, no elevator, laundry service, public Wi-Fi, public Internet* ▭*D, MC, V* ✵*EP.*

$$ 🏨 **Bohio Dive Resort & Spa.** Formerly the Pillory Beach Resort, this resort sits on an otherwise deserted stretch of beach. It's a dream come true for British couple Kelly Shanahan and Nick Gillings, who have created their own retreat on Grand Turk after years of visiting the tiny island. The resort's restaurant is the best on the island. You can relax with yoga sessions or party with the locals at the Sunday sail and kayak races or Thursday-night's "pit party" with roasted meats and music. **Pros:** Has the best restaurant in Grand Turk, on a gorgeous beach, steps away from awesome snorkeling. **Cons:** Rooms are basic and dated, three night minimum. ⌧*Pillory Beach* ☎649/946–2135 ⊕*www.bohio-resort.com* ✍*12 rooms, 4 suites* ⌂*In-room: kitchen (some), no phones. In-hotel: restaurant, bars, pool, spa, beachfront, diving, water sports, no elevator, public Internet* ▭*AE, MC, V* ✍*3-night minimum* ✵*EP.*

$$ 🏨 **Island House.** Owner Colin Brooker gives his guests a personal introduction to the capital island, thanks to his family's long history here. His years of business travel experience have gone into the comfortable, peaceful suites that overlook North Creek. Balcony barbecues, shaded hammocks, and flat-screen TVs are among the diversions from the backdrop of splendid island and ocean views. Suites 3 and 7 command the best sunset views. Graduated terraces descend the hillside to a small pool surrounded by pink-and-white climbing bougainvillea, creating the feel of a Mediterranean hideaway. An array of inflatable toys keeps kids happy. The deserted east beach is a 12-minute walk away. If you stay more than three nights, a car is included in the rental price. **Pros:** Full condo units feel like a home away from home. **Cons:** Not on the beach, you need a car to get around. ⌧*Lighthouse Rd., Box 36* ☎649/946–1519 ⊕*www.islandhouse-tci.com* ✍*8 suites.* ⌂*In-room: kitchen, Wi-Fi. In-hotel: pool, water sports, bicycles, no elevator, laundry facilities, public Wi-Fi, some pets allowed* ▭*AE, D, MC, V* ✵*EP.*

$–$$ 🏨 **Osprey Beach Hotel.** Grand Turk veteran hotelier Jenny Smith has
Fodor'sChoice   transformed this two-story oceanfront hotel with her artistic touches.
★   Palms, frangipani, and deep green azaleas frame it like a painting. Inside, evocative island watercolors, painted through her longtime friend Nashville artist Tupper Saussay, thread through the property. Vaulted ceilings and Indonesian four-poster beds are the highlight of upstairs Suites 51, 52, and 53. Downstairs you can enjoy beach access through your own garden. On the opposite side of Duke Street, the newly built

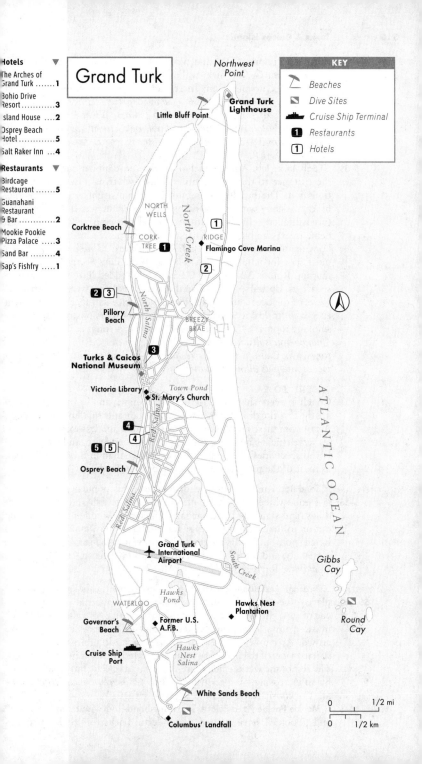

suites have phones, TVs, and Wi-Fi service. **Pros:** Renovated in 2007, best hotel on Grand Turk, walking distance to Front Street, restaurants, and excursions. **Con:** Three-night minimum. ⊠*Duke St., Cockburn Town* ☎649/946–2666 ⊕*www.ospreybeachhotel.com* ⤵*11 rooms, 16 suites* ⚡*In-room: dial-up (some), Wi-Fi (some), kitchen (some). In-hotel: restaurant, bar, pool, beachfront, water sports, no elevator, laundry service, some pets allowed* ▭*AE, MC, V* ⤳*3-night minimum* ⦿*EP.*

\$–\$\$ 🔲 **Salt Raker Inn.** A large anchor on the sun-dappled pathway marks the entrance to this 19th-century house, which is now an unpretentious inn. The building was built by a shipwright and has a large, breezy balcony with commanding views over the sea, but its best feature is hidden behind the facade: a secret garden of tall tamarind and neme trees, climbing vines, hanging plants, potted hibiscus, climbing bougainvillea, and even a pond. The greenery, as well as providing a quiet spot for natural shade, is home to the inn's Secret Garden Restaurant. Rooms A2, B2, and C2 are nicely shaded havens but have no sea views. Upstairs, Rooms G and H share a balcony with unobstructed views of the ocean and Duke Street. **Pros:** Excellent location that is an easy walk to Front Street, restaurants, and excursions. **Cons:** No no-smoking rooms. ⊠*Duke St., Box 1, Cockburn Town* ☎649/946–2260 ⊕*www.hotelsaltraker.com* ⤵*10 rooms, 3 suites* ⚡*In-room: refrigerator, Wi-Fi, dial-up. In-hotel: restaurant, bar, no elevator, laundry service, some pets allowed, public Wi-Fi* ▭*D, MC, V* ⦿*EP.*

WHERE TO EAT

Conch in every shape and form, fresh grouper, and lobster (in season) are the favorite dishes at the laid-back restaurants that line Duke Street. Away from these more-touristy areas, smaller and less-expensive eateries serve chicken and ribs, curried goat, peas and rice, and other native island specialties. Prices are more expensive than in the United States, as most of the produce has to be imported.

AMERICAN
\$–\$\$ ✕**Sand Bar.** Run by two Canadian sisters, this popular beachside bar is a good value, though the menu is limited to fish-and-chips, quesadillas, and similarly basic bar fare. The tented wooden terrace jutting out on to the beach provides shade during the day, making it an ideal lunch spot, but it's also a great place to watch the sunset. The service is friendly, and the local crowd often spills into the street. ⊠*Duke St., Cockburn Town* ☎*No phone* ▭*MC, V.*

CARIBBEAN
\$\$–\$\$\$
★ ✕**Birdcage Restaurant.** At the top of Duke Street, this has become the place to be on Sunday and Wednesday nights, when a sizzling barbecue of ribs, chicken, and lobster combines with live "rake-and-scrape" music from a local group called High Tide to draw an appreciative crowd. Arrive before 8 PM to secure beachside tables and an unrestricted view of the band; the location around the Osprey pool is lovely. The rest of the week, enjoy more-elegant and eclectic fare accompanied by an increasingly impressive wine list. ⊠*Osprey Beach Hotel, Duke St., Cockburn Town* ☎649/946–2666 ▭*MC, V.*

¢–\$ ✕**Mookie Pookie Pizza Palace.** Local husband-and-wife team "Mookie" and "Pookie" have created a wonderful backstreet parlor that has gained well-deserved popularity over the years as much more than a pizza place. At lunchtime, the tiny eatery is packed with locals ordering specials like steamed beef, curried chicken, and curried goat. You can also get burgers and omelets, but stick to the specials if you want fast service, and dine in if you want to get a true taste of island living. By night, the place becomes Grand Turk's one and only pizza take-out and delivery service, so if you're renting a villa or condo, put this spot on speed dial. ⊠*Hospital Rd., Cockburn Town* ☎*649/946–1538* ▭*No credit cards* ☉*Closed Sun.*

ECLECTIC ✗**Guanahani Restaurant & Bar.** Off the town's main drag, this restaurant
$$–$$$ sits on a stunning but quiet stretch of beach. The food goes beyond the
★ usual Grand Turk fare, thanks to the talents of Canadian-born chef Zev Beck, who takes care of the evening meals. His pecan-encrusted mahimahi and crispy sushi rolls are to die for. For lunch, Middle Caicos native Miss Leotha makes juicy jerk chicken to keep the crowd happy. The menu changes daily. The food is the best in Grand Turk, but it's also the island's most expensive restaurant. ⊠*Bohio Dive Resort & Spa, Pillory Beach* ☎*649/946–2135* ▭*MC, V.*

SEAFOOD ✗**Sap's Fishfry.** Down a lesser-known road that runs to the west of
$–$$$ North Creek lies an even lesser-known restaurant. If you survive the potholed road trip, you will undoubtedly feel you deserve a taste of the freshly caught grouper, conch, and lobster specialties served at this small hideaway on the water. This favorite (if slightly scandalous) spot, is where local married men like to bring their "sweethearts." The prices and food are certainly good enough to make it the best choice for a cheap date. Although officially called Sap's, islanders sometimes call it Chubbies. ⊠*North Creek* ☎*No phone* ▭*No credit cards.*

BEACHES

★ Grand Turk is spoiled for choices when it comes to beach options: sunset strolls along miles of deserted beaches, picnics in secluded coves, beachcombing on the coralline sands, snorkeling around shallow coral heads close to shore, and admiring the impossibly turquoise-blue waters. **Governor's Beach,** a beautiful crescent of powder-soft sand and shallow, calm turquoise waters that fronts the official British Governor's residence, called Waterloo, is framed by tall casuarina trees that provide plenty of natural shade. To have it all to yourself, go on a day when cruise ships are not in port. On days when ships are in port, the beach is lined with lounge chairs. For more of a beachcombing experience, **Little Bluff Point Beach,** just west of the Grand Turk Lighthouse, is a low, limestone-cliff-edged, shell-covered beach that looks out onto shallow waters, mangroves, and often flamingos, especially in spring and summer. **Pillory Beach,** with sparkling neon turquoise water, is the prettiest beach on Grand Turk; it also has great off-the-beach snorkeling.

SPORTS & THE OUTDOORS

CYCLING The island's mostly flat terrain isn't very taxing, and most roads have hard surfaces. Take water with you: there are few places to stop for refreshment. Most hotels have bicycles available, but you can also rent them for $10 to $15 a day from **Oasis Divers** (⊠*Duke St., Cockburn Town* ☎649/946–1128 ⊕*www.oasisdivers.com*).

DIVING & SNORKELING

★

In these waters you can find undersea cathedrals, coral gardens, and countless tunnels, but note that you must carry and present a valid certificate card before you'll be allowed to dive. As its name suggests, the **Black Forest** offers staggering black-coral formations as well as the occasional black-tip shark. In the **Library** you can study fish galore, including large numbers of yellowtail snapper. At the Columbus Passage separating South Caicos from Grand Turk, each side of a 22-mi-wide (35-km-wide) channel drops more than 7,000 feet. From January through March, thousands of Atlantic humpback whales swim through en route to their winter breeding grounds. **Gibb's Cay,** a small cay a couple of miles off Grand Turk, makes a great excursion swimming with stingrays.

Dive outfitters can all be found in Cockburn Town. Two-tank boat dives generally cost $60 to $80. **Blue Water Divers** (⊠*Duke St., Cockburn Town* ☎649/946–2432 ⊕*www.grandturkscuba.com*) has been in operation on Grand Turk since 1983 and is the only PADI Gold Palm five-star dive center on the island. Owner Mitch will doubtless put some of your underwater adventures to music in the evenings when he plays at the Osprey Beach Hotel or Salt Raker Inn. **Oasis Divers** (⊠*Duke St., Cockburn Town* ☎649/946–1128 ⊕*www.oasisdivers. com*) specializes in complete gear handling and pampering treatment. It also supplies Nitrox and rebreathers. Besides daily dive trips to the wall, **Sea Eye Diving** (⊠*Duke St., Cockburn Town* ☎649/946–1407 ⊕*www.seaeyediving.com*) offers encounters with friendly stingrays on a popular snorkeling trip to nearby Gibbs Cay.

NIGHTLIFE

On weekends and holidays the younger crowd heads over to the **Nookie Hill Club** (⊠*Nookie Hill* ☎*No phone*) for late-night drinking and dancing. Every Wednesday and Sunday, there's lively "rake-and-scrape" music at the **Osprey Beach Hotel** (⊠*Duke St., Cockburn Town* ☎649/946–2666). On Friday, rake-and-scrape bands play at the **Salt Raker Inn** (⊠*Duke St., Cockburn Town* ☎649/946–2260).

EXPLORING GRAND TURK

Pristine beaches with vistas of turquoise waters, small local settlements, historic ruins, and native flora and fauna are among the sights on Grand Turk. Fewer than 5,000 people live on this 7.5-square-mi (19-square-km) island, and it's hard to get lost, as there aren't many roads.

Cockburn Town. The buildings in the colony's capital and seat of government reflect a 19th-century Bermudian style. Narrow streets are lined with low stone walls and old street lamps, which are now powered by electricity. The once-vital salinas have been restored, and covered benches along the sluices offer shady spots for observing wading birds, including flamingos that frequent the shallows. Be sure to pick up a copy of the tourist board's Heritage Walk guide to discover Grand Turk's rich architecture.

⏱ In one of the oldest stone buildings on the islands, the **Turks & Caicos**
★ **National Museum** houses the Molasses Reef wreck, the earliest ship-
wreck—dating to the early 1500s—discovered in the Americas.
The natural-history exhibits include artifacts left by Taíno, African, North American, Bermudian, French, and Latin American settlers. The museum has a 3-D coral reef exhibit, a walk-in Lucayan
cave with wooden artifacts, and a gallery dedicated to Grand Turk's
little-known involvement in the Space Race (former Senator John
Glenn made his first landfall back on Earth here after his orbit of the
earth). An interactive children's gallery keeps knee-high visitors even
more "edutained." The museum also claims that Grand Turk was
Columbus's first landfall in the New World. ✉ *Duke St., Cockburn
Town* ☎ *649/946–2160* ⊕ *www.tcmuseum.org* ✉ *$5* 🕐 *Mon., Tues.,
Thurs., and Fri. 9–4, Wed. 9–5, Sat. 9–1.*

Grand Turk Lighthouse. More than 150 years old, the lighthouse, built in
the United Kingdom and transported piece by piece to the island, used
to protect ships in danger of wrecking on the northern reefs. Use this
panoramic landmark as a starting point for a breezy cliff-top walk by
following the donkey trails to the deserted eastern beach. ✉ *Lighthouse
Rd., North Ridge.*

6

SALT CAY

Fewer than 100 people live on this 2.5-square-mi (6-square-km) dot of
land, maintaining an unassuming lifestyle against a backdrop of quaint
stucco cottages, stone ruins, and weathered wooden windmills standing sentry in the abandoned salinas. The beautifully preserved island is
bordered by picturesque beaches, where weathered green and blue sea
glass and pretty shells often wash ashore. Beneath the waves, 10 dive
sites are minutes from shore.

There are big plans for Salt Cay, which will change the small island
forever, though probably not for several years. Gone will be the donkeys and chickens roaming the streets; in their place will be a luxurious
resort and new golf course. If you want to see how the Caribbean was
when it was laid back, sleepy and colorful, visit the island now before
it changes.

WHERE TO STAY
*For approximate costs, see the dining and lodging price chart in the
Turks & Caicos Planner, at the beginning of this chapter.*

$–$$ 🏨 **Pirate's Hideaway & Blackbeard's Quarters.** Owner Candy Herwin—
true to her self-proclaimed pirate status—has smuggled artistic treasures across the ocean and even created her own masterpieces to deck
out this lair. Quirkily decorated rooms show her original style and
sense of humor. The African and Crow's Nest suites have private baths;
Blackbeard's Quarters is a four-bedroom house with rooms that can be
rented separately but share a living room and kitchen (one room has
an en-suite bath; the others share a single bath). On a good day, Candy
will cook, but only if you entertain her and other guests—whether by

reading a sonnet or singing a song. If you love eclectic and artisticall inspiring surroundings and want to meet a true pirate queen, this coul well be your perfect hideaway. A freshwater pool and gym have bee recently added. You can rent golf carts to drive around the island. **Pro** Artist workshops are offered during peak season. **Cons:** Not directl on the beach. ⊠ *Victoria St., South District* ☎ 649/946–6909 ⊕ *www saltcay.tc* ⥽ *2 suites, 1 house* ⚘ *In-room: no a/c (some), no phone kitchen (some). In-hotel: beachfront, water sports, bicycles, no eleva tor* ☰ *MC, V* †⊙*IEP.*

$–$$ 🛏 **Sunset Reef.** A blue whale on the rooftop denotes this Victoria Stree property, which has two very basic villas with excellent ocean view and a whale-watching balcony ideal for communal dining. You mus pay extra to use the air-conditioning. **Pros:** Home away from hom feel, great balconies for whale-watching. **Cons:** Extra cost for dail maid service. ⊠ *Victoria St., Balfour Town* ☎ 649/941–7753 ⊕ *www sunsetreef.com* ⥽ *1 1-bedroom villa, 1 2-bedroom villa* ⚘ *In-room: n phone, safe, kitchen, VCR (some). In-hotel: beachfront, water sports no elevator, laundry facilities, some pets allowed* ☰ *MC, V* †⊙*IEP.*

$–$$ 🛏 **Tradewinds Guest Suites.** Yards away from Dean's Dock, a grov of whispering casuarina trees surrounds these five single-story, basi apartments, which offer a moderate-budget option on Salt Cay wit the possibility of all-inclusive and dive packages. Screened porche hammocks overlooking the comings and goings of the small dock and the friendly staff are the best features. **Pros:** Walking distance t diving, fishing, dining, and dancing. **Cons:** Cost of air-conditioning not included in basic rates, some may feel isolated with few nighttim activities and no TVs. ⊠ *Victoria St., Balfour Town* ☎ 649/946–690 ⊕ *www.tradewinds.tc* ⥽ *5 apartments* ⚘ *In-room: no phone, kitche (some), no TV. In-hotel: beachfront, water sports, bicycles, no elevato* ☰ *MC, V* †⊙*IEP.*

WHERE TO EAT

$–$$ ✕ **Island Thyme Bistro.** Owner Porter Williams serves potent alcoholi creations like the "Wolf" and other creatures, as well as fairly sophist cated local and international cuisine. Look for steamed, freshly caugh snapper served in a pepper wine sauce with peas and rice or spicy-ho chicken curry served with a tangy range of chutneys. The airy, tre lis-covered spot overlooks the salinas. This is the best place to eat o Salt Cay and the best place to catch up on island gossip. ⊠ *Nort District* ☎ 649/946–6977 ☰ *MC, V* ⊗ *Closed Wed. mid-May–Jun and Sept.–late Oct.*

$–$$ ✕ **Pat's Place.** Born and bred on the island, Pat Simmons can give yo a lesson in the medicinal qualities of her garden plants and periwinkl flowers as well as excellent native cuisine for a very reasonable pric in her typical Salt Cay home. Home cooking doesn't get any closer t home than this. Try conch fritters for lunch and her steamed groupe with okra rice for dinner. Be sure to call ahead, as she cooks onl when there's someone to cook for. ⊠ *South District* ☎ 649/946–691 ⚘ *Reservations essential* ☰ *No credit cards.*

BEACHES

★ The north coast of **Salt Cay** has superb beaches, with tiny, pretty shells and weathered sea glass. Accessible by boat with the on-island tour operators, **Big Sand Cay,** 7 mi (11 km) south of Salt Cay, is tiny and totally uninhabited, but it's also known for its long, unspoiled stretches of open sand.

SPORTS & THE OUTDOORS

DIVING & SNORKELING
Scuba divers can explore the wreck of the *Endymion,* a 140-foot wooden-hull British warship that sank in 1790. It's off the southern point of Salt Cay. **Salt Cay Divers** (⊠*Balfour Town* ☎*649/946–6906* ⊕*www.saltcaydivers.tc*) conducts daily trips and rents all the necessary equipment. It costs around $80 for a two-tank dive.

WHALE-WATCHING
During the winter months (January through April), Salt Cay is a center for whale-watching, when some 2,500 humpback whales pass close to shore. Whale-watching trips can most easily be organized through your inn or guesthouse.

EXPLORING SALT CAY

Salt sheds and salinas are silent reminders of the days when the island was a leading producer of salt. Now the salt ponds attract abundant birdlife. Island tours are often conducted by motorized golf cart. From January through April, humpback whales pass by on the way to their winter breeding grounds.

Balfour Town. What little development there is on Salt Cay is found here. It's home to several small hotels and a few cozy stores, as well as the main dock and the Green Flash Gazebo, where locals hang out with tourists to watch the sunset and sink a beer.

The grand stone **White House,** which once belonged to a wealthy salt merchant, is testimony to the heyday of Salt Cay's eponymous industry. Still privately owned by the descendants of the original family, it's sometimes opened up for tours. It's worth asking your guesthouse or hotel owner—or any local passerby—if Salt Cay islander "Uncle Lionel" is on-island, as he may give you a personal tour to see the still-intact, original furnishings, books, and medicine cabinet that date back to the early 1800s. ⊠*Victoria St., Balfour Town.*

6

TURKS & CAICOS ISLANDS ESSENTIALS

To research prices, get advice from other travelers, and book travel arrangements, visit www.fodors.com.

■ TRANSPORTATION

BY AIR

The main gateways into the regions are Providenciales International Airport and Grand Turk International Airport. For private planes, Provo Air Center is a full-service FBO (Fixed Base Operator) offering refueling, maintenance, and short-term storage, as well as on-site customs and immigration clearance, a lounge, and concierge services.

Although carriers and schedules can vary according to season, you can find nonstop and connecting flights to Providenciales from several U.S. cities on American, Delta, Spirit Airlines (weekly on Saturday or Sunday depending on the season), and US Airways. There are also flights from other parts of the Caribbean on Air Turks & Caicos and SkyKing; these airlines also fly to some of the smaller islands in the chain from Provo.

Airline Contacts Air Turks & Caicos (☎649/941–5481 ⊕www.airturksandcaicos. com). **American Airlines** (☎649/946–4948 or 800/433–7300). **Delta** (☎800/241–4141). **SkyKing** (☎649/941–5464 ⊕www.skyking. tc). **Spirit Airlines** (☎800/772-7117 ⊕www. spiritair.com). **US Airways** (☎800/622–1015).

Airport Contacts Grand Turk International Airport (GDT ☎649/946–2233). **Providenciales International Airport** (PLS ☎649/941–5670). **Provo Air Center** (☎649/946–4181 ⊕www.provoaircenter.com).

BY BOAT & FERRY

Begun in 2007, there is now scheduled ferry service on Caribbean Cruisin', which offers daily service with several departures between Provo and North Caicos

---

AIRLINE TIP

If you have an afternoon flight, check in your bags early in the morning (keep a change of clothes in a carry-on), then go back to the beach for one last lunch, returning to the airport an hour before your flight departs. It makes for much easier traveling, saves time, and you get your last beach fix.

---

from Walkin Marina in Leeward. There's a twice-weekly ferry from Salt Cay to Grand Turk (weather permitting).

Information Caribbean Cruisin' (✉Walkin Marina, Leeward, Providenciales ☎649/946–5406 or 649/231–4191 ⊕tcimall. tc/northcaicos/images/ferryservice.pdf ✉caribbeancruisin@gmail.com). **Salt Cay Ferry** (☎649/946–6909 ⊕www.turksand caicoswhalewatching.com).

BY CAR

Major reconstruction of Leeward Highway on Providenciales has been completed, and most of the road is now a four-lane divided highway complete with roundabouts. However, the paved two-lane roads through the settlements on Providenciales can be quite rough, although signage is improving. The less-traveled roads in Grand Turk and the family islands are, in general, smooth and paved. Gasoline is expensive, much more so than in the United States.

Driving here is on the left side of the road, British style; when pulling out into traffic, remember to look to your right. Give way to anyone entering a roundabout, as roundabouts are still a relatively new concept in the Turks & Caicos; stop even if you are on what appears to be the primary road. The maximum speed is 40 mph (64 kph), 20 mph (30 kph) through

:lements, and limits, as well as the use
seat belts, are enforced.

s and Budget have offices on the islands.
u might also try local agencies such as
ice Bay Car Rentals, Rent a Buggy, and
ppical Auto Rentals in Provo. Pelican
r Rentals is on North Caicos.

itacts **Avis** (⊠Providenciales
549/946–4705 ⊕www.avis.tc). **Budget**
Providenciales 🕾649/946–4079 ⊕www.
vo.net/budget). **Grace Bay Car Rentals**
Providenciales 🕾649/941–8500 ⊕www.
cebaycarrentals.com). **Pelican Car Rentals**
North Caicos 🕾649/241–8275). **Rent a**
ιgy (⊠Providenciales 🕾649/946–4158
vww.rentabuggy.tc). **Tropical Auto Rentals**
Providenciales 🕾649/946–5300 ⊕www.
vo.net/tropicalauto).

TAXI

bs (actually large vans) in Providencia-
are metered, and rates are regulated by
government at $2 per person per mile
veled. In Provo call the Provo Taxi &
s Group for more information. In the
iily islands, cabs may not be metered,
it's usually best to try to negotiate a
st for your trip when you book your
:i. Many resorts and car-rental agen-
s offer complimentary airport trans-
s. Ask ahead of time.

itact **Provo Taxi & Bus Group**
649/946–5481).

CONTACTS & RESOURCES

NKS & EXCHANGE SERVICES

:es quoted in this chapter are in U.S.
lars, which is the official currency
the islands. Major credit cards and
veler's checks are accepted at many
ablishments. There are ATMs at the
inches, at IGA Supermarket, Ports of
ll shopping center, and Ocean Club
za, all in Provo.

ptiabank and First Caribbean have
ces on Provo, with branches on Grand
rk. Many larger hotels can take care of
your money requests. Bring small denominations to the less-populated islands.

ELECTRICITY

Electricity is fairly stable throughout the
islands, and the current is suitable for all
U.S. appliances (120/240 volts, 60 Hz).

EMERGENCIES

Emergency Services Ambulance & Fire
(🕾999 or 911). **Police** (🕾649/946–2499 in
Grand Turk, 649/946–7116 in North Caicos,
649/946–4259 in Provo, 649/946–3299 in
South Caicos).

Hospitals Associated Medical Practices
(⊠Leeward Hwy., Glass Shack, Providenciales
🕾649/946–4242). **Grand Turk Hospital**
(⊠Hospital Rd., Grand Turk 🕾649/946–2040).

Scuba Diving Emergencies Associated
Medical Practices (⊠Leeward Hwy., Glass
Shack, Providenciales 🕾649/946–4242).

INTERNET, MAIL & SHIPPING

The majority of resorts on the Turks &
Caicos offer Wi-Fi service in their public
areas, if not in the rooms, so you can keep
up with e-mail and the Internet. There are
also several Internet cafés, including one
in the Ports of Call mall on Provo.

The post office is in downtown Provo at
the corner of Airport Road. Collectors
will be interested in the wide selection
of stamps sold by the Philatelic Bureau.
It costs 50¢ to send a postcard to the
United States, 60¢ to Canada and the
United Kingdom, and $1.25 to Australia
and New Zealand; letters, per ½ ounce,
cost 60¢ to the United States, 80¢ to Canada and the United Kingdom, and $1.40
to Australia and New Zealand. When
writing to the Turks & Caicos Islands,
be sure to include the specific island and
"Turks & Caicos Islands, BWI" (British West Indies). Delivery service is provided by FedEx, with offices in Provo and
Grand Turk.

Contacts FedEx (🕾649/946–4682 on Provo).
Philatelic Bureau (🕾649/946–1534).

6

SAFETY

Although crime is not a major concern in the Turks & Caicos Islands, petty theft does occur here, and you're advised to leave your valuables in the hotel safe-deposit box and lock doors in cars and rooms when unattended.

TAXES & SERVICE CHARGES

The departure tax is $35 and is usually built into the cost of your tickets. If not, it's payable only in cash or traveler's checks. Restaurants and hotels add a 10% government tax. Hotels also add 10% to 15% for service.

TELEPHONES

The area code for the Turks & Caicos is 649. Just dial 1 plus the 10-digit number, including area code, from the United States. To make local calls, dial the seven-digit number. To make calls from the Turks & Caicos, dial 0, then 1, the area code, and the number.

All telephone service is provided by Cable & Wireless and Digicel. Many U.S.–based cell phones work on the islands; use your own or rent one from Cable & Wireless. Internet access is available via hotel-room phone connections or Internet kiosks on Provo and Grand Turk. You can also connect to the World Wide Web from any telephone line by dialing C-O-N-N-E-C-T to call Cable & Wireless and using the user name *easy* and the password *access*. Calls from the islands are expensive, and many hotels add steep surcharges for long distance. Talk fast.

Information Digicel TCI (⊕ www.digiceltci. com). **Cable & Wireless** (☎ 649/946–2200, 800/744–7777 for long distance, 649/266–6328 for Internet access, 811 for mobile service ⊕ www.tcimall.tc).

TIPPING

At restaurants, tip 15% if service isn't included in the bill. Taxi drivers also expect a token tip, about 10% of your fare.

CELL PHONE TIPS

You can purchase a cheap cell phone at numerous outlets and simply "top-up" (pay as you go). Incoming calls are free, and with the cheap cell, you'll have service even on secluded and isolated beaches. Have your family call you to save on exorbitant island rates and huge roaming charges. Not all cell phones from home will work in the T&C (some do, but you never know which ones until you're actually on-island), even if the phone company tells you it does.

TOUR OPTIONS

Whether by taxi, boat, or plane, you should try to venture beyond your resort's grounds and beach. The natural environment is one of the main attractions of the Turks & Caicos, yet few people explore beyond the natural wonder of the beach. Big Blue Unlimited has taken ecotouring to a whole new level with educational ecotours, including three-hour kayak trips and more-land-based guided journeys around the family islands. The Coastal Ecology and Wildlife tour is a kayak adventure through red mangroves to bird habitats, rock iguana hideaways, and natural fish nurseries. The North Caicos Mountain Bike Eco Tour gets you on a bike exploring the island, the plantation ruins, the inland lakes, and a flamingo pond with a stop-off at Susan Butterfield's home for lunch. Package costs range from $85 to $225 per person. J&B Tours offers sea and land tours including trips to Middle Caicos, the largest of the islands, for a visit to the caves or to North Caicos to see flamingos and plantation ruins. Nell's Taxi offers taxi tours of the islands, priced between $25 and $30 for the first hour and $25 for each additional hour.

Special day excursions are available from local airline Air Turks & Caicos. Trips include whale-watching in Salt Cay, and if you venture to Middle Caicos and North Caicos, in addition to flights, you get a

ap, water, a lunch voucher, and a moun-
in bike to explore for the day. Trips
art from $99, which includes round-
ip air tickets. Day trips to Grand Turk
e available with SkyKing. For around
179, you get a round-trip flight to the
pital island, a short tour, admission to
e Turks & Caicos National Museum,
stop off for lunch, and time to explore
1 your own.

ntacts **Air Turks & Caicos** (☎649/946–
81 or 649/946–4181 ⊕www.airturks
dcaicos.com). **Big Blue Unlimited**
⊠Leeward Marina, Leeward, Providenciales
☎649/946–5034 ⊕www.bigblue.tc). **J&B**
urs (☎649/946–5047 ⊕www.jbtours.
m). **Nell's Taxi** (☎649/231–0051). **SkyKing**
☎649/941–5464 ⊕www.skyking.tc).

ISITOR INFORMATION

he tourist offices on Grand Turk and
rovidenciales are open daily from 9 to 5.

fore You Leave **Turks & Caicos Islands
urist Board** (954/568–6588 in Ft. Lauder-
le or 800/241–0824 ⊕www.turksandcaicos
urism.com).

Turks & Caicos Islands **Turks & Caicos
lands Tourist Board** (⊠Front St., Cock-
rn Town, Grand Turk ☎649/946–2321
⊠Stubbs Diamond Plaza, The Bight, Provi-
nciales ☎649/946–4970 ⊕www.turks
dcaicostourism.com).

WEDDINGS

Beautiful oceanfront backdrops, endless
starlight nights, and a bevy of romantic
accommodations make the islands an
ideal wedding destination. The residency
requirement is only 24 hours, after which
you can apply for a marriage license to
the registrar in Grand Turk; the ceremony
can take place at any time after the appli-
cation has been granted, generally within
two to three days. You must present a
passport, original birth certificate, and
proof of current marital status, as well
as a letter stating both parties' occupa-
tions, ages, addresses, and fathers' full
names. No blood tests are required, and
the license fee is $50. The ceremony is
conducted by a local minister, justice of
the peace, or the registrar. The marriage
certificate is filed in the islands, although
copies can be sent to your home. There
are a number of wedding coordinators
on-island, and many resorts offer special
wedding packages, which include handling all the details.

Contact **Nila Destinations Wedding
Planning** (☎649/941–4375 ⊕www.
nilavacations.com).

6

UNDERSTANDING
THE BAHAMAS

BAHAMAS AT A GLANCE

FAST FACTS

Type of government: Constitutional parliamentary democracy

Capital: Nassau

Administrative divisions: 21 districts: Acklins and Crooked Islands, Bimini, Cat Island, Exuma, Freeport, Fresh Creek, Governor's Harbour, Green Turtle Cay, Harbour Island, High Rock, Inagua, Kemps Bay, Long Island, Marsh Harbour, Mayaguana, New Providence, Nichollstown and Berry Islands, Ragged Island, Rock Sound, Sandy Point, San Salvador and Rum Cay

Independence: July 10, 1973 (from the United Kingdom)

Legal system: Based on English common law; Privy Council, Supreme Court, Court of Appeal, magistrates courts

Legislature: Bicameral parliament: upper house: 16-member appointed Senate; lower house: 40-member elected House of Assembly

Population: 303, 770

Birth Rate: 17.57 births per 1,000 population

Infant Mortality: 24.68 deaths per 1,000 live births; female: 18.96; male: 30.29

Language: English, Creole (among Haitian immigrants), and strong Bahamian dialect

Ethnic groups: Bahamians are mainly of African descent—85% black, 12% white, and 3% Asian and Hispanic

Life expectancy: Male, 62.24; female, 69.03

Literacy: Total population: 95.6%; male: 94.7%; female, 96.5%

Religion: Dominant religion: Christianity; largest three denominations: Baptist, 35.4%; Anglican, 15.1%; and Roman Catholic, 13.5%

Other denominations and religions represented: Assembly of God, Ba'hai faith, Brethren, Christian and Missionary Alliance, Christian Science, Church of God of Prophecy, Greek Orthodox, Jehovah's Witnesses, Jewish, Latter-day Saint (Mormon), Lutheran, Methodist, Presbyterian, and Seventh Day Adventist

GEOGRAPHY

Location: The archipelago of the island of the Bahamas is in the Atlantic Ocean extending more than 650 miles from the eastern coast of Florida to the southeastern tip of Cuba. Of the some 700 island and almost 2,500 small islets of cays approximately 30 are inhabited.

Coastline: 2,201 mi

Area: Total: 5,382 square mi; land 3,888 square mi; water, 1,494 square mi; about the size of the state of Connecticut in the U.S.

Climate: Tropical marine; moderated by warm waters of the Gulf Stream

Terrain: Long, flat coral formations with some low, rounded hills

Islands: New Providence Island, home to the capital Nassau; Grand Bahama Island and other inhabited islands officially called the Family Islands but commonly known as the Out Islands, including The Abacos, Andros, Cat Island, The Biminis, The Berries, Eleuthera, The Exumas, and Long Island

Natural resources: Salt, aragonite, timber, arable land

Natural hazards: Hurricanes and other tropical storms that cause extensive flooding and wind damage

ECONOMY

Inflation: 1.4%

Unemployment: 10.2%

GDP per capita: $20,200

GDP: $6.1 billion (2005)

Agriculture: Citrus, vegetables, and poultry

Industry: Tourism, banking, cement, salt, rum, oil, transshipment, aragonite, pharmaceuticals, and spiral-welded steel pipe

Work force: Tourism, 50%; other services, 40%; industry, 5%; agriculture, 5%

rrency: Bahamian dollar (U.S. dollar
dely accepted)

change rate: One Bahamian dollar per
S. dollar

bt (external): $342.6 million (2004)

onomic aid: $5 million (2004)

jor export products: Animal products,
m, mineral products and salt, chemi-
ls, fruit and vegetables

port partners U.S., 40.5%; Poland, 13.4;
ain, 12.3; Germany, 5.9%; France,
3%

ports: Machinery and transport equip-
nt, manufactures, chemicals, mineral
els, food and live animals

port partners: U.S., 22.4%; South Korea,
.9%; Brazil, 9.2%; Japan, 7.9%; Italy,
3%; Venezuala 6.6%.

NVIRONMENT

vironmental issues: Coral reef decay,
lid waste disposal

DID YOU KNOW?

■ The Bahamas is a stable, developing nation;
its economy is predominantly dependent
on tourism and offshore banking.

■ Tourism and tourism-driven construction
and manufacturing account for 60% of
the GDP and employ about half of the
labor force.

■ Arawak Indians inhabited the islands
when Christopher Columbus first landed in
the New World on San Salvador in 1492.

■ British settlement of the islands began in
1647; they became a colony in 1783.

■ Since attaining independence from the
U.K. in 1973, the Bahamas has prospered
through tourism, international banking,
and investment management.

■ Because of its geography, the country is
a major transshipment point for illegal
drugs, particularly shipments to the U.S.,
and its territory is used for smuggling illegal migrants into the U.S.

IN THE WAKE OF COLUMBUS: A SHORT HISTORY OF THE BAHAMAS

YOU MIGHT CALL CHRISTOPHER COLUMBUS the first tourist to hit the Bahamas, although he was actually trying to find a route to the East Indies with his *Niña, Pinta,* and *Santa María.* Columbus is popularly believed to have made his first landfall in the New World on October 12, 1492, at San Salvador, in the southern part of the Bahamas. Researchers of the National Geographic Society, however, have come up with the theory that he may first have set foot ashore Samana Cay, some 60 mi southeast of San Salvador. The Bahamians have taken this new theory under consideration, if not too seriously; tradition dies hard in the islands, and they are hardly likely to tear down the New World landfall monument on San Salvador.

The people who met Columbus on his landing day were Arawak Indians, said to have fled from the Caribbean to the Bahamas to escape the depredations of the murderous Caribs around the turn of the 9th century. The Arawaks were a shy, gentle people who offered Columbus and his men their hospitality. He was impressed with their kindness and more than slightly intrigued by the gold ornaments they wore. But the voracious Spaniards who followed in Columbus's footsteps a few years later repaid the Indians' kindness by forcing them to work in the conquistadors' gold and silver mines in Cuba and Haiti; the Bahamas' indigenous peoples were virtually wiped out in the next 30 years, despite the fact that the Spaniards never settled their land.

In 1513 another well-known seafarer stumbled upon the westernmost Bahamian islands. Juan Ponce de León had been a passenger on Columbus's second voyage, in 1493. He conquered Puerto Rico in 1508 and then began searching thirstily for the Fountain of Youth. He thought he had found it on South Bimini, but he changed his mind and moved on to visit the site of St. Augustine, on the northeast coast of Florida.

In 1629 King Charles I claimed the Bahamas for England, though his edict was not implemented until the arrival of English pilgrims in 1648. Having fled the religious repression and political dissension then rocking their country, they settled on the Bahamian island they christened Eleuthera, the Greek word for freedom. Other English immigrants followed, and in 1656 another group of pilgrims, from Bermuda, took over a Bahamian island to the west and named it New Providence because of their links with Providence, Rhode Island. By the last part of the 17th century, some 1,100 settlers were trying to eke out a living, supplemented by the cargoes they salvaged from Spanish galleons that ran aground on the reefs. Many settlers were inclined to give nature a hand by enticing these ships onto the reefs with lights.

Inevitably, the British settlers were joined by a more nefarious subset of humanity, pirates and buccaneers like Edward Teach (better known as Blackbeard, he was said to have had 14 wives), Henry Morgan, and Calico Jack Rackham. Rackham numbered among his crew two violent, cutlass-wielding female members, Anne Bonney and Mary Read, who are said to have disconcerted enemies by swinging aboard their vessels topless. Bonney and Read escaped hanging in Jamaica by feigning pregnancy.

For some 40 years until 1718, pirates in the Bahamas constantly raided the Spanish galleons that carried booty home from the New World. During this period, the Spanish government, furious at the raids, sent ships and troops to destroy the New Providence city of Charles Town, which was later rebuilt and renamed Nassau, in 1695, in honor of King William III, formerly William of Orange-Nassau.

1718 King George I appointed Cap-
Woodes Rogers the first royal gover-
of the Bahamas, with orders to clean
the place. Why the king chose Rog-
for this particular job is unclear—his
king may well have been that it takes
rate to know one, for Woodes Rog-
had been a privateer. But he did take
trol of Nassau, hanging eight pirates
n trees on the site of what was to
ome the British Colonial Hotel.
ay, a statue of the former governor
ds at the hotel entrance, and the
et that runs along the waterfront is
ned after him. Rogers also inspired
saying *Expulsis piratis, restitua
mercia* (Piracy expelled, commerce
ored), which remained the country's
tto until Prime Minister Lynden O.
dling replaced it with the more appro-
te and optimistic Forward, Upward,
ward Together, on the occasion of
pendence from Britain in 1973.

ough the Bahamas enjoyed a certain
sure of tranquillity, thanks to Rogers
the governors who followed him, the
ish colonies in America at the same
e were seething with a desire for
pendence. The peace of the island-
lives was to be shattered during the
olutionary War by a raid in 1778 on
sau by the American navy, which
oined the city's arms and ammuni-
without even firing a shot. Next, in
2, the Spanish came to occupy the
amas until the following year. Under
Treaty of Versailles of 1783, Spain
k possession of Florida, and the Baha-
reverted to British rule.

**BAHAMAS WERE ONCE AGAIN
ERRUN,** between 1784 and 1789,
time by merchants from New Eng-
d and plantation owners from Vir-
a and the Carolinas who had been
l to the British and were fleeing the
th of the American revolutionaries.
king asylum under the British flag,
Southerners brought their families
slaves with them. Many set up new

plantations in the islands, but frustrated
by the islands' arid soil, they soon opted
for greener pastures in the Caribbean.
The slaves they left behind were set free
in 1834, but many retained the names
of their former masters. That is why
you'll find many a Johnson, Saunders,
and Thompson in the towns and villages
throughout the Bahamas.

The land may have been less than fertile,
but New Providence Island's almost perfect climate, marred only by the potential
for hurricanes during the fall, attracted
other interest. Tourism was foreseen as
far back as 1861, when the legislature
approved the building of the first hotel,
the Royal Victoria. Though it was to
reign as the grande dame of the island's
hotels for more than a century, its early
days saw it involved in an entirely different profit-making venture. During
the U.S. Civil War, the Northern forces
blockaded the main Southern ports, and
the leaders of the Confederacy turned to
Nassau, the closest neutral port to the
south. The Royal Victoria became the
headquarters of the blockade-running
industry, which reaped huge profits for
the British colonial government from the
duties it imposed on arms supplies. (In
October 1990, the Royal Victoria Hotel
burned down.)

A similar bonanza, also at the expense
of the United States, was to come in the
1920s, after Prohibition was signed into
U.S. law in 1919. Booze brought into
the Bahamas from Europe was funneled
into a thirsty United States by rumrunners operating out of Nassau, Bimini,
and West End, the community on Grand
Bahama Island east of Palm Beach. Rac-
ing against, and often exchanging gun-
fire with, Coast Guard patrol boats, the
rumrunners dropped off their supplies
in Miami, the Florida Keys, and other
Florida destinations, making their con-
tribution to the era known as the Roaring '20s.

Even then, tourists were beginning to trickle into the Bahamas, many in opulent yachts belonging to the likes of Whitney, Vanderbilt, and Astor. In 1929 a new airline, Pan American, started to make daily flights from Miami to Nassau. The Royal Victoria, shedding its shady past, and two new hotels, the Colonial (now the British Colonial Hilton Nassau) and the Fort Montagu Beach, were all in full operation. Nassau even had instant communication with the outside world: A few miles northwest of the Colonial, a subterranean telegraph cable had been laid linking New Providence with Jupiter, Florida. It took no flash of inspiration to name the area Cable Beach.

One of the most colorful and enigmatic characters of the era, Sir Harry Oakes, came to Nassau in the 1930s from Canada. He built the Bahamas Country Club and the Cable Beach Golf Course; he also built Nassau's first airport in the late '30s to lure the well-heeled and to make commuting easier for the wealthy residents. Oakes Field can still be seen on the ride from Nassau International Airport to Cable Beach.

Oakes was to die in an atmosphere of eerie and mysterious intrigue. Only his good friend, the late Sir Harold Christie, a powerful real-estate tycoon, was in the house at the time that Oakes' body was found, battered and burned. This was a period when all of the news that was fit to print was coming out of the war theaters in Europe and the Far East, but the Miami newspapers and wire services had a field day with the society murder.

Although a gruff, unlikable character, Oakes had no known enemies, but there was speculation that mob hit men from Miami had come over and taken care of him because of his unyielding opposition to the introduction of gambling casinos to the Bahamas. Finally, two detectives brought from Miami pinned the murder on Oakes' son-in-law, Count Alfred de Marigny, for whom the Canadian

was known to have a strong dislike. D Marigny was tried and acquitted in a overcrowded Nassau court. Much of th detectives' research and testimony wa later discredited. For many years after ward, however, the mysterious and stil unsolved crime was a sore point wit New Providence residents.

During World War II, New Providenc also played host to a noble, if unlikely couple. In 1936 the Duke of Windsor ha forsaken the British throne in favor o "the woman I love," an American divor cée named Wallis Warfield Simpson, an the couple temporarily found a carefre life in Paris and the French Riviera. Whe the Nazis overran France, they fled t neutral Portugal. Secret papers reveale after the war suggest that the German had plans to use the duke and duchess, b kidnapping if necessary, as pawns in th German war against Britain. This woul have taken the form of declaring ther king and queen in exile, and seating ther on the throne when Hitler's assumed vic tory was accomplished.

Word of the plot might have reached th ears of Britain's wartime prime minis ter, Winston Churchill, who encourage King George VI, the duke's younge brother and his successor, to send th couple as far away as possible out c harm's way. In 1939 the duke had brief returned to England, offering his service to his brother in the war effort. He wa given a position of perhaps less impor than he had expected, for he and Walli suddenly found themselves in the Baha mas, with the duke as governor an commander in chief.

CHANGES IN THE BAHAMAS' POLIT CAL CLIMATE had to wait for the war end. For more than 300 years, the coun try had been ruled by whites; members c the United Bahamian Party (UBP) wer known as the Bay Street Boys, after Nas sau's main business thoroughfare, becaus they controlled the islands' commerce But the voice of the overwhelmingly blac

ajority was making itself heard. In 1953
London-educated black barrister named
nden O. Pindling joined the opposition
ogressive Liberal Party (PLP); in 1956
e was elected to Parliament.

ndling continued to stir the growing
sentiment most Bahamians now had for
e Bay Street Boys, and his parliamentary
havior became more and more defiant.
1965, during one parliamentary ses-
on, he picked up the speaker's mace and
rew it out the window. Because this
ace has to be present and in sight at
l sessions, deliberations had to be sus-
nded; meanwhile, Pindling continued
s harangue to an enthusiastic throng in
e street below. Two years later, Baha-
ian voters threw the UBP out, and Pin-
ing led the PLP into power.

ndling's magnetism kept him in power
rough independence from Britain in
73 (though loyalty to the mother
untry led the Bahamians to choose to
main within the Commonwealth of
ations, recognize Queen Elizabeth II
their sovereign, and retain a governor-
neral appointed by the queen). For his
rvices to his nation, the prime minister
as knighted by the queen in 1983. His
puty prime minister Clement Maynard
ceived the same accolade in 1989.

In August 1992 there came the biggest
political upset since Pindling took power
in 1967. His Progressive Liberal Party
was defeated in a general election by the
Free National Movement party, headed
by lawyer Hubert Alexander Ingraham.
The 45-year-old former chairman of the
PLP and Cabinet member under Pindling
had been expelled from the party by Pindling in 1986 because of his outspoken
comments on alleged corruption inside
the government. Ingraham's continued
emphasis on this issue during the 1992
campaign did much to lead to Pindling's
defeat and Ingraham's taking over as
prime minister. Ingraham was reelected
for another five-year term in 1996. In
May 2002, the PLP again took the reigns
with the election of the Right Honour-
able Perry G. Christie.

Residents, for the most part, are proud
of their country and are actively involved
in bettering their own lot—the last complete census showed about 27% of the
population was attending school at one
level or another. And in the spirit of their
national motto—Forward, Upward,
Onward Together—they graciously welcome the ever-increasing numbers of
outsiders who have discovered their little
piece of paradise.

—Ian Glass

CASHING IN: A CASINO GAMBLING PRIMER

For a short-form handbook on the rules, the plays, the odds, and the strategies for the most popular casino games—or to decide on the kind of action that's for you and suits your style—read on. You must be 18 to gamble; Bahamians and permanent residents are not permitted to indulge.

The Good Bets

The first part of any viable casino strategy is to risk the most money on wagers that present the lowest edge for the house. Blackjack, craps, video poker, and baccarat are the most advantageous to the bettor in this regard. The two types of bets at baccarat have a house advantage of a little more than 1%. The basic line bets at craps, if backed up with full odds, can be as low as ½%. Blackjack and video poker, at times, can not only put you even with the house (a true 50–50 proposition), but actually give you a slight long-term advantage.

How can a casino possibly provide you with a 50–50 or even a positive expectation at some of its games? First, because a vast number of suckers make the bad bets (those with a house advantage of 5%–35%, such as roulette, keno, and slots) day in and day out. Second, because the casino knows that very few people are aware of the opportunities to beat the odds. Third, because it takes skill—requiring study and practice—to be in a position to exploit these opportunities the casino presents. However, a mere hour or two spent learning strategies for the beatable games will put you light years ahead of the vast majority of visitors who give the gambling industry an average 12% to 15% profit margin.

Baccarat

The most "glamorous" game in the casino, baccarat (pronounced *bah*-kuh-rah) is a version of *chemin de fer*, popular in European gambling halls, and is a favorite with high rollers, because thou sands of dollars are often staked on on hand. The Italian word *baccara* mean "zero"; this refers to the point value o 10s and picture cards. The game is ru by four pit personnel. Two dealers sit sid by side in the middle of the table; the handle the winning and losing bets an keep track of each player's "commission (explained below). The "caller" stands i the middle of the other side of the tabl and dictates the action. The ladderma supervises the game and acts as fina judge if any disputes arise.

How to Play. Baccarat is played wit eight decks of cards dealt from a larg "shoe" (or cardholder). Each player offered a turn at handling the shoe an dealing the cards. Two two-card hand are dealt, the "player" and the "bank hands. The player who deals the card is called the banker, though the hous of course, banks both hands. The playe bet on which hand, player or banker, wi come closest to adding up to 9 (a "natu ral"). The cards are totaled as follow ace through 9 retain face value, whi 10s and picture cards are worth zero. you have a hand adding up to more tha 10, the number 10 is subtracted from th total. For example, if one hand contair a 10 and a 4, the hand adds up to 4. If th other holds an ace and 6, it adds up to If a hand has a 7 and 9, it adds up to 6

Depending on the two hands, the calle either declares a winner and loser (either hand actually adds up to 8 or 9 or calls for another card for the playe hand (if it totals 1, 2, 3, 4, 5, or 10 The bank hand then either stands pat draws a card, determined by a comple series of rules depending on what th player's total is and dictated by the calle When one or the other hand is declared winner, the dealers go into action to pa off the winning wagers, collect the lo ing wagers, and add up the commissi ally 5%) that the house collects on bank hand. Both bets have a house antage of slightly more than 1%.

player-dealer (or banker) contin- to hold the shoe as long as the bank d wins. As soon as the player hand s, the shoe moves counterclockwise ind the table. Players are not required eal; they can refuse the shoe and pass the next player. Because the caller ates the action, the player responsi- ies are minimal. It's not necessary to w any of the card-drawing rules, even u're the banker.

arat Strategy. Making a bet at bac- t is very simple. All you have to do lace your money in either the bank, er, or tie box on the layout, which ears directly in front of where you t the table. If you're betting that the k hand will win, you put your chips e bank box; bets for the player hand n the player box. (Only real suckers on the tie.) Most players bet on the k hand when they deal, since they 'resent" the bank, and to do other- would seem as if they were betting inst" themselves. (This isn't really , but it seems that way.) In the end, ing baccarat is a simple matter of sing whether the player or banker d will come closest to 9, and deciding much to bet on the outcome.

ckjack

to Play. Basically, here's how it works: play blackjack against a dealer, and hever of you comes closest to a card of 21 is the winner. Number cards worth their face value, picture cards worth 10, and aces are worth either 11. (Hands with aces in them are vn as "soft" hands. Always count ice first as an 11; if you also have a our total will be 21, not 11.) If the er has a 17 and you have a 16, you If you have an 18 against a dealer's you win (even money). If both you the dealer have a 17, it's a tie (or h") and no money changes hands. If

you go over a total of 21 (or "bust"), you lose immediately, even if the dealer also busts later in the hand. If your first two cards add up to 21 (a "natural"), you're paid 3 to 2. However, if the dealer also has a natural, it's a push. A natural beats a total of 21 achieved with more than two cards.

You're dealt two cards, either face down or face up, depending on the custom of the particular casino. The dealer also gives herself two cards, one face down and one face up (except in double-expo- sure blackjack, where both the dealer's cards are visible). Depending on your first two cards and the dealer's up card, you can **stand,** or refuse to take another card. You can **hit,** or take as many cards as you need until you stand or bust. You can **double down,** or double your bet and take one card. You can **split** a like pair; if you're dealt two 8s, for example, you can double your bet and play the 8s as if they're two hands. You can **buy insur- ance** if the dealer is showing an ace. Here you're wagering half your initial bet that the dealer *does* have a natural; if so, you lose your initial bet, but are paid 2 to 1 on the insurance (which means the whole thing is a push). You can **surrender** half your initial bet if you're holding a bad hand (known as a "stiff") such as a 15 or 16 against a high-up card like a 9 or 10.

Blackjack Strategy. Playing blackjack is not only knowing the rules—it's also knowing *how* to play. Many people devote a great deal of time to learning complicated statistical schemes. How- ever, if you don't have the time, energy, or inclination to get that seriously involved, the following basic strategies, which cover more than half the situa- tions you'll face, should allow you to play the game with a modicum of skill and a paucity of humiliation:

■ When your hand is a stiff (a total of 12, 13, 14, 15, or 16) and the dealer shows a 2, 3, 4, 5, or 6, always stand.

- When your hand is a stiff and the dealer shows a 7, 8, 9, 10, or ace, always hit.

- When you hold 17, 18, 19, or 20, always stand.

- When you hold a 10 or 11 and the dealer shows a 2, 3, 4, 5, 6, 7, 8, or 9, always double down.

- When you hold a pair of aces or a pair of 8s, always split.

- Never buy insurance.

Craps

Craps is a dice game played at a large rectangular table with rounded corners. Up to 12 players can crowd around the table, all standing. The layout is mounted at the bottom of a surrounding "rail," which prevents the dice from being thrown off the table and provides an opposite wall against which to bounce the dice. It can require up to four pit personnel to run an action-packed, fast-paced game of craps. Two dealers handle the bets made on either side of the layout. A "stickman" wields the long wooden "stick," curved at one end, which is used to move the dice around the table; the stickman also calls the number that's rolled and books the proposition bets made in the middle of the layout. The "boxman" sits between the two dealers and oversees the game; he settles any disputes about rules, payoffs, mistakes, and so on.

How to Play. To play, just stand at the table wherever you can find an open space. You can start betting casino chips immediately, but you have to wait your turn to be the shooter. The dice move around the table in a clockwise fashion: The person to your right shoots before you, the one to the left after (the stickman will give you the dice at the appropriate time). It's important, when you're the "shooter," to roll the dice hard enough so they bounce off the end wall of the table; this ensures a random bounce and shows that you're not trying to control the dice with a "soft roll."

Craps Strategy. Playing craps is fairly straightforward; it's the betting that's complicated. The basic concepts are as follows: If, the first time the shooter rolls the dice, he or she turns up a 7 or 11, that's called a "natural"—an automatic win. If a 2, 3, or 12 comes up on the first throw (called the "come-out roll"), that's termed "craps"—an automatic lose. Each of the numbers 4, 5, 6, 8, 9, or 10 on a first roll is known as a "point": The shooter keeps rolling the dice until the point comes up again. If a 7 turns up before the point does, that's another loser. When either the point or a losing 7 is rolled, this is known as a "decision," which happens on average every 3.3 rolls.

But "winning" and "losing" rolls of the dice are entirely relative in this game, because there are two ways you can bet at craps: "for" the shooter or "against" the shooter. Betting for means that the shooter will "make his point" (win). Betting against means that the shooter will "seven out" (lose). (Either way, you're actually betting against the house, which books all wagers.) If you're betting "for" on the come-out, you'd place your chips on the layout's "pass line." If a 7 or 11 is rolled, you win even money. If a 2, 3, or 12 (craps) is rolled, you lose your bet. If you're betting "against" on the come-out, you place your chips in the "don't pass bar." A 7 or 11 loses, a 2, 3, or 12 wins. A shooter can bet for or against himself or herself, as well as for or against the other players.

There are also roughly two dozen wagers you can make on any single specific roll of the dice. Craps strategy books can give you the details on Come/Don't Come, Odds, Place, Buy, Big Six, Field, and Proposition bets.

Roulette

Roulette is a casino game that utilizes a perfectly balanced wheel with 38 numbers (0, 00, and 1 through 36), a small white ball, a large layout with 11 differ-

betting options, and special "wheel
os." The layout organizes 11 differ-
bets into six "inside bets" (the single
nbers, or those closest to the dealer)
five "outside bets" (the grouped bets,
hose closest to the players).

dealer spins the wheel clockwise and
ball counterclockwise. When the ball
vs, the dealer announces, "No more
." The ball drops from the "back
k" to the "bottom track," caroming
built-in brass barriers and bouncing
nd out of the different cups in the
el before settling into the cup of the
ning number. Then the dealer places a
ker on the number and scoops all the
ng chips into her corner. Depending
now crowded the game is, the casino
count on roughly 50 spins of the
el per hour.

to Play. To buy in, place your cash
he layout near the wheel. Inform the
er of the denomination of the individ-
unit you intend to play (usually 25¢
1, but it can go up as high as $500).
w the table limits (displayed on a sign
ne dealer area)—don't ask for a 25¢
omination if the minimum is $1. The
er gives you a stack of wheel chips
different color from those of all the
r players, and places a chip marker
one of your wheel chips on the rim
he wheel to identify its denomina-
. Note that you must cash in your
el chips at the roulette table before
leave the game. Only the dealer can
y how much they're worth.

ette Strategy. With **inside bets,** you
lay any number of chips (depending
he table limits) on a single number,
rough 36 or 0 or 00. If the number
your payoff is 35 to 1, for a return
36. You could, conceivably, place
chip on all 38 numbers, but the
n of $36 would leave you $2 short,
h divides out to 5.26%, the house
ntage. If you place a chip on the line
veen two numbers and one of those
bers hits, you're paid 17 to 1 for a

return of $18 (again, $2 short of the true
odds). Betting on three numbers returns
11 to 1, four numbers returns 8 to 1, five
numbers pays 6 to 1 (this is the worst bet
at roulette, with a 7.89% disadvantage),
and six numbers pays 5 to 1.

To place an **outside bet,** lay a chip on one
of three "columns" at the lower end
of the layout next to numbers 34, 35,
and 36; this pays 2 to 1. A bet placed
in the first 12, second 12, or third 12
boxes also pays 2 to 1. A bet on red or
black, odd or even, and 1 through 18 or
19 through 36 pays off at even money,
1 to 1. If you think you can bet on red
and black, or odd *and* even, in order to
play roulette and drink for free all night,
think again. The green 0 or 00, which
fall outside these two basic categories,
will come up on average once every 19
spins of the wheel.

Slot Machines

Around the turn of the 20th century,
Charlie Fey built the first mechanical
slot in his San Francisco basement. Slot-
machine technology has exploded in the
past 20 years, and now there are hundreds of different models, which accept
everything from pennies to specially
minted $500 tokens. The major advance
in the game, however, is the progressive
jackpot. Banks of slots within a particular casino are connected by computer, and the jackpot total is displayed
on a digital meter above the machines.
Generally, the total increases by 5%
of the wager. If you're playing a dollar
machine, each time you pull the handle
(or press the spin button), a nickel is
added to the jackpot.

How to Play. To play, insert your penny,
nickel, quarter, silver dollar, or dollar
token into the slot at the far right edge
of the machine. Pull the handle or press
the spin button, then wait for the reels
to spin and stop one by one, and for the
machine to determine whether you're
a winner (occasionally) or a loser (the
rest of the time). It's pretty simple—but

because there are so many different types of machines nowadays, be sure you know exactly how the one you're playing operates.

Slot-Machine Strategy. The house advantage on slots varies widely from machine to machine, between 3% and 25%. Casinos that advertise a 97% payback are telling you that at least one of their slot machines has a house advantage of 3%. Which one? There's really no way of knowing. Generally, $1 machines pay back at a higher percentage than quarter or nickel machines. On the other hand, machines with smaller jackpots pay back more money more frequently, meaning that you'll be playing with more of your winnings.

One of the all-time great myths about slot machines is that they're "due" for a jackpot. Slots, like roulette, craps, keno, and Big Six, are subject to the Law of Independent Trials, which means the odds are permanently and unalterably fixed. If the odds of lining up three sevens on a 25¢ slot machine have been set by the casino at 1 in 10,000, then those odds remain 1 in 10,000 whether the three 7s have been hit three times in a row or not hit for 90,000 plays. Don't waste a lot of time playing a machine that you suspect is "ready," and don't think if someone hits a jackpot on a particular machine only minutes after you've finished playing on it that it was "yours."

Video Poker

Like blackjack, video poker is a game of strategy and skill, and at select times on select machines, the player actually holds the advantage, however slight, over the house. Unlike slot machines, you can determine the exact edge of video poker machines. Like slots, however, video poker machines are often tied into a progressive meter; when the jackpot total reaches high enough, you can beat the casino at its own game. The variety of video poker machines is already large, and it's growing steadily larger. All of the different machines are played in similar fashion, but the strategies are differen[t] This section deals only with straigh[t] draw video poker.

How to Play. The schedule for the pay[-] back on winning hands is posted on th[e] machine, usually above the screen. [It] lists the returns for a high pair (generall[y] jacks or better), two pair, three of a kin[d,] a flush, full house, straight flush, four [of] a kind, and royal flush, depending on th[e] number of coins played—usually 1, 2, [3,] 4, or 5. Look for machines that pay wit[h] a single coin played: one coin for "jack[s] or better" (meaning a pair of jack[s,] queens, kings, or aces; any other pair [is] a stiff), two coins for two pairs, three f[or] three of a kind, six for a flush, nine f[or] a full house, 50 for a straight flush, 10[0] for four of a kind, and 250 for a roy[al] flush. This is known as a 9/6 machine— one that gives a nine-coin payback f[or] the full house and a six-coin paybac[k] for the flush with one coin played. Oth[er] machines are known as 8/5 (8 for the fu[ll] house, 5 for the flush), 7/5, and 6/5.

You want a 9/6 machine because it giv[es] you the best odds: The return from [a] standard 9/6 straight-draw machine [is] 99.5%; you give up only a half perce[nt] to the house. An 8/5 machine return[s] 97.3%. On 6/5 machines, the figu[re] drops to 95.1%, slightly less than ro[u-] lette. Machines with varying paybac[ks] are scattered throughout the casinos. [So] sometimes you'll see an 8/5 machine right ne[xt] to a 9/6, and someone will be blithe[ly] playing the 8/5 machine!

As with slot machines, it's always op[ti-] mum to play the maximum number [of] coins to qualify for the jackpot. Y[ou] insert five coins into the slot and press t[he] "deal" button. Five cards appear on t[he] screen—say, 5, J, Q, 5, 9. To hold the pa[ir] of 5s, you press the hold buttons und[er] the first and fourth cards. The wo[rd] "hold" appears underneath the two 5[s.] You then press the "draw" button (oft[en] the same button as "deal") and three ne[w] cards appear on the screen—say, 10, J, [...]

u have three 5s; with five coins bet, the
chine will give you 15 credits. Now
u can press the "max bet" button: five
its will be removed from your number
credits, and five new cards will appear
the screen. You repeat the hold and
w process; if you hit a winning hand,
proper payback will be added to your
dits. Those who want coins rather
n credit can hit the "cash out" button
any time. Some machines don't have
dit counters and automatically dis-
se coins for a winning hand.

eo-Poker Strategy. Like blackjack, video
ker has a basic strategy that's been for-
lated by the computer simulation of
ndreds of millions of hands. The most
ective way to learn it is with a video
er computer program that deals the
ds on your screen, then tutors you in
w to play each hand properly. If you
't want to devote that much time
the study of video poker, memoriz-
these six rules will help you make

the right decision for more than half the
hands you'll be dealt:

■ **If you're dealt a completely "stiff" hand
(no like cards and no picture cards), draw
five new cards.**

■ **If you're dealt a hand with no like cards
but with one jack, queen, king, or ace,
always hold on to the picture card; if
you're dealt two different picture cards,
hold both. But if you're dealt three different picture cards, only hold two (the two
of the same suit, if that's an option).**

■ **If you're dealt a pair, always hold it, no
matter what the face value.**

■ **Never hold a picture card with a pair of
2s through 10s.**

■ **Never draw two cards to try for a straight
or a flush.**

■ **Never draw one card to try for an inside
straight.**

Bahamas Essentials

PLANNING TOOLS, EXPERT INSIGHT, GREAT CONTACTS

There are planners and there are those who, excuse the pun, fly by the seat of their pants. We happily place ourselves among the planners. Our writers and editors try to anticipate all the issues you may face before and during any journey, and then they do their research. This section is the product of their efforts. Use it to get excited about your trip to Bahamas, to inform your travel planning, or to guide you on the road should the seat of your pants start to feel threadbare.

GETTING STARTED

re really proud of our Web site: ors.com is a great place to begin any ney. Scan Travel Wire for suggested eraries, travel deals, restaurant and el openings, and other up-to-the-min- info. Check out Booking to research es and book plane tickets, hotel ns, rental cars, and vacation pack- . Head to Talk for on-the-ground ters from travelers who frequent message boards. You can also link to s of other travel-related resources.

ESOURCES

LINE TRAVEL TOOLS

About the Bahamas For commercial list- including a comprehensive yellow pages arinas, golf courses, and hotels, visit vw.bahamasgateway.com. Browse ⊕www. masnet.com for general information on slands, including business directories. For ailed list of hotels, B&Bs, and restau- visit ⊕www.bahamas-travel.info. Search vw.the-bahamas-islands.com for down- advice, beach tips, recipes, and message ls. Love films? Read the latest news about ahamas International Film Festival at vw.bintlfilmfest.com. To catch up on social nvironment news, check out ⊕www. lsofthebahamas.com. For general Baha- news, read the online version of Nassau's st newspaper at ⊕ www.thenassau ian.com. Going fishing? Visit ⊕www. g.thebahamian.com before you leave land.

ety Transportation Security Administra- TSA) (⊕www.tsa.gov).

e Zones Timeanddate.com (⊕www.time te.com/worldclock) can help you figure e correct time anywhere in the world.

the Accuweather.com (⊕www. eather.com) is an independent weather- sting service with good coverage of hur- s. **Noaa.gov** (⊕www.noaa.gov) should ir first stop for storm and hurricane ng; go directly to ⊕ www.nhc.noaa.

gov to see detailed tropical storm predictions. **Weather.com** (⊕www.weather.com) is the Web site for the Weather Channel.

Other Resources **CIA World Factbook** (⊕www.cia.gov) has profiles of every country in the world. It's a good source if you need some quick facts and figures.

VISITOR INFORMATION

Contacts **Abacos Tourism Board** (⊕www. abacos.net). **Bahamas Ministry of Tourism** (☎800/224–2627 or 242/302–2000 ⊕www. bahamas.com). **Bahamas Out Islands Pro- motion Board** (☎954/475–8315 ⊕www. myoutislands.com). **Caribbean Tourism Organisation** (☎212/635–9530 ⊕www. doitcaribbean.com). **Exumas Tourist Office** (⊕www.exumabahamas.org). **Grand Bahama Island Tourism Board** (☎800/448–3386 ⊕www.grandbahamavacations.com). **Harbour Island Tourism** (⊕www.harbourislandguide. com). **Nassau/Paradise Island Promotion Board** (☎888/627–7281 or 800/327–9019 ⊕www.nassauparadiseisland.com). **Turks and Caicos Islands Tourist Board** (☎800/241– 0824 ⊕www.turksandcaicostourism.com).

THINGS TO CONSIDER

GEAR

The reason you're going to the Bahamas is to get away from all of that suit-shirt- and-tie turmoil, so your wardrobe should reflect the informality of the experience. Aside from your bathing suit, which will be your favorite uniform, take lightweight clothing (short-sleeve shirts, T-shirts, cot- ton slacks, lightweight jackets for evening wear for men; light dresses, shorts, and T- shirts for women). If you're going during high season, between mid-December and April, toss in a sweater for the occasional cool evening. Cover up in public places and downtown shopping expeditions, and save that skimpy bathing suit for the beach at your hotel.

Some of the more sophisticated hotels require jackets for men and dresses for women at dinner. The Bahamas' casinos do not have dress codes.

PASSPORTS & VISAS

U.S. citizens need a valid passport when entering the Bahamas by air, but do not need a visa. Passports will be required for land and sea travel beginning June 1, 2009.

■TIP→If you're a U.S. citizen traveling abroad, consider registering online with the State Department (https://travelregis-tration.state.gov/ibrs/), so the government will know to look for you should a crisis occur in the country you're visiting.

PASSPORTS

U.S. passports are valid for 10 years. You must apply in person if you're getting a passport for the first time; if your previous passport was lost, stolen, or damaged; or if your previous passport has expired and was issued more than 15 years ago or when you were under 16. All children under 18 must appear in person to apply for or renew a passport. Both parents must accompany any child under 14 (or send a notarized statement with their permission) and provide proof of their relationship to the child.

■TIP→Before your trip, make two copies of your passport's data page (one for someone at home and another for you to carry separately). Or scan the page and e-mail it to someone at home and/or yourself.

There are 13 regional passport offices, as well as 7,000 passport acceptance facilities in post offices, public libraries, and other governmental offices. If you're renewing a passport, you can do so by mail. Forms are available at passport acceptance facilities and online.

The cost to apply for a new passport is $97 for adults, $82 for children under 16; renewals are $67. Allow six weeks for processing, both for first-time passports and renewals. For an expediting fee of $60 you can reduce this time to about two weeks. If your trip is less than two weeks away, you can get a passport even more rapidly by going to a passport office with the necessary documentation. Private expediters can get things done in as little as 48 hours, but charge hefty fees for their services.

U.S. Passport Information U.S. Department of State (☎877/487–2778 ⊕http://travel.state.gov/passport).

U.S. Passport Expediters A. Briggs Passport & Visa Expediters (☎800/806–0581 or 202/464–3000 ⊕www.abriggs.com). **American Passport Express** (☎800/455–5166 or 603/559–9888 ⊕www.americanpassport.com). **Passport Express** (☎800/362–8196 or 401/521–3496 ⊕www.passportexpress.com). **Travel Document Systems** (☎800/874–5100 ⊕www.traveldocs.com). **Travel the World Visas** (☎866/886–8472 ⊕www.world-visa.com).

TRIP INSURANCE

We believe that comprehensive trip insurance is valuable if you're booking a very expensive or complicated trip or when booking far in advance. Who knows what could happen six months down the road? But whether you get insurance has more to do with how comfortable you are assuming all that risk yourself.

Comprehensive travel policies typically cover trip cancellation and interruption, letting you cancel or cut your trip short because of a personal emergency, illness, or, in some cases, acts of terrorism in your destination. Such policies also cover evacuation and medical care. Some also cover you for trip delays because of bad weather or mechanical problems and for lost baggage. Another type of coverage is

ACKING 101

hy do some people travel with a convoy huge suitcases yet never have a thing wear? How do others pack a duffle with week's worth of outfits *and* supplies for ery contingency? We realize that packing a matter of style, but there's a lot to be id for traveling light. These tips help fight e battle of the bulging bag.

ake a list. In a recent Fodor's survey, 29% respondents said they make lists (and ten pack) a week before a trip. You can use ur list to pack and to repack at the end of ur trip. It can also serve as record of the ntents of your suitcase—in case it disapears in transit.

ink it through. What's the weather like? this a business trip? A cruise? Going road? In some places dress may be more less conservative than you're used to. As u create your itinerary, note outfits next to ch activity (don't forget accessories).

lit your wardrobe. Plan to wear every-ing twice (better yet, thrice) and to do undry along the way. Stick to one basic ok—urban chic, sporty casual, etc. Build ound one or two neutrals and an accent g., black, white, and olive green). Women n freshen looks by changing scarves or welry. For a week's trip, you can look nashing with three bottoms, four or five ps, a sweater, and a jacket.

e practical. Put comfortable shoes atop ur list. (Did we need to say this?) Pack htweight, wrinkle-resistant, compact, wash-le items. Stack and roll clothes, so they'll rinkle less. Unless you're on a guided tour a cruise, select luggage you can readily rry. Porters, like good butlers, are hard to d these days.

neck weight and size limitations. In e United States you may be charged extra r checked bags weighing more than 50 unds. Abroad some airlines don't allow u to check bags over 60 to 70 pounds, or ey charge outrageous fees for every excess

pound—or bag. Carry-on size limitations can be stringent, too.

Check carry-on restrictions. Research restrictions with the TSA. Rules vary abroad, so check them with your airline if you're traveling overseas on a foreign carrier. Con-sider packing all but essentials (travel docu-ments, prescription meds, wallet) in checked luggage. This leads to a "pack only what you can afford to lose" approach that might help you streamline.

Rethink valuables. On U.S. flights, airlines are liable for only about $2,800 per person for bags. On international flights, the liabil-ity limit is around $635 per bag. But items like computers, cameras, and jewelry aren't covered, and as gadgetry regularly goes on and of the list of carry-on no-no's, you can't count on keeping things safe by keeping them close. Although comprehensive travel policies may cover luggage, the liability limit is often a pittance. Your home-owner's policy may cover you sufficiently when you travel—or not.

Lock it up. If you must pack valuables, use TSA-approved locks (about $10) that can be unlocked by all U.S. security personnel.

Tag it. Always tag your luggage; use your business address if you don't want people to know your home address. Put the same information (and a copy of your itinerary) inside your luggage, too.

Report problems immediately. If your bags—or things in them—are damaged or go astray, file a written claim with your airline *before leaving the airport*. If the airline is at fault, it may give you money for essentials until your luggage arrives. Most lost bags are found within 48 hours, so alert the airline to your whereabouts for two or three days. If your bag was opened for security reasons in the United States and something is missing, file a claim with the TSA.

Trip Insurance Resources

Insurance Comparison Sites		
Insure My Trip.com	800/487–4722	www.insuremytrip.com
Square Mouth.com	800/240–0369	www.squaremouth.com
Comprehensive Travel Insurers		
Access America	866/807–3982	www.accessamerica.com
CSA Travel Protection	800/873–9855	www.csatravelprotection.com
HTH Worldwide	610/254–8700 or 888/243–2358	www.hthworldwide.com
Travelex Insurance	888/457–4602	www.travelex-insurance.com
Travel Guard International	715/345–0505 or 800/826–4919	www.travelguard.com
Travel Insured International	800/243–3174	www.travelinsured.com
Medical-Only Insurers		
International Medical Group	800/628–4664	www.imglobal.com
International SOS	713/521–7611	www.internationalsos.com
Wallach & Company	800/237–6615 or 540/687–3166	www.wallach.com

financial default—that is, when your trip is disrupted because a tour operator, airline, or cruise line goes out of business. Generally you must buy this when you book your trip or shortly thereafter, and it's only available to you if your operator isn't on a list of excluded companies.

If you're going abroad, consider buying medical-only coverage. Neither Medicare nor some private insurers cover medical expenses anywhere outside of the United States besides Mexico and Canada (including time aboard a cruise ship, even if it leaves from a U.S. port). Medical-only policies typically reimburse you for medical care (excluding that related to pre-existing conditions) and hospitalization abroad, and provide for evacuation. You still have to pay the bills and await reimbursement from the insurer, though.

Expect comprehensive travel insurance policies to cost about 4% to 7% of the total price of your trip (it's more like 12% if you're over age 70). A medical-only policy may or may not be cheaper than a comprehensive policy. Always read the fine print of your policy to make sure that you are covered for the risks that are of most concern to you.

OOKING YOUR TRIP

Online Booking Resources

ggregators

ayak	www.kayak.com	also looks at cruises and vacation packages.
obissimo	www.mobissimo.com	
ixo	www.qixo.com	also compares cruises, vacation packages, and even travel insurance.
destep	www.sidestep.com	also compares vacation packages and lists travel deals.
avelgrove	www.travelgrove.com	also compares cruises and packages.

ooking Engines

heap Tickets	www.cheaptickets.com	a discounter.
xpedia	www.expedia.com	a large online agency that charges a booking fee for airline tickets.
otwire	www.hotwire.com	a discounter.
stminute.com	www.lastminute.com	specializes in last-minute travel; the main site is for the U.K., but it has a link to a U.S. site.
uxury Link	www.luxurylink.com	has auctions (surprisingly good deals) as well as offers on the high-end side of travel.
netravel.com	www.onetravel.com	a discounter for hotels, car rentals, airfares, cruises, and packages.
rbitz	www.orbitz.com	charges a booking fee for airline tickets, but gives a clear breakdown of fees and taxes before you book.
riceline.com	www.priceline.com	a discounter that also allows bidding.
avel.com	www.travel.com	allows you to compare its rates with those of other booking engines.
avelocity	www.travelocity.com	charges a booking fee for airline tickets, but promises good problem resolution.

nline Accommodations

ahamas.com	www.bahamas.com	has packages for destinations throughout the islands.
otelbook.com	www.hotelbook.com	focuses on independent hotels worldwide.
otel Club	www.hotelclub.net	good for major cities worldwide.
otels.com	www.hotels.com	a big Expedia-owned wholesaler that offers rooms in hotels all over the world.
uikbook	www.quikbook.com	offers "pay when you stay" reservations that let you settle your bill at check out, not when you book.

ther Resources

dding For Travel	www.biddingfortravel.com	a good place to figure out what you can get and for how much before you start bidding on, say, Priceline.

Unless your cousin is a travel agent, you're probably among the millions of people who make most of their travel arrangements online. But have you ever wondered just what the differences are between an online travel agent (a Web site through which you make reservations instead of going directly to the airline, hotel, or car-rental company), a discounter (a firm that does a high volume of business with a hotel chain or airline and accordingly gets good prices), a wholesaler (one that makes cheap reservations in bulk and then re-sells them to people like you), and an aggregator (one that compares all the offerings so you don't have to)? Is it truly better to book directly on an airline or hotel Web site? And when does a real live travel agent come in handy?

ONLINE

You really have to shop around. A travel wholesaler such as Hotels.com or Hotel-Club.net can be a source of good rates, as can discounters such as Hotwire or Priceline, particularly if you can bid for your hotel room or airfare. Indeed, such sites sometimes have deals that are unavailable elsewhere. They do, however, tend to work only with hotel chains (which makes them just plain useless for getting hotel reservations outside of major cities) or big airlines (so that often leaves out upstarts like JetBlue and some foreign carriers like Air India). Also, with discounters and wholesalers you must generally prepay, and everything is nonrefundable. And before you fork over the dough, be sure to check the terms and conditions, so you know what a given company will do for you if there's a problem and what you'll have to deal with on your own.

■**TIP➜To be absolutely sure everything was processed correctly, confirm reservations made through online travel agents, discounters, and wholesalers directly with your hotel before leaving home.**

An aggregator site will search many sites and pull the best prices for airfares, hotels, and rental cars from them. Most aggre-gators compare the major travel-booking sites such as Expedia, Travelocity, and Orbitz; some also look at airline Web sites, though rarely the sites of smaller budget airlines. Some aggregators also compare other travel products, including complex packages—a good thing, as you can sometimes get the best overall deal by booking an air-and-hotel package.

WITH A TRAVEL AGENT

If you use an agent—brick-and-mortar or virtual—you'll pay a fee for the service. And know that the service you get from some online agents isn't comprehensive. For example Expedia and Travelocity don't search for prices on budget airlines like JetBlue, Southwest, or small foreign carriers. That said, some agents (online or not) *do* have access to fares that are difficult to find otherwise, and the savings can more than make up for any surcharge.

A knowledgeable brick-and-mortar travel agent can be a godsend if you're booking a cruise, a package trip that's not available to you directly, an air pass, or a complicated itinerary including several overseas flights. What's more, travel agents that specialize in a destination may have exclusive access to certain deals and insider information on things such as charter flights. Agents who specialize in types of travelers (senior citizens, gays and lesbians, naturists) or types of trips (cruises, luxury travel, safaris) can also be invaluable.

■**TIP➜Remember that Expedia, Travelocity, and Orbitz are travel agents, not just booking engines. To resolve any problems with a reservation made through these companies, contact them first.**

Agent Resources American Society of Travel Agents (☎703/739–2782 ⊕www.travelsense.org).

Bahamas Travel Agents Officials at the Bahamas Ministry of Tourism say these four agencies book most Bahamas trips, and can get the best prices, particularly on hotel-air packages: **AAA Travel** (☎800/222–

34 ⊕*www.aaa.com*). **American Express Travel** 800/999–2599 ⊕*www.amttravel.com*). **son Wagonlit** (☎800/335–8747 ⊕*www. lsontravel.com*). **Liberty Travel** (☎888/271– 34 ⊕*www.libertytravel.com*).

ACCOMMODATIONS

hamas accommodations range from ne of the most luxurious in the world, ch as the One & Only Ocean Club on radise Island—favorite of Oprah, Den-, and Ivana—to yoga ashrams and mey Bahamian inns that cost around 00 per night, such as Tingum Village trendy Harbour Island. The Bahamas cializes in dive resorts such as Small pe Bay on Andros Island, and fishing orts like Orange Hill Beach Inn near ssau, where you can catch your fish d ask the chef to cook it for dinner, and Peace and Plenty Bonefish Lodge on uma, where sportsmen such as former seball manager Dusty Baker hunt these sive "greyhounds of the sea."

e lodgings we list are the cream of the p in each price category. We always the facilities that are available—but don't specify whether they cost extra: en pricing accommodations, always what's included.

st hotels and other lodgings require u to give your credit-card details fore they will confirm your reserva-n. If you don't feel comfortable e-mail-this information, ask if you can fax some places even prefer faxes). How-r you book, get confirmation in writ-and have a copy of it handy when a check in.

sure you understand the hotel's can-lation policy. Some places allow you cancel without any kind of penalty—n if you prepaid to secure a discounted e—if you cancel at least 24 hours in vance. Others require you to cancel a ek in advance or penalize you the cost one night. Small inns and B&Bs are st likely to require you to cancel far

in advance. Most hotels allow children under a certain age to stay in their parents' room at no extra charge, but others charge for them as extra adults; find out the cutoff age for discounts.

■TIP➔Assume that hotels operate on the European Plan (EP, no meals) unless we specify that they use the Breakfast Plan (BP, with full breakfast), Continental Plan (CP, Continental breakfast), Full American Plan (FAP, all meals), Modified American Plan (MAP, breakfast and dinner) or are all-inclusive (AI, all meals and most activities).

For lodging price categories, consult the price charts found near the beginning of each chapter.

APARTMENT & HOUSE RENTALS

There has been a huge boom in residential developments, including single-family villas and condominiums, in the Out Islands. Owners usually put these units in the rental pool, generally during hurricane season, June through November. These new properties are listed by the tourist boards, and reservations are made directly with the developments' rental offices. There are also numerous individual homes and villas throughout the country listed by rental agencies.

Contacts Bahamas Home Rentals (☎888/881–2867 or 321/725–9790 ⊕www. bahamasweb.com). **Bahamas Vacation Homes** (☎242/333–4080 ⊕www.bahamasvacationhomes.com). **Hope Town Hideaways** (☎242/366–0224 ⊕www.hopetown.com). **Rent a Villa.com** (☎800/964–1891 ⊕www. rentavilla.com). **Vacation Home Rentals Worldwide** (☎201/767–9393 or 800/633–3284 ⊕www.vhrww.com). **Villas & Apartments Abroad** (☎212/213–6435 ⊕www.vaanyc. com). **Villas International** (☎415/499–9490 or 800/221–2260 ⊕www.villasintl.com). **Villas of Distinction** (☎800/289–0900 ⊕www. villasofdistinction.com). **Wimco** (☎866/850–6140 ⊕www.wimco.com).

10 WAYS TO SAVE

1. Join "frequent guest" programs. You may get preferential treatment in room choice and/or upgrades.

2. Call direct. You can sometimes get a better price if you call a hotel's local toll-free number (if available) rather than a central reservations number.

3. Check online. Check hotel Web sites, as not all chains are represented on all travel sites.

4. Look for specials. Always inquire about packages and corporate rates.

5. Look for price guarantees. For overseas trips, look for guaranteed rates. With your rate locked in you won't pay more, even if the price goes up in the local currency.

6. Look for weekend deals at business hotels. High-end chains catering to business travelers are often busy only on weekdays; to fill rooms they often drop rates dramatically on weekends.

7. Ask about taxes. Check if taxes are included in quoted rates. In some places taxes can add 20% or more to your bill.

8. Read the fine print. Watch for add-ons, including resort fees, energy surcharges, and "convenience" fees for such things as local phone service you won't use or a newspaper in a language you can't read.

9. Know when to go. If high season is December through April and you're trying to book, say, in late April, you might save money by changing your dates by a week or two. Ask when rates go down, though: if your dates straddle peak and nonpeak seasons, a property may still charge peak-season rates for the entire stay.

10. Weigh your options (we can't say this enough). Weigh transportation times and costs against the savings of staying in a hotel that's cheaper because it's out of the way.

BED & BREAKFASTS

There are few traditional bed-and-breakfasts in the Bahamas (only two in Nassau) but more are opening, such as the Bahamas House Inn on Harbour Island and A Stone's Throw Away Bed and Breakfast on New Providence Island.

Reservation Services BedandBreakfast. com (☎512/322–2710 or 800/462–2632 ⊕www.bedandbreakfast.com) lists bed-and-breakfasts in the Bahamas, and also sends out an online newsletter.

HOME EXCHANGES

With a direct home exchange you stay in someone else's home while they stay in yours. Some outfits also deal with vacation homes, so you're not actually staying in someone's full-time residence, just their vacant weekend place.

Exchange Clubs Home Exchange.com (☎800/877–8723 ⊕www.homeexchange. com); $99.95 for a 1-year online listing. **HomeLink International** (☎800/638–3841 ⊕www.homelink.org); $110 yearly for property listing and Web membership; printed catalogs cost an additional $60. **Intervac U.S.** (☎800/756–4663 ⊕www.intervacus. com); $78.88 for Web-only membership; $126 includes Web access and a catalog.

HOTELS

Smaller lodges and resorts offer easier access to local life and are attractive to travelers who want a cultural experience or a sequestered getaway focused on fishing, diving, and other watery pastimes. Many small, family-run hotels throughout the Bahamas, including the occasional B&B, offer low-key, warm accommodations. All hotels listed have private bath unless otherwise noted. But remember: the Bahamas is not particularly known as a budget traveler's destination. Hotel prices reflect the cost of shipping supplies to the islands, which is common in the region, plus the existence of a labor force that is relatively well-paid and well-educated compared to some of the islands in the Caribbean. Finding a decent room for s than $125 a night, especially in high ason, is becoming more and more difult on some islands.

RENTAL CARS

hen you reserve a car, ask about cancelion penalties, taxes, drop-off charges you're planning to pick up the car in e city and leave it in another), and surarges (for being under or over a certain e, for additional drivers, or for driving ross state or country borders or beyond specific distance from your point of ntal). All these things can add substanlly to your costs.

ites are sometimes—but not always— tter if you book in advance or reserve rough a rental agency's Web site. There e other reasons to book ahead, though: r popular destinations, during busy nes of the year, or to ensure that you get rtain types of cars (vans, SUVs, exotic orts cars).

TIP➔ Make sure that a confirmed res-vation guarantees you a car. Agencies metimes overbook, particularly for busy eekends and holiday periods.

nting a car is advised in Nassau and rge Out Islands such as Eleuthera and xuma, where you will want to explore. prepared to drive on the left, which n be easy on country roads, but frusating in Nassau's traffic. International mpanies are generally in Nassau, and u will rent from privately owned comnies on the small islands. Be warned at you might have to settle for a rusty ap that doesn't have working seat belts. ieck it out thoroughly before you leave. id assume companies won't have car ats—bring your own.

 rent a car, you must be 21 years of e or older in both the Bahamas and e Turks and Caicos, the latter of which arges a flat tax of $10 on all rentals.

WORD OF MOUTH

Did the resort look as good in real life as it did in the photos? Did you sleep like a baby, or were the walls paper thin? Did you get your money's worth? Rate hotels and write your own reviews in Travel Ratings or start a discussion about your favorite places in Travel Talk on www. fodors.com. Your comments might even appear in our books. Yes, you, too, can be a correspondent!

CAR-RENTAL INSURANCE

Everyone who rents a car wonders whether the insurance that the rental companies offer is worth the expense. No one—including us—has a simple answer. It all depends on how much regular insurance you have, how comfortable you are with risk, and whether or not money is an issue.

If you own a car, your personal auto insurance may cover a rental to some degree, though not all policies protect you abroad; always read your policy's fine print. If you don't have auto insurance, then seriously consider buying the collision- or loss-damage waiver (CDW or LDW) from the car-rental company, which eliminates your liability for damage to the car. Some credit cards offer CDW coverage, but it's usually supplemental to your own insurance and rarely covers SUVs, minivans, luxury models, and the like. If your coverage is secondary, you may still be liable for loss-of-use costs from the car-rental company. But no credit-card insurance is valid unless you use that card for *all* transactions, from reserving to paying the final bill. All companies exclude car rental in some countries, so be sure to find out about the destination to which you are traveling.

■TIP➔ Diners Club offers primary CDW coverage on all rentals reserved and paid for with the card. This means that Diners Club's company—not your own car insurance—pays in case of an accident. It doesn't

10 WAYS TO SAVE

1. Nonrefundable is best. If saving money is more important than flexibility, then nonrefundable tickets work. Just remember that you'll pay dearly (as much as $100) if you change your plans.

2. Comparison shop. Web sites and travel agents can have different arrangements with the airlines and offer different prices for exactly the same flights.

3. Beware those prices. Many airline Web sites—and most ads—show prices *without* taxes and surcharges. Don't buy until you know the full price.

4. Stay loyal. Stick with one or two frequent-flier programs. You'll get free trips faster and you'll accumulate more quickly the perks that make trips easier. On some airlines these include a special reservations number, early boarding, and upgrades.

5. Watch those ticketing fees. Surcharges are usually added when you buy your ticket anywhere but on an airline Web site (that includes by phone, and paper tickets regardless of how you book).

6. Check early and often. Start looking for cheap fares up to a year in advance, and keep looking until you see something you can live with.

7. Don't work alone. Some Web sites have tracking features that will e-mail you immediately when good deals are posted.

8. Fly mid-week. Look for departures on Tuesday, Wednesday, and Thursday, typically the cheapest days to travel.

9. Be flexible. Check on prices for departures at different times and to and from alternative airports.

10. Weigh your options. What you get can be as important as what you save. A cheaper flight might have a long layover, or it might land at a secondary airport, where your ground transportation costs might be higher.

mean your car-insurance company won't raise your rates once it discovers you had an accident.

Some countries require you to purchase CDW coverage or require car-rental companies to include it in quoted rates. Ask your rental company about issues like these in your destination. In most cases it's cheaper to add a supplemental CDW plan to your comprehensive travel-insurance policy (⇨ *see Trip Insurance under Things to Consider in Getting Started, above*) than to purchase it from a rental company. That said, you don't want to pay for a supplement if you're required to buy insurance from the rental company.

■ TIP➡ You can decline the insurance from the rental company and purchase it through a third-party provider such as Travel Guard (www.travelguard.com)—$9 per day for $35,000 of coverage. That's sometimes just under half the price of the CDW offered by some car-rental companies.

■ VACATION PACKAGES

Packages *are not* guided excursions. Packages combine airfare, accommodations, and perhaps a rental car or other extras (theater tickets, guided excursions, boat trips, reserved entry to popular museums, transit passes), but they let you do your own thing. During busy periods packages may be your only option, as flights and rooms may be sold out otherwise. Packages will definitely save you time. They can also save you money, particularly in peak seasons, but—and this is a really big "but"—you should price each part of the package separately to be sure. And be aware that prices advertised on Web sites and in newspapers rarely include service charges or taxes, which can up your costs by hundreds of dollars.

■ TIP➡ Some packages and cruises are sold only through travel agents. Don't always assume that you can get the best deal by booking everything yourself.

ıch year consumers are stranded or
se their money when packagers—even
ırge ones with excellent reputations—
› out of business. How can you protect
ourself? First, always pay with a credit
rd; if you have a problem, your credit
rd company may help you resolve it.
cond, buy trip insurance that cov-
s default. Third, choose a company
ıat belongs to the United States Tour
perators Association, whose members
ust set aside funds to cover defaults.
nally, choose a company that also par-
:ipates in the Tour Operator Program
the American Society of Travel Agents
STA), which will act as mediator in
ıy disputes. You can also check on the
ur operator's reputation among travel-
s by posting an inquiry on one of the
›dors.com forums.

ckage tours are usually the way to go in
e Bahamas. Even small inns in the Out
ands offer air-room packages and even
-room-dive and air-room-fish packages
ıat are cheaper than paying separately.

ganizations **American Society of Travel**
ents ([ASTA] ☎703/739–2782 ⊕www.
anet.com). **United States Tour Opera-**
's Association ([USTOA] ☎212/599–6599
www.ustoa.com).

■TIP→**Local tourism boards can provide
information about lesser-known and small-
niche operators that sell packages to only a
few destinations.**

▌ CRUISES

A cruise can be one of the most pleasur-
able ways to see the islands. A multi-
island excursion allows for plenty of land
time because of the short travel times
between destinations. Be sure to shop
around before booking.

Cruise Lines **Carnival Cruise Line**
(☎888/227–6482). **Celebrity Cruises** (☎
800/647–2251). **Costa Cruises** (☎800/445–
8020). **Crystal Cruises** (☎866/446–6625).
Discovery Cruise Line (☎800/259–1579).
Disney Cruise Line (☎800/951–3532). **Hol-
land America Line** (☎206/281–3535 or
877/724–5425). **Mediterranean Shipping
Cruises** (☎800/666–9333). **Norwegian
Cruise Line** (☎866/234–0292). **Oceania
Cruises** (☎305/514–2300 or 800/531–5619).
Princess Cruises (☎800/774–6237). **Regent
Seven Seas Cruises** (☎877/505–5370).
Royal Caribbean International (☎866/562–
7625). **Seabourn Cruise Line** (☎305/463–
3000 or 800/929–9391). **SeaDream Yacht
Club** (☎305/631–6110 or 800/707–4911).
Silversea Cruises (☎954/522–4477 or
800/722–9955).

TRANSPORTATION

▮ BY AIR

Most international flights to the Bahamas connect through airports in Florida, New York, Charlotte, Atlanta, Newark, or Philadelphia. Most domestic flights make a quick stop in Miami or Fort Lauderdale. If you're flying to the Out Islands, you may have to make a connection in both Florida and Nassau—and you still may have to take a ferry or a water taxi to your final destination, as many of the smaller islands do not have airports.

A direct flight from New York City to Nassau takes approximately three hours. The flight from Charlotte to Nassau is two hours, and the flight from Miami to Nassau takes about an hour. It's about a 35-minute flight from Fort Lauderdale to Freeport; about 25 minutes from West Palm Beach to Freeport; and traveling from Miami or Fort Lauderdale to Marsh Harbour takes about an hour. Most flights between the islands of the Bahamas take less than 90 minutes. You'll most likely spend more time on the ground waiting than in the air.

▮**TIP➜If you travel frequently, look into the TSA's Registered Traveler program. The program, which is still being tested in several U.S. airports, is designed to cut down on gridlock at security checkpoints by allowing prescreened travelers to pass quickly through kiosks that scan an iris and/or a fingerprint. How sci-fi is that?**

Airlines & Airports Airline and Airport Links.com has links to many of the world's airlines and airports.

Airline Security Issues Transportation Security Administration (⊕www.tsa.gov) has answers for almost every question that might come up.

AIRPORTS

The major gateways to the Bahamas include Freeport Grand Bahama International Airport (FPO), on Grand Bahama Island, and Nassau International Airport (NAS), on New Providence Island. There are no hotels next to the Freeport and Nassau airports, so expect to spend at least $15 to get to the nearest hotel or resort. Nassau International Airport has a nice restaurant with Bahamian dishes in the international concourse on the second floor and one gift shop–newsstand. There are several small gift stores, a newsstand, and a money exchange office at the check-in area. There's a small café in the domestic terminal, a newsstand, and several small gift stores. *For more airports, ➪ see Essentials in individual chapters.*

Airport Information Grand Bahama International Airport (☎242/352–8881).Nassau International Airport (☎242/377–1759).

GROUND TRANSPORTATION

At each of the country's two largest airports, Nassau and Freeport, there is one taxi stand and an airport official who tells you the price of the taxi and points out your driver. The process is very efficient and orderly. Fares from the airport are set. Some sample fares from Nassau's airport: to Cable Beach, $15; to Paradise Beach, $27; to downtown, $22. The cost from the Freeport airport in Grand Bahama to Lucaya is $19. These prices are for two passengers; each additional passenger costs another $3. Taxis come in all shapes—compact cars and big vans—so there is no uniform look, but most will display a number in the windshield or on the front license plate. And inside there is a laminated driver identification tag posted on the dash or hanging from the rearview mirror. On small islands, the fare, which is also set by the government, can be negotiated a little.

ntacts The following taxi companies oper-
e in Nassau. Elsewhere in the Bahamas,
xis are individually owned. **Four Season
ecutive Service** (☎242/423–3777). **God-
ey Simms Taxi Service** (☎242/324–5050
www.taxi516.com). **Taxi & City/Country
urs** (☎242/323–5818).

IGHTS

ir service to the Bahamas varies season-
ly, with the biggest choice of flights usu-
ly available in the Christmas-to-Easter
indow. Things can change substantially
om year to year. Carriers come and
, especially in the Out Islands, which
e served mostly by smaller commuter
rlines and charters. Schedules change
equently. The smallest cays may have
heduled service only a few days a week,
may rely mostly on charters. In the
ut Islands, ask your hotel for flight rec-
mmendations, as they are likely to have
e most up-to-date information on car-
rs and schedules; some can even help
u book air travel.

rline Contacts **Air Canada** (☎888/247–
62). **American Airlines** (☎800/433–7300).
merican Eagle (☎800/433–7300). **Con-
ental Airlines** (☎800/523–3273 for U.S.
d Mexico reservations, 800/231–0856 for
ernational reservations). **Delta Airlines**
☎800/221–1212 for U.S. reservations,
0/241–4141 for international reservations).
tBlue (☎800/538–2583). **Northwest
rlines** (☎800/225–2525). **Spirit Airlines**
☎800/772–7117 or 586/791–7300). **USAir-
ys** (☎800/428–4322 for U.S. and Canada
ervations, 800/622–1015 for international
ervations).

naller Airlines **Air Sunshine** (☎800/327–
00 or 954/434–8900). **Bahamasair**
☎800/222–4262). **Chalks Ocean Air-
ys** (☎877/924–2557). **Cherokee Air**
☎242/367–3450). **Comair** (☎800/221–
12). **Gulfstream International Air-
ys** (☎800/231–0856). **Island Express**
☎954/359–0380). **Lynx Air International**
☎888/596–9247). **Twin Air** (☎954/359–
56). **Vintage Props and Jets** (☎800/852–
75). **Yellow Air Taxi** (☎ 954/321–0292).

**Within the Bahamas Air Charter Baha-
mas** (☎866/359–4752). **Bahamasair**
(☎242/377–8451). **LeAir** (☎242/377–2356).
Take Flight Air Charters (☎242/362–1877).

**Within the Turks & Caicos Air Turks and
Caicos** (☎649/941–5481). **Global Airways**
(☎649/941–3222 ⊕www.globalairways.tc).
Sky King (☎649/941–5464 ⊕www.skyking.tc).

■ BY BOAT & FERRY

If you're of an adventurous frame of
mind, and have time to spare, take a ferry
or traditional mail boat, which regularly
leave Nassau from Potter's Cay, under
the Paradise Island bridge. Although
fast, modern, air-conditioned boats now
make some of the trips, some remote
destinations are still served by slow, old-
fashioned craft. Especially if you choose
the mail boat route, you may even find
yourself sharing company with goats or
chickens, and making your way on deck
through piles of lumber and crates of
cargo; on these lumbering mail boats,
expect to spend 5 to 12 or more hours
slowly making your way between island
outposts. These boats operate on Bahamian time, which is a casual, unpredict-
able measure, and the schedules can be
thrown off by bad weather. The larger
ferries now can be booked ahead of time,
and even online, but mail boats cannot
generally be booked in advance, and services are limited. In Nassau, check details
with the dockmaster's office at Potter's
Cay. You can purchase tickets from the
dockmaster or from the captain or mate
just before departure; one-way trips are
generally about $35.

From Florida, the Discovery Cruise Line
travels to Grand Bahama Island daily
with its 1,100-passenger *Discovery Sun*,
complete with swimming pool, casino,
live entertainment, disco, and buffets.
Passengers can either make it just a day
trip, arriving in the Bahamas in the morning and departing that afternoon, or stay

on the island for a few days. Round-trip fares start at about $140.

Within the Bahamas, Bahamas Ferries has the most, and most comfortable, options for island-hopping, with air-conditioned boats that offer food and beverages served by cabin attendants. Schedules do change rather frequently; if you're planning to ferry back to an island to catch a flight, check and double-check the departure times, and build in extra time in case the weather's bad or the boat inexplicably doesn't make the trip you'd planned on. Ferries serve most of the major tourist destinations from Nassau, including Spanish Wells, Governor's Harbour, Harbour Island, Abaco, Exuma, and Andros. The high-speed ferry that runs between Nassau and Spanish Wells, Governor's Harbour, and Harbour Island costs $70 one way, and takes about two hours each way.

Local ferries in the Out Islands transport islanders and visitors from the main island to smaller cays. Usually, these ferries make several round-trips daily, and keep a more punctual schedule than the longer-haul ferry. The Out Island ferry captains keep in close touch with the airports, so, for instance, if your flight is delayed, the last ferry of the day might wait around a while for stragglers. (Or, it might not. Check with your hotel or rental villa to see what types of alternate transportation they can arrange in case you miss the day's last ferry.) From the ferry docks, if you've missed the boat, so to speak, you can sometimes catch a ride to outlying cays with locals, but if you do, always offer to chip in for gas, which is expensive in the Bahamas.

If you're setting sail yourself, note that cruising boats must clear customs at the nearest port of entry before beginning any diving or fishing. The fee is $150 for boats 35 feet and under and $300 for boats 36 feet and longer, which includes fishing permits and departure tax for up to four persons. Each additional person

above the age of four will be charged the $15 departure tax. Stays of longer than 12 months must be arranged with Bahamas customs and immigration officials.

Information Bahamas Ferries (☎242/323–2166 ⊕www.bahamasferries.com). **Discovery Cruise Line** (☎888/213–8253 ⊕www.discoverycruise.com). **Potter's Cay Dockmaster** (☎242/393–1064).

▮ BY BUS

Buses on New Providence Island and Grand Bahama are called jitneys, and are actually vans. Route numbers are clearly marked, and there's usually service from early morning until dusk. Exact change ($1 around town; $2 for travel outside the city) is required, and although there are established stops, you can sometimes hail a jitney. Let the driver know where you would like to get off. There's no bus service on most of the Out Islands.

▮ BY CAR

Renting a car is usually advisable on large islands such as Grand Bahama, Exuma, Long Island, Eleuthera, and Andros, where bus service is sparse or nonexistent. You can't take a car to the Bahamas unless it is shipped as cargo, and to do that, you will pay a very high price.

It's common to hire a driver with a van on most islands, and prices are negotiable. Most drivers charge by the half day or full day, and prices depend on the stops and distance, although half-day tours are generally $50 to $100 for one to four people, more for more than four. Full-day tours are $100 to $200. It's customary to pay for the driver's lunch. All tour guides in the Bahamas are required to take a tourism course, pass a test to be a guide, and are required to get a special license to operate a taxi.

GASOLINE

The cost of fuel in the Bahamas is usually about twice that in the United States, and prepare to pay in cash. Gas stations may be few and far between in the Out Islands such as Andros and Eleuthera. Keep the car full. You can ask for a handwritten receipt if printed ones are not available. Gas stations may be closed on Sunday.

PARKING

There are few parking meters in the Bahamas, none in downtown Nassau. Police are lenient with visitors' rental cars parked illegally, and will generally just ask the driver to move it. Parking spaces are hard to find in Nassau, so be prepared to park on a side street and walk. Most hotels offer off-street parking for guests. There are few parking lots not associated with hotels.

ROAD CONDITIONS

In and around Nassau, roads are good, although a bit crowded in peak season. From 7 to 10 AM and 3 to 6 PM, downtown Nassau and most major arteries are congested with cars and pedestrians. When cruise ships are in, pedestrian traffic further stifles the flow. On Grand Bahama Island and the Out Islands, conditions vary from the perfectly paved and manicured boulevards in Freeport to narrow and winding countryside roads that are filled with potholes. Make sure you have a spare tire in good condition and necessary tools.

ROADSIDE EMERGENCIES

In case of road emergency, stay in your vehicle with emergency flashers engaged and wait for help, especially after dark. If someone stops to help, relay information through a small opening in the window. If it's daylight and help does not arrive, walk to the nearest phone and call for help. In the Bahamas, motorists readily stop to help drivers in distress. Ask for emergency numbers at the car rental office when you pick up your car. These numbers vary from island to island. On smaller islands, the owner of the company may want you to call him at his home.

Emergency Services **Bahamas Police** (☎919).

RULES OF THE ROAD

Remember, like the British, islanders drive on the left side of the road, which can be confusing because most cars are American with the steering wheel on the left. It is illegal, however, to make a left-hand turn on a red light. Many streets in downtown Nassau are one-way. Round-abouts pose further confusion to Americans. Remember to keep left and yield to oncoming traffic as you enter the round-about and at GIVE WAY signs.

■ BY TAXI

There are taxis waiting at every airport, in Nassau along Bay Street, and outside all of the main hotels and cruise-ship docks. Beware of "hackers"—drivers who don't display their license (and may not have one). Sometimes you can negotiate a fare, but you must do so before you enter the taxi. On Grand Bahama and New Providence, taxi rates are usually zoned, but they may also be metered; again, check before getting in. Some sample fares around Nassau: airport to Cable Beach, $15; airport to Paradise Beach, $27; airport to downtown, $22. Sample fares around Grand Bahama: airport to Lucaya, $19; harbor to Port Lucaya Marketplace, $24. These prices are for two passengers; each additional passenger costs another $3. In the Out Islands, rates are negotiated, but drivers usually don't want to budge by more than a few dollars on their prices (and you might find that renting a car is more economical). You'll find that Bahamian taxi drivers are more talkative than their U.S. counterparts. When you take a taxi to dinner or to town, it's common for the driver to wait and take you back, which doesn't cost more. A 15% tip is suggested.

ON THE GROUND

■ COMMUNICATIONS

INTERNET

Wireless Internet service is becoming more available throughout the islands, but there are still pockets where service is impossible or difficult to get, and it's likely to be slower than you may be accustomed to. If Internet service is an important consideration to you, ask your hotel representative about service before traveling.

If you're carrying a laptop into the Bahamas, you must fill out a Declaration of Value form upon arrival, noting make, model, and serial number. Bring an extra battery, as they're not always readily available in out-of-the-city locations. The Bahamian electrical current is compatible with U.S. computers.

Contacts Cybercafes (⊕ www.cybercafes. com) lists over 4,000 Internet cafés worldwide.

PHONES

The good news is that you can now make a direct-dial telephone call from virtually any point on earth. The bad news? You can't always do so cheaply. Calling from a hotel is almost always the most expensive option; hotels usually add huge surcharges to all calls, particularly international ones. Calling cards usually keep costs to a minimum, but only if you purchase them locally. And then there are mobile phones (⇨ see below); they may be a much cheaper option than calling from your hotel.

Bahamas Telecommunications Company (BTC) is the phone company in the Bahamas. Most public phones require BTC phone cards (available at outlets throughout the islands). Check with your calling card provider before traveling to see if your card will work in the islands (on the smaller cays, it almost certainly won't) and to see about surcharges. And always ask at your hotel desk about what

charges will apply when you make card calls from your room. There's usually a charge for making toll-free calls to the United States.

When you're calling the Bahamas, the country code is 242. The country code for the Turks and Caicos is 649. You can dial either number from the United States as you would make an interstate call. The country code is 1 for the United States.

CALLING WITHIN THE BAHAMAS

Within the Bahamas, to make a local call from your hotel room, dial 9, then the number. If your party doesn't answer before the fifth ring, hang up or you'll be charged for the call. Some 800 and 888 numbers—particularly airline and credit card numbers—can be called from the Bahamas. Others can be reached by substituting an 880 prefix and paying for the call.

Dial 916 for directory information and 0 for operator assistance.

CALLING OUTSIDE THE BAHAMAS

In big resorts, instructions are given by the room phones on how to make international calls and the costs, which differ from resort to resort. In small inns, especially those in the Out Islands, you may not be able to get an AT&T, Sprint, or other operator or international operator, but the hotel front desk can usually do it for you.

Access Codes AT&T USADirect (☎ 800/872–2881). **MCI Call USA** (☎ 800/888–8000). **Sprint Express** (☎ 800/389–2111).

CALLING CARDS

Prepaid phone cards are plentiful in stores throughout the islands. The national company is Bahamas Telecommunications Company.

To place a call from a public phone using your own calling card, dial 0 for the oper-

or, who will then place the call using ur card number. These sometimes can- t be used on more remote islands.

y phones accept Bahamas Direct Pre- id cards purchased from BTC at vend- g machines, stores, and BTC offices. u can use these cards to call within the untry or to the United States.

ntact **Bahamas Telecommunications mpany (BTC)** (☏242/323–6414 ⊕www. bahamas.com).

BILE PHONES

you have a multiband phone (some untries use different frequencies than at's used in the United States) and your vice provider uses the world-standard M network (as do T-Mobile, Cingu- , and Verizon), you can probably use ur phone abroad. Roaming fees can be ep, however: 99¢ a minute is consid- d reasonable. And overseas you nor- lly pay the toll charges for incoming ls. It's almost always cheaper to send ext message than to make a call, since t messages have a very low set fee ten less than 5¢).

ou just want to make local calls, con- er buying a new SIM card (note that ur provider may have to unlock your one for you to use a different SIM d) and a prepaid service plan in the tination. You'll then have a local num- and can make local calls at local rates. your trip is extensive, you could also ply buy a new cell phone in your des- ation, as the initial cost will be offset r time.

IP→If you travel internationally fre- ntly, save one of your old mobile phones uy a cheap one on the Internet; ask your phone company to unlock it for you, and e it with you as a travel phone, buying a w SIM card with pay-as-you-go service in h destination.

ne U.S. cell phones work in the Baha- s, but you won't know until you get re; check with your provider before your trip, but be prepared to be surprised. The Bahamas Telephone Company has roaming agreements with many U.S. companies, including Cingular, T-Mobile, and Sprint Nextel. Roaming rates are $3 per day and 99¢ per minute. In order for non-BaTelCo subscribers to receive calls while in the Bahamas, the caller must dial 1–242–359–7626, wait for the second tone and then dial your number. How- ever, service can be spotty everywhere, and on the Out Islands, don't expect cell phones to work at all. In Nassau, you can rent phones from BTC on a variety of packages. You can rent GMS cellular phones from companies such as Cellular Abroad, which charges 74¢ a minute on calls to the United States plus the rental of the phone.

Contacts Cellular Abroad (☏800/287–5072) rents and sells GMS phones and sells SIM cards that work in many countries. **Mobal** (☏888/888–9162) rents mobiles and sells GSM phones (starting at $49) that will operate in 140 countries. Per-call rates vary throughout the world. **Planet Fone** (☏888/988–4777) rents cell phones that will operate in more than 150 countries.

▌ CUSTOMS & DUTIES

You're always allowed to bring goods of a certain value back home without hav- ing to pay any duty or import tax. But there's a limit on the amount of tobacco and liquor you can bring back duty-free, and some countries have separate limits for perfumes; for exact figures, check with your customs department. The val- ues of so-called "duty-free" goods are included in these amounts. When you shop abroad, save all your receipts, as customs inspectors may ask to see them as well as the items you purchased. If the total value of your goods is more than the duty-free limit, you'll have to pay a tax (most often a flat percentage) on the value of everything beyond that limit.

Customs allows you to bring in 1 liter of wine or liquor and five cartons of cigarettes in addition to personal effects, purchases up to $100, and all the money you wish. Certain types of personal belongings may get a raised eyebrow—an extensive collection of CDs or DVDs, for instance—if they suspect you may be planning to sell them while in the country. However, real hassles at immigration are rare, since officials realize tourists are the lifeblood of the economy. But don't even think of smuggling in marijuana or any kind of narcotic. Justice is swift and severe in the Bahamas.

You would be well advised to leave pets at home, unless you're considering a prolonged stay in the islands. An import permit is required from the Ministry of Agriculture and Fisheries for all animals brought into the Bahamas. The animal must be more than six months old. You'll also need a veterinary health certificate issued by a licensed vet. The permit is good for one year from the date of issue, costs $15, and the process must be completed immediately before departure. U.S. residents who have been out of the country for at least 48 hours may bring home $800 worth of foreign goods duty-free, as long as they have not used the $800 allowance or any part of it in the past 30 days.

Information in the Bahamas and Turks & Caicos Ministry of Agriculture and Fisheries (☎ 242/325–7502). **U.S. Embassy** (☎ 242/322–1181).

U.S. Information U.S. Customs and Border Protection (⊕ www.cbp.gov).

▌EATING OUT

The restaurants we list are the cream of the crop in each price category. You'll find all types, from cosmopolitan to the most casual restaurants, serving all types of cuisine. Children will like the outdoor restaurants such as The Poop Deck and Traveller's Rest in Nassau, where they can watch the water. Order the Bahamian children's favorite dessert, guava duff. Vegetarians will find plenty of vegetables on the menu, but the Bahamas' signature dishes are fish and conch.

For information on food-related health issues, see Health below.

MEALS & MEALTIMES
Breakfast, generally served from 8 until 10, is typically grits, eggs, bacon, or little whole snappers boiled with pepper and onions served with grits and johnnycakes (thick homemade bread). Lunch is usually fried fish sandwiches and conch salad. Dinner is served 6 until 10 or 11, with a variety of grilled or fried fish, salads, and vegetables. Overall, you may end up eating more fried food than you are used to. Restaurants are busiest Friday and Saturday nights.

Unless otherwise noted, the restaurants listed in this guide are open daily for lunch and dinner.

PAYING
The U.S. dollar is on par with the Bahamian dollar and both currencies are accepted in restaurants. Most credit cards are also widely accepted in most restaurants. Typically, you will have to ask for your check when you are finished.

For dining price categories, consult the price charts found near the beginning of each chapter. For guidelines on tipping, see Tipping below.

RESERVATIONS & DRESS
Regardless of where you are, it's a good idea to make a reservation if you can. We only mention them specifically when reservations are essential (there's no other way you'll ever get a table) or when they are not accepted. For popular restaurants, book as far ahead as you can (often 30 days), and reconfirm as soon as you arrive. (Large parties should always call ahead to check the reservations policy.) We mention dress only when men are required to wear a jacket or a jacket and

LOCAL DO'S & TABOOS

CUSTOMS OF THE COUNTRY

Humor is a wonderful way to relate to the islanders, but don't force it. Don't try to talk their dialect unless you are adept at it. Though most Bahamians are too polite to show it, you may offend them if you make a bad attempt at local lingo. Church is central in the lives of the Bahamians. They dress up in their fanciest finery; it's a sight to behold on Saturday evening and Sunday morning. To show respect, dress accordingly if you plan to attend religious ceremonies. No doubt you'll be outdone, but do dress up regardless.

GREETINGS

Bahamians greet people with a proper British "good morning," "good afternoon," or "good evening." When approaching an islander to ask directions or information, preface your request with such a greeting, and ask "how are you?" Smile, and don't rush into a conversation, even if you're running late.

LANGUAGE

Islanders speak English with a lilt influenced by their British and/or African ancestry. When locals talk among themselves in local dialect, it's virtually impossible for the unaccustomed to understand them. They take all sorts of shortcuts and pepper the language with words all their own. When islanders speak to visitors, they will use standard English.

OUT ON THE TOWN

When you hail a waiter, say sir or miss. Your check usually will not be brought until you ask for it. Bahamians do not like drunkenness, and, unfortunately, frequently have to put up with drunken Americans. Bahamians generally are not smokers, so smokers should choose outdoor cafés and terraces at restaurants. And all you honeymooners, save the displays of affection for the hotel. PDAs are not accepted here—although Americans will blush at the way Bahamians dance, even the middle-aged, which is pelvis to pelvis.

Bahamians love to dress up, and will wear Sunday suits and dresses to dinner at nice restaurants and clubs.

SIGHTSEEING

Visitors should dress conservatively when going to houses of worship. Bahamians love hats, and you will see quite a parade of fancy hats at church even on small islands. You should not wear swimsuits into stores and restaurants, even those on the beach. There are very few homeless Bahamians and on the few occasions when people ask for money, just shake your head and keep walking. Polite children in school uniforms will often have fund-raisers in tourist areas, and parents and teachers will be there. Donations are greatly appreciated and help local schools. A decade ago, drug dealers frequently approached visitors on Nassau's streets, but police have cracked down, especially in tourist areas. Most likely you'll only be asked if you want your hair braided. It's customary to address people by Mr., Miss, and Mrs. in business situations, and with taxi drivers, concierges, hotel managers, guides, and tour desk operators. Bahamians are more formal than Americans, and they value good manners; always remember your please and thank-yous.

TIME

Bahamians tend to have a more casual attitude about time than visitors may be used to, which islanders say is because they've long lived a good life in a land where nature provided just about every need for housing, food, and livelihood. Bahamians believe there is always time to worry about the bad things tomorrow. Don't take it personally; things DO get done, though perhaps not at the rate you'd expect. Asking a Bahamian to hurry, especially if done rudely, however, may just slow things down. Stay polite, keep your humor, and try to slow down yourself—you'll have a better island experience.

tie. Otherwise, you can assume that dining out is a casual affair.

Kalik beer is made in the Bahamas and is available at most restaurants for lunch and dinner.

■ ELECTRICITY

Electricity is 120 volts/60 cycles AC, which is compatible with all U.S. appliances.

■ EMERGENCIES

The emergency telephone number in the Bahamas is 919 or 911. Pharmacies usually close at 6 PM. Emergency medicine after hours is available only at hospitals, or on remote Out Islands, at clinics.

General Emergency Contacts Aircraft Rescue (☎ 242/377–7077). **Doctor's Hospital Acute Care in Nassau** (☎ 242/322–8411). **Princess Margaret Hospital Acute Care** (Nassau) (☎ 242/322–2861). **Rand Memorial Hospital** (☎ 242/352–6735). **United States Embassy** (☎ 242/322–1181).

■ HEALTH

For information on travel insurance, shots and medications, and medical-assistance companies see Shots & Medications under Things to Consider in Before You Go, above.

The major health risk in the Bahamas is traveler's diarrhea. This is most often caused by ingesting fruits, shellfish, and drinks to which your body is unaccustomed. Go easy at first on new foods such as mangoes, conch, and rum punch. There are rare cases of contaminated fruit, vegetables, or drinking water. If you're susceptible to digestive problems, avoid ice, uncooked food, and unpasteurized milk and milk products, and drink bottled water, or water that has been boiled for several minutes, even when brushing your teeth. Mild digestive treatments might include Imodium (known generically as loperamide) or Pepto-Bismol, both of which can be purchased over the counter. Travelers prone to travel-related stomach disorders who are comfortable with alternative medicine might pick up some *po chai* tablets from a doctor of Eastern medicine or Asian pharmacy—it's a great stomach cure-all. Drink plenty of purified water or tea; chamomile is a good folk remedy. In severe cases, rehydrate yourself with a salt-sugar solution (½ teaspoon salt and 4 tablespoons sugar per quart of water).

No-see-ums (sand fleas) and mosquitoes can be bothersome. Some travelers have allergies to sand-flea bites, and the itching can be extremely annoying. To prevent the bites, use a recommended bug repellent. To ease the itching, rub alcohol on the bites. Some Out Island hotels provide sprays or repellents but it's a good idea to bring your own.

Hospitals and other health care facilities are readily available in Nassau, Freeport, and Grand Turk. In the Out Islands, facilities range from clinics to private practitioners. For more serious emergencies, an airlift can be arranged from any location. The most serious accidents and illnesses may require treatment in the United States, most likely in a hospital in Florida; less severe emergency cases will be sent to Nassau or Freeport. The costs of a medical evacuation, especially to the United States, can quickly run into the thousands of dollars, and your personal health insurance may not cover such costs. If you're planning on pursuing inherently risky activities, such as scuba diving, or if you have an existing medical condition, check your existing policy. You may want to consider buying a medical insurance policy that lasts the duration of your trip.

Do not fly within 24 hours of scuba diving. Always know where your nearest decompression chamber is *before* you embark on a dive expedition, and how you would get there in an emergency.

sking in the sun is one of the great easures of a Bahamian vacation, but cause the sun is closer to Earth the farer south you go, it will burn your skin ore quickly, so take precautions against nburn and sunstroke. On a sunny day, en people who are not normally bothd by strong sun should cover up with ong-sleeve shirt, a hat, and pants or a ach wrap while on a boat or midday the beach. Carry UVA/UVB sunblock ith an SPF of at least 15) for your face d other sensitive areas. If you're engag- ; in water sports, be sure the sunscreen waterproof. Wear sunglasses because es are particularly vulnerable to direct n and reflected rays. Be sure to drink ough liquids—water or fruit juice pref- bly—and avoid coffee, tea, and alco- l. Above all, limit your sun time for first few days until you become accus- ned to the rays. Do not be fooled by overcast day. Quite often you will get worst sunburns when you least expect m. The safest hours for sunbathing are 6 PM, but even then it's wise to limit tial exposure.

compression Chamber **Bahamas Hyper-
ic Centre** (☎242/362–5765).

VER-THE-COUNTER REMEDIES

armacies carry most of the same pain ief products you find in the United tes, but often at a higher price, so pack y over-the-counter medications you ularly use. They also sell a product led 2-2-2, which is equal parts aspi- , caffeine, and codeine. It's an effective nkiller but can cause upset stomach.

HOURS OF OPERATION

nks are generally open Monday–Thurs- y 9 or 9:30 to 3 or 4 and Friday 9 to 5. wever, on the Out Islands, banks may ep shorter hours—on the smallest cays, y may be open only a day or two each ek. ATMs are common on the larger d more heavily populated islands, but n't count on finding one when you

need it on some of the more remote cays. (Most ATMs, by the way, dispense Baha- mian dollars.) Most Bahamian offices observe bank hours.

Hours for attractions vary. Most open between 9 and 10 and close around 5.

Though most drugstores typically abide by normal store hours, some stay open 24 hours.

Shops in downtown Nassau are open Monday–Saturday 9 to 5. Grand Baha- ma's International Bazaar and Port Lucaya Marketplace are open 10 to 6. Most stores, with the exception of straw markets and malls, close on Sunday. Shop in the morning, when streets are less crowded. Remember that when you're shopping in Nassau, Freeport, and Port Lucaya, you may be competing with the hordes of passengers that pour off cruise ships daily.

HOLIDAYS

The grandest holiday of all is Junkanoo, a carnival that came from slaves who made elaborate costumes and instruments such as goatskin drums. Junkanoo is celebrated on Boxing Day, the day after Christmas, and New Year's Day (the bands compete in all-night parades that start in the wee hours). Don't expect to conduct any busi- ness during the week of festivities. Dur- ing other legal holidays, most offices close, and some may extend the holiday by keeping earlier (or no) hours the day before or after. In the Bahamas, official holidays include New Year's Day, Good Friday, Easter, Whit Monday (last Mon. in May), Labour Day (1st Mon. in June), Independence Day (July 10), Emancipation Day (1st Mon. in Aug.), Discovery Day (Oct. 12), Christmas Day, and Boxing Day (Dec. 26). In Turks and Caicos, islanders also celebrate Commonwealth Day (Mar.), Easter Monday, National Heroes Day (May), the Queen's Birthday (June), National Youth Day (Sept.), and International Human Rights Day (Oct.). They celebrate Emancipation Day (Aug. 1) but do not celebrate Whit Monday, Labour Day, or Independence Day.

▌ MAIL

Regardless of whether the term "snail mail" was coined in the Bahamas, you're likely to arrive home long before your postcards do—it's not unheard of for letters to take two to four weeks to reach their destinations. No postal (zip) codes are used in the Bahamas—all mail is collected from local area post office boxes.

First-class mail to the United States is 65¢ per half ounce. Airmail postcards to the United States require a 50¢ stamp in the Bahamas; the stamps must be Bahamian. In Turks and Caicos, prices are comparable. Postcard stamps good for foreign destinations are usually sold at shops selling postcards, so you don't have to make a special trip.

Mailing time to the United States from the Bahamas is 4 to 15 days—but this is only an estimate. Don't be surprised if it takes longer. From the United States, a postcard or a letter sent to the Bahamas costs 90¢.

SHIPPING PACKAGES

If you want to ship purchases home, take the same precautions you take in the United States—don't pack valuables or fragile items.

Express Services Copimaxx (☎242/328–2679). **FedEx** (☎242/352–3402 or

242/352–3403 Freeport; 242/322–5656 or 242/322–5657 Nassau; 242/367–2817 Abaco; 242/368–2540 Andros; 242/332–2720 Eleuthera;242/337–6786 Long Island; 649/946–2542 Grand Turk; 649/946–4682 Providenciales; 800/247–4747 U.S. international customer service). **Mail Boxes Etc.** (☎242/394–1506).

ITEM	AVERAGE COST
Cup of Coffee	$2
Glass of Wine	$6
Glass of Beer	$5
Sandwich	$8
One-Mile Taxi Ride in Capital City	$4
Museum Admission	$5

▌ MONEY

Generally, prices in the Bahamas are about the same as in the United States. A hotel can cost anywhere from $75 a night (for cottages and apartments in downtown Nassau and in the Out Islands) to $400 and up (at the ritzier resorts on Paradise Island, Harbour Island, Freeport, and Lucaya), depending on the season. Add at least $35 per person per day for meals at an absolute minimum. Three-night and seven-night package stays offered by most hotels can cut costs considerably. You generally don't get a break for paying with cash. Businesses usually don't care if you pay in U.S. dollars or Bahamian dollars since they're the same value. In the Out Islands, you'll notice that meals and simple goods can be expensive; prices are high due to the remoteness of the islands and the costs of importing. ATMs are widely available, except on the most remote islands, but often the currency dispensed is Bahamian. If you have any left at the end of your stay you can exchange it at the airport.

Prices throughout this guide are given for adults. Substantially reduced fees are most always available for children, students, and senior citizens.

TIP→Banks never have every foreign currency on hand, and it may take as long as a week to order. If you're planning to change funds before leaving home, don't wait till the last minute.

ATMS & BANKS

Your own bank will probably charge a fee for using ATMs abroad; the foreign bank you use may also charge a fee. Nevertheless, you'll usually get a better rate of exchange at an ATM than you will at a currency-exchange office or even when changing money in a bank. And extracting funds as you need them is a safer option than carrying around a large amount of cash.

TIP→PINs with more than four digits are not recognized at ATMs in the Bahamas. If yours has five or more, remember to change it before you leave.

There are ATMs at banks, malls, resorts, and shops throughout the major islands. However, in more remote locations, be sure to take a bit more cash than you think you might need; there are few or no ATMs on some small cays, and on weekends or holidays, those that exist may run out of cash. Banking hours are Monday–Thursday 9:30 to 3 and Friday from 9:30 to 5. There are ATM machines at both Paradise Island and Cable Beach casinos, at Rawson Square on Bay Street, and at the British Colonial Hotel in Nassau. These machines are on the Plus and Cirrus systems. Bahamas banks include Scotiabank and Royal Bank of Canada.

ATM Locations MasterCard/Cirrus (☎800/622–7747) provides locations in the Bahamas and worldwide. **Visa/Plus** (☎800/847–2911) has information for locations in the United States and international destinations.

CREDIT CARDS

Throughout this guide, the following abbreviations are used: **AE**, American Express; **D**, Discover; **DC**, Diners Club; **MC**, MasterCard; and **V**, Visa.

It's a good idea to inform your credit-card company before you travel, especially if you're going abroad and don't travel internationally very often. Otherwise, the credit-card company might put a hold on your card owing to unusual activity—not a good thing halfway through your trip. Record all your credit-card numbers—as well as the phone numbers to call if your cards are lost or stolen—in a safe place, so you're prepared should something go wrong. Both MasterCard and Visa have general numbers you can call (collect if you're abroad) if your card is lost, but you're better off calling the number of your issuing bank, since MasterCard and Visa usually just transfer you to your bank; your bank's number is usually printed on your card.

If you plan to use your credit card for cash advances, you'll need to apply for a PIN at least two weeks before your trip. Although it's usually cheaper (and safer) to use a credit card abroad for large purchases (so you can cancel payments or be reimbursed if there's a problem), note that some credit-card companies *and* the banks that issue them add substantial percentages to all foreign transactions, whether they're in a foreign currency or not. Check on these fees before leaving home, so there won't be any surprises when you get the bill.

When you book your hotel accommodations, be sure to ask if credit cards are accepted; some smaller hotels in the islands do not take plastic.

Reporting Lost Cards American Express (☎800/297–2977 in the U.S. or 336/393–1111 collect from abroad). **Diners Club** (☎800/234–6377 in the U.S. or 303/799–1504 collect from abroad). **Discover** (☎800/347–2683 in the U.S. or 801/902–

3100 collect from abroad). **MasterCard** (☎800/622–7747 in the U.S. or 636/722–7111 collect from abroad). **Visa** (☎800/847–2911 in the U.S. or 410/581–9994 collect from abroad).

CURRENCY & EXCHANGE

The U.S. dollar is on par with the Bahamian dollar and is accepted all over the Bahamas. Bahamian money runs in bills of $1, $5, $10, $20, $50, and $100. The U.S. dollar is the currency of the Turks and Caicos. Since the U.S. currency is accepted throughout, there really is no need to change to Bahamian. Also, you won't incur any transaction fees for currency exchange, or worry about getting stuck with unspent Bahamian dollars. Carry small bills when bargaining at straw markets.

■**TIP**➔**Even if a currency-exchange booth has a sign promising no commission, rest assured that there's some kind of huge, hidden fee. (Oh … that's right. The sign didn't say no fee.) And as for rates, you're almost always better off getting foreign currency at an ATM or exchanging money at a bank.**

TRAVELER'S CHECKS

Some consider this the currency of the cave man, and it's true that fewer establishments accept traveler's checks these days. Nevertheless, they're a cheap and secure way to carry extra money, particularly on trips to urban areas. Both Citibank (under the Visa brand) and American Express issue traveler's checks in the United States, but Amex is better known and more widely accepted; you can also avoid hefty surcharges by cashing Amex checks at Amex offices. Whatever you do, keep track of all the serial numbers in case the checks are lost or stolen.

In the Bahamas, traveler's checks are widely used, but often need to be cashed at banks. ATM machines are scarce on small islands, so keep that in mind. You will need cash for taxi drivers and small restaurants.

Contacts American Express (☎800/297–2977 or 800/528–4800).

▌RESTROOMS

Most attractions, restaurants, and shopping areas have reasonably clean, and sometimes attended, public restrooms. Beaches away from the resorts often have no facilities. Headquarter your beach escape near a bar or restaurant for restroom access.

Find a Loo The Bathroom Diaries (⊕www. thebathroomdiaries.com) is flush with unsanitized info on restrooms the world over—each one located, reviewed, and rated.

▌SAFETY

Crime against tourists is rare, and, unlike some of the Caribbean countries, the Bahamas has little panhandling. But take the precautions you would in any foreign country: be aware of your wallet or handbag at all times, and keep your jewelry in the hotel safe. Be especially wary in remote areas, always lock your rental vehicle, and don't keep any valuables in the car, even in the locked trunk.

Women traveling alone should not go out walking unescorted at night in Nassau or in remote areas. Crime is low, but there's no need to take unnecessary risks. In most other cases, women are safe and treated with respect. To avoid unwanted attention, dress conservatively and cover up swimsuits off the beach.

■**TIP**➔**Distribute your cash, credit cards, IDs, and other valuables between a deep front pocket, an inside jacket or vest pocket, and a hidden money pouch. Don't reach for the money pouch once you're in public.**

▌TAXES

There's no sales tax in the Bahamas, and no departure tax. The departure tax from Turks and Caicos is $35 for persons older than age two, to be paid in either cu

cy at the airport upon departure. Tax
your hotel room is 6%–12%, depend-
g on the island visited; at some resorts,
mall service charge of up to 5% may
added to cover housekeeping and bell-
n service. U.S. visitors can take home
00 worth of duty-free goods. The next
,000 is taxed at 10% (⇨ see *Customs
Duties, above*).

TIME

e Bahamas and the Turks and Caicos
within the Eastern Standard Time
iT) Zone, which means that it's 7 AM
the Bahamas (or New York) when it's
on in London and 10 PM in Sydney.
summer, the islands switch to Eastern
ylight Time (EDT).

TIPPING

e usual tip for service from a taxi driver
waiter is 15% and $1–$2 a bag for por-
s. Many hotels and restaurants auto-
tically add a 15% gratuity to your bill.

TIPPING GUIDELINES FOR THE BAHAMAS	
Bartender	$1–$2 per drink
Bellhop	$1–$5 per bag, depending on the level of the hotel
Coat Check	$1–$2 per item checked unless there is a fee, then nothing
Hotel Concierge	$5 or more, if he or she performs a service for you
Hotel Doorman	$1–$2 if he helps you get a cab
Hotel Maid	$1–$3 a day (either daily or at the end of your stay, in cash)
Hotel Room-Service Waiter	$1–$2 per delivery, even if a service charge has been added
Porter at Airport or Train Station	$1 per bag
Restroom Attendant	Small change or $1 in more expensive restaurants
Skycap at Airport	$1–$3 per bag checked
Taxi Driver	15%–20%, but round up the total to the next dollar amount
Tour Guide	10% of the cost of the tour
Valet Parking Attendant	$1–$2, but only when you get your car
Waiter	15%–20%, with 20% being the norm at high-end restaurants

INDEX

ABOUT OUR WRITERS

Grand Bahama Island writer Chelle Koster Walton admits she's a "fair-weather writer"—her specialty is travel to Florida and the Caribbean. She has written for such publications as *FamilyFun, Bridal Guide, The St. Petersburg Times, National Geographic Traveler,* and the *Miami Herald.* A resident of Sanibel Island, Florida, for 25 years, she is the author of several Florida guidebooks, including *Sarasota, Sanibel Island & Naples, Fun with the Family in Florida,* and *Adventure Guide to Tampa Bay & Florida's West Coast.*

Kevin Kwan, our Harbour Island guru, is a writer, photographer, and creative consultant who considers himself a perpetual islander. Born on the island of Singapore, he is now based on the island of Manhattan, but spends as much time as he can discovering other islands around the globe. Books he's authored include *I Was Cuba* and *Luck: The Essential Guide.*

Born in England and bred in the Bahamas, Jessica Robertson has traveled the world for work and play but calls Nassau home. Our New Providence Island expert has visited just about all of the populated islands in the Bahamas, as well as some occupied only by hermit crabs and seagulls, and works as the news director of the Broadcasting Corporation of the Bahamas.

Patricia Rodriguez Terrell lived in the Caribbean for nearly three years, including a stretch on a tiny cay in the Abacos, where everyone got around by golf cart or fishing boat and where she developed a deep love of grouper burgers and cracked conch. She, her husband (a chef), and their young son—who learned how to walk on the soft beaches of the Bahamas—now live in Texas, where she works as a writer and editor. Patricia updated our Bahamas Essentials section.

On a quest to find the best beaches in the world, Ramona Settle chose Providenciales in the Turks & Caicos Islands—where each beach has more beautiful turquoise water than the last—to be her second home. She photographs its beauty in her spare time.

A fly-fishing and powder-skiing junkie, Stephen F. Vletas is based in Jackson Hole, Wyoming. Vletas was the owner of an international fly-fishing company for 16 years, is the author of *The Bahamas Fly Fishing Guide,* and has recently published a novel, *Tight Loop.* He has also written many articles for national publications including *Fly Rod & Reel, Fly Fisherman, Fly Fishing in Salt Waters,* and *Scientific Anglers Quarterly.* Vletas and his wife, Kim, consider Andros Island their second home, making him the perfect person to update our Out Islands and Abacos chapters.